THE WESTERN WORLD IN THE

TWENTIETH CENTURY

A SOURCE BOOK

THE Western World in the Twentieth Century

A SOURCE BOOK FROM THE

CONTEMPORARY CIVILIZATION PROGRAM IN

COLUMBIA COLLEGE, COLUMBIA UNIVERSITY

Edited by Bernard Wishy

NEW YORK · Columbia University Press

 1961

COPYRIGHT © 1961, COLUMBIA UNIVERSITY PRESS

PUBLISHED IN GREAT BRITAIN, INDIA, AND PAKISTAN
BY THE OXFORD UNIVERSITY PRESS
LONDON, BOMBAY, AND KARACHI

LIBRARY OF CONGRESS CATALOG CARD NUMBER: 61:8987
MANUFACTURED IN THE UNITED STATES OF AMERICA

PREFACE

This volume is based on the Contemporary Civilization program in Columbia College. The most recent (third) edition of Columbia's two source volumes, *Introduction to Contemporary Civilization in the West,* ends on the eve of the First World War. The wide use of the earlier editions in schools other than Columbia seemed to justify a third volume of source documents on the world since 1900. Many of the principal political and economic documents on the period after 1900 in the second edition of Volume II are included in this collection. There is, however, an even wider variety of additional sources. Every effort has been made to produce a book similar in format to the preceding volumes in the Columbia series. New selections have replaced those that proved less successful than others for classroom discussion and analysis. In a few cases selections from the old Volume II have been retitled for the sake of coherence with the new documents.

The Western World in the Twentieth Century owes a great debt to the traditions and prestige of two generations of work in Contemporary Civilization at Columbia carried on by many scholars.

Barry Augenbraun carried a great weight of responsibility in research on the sources. His fine scholarship matched his taste and intelligence. Benjamin K. Bennett provided several translations from the German. Jane Slater, Daisy Grandison, and Phyllis Holbrook shared the heavy job of typing the manuscript.

John G. Palfrey, Dean of Columbia College, concurred in the decision to prepare these additional sources for publication.

BERNARD WISHY

CONTENTS

I HOPES AND FEARS FOR THE TWENTIETH CENTURY

H. G. WELLS

ERBERT GEORGE WELLS (1866–1946) was one of the spokesmen for the generation of liberals that came to maturity between 1890 and 1914. Like them Wells looked forward confidently to the world-wide triumph of science, industrialism, and social justice. He was the son of an English cricket player and all his education through the University of London was financed by scholarships. He was active in the early work of the Fabian socialists but soon clashed with the highly individualistic leaders of that sect. He also developed a growing antipathy for what seemed their excessive dedication to efficiency and élitism.

Most of Wells' ideas were expressed in his novels, but he was also a prolific writer of articles and tracts. For most of his life he was a republican, opposed to the continuation of the English monarchy. He was most successful as a writer of science fiction and such books as *The Time Machine, The War of the Worlds,* and *The Invisible Man* have become classics in that genre. Social history and social prophecy were also Wellsian genres; he was an early champion of the "new woman" and of the "new man" of science, efficiency, and intense practicality.

Wells was not a profound thinker, but at his best he exemplified the humane cosmopolitanism of the enlightened classes in the West at the beginning of this century. Like many members of his generation he was shocked by the potentialities for senseless violence revealed by the First World War but his immensely popular *The Outline of History* (1920) still expressed faith in the ultimate triumph of reason and decency.

This selection is one of many similar declarations of faith in Western ideals that were published in Europe and America on the eve of Sarajevo. It is taken from *The Great State* (New York: Harper and Brothers, 1912).

THE PAST AND THE GREAT STATE

THE NORMAL SOCIAL LIFE is a type of human association and employment, of extreme prevalence and antiquity, which appears to have been the lot of the enormous majority of human beings as far back as history or tradition or the vestiges of material that supply our conceptions of the neolithic period can carry us. It has never been the lot of all humanity at any time, today it is perhaps less predominant than it has ever been, yet even to-day it is probably the lot of the greater moiety of mankind.

Essentially this type of association presents a localized community, a community of which the greater proportion of the individuals are engaged more or less directly in the cultivation of the land. With this there is also associated the grazing or herding over wider or more restricted areas, belonging either collectively or discretely to the community, of sheep, cattle, goats, or swine, and almost always the domestic fowl is a commensal of man in this life. The cultivated land at least is usually assigned, temporarily or inalienably, as property to specific individuals, and the individuals are grouped in generally monogamic families of which the father is the head. Essentially the social unit is the Family, and even where as in Mahomedan countries there is no legal or customary restriction upon polygamy, monogamy still prevails as the ordinary way of living. Unmarried women are not esteemed, and children are desired. According to the dangers or securities of the region, the nature of the cultivation and the temperament of the people, this community is scattered either widely in separate steadings or drawn together into villages. At one extreme, over large areas of thin pasture this agricultural community may verge on the nomadic; at another, in proximity to consuming markets it may present the concentration of intensive culture. There may be an adjacent Wild supplying wood, and perhaps controlled by a simple forestry. The law that holds this community together is largely traditional and customary, and almost always as its primordial bond there is some sort of temple and some sort of priest. Typically the temple is devoted to a local God or a localized saint, and its position indicates the central point of the locality, its assembly place and its market. Associated with the agriculture there are usually a few imperfectly specialised tradesmen, a smith, a garment-maker perhaps, a basket-maker or potter, who group about the church or temple. The community may maintain itself in a state of complete isolation, but more usually there are tracks or roads to the centres of adjacent communities, and a certain drift of travel, a certain trade in nonessential things. In the fundamentals of life this normal community is independent and self-subsisting, and where it is not beginning to be modified by the novel forces of the new times it produces its own food and drink, its own clothing, and largely intermarries within its limits.

This in general terms is what is here intended by the phrase the Normal Social Life. It is still the substantial part of the rural life of all Europe and most of Asia and Africa, and it has been the life of the great majority of human beings for immemorial years. It is the root life. It rests upon the soil, and from that soil below and its reaction to the seasons and the moods of the sky overhead have grown most of the traditions, institutions, sentiments, beliefs, superstitions, and fundamental songs and stories of mankind.

But since the very dawn of history at least this Normal Social Life has never been the whole complete life of mankind. Quite apart from the marginal life of the savage hunter, there have been a number of forces and influences within men and women and without that have produced abnormal and surplus ways of living, supplemental, additional, and even antagonistic to this normal scheme. . . .

Indeed all recorded history is in a sense the history of these surplus and supplemental activities of mankind. The Normal Social Life flowed on in its immemorial fashion, using no letters, needing no records, leaving no history. Then, a little minority, bulking disproportionately in the record, come the trader and sailor, the slave, the landlord and the tax-compeller, the townsman and the king. . . .

Now this human over-life may take either beneficent or maleficent or neutral aspects towards the general life of humanity. It may present itself as law and pacification, as a positive addition and superstructure to the Normal Social Life, as roads and markets and cities, as courts and unifying monarchies, as helpful and directing religious organisations, as literature and art and science and philosophy, reflecting back upon the individual in the Normal Social Life from which it arose, a gilding and refreshment of new and wider interests and added pleasures and resources. One may define certain phases in the history of various countries when this was the state of affairs, when a country-side of prosperous communities with a healthy family life and a wide distribution of property, animated by roads and towns and unified by a generally intelligible religious belief, lived in a transitory but satisfactory harmony under a sympathetic government. . . .

But the general effect of history is to present these phases as phases of exceptional good luck, and to show the surplus forces of humanity as on the whole antagonistic to any such equilibrium with the Normal Social Life. . . . But it never returns in precisely its old form. The surplus forces have always produced some traceable change; the rhythm is a little altered. As between the Gallic peasant before the Roman conquest, the peasant of the Gallic province, the Carlovingian peasant, the French peasant of the thirteenth, the seventeenth, and the twentieth centuries, there is, in spite of a general uniformity of life, of a common atmosphere of cows, hens, dung, toil, ploughing, economy, and domestic intimacy, an effect of accumulating generalising influences and of wider relevancies. And the oscillations of empires and kingdoms, religious movements, wars, invasions, settlements leave upon the mind an impression that the surplus life of mankind, the less-localised life of mankind, that life of mankind which is not directly connected with the soil but which has become more or less detached from and independent of it, is becoming proportionately more important in relation to the Normal Social Life. It is as if a different way of living was emerging from the Normal Social Life and freeing itself from its traditions and limitations.

And this is more particularly the effect upon the mind of a review of the history of the past two hundred years. . . .

The Normal Social Life has been overshadowed as it has never been overshadowed before by the concentrations and achievements of the surplus life. Vast new possibilities open to the race; the traditional life of mankind, its traditional systems of association, are challenged and threatened; and all the social thought, all the political activity of our time turns in reality upon the conflict of this ancient system whose essentials we have here defined and termed the Normal Social Life with the still vague and formless impulses that seem destined either to involve it and men in a final destruction or to replace it by some new and probably more elaborate method of human association. . . .

Now most of the political and social discussion of the last hundred years may be regarded and rephrased as an attempt to apprehend this defensive struggle of the Normal Social Life against waxing novelty and innovation, and to give a direction and guidance to all of us who participate. And it is very largely a matter of temperament and free choice still, just where we shall decide to place ourselves. Let us consider some of the key words of contemporary thought, such as Liberalism, Individualism, Socialism, in the light of this broad generalisation we have made; and then we shall find it easier to explain our intention in employing as a second technicality the phrase of The Great State as an opposite to the Normal Social Life, which we have already defined.

II

The Normal Social Life has been defined as one based on agriculture, traditional and essentially unchanging. It has needed no toleration and displayed no toleration for novelty and strangeness. Its beliefs have been of such a nature as to justify and sustain itself, and it has had an intrinsic hostility to any other beliefs. The god of its community has been a jealous god even when he was only a tribal and local god. Only very occasionally in history until the coming of the modern period do we find any human community relaxing from this ancient and more normal state of entire intolerance towards ideas or practices other than its own. . . .

But with the steady development of innovating forces in human affairs, there has actually grown up a cult of receptivity, a readiness for new ideas, a faith in the probable truth of novelties. Liberalism—I do not of course refer in any way to the political party which makes this profession—is essentially anti-traditionalism; its tendency is to commit for trial any institution or belief that is brought before it. It is the accuser and antagonist of all the fixed and ancient values and imperatives and prohibitions of the Normal Social Life. And growing up in relation to Liberalism and sustained by it is the great body of scientific knowledge, which professes at least to be absolutely undogmatic and perpetually on its trial and under assay and re-examination.

Now a very large part of the advanced thought of the past century is no more than the confused negation of the broad beliefs and institutions which have been the heritage and social basis of humanity for immemorial years. This is as true of the extremest Individualism as of the extremest Socialism. The former denies that element of legal and customary control which has always subdued the individual to the needs of the Normal Social Life, and the latter that qualified independence of distributed property which is the basis of family autonomy. Both are movements against the ancient life, and nothing is more absurd than the misrepresentation which presents either as a conservative force. They are two divergent schools with a common disposition to reject the old and turn towards the new. The Individualist professes a faith for which he has no rational evidence, that the mere abandonment of traditions and controls must ultimately produce a new and beautiful social order; while the Socialist, with an equal liberalism, regards the outlook with a kind of hopeful dread and insists upon an elaborate legal readjustment, a new and untried scheme of social organisation to replace the shattered and weakening Normal Social Life.

Both these movements, and indeed all movements that are not movements for the subjugation of innovation and the restoration of tradition, are vague in the prospect they contemplate. They produce no definite forecasts of the quality of the future towards which they so confidently indicate the way. But this is less true of modern socialism than of its antithesis, and it becomes less and less true as socialism, under an enormous torrent of criticism, slowly washes itself clean from the mass of partial statement, hasty misstatement, sheer error and presumption, that obscured its first emergence.

But it is well to be very clear upon one point at this stage, and that is, that this present time is not a battle-ground between individualism and socialism; it is a battle-ground between the Normal Social Life on the one hand and a complex of forces on the other which seek a form of replacement and seem partially to find it in these and other doctrines. . . .

Nearly every individual nowadays is at least a little confused, and will be found to wobble in the course even of a brief discussion between one attitude and the other. This is a separation of opinions rather than of persons. And particularly that word Socialism has become so vague and incoherent that for a man to call himself a socialist nowadays is to give no indication whatever whether he is a Conservator like William Morris, a non-Constructor like Karl Marx, or a Constructor of any of half a dozen different schools. On the whole, however, modern socialism tends to fall towards the Conservative wing. So, too, do those various movements in England and Germany and France called variously nationalist and imperialist, and so do the American civic and social reformers. All these movements are agreed that the world is progressive towards a novel and unprecedented social order, not necessarily and fatally better, and that it needs organised and even institutional guidance thither, however much they differ as to the form that order should assume. . . .

With less arrogance and confidence, but it may be with a firmer faith than our predecessors of the Fabian essays, we declare that we believe a more spacious social order than any that exists or ever has existed, a Peace of the World in which there is an almost universal freedom, health, happiness, and well-being, and which contains the seeds of a still greater future, is possible to mankind. We propose to begin again with the recognition of those same difficulties the Fabians first realised. But we do not propose to organise a society, form a group for the control of the two chief political parties, bring about "socialism" in twenty-five years, or do anything beyond contributing in our place and measure to that constructive discussion whose real magnitude we now begin to realise.

We have faith in a possible future, but it is a faith that makes the quality of that future entirely dependent upon the strength and clearness of purpose that this present time can produce. We do not believe the greater social state is inevitable. Yet there is, we hold, a certain qualified inevitability about this greater social state because we believe any social state not affording a general contentment, a general freedom, and a general and increasing fulness of life, must sooner or later collapse and disintegrate again, and revert more or less completely to the Normal Social Life, and because we believe the Normal Social Life is itself thick-sown with the seeds of fresh beginnings. The Normal Social Life has never at any time been absolutely permanent, always it has carried within itself the germs of enterprise and adventure and exchanges that finally attack its stability. The superimposed social order of to-day, such as it is, with its huge development of expropriated labour, and the schemes of the later Fabians to fix this state of affairs in an organised form and render it plausibly tolerable, seem also doomed to accumulate catastrophic tensions. Bureaucratic schemes for establishing the regular life-long subordination of a labouring class, enlivened though they may be by frequent inspection, disciplinary treatment during seasons of unemployment, compulsory temperance, free medical attendance, and a cheap and shallow elementary education, fail to satisfy the restless cravings in the heart of man. They are cravings that even the baffling methods of the most ingeniously worked Conciliation Boards cannot permanently restrain. The drift of any Servile State must be towards a class revolt, paralysing sabotage, and a general strike. The more rigid and complete the Servile State becomes, the more thorough will be its ultimate failure. Its fate is decay or explosion. From its débris we shall either revert to the Normal Social Life and begin again the long struggle towards that ampler, happier, juster arrangement of human affairs which we . . . at any rate believe to be possible, or we shall pass into the twilight of mankind.

This greater social life we put, then, as the only real alternative to the Normal Social Life from which man is continually escaping. For it we do not propose to use the expressions the "socialist state" or "socialism," because we believe those terms have now by constant confused use become so battered and bent and discoloured by irrelevant associations as to be rather misleading than expressive. We propose to use the term The Great State to express this ideal of a social system no longer localised, no longer immediately tied to and conditioned by the cultivation of the land, world-wide in its interests and outlook and catholic in its tolerance and sympathy, a system of great individual freedom with a universal understanding among its citizens of a collective thought and purpose.

Now the difficulties that lie in the way of humanity in its complex and toilsome journey through the coming centuries towards this Great State are fundamentally difficulties of adaptation and adjustment. To no conceivable social state is man inherently fitted: he is a creature of jealousy and suspicion, unstable, restless, acquisitive, aggressive, intractible, and of a most subtle and nimble dishonesty. Moreover, he is imaginative, adventurous, and inventive. His nature and instincts are as much in conflict with the necessary restrictions and subjugation of the Normal Social Life as they are likely to be with any other social net that necessity may weave about him. But the Normal Social Life had this advantage, that it has a vast accumulated moral tradition and a minutely worked-out material method. All the fundamental institutions have arisen in relation to it and are adapted to its conditions. To revert to it after any phase of social chaos and distress is and will continue for many years to be the path of least resistance for perplexed humanity. . . .

Let us briefly recapitulate the main problems which have to be attacked in the attempt to realise the outline of the Great State. At the base of the whole order there must be some method of agricultural production, and if the agricultural labourer and cottager and the ancient life of the small house-holder on the holding, a life laborious, prolific, illiterate, limited, and in immediate contact with the land used, is to recede and disappear, it must recede and disappear before methods upon a much larger scale, employing wholesale machinery and involving great economies. . . . A fully developed civilisation employing machines in the hands of highly skilled men will minimise toil to the very utmost, no man will shove where a machine can shove, or carry where a machine can carry; but there will remain, more particularly in the summer, a vast amount of hand operations, invigorating and even attractive to the urban population. Given short hours, good pay, and all the jolly amusement in the evening camp that a free, happy, and intelli-gent people will develop for themselves, and there will be little difficulty about this particular class of work to differentiate it from any other sort of necessary labour.

One passes, therefore, with no definite transition from the root problem of agricultural production in the Great State to the wider problem of labour in general. . . .

We who look to the Great State as the present aim of human progress believe a state may solve its economic problem without any section what-ever of the community being condemned to lifelong labour. And contem-porary events, the phenomena of recent strikes, the phenomena of sabotage carry out the suggestion that in a community where nearly every one reads extensively, travels about, sees the charm and variety in the lives of pros-perous and leisurely people, no class is going to submit permanently to modern labour conditions without extreme resistance, even after the most elaborate Labour Conciliation schemes and social minima are established. Things are altogether too stimulating to the imagination nowadays. Of all impossible social dreams that belief in tranquillised and submissive and virtuous Labour is the wildest of all. No sort of modern men will stand it. They will as a class do any vivid and disastrous thing rather than stand it. Even the illiterate peasant will only endure lifelong toil under the stimulus of private ownership and with the consolations of religion; and the typical modern worker has neither the one nor the other. For a time, indeed, for a generation or so even, a labour mass may be fooled or coerced, but in the end it will break out against its subjection even if it breaks out to a general social catastrophe.

We have, in fact, to invent for the Great State, if we are to suppose any Great State at all, an economic method without any specific labour class. . . .

Adhesion to the conception of the Great State involves adhesion to the belief that the amount of regular labour, skilled and unskilled, required to produce everything necessary for every one living in its highly elaborate civilisation may, under modern conditions, with the help of scientific economy and power-producing machinery, be reduced to so small a number of working hours per head in proportion to the average life of the citizen, as to be met as regards the greater moiety of it by the payment of wages over and above the gratuitous share of each individual in the general output; and as regards the residue, a residue of rough, disagreeable, and monotonous operations, by some form of conscription, which will devote a year, let us say, of each person's life to the public service. If we reflect that in the contemporary state there is already food, shelter, and clothing of a sort for every one, in spite of the fact that enormous numbers of people do no productive work at all because they are too well off, that great numbers are out of work, great numbers by bad nutrition and training incapable of work, and that an enormous amount of the work actually done is the overlapping production of competitive trade and work, upon such politically necessary but socially use-less things as Dreadnoughts, it becomes clear that the absolutely unavoidable labour in a modern community and its ratio to the available vitality must be of very small account indeed. But all this has still to be worked out even in the most general terms. An intelligent science of Economics should afford standards and technicalities and systematised facts upon which to base an estimate. . . .

But behind all these conceivable triumphs of scientific adjustment and direction lies the infinitely greater difficulty on our way to the Great State, the difficulty of direction. What sort of people are going to distribute the work of the community, decide what is or is not to be done, determine wages, initiate enterprises; and under what sort of criticism, checks, and controls are they going to do this delicate and extensive work? With this we open the whole problem of government, administration, and officialdom. . . .

Whatever else may be worked out in the subtler answers our later time prepares, nothing can be clearer than that the necessary machinery of government must be elaborately organised to prevent the development of a managing caste, in permanent conspiracy, tacit or expressed, against the normal man. Quite apart from the danger of unsympathetic and fatally irritating government, there can be little or no doubt that the method of making men officials for life is quite the worst way of getting official duties done. Officialdom is a species of incompetence. The rather priggish, timid, teachable and well-behaved sort of boy who is attracted by the prospect of assured income and a pension to win his way into the civil service, and who then by varied assiduities rises to a sort of timidly vindictive importance, is the last person to whom we would willingly intrust the vital interests of a nation. We want people who know about life at large, who will come to the public service seasoned by experience, not people who have specialised and acquired that sort of knowledge which is called, in much the same spirit of qualification as one speaks of German Silver, Expert Knowledge. It is clear our public servants and officials must be so only for their periods of service. . . .

And since the Fabian socialists have created a wide-spread belief that in their projected state every man will be necessarily a public servant or a public pupil because the state will be the only employer and the only educator, it is necessary to point out that the Great State presupposes neither the one nor the other. It is a form of liberty and not a form of enslavement. We agree with the bolder forms of socialism in supposing an initial proprietary independence in every citizen. The citizen is a shareholder in the state. Above that and after that, he works if he chooses. But if he likes to live on his minimum and do nothing—though such a type of character is scarcely conceivable—he can. His earning is his own surplus. . . .

I would like to underline in the most emphatic way that it is possible to have this Great State, essentially socialistic, owning and running the land and all the great public services, sustaining everybody in absolute freedom at a certain minimum of comfort and well-being, and still leaving most of the interests, amusements, and adornments of the individual life, and all sorts of collective concerns, social and political discussion, religious worship, philosophy, and the like to the free personal initiatives of entirely unofficial people. . . .

The whole spirit of the Great State is against any avoidable subjugation; but the whole spirit of that science which will animate the Great State forbids us to ignore woman's functional and temperamental differences. A new status has still to be invented for women, a Feminine Citizenship differing in certain respects from the normal masculine citizenship. Its conditions remain to be worked out. We have indeed to work out an entire new system of relations between men and women, that will be free from servitude, aggression, provocation, or parasitism. The public Endowment of Motherhood as such may perhaps be the first broad suggestion of the quality of this new status. A new type of family, a mutual alliance in the place of a subjugation, is perhaps the most startling of all the conceptions which confront us directly we turn ourselves definitely towards the Great State. . . .

As our conception of the Great State grows, so we shall begin to realise the nature of the problem of transition, the problem of what we may best do in the confusion of the present time to elucidate and render practicable this new phase of human organisation. Of one thing there can be no doubt, that whatever increases thought and knowledge moves towards our goal; and equally certain is it that nothing leads thither that tampers with the freedom of spirit, the independence of soul in common men and women. In many directions, therefore, the believer in the Great State will display a jealous watchfulness of contemporary developments rather than a premature constructiveness. We must watch wealth; but quite as necessary it is to watch the legislator, who mistakes propaganda for progress and class exasperation to satisfy class vindictiveness for construction. Supremely important is it to keep discussion open, to tolerate no limitation on the freedom of speech, writing, art and book distribution, and to sustain the utmost liberty of criticism upon all contemporary institutions and processes.

This briefly is the programme of problems and effort to which this idea of the Great State, as the goal of contemporary progress, directs our minds.

DAVID LLOYD GEORGE

THE BRITISH statesman David Lloyd George (1863–1945) was one of the most dramatic English political leaders in the early twentieth century. He came from obscurity in Wales into the House of Commons at the age of twenty-seven. Behind him lay poverty, a small-town solicitorship, and the Welsh tradition of great speaking for Godly causes. Within ten years he was the most flamboyant of the Welsh radicals in the Liberal party group in the House who gave their support in return for favors to Wales.

Lloyd George was a controversial person whose sincerity and high style were often suspected. He came into prominence first during the Boer War (1899) when he practiced a favorite pastime of preaching political morality to England, "While England and Scotland are drunk with blood the Welsh continue sane; they are walking along the road of progress and liberty."

Previous cabinet experience under the Liberals brought him the chancellorship of the exchequer (1908–15) under the Asquith ministry. In 1909 Lloyd George introduced the first welfare-state budget in English history. Although it was by no means the first proposal for English social legislation, his speech did mark the emergence of a new liberalism as high public policy. When this budget was rejected by the House of Lords later in 1909, there was precipitated a notable constitutional crisis that ended in 1911 with new limits on the Lords' powers.

Lloyd George's ministerial performance in the early years of the war was outstanding and in 1916 he became prime minister. At the Paris Peace Conference he was as vigorous in defending British interests as he had been in helping to prosecute the war but he was overshadowed by Clemenceau and Woodrow Wilson. His ministry fell in 1922 and he never again returned to political power, however powerful a figure he remained in the Liberal party and in House debates. Auspiciously enough, his last impressive moment in the House came on May 8, 1940 when he urged Neville Chamberlain to resign. When this was accomplished, Lloyd George's former first lord of the admiralty, Winston Churchill, was brought to power. Near the end of his life, the former Welsh radical entered the House of Lords as an earl.

The following extract from the budget speech of 1909 is from the collection of Lloyd George's speeches in *Better Times* (London: Hodder and Stoughton, 1910).

THE PEOPLE'S BUDGET, 1909

I COME to the consideration of the social problems which are urgently pressing for solution—problems affecting the lives of the people. The solution of all these questions involves finance. What the Government have to ask themselves is this: Can the whole subject of further social reform be postponed until the increasing demands made upon the National Exchequer by the growth of armaments have ceased? Not merely can it be postponed, but ought it to be postponed? Is there the slightest hope that if we deferred consideration of the matter we are likely within a generation to find any more favourable moment for attending to it? And we have to ask ourselves this further question. If we put off dealing with these social sores, are the evils which arise from them not likely to grow and to fester, until finally the loss which the country sustains will be infinitely greater than anything it would have to bear in paying the cost of an immediate remedy?

There are hundreds of thousands of men, women, and children in this country now enduring hardships for which the sternest judge would not hold them responsible; hardships entirely due to circumstances over which they have not the slightest command; the fluctuations and changes of trade, even of fashions; ill-health and the premature breakdown or death of the breadwinner. Owing to events of this kind, all of them beyond human control—at any rate beyond the control of the victims—thousands, and I am not sure I should be wrong if I said millions, are precipitated into a condition of acute distress and poverty. How many people there are of this kind in this wealthy land the figures as to Old Age Pensions have thrown a very unpleasant light upon. Is it fair, is it just, is it humane, is it honourable, is it safe to subject such a multitude of our poor fellow-countrymen and countrywomen to continued endurance of these miseries until nations have learnt enough wisdom not to squander their resources on these huge machines for the destruction of human life? I have no doubt as to the answer which will be given to that question by a nation as rich in humanity as it is in store. . . .

What are the dominating causes of poverty amongst the industrial classes? For the moment I do not refer to the poverty which is brought about by a man's own fault. I am only alluding to causes over which he has no control. Old age, premature breakdown in health and strength, the death of the breadwinner, and unemployment due either to the decay of industries and seasonable demands, or to the fluctuations or depressions in trade. The distress caused by any or either of these causes is much more deserving of immediate attention than the case of a healthy and vigorous man of 65 years of age, who is able to pursue his daily avocation, and to earn without undue strain an income which is quite considerable enough to provide him and his wife with a comfortable subsistence.

When Bismarck was strengthening the foundations of the new German Empire one of the very first tasks he undertook was the organisation of a scheme which insured the German workmen and their families against the worst evils arising from these common accidents of life. And a superb scheme it is. It has saved an incalculable amount of human misery to hundreds of thousands and possibly millions of people.

Wherever I went in Germany, north or south, and whomever I met, whether it was an employer or a workman, a Conservative or a Liberal, a Socialist or a Trade Union leader—men of all ranks, sections and creeds, with one accord joined in lauding the benefits which have been conferred upon Germany by this beneficent policy. Several wanted extensions, but there was not one who wanted to go back. The employers admitted that at first they did not quite like the new burdens it cast upon them, but they now fully realised the advantages which even they derived from the expenditure, for it had raised the standard of the workman throughout Germany.

By removing that element of anxiety and worry from their lives it had improved their efficiency. Benefits which in the aggregate amounted to 40 millions a year were being distributed under this plan. . . .

At the present moment there is a network of powerful organisations in this country, most of them managed with infinite skill and capacity, which have succeeded in inducing millions of workmen in this country to make something like systematic provision for the troubles of life. But in spite of all the ability which has been expended upon them, in spite of the confidence they generally and deservedly inspire, unfortunately there is a margin of people in this country amounting in the aggregate to several millions who either cannot be persuaded or perhaps cannot afford to bear the expense of the systematic contributions which alone make membership effective in these great institutions. And the experience of this and of every other country is that no plan or variety of plans short of an universal compulsory system can ever hope to succeed in coping adequately with the problem. In this country we have trusted until recently to voluntary effort, but we found that for old age and accidents it was insufficient.

In Belgium they have resorted to the plan of granting heavy subsidies to voluntary organisations, and they have met with a certain amount of success. But whether here or in Belgium, or in any other land, success must be partial where reliance is absolutely placed upon the readiness of men and women to look ahead in the days of abounding health and strength and buoyancy of spirit to misfortunes which are not even in sight, and which may be ever averted.

The Government are now giving careful consideration to the best methods for making such a provision. We are investigating closely the plans adopted by foreign countries, and I hope to circulate papers on the point very soon. We have put ourselves into communication with the leaders of some of the principal friendly societies in the country with a view to seeking their invaluable counsel and direction. We could not possibly get safer or more experienced advisers. We are giving special attention to the important reports of the Poor Law Commission, both Majority and Minority, which advise that the leading principle of Poor Law legislation in future should be the drawing of a clear and definite line between those whose poverty is the result of their own misdeeds and those who have been brought to want through misfortune.

All I am in a position now to say is that, at any rate, in any scheme which we may finally adopt we shall be guided by these leading principles or considerations. The first is that no plan can hope to be really comprehensive or conclusive which does not include an element of compulsion. The second is that for financial as well as for other reasons, which I do not wish to enter into now, success is unattainable in the near future, except on the basis of a direct contribution from the classes more immediately concerned. The third is that there must be a State contribution substantial enough to enable those whose means are too limited and precarious to sustain adequate premiums to overcome that difficulty without throwing undue risks on other contributors. The fourth, and by no means the least important, is that in this country, where benefit and provident societies represent such a triumph of organisation of patience and self-government, as probably no other country has ever witnessed, no scheme would be profitable, no scheme would be tolerable, which would do the least damage to those highly beneficent organisations. On the contrary, it must be the aim of every well-considered plan to encourage, and, if practicable, as I believe it is, to work through them. . . .

We recognise in this matter that we must walk with caution, and that it will be best to begin with certain groups of trades peculiarly liable to the fluctuations I have referred to and in other respects suitable for insurance, rather than to attempt to cover the entire area of industry. The Royal Commission were emphatic in recommending that any scheme of unemployment insurance should have a trade basis, and we propose to adopt this principle. Within the selected trades, however, the scheme will apply universally to all adult workers. Any insurance schemes of this kind must necessarily require contributions from those engaged in the insured trades, both as employers and employed; but we recognise the necessity of supplementing these contributions by a State grant and guarantee. We cannot, of course, attempt to pass the necessary Bill to establish unemployment insurance during the present Session. But the postponement will not involve any real delay, for the establishment of labour exchanges is a necessary preliminary to the work of insurance, and this will occupy time which may also be advantageously employed in consulting the various interests upon the details of the scheme and in coordinating its financial provisions with the machinery of invalidity and other forms of insurance.

So much for the provision which we hope to be able to make for those who, under the changing conditions which are inevitable in trade and commerce, are temporarily thrown out of employment. We do not put this forward as a complete or an adequate remedy for all the evils of unemployment, and we do not contend that when this insurance scheme has been set up and financed the State has thereby done all in its power to help towards solving the problem. After all, it is infinitely better, in the interests both of the community and of the unemployed themselves, that the latter should be engaged on remunerative work, than that they should be drawing an allowance from the most skillfully contrived system of insurance. This country is small—I suppose it is the smallest great country in the world— but we have by no means exhausted it possibility for healthy and productive employment. It is no part of the function of a Government to create work; but it is an essential part of its business to see that the people are equipped to make the best of their own country, are permitted to make the best of their own country, and, if necessary, are helped to make the best of their own country.

A State can and ought to take a longer view and a wider view of its investments than individuals. The resettlement of deserted and impoverished parts of its own territories may not bring to its coffers a direct return which would reimburse it fully for its expenditure; but the indirect enrichment of its resources more than compensates it for any apparent and immediate loss. The individual can rarely afford to wait, a State can; the individual must judge of the success of his enterprise by the testimony given for it by his bank book; a State keeps many ledgers, not all in ink, and when we wish to judge of the advantage derived by a country from a costly experiment we must examine all those books before we venture to pronounce judgment. . . .

The State can help by instruction, by experiment, by organisation, by direction, and even, in certain cases which are outside the legitimate sphere of individual enterprise, by incurring direct responsibility. I doubt whether there is a great industrial country in the world which spends less money on work directly connected with the development of its resources than we do. Take, if you like, and purely as an illustration, one industry alone—agriculture—of all industries the most important for the permanent well-being of any land. Examine the Budgets of foreign countries—we have the advantage in other directions—but examine and compare them with our own, and hon.

Members will be rather ashamed at the contrast between the wise and lavish generosity of countries much poorer than ours and the short-sighted and niggardly parsimony with which we dole out small sums of money for the encouragement of agriculture in our country.

We are not getting out of the land anything like what it is capable of endowing us with. Of the enormous quantity of agricultural and dairy produce and fruit, and of the timber imported into this country, a considerable portion could be raised on our own lands. On this, hon. Members opposite and ourselves will agree. The only difference is as to the remedy. In our opinion, the remedy which they suggest would make food costlier and more inaccessible for the people; the remedies which we propose, on the other hand, would make food more abundant, better, and cheaper. What is it we propose?—and, let the Committee observe, I am only dealing with that part of the problem which affects finance.

I will tell the House therefore, briefly, what I propose doing in regard to this and all kindred matters I have dwelt upon. There is a certain amount of money—not very much—spent in this country in a spasmodic kind of way on what I call the work of national development—in light railways, in harbours, in indirect but very meagre assistance to agriculture. I propose to gather all these grants together into one Development Grant, and to put in this year an additional sum of £200,000. Legislation will have to be introduced, and I will then explain the methods of administration and the objects in greater detail, but the grant will be utilised in the promotion of schemes which have for their purpose the development of the resources of the country. It will include such objects as the institution of schools of forestry, the purchase and preparation of land for afforestation, the setting up of a number of experimental forests on a large scale, expenditure upon scientific research in the interests of agriculture, experimental farms, the improvement of stock—as to which there have been a great many demands from people engaged in agriculture—the equipment of agencies for disseminating agricultural instruction, the encouragement and promotion of co-operation, the improvement of rural transport so as to make markets more accessible, the facilitation of all well-considered schemes and measures for attracting labour back to the land by small holdings or reclamation of wastes. . . .

We have . . . during the last 60 years, in this country accumulated wealth to an extent which is almost unparalleled in the history of the world, but we have done it at an appalling waste of human material. We have drawn upon the robust vitality of the rural areas of Great Britain, and especially of Ireland, and spent its energies recklessly in the devitalising atmosphere of urban factories and workshops as if the supply were inexhaustible. We are now beginning to realise that we have been spending our capital, and at a disastrous rate, and it is time we should make a real, concerted, national effort to replenish it. I put forward this proposal, not a very extravagant one, as a beginning. . . .

Now what are the principles upon which I intend to proceed in getting [the necessary] taxes? The first principle on which I base my financial proposals is this—that the taxation which I suggest, while yielding in the present year not more than sufficient to meet this year's requirements, should be of such a character that it will produce enough revenue in the second year to cover the whole of our estimated liabilities for that year; and, moreover, that it will be of such an expansive character as to grow with the growing demand of the social programme which I have sketched without involving the necessity for imposing fresh taxation in addition to what I am asking Parliament to sanction at the present time.

The second principle on which I base my proposals is that the taxes should be of such a character as not to inflict any injury on that trade or commerce which constitutes the sources of our wealth.

My third principle is this, that all classes of the community in this financial emergency ought to be called upon to contribute. I have never been able to accept the theory which I have seen advanced that you ought to draw a hard-and-fast line at definite incomes and say that no person under a certain figure should be expected to contribute a penny towards the burden of the good government of the country. In my judgment all should be called upon to bear their share. No voluntary associations, religious, philanthropic or provident, have ever been run on the principle of exempting any section of their membership from subscription. They all contribute, even to the widow's mite. It is considered not merely the duty, but the privilege and pride of all to share in the common burden, and the sacrifice is as widely distributed as is the responsibility and the profit.

At the same time, when you come to consider whether the bulk of the taxation is to be raised by direct or indirect means, I must point out at this stage—I shall have a little more to say on this subject later on—that the industrial classes, in my judgment, upon a close examination of their contributions to local and Imperial finance, are paying more in proportion to their incomes than those who are better off. Their proportion to local finances especially is heavier, because, although nominally the rates are not paid by them, as everyone knows, they are really. For that reason the burden at the present moment of new taxation bears much more heavily in proportion to their income on that class than it does upon the wealthier and better-to-do classes. . . .

Now I come to my direct taxation. It must be obvious that in meeting a large deficit of this kind I should be unwise to trust to speculative or fancy taxes. I therefore propose, first of all, to raise more money out of the income tax and estate duties. Income tax in this country only begins when the margin of necessity has been crossed and the domain of comfort and even of gentility has been reached. A man who enjoys an income of over £3 a week need not stint himself or his family of reasonable food or of clothes and shelter. There may be an exception in the case of a man with a family, whose gentility is part of his stock in trade or the uniform of his craft. Then, I agree, things often go hard.

When you come to estate duties, what a man bequeaths, after all, represents what is left after he has provided for all his own wants in life. Beyond a certain figure it also represents all that is essential to keep his family in the necessaries of life. The figure which the experience of 70 years has sanctified as being that which divides sufficiency from gentility is £150 to £160 a year. A capital sum that would, if invested in safe securities, provide anything over that sum ought to be placed in a different category from any sum which is below that figure.

There is one observation which is common to income tax and the death duties, more especially with the higher scales. What is it that has enabled the fortunate possessors of these incomes and these fortunes to amass the wealth they enjoy or bequeath? The security ensured for property by the agency of the State, the guaranteed immunity from the risks and destruction of war, ensured by our natural advantages and our defensive forces. This is an essential element even now in the credit of the country; and, in the past, it means that we were accumulating great wealth in this land, when the industrial enterprises of less fortunately situated countries were not merely at a standstill, but their resources were being ravaged and destroyed by the havoc of war.

What, further, is accountable for this growth of wealth? The spread of intelligence amongst the masses of the people, the improvements in sanitation and in the general condition of the people. These have all contributed towards the efficiency of the people, even as wealth-producing machines. Take, for instance, such legislation as the Education Acts and the Public Health Acts: they have cost much money, but they have made infinitely more. That is true of all legislation which improves the conditions of life for the people. An educated, well-fed, well-clothed, well-housed people invariably leads to the growth of a numerous well-to-do class. If property were to grudge a substantial contribution towards proposals which ensure the security which is one of the essential conditions of its existence, or towards

keeping from poverty and privation the old people whose lives of industry
and toil have either created that wealth or made it productive, then property
would be not only shabby, but shortsighted.

Now what do I propose? When it is remembered that the total yield of
income tax on its present basis amounts to little more than five years' normal
growth of the aggregate income upon which income tax is payable (which
increased from £607,500,000 in 1901–2 to £640,000,000 in 1906–7), it will be
seen that our present reserve of taxable capacity is as great at the present
moment with the existing rate of the tax as it would have been five years ago
if there had been no tax at all. If the tax were doubled in the present year
income tax payers would, in the aggregate, after payment of the double rate,
be in the enjoyment of almost exactly the same net income as five years ago.
A careful consideration of these figures ought to convince the most sceptical
that the maximum rate of the tax may be retained at 1s., or even increased,
without seriously encroaching upon our available reserves for national
emergencies. The time, however, has gone by when a simple addition of
pence to the poundage of the tax, attractive as the simplicity of that expedient
is, can be regarded as a satisfactory solution of a financial difficulty. . . .

In the case of incomes not exceeding £500, the pressure of the tax, notwithstanding the abatements at present allowed, is sorely felt by taxpayers
who have growing families to support, and although a comparatively trifling
additional burden will be imposed upon them by the increased rate, since the
aggregate income of this class is to the extent of at least four-fifths exclusively earned income, I think that even upon the present basis they have
a strong claim to further relief. Even from the purely fiscal point of view
there is this essential difference between the position of a man with a family
and that of the taxpayer who has no such responsibilities. The family man
is, generally speaking, a much heavier contributor to that portion of the
revenue which is derived from indirect taxation and inhabited house duty,
so that in comparison with the bachelor he is taxed not so much in proportion to his income as in proportion to his outgoings.

There is no class of the community which has a much harder struggle or a
more anxious time than that composed of the men whose earnings just
bring them within the clutches of the income tax collector. On a small income they have not merely to maintain themselves, but to exhaust a large
proportion of their limited resources in that most worrying and wasteful of
all endeavours known as "keeping up appearances." They are often much
worse off and much more to be pitied than the artisan who earns half their
wages. If they have only themselves to think about they do well, but when
they have a family dependent upon them the obligation to keep up the

appearance of respectability of all their dependents is very trying. I am strongly of opinion that they deserve special consideration in the rearrangement of our finances.

Continental countries recognise their claim, and I propose that for all incomes under £500, in addition to the existing abatements, there shall be allowed from the income in respect of which the tax is paid a special abatement of £10 for every child under the age of 16 years. Take the case of the widow with a family, which is always cited in reference to proposals to tax income or property: she will in most cases be better off with this abatement, should her family be of average numbers, even though she is rated at 1s. 2d., than she was before. The new abatement will, like the existing abatements, be allowed irrespective of the source from which the income is derived, and earned incomes, upon which no new burden is to be imposed, as well as unearned incomes, will enjoy the advantage of the concession. . . .

The imposition of a super-tax, however, upon large incomes, on the lines suggested by the Select Committee of 1906, is a more practicable proposition [than a complete system of graduation], and it is upon this basis that I intend to proceed. Such a super-tax might take the form of an additional poundage charged at a uniform rate upon the whole income of persons whose total income exceeds the maximum above which the tax is to be applied, or the poundage might be varied according to the amount of the income to be taxed. A third, and I think preferable, alternative is to adopt a uniform poundage, but to charge the tax not upon the total income, but upon the amount only by which the income exceeded a certain fixed amount, which would naturally, but need not necessarily, be the amount of the minimum income which attracts the tax. We might begin, say, at £3,000, and levy the new tax upon all income in excess of £3,000, or at £5,000, and levy the tax upon income in excess of £5,000. In the former case some 25,000 assessments would be required, in the latter only 10,000—from the point of view of administration a very strong argument in favour of the adoption of the higher figure, at any rate, in the first instance. On the other hand, a general abatement of £5,000 per taxpayer would be extremely costly, and though it would have the effect of largely reducing the actual as compared with the nominal rate of the tax, except in the case of very large incomes indeed, the nominal rate necessary to produce an adequate revenue—though in reality no measure of the general burden—would tend to appear somewhat alarming. . . .

Now I come to the question of land. The first conviction that is borne in upon the Chancellor of the Exchequer who examines land as a subject for taxation is this: that in order to do justice he must draw a broad distinction between land whose value is purely agricultural in its character and composition, and land which has a special value attached to it owing either to the fact of its covering marketable mineral deposits or because of its proximity to any concentration of people.

Agricultural land has not, during the past 20 or 30 years, appreciated in value in this country. In some parts it has probably gone down. I know parts of the country where the value has gone up. But there has been an enormous increase in the value of urban land and of mineral property. And a still more important and relevant consideration in examining the respective merits of these two or three classes of claimants to taxation is this. The growth in the value, more especially of urban sites, is due to no expenditure of capital or thought on the part of the ground owner, but entirely owing to the energy and the enterprise of the community. Where it is not due to that cause, and where it is due to any expenditure by the urban owner himself, full credit ought to be given to him in taxation, and full credit will be given to him in taxation. I am dealing with cases which are due to the growth of the community, and not to anything done by the urban proprietor. It is undoubtedly one of the worst evils of our present system of land tenure that instead of reaping the benefit of the common endeavour of its citizens a community has always to pay a heavy penalty to its ground landlords for putting up the value of their land. . . .

And yet, although the landlord, without any exertion of his own, is now in these cases in receipt of an income which is ten or even a hundredfold of what he was in the habit of receiving when these properties were purely agricultural in their character, and although he is in addition to that released from all the heavy financial obligations which are attached to the ownership of this land as agricultural property, he does not contribute a penny out of his income towards the local expenditure of the community which has thus made his wealth, in the words of John Stuart Mill, "whilst he was slumbering." Is it too much, is it unfair, is it inequitable, that Parliament should demand a special contribution from these fortunate owners towards the defence of the country and the social needs of the unfortunate in the community, whose efforts have so materially contributed to the opulence which they are enjoying?

There is another aspect of this matter which I should like to say a word upon before I come to the actual proposals of the Government. I have dwelt upon the fundamental difference in the demeanour of landowners towards their urban tenants, and that which under the inspiration of more high-minded and public-spirited principles marks their conduct towards their agricultural tenants. There is no doubt that the spirit of greed is unconsciously much more dominant and unrestrained in the former case.

One disastrous result of this is that land which is essential to the free and healthy development of towns is being kept out of the market in order to enhance its value, and that towns are cramped and their people become overcrowded in dwellings which are costly without being comfortable. You have only to buy an ordnance survey map and put together the sheets which include some town of your acquaintance and the land in its immediate vicinity, and you will see at once what I mean. You will find, as a rule, your town or village huddled in one corner of the map, dwellings jammed together as near as the law of the land will permit, with an occasional courtyard, into which the sunshine rarely creeps, but with nothing that would justify the title of "garden." For it is the interest of the landlord to pile together on the land every scrap of bricks and mortar that the law will allow; and yet, outside, are square miles of land unoccupied, or at least rebuilt upon. Land in the town seems to let by the grain, as if it were radium. Not merely towns, but villages (and by villages and towns I mean the people who dwell in them) suffer extremely from the difficulty which is experienced in obtaining land, and by the niggardliness with which sites are measured out.

You cannot help feeling how much healthier and happier the community could have been made in these towns and villages if they had been planned on more spacious and rational principles, with a reasonable allowance of garden for every tenant, which would serve as a playground, as vegetable and flower garden, for the workman and his family, and which would even, in many districts, help materially to solve the problem of unemployment.

The same observations apply to the case of mineral royalties. There, all the expenditure is incurred by the capitalist, who runs the risk of losing his capital, while the miner risks his life; and I do not think it is too much to ask the royalty owner, who has contributed no capital and runs no risk, to share in this emergency in bearing the large burden that is cast upon us for the defence of the country, and to help to pay the large sum of money needed to make provision for social needs, for the aged, and for those who have been engaged in digging out mining royalties all their lives. . . .

This is a War Budget. It is for raising money to wage implacable warfare against poverty and squalidness. I cannot help hoping and believing that before this generation has passed away we shall have advanced a great step towards that good time when poverty, and the wretchedness and human degradation which always follow in its camp will be as remote to the people of this country as the wolves which once infested its forests.

GEORGES SOREL

GEORGES SOREL (1847–1922) was until 1892 a respectable bourgeois, the chief engineer of highways and bridges for the French government and a recipient of a ribbon of the Legion of Honor. After 1892 he devoted himself exclusively to writing, and in 1908 published his best-known work *Reflections on Violence*. Sorel, during his lifetime and since his death, has become many things to many men. He was at one time a defender of Dreyfus but in his later days became a convinced anti-Semite. Content at one time to accept the alliance of democratic and socialist thought, he became eventually an ever more outspoken enemy of democracy; in endeavors to effect an alliance of radicals and reactionaries against democracy, he even became friendly with extreme royalists. Aligned with proletarian groups he nevertheless was not unsympathetic to attempts to translate his philosophy into bourgeois terms. And while Lenin called him "that notorious muddlehead," he looked with favor (though always pessimistically) on the Russian Revolution.

Sorel's philosophy drew on many of the systems of thought current in his day. He regarded Proudhon as a precursor of his moralistic critique of contemporary society. Eduard von Hartmann's philosophy of the unconscious, a compound of Hegel and Schopenhauer, strengthened his belief that capitalism could be understood as the play of blind and irrational forces. Sorel considered the kernel of Marxism to be the conception of class struggle, but believed it important to remove from that idea any claim to scientific prediction of the future. In *Reflections on Violence* Sorel combines key Marxist ideas with an intuitionism borrowed from his contemporary, the idealist philosopher Henri Bergson, by whom he was also very much impressed.

The *Reflections* gave vigorous expression to a syndicalist faith in direct action, the enmity felt towards the state as such, and a regard for placing "the forces of production in the hands of *free men*." Sorel was not seriously involved in the day to day work of rank and file syndicalists, but he was disappointed when the faith in the general strike waned in France. In his last days, he returned for comfort to the "myths" of Christianity. The following passage is from *Reflections on Violence* (Glencoe, Illinois: The Free Press, 1950), translated from the French by T. E. Hulme and J. Roth, and reprinted here with the permission of the publisher.

REFLECTIONS ON VIOLENCE

ACCORDING TO Marx, capitalism, by reason of the innate laws of its own nature, is hurrying along a path which will lead the world of to-day, with the inevitability of the evolution of organic life, to the doors of the world of to-morrow. This movement comprises a long period of capitalistic construction, and it ends by a rapid destruction, which is the work of the proletariat. Capitalism creates the heritage which Socialism will receive, the men who will suppress the present régime, and the means of bringing about this destruction, at the same time that it preserves the results obtained in production. Capitalism begets new ways of working; it throws the working class into revolutionary organizations by the pressure it exercises on wages; it restricts its own political basis by competition, which is constantly eliminating industrial leaders. Thus, after having solved the great problem of the organization of labour, to effect which Utopians have brought forward so many naïve or stupid hypotheses, capitalism provokes the birth of the cause which will overthrow it, and thus renders useless everything that Utopians have written to induce enlightened people to make reforms; and it gradually ruins the traditional order, against which the critics of the idealists had proved themselves to be so deplorably incompetent. . . . Without any co-ordinated plan, without any directive ideas, without any ideal of a future world, it is the cause of an inevitable evolution; it draws from the present all that the present can give towards historical development; it performs in an almost mechanical manner all that is necessary, in order that a new era may appear, and that this new era may break every link with the idealism of the present times, while preserving the acquisitions of the capitalistic economic system.

Socialists should therefore abandon the attempt (initiated by the Utopians) to find a means of inducing the enlightened middle class to prepare the *transition to a more perfect system of legislation;* their sole function is that of explaining to the proletariat the greatness of the revolutionary part they are called upon to play. By ceaseless criticism the proletariat must be brought to perfect their organizations; they must be shown how the embryonic forms which appear in their unions [1] may be developed, so that, finally, they may build up institutions without any parallel in the history of the middle class; that they may form ideas which depend solely on their position as producers in large industries, and which owe nothing to middle-class thought; and that they may acquire *habits of liberty* with which the middle class nowadays are no longer acquainted.

This doctrine will evidently be inapplicable if the middle class and the proletariat do not oppose each other implacably, with all the forces at their disposal; the more ardently capitalist the middle class is, the more the proletariat is full of a warlike spirit and confident of its revolutionary strength,

---

[1] [The French is *sociétés de résistance.* What is meant is the syndicate, considered principally as a means of combining workmen against the employers.—*Trans. Note.*]

the more certain will be the success of the proletarian movement. . . .

It is often urged, in objection to the people who defend the Marxian conception, that it is impossible for them to stop the movement of degeneration which is dragging both the middle class and the proletariat far from the paths assigned to them by Marx's theory. They can doubtless influence the working classes, and it is hardly to be denied that strike violences do keep the revolutionary spirit alive; but how can they hope to give back to the middle class an ardor which is spent?

It is here that the rôle of violence in history appears to us as singularly great, for it can, in an indirect manner, so operate on the middle class as to awaken them to a sense of their own class sentiment. Attention has often been drawn to the danger of certain acts of violence which compromised *admirable social works,* disgusted employers who were disposed to arrange the happiness of their workmen, and developed egoism where the most noble sentiments formerly reigned.

To repay with *black ingratitude* the *benevolence* of those who would protect the workers, to meet with insults the homilies of the defenders of human fraternity, and to reply by blows to the advances of the propagators of social peace—all that is assuredly not in conformity with the rules of fashionable Socialism . . . but it is a very practical way of indicating to the middle class that they must mind their own business and only that.

I believe also that it may be useful to thrash the orators of democracy and the representatives of the Government, for in this way you insure that none shall retain any illusions about the character of acts of violence. But these acts can have historical value only if they are the *clear and brutal expression of the class war:* the middle classes must not be allowed to imagine that, aided by cleverness, social science, or high-flown sentiments, they might find a better welcome at the hands of the proletariat.

The day on which employers perceive that they have nothing to gain by works which promote social peace, or by democracy, they will understand that they have been ill-advised by the people who persuaded them to abandon their trade of creators of productive forces for the noble profession of educators of the proletariat. Then there is some chance that they may get back a part of their energy, and that moderate or conservative economics may appear as absurd to them as they appeared to Marx. In any case, the separation of classes being more clearly accentuated, the proletarian movement will have some chance of developing with greater regularity than to-day. . . .

Every time that we attempt to obtain an exact conception of the ideas behind proletarian violence we are forced to go back to the notion of the general strike. . . .

The *new school,* which calls itself Marxist, Syndicalist, and revolutionary, declared in favor of the idea of the general strike as soon as it became clearly conscious of the true sense of its own doctrine, of the consequences of its activity, and of its own originality. It was thus led to leave the old official, Utopian, and political tabernacles, which hold the general strike in horror, and to launch itself into the true current of the proletarian revolutionary movement; for a long time past the proletariat had made adherence to the principle of the general strike the *test* by means of which the Socialism of the workers was distinguished from that of the amateur revolutionaries.

Parliamentary Socialists can only obtain great influence if they can manage, by the use of a very confused language, to impose themselves on very diverse groups; for example, they must have working-men constituents simple enough to allow themselves to be duped by high-sounding phrases about future collectivism; they are compelled to represent themselves as profound philosophers to stupid middle-class people who wish to appear to be well informed about social questions; it is very necessary also for them to be able to exploit rich people who think that they are earning the gratitude of humanity by taking shares in the enterprises of Socialist politicians. . . .

Against this noisy, garrulous, and lying Socialism, which is exploited by ambitious people of every description, which amuses a few buffoons, and which is admired by decadents—revolutionary Syndicalism takes its stand, and endeavors, on the contrary, to leave nothing in a state of indecision; its ideas are honestly expressed, without trickery and without mental reservations; no attempt is made to dilute doctrines by a stream of confused commentaries. Syndicalism endeavors to employ methods of expression which throw a full light on things, which put them exactly in the place assigned to them by their nature, and which bring out the whole value of the forces in play. Oppositions, instead of being glozed over, must be thrown into sharp relief if we desire to obtain a clear idea of the Syndicalist movement; the groups which are struggling one against the other must be shown as separate and as compact as possible; in short, the movements of the revolted masses must be represented in such a way that the soul of the revolutionaries may receive a deep and lasting impression.

These results could not be produced in any very certain manner by the use of ordinary language; use must be made of a body of images which, *by intuition alone,* and before any considered analyses are made, is capable of evoking as an undivided whole the mass of sentiments which corresponds to the different manifestations of the war undertaken by Socialism against modern society. The Syndicalists solve this problem perfectly, by concentrating the whole of Socialism in the drama of the general strike; there is thus no longer any place for the reconciliation of contraries in the equivocations of the professors; everything is clearly mapped out, so that only one interpretation of Socialism is possible. This method has all the advantages which "integral" knowledge has over analysis, according to the doctrine of Bergson; and perhaps it would not be possible to cite another example which would so perfectly demonstrate the value of the famous professor's doctrines.

The possibility of the actual realization of the general strike has been much discussed; it has been stated that the Socialist war could not be decided in one single battle. To the people who think themselves cautious, practical, and scientific the difficulty of setting great masses of the proletariat in motion at the same moment seems prodigious; they have analyzed the difficulties of detail which such an enormous struggle would present. It is the opinion of the Socialist-sociologists, as also of the politicians, that the general strike is a popular dream, characteristic of the beginnings of a working-class movement; we have had quoted against us the authority of Sidney Webb, who has decreed that the general strike is an illusion of youth, of which the English workers—whom the monopolists of sociology have so often presented to us as the depositaries of the true conception of the working-class movement —soon rid themselves.

That the general strike is not popular in contemporary England, is a poor argument to bring against the historical significance of the idea, for the English are distinguished by an extraordinary lack of understanding of the class war; their ideas have remained very much dominated by medieval influences: the guild, privileged, or at least protected by laws, still seems to them the ideal of working-class organization; it is for England that the term *working-class aristocracy,* as a name for the trades unionists, was invented, and, as a matter of fact, trades unionism does pursue the acquisition of legal privileges. (This is seen, for example, in the efforts made by the trades unions to obtain laws absolving them from the civil responsibilities of their acts.) We might therefore say that the aversion felt by England for the general strike should be looked upon as strong presumptive evidence in favor of the latter by all those who look upon the class war as the essence of Socialism.

Moreover, Sidney Webb enjoys a reputation for competence which is very much exaggerated; all that can be put to his credit is that he has waded through uninteresting blue-books, and has had the patience to compose an extremely indigestible compilation on the history of trades unionism; he has a mind of the narrowest description, which could only impress people unaccustomed to reflection. Those who introduced his fame into France knew nothing at all about Socialism; and if he is really in the first rank of contemporary authors of economic history, as his translator affirms, it is because the intellectual level of these historians is rather low; moreover, many examples show us that it is possible to be a most illustrious professional historian and yet possess a mind something less than mediocre.

Neither do I attach any importance to the objections made to the general strike based on considerations of a practical order. The attempt to construct hypotheses about the nature of the struggles of the future and the means of suppressing capitalism, on the model furnished by history, is a return to the old methods of the Utopists. There is no process by which the future can be predicted scientifically, nor even one which enables us to discuss whether one hypothesis about it is better than another; it has been proved by too many memorable examples that the greatest men have committed prodigious errors in thus desiring to make predictions about even the least distant future. (The errors committed by Marx are numerous and sometimes enormous. . . .)

And yet without leaving the present, without reasoning about this future, which seems for ever condemned to escape our reason, we should be unable to act at all. Experience shows that the *framing of a future, in some indeterminate time,* may, when it is done in a certain way, be very effective, and have very few inconveniences; this happens when the anticipations of the future take the form of those myths, which enclose with them, all the strongest inclinations of a people, of a party or of a class, inclinations which recur to the mind with the insistence of instincts in all the circumstances of life; and which give an aspect of complete reality to the hopes of immediate action by which, more easily than by any other method, men can reform their desires, passions, and mental activity. We know, moreover, that these social myths in no way prevent a man profiting by the observations which he makes in the course of his life, and form no obstacle to the pursuit of his normal occupations. (It has so often been remarked that English or American sectarians whose religious exaltation was fed by the apocalyptic myths were often none the less very practical men.)

The truth of this may be shown by numerous examples.

The first Christians expected the return of Christ and the total ruin of the pagan world, with the inauguration of the kingdom of the saints, at the end of the first generation. The catastrophe did not come to pass, but Christian thought profited so greatly from the apocalyptic myth that certain contemporary scholars maintain that the whole preaching of Christ referred solely to this one point. The hopes which Luther and Calvin had formed of the religious exaltation of Europe were by no means realized; these fathers of the Reformation very soon seemed men of a past era; for present-day Protestants they belong rather to the Middle Ages than to modern times, and the problems which troubled them most occupy very little place in contemporary

Protestantism. Must we for that reason deny the immense result which came from their dreams of Christian renovation? It must be admitted that the real developments of the Revolution did not in any way resemble the enchanting pictures which created the enthusiasm at its first adepts; but without those pictures would the Revolution have been victorious? Many Utopias were mixed up with the Revolutionary myth, because it had been formed by a society passionately fond of imaginative literature, full of confidence in the "science," and very little acquainted with the economic history of the past. These Utopias came to nothing; but it may be asked whether the Revolution was not a much more profound transformation than those dreamed of by the people who in the eighteenth century had invented social Utopias. In our own times Mazzini pursued what the wiseacres of his time called a mad chimera; but it can no longer be denied that, without Mazzini, Italy would never have become a great power, and that he did more for Italian unity than Cavour and all the politicians of his school.

A knowledge of what the myths contain in the way of details which will actually form part of the history of the future is then of small importance; they are not astrological almanacs; it is even possible that nothing which they contain will ever come to pass,—as was the case with the catastrophe expected by the first Christians. In our own daily life, are we not familiar with the fact that what actually happens is very different from our preconceived notion of it? And that does not prevent us from continuing to make resolutions. Psychologists say that there is heterogeneity between the ends in view and the ends actually realized: the slightest experience of life reveals this law to us, which Spencer transferred into nature, to extract therefrom his theory of the multiplication of effects.

The myth must be judged as a means of acting on the present; any attempt to discuss how far it can be taken literally as future history is devoid of sense. *It is the myth in its entirety which is alone important:* its parts are only of interest in so far as they bring out the main idea. No useful purpose is served, therefore, in arguing about the incidents which may occur in the course of a social war, and about the decisive conflicts which may give victory to the proletariat; even supposing the revolutionaries to have been wholly and entirely deluded in setting up this imaginary picture of the general strike, this picture may yet have been, in the course of the preparation for the Revolution, a great element of strength, if it has embraced all the aspirations of Socialism, and if it has given to the whole body of Revolutionary thought a precision and a rigidity which no other method of thought could have given.

To estimate, then, the significance of the idea of the general strike, all the methods of discussion which are current among politicians, sociologists, or people with pretensions to political science, must be abandoned. Everything which its opponents endeavor to establish may be conceded to them, without reducing in any way the value of the theory which they think they have refuted. The question whether the general strike is a partial reality, or only a product of popular imagination, is of little importance. All that it is necessary to know is, whether the general strike contains everything that the Socialist doctrine expects of the revolutionary proletariat.

To solve this question we are no longer compelled to argue learnedly about the future; we are not obliged to indulge in lofty reflections about philosophy, history, or economics; we are not on the plane of theories, and we can remain on the level of observable facts. We have to question men who take a very active part in the real revolutionary movement amidst the proletariat, men who do not aspire to climb into the middle class and whose mind is not dominated by corporative prejudices. These men may be deceived about an infinite number of political, economical, or moral questions; but their testimony is decisive, sovereign, and irrefutable when it is a question of knowing what are the ideas which most powerfully move them and their comrades, which most appeal to them as being identical with their socialistic conceptions, and thanks to which their reason, their hopes, and their way of looking at particular facts seem to make but one indivisible unity.

Thanks to these men, we know that the general strike is indeed what I have said: the *myth* in which Socialism is wholly comprised, *i.e.,* a body of images capable of evoking instinctively all the sentiments which correspond to the different manifestations of the war undertaken by Socialism against modern society. Strikes have engendered in the proletariat the noblest, deepest, and most moving sentiments that they possess; the general strike groups them all in a co-ordinated picture, and, by bringing them together, gives to each one of them its maximum of intensity; appealing to their painful memories of particular conflicts, it colors with an intense life all the details of the composition presented to consciousness. We thus obtain that intuition of Socialism which language cannot give us with perfect clearness—and we obtain it as a whole, perceived instantaneously. . . .

[The] class war . . . is the point of departure for all Socialistic thought and stands in such great need of elucidation, since sophists have endeavored to give a false idea of it.

Marx speaks of society as if it were divided into two fundamentally antagonistic groups; observation, it has often been urged, does not justify this division, and it is true that a certain effort of will is necessary before we can find it verified in the phenomena of everyday life.

The organization of a capitalistic workshop furnishes a first approximation, and piece-work plays an essential part in the formation of the class idea; in fact, it throws into relief the very clear opposition of interest about the price of commodities; the workers feel themselves under the thumb of the employers in the same way that peasants feel themselves in the power of the merchants and the money-lenders of the towns; history shows that no economic opposition has been more clearly felt than the latter; since civilization has existed, country and town have formed two hostile camps. Piece-work also shows that in the wage-earning world there is a group of men somewhat analogous to the retail shopkeepers, possessing the confidence of the employer, and not belonging to the proletariat class.

The strike throws a new light on all this; it separates the interests and the different ways of thinking of the two groups of wage-earners—the foremen, clerks, engineers, etc., as contrasted with the workmen who alone go on strike—much better than the daily circumstances of life do; it then becomes clear that the administrative group has a natural tendency to become a little aristocracy; for these people, State Socialism would be advantageous, because they would go up one in the social hierarchy.

MAX WEBER

THE NAME OF Max Weber (1864–1920) is preeminent among an extraordinary group of German social scientists of the era before the First World War. His father was a prominent well-to-do member of the National Liberal party and a Reichstag member under Bismarck. Weber inherited from him a lifelong interest in political affairs which he combined with a brilliant academic career. Raised and educated in Berlin for the bar, his first teaching post was at the University of Berlin. Thereafter he held high posts in economics at Freiburg, Heidelberg, and Munich. Constantly plagued by poor health from his early days at Heidelberg, he nevertheless was able to write many essays and longer studies of which the most famous is *The Protestant Ethic and the Spirit of Capitalism* (1904–5).

Weber knew intimately many of the important political figures of his time and often served as their adviser. His most notable political labors came at the end of the war when he helped draft a memorandum denying German war guilt at the Paris Peace Conference, and later when he exercised a strong voice in the preliminary work on the Weimar Constitution.

Weber was intellectually antipathetic to the traditions of German idealist philosophy and to the concern of his contemporaries with narrow historical fact. Early in his academic career he developed strong sympathies for Marxism, but then abandoned its emphasis on the paramount importance of economic forces in history and began to stress instead the interplay of army, bureaucracy, economy, and religion. His study of the influence of Calvinism on the growth of capitalism was, in fact, the first part of an incomplete three-volume work on the relation of various religious movements to economic organization.

Although humane and progressive in his political beliefs, Weber was skeptical that there were any inherently liberating tendencies in the growth of modern science, industry, and the secular bureaucratic state. A cautious liberalism is the underlying personal creed in most of his topical works. The combination of this faith with his typical dramatic generalizations can be found in this selection from Weber's essay, "On the Status of Middle-Class Democracy in Russia" (1906), inspired by the Russian Revolution of 1905 and published in the *Archiv für Sozialwissenschaft und Sozialpolitik*. This portion of that essay has been translated by Benjamin K. Bennett for this volume and has been specially titled.

THE NEW DESPOTISM

THE DEVELOPMENT of capitalism [in Russia] will effect the destruction of "folk" Romanticism, whose place for the most part will doubtless be taken by

Marxism. But the latter's intellectual tools are entirely unequal to the pressing and fundamental agrarian problem, and it is precisely the encounter with this problem that can draw the two factions of the intelligentsia together again. The challenge can clearly be met only through the organs of self-government, and for this reason alone it seems that, in order to survive, Liberalism must find its calling, now as before, in struggling against bureaucratic as well as Jacobin *centralism,* and in striving to fill the masses with the basic individualistic idea of the "inalienable rights of men,"—which idea has become as matter-of-fact to us west Europeans as black bread is to the man who has plenty to eat.

Just as they do not indicate a *single* social and economic program, neither are these individualistic axioms of "natural law" produced *exclusively* by a *single* set of economic conditions—least of all by "modern" conditions.

Quite the contrary: as much as the fight for such "individualistic" values has to reckon at every step with the "material" conditions of its environment—so much the less can their "realization" be left to "economic development." The chances for "democracy" or "individualism" would be very poor if we relied for their development upon the "automatic" workings of *material* interests. For these interests tend, as obviously as one could desire, in the opposite direction: in the American "benevolent feudalism," in the German so-called "welfare measures," in the Russian factory system—everywhere has been erected *the shell of the new despotism:* and it requires only, in order to finally be filled and completed, that the masses be rendered docile by the slowing of technological-economic "progress" and the victory of "revenue" over "profit" in connection with the eventual exhaustion of "free" land and "free" markets. At the same time, increasing complexity of economic management, partial nationalization and municipalization and the territorial extent of populations all continually create new paperwork, further specialization and division of labor, and job-training in government —in other words, a caste system. Those American workers who were *against* the "Civil Service Reform" knew what they were about: they would rather have been managed by ambitious climbers of doubtful morals then by a hallowed society of mandarins—but their protest is futile. . . .

In the face of this fact, let those who live in constant fear that there could be in the future *too much* "democracy" and "individualism" and too little "authority," "aristocracy," "respect for office" and such like, let them finally calm themselves; it is all too inevitable that the trees of democratic individualism shall not grow to heaven. All experience teaches us that "history" relentlessly produces new "aristocracies" and "authorities" to which whoever finds it necessary for himself—or for the "people"—can cling.

If it were *only* a question of "material" conditions and of the constellations of interest "created" by them, then any sober observer would have to say: all economic signs forecast increasing "un-freedom." It is completely ridiculous to ascribe to present-day capitalism, as it is imported in Russia and exists in America,—to ascribe to this "inevitability" of our economic development—a natural affinity for "democracy" or, as some go so far as to assert, "freedom" (in some sense or other of the word), when after all the real question can only be: under capitalism, are these things at all "possible?" In fact they are possible only where the definite *will* of a nation, not to let itself be run like a herd of sheep, constantly supports them. We are "individualists" and partisans of "democratic" institutions in that we strive "against the stream" of material circumstances. Whoever would be a weather-vane for "developmental tendencies," let him, as quickly as possible, forsake these old-fashioned ideals.

The historical growth of modern "freedom" had unique, never-to-be-repeated circumstances as a precondition. Let us enumerate the most important.

First, Transoceanic expansion: in the armies of Cromwell, in the French Constituent Assembly, still today in our entire economic life, this wind is blowing from across the sea:—but there are no longer any new continents for expansion. It is the great land masses, North America on one side and Russia on the other, toward whose monotonous plains, so conducive to being parcelled out, the bulk of the civilized West's population increasingly tends, as once before in late antiquity.

Second, the peculiar economic and social structure of the "early capitalist" epoch in Western Europe; and third, the victory of science over existence, the "self-realization of the spirit." But the rational ordering of objective existence has today, doubtless after the destruction of innumerable "values," at least "in principle" done its work. The increasingly uniform way of life, going hand in hand with "standardization" of production, is, under the present conditions of "commercial" existence, the universal result of this ordering,—and "science" as such is today creating no more "universal personality." . . .

Finally: certain ideal notions of value which grew out of the concrete historical character of an established set of religious conceptions and which, working together with many equally characteristic political constellations and with the above-mentioned material preconditions, formed the "ethical" character and the "cultural values" of modern man.

Can any material development as such, especially the present-day late-capitalist development, preserve or even perhaps create anew these unique historical conditions? This question need only be posed in order to be answered. Not a shadow of probability indicates that economic "socialization" as such must bear in its womb the development of either essentially "free" personalities or "altruistic" ideals. Are we supposed to find the germ of something like this among those who, in their opinion, will be carried to inevitable victory by "material development?" A "correct" Social-Democracy drills into the masses a spiritual parade march, and prods them not toward the eternal paradise (which, in Puritanism, *also* had many quite respectable services to offer in the cause of temporal "freedom") but toward the temporal paradise,—and, in so doing, turns this paradise into a sort of protective vaccination for those interested in the *status quo*. It accustoms its wards to docility before dogmas and party-authority, it accustoms them to the futile spectacle of the mass-strike and to the sedentary pleasure of listening to the unnerving shrieks of their journalistic prebendaries, which noise, however, in the eyes of its opponent, is as harmless as it is ultimately silly,—it accustoms them, in short, to a "hysterical affective enjoyment," which both replaces and represses all economic or political thought and action. In this barren soil, after the "eschatological" era of the movement has passed and generation after generation has clenched its fists in its pocket or bared its teeth toward heaven, only spiritual numbness can grow.

And yet, the time presses us "to act while the day lasts." For the problem will remain open only during the next few generations, only so long as economic and spiritual "revolution," much-reviled "anarchy" in production and equally reviled "subjectivism" maintain an unbroken existence. By means of these movements, and *only* by means of them, can the life of the huge masses be made self-dependent. Whatever, in the way of "inalienable" rights of personality and freedom, is not won while these movements last, will then, when the world has once become economically "full" and intellectually "sated," will then perhaps never be won. Perhaps: so far, at least, as our feeble eyes can penetrate the obscuring mists of man's future. . . .

No matter how strong the retrogressions of the near future, Russia is entering upon the path of specifically European development: the mighty influx of Western ideas is destroying both patriarchal and communal conservatism here, just as, conversely, the mighty immigration of Europeans, and specifically east Europeans, into the United States is at work undermining there the old democratic traditions—both of which movements are supported by the forces of capitalism. Despite the tremendous difference between them, the economic natures of capitalist development in both of these "communizing" population reservoirs are, in many respects, comparable (which idea admits of expansion sometime in the future). The emancipation from the "historical," especially, is in both cases inescapable and fits with the "continental" character of the nearly boundless geographical stage. Upon both developments, however,—and this is the more important comparison—depends the same thing: in a certain sense, both are perhaps "last chances" for the erection, "from the ground up," of "free" cultures. —"Millennia passed before you began life, and still more millennia await silently what you will do with that life,"—this thought, which Carlyle's passionate belief in personality would cry out to each new human being, can be applied without exaggeration not only to the present situation of the United States but also to that of Russia: Russia, partly as she is now and partly as she evidently will be after another generation. Therefore, leaving aside all differences in national character and—let us admit them—in national interest, we cannot but look with deep emotion and sympathy upon the fight for freedom in Russia and its fighters—of whatever "leaning" or "class" they may be.

JOHN A. HOBSON

J. A. HOBSON (1858–1940) was among those European socialists who, even before Lenin, analyzed the nature of modern imperialism. An Englishman, he became an economist and socialist early in life, and is known as one of the pioneers of "welfare economics." He published many books on subjects other than imperialism and economic policy.

Hobson shared with writers like Lenin the now classic, and still popular, view that after 1870 the fundamental cause of imperialism was a deliberately sought expansion of Western capitalism overseas. He differed from Lenin by hoping that moral suasion and peaceful reform might turn the West from what seemed its ruinous course.

Despite its seeming plausibility, Hobson's analysis does not square with the facts. Imperialism after 1870 was initially an enthusiasm of Western conservative and landed political parties; it was not the demand of industrialists. It did not have economic sources exclusively but was adopted at first as a political device to win votes and glories of empire for groups in the West losing prestige and power at home at the hands of challenging industrial and working-class forces. Trade undoubtedly followed the flag, however unevenly, but available evidence suggests that industrial and finance capital did not push Europe into its last round of imperial adventures or even into the First World War.

By 1902, when Hobson published the first edition of *Imperialism,* the major European powers and the United States were cutting up the untaken regions of the world into spheres of influence. The rivalry for empire dangerously increased antagonism between the nations but in areas like China, Persia, the Sudan, and elsewhere, where rival Western powers clashed, accommodations were often worked out. It is noteworthy that when general war broke out in 1914 it was over an issue in Europe and involved, most directly, three of the least industrialized European nations.

By 1914 few areas of the world were left for claims by Western powers. By 1918 the high tide of Western power in the non-Western world had passed. During the war the forces that eventually brought colonial nations their freedom were set in more rapid motion, but did not come to their final results until a generation or two later.

This selection is from Hobson's *Imperialism* (London: Nisbet, 1902).

IMPERIALISM

THE POLITICAL SIGNIFICANCE OF IMPERIALISM

The curious ignorance which prevails regarding the political character and tendencies of Imperialism cannot be better illustrated than by the following passage from a learned work upon "The History of Colonization":

The extent of British dominion may perhaps be better imagined than described, when the fact is appreciated that, of the entire land surface of the globe, approximately one-fifth is actually or theoretically under that flag, while more than one-sixth of all the human beings living in this planet reside under one or the other type of English colonization. The names by which authority is exerted are numerous, and processes are distinct, but the goals to which this manifold mechanism is working are very similar. According to the climate, the natural conditions and the inhabitants of the regions affected, procedure and practice differ. The means are adapted to the situation: there is not any irrevocable, immutable line of policy: from time to time, from decade to decade, English statesmen have applied different treatments to the same territory. Only one fixed rule of action seems to exist; it is to promote the interests of the colony to the utmost, to develop its scheme of government as rapidly as possible, and eventually to elevate it from the position of inferiority to that of association. Under the charm of this beneficent spirit the chief colonial establishments of Great Britain have already achieved substantial freedom, without dissolving nominal ties; the other subordinate possessions are aspiring to it, while, on the other hand, this privilege of local independence has enabled England to assimilate with ease many feudatory States into the body politic of her system.

Here then is the theory that Britons are a race endowed, like the Romans, with a genius for government, that our colonial and imperial policy is animated by a resolve to spread throughout the world the arts of free self-government which we enjoy at home, and that in truth we are accomplishing this work.

Now, without discussing here the excellencies or the defects of the British theory and practice of representative self-government, to assert that our "fixed rule of action" has been to educate our dependencies in this theory and practice is quite the largest misstatement of the facts of our colonial and imperial policy that is possible. Upon the vast majority of the populations throughout our Empire we have bestowed no real powers of self-government, nor have we any serious intention of doing so, or any serious belief that it is possible for us to do so.

Of the three hundred and sixty-seven millions of British subjects outside these isles, not more than eleven millions, or one in thirty-four, have any real self-government for purposes of legislation and administration.

Political freedom, and civil freedom, so far as it rests upon the other, are simply non-existent for the overwhelming majority of British subjects. In the self-governing colonies of Australasia and North America alone is responsible representative government a reality, and even there considerable populations of outlanders, as in West Australia, or servile labour, as in Queensland, have tempered the genuineness of democracy. In Cape Colony and Natal events testify how feebly the forms and even the spirit of the free British institutions have taken root in States where the great majority of the population were always excluded from political rights. The franchise and the rights it carries remain virtually a white monopoly in so-called self-governing colonies, where the coloured population was, in 1903, to the white as four to one and ten to one respectively. . . .

The overwhelming majority of the subjects of the British Empire are under Crown colony government, or under protectorates. In neither case do they enjoy any of the important political rights of British citizens; in neither case are they being trained in the arts of free British institutions. In the Crown colony the population exercises no political privileges. The governor, appointed by the Colonial office, is absolute, alike for legislation and administration; he is aided by a council of local residents usually chosen by himself or by home authority, but its function is merely advisory, and its advice can be and frequently is ignored. In the vast protectorates we have assumed in Africa and Asia there is no tincture of British representative government; the British factor consists in arbitrary acts of irregular interference with native government. Exceptions to this exist in the case of districts assigned to Chartered Companies, where business men, animated avowedly by business ends, are permitted to exercise arbitrary powers of government over native populations under the imperfect check of some British Imperial Commissioner.

Again, in certain native and feudatory States of India our Empire is virtually confined to government of foreign relations, military protection, and a veto upon grave internal disorder, the real administration of the countries being left in the hands of native princes or headmen. However excellent this arrangement may be, it lends little support to the general theory of the British Empire as an educator of free political institutions.

Where British government is real, it does not carry freedom or self-government; where it does carry a certain amount of freedom and self-government, it is not real. Not five per cent of the population of our Empire are possessed of any appreciable portion of the political and civil liberties which are the basis of British civilization. Outside the eleven millions of British subjects in Canada, Australia, and New Zealand, no considerable body is endowed with full self-government in the more vital matters, or being "elevated from the position of inferiority to that of association." . . .

The present condition of the government under which the vast majority of our fellow-subjects in the Empire live is eminently un-British in that it is based, not on the consent of the governed, but upon the will of imperial officials; it does indeed betray a great variety of forms, but they agree in the essential of un-freedom. Nor is it true that any of the more enlightened methods of administration we employ are directed towards undoing this character. Not only in India, but in the West Indies, and wherever there exists a large preponderance of coloured population, the trend, not merely of ignorant, but of enlightened public opinion, is against a genuinely representative government on British lines. It is perceived to be incompatible with the economic and social authority of a superior race. . . .

II

Now this large expansion of British political despotism is fraught with reactions upon home politics which are deserving of most serious consideration. A curious blindness seems to beset the mind of the average educated Briton when he is asked to picture to himself our colonial Empire. Almost instinctively he visualises Canada, Australasia, and South Africa—the rest he virtually ignores. Yet the Imperialism which is our chief concern, the expansion of the last quarter of the nineteenth century, has nothing in common with Canada and Australasia, and very little with "white man's Africa."

When Lord Rosebery uttered his famous words about "a free, tolerant and unaggressive Empire," he can scarcely have had in mind our vast encroachments in West and Central Africa, in the Soudan, on the Burmese frontier, or in Matabeleland. But the distinction between genuine Colonialism and Imperialism, important in itself, is vital when we consider their respective relations to domestic policy.

Modern British colonialism has been no drain upon our material and moral resources, because it has made for the creation of free white democracies, a policy of informal federation, of decentralisation, involving no appreciable strain upon the governmental faculties of Great Britain. Such federation, whether it remains informal with the slight attachment of imperial sovereignty which now exists, or voluntarily takes some more formal shape, political or financial, may well be regarded as a source of strength, political and military.

Imperialism is the very antithesis of this free, wholesome colonial connection, making, as it ever does, for greater complications of foreign policy, greater centralisation of power, and a congestion of business which ever threatens to absorb and overtax the capacity of parliamentary government.

The true political nature of Imperialism is best seen by confronting it with the watchwords of progress accepted in the middle of the nineteenth century by moderate men of both great parties in the State, though with interpretations, varying in degree—peace, economy, reform, and popular self-government. Even now we find no formal abandonment of the principles of government these terms express, and a large section of professed Liberals believe or assert that Imperialism is consistent with the maintenance of all these virtues.

This contention, however, is belied by facts. The decades of Imperialism have been prolific in wars; most of these wars have been directly motived by aggression of white races upon "lower races," and have issued in the forcible seizure of territory. Every one of the steps of expansion in Africa, Asia, and the Pacific has been accompanied by bloodshed; each imperialist Power keeps an increasing army available for foreign service; rectification of frontiers, punitive expeditions, and other euphemisms for war have been in incessant progress. The Pax Britannica, always an impudent falsehood, has become a grotesque monster of hypocrisy; along our Indian frontiers, in West Africa, in the Soudan, in Uganda, in Rhodesia fighting has been well-nigh incessant. Although the great imperialist Powers kept their hands off one another, save where the rising empire of the United States found its opportunity in the falling empire of Spain, the self-restraint has been costly and precarious. Peace as a national policy is antagonized not merely by war, but by militarism, an even graver injury. Apart from the enmity of France and Germany, the main cause of the vast armaments which have drained the resources of most European countries is their conflicting interests in territorial and commercial expansion. Where thirty years ago there existed one sensitive spot in our relations with France, or Germany, or Russia, there are a dozen now; diplomatic strains are of almost monthly occurrence between Powers with African or Chinese interests, and the chiefly business nature of the national antagonisms renders them more dangerous, inasmuch as the policy of Governments passes under the influence of distinctively financial juntos.

The contention of the *si pacem vis para bellum* (if you wish peace prepare for war) school, that armaments alone constitute the best security for peace, is based upon the assumption that a genuine lasting antagonism of real interests exists between the various peoples who are called upon to undergo this monstrous sacrifice.

Our economic analysis has disclosed the fact that it is only the interests of competing cliques of business men—investors, contractors, export manufacturers, and certain professional classes—that are antagonistic; that these cliques, usurping the authority and voice of the people, use the public resources to push their private interests, and spend the blood and money of the people in this vast and disastrous military game, feigning national antagonisms which have no basis in reality. It is not to the interest of the British people, either as producers of wealth or as tax-payers, to risk a war with Russia and France in order to join Japan in preventing Russia from seizing Corea; but it may serve the interests of a group of commercial politicians to promote this dangerous policy. The South African war, openly fomented by gold speculators for their private purposes, will rank in history as a leading case of this usurpation of nationalism. . . . The patent admitted fact that, as a result of imperial competition, an ever larger proportion of the time, energy, and money of "imperialist" nations is absorbed by naval and military armaments, and that no check upon further absorption is regarded as practicable by Imperialists, brings "militarism" into the forefront of practical politics. Great Britain and the United States, which have hitherto congratulated themselves on escaping the militarism of continental Europe, are now rapidly succumbing. Why? Does any one suggest that either nation needs a larger army for the protection of its own lands or of any of its genuine white settlements in other lands? Not at all. It is not pretended that the militarization of England is required for such protective work. Australia and New Zealand are not threatened by any power, nor could a British army render them adequate assistance if they were; equally impotent would British land forces be against the only Power which could conceivably attack our Canadian Dominion; even South Africa, which lies on the borderland between colony and tropical dependency, cannot ultimately be secured by the military power of England. It is our mistaken annexation of tropical and sub-tropical territories, and the attempt to govern "lower races," that is driving us down the steep road to militarism. . . .

Imperialism—whether it consists in a further policy of expansion or in the rigorous maintenance of all those vast tropical lands which have been earmarked as British spheres of influence—implies militarism now and ruinous wars in the future. This truth is now for the first time brought sharply and nakedly before the mind of the nation. The kingdoms of the earth are to be ours on condition that we fall down and worship Moloch. . . .

So far, I have regarded the issue on its narrowly economic side. Far more important are the political implications of militarism. These strike at the very root of popular liberty and the ordinary civic virtues. A few plain reflections serve to dispel the sophistical vapours which are used to form a halo round the life of the soldier. *Respice finem.* There exists an absolute antagonism between the activity of the good citizen and that of the soldier. The end of the soldier is not, as is sometimes falsely said, to die for his country; it is to kill for his country. In as far as he dies he is a failure; his work is to kill, and he attains perfection as a soldier when he becomes a perfect killer. This end, the slaughter of one's fellow-men, forms a professional character, alien from, and antagonistic to, the character of our ordinary citizen, whose work conduces to the preservation of his fellow-men. If it be contended that this final purpose, though informing and moulding the structure and functions of an army, operates but seldom and slightly upon the consciousness of the individual soldier, save upon the battlefield, the answer is that, in the absence from consciousness of this end, the entire routine of the soldier's life, his drill, parades, and whole military exercise, is a useless, purposeless activity, and that these qualities exercise a hardly less degrading influence on character than the conscious intention of killing his fellowmen. . . .

The order and progress of Great Britain during the nineteenth century was secured by the cultivation and practice of the ordinary civic and industrial virtues, assisted by certain advantages of natural resources and historical contingencies. Are we prepared to substitute the military code of ethics or to distract the national mind and conduct by a perpetual conflict of two warring principles, the one making for the evolution of the good citizen, the other for the evolution of the good soldier?

Ignoring, for the present, the distinctively moral degradation of this reversion from industrial to military ethics, we cannot but perceive that the damage done to commercial morality must react disastrously upon the wealth-producing power of the nation, and sap the roots of imperial expenditure.

But one loophole of escape from this dilemma presents itself, an escape fraught with still graver peril. The new Imperialism has been, we have seen, chiefly concerned with tropical and sub-tropical countries where large "lower races" are brought under white control. Why should Englishmen fight the defensive or offensive wars of this Empire, when cheaper, more numerous, and better-assimilated fighting material can be raised upon the spot, or transferred from one tropical dominion to another? As the labour of industrial development of tropical resources is put upon the "lower races" who reside there, under white superintendence, why should not militarism be organized upon the same basis, black or brown or yellow men, to whom military discipline will be "a wholesome education," fighting for the British Empire under British officers? Thus can we best economize our own limited military material, keeping most of it for home defence. This simple solution —the employment of cheap foreign mercenary armies—is no new device. The organization of vast native forces, armed with "civilized" weapons, drilled on "civilized" methods, and commanded by "civilized" officers, formed one of the most conspicuous features of the latest stages of the great Eastern Empires, and afterwards of the Roman Empire. It has proved one of the most perilous devices of parasitism, by which a metropolitan population entrusts the defence of its lives and possessions to the precarious fidelity of "conquered races," commanded by ambitious pro-consuls. . . .

This mode of militarism, while cheaper and easier in the first instance implies less and less control from Great Britain. Though reducing the strain of militarism upon the population at home, it enhances the risks of wars, which become more frequent and more barbarous in proportion as they involve to a less degree the lives of Englishmen. The expansion of our Empire under the new Imperialism has been compassed by setting the "lower races" at one another's throats, fostering tribal animosities and utilising for our supposed benefit the savage propensities of the peoples to whom we have a mission to carry Christianity and civilization.

That we do not stand alone in this ignominious policy does not make it better, rather worse, offering terrible prophetic glimpses into a not distant future, when the horrors of our eighteenth century struggle with France in North America and India may be revived upon a gigantic scale, and Africa and Asia may furnish huge cock-pits for the struggles of black and yellow armies representing the imperialist rivalries of Christendom. The present tendencies of Imperialism plainly make in this direction, involving in their recoil a degradation of Western States and a possible débâcle of Western civilization.

In any event Imperialism makes for war and for militarism, and has brought a great and limitless increase of expenditure of national resources upon armaments. It has impaired the independence of every nation which has yielded to its false glamour. Great Britain no longer possesses a million pounds which it can call its own; its entire financial resources are mortgaged to a policy to be dictated by Germany, France, or Russia. A move from any of these Powers can force us to expend upon more battleships and military preparations the money we had designed to use for domestic purposes. The priority and reckless magnitude of our imperial expansion has made the danger of an armed coalition of great Powers against us no idle chimera.

The development of their resources along the lines of the new industrialism, on the one hand, by driving them to seek foreign markets, brings them in all parts of the world against the vexatious barriers of British possessions; on the other, has furnished them with ample means of public expenditure. The spread of modern industrialism tends to place our "rivals" on a level with ourselves in their public resources. Hence, at the very time when we have more reason to fear armed coalition than formerly, we are losing that superiority in finance which made it feasible for us to maintain a naval armament superior to any European combination.

All these perils in the present and the future are the fruits of the new Imperialism, which is thus exposed as the implacable and mortal enemy of Peace and Economy. . . .

Every important social reform, even if it does not directly involve large public expenditure, causes financial disturbances and risks which are less tolerable at times when public expenditure is heavy and public credit fluctuating and embarrassed. Most social reforms involve some attack on vested interests, and these can best defend themselves when active Imperialism absorbs public attention. When legislation is involved, economy of time and of governmental interest is of paramount importance. Imperialism, with its "high politics," involving the honour and safety of the Empire, claims the first place, and, as the Empire grows, the number and complexity of its issues, involving close, immediate, continuous attention, grow, absorbing the time of the Government and of Parliament. It becomes more and more impossible to set aside parliamentary time for the full unbroken discussion of matters of most vital domestic importance, or to carry through any large serious measure of reform.

It is needless to labour the theory of this antagonism when the practice is apparent to every student of politics. Indeed, it has become a commonplace of history how Governments use national animosities, foreign wars, and the glamour of empire-making, in order to bemuse the popular mind and divert rising resentment against domestic abuses. The vested interests, which, on our analysis, are shown to be chief prompters of an imperialist policy, play for a double stake, seeking their private commercial and financial gains at the expense and peril of the commonwealth. They at the same time protect their economic and political supremacy at home against movements of popular reform. The city ground landlord, the country squire, the banker, the usurer, and the financier, the brewer, the mine-owner, the ironmaster, the ship-builder, and the shipping trade, the great export manufacturers and merchants, the clergy of the State Church, the universities, and great public schools, the legal trade unions and the services have, both in Great Britain and on the Continent, drawn together for common political resistance against attacks upon the power, the property, and the privileges which in various forms and degrees they represent. Having conceded under pressure the form of political power in the shape of elective institutions and a wide franchise to the masses, they are struggling to prevent the masses from gaining the substance of this power and using it for the establishment of equality of economic opportunities. The collapse of the Liberal party upon the Continent, and now in Great Britain, is only made intelligible in this way. Friends of liberty and of popular government so long as the new industrial and commercial forces were hampered by the economic barriers and the political supremacy of the noblesse and the landed aristocracy, they have come to temper their "trust" of the people by an ever-growing quantity of caution, until within the last two decades they have either sought political fusion with the Conservatives or have dragged on a precarious existence on the strength of a few belated leaders with obsolescent principles. Where Liberalism preserves any real strength, it is because the older struggle for the franchise and the primary liberties has been delayed, as in Belgium and in Denmark, and a modus vivendi has been possible with the rising working-class party. In Germany, France, and Italy the Liberal party as a factor in practical politics has either disappeared or is reduced to impotence; in England it now stands convicted of a gross palpable betrayal of the first conditions of liberty, feebly fumbling after programmes as a substitute for principles. Its leaders, having sold their party to a confederacy of stock gamblers and jingo sentimentalists, find themselves impotent to defend Free Trade, Free Press, Free Schools, Free Speech, or any of the rudiments of ancient Liberalism. They have alienated the confidence of the people. For many years they have been permitted to conduct a sham fight and to call it politics; the people thought it real until the South African war furnished a decisive dramatic test, and the unreality of Liberalism became apparent. It is not that Liberals have openly abandoned the old principles and traditions, but that they have rendered them of no account by dallying with an Imperialism which they have foolishly and futilely striven to distinguish from the firmer brand of their political opponents. This surrender to Imperialism signifies that they have preferred the economic interests of the possessing and speculative classes, to which most of their leaders belong, to the cause of Liberalism. . . .

IV

The antagonism with democracy drives to the very roots of Imperialism as a political principle. Not only is Imperialism used to frustrate those measures of economic reform now recognized as essential to the effectual working of all machinery of popular government, but it operates to paralyse the working of that machinery itself. Representative institutions are ill-adapted for empire, either as regards men or methods. The government of a great heterogeneous medley of lower races by departmental officials in London and their nominated emissaries lies outside the scope of popular knowledge and popular control. The Foreign, Colonial, and Indian Secretaries in Parliament, the permanent officials of the departments, the governors and staff who represent the Imperial Government in our dependencies, are not, and cannot be, controlled directly or effectively by the will of the people. This subordination of the legislative to the executive, and the concentration of executive power in an autocracy, are necessary consequences of the predominance of foreign over domestic politics. The process is attended by a decay of party spirit and party action, and an insistence on the part of the autocracy, whether it be a Kaiser or a Cabinet, that all effective party criticism is unpatriotic and verges on treason. An able writer, discussing the new foreign policy of Germany, summarises the point of view of expansionists: "It is claimed by them that in foreign affairs the nation should stand as one man, that policies once entered upon by the Government should not be repudiated, and that criticism should be avoided as weakening the influence of the nation abroad. . . . It is evident that when the most important concerns of a nation are thus withdrawn from the field of party difference, party government itself must grow weak, as dealing no longer with vital affairs. . . . Thus, as the importance of the executive is enhanced, that of the legislative is lowered, and parliamentary action is looked down upon as the futile and irritating activity of unpractical critics. If the governmental measures are to be adopted inevitably, why not dispense with the irritating delay of parliamentary discussion?" . . .

In Great Britain the weakening of "party" is visibly attended by a decline of the reality of popular control. Just in proportion as foreign and colonial policy bulks more largely in the deliberative and administrative work of the State is government necessarily removed from the real control of the people. It is no mere question of economy of the time and energy of Parliament, though the dwindling proportion of the sessions devoted to consideration of domestic questions represents a corresponding decline of practical democracy. The wound to popular government penetrates far deeper. Imperialism, and the military, diplomatic, and financial resources which feed it, have become so far the paramount considerations of recent Governments that they mould and direct the entire policy, give point, colour and character to the conduct of public affairs, and overawe by continual suggestions of unknown and incalculable gains and perils the nearer and more sober processes of domestic policy. The effect on parliamentary government has been great, quick, and of palpable import, making for the diminution of the power of representative institutions. At elections the electorate is no longer invited to exercise a free, conscious, rational choice between the representatives of different intelligible policies; it is invited to endorse, or to refuse endorsement, to a difficult, intricate, and hazardous imperial and foreign policy, commonly couched in a few well-sounding general phrases, and supported by an appeal to the necessity of solidarity and continuity of national conduct—virtually a blind vote of confidence. In the deliberations of the House of Commons the power of the Opposition to oppose has been seriously and progressively impaired: partly by alteration in the rules of the House, which have diminished the right of full discussion of legislative measures in their several stages, and impaired the privileges of the Commons, viz., the right of discussing grievances upon votes of Supply, and of questioning ministers regarding the conduct of their offices; partly by a forcible encroachment of the Government upon the rights and privileges formerly enjoyed by private members in moving resolutions and in introducing bills. This diminution of the power of opposition is only the first of a series of processes of concentration of power. The Government now claims for its measures the complete disposal of the time of the House whenever it judges such monopoly to be desirable. . . .

Amid this general decline of parliamentary government the "party system" is visibly collapsing, based as it was on plain cleavages in domestic policy which have little significance when confronted with the claims and powers of Imperialism. If the party system is destined to survive in British politics, it can only do so by the consolidation of all sections opposed to the "imperialist" practices to which Liberal as well as Conservative ministries have adhered during recent years. So long as Imperialism is allowed to hold the field, the only real political conflict is between groups representing the divergent branches of Imperialism, the men upon the spot and the Home Government, the Asiatic interests of India and China and the forward policy in Africa, the advocates of a German alliance or a Franco-Russian alliance. . . .

The political effects, actual and necessary, of the new Imperialism, as illustrated in the case of the greatest of imperialist Powers, may be thus summarised. It is a constant menace to peace, by furnishing continual temptations to further aggression upon lands occupied by lower races and by embroiling our nation with other nations of rival imperial ambitions; to the sharp peril of war it adds the chronic danger and degradation of militarism, which not merely wastes the current physical and moral resources of the nations, but checks the very course of civilization. It consumes to an illimitable and incalculable extent the financial resources of a nation by military preparation, stopping the expenditure of the current income of the State upon productive public projects and burdening posterity with heavy loads of debt. Absorbing the public money, time, interest and energy on costly and unprofitable work of territorial aggrandisement, it thus wastes those energies of public life in the governing classes and the nations which are needed for internal reforms and for the cultivation of the arts of material and intellectual progress at home. Finally, the spirit, the policy, and the methods of Imperialism are hostile to the institutions of popular self-government, favouring forms of political tyranny and social authority which are the deadly enemies of effective liberty and equality.

THE HAGUE PEACE CONFERENCES

THE HAGUE Conference of 1907, like its predecessor of 1899, showed the conflicting tendencies at work in the foreign relations of the Western nations. The hopes of men of good will for the peaceful settlement of disputes, for the triumph of law over force, for the reduction of armaments, and for humane policies during war conflicted with the growing stake of the nations in protecting their sovereignty and in surrendering no vital interests to any supernational authority or potential enemies.

The first conference of 1899 had been called, on the surprising initiative of Tsar Nicholas II, to consult on "the advantages of a genuine and lasting peace" and "to fix a limit to the continually increasing growth of armaments." The most notable direct results of the meeting were the establishment of the Permanent Court of Arbitration, called the Hague Tribunal, and the codification of the laws of war and the rules and procedures of arbitration. The extraordinary side-effect of the meeting was to spark world-wide demands for peace by a growing number of peace societies and organizations.

The second conference, eight years later, from whose proceedings the following selection is extracted, met as the European balance of power grew more precarious and the pleas for peace and limitation of arms increased in number and intensity. Like the first meeting, the second came to nothing on matters of vital national interest, for without political security it was apparent that nations would not willingly risk their claims even to impartial adjudications; yet the most hopeful of the partisans of peace at the Hague wanted to transform political conflicts into legal ones.

Despite unsuccessful British and American efforts to secure a convention on compulsory arbitration, the gathering of 1907 completed a reworking of the rules of land and naval warfare covering such matters as the rights of neutrals, the treatment of war prisoners and of occupied territories, and the limits of bombardments. Although a third conference, scheduled for 1916, could not meet because of the bitter war that the earlier conferences had not prevented, the two meetings that were held were the first united international effort in modern times to deal with complex world problems before they exploded into war. Undoubtedly, the Hague meetings also led the way to the greater postwar world organizations for peace.

This selection comes from *The Proceedings of the Hague Peace Conferences, The Conference of 1907* (New York: Carnegie Endowment for International Peace, 1920), Volume I.

THE PROCEEDINGS OF THE HAGUE
PEACE CONFERENCE, 1907

His Excellency Mr. Nelidow takes the presidential chair and delivers the following address:

Gentlemen: Permit me first of all to perform an agreeable duty—to express to you my profound gratitude for the honor which you do me by entrusting me with the direction of your labors.

In seeing the representatives of nearly all constituted States gathered together here in one assembly, I cannot help feeling a great and deep emotion. This is the first time that such a thing has happened, and it was the idea of peace which brought the Governments to delegate from every quarter of the globe the most eminent men of their countries to discuss together the most cherished interests of mankind—conciliation and justice. May I venture to consider this a good omen for the progress of our labors and to express the hope that the same sentiments of concord which have animated the Governments, will likewise prevail among their representatives, and thus contribute to the success of the task which is imposed upon us?

This task, gentlemen, which has been accepted by all the Governments, consists of two parts: on the one hand, we must endeavor to discover a method of settling amicably differences which may arise between States, and thus prevent ruptures and armed conflict. On the other hand, we must endeavor to lighten the burdens of war—in case it breaks out—both as regards the combatants and those who may be indirectly affected by it. These two problems have sometimes appeared to be incompatible. When during the war of secession in the United States, a professor—Dr. Lieber, I believe— drew up a plan of instructions to commanders of troops occupying enemy territory and to the local authorities of the occupied territory, with a view to lessening the difficulties of both and the burdens of this abnormal condition of affairs, I heard the opinion expressed that it was absolutely wrong to endeavor to alleviate the horrors of war. "To make war short and infrequent," I was told, "the inhabitants of the countries engaged in it must be made to feel its full burden, so that they will seek to end it as soon as possible and be loth to begin again." It seems to me, gentlemen, that this notion is absolutely specious. The horrors of the conflicts in ancient times and the wars of the Middle Ages lessened neither their length nor their frequency, whilst the alleviating regulations, which were adopted in the second half of the last century, for the carrying on of war, for the treatment of prisoners and wounded, and, in short, the whole series of humanitarian measures—

which were the honor of the First Peace Conference, and which are to be completed by the labors we are beginning—have in nowise contributed to a development of a taste for war. On the contrary, they have spread throughout the whole civilized world a sentiment of international amenity and have created a peaceable current which reveals itself in the manifestations of sympathy with which public opinion welcomes and will, I hope, accompany our labors. We shall therefore have to persevere in this respect along the road opened by our predecessors of 1899.

As for the other part of our task—the means of preventing and avoiding conflicts between States—it seems to me unnecessary to dwell upon the services which the institutions and provisions established by the First Conference have already rendered to the cause of peace and law. The opinion has been expressed that the differences adjusted as a result of the First Hague Conference were no more important than what might be called international "justice of the peace" cases. Well! gentlemen, justices of the peace render important services to public order and tranquility. They settle private quarrels amicably and help to keep the atmosphere calm by removing petty causes of irritation between individuals, which by accumulating sometimes produce serious hostility. It is the same with nations. It is by preventing trifling dissensions in their relations that the way is prepared for good understanding when greater interests are at stake. The official recognition of arbitration has already created a disposition on the part of the various States to have recourse to it for settling disputes in a field whose boundaries are constantly growing wider. Thus, since 1899 thirty-three arbitration conventions have been concluded between different States. But, more than that, four serious and complicated cases, capable of creating irritation between the Powers, have been brought before the Hague Court of Arbitration. Likewise the commission of inquiry created by the act of 1899 was, as everybody remembers, called upon to take up a most serious case, which without this fortunate Convention might have had the most dangerous consequences.

Therefore, gentlemen, we can look with respect upon the results of our predecessors' activity at the Hague. They should encourage us to persevere in the work already accomplished and to give it a broader development. All the friends of civilization follow with sympathetic interest the progress of international institutions emanating from the First Hague Conference, and a generous citizen of the United States has even made gift of a fortune to erect here a sumptuous palace, where the Peace Conference may have a permanent home. It is our duty to make them worthy of this act of munificence. We can in this way show our gratitude to Mr. Carnegie.

However, let us not be too ambitious, gentlemen. Let us not forget that our means of action are limited; that nations are living beings, just like the individuals of which they are composed; that they have the same impulses; that, if in daily life the judicial organs, in spite of the stern authority with which they are invested, do not succeed in preventing quarrels, altercations, and violence between individuals, it will be the same between nations, although the progress of conciliation and the increasing humanization of manners and customs will certainly diminish the number of such cases. Above all, gentlemen, let us not forget that there is a whole series of cases, where honor, dignity, and essential interests are involved, where individuals are concerned as well as where nations are concerned, and in which neither, whatever may be the consequences, will recognize any other authority than that of their own judgment and personal feelings.

But let that not discourage us from dreaming of the ideal of universal peace and the brotherhood of nations, which are after all only the higher aspirations of the human soul. Is not the pursuit of an ideal, toward which we continually strive without ever being able to reach it, essential to all progress? A tangible goal once reached kills the impulse, while progress in any undertaking requires the constant stimulation of an aspiration toward something higher. Excelsior is the device of progress. Let us set bravely to work, our way lighted by the bright star of universal peace and justice, which we shall never reach, but which will always guide us for the good of mankind. For whatever we can do within the modest limit of our means in the interest of individuals by lightening the burdens of war and on behalf of States by avoiding conflicts, will constitute so many titles to the gratitude of humanity, which we shall have won for the Governments that we represent. (Unanimous applause.)

Mr. de Beaufort takes the floor:
The Commission appointed to attend to the communications, etc., sent to the Conference, commenced its work by first examining those documents which seemed to be of greatest importance, and which contain the wishes expressed by numerous associations, educational institutions, or societies which endeavor to develop more and more sympathetic sentiments in favor of universal peace.

These telegrams, letters, petitions, books, pamphlets, etc., of which there are rather a large number, are naturally all inspired by the same principles. They are in general warm wishes for the success of the work of the Conference, enthusiastic greetings sent from several parts of the world, words of encouragement for the accomplishment of the high mission of the Conference, and means, more or less practical, offered to our consideration upon the questions whose study now occupies our attention.

Thus, for example, it may be stated that most of these communications contain petitions in favor of arbitration as the most effective means for the settlement of international disputes; some among them express the desire of seeing submitted to arbitration the difficulties which may arise between nations and to give it an obligatory character; others deal with the declaration of war, the inviolability of private property, the amelioration of the condition of the wounded and, in general, all those who suffer from the inevitable misfortunes caused by war. There are also communications concerning the lightening of military burdens, and even those advocating disarmament.

The Commission, although it appreciates equally the humanitary manifestations of which a sketch has just been given, finds it necessary to point out to the Conference especially:

The document presented by the Conseil international des femmes, to which are joined two million signatures affixed in twenty different countries;

Those remitted by Pastor Richmond as the mandatory of six religious associations of the United States;

Those which contain the resolutions adopted, either by the professors and students of twenty-three colleges of North America, or at a meeting which took place in Chicago, or by the Piatt County Society, representing in all the pacific opinions of over twenty-seven thousand persons; we received these resolutions through the intermediary of Mr. George Fulk.

The Commission considers it its duty likewise to point out to the Conference the communications of several Churches of Germany, Austria-Hungary, France, the Netherlands and Switzerland (grouped in a single document), Great Britain and the United States. The diversity of Churches represented by these communications, as well as the number and importance of the signatures seen therein, give a very special value to the words used by their authors to express their *vœux* in favor of peace.

Although fearing that this enumeration becomes a little long, one cannot pass by in silence the manifestations of over fifteen thousand Swedish citizens, men and women, who met in several places in their country and adopted resolutions favorable to the work of the Conference;

Those sent to us by the International Peace Bureau established at Berne, coming from three societies of the United States;

Those brought to our attention by l'Unione Lombarda and the Société Internationale de la Paix; and

The communications sent by l'Alliance universelle des femmes pour la

Paix par l'education, La Ligue internationale de la Paix et de la Liberté, and
the Vrije Gemeente d'Amsterdam, among others.

In this report cannot be neglected the telegrams, which, since the opening
of the Conference, have been sent auguring splendid results from it, from
the Société Internationale de la Paix of the Republic of San Marino, the
Société japonaise de la Paix at Tokio, the British Council of Peace Society of
Great Britain, the Portuguese association Paix et desarmement of Lisbon,
the Dutch members of the student body Corda fratres of Leiden, the Delegation permanente des Sociétés de la Paix de France, etc., etc.

As to the books and pamphlets received by the Conference, those of which
were a sufficient number have already been distributed among the delegates; the others are kept in the archives of the Secretariat, where the delegates may find them. There may also be found there an itemized list upon
which are inscribed all the communications whose examination has constituted the work of this Commission.

The President: The first delegate of Great Britain has the floor.

His Excellency Sir Edward Fry: Mr. President, I have the honor to submit
to you in behalf of the Government of His Britannic Majesty a proposal of
the highest importance.

When His Imperial Majesty of Russia convoked the First Peace Conference at The Hague he proposed as the prime object of its work that "of
seeking without delay means for putting a limit to the progressive increase
of military and naval armaments, a question the solution of which becomes
evidently more and more urgent in view of the fresh extension given to
these armaments."

After having taken into consideration the report of the First Commission
of the Conference, which had been charged with the examination of the
question, the Conference unanimously adopted the following resolution:

The Conference is of opinion that the restriction of military charges,
which are at present a heavy burden on the world, is extremely desirable
for the increase of the material and moral welfare of mankind.

Count Mouravieff, in his memorandum of August, 1898, addressed to
Europe in the name of His Majesty the Emperor of Russia, said:

The ever-increasing financial charges strike and paralyze public prosperity at
its source; the intellectual and physical strength of the nations, their labor and
capital, are for the most part diverted from their natural application and un-
productivity consumed; hundreds of millions are spent in acquiring terrible
engines of destruction, which though to-day regarded as the last word of science
are destined to-morrow to lose value in consequence of some fresh discovery

in the same field. National culture, economic progress, and the production of wealth are either paralyzed or perverted in their development.

Moreover, in proportion as the armaments of each Power increase, so do they less and less attain the object aimed at by the Governments. Economic crises, due in great part to the system of amassing armaments to the point of exhaustion, and the continual danger which lies in this accumulation of war material, are transforming the armed peace of our days into a crushing burden which the peoples have more and more difficulty in bearing. It appears evident, then, that if this state of affairs be prolonged, it will inevitably lead to the very cataclysm which it is desired to avert, and the impending horrors of which are fearful to every human thought.

These words, so eloquent and so true when they were first uttered, are to-day still more forcible and more true. For, Mr. President, since that date military expenditure upon armies as well as upon navies has considerably increased. Thus, according to the most exact information which I have received, this expenditure reached in 1898—that is to say, in the year which immediately preceded the First Conference at The Hague—a total of more than £251,000,000 for the countries of Europe—with the exception of Turkey and Montenegro (regarding which I have no information),—the United States of America, and Japan; while in the year 1906 the similar expenditure of the same countries exceeded a total of £320,000,000.

It will thus be seen that in the interval between the two Conferences annual military expenditure has been augmented by the sum of £69,000,000, or more than 1,725 millions of francs, which is an enormous increase.

Such is this excessive expenditure, which might be employed for better ends; such, Mr. President, is the burden under which our populations are groaning; such is the Christian peace of the civilized world in the twentieth century.

I will not speak of the economic aspect of the question, of the great mass of men who are compelled by these preparations for war to leave their occupations, and of the prejudicial effect of this state of things upon the general prosperity. You know this aspect of the question better than I do.

I am, therefore, quite sure that you will agree with me in the conclusion that the realization of the desire expressed by the Emperor of Russia and by the First Conference would be a great blessing for the whole of humanity. Is this desire capable of being realized? This is a question to which I cannot supply a categorical answer. I can only assure you that my Government is a convinced supporter of these high aspirations, and that it charges me to invite you to work together for the realization of this noble desire.

In ancient times, Mr. President, men dreamed of an age of gold which had existed on earth in the distant past; but in all ages and among all nations poets, sibyls, prophets, and all noble and inspired souls have always cherished the hope of the return of this golden age under the form of the reign of universal peace. . . . but to-day the sense of the solidarity of the human race has more than ever spread over the whole world. It is this sentiment that has rendered possible the convocation of the present Conference; and it is in the name of this sentiment that I request you not to separate without having asked that the Governments of the world should devote themselves very earnestly to the question of the limitation of military charges.

My Government recognizes that it belongs to the duty of every country to protect itself against its enemies and against the dangers by which it may be threatened, and that every Government has the right and the duty to decide what its own country ought to do for this purpose. It is, therefore, only by means of the good-will, the free-will, of each Government, acting in its own right, for the welfare of its own country, that the object of our desires can be realized.

The Government of His Britannic Majesty, recognizing that several Powers desire to restrict their military expenditure, and that this object can only be realized by the independent action of each Power, has thought it to be its duty to inquire whether there are any means for satisfying these aspirations. My Government has therefore authorized us to make the following declaration:

The Government of Great Britain will be prepared to communicate annually to Powers which would pursue the same course the program for the construction of new ships of war and the expenditure which this program would entail. This exchange of information would facilitate an exchange of views between the Governments on the subject of the reductions which it might be possible to effect by mutual agreement.

The British Government believes that in this way it might be possible to arrive at an understanding with regard to the expenditure which the States which should undertake to adopt this course would be justified in incorporating in their estimates.

In conclusion, therefore, Mr. President, I have the honor to propose to you the adoption of the following resolution:

The Conference confirms the resolution adopted by the Conference of 1899 in regard to the limitation of military expenditure; and inasmuch as military expenditure has considerably increased in almost every country since that time, the Conference declares that it is eminently desirable that the Governments should resume the serious examination of this question. (Repeated applause.)

The President: . . . . The eloquence of his Excellency the first British delegate, and the proposal with which it concluded, as well as the communications with which I have just acquainted you, cannot, it seems to me, fail to meet with a sympathetic reception on our part. The idea of diminishing the charges which weigh upon the populations owing to the fact of wars, by seeking the means of putting an end to the progressive increase of armaments on land and on sea, constituted the chief motive of the initiative taken by the Emperor of Russia in order to bring about the meeting of the Peace Conferences. This thought has been, so to speak, the corner-stone of that action. It formed the starting-point of the Russian circular of August 12/24, 1898, and was placed at the head of the program which the Cabinet of St. Petersburg proposed to the Powers in its circular of December 30, 1898/January 11, 1899. All the Governments gave their adherence, and the Conference, from the outset, had to occupy itself with a proposal of the Russian delegation which aimed at preventing the increase of armaments.

Contact with reality, however, was not long in revealing all the practical difficulties which this generous thought involved when the question of applying it arose. In the Commission which was entrusted with the consideration of the subject very keen differences of opinion soon broke out, and the debates assumed such character that, instead of the desired understanding, there was a danger of a disagreement which might have proved fatal to the rest of the labors of the Conference. It had to be acknowledged that the question was not ripe, that it required further study on the part of the different Governments at home; and it was in this sense that, after having unanimously adopted the resolution which has just been recalled by the first delegate of Great Britain, the Commission expressed the wish that "the Governments, taking into consideration the proposals made at the Conference," should "examine the possibility of an agreement as to the limitation of armed forces by land and sea, and of war budgets."

But here once more practical experience was not destined to correspond with the ideal nature of the wish. As I have just intimated, only two States, the Argentine Republic and Chile, have been able to give effect to that wish by concluding a convention of disarmament, which I have had the honor of reading to you. The majority of the Powers of Europe had other preoccupations. Scarcely had the Conference terminated its labors when troubles which arose in an empire of eastern Asia obliged the Governments to intervene with armed force. A short time afterwards one of the great European Powers found itself engaged in South Africa in a struggle which necessitated on its part a great military effort. Finally, during these last years, the Far East was the theatre of a gigantic war, the liquidation of which is barely finished. Need I also mention the colonial struggles and diplomatic difficulties which may have temporarily compelled one Power or another to increase its armaments? The result was that the Governments, far from having been able to occupy themselves, in conformity with the desire expressed by the Conference, with the means of limiting armaments, had, on the contrary, to increase their armaments to an extent which has just been shown you by the figures adduced by Sir Edward Fry.

It was in consideration of these circumstances, gentlemen, that the Russian Government this time refrained from placing the limitation of armaments upon the program of the Conference which it proposed to the Powers. To begin with, it considered that this question was not ripe for fruitful discussion. In the second place, it did not desire to provoke discussions which, as the experience of 1899 showed, could only, in opposition to the aim of our common endeavors, accentuate a disagreement among the Powers by giving occasion for irritating debates. The Russian Government, for its part, was determined not to take part in such discussions, and it knew that this was likewise the determination of some other Great Powers.

Yet the seed sown at the time of the First Conference has germinated independently of the action of the Governments. A very emphatic movement of public opinion has arisen in different countries in favor of the limitation of armaments, and the Governments, whose sympathies for the principle have not diminished, in spite of the difficulties of carrying it out, find themselves confronted with manifestations which they are not in a position to satisfy. Thus it is, gentlemen, that the British Government, giving expression to its own preoccupations, and making itself the organ of public feeling, evinced its intention of nevertheless calling the attention of the Powers assembled in Conference at The Hague to the question of the limitation of armaments, and that its first delegate has just brought before us the wish which the cabinet of London would like to see adopted by us.

I for my part am unable to discover any other means of evincing the interest which the Powers take in this question. If the question was not ripe in 1899, it is not any more so in 1907. It has not been possible to do anything on these lines, and the Conference to-day finds itself as little prepared to enter upon them as in 1899. Any discussion which should in itself prove sterile could only be harmful to the cause which was in view by accentuating differences of opinion on questions of fact, while there exists unity of general intentions which might one day meet with their realization. It is for this reason, gentlemen, that the proposal now made to us by the British delegation, to confirm the resolution adopted by the Conference of 1899 by formulating anew the desire which was then expressed, is what best corresponds with the present state of the question and with the interest which we all have in seeing it directed into a channel where the unanimity of the Powers could alone constitute a guarantee of its further progress. And it will be an honor for the Second Peace Conference to have contributed to this end by its immediate vote.

I therefore can only applaud the English initiative, and recommend you to unite in accepting the resolution, as it has been proposed to us by Sir Edward Fry, with unanimous acclamation. (Unanimous applause.)

II WORLD WAR AND PEACE

RESOLUTIONS OF THE SECOND
INTERNATIONAL: 1912

FOUNDED in 1889, the Second International was an organization of the leading socialist parties in Europe and America. By 1910 it was predominantly pacifist in its attitude toward any prospective European war, mainly because the members staunchly believed that the working people of the nations had a common stake in peace and justice while the capitalist and militarist governments were engaged in a life and death struggle for markets and national supremacy. The socialist cry was "The worker has no country."

There were many ideological and practical difficulties in the socialist position. The pacifist impulse clashed with the socialist admiration for progressive and humane heroes of the past who had fought in patriotic wars; it did not allow for participation in defensive wars; it held out no hope for groups such as the Czech and Polish workers who might have to wage a civil war or who depended on an international war to throw off Austro-Hungarian rule; it underestimated the force of patriotism in working people once a nation was at war; and, in the peaceful struggle for socialism through electoral victories, it left socialists open to charges of treason or disloyalty to the nation, and would perhaps drive workers to desert socialist ranks for more nationalistic parties. The strongest general argument against pacifism was that it was a sign to reactionary and aggressive groups that they could dare all against the working class—no force would be used to stop them.

The 1910 meeting of the Second International at Copenhagen accepted the principle of peace above all and, unrealistically, declared that the liberty of subjugated peoples was to be achieved peacefully and without disrupting Socialist forces. Socialists were asked to agitate and vote in their parliaments for compulsory arbitration of all international disputes, for reduction of armaments, and against further arms appropriations. The basic issue—calling an international general strike in the event of war—was tabled for the International's next meeting.

At Basel, Switzerland, an emergency meeting took place because of the growing fear that the First Balkan War (1912) would spread to the major powers. The hope was that socialists in the Balkans would move their nations to federate and to drop expansionist plans that might cause a world war. Socialists in the major nations were urged to take every step to prevent their governments from intervening in Balkan problems. As usual, much brilliant oratory covered the divisions among the socialists along national lines and the brave words disguised the fact that socialists lacked the power to prevent war, except by strikes or actual revolutions. But among the socialists, their belief in "revisionism," a gradual, peaceful parliamentary approach to socialism, opposed the very measures that might have maintained peace, for the price of peace was possibly to start civil wars.

On the very eve of the war (July, 1914), by a small majority, the International finally accepted the principle of a general strike in all nations in order to prevent hostilities, but socialist efforts to block the conflict came to nothing.

This selection comes from *Ausserordentlicher Internationaler Sozialisten-Kongress* (Berlin, 1912) and has been translated by Barry Augenbraun.

ૐ

PROCEEDINGS OF THE SECOND
INTERNATIONAL, *1912*

JEAN JAURÈS [France]: I am here to present to you the resolution unanimously adopted, after the most intense study, by the International Bureau and hereby recommended to your attention. (The speaker reads the [following] resolution):

In its Stuttgart and Copenhagen Congresses, the International has set down, as guiding principles for the proletariat of all nations in its opposition to war, the following:

Manifesto of the International on the Current Situation

Whenever war threatens to break out, the duty of the working classes and their parliamentary representatives in the nations concerned, aided by the co-ordinating activity of the International Bureau, shall be: to exert *all possible force* in order, *by whatever means shall seem most effective, to hinder the outbreak of war*. The means used may naturally be expected to vary in accordance with the intensification of the class-struggle and of the general political situation.

In the event that war should nevertheless break out, the workers' duty shall become: *to labour toward its termination* and, with all their powers, to strive *to utilise the wartime economic and political crisis for the purpose of arousing the people and thereby expediting the removal of capitalistic class-domination.*

Recent events have more than ever impressed upon the proletariat this duty: to impart to its planned, co-operative efforts the greatest power and energy. On one hand, the general insanity of armament has caused the cost of living to rise more sharply and has thereby increased class-contradictions, irrevocably angering the working class. The workers wish to set a limit to this system of unrest and extravagance. On the other hand, the continually recurring threats of war are becoming more and more irritating. Europe's great peoples are every instant on the point of being driven against one another. Moreover, not an atom of popular interest has been cited which could excuse this outrage against humanity and reason.

The Balkan crisis, which hitherto has brought about such frightful abominations, would become, if allowed to spread, the most terrifying of dangers to civilisation and to the proletariat. At the same time it would become, because of the crying contradiction between the hugeness of the catastrophe and the pettiness of the participating interests, the greatest disgrace in world history.

For this reason, the Congress confirms with satisfaction a complete unity among socialist parties and trade-unions of all lands, in this war against war.

While the proletarians of all nations were simultaneously joining the fight against imperialism, each section of the International was setting up proletarian resistance against its own government and mobilising national public opinion against all warlike ambitions. In this way was created a magnificent co-operative effort on the part of the workers of all nations, which co-operation has already contributed a great deal toward preserving a threatened world peace. The ruling classes' fear of a proletarian revolution consequent upon world conflict has proven itself an important surety against war.

The Congress therefore encourages the social-democratic parties to continue their struggle with all applicable means. The Congress will indicate the particular rôle of each socialist party in the co-operative effort. . . .

The International's most important assignment falls to the working class of Germany, France and England. For the moment, the duty of the workers of these nations is as follows: to demand of their governments that they refrain from giving any assistance to Russia or Austria-Hungary, that they avoid any involvement in the Balkan confusion, and that they maintain absolute neutrality. A war among the world's three culturally leading nations on account of the Serbo-Austrian controversy over ports, would be criminal madness. The workers of Germany and France do not recognise the existence of any secretly concluded treaty-obligation to step into the Balkan conflict.

If, however, Turkey's military ruin should further lead to a wavering of Ottoman predominance in the Near East, then it shall become the duty of England's, France's and Germany's socialists to oppose the policy of Near Eastern conquest, which policy would doubtless lead directly to world conflict.

The Congress regards the artificially maintained antagonism between Great Britain and the German Reich as the greatest danger to Europe's peace. The Congress therefore applauds the efforts of both nations' working classes to bridge this antagonism. It considers that the best means to this end would be the conclusion of an agreement between Germany and England on the cessation of naval armament and the abolition of the right of capture at sea. The Congress encourages the socialists of England and Germany to continue their agitation for such an agreement.

The overcoming of antagonism between, on one side, Germany, and on the other, England and France, would remove the greatest danger to world peace. It would, moreover, shake the power of Czarism, which profits from this antagonism; it would render impossible an Austro-Hungarian attack on Serbia; in short, it would ensure peace for the world. It is this goal, therefore, toward which the International's efforts are primarily to be directed.

The Congress affirms that the entire Socialist International is united upon these fundamental points of world policy. It encourages the workers of all nations to oppose capitalistic imperialism with the force of international proletarian solidarity. It warns the ruling classes of all states against further increasing the mass-misery brought about by capitalistic production methods. It emphatically demands peace. Let governments not forget that, in the present condition of Europe and the present mood of the working class, they cannot unleash war without endangering themselves. Let governments remember that the Franco-German War occasioned a revolutionary outbreak of the commune, that the Russo-Japanese War set into motion the revolutionary forces of the Russian peoples, that the military and maritime preparedness race has enormously sharpened the class-struggle in England and on the Continent, and has caused gigantic work-stoppages. It would be madness for governments not to comprehend that the thought alone of the monstrousness of world conflict must call forth wrath and rebellion from the working class. Proletarians feel it a crime to shoot at one another for the profit of capitalists, the ambition of dynasties, or the credit of secret diplomatic treaties.

If governmental powers should cut off every avenue of normal development and thereby drive the proletariat to drastic measures, they themselves would have to bear all responsibility for the consequences of the crisis they had brought about.

The International will double its efforts to avert this crisis; it will raise its protest with ever greater vigour: it will make its propaganda ever more energetic and comprehensive. The Congress therefore instructs the International Socialist Bureau to follow the course of events ever more alertly and, no matter what might occur, to maintain and strengthen the relationship among proletarian parties.

The proletariat is conscious of its current rôle as the bearer of man's future. The proletariat will utilise all its energies toward hindering that slaughter of the flower of all peoples with which the horrors of mass-murder, starvation and pestilence threaten the world.

Thus the Congress turns to you, proletarians and socialists of all nations, and begs you let your voice be heard in this critical hour! Make your will known in all forms and in all places, raise your protest full-force in the parliaments, gather and demonstrate in huge masses, make use of all means which the organisation and strength of the proletariat put into your hands! Make certain that governments are incessantly reminded of the alert and passionate will to peace of the proletariat! To the capitalistic world of exploitation and mass-murder, oppose the proletarian world of peace and brotherhood among peoples!

I should like to add just a word of my own, to the end that our French comrades be more disposed to accept the resolution. The gist of the resolution is threefold. First, it defines the world policy common to all sections of the International. In doing so, it performs a positive task. It demonstrates to governments that, if they were to relinquish their selfish ambitions, a policy of international solidarity would be possible. Next: though our resolution foresees, in the welter of possibilities, no single course for our action, neither does it prohibit any possible course of action. It warns the world's governments and makes clear to them that they could easily create a revolutionary situation, indeed the most revolutionary situation conceivable. (Hearty applause.) If the monstrous crime of a world war were actually committed, then rulers would have to count on their workers' sacrificing not only life but also conscience. For proletarians shall be solidly united in thought and feeling. Finally, the resolution confirms the unity and power of our campaign.

Comrades, this Congress is already a noble event and an historic action. It has not been satisfied simply to establish the principles common to the entire International; rather, it has emphasized the necessity for, and unity of, our struggle. We must continue to do this in the parliaments and in the masses, as is indicated by the Manifesto. In so doing, we shall operate effectively toward rendering impossible the horror of war. And at the same time, we shall be showing proof that the interests of the proletariat coincide with the interests of all civilisation and humanity. (Wild applause.)

The International represents all the ethical forces in the world! And if that tragic hour should ever strike, in which we must give our all, this awareness shall support us and give us strength. Not superficially, no, from the profoundest depths of our nature do we declare: we are prepared to make any and all sacrifices! (Great commotion and a long period of wild applause.)

THE CROWE MEMORANDUM

FOR ALL his Machiavellianism the policy of Bismarck as chancellor of Germany was based on a sense of need for general European peace. Even his more aggressive moves had definitely limited goals, and there is little evidence to suggest that he had plans for German mastery of Europe. With the accession of Kaiser Wilhelm II to the German throne in 1888 conflicts with the European powers sharpened and Bismarck was dismissed.

The document that follows was prepared for confidential circulation in the British Foreign Office late in 1906 by Mr. (later Sir) Eyre Crowe. There is much evidence to indicate that the Crowe memorandum helped solidify the growing beliefs of British officials that Germany was deliberately challenging the balance of power and England's dominance in the world.

Following the circulation of Crowe's paper, Lord Sanderson of the Foreign Office prepared a different summary of Anglo-German relations and his memorandum was also passed around. Crowe defended his position by annotating Sanderson's note, which, though dated February 21, 1907, was not printed for confidential circulation until September 1908.

The Crowe memorandum was printed in the series *British Documents on the Origins of the War,* edited by G. P. Gooch and H. Temperley (London: His Majesty's Stationery Office, 1928), Vol. III.

THE CROWE MEMORANDUM

THE MAINTENANCE of a state of tension and antagonism between third Powers had avowedly been one of the principal elements in Bismarck's political combinations by which he first secured and then endeavoured to preserve the predominant position of Germany on the continent. It is now no longer denied that he urged England to occupy Egypt and to continue in occupation, because he rightly foresaw that this would perpetuate the antagonism between England and France. Similarly, he consistently impressed upon Russia that it would be to her interest to divert her expansionist ambitions from the Balkan countries to Central Asia, where he hoped both Russia and England would, owing to the inevitable conflict of interests, keep one another fully occupied. The Penjdeh incident, which nearly brought about a war, was the outcome of his direct suggestion that the moment was favourable for Russia to act. Prince Bismarck had also succeeded by all sorts of devices—including the famous reinsurance Treaty with Russia—in keeping France and Russia apart so long as he remained in office. The conclusion of the Franco-Russian alliance some time after Bismarck's fall filled Germany with concern and anxiety, and she never ceased in her efforts at least to neutralise it by establishing the closest possible relations with Russia for herself. From this point of view the weakening of Russia's general position presented simultaneously two advantages. It promised to free Germany for some time to come from any danger of aggression on her eastern frontier, and it deprived France of the powerful support which alone had hitherto enabled her to stand up to Germany in the political arena on terms of equality. It is only natural that the feeling of satisfaction derived from the relative accession of strength due to these two causes should have been somewhat rudely checked by the unexpected intelligence that France had come to an understanding with England.

It was, in fact, soon made apparent that, far from welcoming, as Prince Bülow pretended, an Anglo-French rapprochement, the Emperor's Government had been thoroughly alarmed at the mere disappearance of all causes of friction between the two Western Powers, and was determined to resort to any measures likely to bring about the dissolution of a fresh political combination, which it was felt might ultimately prove another stumbling-block in the way of German supremacy, as the Franco-Russian alliance had previously been regarded. Nor is it possible to be blind to the fact that Germany is bound to be as strongly opposed to a possible Anglo-Russian understanding; and, indeed, there is already conclusive evidence of German activity to prevent any such contingency from happening in the near future.

The German view on this subject cannot be better stated than was done by Herr von Tschirschky, now Foreign Secretary at Berlin, then Prussian Minister at Hamburg, in speaking on New Year's Day 1906 to His Majesty's Consul-General at that place. He said:—

Germany's policy always had been, and would be, to try to frustrate any coalition between two States which might result in damaging Germany's interests and prestige; and Germany would, if she thought that such a coalition was being formed, even if its actual results had not yet been carried into practical effect, not hesitate to take such steps as she thought proper to break up the coalition.

In pursuance of this policy, which, whatever its merits or demerits, is certainly quite intelligible, Germany waited for the opportune moment for taking action, with the view of breaking up, if possible, the Anglo-French entente. When Russia was staggering under the crushing blows inflicted by Japan, and threatened by internal revolution, the German campaign was opened. The object of nipping in the bud the young friendship between France and England was to be attained by using as a stalking-horse those very interests in Morocco which the Imperial Chancellor had, barely a year before, publicly declared to be in no way imperilled. . . .

When the signature of the Algeciras Act brought to a close the first chapter of the conflict respecting Morocco, the Anglo-French entente had acquired a different significance from that which it had at the moment of its inception. Then there had been but a friendly settlement of particular outstanding differences, giving hope for future harmonious relations between two neighbouring countries that had got into the habit of looking at one another askance; now there had emerged an element of common resistance to outside dictation and aggression, a unity of special interests tending to develop into active co-operation against a third Power. It is essential to bear in mind that this new feature of the entente was the direct effect produced by Germany's effort to break it up, and that, failing the active or threatening hostility of Germany, such anti-German bias as the entente must be admitted to have at one time assumed, would certainly not exist at present, nor probably survive in the future. But whether the antagonism to Germany into which England had on this occasion been led without her wish or intention was but an ephemeral incident, or a symptomatic revelation of some deep-seated natural opposition between the policies and interests of the two countries is a question which it clearly behoves British statesmen not to leave in any obscurity. To this point, then, inquiry must be directed.

The general character of England's foreign policy is determined by the immutable conditions of her geographical situation on the ocean flank of Europe as an island State with vast oversea colonies and dependencies, whose existence and survival as an independent community are inseparably bound up with the possession of preponderant sea power. The tremendous influence of such preponderance has been described in the classical pages of Captain Mahan. No one now disputes it. Sea power is more potent than land power, because it is as pervading as the element in which it moves and has its being. Its formidable character makes itself felt the more directly that a maritime State is, in the literal sense of the word, the neighbour of every country accessible by sea. It would, therefore, be but natural that the power of a State supreme at sea should inspire universal jealousy and fear, and be ever exposed to the danger of being overthrown by a general combination of the world. Against such a combination no single nation could in the long run stand, least of all a small island kingdom not possessed of the military strength of a people trained to arms, and dependent for its food supply on oversea commerce. The danger can in practice only be averted—and history shows that it has been so averted—on condition that the national policy of the insular and naval State is so directed as to harmonize with the general desires and ideals common to all mankind, and more particularly that it is closely identified with the primary and vital interests of a majority, or as many as possible, of the other nations. Now, the first interest of all countries is the preservation of national independence. It follows that England, more than any other non-insular Power, has a direct and positive interest in the maintenance of the independence of nations, and therefore must be the natural enemy of any country threatening the independence of others, and the natural protector of the weaker communities.

Second only to the ideal of independence, nations have always cherished the right of free intercourse and trade in the world's markets, and in proportion as England champions the principle of the largest measure of general freedom of commerce, she undoubtedly strengthens her hold on the interested friendship of other nations, at least to the extent of making them feel apprehensive of naval supremacy in the hands of a free trade England than they would in the face of a predominant protectionist Power. This is an aspect of the free trade question which is apt to be overlooked. It has been well said that every country, if it had the option, would, of course, prefer itself to hold the power of supremacy at sea, but that, this choice being excluded, it would rather see England hold that power than any other State.

History shows that the danger threatening the independence of this or that nation has generally arisen, at least in part, out of the momentary predominance of a neighbouring State at once militarily powerful, economically efficient, and ambitious to extend its frontiers or spread its influence, the danger being directly proportionate to the degree of its power and efficiency, and to the spontaneity or "inevitableness" of its ambitions. The only check on the abuse of political predominance derived from such a position has always consisted in the opposition of an equally formidable rival, or of a combination of several countries forming leagues of defence. The equilibrium established by such a grouping of forces is technically known as the balance of power, and it has become almost an historical truism to identify England's secular policy with the maintenance of this balance by throwing her weight now in this scale and now in that, but ever on the side opposed to the political dictatorship of the strongest single State or group at a given time.

If this view of British policy is correct, the opposition into which England must inevitably be driven to any country aspiring to such a dictatorship assumes almost the form of a law of nature, as has indeed been theoretically demonstrated, and illustrated historically, by an eminent writer on English national policy.

By applying this general law to a particular case, the attempt might be made to ascertain whether, at a given time, some powerful and ambitious State is or is not in a position of natural and necessary enmity towards England; and the present position of Germany might, perhaps, be so tested. Any such investigation must take the shape of an inquiry as to whether Germany is, in fact, aiming at a political hegemony with the object of promoting purely German schemes of expansion, and establishing a German primacy in the world of international politics at the cost and to the detriment of other nations. . . .

With the events of 1871 the spirit of Prussia passed into the new Germany. In no other country is there a conviction so deeply rooted in the very body and soul of all classes of the population that the preservation of national rights and the realization of national ideals rest absolutely on the readiness of every citizen in the last resort to stake himself and his State on their assertion and vindication. With "blood and iron" Prussia had forged her position in the councils of the great Powers of Europe. In due course it came to pass that, with the impetus given to every branch of national activity by the newly-won unity, and more especially by the growing development of oversea trade flowing in ever-increasing volume through the now Imperial ports of the formerly "independent" but politically insignificant Hanse Towns, the young empire found opened to its energy a whole world outside Europe, of which it had previously hardly had the opportunity to become more than dimly conscious. Sailing across the ocean in German ships, German merchants began for the first time to divine the true position of countries such as England, the United States, France, and even the Netherlands, whose political influence extends to distant seas and continents. The colonies and foreign possessions of England more especially were seen to give to that country a recognized and enviable status in a world where the name of Germany, if mentioned at all, excited no particular interest. The effect of this discovery upon the German mind was curious and instructive. Here was a vast province of human activity to which the mere title and rank of a European Great Power were not in themselves a sufficient passport. Here in a field of portentous magnitude, dwarfing altogether the proportions of European countries, others, who had been perhaps rather looked down upon as comparatively smaller folk, were at home and commanded, whilst Germany was at best received but as an honoured guest. Here was distinct inequality, with a heavy bias in favour of the maritime and colonizing Powers.

Such a state of things was not welcome to German patriotic pride. Germany had won her place as one of the leading, if not, the foremost Power on the European continent. But over and beyond the European Great Powers there seemed to stand the "World Powers." It was at once clear that Germany must become a "World Power." The evolution of this idea and its translation into practical politics followed with singular consistency the line of thought that had inspired the Prussian Kings in their efforts to make Prussia great. "If Prussia," said Frederick the Great, "is to count for something in the councils of Europe, she must be made a Great Power." And the echo: "If Germany wants to have a voice in the affairs of the larger oceanic world she must be made a 'World Power.'" "I want more territory," said Prussia. "Germany must have Colonies," said the new world-policy. And Colonies were accordingly established, in such spots as were found to be still unappropriated, or out of which others could be pushed by the vigorous assertion of a German demand for "a place in the sun": Damaraland, Cameroons, Togoland, German East Africa, New Guinea, and groups of other islands in the Pacific. The German example, as was only natural, found ready followers, and the map of unclaimed territories was filled up with surprising rapidity. When the final reckoning was made up the actual German gain seemed, even in German eyes, somewhat meagre. A few fresh possessions were added by purchase or by international agreement—the Carolines, Samoa, Heligoland. A transaction in the old Prussian style secured Kiao-chau. On the whole, however, the "Colonies" have proved assets of somewhat doubtful value.

Meanwhile the dream of a Colonial Empire had taken deep hold on the German imagination. Emperor, statesmen, journalists, geographers, economists, commercial and shipping houses, and the whole mass of educated and uneducated public opinion continue with one voice to declare: We *must* have real Colonies, where German emigrants can settle and spread the national ideals of the Fatherland, and we *must* have a fleet and coaling stations to keep together the Colonies which we are bound to acquire. To the question, "why *must?*" the ready answer is: "A healthy and powerful State like Germany, with its 60,000,000 inhabitants, must expand, it cannot stand still, it must have territories to which its overflowing population can emigrate without giving up its nationality." When it is objected that the world is now actually parcelled out among independent States, and that territory for colonization cannot be had except by taking it from the rightful possessor, the reply again is: "We cannot enter into such considerations. Necessity has no law. The world belongs to the strong. A vigorous nation cannot allow its growth to be hampered by blind adherence to *status quo*. We have no designs on other people's possessions, but where States are too feeble to put their territory to the best possible use, it is the manifest destiny of those who can and will do so to take their places." . . .

So long, then, as Germany competes for an intellectual and moral leadership of the world in reliance on her own national advantages and energies England can but admire, applaud, and join in the race. If, on the other hand, Germany believes that greater relative preponderance of material power, wider extent of territory, inviolable frontiers, and supremacy at sea are the necessary and preliminary possessions without which any aspirations to such leadership must end in failure, then England must expect that Germany will surely seek to diminish the power of any rivals, to enhance her own by extending her dominion, to hinder the co-operation of other States, and ultimately to break up and supplant the British Empire.

Now, it is quite possible that Germany does not, nor ever will, consciously cherish any schemes of so subversive a nature. Her statesmen have openly repudiated them with indignation. Their denial may be perfectly honest, and their indignation justified. If so, they will be most unlikely to come into any kind of armed conflict with England, because, as she knows of no causes of present dispute between the two countries, so she would have difficulty in imagining where, on the hypothesis stated, any such should arise in the future. England seeks no quarrels, and will never give Germany cause for legitimate offence.

But this is not a matter in which England can safely run any risks. The assurances of German statesmen may after all be no more genuine than they were found to be on the subject of the Anglo-French *entente* and German interests in Morocco, or they may be honestly given but incapable of fulfilment. It would not be unjust to say that ambitious designs against one's neighbours are not as a rule openly proclaimed, and that therefore the absence of such proclamation, and even the profession of unlimited and universal political benevolence are not in themselves conclusive evidence for or against the existence of unpublished intentions. The aspect of German policy in the past, to which attention has already been called, would warrant a belief that a further development on the same general lines would not constitute a break with former traditions, and must be considered as at least possible. In the presence of such a possibility it may well be asked whether it would be right, or even prudent, for England to incur any sacrifices or see other, friendly, nations sacrificed merely in order to assist Germany in building up step by step the fabric of a universal preponderance, in the blind confidence that in the exercise of such preponderance Germany will confer unmixed benefits on the world at large, and promote the welfare and happiness of all other peoples without doing injury to any one. There are, as a matter of fact, weighty reasons which make it particularly difficult for England to entertain that confidence. These will have to be set out in their place. . . .

It has been so often declared, as to have become almost a diplomatic platitude, that between England and Germany, as there has never been any real clashing of material interests, so there are no unsettled controversies over outstanding questions. Yet for the last twenty years, as the archives of our Foreign Office show, German Governments have never ceased reproaching British Cabinets with want of friendliness and with persistent opposition to German political plans. A review of British relations during the same period with France, with Russia, and with the United States reveals ancient and real sources of conflict, springing from imperfectly patched-up differences of past centuries, the inelastic stipulations of antiquated treaties, or the troubles incidental to unsettled colonial frontiers. Although with these countries England has fortunately managed to continue to live in peace, there always remained sufficient elements of divergence to make the preservation of good, not to say cordial, relations an anxious problem requiring constant alertness, care, moderation, good temper, and conciliatory disposition. When particular causes of friction became too acute, special arrangements entered into succeeded as a rule in avoiding an open rupture without, however, solving the difficulties, but rather leaving the seed of further irritation behind. This was eminently the case with France until and right up to the conclusion of the Agreement of the 8th April, 1904.

A very different picture is presented by the succession of incidents which punctuate the record of contemporary Anglo-German relations. From 1884 onward, when Bismarck first launched his country into colonial and maritime enterprise, numerous quarrels arose between the two countries. They all have in common this feature—that they were opened by acts of direct and unmistakable hostility to England on the part of the German Government, and this hostility was displayed with a disregard of the elementary rules of straightforward and honourable dealing, which was deeply resented by successive British Secretaries of State for Foreign Affairs. But perhaps even more remarkable is this other feature, also common to all these quarrels, that the British Ministers, in spite of the genuine indignation felt at the treatment to which they were subjected, in each case readily agreed to make concessions or accept compromises which not only appeared to satisfy all German demands, but were by the avowal of both parties calculated and designed to re-establish, if possible, on a firmer basis the fabric of Anglo-German friendship. To all outward appearance absolute harmony was restored on each occasion after these separate settlements, and in the intervals of fresh outbreaks it seemed true, and was persistently reiterated, that there could be no further occasion for disagreement.

The peculiar diplomatic methods employed by Bismarck in connection with the first German annexation in South-West Africa, the persistent way in which he deceived Lord Ampthill up to the last moment as to Germany's colonial ambitions, and then turned round to complain to the want of sympathy shown for Germany's "well-known" policy; the sudden seizure of the Cameroons by a German doctor armed with officially-obtained British letters of recommendation to the local people, at a time when the intention of England to grant the natives' petition for a British Protectorate had been proclaimed; the deliberate deception practised on the Reichstag and the German public by the publication of pretended communications to Lord Granville which were never made, a mystification of which Germans to this day are probably ignorant; the arousing of a profound outburst of anti-English feeling throughout Germany by Bismarck's warlike and threatening speeches in Parliament; the abortive German raid on St. Lucia Bay, only just frustrated by the vigilance of Mr. Rhodes; the dubious proceedings by which German claims were established over a large portion of the Sultan of Zanzibar's dominions; the hoisting of the German flag over vast parts of New Guinea, immediately after inducing England to postpone her already-announced intention to occupy some of those very parts by representing that a friendly settlement might first determine the dividing line of rival territorial claims; the German pretensions to oust British settlers from Fiji and Samoa: these incidents constitute the first experience by a British Cabinet of German hostility disguised as injured friendship and innocence. It was only England's precarious position resulting from the recent occupation of Egypt (carefully encouraged by Bismarck), the danger of troubles with Russia in Central Asia (directly fomented by a German special mission to St. Petersburgh), and the comparative weakness of the British navy at the time, which prevented Mr. Gladstone's Government from contemplating a determined resistance to these German proceedings. It was, however, felt rightly that, apart from the offensiveness of the methods employed, the desires entertained by Germany, and so bluntly translated into practice, were not seriously antagonistic to British policy. Most of the territory ultimately acquired by Bismarck had at some previous time been refused by England, and in the cases where British occupation had lately been contemplated, the object had been not so much to acquire fresh provinces, as to prevent their falling into the hands of protectionist France, who would inevitably have killed all British trade. It seems almost certain that had Germany from the outset sought to gain by friendly overtures to England what she eventually secured after a display of unprovoked aggressiveness, there would have been no difficulty in the way of an amicable arrangement satisfactory to both parties.

As it was, the British Cabinet was determined to avoid a continuance of the quarrel, and having loyally accepted the situation created by Germany's violent action, it promptly assured her of England's honest desire to live with her on terms of absolute neighbourliness, and to maintain the former cordial relations. The whole chapter of these incidents was typical of many of the fresh complications of a similar nature which arose in the following years. With the advent of Lord Salisbury's administration in 1885, Bismarck thought the moment come for inviting England to take sides with the Triple Alliance. Repeated and pressing proposals appear to have been made thenceforward for some considerable time with this end. Whilst the British Government was too prudent to abandon altogether the traditional policy of holding the balance between the continental Powers, it decided eventually, in view of the then threateningly hostile attitude of France and Russia, to go so far in the direction of co-operation with the Triple Alliance as to conclude the two secret Mediterranean Agreements of 1887. At the same time Lord Salisbury intimated his readiness to acquiesce in the German annexation of Samoa, the consummation of which was only shipwrecked owing to the refusal of the United States on their part to abandon their treaty rights in that group of islands in Germany's favour. These fresh manifestations of close relations with Germany were, however, shortly followed by the serious disagreements caused by the proceedings of the notorious Dr. Carl Peters and other German agents in East Africa. Uganda, athwart the line of communication running from Egypt to the head-waters of the Nile, failed, but England, having previously abandoned the Sultan of Zanzibar to Germany's territorial ambitions, now recognised the German annexation of extensive portions of his mainland dominions, saving the rest by the belated declaration of a British protectorate. The cession of Heligoland sealed the reassertion of Anglo-German brotherhood, and was accompanied by the customary assurance of general German support to British policy, notably in Egypt.

On this and on other occasions England's spirit of accommodation went so far as to sacrifice the career of subordinate British officials, who had done no more than carry out the policy of their Government in as dignified a manner as circumstances allowed, and to whose conduct that Government attached no blame, to the relentless vindictiveness of Germany, by agreeing to their withdrawal as one of the conditions of a settlement. In several instances the German Government admitted that no fault attached to the British official, whilst the German officer alone was acknowledged to be at fault, but asked that the latter's inevitable removal should be facilitated, and the outside world misled, by the simultaneous withdrawal of his British colleagues. In one such case, indeed, a German Consul, after being transferred with promotion to another post, was only a few years afterwards reinstated on the scene of his original blunders with the higher rank of Consul-General without any British protest being made.

The number of British officials innocently branded in this manner in the course of some years is not inconsiderable, and it is instructive to observe how readily and *con amore* the German Government, imitating in this one of the great Bismarck's worst and least respectable foibles, habitually descend to attacking the personal character and position of any agents of a foreign State, often regardless of their humble rank, whose knowledge, honesty, and efficient performance of their duties are thought to be in the way of the realization of some particular, probably not very straightforward, piece of business. Such machinations were conspicuous in connection with the fall of M. Delcassé, but tales could be told of similar efforts directed against men in the service of the Spanish, Italian, and Austrian, as well as of the British Government.

It seems unnecessary to go at length into the disputes about the frontiers of the German Colonies in West Africa and the hinterland spheres of influence in 1903–1904, except to record the ready sacrifice of undoubted British treaty rights to the desire to conciliate Germany, notwithstanding the provocative and insulting proceedings of her agents and officials; nor into the agreement entered into between Germany and France for giving the latter access to the Niger, a transaction which, as the German Government blandly informed the British Embassy at Berlin, was intended to show how unpleasant it could make itself to England if she did not manifest greater alacrity in meeting German wishes.

It was perhaps partly the same feeling that inspired Germany in offering determined resistance to the scheme negotiated by Lord Rosebery's Government with the Congo Free State for connecting the British Protectorate of Uganda by a railway with Lake Tanganyika. No cession of territory was involved, the whole object being to allow an all-British through communication by rail and lake steamers from the Cape to Cairo. It was to this that Germany objected, although it was not explained in what way her interests would be injuriously affected. She adopted on this occasion a most minatory tone towards England, and also joined France, who objected to other portions of the Anglo-Congolese Agreement, in putting pressure on King Leopold. In the end the British Government consented to the cancellation of the clauses respecting the lease of the strip of land required for the construction of the railway, and Germany declared herself satisfied.

More extraordinary still was the behaviour of the German Government in respect to the Transvaal. The special treaty arrangements, which placed the foreign relations of that country under the control of England, were, of course, well known and understood. Nevertheless, it is certain that Germany believed she might by some fortuitous circumstances hope some day to establish her political dominion over the Boers, and realize her dream of occupying a belt of territory running from east to west right across Africa. She may have thought that England could be brought amicably to cede her rights in those regions as she had done before in other quarters, but, meanwhile, a good deal of intriguing went on which cannot be called otherwise than actively hostile. Opposition to British interests was deliberately encouraged in the most demonstrative fashion at Pretoria, which went so far in 1895 that the British Ambassador at Berlin had to make a protest. German financial assistance was promised to the Transvaal for the purpose of buying the Delagoa Bay Railway, a British concern which had been illegally confiscated by the Portuguese Government, and was then the subject of an international arbitration. When this offer failed, Germany approached the Lisbon Cabinet direct with the demand that, immediately on the arbitration being concluded, Germany and Portugal should deal with the railway by common agreement. It was also significant that at the time of the British annexation of Amatongaland (1895), just south of the Portuguese frontier on the East Coast, Germany thought it necessary to warn England that this annexation was not recognised by the Transvaal, and that she encouraged the feverish activity of German traders to buy up all available land round Delagoa Bay. In the same year, following up an intimation that England's "opposition to German interests at Delagoa Bay"—interests of which no British Government had ever previously been informed—was considered by Germany as one of the legitimate causes of her ill-will towards England, the German Government went out of its way to declare the maintenance of the independence of the Transvaal to be a German national interest. Then followed the chapter of the Jameson raid and the Emperor's famous telegram to President Krüger. The hostile character of that demonstration was thoroughly understood by the Emperor's Government, because we know that preparations were made for safe-guarding the German fleet in the contingency of a British attack. But in a way the most important aspect of the incident was that for the first time the fact of the hostile character of Germany's official policy was realized by the British public, who up to then, owing to the anxious care of their Government to minimize the results of the perpetual friction with Germany, and to prevent any aggravation of that friction by concealing as far as possible the unpleasant details of Germany's aggressive behaviour, had been practically unaware of the persistently contemptuous treatment of their country by their Teutonic cousins. The very decided view taken by British public opinion of the nature of any possible German intervention in South Africa led the German Government, though not the German public, to abandon the design of supplanting England at Pretoria. But for this "sacrifice" Germany, in accordance with her wont, demanded a price—namely, British acquiescence in the reversion to her of certain Portuguese Colonies in the event of their eventual division and appropriation by other Powers. The price was paid. But the manner in which Germany first bullied the Portuguese Government and then practically drove an indignant British Cabinet into agreeing in anticipation to this particular scheme of spoliation of England's most ancient ally, was deeply resented by Lord Salisbury, all the more, no doubt, as by this time he was fully aware that this new "friendly" settlement of misunderstandings with Germany would be no more lasting than its many predecessors. When, barely twelve months later, the Emperor, unabashed by his recent formal "abandonment of the Boers," threatened that unless the question of the final ownership of Samoa, then under negotiation, was promptly settled in Germany's favour, he would have to reconsider his attitude in the British conflict with the Transvaal which was then on the point of being submitted to the arbitrament of war, it cannot be wondered at that the British Government began to despair of ever reaching a state of satisfactory relations with Germany by continuing in the path of friendly concessions and compromises. Yet no attempt was even then made to seek a new way. The Agreement by which Samoa definitely became German was duly signed, despite the serious protests of our Australian Colonies, whose feelings had been incensed by the cynical disregard with which the German agents in the group, with the open support of their Government, had for a long time violated the distinct stipulations of the Samoan Act agreed to at Berlin by the three interested Powers in 1889. And when shortly after the outbreak of the South African war, Germany threatened the most determined hostility unless England waived the exercise of one of the most ancient and most firmly-established belligerent rights of naval warfare, namely, the search and citation before a Prize Court of neutral mercantile vessels suspected of carrying contraband, England once more preferred an amicable arrangement under which her undoubted rights were practically waived, to embarking on a fresh quarrel with Germany. The spirit in which this more than conciliatory attitude was appreciated at Berlin became clear when immediately afterwards the German Chancellor openly boasted to the Reichstag that he had compelled England by the display of German firmness to abandon her absolutely unjust claim to interference with the unquestioned rights of neutrals, and when the Emperor subsequently appealed to his nation to hasten on the building of an overwhelming German fleet, since the want of superior naval strength alone had on this occasion prevented Germany from a still more drastic vindication of Germany's interests. . . .

As if none of these things had happened, fresh German demands in another field, accompanied by all the same manifestations of hostility, were again met, though with perhaps increasing reluctance, by the old willingness to oblige. The action of Germany in China has long been distinctly unfriendly to England. In 1895 she tried to obtain from the Chinese Government a coaling station in the Chusan Islands, at the mouth of the Yang-tsze, without any previous communication with the British Government, whose preferential rights over the group, as established by Treaty, were of course well known. The manner in which Kiao-chau was obtained, however unjustifiable it may be considered by any recognized standard of political conduct, did not concern England more than the other Powers who professed in their Treaties to respect China's integrity and independence. But Germany was not content with the seizure of the harbour, she also planned the absorption of the whole of the large fertile province of Shantung. The concession of the privileged rights which she wrung from the Chinese Government was obtained owing in no small degree to her official assurance that her claims had the support of England who, needless to say, had never been informed or consulted, and who was, of course, known to be absolutely opposed to stipulations by which, contrary to solemn British treaty rights, it was intended to close a valuable province to British trade and enterprise.

About this time Germany secretly approached Russia with a view to the conclusion of an Agreement, by which Germany would have also obtained the much desired foothold on the Yang-tsze, then considered to be practically a British preserve. These overtures being rejected, Germany wished at least to prevent England from obtaining what she herself had failed to secure. She proposed to the British Cabinet a self-denying Agreement stipulating that neither Power should endeavour to obtain any territorial advantages in Chinese dominions, and that if any third Power attempted to do so both should take common action.

The British Government did not conceal their great reluctance to this arrangement, rightly foreseeing that Germany would tacitly exempt from its operation her own designs on Shantung, and also any Russian aggression in Manchuria, whilst England would solemnly give up any chances she might have of establishing on a firm basis her well-won position on the Yang-tsze. That is, of course, exactly what subsequently did happen. There was no obvious reason why England should lead herself to this gratuitous tying of her own hands. No counter-advantage was offered or even suggested, and the British taste for these one-sided transactions had not been stimulated by past experience. Nevertheless, the policy of conciliating Germany by meeting her expressed wishes once more triumphed, and the Agreement was signed —with the foreseen consequences: Russian aggression in Manchuria was declared to be altogether outside the scope of the stipulations of what the German Chancellor took care to style the "Yang-tsze" Agreement, as if its terms had referred specially to that restricted area of China, and the German designs on Shantung continue to this day to be tenaciously pursued. . . .

There is no pretence to completeness in the foregoing survey of Anglo-German relations, which, in fact, gives no more than a brief reference to certain salient and typical incidents that have characterized those relations during the twenty years. The more difficult task remains of drawing the logical conclusions. The immediate object of the present inquiry was to ascertain whether there is any real and natural ground for opposition between England and Germany. It has been shown that such opposition has, in fact, existed in an ample measure for a long period, but that it has been caused by an entirely one-sided aggressiveness, and that on the part of England the most conciliatory disposition has been coupled with never-failing readiness to purchase the resumption of friendly relations by concession after concession.

It might be deduced that the antagonism is too deeply rooted in the relative position of the two countries to allow of its being bridged over by the kind of temporary expedients to which England has so long and so patiently resorted. On this view of the case it would have to be assumed that Germany is deliberately following a policy which is essentially opposed to vital British interests, and that an armed conflict cannot in the long run be averted, except by England either sacrificing those interests, with the result that she would lose her position as an independent Great Power, or making herself too strong to give Germany the chance of succeeding in a war. This is the opinion of those who see in the whole trend of Germany's policy conclusive evidence that she is consciously aiming at the establishment of a German hegemony, at first in Europe, and eventually in the world.

DIPLOMACY: 1914

NEARLY a half century after the events there is still no clear consensus among scholars on the causes of the World War that began in 1914. Imperialism, armament races, the alliance system, yellow journalism have all been suggested as the general or immediate reasons for the conflict.

Despite the growing tension between the nations and the build-up of alliances leaving little room for maneuvering, all the disputes between the powers before 1914 were peacefully settled, but with increasing difficulty and fears that the next crisis would permit no compromises. Those wars that did break out before 1914, especially in the Balkans, were successfully limited and contained.

The following collection of diplomatic letters, telegrams, and dispatches attempts to clarify how the men of "that fateful beautiful summer" of 1914 understood each other's intentions and perhaps only blundered into war despite the alleged "inevitable forces" making over the years for a fatal final conflict. Although the German government has often been accused of making the war possible by its so-called blank check to Austria-Hungary to settle its Balkan problems, the hope and understanding at Berlin was that the Serbian–Austro-Hungarian conflict would be localized. Unfortunately, the balance of power had been brought to so fine a point by 1914 that Russia, tied to France and England by treaty, feared that the next move by its rival in the Balkans, Austria-Hungary, would tip the balance irretrievably to her disadvantage. The balance of power had worked for generations for general European peace, but as it reached perfection in 1914 its paradoxical result was war. Had any of the men of 1914 understood the fundamental transformation of Western civilization that their war was to bring, it seems difficult to believe that they would have taken what risks they did. In any case, by 1918 Europe and its best ideals had received blows from which they never recovered and the zenith of Western confidence and influence in the world may well prove to have passed.

The selections have been arranged in chronological order from three of the many collections of documents published by the European governments during and after the war. The volumes are: *Collected Diplomatic Documents Relating to the Outbreak of the European War* (London: His Majesty's Stationery Office, 1915); *Outbreak of the World War*, edited by Karl Kautsky (New York: Oxford University Press, 1924); and *British Documents on the Origins of the War, 1898–1914*, edited by G. P. Gooch and A. Temperley (London: His Majesty's Stationery Office, 1926), Vol. XI.

DIPLOMATIC DOCUMENTS

Consul Jones to Sir Edward Grey [1]

Serajevo, June 28, 1914.
D. 12:30 P. M.
R. 4 P. M.

Tel.

According to news received here heir apparent and his consort assassinated this morning by means of an explosive nature.

M. Dumaine, French Ambassador at Vienna, to Mr. René Viviani,
President of the Council, Minister for Foreign Affairs

Vienna, July 2, 1914.

The crime of Serajevo arouses the most acute resentment in Austrian military circles, and among all those who are not content to allow Servia to maintain in the Balkans the position which she has acquired.

The investigation into the origin of the crime which it is desired to exact from the Government at Belgrade under conditions intolerable to their dignity would, in case of a refusal, furnish grounds of complaint which would admit of resort to military measures.

Dumaine

The [German] Ambassador at Vienna to the [German]
Imperial Chancellor

Vienna, July 2, 1914.

Confidential.

In connection with my previous report I have the honor of further reporting as follows concerning my audience of today with His Majesty the Emperor Franz Joseph. . . .

His Majesty, in conclusion, returned once more to the subject of his Serbian neighbor. The intrigues at Belgrade were intolerable. There was nothing to be accomplished by kindness to those people. His Majesty here referred to the position which Mr. von Hartwig occupied at Belgrade, and to the worry caused him by the so-called practise mobilization of the Russians in the fall, just at the time when the recruits are being enlisted here and

[1] British foreign secretary.

the Army is not entirely prepared for the field. He hoped that my Emperor and the Imperial Government appreciated the dangers which threatened the Monarchy by reason of the neighborhood of Serbia. As he had said, it was necessary to plan for the future and to guard the status of the countries connected by the Triple Alliance. At this remark of the Emperor, I took occasion to say to His Majesty himself—as a few days before I had already stated very emphatically to Count Berchtold—that His Majesty could count absolutely on finding Germany solidly behind the Monarchy whenever it came to the point of defending one of the latter's vital interests. The decision on the question as to where and when such a vital interest was at stake, must be left to Austria herself. A responsible policy could not be founded on wishes or opinions, however comprehensible they might be. Before any decisive step was taken, it would have to be determined very carefully just how far one wished or would have to go, and by what means the goal aimed at was to be reached. First of all, before taking any step that might be fraught with weighty consequences, the general political situation should be considered, the probable attitude of the other Powers and nations estimated, and the ground carefully leveled and prepared. I could only repeat that my Emperor would stand behind every firm determination arrived at by Austria-Hungary. His Majesty eagerly agreed to my every word, and said that I was quite right.

The [German] Imperial Chancellor to the Ambassador at Vienna

Telegram 113.
Confidential. For Your Excellency's personal information and guidance.
Berlin, July 6, 1914.

The Austro-Hungarian Ambassador yesterday delivered to the Emperor a confidential personal letter from the Emperor Franz Joseph, which depicts the present situation from the Austro-Hungarian point of view, and describes the measures which Vienna has in view. A copy is now being forwarded to Your Excellency.

I replied to Count Szögyeny[2] today on behalf of His Majesty that His Majesty sends his thanks to the Emperor Franz Joseph for his letter and would soon answer it personally. In the meantime His Majesty desires to say that he is not blind to the danger which threatens Austria-Hungary and thus the Triple Alliance as a result of the Russian and Serbian Panslavic agitation. Even though His Majesty is known to feel no unqualified confidence in Bulgaria and her ruler, and naturally inclines more toward our

[2] Austro-Hungarian ambassador to Germany.

old ally Roumania and her Hohenzollern prince, yet he quite understands that the Emperor Franz Joseph, in view of the attitude of Roumania and of the danger of a new Balkan alliance aimed directly at the Danube Monarchy, is anxious to bring about an understanding between Bulgaria and the Triple Alliance. His Majesty will, therefore, direct his minister at Sofia to lend the Austro-Hungarian representative such support as he may desire in any action taken to this end. His Majesty will, furthermore, make an effort at Bucharest, according to the wishes of the Emperor Franz Joseph, to influence King Carol to the fulfilment of the duties of his alliance, to the renunciation of Serbia, and to the suppression of the Roumanian agitations directed against Austria-Hungary.

Finally, as far as concerns Serbia, His Majesty, of course, can not interfere in the dispute now going on between Austria-Hungary and that country, as it is a matter not within his competence. The Emperor Franz Joseph may, however, rest assured that His Majesty will faithfully stand by Austria-Hungary, as is required by the obligations of his alliance and of his ancient friendship.

Bethmann-Hollweg

The [German] Ambassador at Vienna to the Foreign Office

Telegram 85.

Absolutely confidential. Vienna, July 10, 1914.

Count Berchtold[3] gives me the following information concerning his yesterday's conference with His Majesty the Emperor Franz Joseph at Ischl:

His Majesty the Emperor discussed the state of affairs with great calmness. He first gave expression of his warm gratitude for the attitude of our Most Gracious Master and of the Imperial Government, and stated that he was quite of our opinion that it was necessary *now* to come to some *determination,* in order to put an end to the intolerable conditions in connection with Serbia. His Majesty was quite clear as to the importance of such a determination, added Count Berchtold.

The Minister then informed the Emperor of the two methods under discussion here as to the approaching action against Serbia. His Majesty seemed to think that the difference between them might be bridged over. On the whole, however, His Majesty had shown himself more inclined to the view that *concrete demands should be* leveled at Serbia. Nor could he, the Minister, deny the advantages of such procedure. The odium of an unexpected attack on Serbia, which would otherwise fall upon the Monarchy, would

[3] Austro-Hungarian foreign minister.

thus be avoided and Serbia would be put in the wrong. This procedure would also make an attitude of neutrality at least, materially easier both for Roumania and for England. At present the formulation of appropriate demands on Serbia constituted the principal source of anxiety here, and Count Berchtold said that he would be glad to know what they thought about it in Berlin. He thought that among other things, it might be demanded that an agency of the Austro-Hungarian Government be established at Belgrade in order to keep an eye from there on the Greater-Serbia machinations, perhaps, also, to insist upon the dissolution of the associations and the dismissal of *some compromised officers.* The respite allowed for the reply must be made as brief as possible, say forty-eight hours. It is true, that even so short a respite would suffice to enable Belgrade to get advice from Petersburg. If the Serbs should accept all the demands made on them, it would prove a solution which would be "very disagreeable" to him, and he was still considering what *demands* could *be put* that would be *wholly impossible for the Serbs to accept.*

Finally, the Minister complained again about the attitude of Count Tisza,[4] which made energetic procedure against Serbia difficult for him. Count Tisza asserted that they must proceed "like gentlemen," but that was scarcely possible to accomplish when such important national interests were concerned and *especially against such an opponent as Serbia.*

The Minister would be glad to follow the suggestion of the Imperial Government about commencing even now to set public opinion in England against Serbia by means of the press—about which Count Szögyeny had telegraphed. But this must be done cautiously, in his opinion, in order not to alarm Serbia prematurely.

The Minister of War is going on his leave tomorrow, and Baron Conrad von Hotzendorf[5] is also going to Vienna for a time. This is being done, as Count Berchtold told me, *on purpose,* in order to *prevent any disquiet.*

                                                        Tschirschky

The [German] *Ambassador at Vienna to the Imperial Chancellor*

Absolutely confidential.   Vienna, July 14, 1914.

Count Tisza came to see me today after his conference with Count Berchtold. The Count said that he had always been the one who had advised caution, but that every day had strengthened him in the conviction more and more *that the Monarchy would have to come to an energetic decision* in order to prove its vitality and *to put an end to the intolerable conditions*

---

[4] Hungarian prime minister.   [5] Austrian chief of staff.

in the south-east. The tone of the Serbian press and of the Serbian diplomats was so *presumptuous as simply not to be borne.* "It was very hard for me to come to the decision," said the Minister, "to give my advice for war, but I am now firmly *convinced of its necessity,* and I shall stand up for the greatness of the Monarchy to the utmost of my ability."

Fortunately *full agreement and determination* prevail among the authorities here. His Majesty Franz Joseph judges very calmly of the situation, as Baron Burian, too, who has talked with His Majesty at Ischl during the last day or two, reports, and will certainly hold out to the bitter end. Count Tisza added that *Germany's* unconditional assumption of a stand *by the side of the Monarchy* had a great influence on the firm attitude of the Emperor.

The note to be forwarded to Serbia had not yet been completed today in its final wording. This will not be done before Sunday. With regard to the time of its delivery to Serbia, it was decided today that it would be better to wait until Poincaré's [6] departure from Petersburg, that is until the twenty-fifth. Then, however, immediately upon the expiration of the respite granted Serbia, in case the latter should not submit to all the demands, *mobilization* would follow. The note is being composed so that the possibility of its acceptance is *practically excluded.* It was considered particularly important that it should demand not only assurances and promises, *but deeds.* In the composition of the note it was necessary, according to his view, to take care that it should be intelligible to the great general public—particularly in England—and that it should put Serbia plainly and clearly in the wrong.

Baron *Conrad* had made a *very good impression* on him at the last conference. He had spoken with great decision and calmness. Within the next few days they must, it was true, be prepared to have the people begin complaining again that *indecision and delay held sway here.* But that mattered little, if they only knew in Berlin that such was not the case.

In conclusion Count Tisza pressed my hand warmly, and said: "Together we shall now look the future calmly and firmly in the face."

Von Tschirschky

---

[6] President of France.

The [German] Secretary of State for Foreign Affairs to the
Ambassador at Rome and to the Chargé d'Affaires at Bucharest [7]

Telegrams 4, 36.
Confidential.   Berlin, July 14, 1914.

Should the outcome of the inquiry into the assassination at Serajevo cause
Austria-Hungary to adopt severe measures against Serbia, we, like the rest
of Europe, should be greatly interested in localizing any conflict that might
eventually result. This would depend on public opinion throughout Europe
making it possible for the various Governments to look on inactively while
Austria and Serbia settled their difference. For this purpose it is necessary
that the press in your locality should give space to the view that the conflict
involves a matter which concerns only the two participants. Austria should
not be blamed for placing herself in a position of defense against the continual menace to her existence contained in the harassing mischief-making
of a neighboring country. The sympathies of the whole civilized world
should be on her side in this struggle, as it is a struggle for the purpose of
finally strangling a propaganda that does not hesitate at assassination as a
weapon for war, and that constitutes a stain upon European culture and an
enduring menace to European peace by the unscrupulous and criminal manner in which it operates.

Kindly use your influence to the best of your ability on the local press in
line with these suggestions, carefully avoiding, however, in so doing, everything that might arouse the impression that we were instigating the Austrians
to war.

                                                              Jagow

Telegram from His Imperial Majesty the Emperor of Russia
to His Royal Highness Prince Alexander of Servia,
July 14 (27), 1914

When your Royal Highness applied to me at a time of especial stress,
you were not mistaken in the sentiments which I entertain for you, or in my
cordial sympathy with the Servian people.

The existing situation is engaging my most serious attention, and my
Government are using their utmost endeavour to smooth away the present
difficulties. I have no doubt that your Highness and the Royal Servian
Government wish to render that task easy by neglecting no step which

[7] A similar telegram was dispatched two days earlier to the German ambassador at London.

might lead to a settlement, and thus both prevent the horrors of a new war and safeguard the dignity of Servia.

So long as the slightest hope exists of avoiding bloodshed, all our efforts must be directed to that end; but if in spite of our earnest wish we are not successful, your Highness may rest assured that Russia will in no case disinterest herself in the fate of Servia.

The [German] Secretary of State for Foreign Affairs to the Ambassador at Rome

Telegram 5.
Confidential.   Berlin, July 15, 1914.
   Please report by wire whether Your Excellency needs funds for influencing local press, and if so, what sum?

                                                                    Jagow

The [German] Secretary of State for Foreign Affairs to the Ambassador at London

Private letter.   Berlin, July 18, 1914.
Dear Lichnowsky:
   Your opinion on our policy as contained in your Serbian report is always appreciated by me, and I am sure that the Imperial Chancellor feels the same way about it. Nor do I hesitate to admit that many of your remarks are justified. But after all, we are allied to Austria: *hic Rhodus, hic salta*. There may also be different opinions as to whether we get all our money's worth from an alliance with that ever disintegrating composition of nations beside the Danube, but there I say with the poet—Busch, I think it was—"If no longer you like your company, look for another, if any there be." And, unfortunately, we have not yet been able to arrive at a relationship with England that promises complete satisfaction, nor could we, after all that has passed, arrive at it, if, indeed, we shall ever be able to arrive at it.

   Austria, which has forfeited more and more prestige as a result of her lack of vigor, hardly counts any longer as a really Great Power. The Balkan crisis weakened her position still further. Our alliance federation has also been weakened by this retrogression of Austria's position as a Power.

   Austria no longer intends to tolerate the sapping activities of the Serbians, and just as little does she intend to tolerate longer the continuously provocative attitude of her small neighbor at Belgrade—see the talk in the Serbian press—and that of Mr. Pashitch.[8] She fully realizes that she has neglected

_____
[8] Serbian prime minister.

many opportunities, and that she is still able to act, though in a few years she may no longer be able to do so. Austria is now going to come to an understanding with Serbia, and has told us so. During the whole Balkan crisis we mediated successfully in the interest of peace, without forcing Austria to passivity at any of the critical moments. The fact that notwithstanding that we have often, with injustice, been accused of trimming and shuffling, makes no difference to me. Nor have we at the present time forced Austria to her decision. But we neither could nor should attempt to stay her hand. If we should do that, Austria would have the right to reproach us (and we ourselves) with having deprived her of her last chance of political rehabilitation. And then the process of her wasting away and of her internal decay would be still further accelerated. Her standing in the Balkans would be gone forever. You will undoubtedly agree with me that the absolute establishment of the Russian hegemony in the Balkans is, indirectly, not permissible, even for us. The maintenance of Austria, and, in fact, of the most powerful Austria possible, is a necessity for us both for internal and external reasons. That she can not be maintained forever, I will willingly admit. But in the meantime we may perhaps be able to arrange other combinations.

We must attempt to localize the conflict between Austria and Serbia. Whether we shall succeed in this will depend first on Russia, and secondly on the moderating influence of Russia's Allies. The more determined Austria shows herself, the more energetically we support her, so much the more quiet will Russia remain. To be sure, there will be some agitation in Petersburg, but, on the whole, Russia is not ready to strike at present. Nor will France or England be anxious for war at the present time. According to all competent observation, Russia will be prepared to fight in a few years. Then she will crush us by the number of her soldiers; then she will have built her Baltic Sea fleet and her strategic railroads. Our group, in the meantime, will have become weaker right along. In Russia this is well known, and they are therefore determined to have peace for a few years yet. I readily believe your cousin Benckendorff when he says that Russia wants no war with us at present. Sazonoff assures us of the same thing, but the Government of Russia, which is still attached to peace and half-way friendly to Germany today, is constantly growing weaker, while the feeling of the Slavic element is rapidly becoming more hostile to Germany. Russia's fundamental treatment of us was clearly indicated last fall. During the Balkan crisis she could not thank us enough for our peaceful influence. But no sooner had the crisis passed, than her unfriendly behavior recommenced —on account of Liman, etc. If we can not attain localization (of the conflict) and Russia attacks Austria, a *casus foederis*[9] will then arise; we could not throw Austria over then. We stand in the midst of an isolation that can scarcely be called "proud." I desire no preventive war, but if war should come, we can not hide behind the fence.

I still hope and believe, even today, that the conflict can be localized. In this matter the attitude of England will prove of great significance. I am fully convinced that local opinion in that country will not be enthusiastic over Austria's procedure, and I admit that all your arguments in this line are correct. But we must do all that is possible to prevent her becoming too enthusiastic in the Serbian cause, for it is a long road from either sympathy or antipathy to the fanning of the flames of a world-conflagration. Sir Grey is always talking of the balance of power represented by the two groups of Powers. It should, therefore, be perfectly obvious to him that this balance of power would be utterly destroyed if we should desert Austria and she should be demolished by Russia, and also that the balance of power would be made to totter considerably by a world-conflagration. Therefore, if he is honorable and logical, he must stand by us in attempting to localize the conflict. But now, *satis superque;*[10] it is one o'clock in the morning. If these arguments in favor of our policy are, perhaps, not sufficient to convince you, I know, nevertheless that you will stand behind them.

With the warmest greeting, sincerely yours,

Jagow

Sir H. Rumbold[11] to Sir Edward Grey

Berlin, July 22, 1914.

MINUTES

It is difficult to understand the attitude of the German Government. On the face of it, it does not bear the stamp of straight-forwardness. If they really are anxious to see Austria kept reasonably in check, they are in the best position to speak at Vienna. All they are doing is to inflame the passions at Belgrade and it looks very much like egging on the Austrians when they openly and persistently threaten the Servian Government through their official newspapers.

It may be presumed that the German Government do not believe that there is any real danger of war. They appear to rely on the British Govern-

[9] Collapse of the treaty.   [10] Enough and more than enough.
[11] British *chargé d'affaires* at Berlin.

ment to reinforce the German and Austrian threats at Belgrade; it is clear that if the British Government did intervene in this sense, or by addressing admonitions to St. Petersburg, the much desired breach between England and Russia would be brought one step nearer realisation.

But I admit that all this is speculation. We do not know the facts. The German Government clearly do know. They know what the Austrian Government is going to demand, they are aware that those demands will raise a grave issue, and I think we may say with some assurance that they have expressed approval of those demands and promised support, should dangerous complications ensue. So much can, I think, be read in the present telegram.

Prince Lichnowsky's vague hints and apprehensions do not quite correspond to the actual situation which his Government is helping to create. —E.A.C. July 22.

Sir R. Rodd [12] to Sir Edward Grey

Rome, July 22, 1914.
D. 2:35 P.M.
Tel. (No. 116) R. 6 P.M.

Minister of Foreign Affairs, who is in constant touch with Austrian Embassy, told me that he feared that communication to be made to Servia had been drafted in terms which must inevitably be inacceptable. He had hopes that they might have been modified at Ischl. He is convinced that a party in Austria are determined to take this opportunity of crushing Servia, which would be quite against the interests of Italy.

(Repeated to Vienna and Belgrade.)

Russian Ambassador to Sir A. Nicholson

Wednesday, July 29.
ENCLOSURE (2)

M. Sazanoff's telegram to the Russian Ambassador at Berlin, 15/28 July, 1914.

Chesham House, Chesham Place, S.W.

In consequence of the declaration of war addressed by Austria-Hungary to Serbia, the Imperial Government will order mobilization tomorrow in the military districts of Odessa, Kiev, Moscow and Kazan. Kindly convey

---

[12] British ambassador to Italy.

this information to the German Government, while making clear the absence in Russia of any aggressive designs against Germany. The Russian ambassador at Vienna has not yet been recalled from his post.

Main Text of Austrian Ultimatum to Serbia, July 23

In order to give a formal character to this undertaking the Royal Servian Government shall publish on the front page of their "Official Journal" of the 13/26 July the following declaration:—

"The Royal Government of Servia condemn the propaganda directed against Austria-Hungary—*i.e.,* the general tendency of which the final aim is to detach from the Austro-Hungarian Monarchy territories belonging to it, and they sincerely deplore the fatal consequences of these criminal proceedings.

"The Royal Government regret that Servian officers and functionaries participated in the above-mentioned propaganda and thus compromised the good neighbourly relations to which the Royal Government were solemnly pledged by their declaration of the 31st March, 1909.

"The Royal Government, who disapprove and repudiate all idea of interfering or attempting to interfere with the destinies of the inhabitants of any part whatsoever of Austria-Hungary, consider it their duty formally to warn officers and functionaries, and the whole population of the kingdom, that henceforward they will proceed with the utmost rigour against persons who may be guilty of such machinations, which they will use all their efforts to anticipate and suppress.

"This declaration shall simultaneously be communicated to the Royal army as an order of the day by His Majesty the King and shall be published in the 'Official Bulletin' of the Army.

"The Royal Servian Government further undertake:

"1. To suppress any publication which incites to hatred and contempt of the Austro-Hungarian Monarchy and the general tendency of which is directed against its territorial integrity;

"2. To dissolve immediately the society styled 'Narodna Odbrana,' to confiscate all its means of propaganda, and to proceed in the same manner against other societies and their branches in Servia which engage in propaganda against the Austro-Hungarian Monarchy. The Royal Government shall take the necessary measures to prevent the societies dissolved from continuing their activity under another name and form:

"3. To eliminate without delay from public instruction in Servia, both as regards the teaching body and also as regards the methods of instruction, everything that serves, or might serve, to foment the propaganda against Austria-Hungary;

"4. To remove from the military service, and from the administration in general, all officers and functionaries guilty of propaganda against the Austro-Hungarian Monarchy, whose names and deeds the Austro-Hungarian Government reserve to themselves the right of communicating to the Royal Government;

"5. To accept the collaboration in Servia of representatives of the Austro-Hungarian Government for the suppression of the subversive movement directed against the territorial integrity of the Monarchy;

"6. To take judicial proceedings against accessories to the plot of the 28th June who are on Servian territory; delegates of the Austro-Hungarian Government will take part in the investigation relating thereto;

"7. To proceed without delay to the arrest of Major Voija Tankositch and of the individual named Milan Ciganovitch, a Servian State employé, who have been compromised by the results of the magisterial enquiry at Serajevo;

"8. To prevent by effective measures the co-operation of the Servian authorities in the illicit traffic in arms and explosives across the frontier, to dismiss and punish severely the officials of the frontier service at Schabatz and Ložnica guilty of having assisted the perpetrators of the Serajevo crime by facilitating their passage across the frontier;

"9. To furnish the Imperial and Royal Government with explanations regarding the unjustifiable utterances of high Servian officials, both in Servia and abroad, who, notwithstanding their official position, have not hesitated since the crime of the 28th June to express themselves in interviews in terms of hostility to the Austro-Hungarian Government; and, finally,

"10. To notify the Imperial and Royal Government without delay of the execution of the measures comprised under the preceding heads.

"The Austro-Hungarian Government expect the reply of the Royal Government at the latest by 6 o'clock on Saturday evening, the 25th July."

Russian Chargé d'Affaires at Vienna to Russian Minister for Foreign Affairs

Vienna, July 12 (25), 1914.

(Telegram.)

Count Berchtold is at Ischl. In view of the impossibility of arriving there in time, I have telegraphed to him our proposal to extend the time limit of the ultimatum, and I have repeated this proposal verbally to Baron Macchio.

The latter promised to communicate it in time to the Minister for Foreign Affairs but added that he had no hesitation in predicting a categorical refusal.

Note of the Serbian Government in reply to the Austro-Hungarian Ultimatum, July 25

The Royal Government of Serbia condemns all propaganda which may be directed against Austria-Hungary, that is to say, all such tendencies as aim at ultimately detaching from the Austro-Hungarian Monarchy territories which form part thereof, and it sincerely deplores the baneful consequences of these criminal movements. The Royal Government regrets that, according to the communication from the Imperial and Royal Government, certain Serbian officers and officials should have taken part in the above-mentioned propaganda, and thus compromised the good-neighborly relations to which the Royal Serbian Government was solemnly engaged by the declaration of the 18th (31st) March, 1909, which declaration disapproves and repudiates all idea or attempt at interference with the destiny of the inhabitants of any part whatsoever of Austria-Hungary, and it considers it a duty formally to warn the officers, officials and entire population of the Kingdom that henceforth it will take the most rigorous steps against all such persons as are guilty of such acts, to prevent and to repress which it will use its utmost endeavor.

This declaration will be brought to the knowledge of the Royal Army in an order of the day, in the name of His Majesty the King, by his Royal Highness the Crown Prince Alexander, and will be published in the next official army bulletin.

The Royal Government further undertakes:

1. To introduce at the first regular convocation of the Skuptchina a provision into the press law providing for the most severe punishment of incitement to hatred or contempt of the Austro-Hungarian Monarchy, and for taking action against any publication the general tendency of which is directed against the territorial integrity of Austria-Hungary. The Government engages at the approaching revision of the Constitution to cause an amendment to be introduced into Article 22 of the Constitution of such a nature that such publication may be confiscated, a proceeding at present impossible under the categorical terms of Article 22 of the Constitution.

2. The Government possesses no proof, nor does the note of the Imperial and Royal Government furnish it with any, that the *Narodna Odbrana* and other similar societies have committed up to the moment any criminal act

of this nature through the proceedings of any of their members. Nevertheless, the Royal Government will accept the demand of the Imperial and Royal Government and will dissolve the Narodna Odbrana society and every other society which may be directing its efforts against Austria-Hungary.

3. The Royal Serbian Government undertakes to remove without delay from its public educational establishments in Serbia all that serves or could serve to foment propaganda against Austria-Hungary, whenever the Imperial and Royal Government furnishes them with facts and proofs of this propaganda.

4. The Royal Government also agrees to remove from military service all such persons as the judicial inquiry may have proved to be guilty of acts directed against the integrity of the territory of the Austro-Hungarian Monarchy, and it expects the Imperial and Royal Government to communicate to it at a later date the names and the acts of these officers and officials for the purposes of the proceedings which are to be taken against them.

5. The Royal Government must confess that it does not clearly grasp the meaning or the scope of the demand made by the Imperial and Royal Government that Serbia shall undertake to accept the collaboration of the organs of the Imperial and Royal Government upon its territory, but it declares that it will admit such collaboration as agrees with the principle of international law, with criminal procedure, and with good-neighborly relations.

6. It goes without saying that the Royal Government considers it its duty to open an inquiry against all such persons as are, or eventually may be, implicated in the plot of the 15th (28th) June, and who happen to be within the territory of the Kingdom. As regards the participation in this inquiry of Austro-Hungarian agents or authorities appointed for this purpose by the Imperial and Royal Government, the Royal Government cannot accept such an arrangement, as it would be a violation of the Constitution and of the law of criminal procedure; nevertheless, in concrete cases communications as to the results of the investigation in question might be given to the Austro-Hungarian agents.

7. The Royal Government proceeded, on the very evening of the delivery of the note, to arrest Commandant Voislav Tankositch. As regards Milan Ciganovitch, who is a subject of the Austro-Hungarian Monarchy and who up to the 15th (28th) June was employed (on probation) by the directorate of railways, it has not yet been possible to arrest him.

The Austro-Hungarian Government is requested to be so good as to supply as soon as possible, in the customary form, the presumptive evidence of guilt, as well as the eventual proofs of guilt which have been collected up to the present, at the inquiry of Serajevo, for the purposes of the latter inquiry.

8. The Serbian Government will reinforce and extend the measures which have been taken for preventing the illicit traffic of arms and explosives across the frontier. It goes without saying that it will immediately order an inquiry and will severely punish the frontier officials on the Schabatz-Ložnica line who have failed in their duty and allowed the authors of the crime of Serajevo to pass.

9. The Royal Government will gladly give explanations of the remarks made by its officials, whether in Serbia or abroad, in interviews after the crime, and which, according to the statement of the Imperial and Royal Government, were hostile towards the Monarchy, as soon as the Imperial and Royal Government has communicated to them the passages in question in these remarks, and as soon as they have shown that the remarks were actually made by the said officials, although the Royal Government will itself take steps to collect evidence and proofs.

10. The Royal Government will inform the Imperial and Royal Government of the execution of the measures comprised under the above heads, in so far as this has not already been done by the present note, as soon as each measure has been ordered and carried out.

If the Imperial and Royal Government is not satisfied with this reply, the Serbian Government, considering that it is not to the common interest to precipitate the solution of this question, are ready, as always, to accept a pacific understanding, either by referring this question to the decision of the International Tribunal of The Hague, or to the Great Powers which took part in the drawing up of the declaration made by the Serbian Government on the 18th (31st) March, 1909.[13]

A brilliant performance for a time-limit of only forty-eight hours. This is more than one could have expected! A great moral victory for Vienna; but with it every reason for war drops away, and Giesl might have remained quietly in Belgrade. On the strength of this I should never have ordered mobilization!

W.[14]

[13] Serbian reply ends here.

[14] Marginal comment of the Kaiser on the copy of the Serbian reply in the German archives.

The [German] Ambassador at Vienna to the Foreign Office

Telegram 104.   Vienna, July 25, 1914.
Baron Macchio [15] tells me over the telephone: As several points in the
Serbian reply are unsatisfactory, Baron Giesl [16] has left. General mobilization
said to have been going on in Serbia since three o'clock this afternoon.

Tschirschky

The [German] Ambassador at Petersburg to the Foreign Office

Telegram 153.   Petersburg, July 25, 1914.
General von Chelius [17] reports for His Majesty:
The troop maneuvers at Drasnoje Camp were broken off suddenly today,
the regiments are returning at once to their garrisons; maneuvers are called
off, military students were commissioned as officers today instead of in the
fall. Grand Headquarters are in the throes of great excitement over Austria's
procedure. I have the impression that all preparations are being made for
mobilization against Austria.

Pourtalès

M. Bienvenu-Martin, Acting Minister for Foreign Affairs to the French Ambassadors at London, St. Petersburg, Berlin, Vienna, Rome

Paris, July 27, 1914.
The Austro-Hungarian Ambassador came to see me to hand me a memorandum which amounted to an indictment of Servia; he was instructed by
his Government to state that since Servia had not given a satisfactory reply
to the requirements of the Imperial Government, the latter found themselves
obliged to take strong measures to induce Servia to give the satisfaction and
guarantees that are required of her. To-morrow the Austrian Government
will take steps to that effect.

I asked the Ambassador to acquaint me with the measures contemplated
by Austria, and Count Scézsen [18] replied that they might be either an
ultimatum, or a declaration of war, or the crossing of the frontier, but he had
no precise information on this point.

I then called the Ambassador's attention to the fact that Servia had accepted

---

[15] Undersecretary, Austrian foreign office.   [16] Austro-Hungarian minister to Serbia.
[17] German military plenipotentiary at St. Petersburg.
[18] Austro-Hungarian ambassador to France.

Austria's requirements on practically every point, and that the differences that remained on certain points might vanish with a little mutual goodwill, and with the help of the Powers who wished for peace; by fixing to-morrow as the date for putting her resolution into effect, Austria for the second time was making their co-operation practically impossible, and was assuming a grave responsibility in running the risk of precipitating a war the limits of which it was impossible to foresee.

I enclose for your information the memorandum that Count Scézsen handed to me.

Bienvenu-Martin

The Imperial Chancellor to the [German] Emperor

Telegram 151.   Berlin, July 27, 1914.

Austria does not appear to be able to enter upon military activities before the 12th of August, and Serbia appears to intend to confine herself exclusively to the defensive. Serbia's answer to the ultimatum, the text of which we have not yet been able to get hold of, is said to agree to nearly all the points, even the punishment of all officers, outside of a general order; cooperation only with certain reservations.

Your most humble servant,

Bethmann-Hollweg

M. Paléologue, French Ambassador at St. Petersburgh, to M. Bienvenu-Martin, Acting Minister for Foreign Affairs

St. Petersburgh, July 28, 1914.

The Austro-Hungarian Government has not yet replied to the proposal of the Russian Government suggesting the opening of direct conversations between St. Petersburgh and Vienna.

Mr. Sazonoff [19] received the German and Austro-Hungarian Ambassadors this afternoon. The impression which he got from this double interview is a bad one; "Certainly," he said to me, "Austria is unwilling to converse."

As the result of a conversation which I have just had with my two colleagues I have the same impression of pessimism.

Paléologue

[19] Russian foreign minister.

The [German] Ambassador at London to the Foreign Office

Telegram 171.   London, July 28, 1914.

The members of the local Austrian Embassy, including Count Mensdorff,[20] have, in their talks with members of this Embassy and with me, never attempted the least concealment of the fact that Austria was solely concerned with the destruction of Serbia, and that the note was intentionally so constructed that it would have to be rejected. When the news that Serbia had submitted was published Saturday night by the *Central News,* these gentlemen were actually stunned. Count Mensdorff told me only yesterday in confidence that in Vienna they were absolutely set on war, as Serbia was to be "beaten to the earth."

Lichnowsky

The [German] Ambassador at Vienna to the Foreign Office

Telegram 118.   Vienna, July 28, 1914.

Declaration of war sent by telegraph today at eleven o'clock to the Serbian Ministry of Foreign Affairs.

Tschirschky

M. N. Pashitch, [Serbian] Prime Minister and Minister for Foreign Affairs, to all the Serbian Legations abroad

(Telegraphic.)   Nish, July 15/28, 1914.

The Austro-Hungarian Government declared war on Serbia at noon to-day by an open telegram to the Serbian Government.

The Czar to the Emperor

Peterhof Palace, July 29, 1914.

Telegram (unnumbered).

His Majesty the Emperor, New Palace.

Am glad you are back. In this most serious moment I appeal to you to help me. An *ignoble* war has been declared to a *weak* country. The *indignation* in Russia, *shared fully by me,* is *enormous.* I foresee that very soon I shall be *overwhelmed* by the *pressure* brought upon me, and be *forced* to take extreme measures which will *lead to war.* To try and avoid such a

---

[20] Austro-Hungarian ambassador to England.

calamity as a European war, I beg you in the name of our old friendship to do what you can to *stop* your *allies* from *going too far*.

Nicky

(following in italics) A confession of his own weakness, and an attempt to put the responsibility on my shoulders. The telegram contains a concealed threat and an order-like summons to tie the hands of our ally. . . . The expression "ignoble war" does not indicate any sense of monarchical unity in the czar, but rather a Panslavic conception; i.e., worry over a *capitis diminutio* [21] in the Balkans in case of an Austrian victory. This might well first be waited for in its collective result. There will always be time later for negotiation and eventually for mobilization, for which now Russia has no reason at all. Instead of summoning us to check our allies, His Majesty should turn to the Emperor Franz Joseph and deal with him in order to learn His Majesty's intentions. Should not copies of both the telegrams be sent to His Majesty the King at London for his information? The Socialists are making anti-military demonstrations in the streets; that must not be tolerated, in any event, not now; in case they are repeated, I shall proclaim a state of martial law and have the leaders one and all *tutti quanti* [22] locked up. Instruct Loebell and Jagow about this. We can tolerate no Socialist propaganda now! [23]

Wilhelm

The [German] Imperial Chancellor to the Ambassador at Paris

Telegram 172.

Urgent   Berlin, July 29, 1914.

Reports of French preparations for war are becoming more frequent. Kindly take up the matter with the French Government and call its attention to the fact that such activities would force us to take measures for self-protection. We should have to proclaim a state of "risk of war," which, although it would not yet mean mobilization or the calling in of any reserves to the colors, would nevertheless increase the tension. We continue to hope for the preservation of peace.

Bethmann-Hollweg

---

[21] A loss of rights.   [22] All of them.
[23] Marginal notes by the Kaiser.

Sir G. Buchanan[24] to Sir Edward Grey

St. Petersburg, July 30, 1914.
D. 6:40 P.M.
Tel.   R. 5:20 P.M.

It has been decided to issue orders for general mobilisation.

This decision was taken in consequence of report received from Russian Ambassador in Vienna to the effect that Austria is determined not to yield to intervention of Powers, and that she is moving troops against Russia, as well as against Servia.

Russia has also reason to believe that Germany is making active military preparations and she cannot afford to let her get a start.

The [German] Ambassador at Paris to the Foreign Office

Telegram 233.   Paris, July 30, 1914.

Embassy and General Consulate are being stormed by Germans asking for advice about leaving. In view of the possibility that the French Government might at the outbreak of hostilities intern or expel to Spain, Germans capable of bearing arms, we think immediate return home of men liable to service advisable. Other Germans settled here can wait, as far as they are not dismissed from their places, which so far has happened very rarely.

Does Your Excellency agree?

Schoen

The Secretary of State for Foreign Affairs to the Ambassador at Paris

Telegram 175.   Berlin, July 31, 1914.

Departure of Germans advisable.

Jagow

The Emperor to the Czar

Telegram (unnumbered).   Berlin, July 31, 1914.

On your appeal to my friendship and your call for assistance began to mediate between your and the Austro-Hungarian Government. While this action was proceeding your troops were mobilized against Austria-Hungary, my ally. Thereby, as I have already pointed out to you, my mediation has been made almost illusory.

[24] British ambassador to Russia.

I have nevertheless continued my action. I now receive authentic news of serious preparations for war on my eastern frontier. Responsibility for the safety of my Empire forces preventive measures of defense upon me. In my endeavors to maintain the peace of the world I have gone to the utmost limit possible. The responsibility for the disaster which is now threatening the whole civilized world will not be laid at my door. In this moment it still lies in your power to avert it. Nobody is threatening the honor or power of Russia who can well afford to await the result of my mediation. My friendship for you and your Empire, transmitted to me by my grandfather on his deathbed, has always been sacred to me and I have honestly often backed up Russia when she was in serious trouble, especially in her last war.

The peace of Europe may still be maintained by you, if Russia will agree to stop the military measures which must threaten Germany and Austria-Hungary.

WILLY

Secret Telegram [from Russian Foreign Minister] to Russian Representatives abroad

August 1, 1914.

(Telegram.)

At midnight the German Ambassador announced to me, on the instruction of his Government, that if within 12 hours, that is by midnight on Saturday, we had not begun to demobilise, not only against Germany, but also against Austria, the German Government would be compelled to give the order for mobilisation. To my enquiry whether this meant war, the Ambassador replied in the negative, but added that we were very near it.

Sir G. Buchanan to Sir Edward Grey

St. Petersburg, August 1, 1914.
D. 1:20 P.M.
R. 11:15 P.M.

Tel. (No. 201.)

German Ambassador handed to Minister for Foreign Affairs formal declaration of war this evening at 7 o'clock.

The [German] Ambassador at Paris to the Foreign Office

Telegram 240.   Paris, August 1, 1914.
Mobilization of the entire French army ordered Saturday at 5 p.m. Sunday, first day of mobilization.

Military Attaché Klüber
Schoen

The Grand Duchess of Luxemburg to the Emperor

Telegram (unnumbered).   Luxemburg, August 2, 1914.
His Majesty the German Emperor, Berlin
At this moment the Grand Duchy is being occupied by German troops. My Government has lodged a protest in the proper quarter and has demanded an explanation of the occurrence. I beg Your Majesty to hasten this explanation and to respect the country's rights.

Marie Adelheid

The [German] Imperial Chancellor to the Minister at Luxemburg

Telegram 12.   Berlin, August 2, 1914.
Our military measures in Luxemburg indicate no hostile action against Luxemburg, but are solely measures for the protection of the railroads under our management there, against an attack by the French. Luxemburg will receive full compensation for any possible damages. Kindly inform local Government.

Bethmann-Hollweg

Sir F. Villiers [25] to Sir Edward Grey

Brussels, August 2, 1914.
D. 12:15 P.M.
R. 1:25 P.M.
Tel. (No. 101.)
Minister for Foreign Affairs states that Belgian Government have no reason whatever to suspect Germany of an intention to violate neutrality. He says that Belgian Government have not considered idea of appeal to other guarantee Powers, nor of intervention should a violation occur; they would

[25] British minister-plenipotentiary to Belgium.

rely upon their own armed force as sufficient to resist aggression, from whatever quarter it might come.

The [German] Ambassador at London to the Foreign Office

Telegram 218.   London, August 2, 1914

The question as to whether we are going to violate Belgian territory in our war with France may be of decisive importance in determining that of England's neutrality. This impression of mine is decidedly corroborated, not alone by Sir E. Grey's statements, but by information from the Austrian Embassy and by the local press. Should we violate the neutrality of Belgium and a war with the Belgians were to result from it, I believe that the Government would be unable to remain neutral much longer, in the face of the storm that could then be expected from aroused local public opinion. On the other hand, should we respect Belgian neutrality, it is always possible that England would remain neutral, if, in the event of victory over France, we should proceed with moderation. But since it is beginning to be believed here that a violation of Belgian neutrality is to be reckoned with, I think it not impossible that England will take a stand against us within a very short time. Today, Sunday, a meeting of the Cabinet takes place, and I assume that this question will undoubtedly be taken up at it.

                                                    Lichnowsky

Sir F. Villiers to Sir Edward Grey

                                        Brussels, August 4, 1914.
                                        D. August 4, 4 P.M.
                                        R. August 5, 12:50 A.M.

Tel. (No. 29.)

I have just received from Minister for Foreign Affairs a note of which following is a literal translation:—

"Belgian Government regret to have to inform His Majesty's Government that this morning armed forces of Germany penetrated into Belgian territory in violations of engagements assumed by treaty. Belgian Government are firmly resolved to resist by all means in their power. Belgium appeals to Great Britain and France and Russia to co-operate, as guarantors, in defence of her territory.

"There would be concerted and common action with the object of resisting the forcible measures employed by Germany against Belgium and at the same time of guarding the maintenance for future of the independence and integrity of Belgium.

"Belgium is happy to be able to declare that she will assume defence of her fortified places."

M. René Viviani, President of the Council, Minister for Foreign Affairs, to M. Jules Cambon, French Ambassador at Berlin

TELEGRAM COMMUNICATED TO FRENCH REPRESENTATIVES ABROAD

Paris, August 3, 1914.

I request you to ask for your passports and to leave Berlin at once with the staff of the Embassy, leaving the charge of French interests and the care of the archives to the Spanish Ambassador. I request you at the same time to protest in writing against the violation of the neutrality of Luxemburg by German troops, of which notice has been given by the Prime Minister of Luxemburg; against the ultimatum addressed to the Belgian Government by the German Minister at Brussels to force upon them the violation of Belgian neutrality and to require of that country that she should facilitate military operations against France on Belgian territory; finally against the false allegation of an alleged projected invasion of these two countries by French armies, by which he has attempted to justify the state of war which he declares henceforth exists between Germany and France.

René Viviani

The King of the Belgians to the [German] Emperor

Telegram (Unnumbered).   Brussels, August 4, 1914.
To His Majesty the Emperor, Berlin.

The feelings of friendship which I have expressed to Your Majesty and those of which you have so often asssured me, the most cordial relations between our two Governments, the constantly correct attitude of Belgium against which Germany has never been able to formulate the least reproach, did not permit me to assume for a single moment that Your Majesty would force us, in the face of all Europe, to the cruel choice between war and dishonor, between fidelity to treaties and faithlessness to our international obligations.

Albert

*Count de Lalaing, Belgian Minister at London, to M. Davignon,
Belgian Minister for Foreign Affairs*

London, August 5, 1914.

(Telegram.)

Germany having rejected the British proposals, Great Britain has informed her that a state of war existed between the two countries as from 11 o'clock.

The Austro-Hungarian Embassy to the Foreign Office

Berlin, August 5, 1914.

NOTIFICATION

Count Szapary [26] was instructed by Count Berchtold yesterday to notify the Russian Government that, in view of the war that has broken out between Germany and Russia as a result of Russian aggression, as well as in view of Russia's threatening attitude toward our conflict with Serbia, we consider ourselves to be at war with Russia.

Sir Edward Grey to Sir M. de Bunsen [at Vienna]

Foreign Office, August 12, 1914.

Tel. (No. 213) *En clair.*   D. 7:15 P.M.

At the request of the French Government, who have no diplomatic means of communicating with Austria direct, I have made to the Austrian Ambassador a communication that amounts to a complete rupture between France and Austria, on the ground that Austria declared war on Russia, who was already fighting on the side of France, and that Austria has sent troops over the German frontier under conditions that are a direct menace to France.

The rupture having been brought about with France in this way, His Majesty's Government are obliged to instruct you to ask for your passports, and I have announced to the Austrian Ambassador that a state of war exists between the two countries from midnight.

[26] Austro-Hungarian ambassador to Russia.

Declaration of the Triple Entente (September 4, 1914)

DECLARATION

*M. Delcassé, Minister for Foreign Affairs, to the
French Ambassadors and Ministers abroad*

Paris, September 4, 1914.

The following declaration has this morning been signed at the Foreign Office at London:—

"The undersigned duly authorized thereto by their respective Governments hereby declare as follows:—

"The British, French and Russian Governments mutually engage not to conclude peace separately during the present war. The three Governments agree that when terms of peace come to be discussed, no one of the Allies will demand terms of peace without the previous agreement of each of the other Allies."

(*Signed*)   Paul Cambon
Count Benckendorff
Edward Grey

This declaration will be published today.

Delcassé

JULES ROMAINS

Although the American Civil War had given some hint of things to come in warfare, few, if any, of the men who took Europe into war in 1914 could have gauged the scale of the ensuing carnage. A wave of patriotic fervor at first swept through the principal belligerent nations and made nonsense of the prewar hopes of socialist leaders for working-class pacifism. By interpreting the war as a defensive struggle the masses were able to become violently patriotic. Initial German victories greatly strengthened German nationalist feeling and, together with atrocity stories, and actual brutality, drove the French and English into positive fury against the "Huns."

Then came the "technical surprise"—an incredible concentration of fire power at the fronts, made possible by mass production of armaments. Dreadful battles often yielded only a few hundred yards while tens of thousands fell dead or wounded. A vicious self-reinforcing process was set in motion. Firepower made for hideous casualties but, paradoxically, it sometimes gave opposing soldiers a feeling of camaraderie in death. Ever heightening civilian war fever stimulated by the slaughter diminished any chance for diplomatic negotiation and compromise. War aims were thus inflated and, with the determination that a battle for civilization itself was being fought, all-out efforts were made to increase firepower and the size of armies at the fronts. And the cycle began again. The process could not go on indefinitely: As the blood-bath continued patriotism began to sag and suppressed claims of class and of interest groups came again to the surface. Serious mutinies broke out at the front. Europe was bleeding to death.

American manpower and Allied armaments finally turned the tide in the summer of 1918 against a nearly successful final German offensive. Those men still alive in 1918, who had gone to war unaware of what the trenches were to mean, could no longer confidently believe in life or in European civilization. The shattering experience of the trenches inspired a number of war novels in Europe and America long after the Armistice. John Dos Passos and Ernest Hemingway in the United States, Ford Madox Ford in England, and Erich Maria Remarque in Germany were a few of the writers who helped make their reputations by their description of the horrors of the war.

Of all the accounts of life in the trenches none was as powerful as Jules Romains' *Verdun*. The title was well chosen, for Verdun was perhaps the longest and worst of the battles on the Western front. The countryside around the French fortress city looked like the cratered areas on the moon at the war's end and the scars were visible twenty years later. The number of casualties was beyond belief. *Verdun* is one of a series of novels by Romains entitled *Men of Good Will*, attempting to depict various aspects of European culture in the twentieth century. The selection below is a chapter in the form of a letter by one of the chief characters in the novel to a friend. The letter tells what the battle at Verdun has done to him and his ideals and analyzes what the war will do to Europe.

Verdun was translated from the French by Gerard Hopkins (New York: Alfred A. Knopf, 1940).

VERDUN

CHAPTER 15. A LETTER FROM JERPHANION TO JALLEZ. HOW ONE MANAGES TO CARRY ON

I can't tell you how pleased I was to get your long letter; not so much because of its news—you don't tell me much about yourself (more's the pity!) but because it serves as a link, a life-line, connecting me with what I still insist on regarding as the only reality.

I am tempted, instead of answering your questions, to ask a few of my own, such as: "Is it, then, really possible still to find something that resembles a genuine existence? Did the 2nd of December 1915 actually happen, or was it like something one finds fossilized in books? How can it possibly fit in with the rest of the picture?"

I suppose you'll say to yourself: "He's working himself into one of his states—it's all just words." There, alas, you're wrong. . . . But, all the same, you won't be able to give an answer to my rather absurd and self-pitying question, because you can't know what it's like to suffer from the sort of intellectual atrophy, the pernicious mental scurvy, that comes of long privation of all the things that make life real; because even the analogy of thirst can't possibly give you an inkling of what it's like to be tortured by the absence of everything that makes life worth living.

I don't mean that the things you ask aren't difficult enough in all conscience to answer. Here we just don't let ourselves think of them, and I have a feeling that, just because you guessed as much, you put off raising these particular questions until now. It is natural, indeed inevitable, that you should be infinitely curious. Incidentally, let me say that you've missed something in not having had that experience for yourself. No letter, no amount of talk, and still more, no literary descriptions in second-rate books—and books on the war cannot but be second-rate—could ever give you the faintest idea of the reality. You, perhaps, with your acute sensibility and your long training in coming to terms with the inexpressible, might succeed in bringing into consciousness what the average consciousness refuses to register. This I say sincerely and with no intention whatever of irony.

The most one can do is to throw one's line at a venture in the hope of hooking some fragment of experience that may serve as evidence, or, rather, as one scrap of evidence among others. I try to think forward to the day when some man will try to put together the thousand and one statements of those who were witnesses of these events which at present are beyond the power of thought to compass. What will he make of them? God knows!

You must take everything I say as no more than a purely personal version. I no sooner write down a phrase than I want to scratch it out again as false, conventional, intolerably one-sided, as a wholly distorted view of the facts.

What you want to know most of all is how a man, brought up as we have been brought up, can put up with this life, day in, day out, week after week, month after month. "What is his attitude of mind?" were your actual words. What attitude will give him least sense of pain? To put it more simply still, what is this life of mine like, you ask, and whence do I draw sufficient courage to endure it?

Need I remind you of the enthusiasm of the first days? I shared in it. I don't attempt to deny the fact. What produced it? Ignorance; love of the dramatic; an accumulated spiritual vitality which found no employment in the things of every day and so was ready for anything out of the ordinary; belief, too, that enthusiasm, given its head, could irresistibly mould events. What it comes to is this: on the 2nd of August I felt convinced that victory would be ours by the 1st of September, and that the only real problem would be how best to use it in the interests of humanity.

I admit that I was rather ashamed of my share in that enthusiasm, that I recognized it as something irrational, but you yourself felt something of the same sort, you told me, for about forty-eight hours, which proves that it must have been terribly contagious, a kind of acute form of influenza. With me it lasted longer. How long? Three weeks? Six weeks? Let us say three weeks at its most violent stage, with a few weeks longer allowed for slow convalescence and occasional relapses. Looking back, I realize that enthusiasm of that kind could not stand up to the proof that enthusiasm alone is quite incapable of winning a war.

How much of it do I retain today? With my hand on my heart, and not at all wishing to pose, by reaction, as "hard-boiled," I can say: almost exactly nothing.

Sometimes I try to fan it once more into flame, because, in a way, it would be a help. But it's difficult. I cannot now begin to conceive how this war can possibly turn out "well," meaning by "well" something that our idealism could accept. Its main consequences, so far as I can see, will be something of this sort: Entry of the Tsar into Constantinople; or the unchallenged supremacy of Great Britain from Liverpool to Singapore. Nor does my egotism as a Frenchman see anything really comforting ahead. I know perfectly well that my country will be far too exhausted to impose its will on Europe, even assuming that will to be good. Meanwhile I see only too clearly what the positive results—I'm not speaking now of intangible things—have so far been: a rich harvest of profiteers; a baseness of soul in people at the rear which leads them to find it perfectly natural that we should continue to act as a bulwark behind which they can carry on their filthy little lives, their filthy little activities of buying and selling. Nor am I forgetting what may be a comparatively unimportant detail, though to me it means a lot—the gutter stupidity of all those gentlemen of letters, those so-called intellectuals, whose words and attitudes are a constant insult to the spirit, to ordinary common sense, to any reasons we may have for continuing the struggle, to us who are continuing it. Never—and I can't stress this too strongly—never shall I forget the feeling of shame that these oafs induce in me.

Add to all this the bestiality, the gloomy bestiality, into which this business has flung us so that it has become our daily food.

I've just thought of three sentences (I'm writing this by the light of a candle, in my dug-out, with a board across my knees) which sum up my present state of mind: (1) I no longer believe that a "crushing" victory would be an advantage. (2) If all we can hope for is an inconclusive peace, what is the use of going on? (3) Meanwhile, everything we see happening, whether at the front or in the rear, is horrible.

But, above all, these five words seem written in fire on the walls of my dug-out: *Nothing can be worth this.* Nothing = any conceivable argument. This = the kind of life we are leading (with a hideous death for ever hanging over our heads). That is the final word of wisdom so far as the war is concerned. Everything else is mere fine writing.

You will say: "If you feel like that you must be a very bad soldier."

No, I'm rather a good one. Or so I think, and my colleagues and superiors think so too. I have been given a company over the heads of a good many others, and in spite of the fact that I have been away from the line for several months. Since I'm certainly not "as brave as a lion," and have never captured an enemy battery and pinned the gunners to their guns with my bayonet (which is the least of the noble exploits with which M. Henri Lavedan regales the ladies and gentlemen at home), I can only assume that a sort of pigheaded mediocrity is all that I have to recommend me. Odd, isn't it?

What helps me to carry on (me, regarded as typical of all the others)?

Perhaps the thought that I might be worse off. You may laugh, but it's probably true. I might be in a worse part of the line, where hard fighting was going on all the time. I might have had both my legs blown off. I might be dead. I might be a private.

This last consideration has a slightly comic look; a week ago I quite likely shouldn't have included it. But it so happens that I've got in my company a rather extraordinary man. His name is Griollet, a Parisian from the 9th arrondissement. In civil life he's a leather-worker (with his own little business). I couldn't make him out at first, because he doesn't say much. He's one of the very few among my men to whom I can talk freely without any danger of his taking advantage of the fact. For instance, he's the only man I've dared question on what he really thinks and feels. The day before yesterday we were having a chat. In the course of the conversation he suddenly said, without the slightest trace of impertinence, like someone who has been thinking out a problem and weighing the pros and cons: "You officers do have certain advantages, but I'm not sure that they amount to much compared with all the worry and responsibility. Still, they're something. And your work's more interesting." Another of his remarks was: "Even though an officer runs the same risks as us, it's easier, in a way, for him to be brave."

I've been thinking a good deal since about the truth of what he said. It's certainly a fact that having to bother about my men is a "diversion" in the Pascalian sense of the word. You have no idea how much office work there is in the trenches. I have endless reports to render, some daily, others at short and recurrent intervals: a report every forty-eight hours—trench state, list of casualties (even in quiet times we have casualties, alas!), lists of this, that, and the other; suggestions for decorations and promotion (*sic*). I have to go and take a look as often as possible at the sort of second-hand dealer's, or rather ironmonger's, shop which we've rigged up here in the bowels of the earth, for which I'm responsible. It really is like the sort of old-iron store one sees at Belleville or Vaugirard, and I'm the proprietor who's for ever looking at his shelves and nosing into the corners wondering: "Have I got enough stove-pipes? Has Alfred, my clerk, forgotten to let me know that we're short of wrenches or screw-drivers?" But my stock is rather different. It consists of rifle ammunition, bombs, grenades, tools, signal rockets, steel plates, and anti-gas sprays, pails of hyposulphite, boxes of biscuit, and all the hundred and one gadgets we need for killing or to avoid being killed. At any moment when there's a chance of my being left to myself, free, that's to say, to take a plunge into the dark waters of the rivar Kafar (the oued-el-Kafir, as one of my friends is fond of saying), I suddenly remember that I've got to find a working party, and twenty minutes later a fatigue, and that that's going to leave me short of sentries, because, of course, half the men are having their time off for sleep. All that, and numerous other details, divides my waking hours into small sections, each one of which is thus made easier to swallow and contains only a dose of poison so small that the organism can absorb it.

And what about your physical condition? you'll ask. Surely that bulks pretty large? How do you manage? For instance, what about cold? I don't mind telling you that all last winter it was a haunting obsession for everyone in the line, with its refinements of torture such as frost-bitten feet, or, rather, mortified feet, feet rotting to pieces with a sort of pallid corruption. A living man might at any moment discover that his feet were those of a corpse in an advanced stage of decomposition. Today we mind rather less about the cold. We have woolens and blankets, trench boots—a whole primitive technique of living which has turned us into the semblance of prehistoric man.

Food? So far as that's concerned, we obviously have less to complain of than the men. They're pretty badly off just now, worse off than they were during the first winter of the war. God alone knows why! They're issued a sort of prison gruel, and not enough of it to satisfy a hungry man. If they didn't get parcels from home. . . . But a number of mine are from the occupied territories and consequently get nothing of that sort. It's terrible to see the poor devils weighed down with this load of purely animal misery in addition to everything else. We officers don't do so badly. The cook concocts some sort of stew for us while we're in the line. It tastes pretty funny, but at least there's enough of it. When we're in billets, things are better for everyone, the men included. After all, if the war had nothing worse than bad food to offer, it wouldn't be so terrible.

Dirt. I've got a few things to say about that. It's a subject worth a certain amount of thought. Here, for the moment, as a result of various causes which have to do with the nature of the place, the permanence of the line, the relative state of quiet, we are not experiencing degree of dirt No. I; I have experienced it, though, and I shall experience it again: having to go, I mean, four or five days without washing so much as one's face. Under present conditions I manage to get my face clean every morning, and my hands about twice a day. Naturally, one goes to bed with one's clothes on, though one can usually unlace one's boots. (Sometimes, in an access of daring, I take mine right off.) The result is rather less foul than the evidence of your nose might lead you to guess. Out at rest we have a thorough clean-up. This open-air life solves a good many problems. We don't overeat and our skins act pretty freely. Many impurities, both internal and external, evaporate or undergo a sea-change. On the whole I probably stink rather less than did Louis

XIV. I've noted one or two odd things. I don't deny that the men I meet in the trenches do smell pretty strong, but it's the kind of smell I've often come across, at home, among the peasants who work in the fields, a sort of animal smell (animals don't wash much, either); a smell that has about it something earthy and alive. Far from being repulsive, it gives one an idea of what men, mankind in general, would be if one had to rely for one's impressions on the sense of smell alone, a counterbalancing impression to the one that comes through the eyes. Since we do not, as a rule, mind the shape of a man, why should we object to his smell? I'll even whisper a private little theory of my own. Imagine a few young women living here in the same physical conditions as ourselves, and as healthy as most of us are. Not only should we find their open-air smell quite definitely not unpleasing, but I have an idea that it might be positively attractive, that it might set us dreaming, might wake our desires and exercise upon us a magic charm.

Lice . . . it's hard, I must confess, to find anything much to say for them. In my own little cubby-hole I'm fairly free of them, but they exist none the less. There are trenches no more than five hundred yards away to our right which are infested with them, and by a giant species too, which bear about the same resemblance to the ordinary decent louse as the gutter rat does to the fieldmouse. Fortunately, the louse does not believe much in walking. He uses carriages (ourselves, to wit), and when the carriages move, he moves too. I've told my men to keep as far as possible from their pals in the trenches to our right, and when they do meet, to avoid "transfers."

All the same—since I'm being honest with you—I do have a few lice, not all the time I'm in the line, but almost. I don't attract them much, it seems (though I've always been a happy hunting ground for fleas. I've known dog-fleas to smell me out across a room and rush pell-mell from their master to make my acquaintance). Shall I pretend that one gets used to lice? Certainly not! But, provided there are not too many of them, one does find oneself regarding them as among the less important trials of the human state. When I was in La Rochelle one June, we had a plague of tiny mosquitoes. Especially between six and eleven at night, they used to come in at the windows, and when I was working at my table they worried me incessantly. They had a way of making a dead set at my elbows, my ankles, and round my knees. Well, I got into the habit of working through it all, of concentrating on what I was doing, of reading poetry without losing my sense of form or of content, while all the time scratching away at my ankles and my elbows, and smacking away at the little beasts—a game at which I developed considerable skill.

I've even come to believe that man is so made that the presence of a small

superficial irritation, provided the sensation is acute without being symptomatic of any serious trouble, is a definite aid to his mental equilibrium and
serves to keep occupied the restless margin of his consciousness. He regards
it, too, as a sort of ring of Polycrates, for I suspect that there is in all of us,
always, an obscure sense of fate, inherited from numberless ancestral misfortunes, which whispers: "We are not sent into this world to live peacefully. When there's nothing to worry us, it's not natural, it's a bad sign." A
small irritation gives us the assurance that we are paying our "residence
tax" so far as this world is concerned—not much, to be sure, but enough to
ensure us against the jealousy and the thunderbolts of Heaven. (Do you
think mankind will ever get over this hereditary mistrust of everything that
looks at all like happiness? This war will have intensified the feeling of
nervousness for at least a century to come.) Well then, I want you to understand that the presence of lice in the trenches has served to inoculate me
sometimes against that vague uneasiness of which I am conscious when we
have been left too long without being bombarded. (To cover the ground completely, I ought to mention the rats. But they're not really worth worrying
about—merely one source of irritation the more.)

I have written about the smell of the living. Now I've got to send you a
few words about the smell of the dead. I'm sorry, but you've got only yourself to thank: you asked me for a complete picture of my days, and I shall
spare you nothing. Don't worry, though, I'm not going to start being romantic. We no more live in "the odour of death" than during the spring of
1914 in Paris we lived in "the odour of gasoline." But the smell of corpses is
all part of our daily existence. We can never entirely forget it. Sometimes,
and without warning, unfortunately, it takes the centre of the stage—and that
means that we've got to be ready at all times to face the possibility with
steadfastness and unconcern.

Generally speaking, our attitude to death and its trappings is symptomatic
of a really remarkable change in outlook. It makes one realize, looking back,
how much quiet efficiency went, in the old pre-war days, to keep the living
from being obsessed by the idea of mortality, from finding themselves suddenly face to face with its material evidence. Sanitary precautions were admirably organized, so admirably that we never really gave the question a
moment's thought. In the world of our present existence they are badly
handicapped by circumstances—have, in fact, been literally overthrown. I
don't mean that there's any deliberate attempt to force the dead on the attention of the living, but we can't help spending our days next door to them or
constantly meeting the signs of their proximity.

The oddest aspect of the business is the way the men treat it. It's not at all simple. The constant reminder of death seems to nag at their consciousness, to provoke and awake in them sentiments of a very different kind, many of which are rather surprising. In the first place, and this is almost too obvious to mention, the living have become extremely familiar with the look of death. They are not easily moved to a display of emotion. When the wind brings to their nostrils the smell of corpses, they say almost jokingly: "God, what a stench!" rather as though they were in some workshop while the sanitary men were emptying a neighbouring cesspool. When, at some turn in the trench, they happen to see sticking from the earth two feet still in their boots (a very frequent sight), they're as likely as not to remark, if the feet in question are pretty large: "That chap took an out size, I'll warrant." The very sanity of their outlook gives it a sort of human quality. The fact that the feet are French no more moves them to pious reflection or sentimental silence than if they were Boche—though Maurice Barrès would like to have us believe it does. But side by side with that attitude there goes a tendency to be disgusted, and a very real superstitious dread. I've seen men stand up to a cursing and to threat of punishment rather than use their shovels to move a few fragments of corpse that happened to turn up in a parapet or trench wall. But I've seen another knock out his pipe against the head of a tibia, fleshless of course, but quite obviously human, which was sticking out of the earth near where he was sitting. A friend of mine told me that when he was in the line near Soissons last winter, his men used regularly to hang their caps or sling their haversacks on a blackened and dried-up human hand that jutted out from the trench wall at a convenient height, close to the entrance to a listening-post, but that when, disgusted by the sight, he gave orders for the hand to be cut off and buried, he could find no one willing to do the job. This blackened hand, which they treated with complete unconcern so long as it was merely a question of using it in a friendly way, became suddenly an object of superstitious terror when the question arose of doing it violence. You will tell me that the reason is obvious, that for the simple souls of common soldiers, unconcern has nothing in common with profanation, while cruelty has. Maybe. It's important, though, to stress the degree of malice or deliberate cruelty which might be held to be sufficient excuse for the calling forth of a spirit of vengeance from the dead; and, in other cases, to take into account the far more obscure thought that it is bad luck to touch a dead man, or bits of a dead man, and still more to move them from their chosen resting-place. So far from the idea of profanation, taken in its widest sense, always acting as a deterrent, I'm pretty sure that it quite often is an actual stimulus. I've noticed that the men are not content with having gained a familiarity with death which hardens them and renders them less susceptible to being shocked, if, indeed, shocked at all, at the idea of doing things that in the old days would have sickened them. Such an attitude is an inevitable result of the deadening effects of war on human sensibilities. But their moral deterioration goes much further than that. In many cases they seem actually relieved at being freed from the particular attitude of respect for human life in which most of them have been brought up. That is something quite different from a mere deadening of sensibility. It is an active satisfaction in loosening the bonds of sentiment, and it worries me very considerably. It's hard to mark the subtle difference without being guilty of exaggeration. Don't believe the people who tell you that war has made the average man more ferocious. They're either lying or letting mere words go to their head. When my men, as occasionally happens, talk of "hating" the enemy, it's really only so much talk (unless, perhaps, they are from the occupied territories, or are suffering from a species of shell-shock). If they never let a chance of retaliation slip, that's because they feel their self-respect involved. I've never known the joyous anticipation of jabbing his enemy's guts out get a man over the top a moment sooner than he can help. On the other hand, there's no doubt whatever that they are delighted at the thought that they need no longer approach life with kid gloves, and that they do derive a sort of gutter satisfaction from treating life and its manifestation in the bits and pieces of human beings like so much dirt. Nor can there be any doubt that such an attitude can, superficially at least, be confused with ferocity.

The whole business reminds me vividly of the Middle Ages. We are rapidly taking on again the mental outlook of the Middle Ages: lack of reverence for the human carcass and for mere flesh whether living or dead; the very large part, on the other hand, which we accord, in our preoccupations, to this same flesh; the mocking unconcern which we show for those aspects of the human body which are most degrading, such as excreta, carrion, skeletons; the whole side of mediaeval consciousness which produced the *danse macabre* and found delight in setting charnel-houses, gargoyles, obscene bas-reliefs, and latrines in the shadow of the great cathedrals. We of the fighting services seem to be saying: "We've been poisoned ever since we were children with a hundred and one sugary refinements, shamefaced prejudices, and lies. What nonsense it all is! We're nothing but a mass of guts after all, damned useless guts, which only stop rotting inside us the better to rot on the ground." *Quia pulvis es* (Because you are dust). The real hymn of the trenches is the *Dies Irae,* which, as you once pointed out to me, ought to be sung to a brisk and brutal rhythm with a touch of crude joviality and insolence, a sort of triumphal challenge to the whole beastly business of living from which at last we are to be set free.

The same attitude, I am convinced, accounts for the courage with which we go into action when we can no longer help ourselves. Courage is by no means incompatible with terror, with the general nervousness of the trenches. The irreverent laughter induced in us by the spectacle of life prevents us from taking our own individual lives too seriously. Men in the mass are seen to be like a shoal of fish or cloud of locusts swarming to destruction. The individual man is less than nothing—certainly not worth worrying about. The act of clinging to life is merely so much extra and useless trouble. We just let ourselves be swept along; the tide of danger picks us up and carries us with it. It will leave us high and dry precisely where it chooses and how it chooses: dead, mutilated, made prisoner, or even still living—not that that really settles anything.

This, it seems to me, is the one irreparable loss. It has taken civilization centuries of patient fumbling to teach men that life, their own and that of others, is something sacred. Well, it's been so much work thrown away. We shan't, you'll see, get back to that attitude in a hurry.

For people like us, this particular disaster is but one aspect of a far more extensive disaster, from the effects of which I, for one, shall never recover. How can I explain what I mean without making the sceptics smile? (But you're no sceptic.) Let me put it this way: Without subscribing to the cruder forms of the belief in progress, we did think—I hope you don't mind my saying "we"—that the last few centuries of Western civilization had given to human nature an orientation, a culture, that, no matter how one viewed it from the point of view of metaphysics, had had certain very important practical results. If we anticipated a continuance of the process, we could not, I think, be accused of undue stupidity. But that's a thing of the past. The anticipation, like everything else, has been swept away. My most haunting horror is not that I see men now willing to suffer and to act as they do, but that having so seen them, I shall never again be able to believe in their good intentions. Look at the thing how you will, it is now proved beyond power of contradiction that millions of men can tolerate, for an indefinite period and without spontaneously rising in revolt, an existence more terrible and more degrading than any that the numberless revolutions of history were held to have terminated for ever. They obey and they suffer as unquestioningly as the slaves and victims of the most bestial periods known to us. Don't let us blind ourselves to the truth by saying that at least they know why they are doing it, and that the fact of their free will saves their human dignity. We have no reason to affirm that the slaves and victims of past societies did not, between their rations of stripes, receive doses of moral drugs, injections of powerful suggestion, which created in them an attitude of consent. The slaves of the Pyramids may have been filled with admiration for the architectural ambitions of Pharaoh. The Hindu widows who were burned on the funeral pyres of their husbands were no doubt persuaded that those who hoisted them on to the piles of aromatic wood were only helping them to accomplish a painful duty. All our talk of man's dignity is but mockery unless and until a day comes when certain things will under no circumstances be required of him or accepted by him as inevitable. I can no longer believe that any such day will ever come. You have often laughed at my optimism, at my Rousseauism; well, I am now in a state of mind that forces me to a deep distrust of man, of everything he may enforce as master or consent either to do or to endure as slave.

We know now that men can be made to do exactly anything—after a hundred years of democracy and eighteen centuries of the Christian faith. It's all a question of finding the right means. If only we take enough trouble and go sufficiently slowly, we can make him kill his aged parents and eat them in a stew. I foresee appalling developments. We may live to witness the revival of human sacrifice. We may see thinkers sent to the stake or the electric chair for having preached heresy. We may see witch trials and per-secution of the Jews as bad as any that took place in the Middle Ages. We may see crowds yelling themselves into a hysteria of adoration as the despot passes, and the sons of those who now vote Socialist rolling on the ground and crying: "Crush us, O living God!" But there is this grain of comfort: we may be dead by that time, or at least I may. Don't kid yourself that your old friend Jerphanion is playing the prophet. Everything he says is clearly visible by the cold light of common sense in what is going on before our eyes.

I can hear your comment: "It isn't as bad as that yet; the old boy is exag-gerating as usual. He wants to punish himself for having believed too blindly in mankind and in the future, so he's just diving headlong into despair."

No, it isn't as bad as that yet, I agree. But we have crossed the Rubicon. However short a time ago the attack began, the fact remains that our de-fences have been shattered, and we are now in a world where all these things are natural, simple, and, I repeat, only too much a matter of practical politics. It was on the 2nd of August 1914 that the real front was broken, the front held by civilization against barbarism.

But I must be fair. The war has brought us one positive advantage. It could hardly do less. Its name is comradeship—a rough kindness of man to man, a touching confidence of the soldier in his junior officers (not always, and it stops before it has got very far in the hierarchy); unselfishness; an absence, or a diminution, of the tendency to look ahead, at least very far ahead; a carelessness, though it is bred of despair; a clinging, sometimes a blind clinging, to the minute and the possible happiness it may offer.

I was going to add, in my desire to hold the scales even, that from these temporary virtues—for they all spring from our present discontents—durable benefits might result: such, for instance, as physical hardness; a definite incapacity to make mountains out of molehills; a willingness to seize the passing moment and enjoy what it has to give; a refusal to spoil one's life by indulging in trivial anxieties; and, chief of all, a readiness to accept as an incomprehensible miracle the mere fact of breathing and living, of being able to drink a glass of wine under a tree, of being able to go to sleep in a bed, without the ever haunting fear of shells.

But let me tell you what happened on the occasion of my last leave, my second, as it happens (the one when I so much regretted missing you. The first when I was convalescing, I spent, as you probably remember, in the Charente-Inférieure, so that the same situation didn't arise). Well, when I got home, when I saw my apartment and my wife just as they had always been, all the familiar things of my life, I was so deeply moved that I believe I actually cried. That is all perfectly natural; but now mark the sequel. Suddenly, I found myself feeling that the apartment was small(!). My study, in particular, seemed airless, without light, melancholy. I was worried by some feeling for which I could not find words. Put crudely, it was like this: "Is it worth while going through all I'm going through if this is what I've got to come back to?"

I had been drunk with delight at seeing my wife again. But that didn't prevent me, the very next morning, from being persnickety, almost ill-humoured, like a man who has never had to do without the petty comforts of life. All my old habits, even the most trivial, closed down on me again. The only difference was that I was rather more impatient, more sensitive than I used to be. A spoiled cup of coffee sent me off into a rage. You understand what I mean? Nothing seemed to me to be good enough for a man who had to make up for so much lost time. The change from the life of the trenches wasn't complete, wasn't dramatic, enough. Do you know, I believe that if the war really does end one day, the men who have fought it, so far from feeling thankful that they have been able to get back to the humble conditions of their former homes, will see everything with a disillusioned and disgusted eye. They will say, as I almost said the other day: "Is this all?" Nothing short of the life of a prince, a cardinal, or perhaps a millionaire with a villa on the Riviera will convince them that they're not being fooled.

And at the same time there are moments when I am haunted by a vision of life as it used to be when it was real and lovely (for what we find, when we're lucky, on leave is not the real life; somehow it's all different). I see the Grands Boulevards on a June day; I see

> A busy harbour where my soul
> Can drink its fill . . .

remembering the sauntering days of love, or one of our strolls about the out-lying suburbs. At such times I pay, with a sense of delicious, overwhelming melancholy, my tribute to life as once it was. I don't really believe it can ever be like that again. I wear its picture on my heart as I might the portrait of some dear dead woman of the past.

WOODROW WILSON

THOMAS WOODROW WILSON was born in 1856 in Virginia and was educated at Princeton, the University of Virginia, and the Johns Hopkins University. He entered academic life in 1883 after a year of legal practice. For the next twenty years he seemed destined for a distinguished university career; in 1902 he became the president of Princeton University.

But his safe political and social opinions in a time of growing reform sentiment attracted the attention of important conservatives and his intense ambitiousness and equally strong conviction of his righteousness soon made Princeton too small a place for his powers. Deftly but surely Wilson edged forward into politics. A defeat on a major policy proposal at Princeton and a rising reform movement in New Jersey with a need for a seemingly non-political new man to counter popular disgust with machines were influential in bringing him the Democratic nomination for governor of New Jersey in 1910. Pushed, however, by progressive leaders in the state, Wilson abandoned his earlier conservative ideas and almost overnight adopted the reform position.

As governor Wilson broke a bargain with the New Jersey bosses, captured control of his state party, and in 1912 the Democrats nominated him for the presidency. He campaigned largely for a return to the American traditions of individualism, for a fair chance for "the man on the make." Elected after a three-way contest against President W. H. Taft and ex-President Theodore Roosevelt, Wilson by the end of 1913 had signed three modest laws supposedly embodying the substance of his pledges to a "New Freedom." Election reverses, his own capacity to grow politically, and the demands of progressives soon made him move further along the road of reform. He was narrowly re-elected as a peace and prosperity candidate in 1916.

Wilson pleaded publicly with the American people for full neutrality on the outbreak of the First World War. Privately, he was rapidly convinced that the Allied cause must win, but, during the years of neutrality, he did little to educate the public about the nature and purposes of the Allied cause. Anger at the Germans' ruthless use of the submarine played increasingly against Wilson's fear of responsibility for the consequences of entering the war. America went into the struggle in April, 1917, according to Wilson, only to make it unnecessary ever to go to war again. The high ideals expressed in his war aims, the famous "Fourteen Points" were not forced onto the weary, vengeful Allies; the American people expected a utopian peace.

At the Paris Peace Conference an unwilling Wilson was forced to play "power politics" on many key issues. He saved some principle; the compromises he most regretted he thought would be corrected by the proposed League of Nations. When he returned home with the treaty in the summer of 1919 he could compromise no more.

Skillful work by a small group of senators managed to prevent rapid approval of the treaty despite the seeming initial public approval. Knowing that he had a fight on his hands, Wilson went to the people to explain the treaty and to insist that it be ratified without any reservations. During the grueling trip in September, 1919 Wilson collapsed from a stroke from which he never fully recovered. From his sickroom isolation in the White House came a command to Democrats for no-compromise with the senatorial opposition led by Henry Cabot Lodge. Had Wilson relented, the treaty with only minor reservations would have been saved. In its pure Wilsonian form it was rejected by the Senate, to the relief of isolationists and jingoes, but also of many liberals who believed that Wilson and his "monstrous" treaty had betrayed his ideal of "peace without victory."

The election of 1920 settled the final fate of the treaty and of direct American participation in the new League of Nations. President Harding, despite vague promises in his campaign to provide something like the treaty, declared it a closed issue. Wilson, a tragic figure of a great man brought low by his own pride, lived for three years after retiring from office. He died in Washington in 1924, still bitterly convinced of the rightness of his stand and in the view of many, a prophet before his time of a world made peaceful and just by law.

The following is taken from one of Wilson's more notable speeches in his 1919 campaign to rally support for the treaty. The full text is in *Addresses of President Wilson* (Washington, D.C.: Government Printing Office, 1919).

ADDRESS AT COLUMBUS, OHIO, SEPTEMBER 4, 1919

MR. CHAIRMAN, Gov. Campbell, my fellow citizens, it is with very profound pleasure that I find myself face to face with you. I have for a long time chafed at the confinement of Washington. I have for a long time wished to fulfill the purpose with which my heart was full when I returned to our beloved country, namely, to go out and report to my fellow countrymen concerning those affairs of the world which now need to be settled. The only people I owe any report to are you and the other citizens of the United States.

And it has become increasingly necessary, apparently, that I should report to you. After all the various angles at which you have heard the treaty held up, perhaps you would like to know what is in the treaty. I find it very difficult in reading some of the speeches that I have read to form any conception of that great document. It is a document unique in the history of the world for many reasons, and I think I can not do you a better service, or the peace of the world a better service, than by pointing out to you just what this treaty contains and what it seeks to do.

In the first place, my fellow countrymen, it seeks to punish one of the greatest wrongs ever done in history, the wrong which Germany sought to do to the world and to civilization; and there ought to be no weak purpose with regard to the application of the punishment. She attempted an intolerable thing, and she must be made to pay for the attempt. The terms of the treaty are severe, but they are not unjust. I can testify that the men associated with me at the peace conference in Paris had it in their hearts to do justice and not wrong. But they knew, perhaps, with a more vivid sense of what happened than we could possibly know on this side of the water, the many solemn covenants which Germany had disregarded, the long preparation she had made to overwhelm her neighbors, and the utter disregard which she had shown for human rights, for the rights of women, of children, of those who were helpless. They had seen their lands devastated by an enemy that devoted himself not only to the effort at victory, but to the effort at terror—seeking to terrify the people whom he fought. And I wish to testify that they exercised restraint in the terms of this treaty. They did not wish to overwhelm any great nation. They acknowledged that Germany was a great nation, and they had no purpose of overwhelming the German people, but they did think that it ought to be burned into the consciousness of men forever that no people ought to permit its government to do what the German Government did.

In the last analysis, my fellow countrymen, as we in America would be the first to claim, a people are responsible for the acts of their government. If their government purposes things that are wrong, they ought to take measures to see to it that that purpose is not executed. Germany was self-governed; her rulers had not concealed the purposes that they had in mind, but they had deceived their people as to the character of the methods they were going to use, and I believe from what I can learn that there is an awakened consciousness in Germany itself of the deep iniquity of the thing that was attempted. When the Austrian delegates came before the peace conference, they in so many words spoke of the origination of the war as a crime and admitted in our presence that it was a thing intolerable to contemplate. They knew in their hearts that it had done them the deepest conceivable wrong, that it had put their people and the people of Germany at the judgment seat of mankind, and throughout this treaty every term that was applied to Germany was meant, not to humiliate Germany, but to rectify the wrong that she had done.

Look even into the severe terms of reparation—for there was no indemnity. No indemnity of any sort was claimed, merely reparation, merely paying for the destruction done, merely making good the losses so far as such losses could be made good which she had unjustly inflicted, not upon the goverments, for the reparation is not to go to the governments, but upon the people whose rights she had trodden upon with absolute absence of everything that even resembled pity. There was no indemnity in this treaty, but there is reparation, and even in the terms of reparation a method is devised by which the reparation shall be adjusted to Germany's ability to pay it.

I am astonished at some of the statements I hear made about this treaty. The truth is that they are made by persons who have not read the treaty or who, if they have read it, have not comprehended its meaning. There is a method of adjustment in that treaty by which the reparation shall not be pressed beyond the point which Germany can pay, but which will be pressed to the utmost point that Germany can pay—which is just, which is righteous. It would have been intolerable if there had been anything else. For, my fellow citizens, this treaty is not meant merely to end this single war. It is meant as a notice to every government which in the future will attempt this thing that mankind will unite to inflict the same punishment. There is no national triumph sought to be recorded in this treaty. There is no glory sought for any particular nation. The thought of the statesmen collected around that table was of their people, of the sufferings that they had gone through, of the losses they had incurred—that great throbbing heart which was so depressed, so forlorn, so sad in every memory that it had had of the five tragical years that have gone. Let us never forget those years, my fellow countrymen. Let us never forget the purpose—the high purpose, the disinterested purpose—with which America lent its strength not for its own glory but for the defense of mankind.

As I said, this treaty was not intended merely to end this war. It was intended to prevent any similar war. I wonder if some of the opponents of the league of nations have forgotten the promises we made our people before we went to that peace table. We had taken by processes of law the flower of our youth from every household, and we told those mothers and fathers and sisters and wives and sweethearts that we were taking those men to fight a war which would end business of that sort; and if we do not end it, if we do not do the best that human concert of action can do to end it, we are of all men the most unfaithful, the most unfaithful to the loving hearts who suffered in this war, the most unfaithful to those households bowed in grief and yet lifted with the feeling that the lad laid down his life for a great thing and, among other things, in order that other lads might never have to do the same thing. That is what the league of nations is for, to end this war justly, and then not merely to serve notice on governments which would contemplate the same things that Germany contemplated that they will do it at their peril, but also concerning the combination of power which will prove to them that that they will do it at their peril. It is idle to say the world will combine against you, because it may not, but it is persuasive to say the world is combined against you, and will remain combined against the things that Germany attempted. The league of nations is the only thing that can prevent the recurrence of this dreadful catastrophe and redeem our promises.

The character of the league is based upon the experience of this very war. I did not meet a single public man who did not admit these things, that Germany would not have gone into this war if she had thought Great Britain was going into it, and that she most certainly would never have gone into this war if she dreamed America was going into it. And they all admitted that a notice beforehand that the greatest powers of the world would combine to prevent this sort of thing would prevent it absolutely. When gentlemen tell you, therefore, that the league of nations is intended for some other purpose than this, merely reply this to them: If we do not do this thing, we have neglected the central covenant that we made to our people, and there will then be no statesman of any country who can thereafter promise his people alleviation from the perils of war. The passions of this world are not dead. The rivalries of this world are not cooled. They have been rendered hotter than ever. The harness that is to unite nations is more necessary now than it ever was before, and unless there is this assurance of combined action before wrong is attempted, wrong will be attempted just so soon as the most ambitious nations can recover from the financial stress of this war.

Now, look what else is in the treaty. This treaty is unique in the history of mankind, because the center of it is the redemption of weak nations. There never was a congress of nations before that considered the rights of those who could not enforce their rights. There never was a congress of nations before that did not seek to effect some balance of power brought about by means of serving the strength and interest of the strongest power concerned; whereas this treaty builds up nations that never could have won their freedom in any other way; builds them up by gift, by largess, not by obligations; builds them up because of the conviction of the men who wrote the treaty that the rights of people transcend the rights of governments, because of the conviction of the men who wrote that treaty that the fertile source of war is wrong. The Austro-Hungarian Empire, for example, was held together by military force and consisted of peoples who did not want to live together, who did not have the spirit of nationality as toward each other, who were constantly chafing at the bands that held them. Hungary, though a willing partner of Austria, was willing to be a partner because she could share Austria's strength to accomplish her own ambitions, and her own ambitions were to hold under her the Jugo-Slavic peoples that lay to the south of her; Bohemia, an unhappy partner, a partner by duress, beating in all her veins the strongest national impulse that was to be found anywhere in Europe; and north of that, pitiful Poland, a great nation divided up among the great powers of Europe, torn asunder, kinship disregarded, natural ties treated with contempt, and an obligatory division among sovereigns imposed upon her—a part of her given to Russia, a part of her given to Austria, a part of her given to Germany—great bodies of Polish people never permitted to have the normal intercourse with their kinsmen for fear that that fine instinct of the heart should assert itself which binds families together. Poland could never have won her independence. Bohemia never could have broken away from the Austro-Hungarian combination. The Slavic peoples to the south, running down into the great Balkan Peninsula, had again and again tried to assert their nationality and independence, and had as often been crushed, not by the immediate power they were fighting, but by the combined power of Europe. The old alliances, the old balances of power, were meant to see to it that no little nation asserted its right to the disturbance of the peace of Europe, and every time an assertion of rights was attempted they were suppressed by combined influence and force.

This treaty tears away all that: says these people have a right to live their own lives under the governments which they themselves choose to set up. That is the American principle, and I was glad to fight for it. When strategic claims were urged, it was matter of common counsel that such considerations were not in our thought. We were not now arranging for future wars. We were giving people what belonged to them. . . .

The heart of this treaty then, my fellow citizens, is not even that it punishes Germany. That is a temporary thing. It is that it rectifies the age-long wrongs which characterized the history of Europe. There were some of us who wished that the scope of the treaty would reach some other age-long wrongs. It was a big job, and I do not say that we wished that it were bigger, but there were other wrongs elsewhere than in Europe and of the same kind which no doubt ought to be righted, and some day will be righted, but which we could not draw into the treaty because we could deal only with the countries whom the war had engulfed and affected. But so far as the scope of our authority went, we rectified the wrongs which have been the fertile source of war in Europe. . . .

Here [shows map] are two neighboring peoples. The one people have not stopped at a sharp line, and the settlements of the other people or their migrations have not begun at a sharp line. They have intermingled. There are regions where you can not draw a national line and say there are Slavs on this side [illustrating] and Italians on that [illustrating]. It can not be done. You have to approximate the line. You have to come as near to it as you can, and then trust to the processes of history to redistribute, it may be, the people that are on the wrong side of the line. There are many such lines drawn in this treaty and to be drawn in the Austrian treaty, where there are perhaps more lines of that sort than in the German treaty. When we came to draw the line between the Polish people and the German people—not the line between Germany and Poland; there was no Poland, strictly speaking, but the line between the German and the Polish people—we were confronted by such problems as the disposition of districts like the eastern part of Silesia, which is called Upper Silesia because it is mountainous and the other part is not. Upper Silesia is chiefly Polish, and when we came to draw the line of what should be Poland it was necessary to include Upper Silesia if we were really going to play fair and make Poland up of the Polish peoples wherever we found them in sufficiently close neighborhood to one another, but it was not perfectly clear that Upper Silesia wanted to be part of Poland. At any rate, there were Germans in Upper Silesia who said that it did not, and therefore we did there what we did in many other places. We said, "Very well, then, we will let the people that live there decide. We will have a referendum. Within a certain length of time after the war, under the supervision of an international commission which will have a sufficient armed force behind it to preserve order and see that nobody interferes with the elections, we will have an absolutely free vote and Upper Silesia shall go either to Germany or to Poland, as the people in Upper Silesia prefer." That illustrates many other cases where we provided for a referendum, or a plebiscite, as they chose to call it. We are going to leave it to the people themselves, as we should have done, what government they shall live under. It is none of my prerogative to allot peoples to this government or the other. It is nobody's right to do that allotting except the people themselves, and I want to testify that this treaty is shot through with the American principle of the choice of the governed. . . .

But we did much more than that. This treaty contains among other things a Magna Charta of labor—a thing unheard of until this interesting year of grace. There is a whole section of the treaty devoted to arrangements by which the interests of those who labor with their hands all over the world, whether they be men or women or children, are sought to be safeguarded; and next month there is to meet the first assembly under this section of the league. Let me tell you, it will meet whether the treaty is ratified by that time or not. There is to meet an assembly which represents the interests of laboring men throughout the world. Not their political interests; there is nothing political about it. It is the interests of men concerning the conditions of their labor; concerning the character of labor which women shall engage in, the character of labor which children shall be permitted to engage in; the hours of labor; and, incidentally, of course, the remuneration of labor; that labor shall be remunerated in proportion, of course, to the maintenance of the standard of living, which is proper, for the man who is expected to give his whole brain and intelligence and energy to a particular task. I hear very little said about the Magna Charta of labor which is embodied in this treaty. It forecasts the day, which ought to have come long ago, when statesmen will realize that no nation is fortunate which is not happy and that no nation can be happy whose people are not contented; contented in their lives and fortunate in the circumstances of their lives.

If I were to state what seems to me the central idea of this treaty, it would be this: It is almost a discovery in international conventions that nations do not consist of their governments but consist of their people. That is a rudimentary idea. It seems to us in America to go without saying, but, my fellow citizens, it was never the leading idea in any other international congress that I ever heard of; that is to say, any international congress made up of the representatives of governments. They were always thinking of national policy, of national advantage, of the rivalries of trade, of the advantages of territorial conquest. There is nothing of that in this treaty. You will notice that even the territories which are taken away from Germany, like her colonies, are not given to anybody. There is not a single act of annexation in this treaty. Territories inhabited by people not yet to govern themselves, either because of economical or other circumstances, are put under the care of powers, who are to act as trustees—trustees responsible in the form of the world at the bar of the league of nations, and the terms upon which they are to exercise their trusteeship are outlined. They are not to use those people by way of draft to fight their wars for them. They are not to permit any form of slavery among them, or enforced labor. They are to see to it that there are humane conditions of labor with regard not only to the women and children but to the men also. They are to establish no fortifications. They are to regulate the liquor and the opium traffic. They are to see to it, in other words, that the lives of the people whose care they assume—not sovereignty over whom they assume—are kept clean and safe and wholesome. There again the principle of the treaty comes out, that the object of the arrangement is the welfare of the people who live there, and not the advantage of the trustee.

It goes beyond that. It seeks to gather under the common supervision of the league of nations the various instrumentalities by which the world has been trying to check the evils that were in some places debasing men, like the opium traffic, like the traffic—for it was a traffic—in women and children, like the traffic in other dangerous drugs, like the traffic in arms among uncivilized people who could use arms only for their own detriment. It provides for sanitation, for the work of the Red Cross. Why, those clauses, my fellow citizens, draw the hearts of the world into league, draw the noble impulses of the world together and make a team of them.

I used to be told that this was an age in which mind was monarch, and my comment was that if that was true, the mind was one of those modern monarchs that reigns and does not govern; that, as a matter of fact, we were governed by a great representative assembly made up of the human passions, and that the best we could manage was that the high and fine passions should be in a majority so that they could control the baser passions, so that they could check the things that were wrong. This treaty seeks something like that. In drawing the humane endeavors of the world together it makes a league of the fine passions of the world, of its philanthropic passions, of its passion of pity, of its passion of human sympathy, of its passion of human friendliness and helpfulness, for there is such a passion. It is the passion which has lifted us along the slow road of civilization. It is the passion which made ordered government possible. It is the passion which has made justice and established it in the world.

That is the treaty. Did you ever hear of it before? Did you ever know before what was in this treaty? Did anybody before ever tell you what the treaty was intended to do? I beg, my fellow citizens, that you and the rest of those Americans with whom we are happy to be associated all over this broad land will read the treaty yourselves, or, if you will not take the time to do that—for it is a technical document—that you will accept the interpretation of those who made it and know what the intentions were in the making of it. I hear a great deal, my fellow citizens, about the selfishness and the selfish ambitions of other governments, and I would not be doing justice to the gifted men with whom I was associated on the other side of the water if I did not testify that the purposes that I have outlined were their purposes. We differed as to the method very often. We had discussions as to the details, but we never had any serious discussion as to the principle. While we all acknowledged that the principles might perhaps in detail have been better realized, we are all back of those principles. There is a concert of mind and of purpose and of policy in the world that was never in existence before. I am not saying that by way of credit to myself or to those colleagues to whom I have alluded, because what happened to us was that we got messages from our people. We were under instructions, whether they were written down or not, and we did not dare come home without fulfilling those instructions. If I could not have brought back the kind of treaty that I did bring back, I never would have come back, because I would have been an unfaithful servant, and you would have had the right to condemn me in any way that you chose to use. So that I testify that this is an American treaty not only, but it is a treaty that expresses the heart of the great peoples who were associated together in the war against Germany.

I said at the opening of this informal address, my fellow citizens, that I had come to make a report to you. I want to add to that a little bit. I have not come to debate the treaty: It speaks for itself, if you will let it. The arguments directed against it are directed against it with a radical misunderstanding of the instrument itself. Therefore, I am not going anywhere to debate the treaty. I am going to expound it, and I am going, as I do here, now, to-day, to urge you in every vocal method that you can use to assert the spirit of the American people in support of it. Do not let men pull it down. Do not let them misrepresent it. Do not let them lead this Nation away from the high purposes with which this war was inaugurated and fought. As I came through that line of youngsters in khaki a few minutes ago I felt that I could salute them because I had done the job in the way I promised them I would do it, and when this treaty is accepted, men in khaki will not have to cross the seas again. That is the reason I believe in it.

I say "when it is accepted," for it will be accepted. I have never entertained a moment's doubt of that, and the only thing I have been impatient of has been the delay. It is not dangerous delay, except for the temper of the peoples scattered throughout the world who are waiting. Do you realize, my fellow citizens, that the whole world is waiting on America? The only country in the world that is trusted at this moment is the United States, and the peoples of the world are waiting to see whether their trust is justified or not. That has been the ground of my impatience. I knew their trust was justified, but I begrudged the time that certain gentlemen wish to take in telling them so. We shall tell them so in a voice as authentic as any voice in history, and in the years to come men will be glad to remember that they had some part in the great struggle which brought this incomparable consummation of the hopes of mankind.

JOHN MAYNARD KEYNES

THE MOST FAMOUS of a long line of modern English economists, John Maynard Keynes (1883–1946) combined a brilliant academic career at Cambridge University with high influence on government policies in England and the United States. Keynes made perhaps the most notable contributions to the recent revision of liberal economic theory that justifies the state's responsibility and power to prevent or cure depressions. His criticisms of *laissez-faire*, especially after 1929, did not prevent him from using his knowledge of its shrine, the stockmarket, to good advantage. He earned a large fortune for himself and his college by shrewd investments. A man of great urbanity and taste, he was also at the center of the famous Bloomsbury group of London intellectuals that included Virginia Woolf, E. M. Forster, and Lytton Strachey.

Keynes was asked to serve with the British experts at the Paris Peace Conference of 1919. His anger and dismay with what he called the Carthaginian peace with Germany forced him to resign. He then wrote the most famous and most discussed analysis of the treaty, *The Economic Consequences of the Peace* (1919). The title did not completely reveal the book's scope for the essay was a broad analysis of the recent history of the West. Although later proven incorrect on specific predictions, Keynes had a keen and accurate sense of the general effect of the treaty on the revolutionary era already begun in Europe by the Bolsheviks. His analysis contrasted radically with Woodrow Wilson's prediction that the treaty brought peace with justice.

Keynes spent the years after the war teaching, writing, and advising on public policy. During the Great Depression he published his *General Theory of Employment, Interest, and Money* (1936), the best-known reformulation of liberal economic theory and, to many economists, the basic guide to understanding the economics of the non-socialist welfare state. Its triumph at major American and English universities increased the number of Keynesian economists called into government service.

As the Second World War neared its end Keynes played a large role in the conferences and discussions planning the postwar international economy. Although a newer generation of economists was becoming critical of certain aspects of Keynes work or reformulating his ideas to meet new problems and conditions, the great influence of the "Keynesian revolution" was an established fact.

The following selection comes from *The Economic Consequences of the Peace* (New York: Harcourt, Brace, and Howe, 1920).

THE ECONOMIC CONSEQUENCES OF THE PEACE

CHAPTER I. INTRODUCTORY

The power to become habituated to his surroundings is a marked characteristic of mankind. Very few of us realize with conviction the intensely unusual, unstable, complicated, unreliable, temporary nature of the economic organization by which Western Europe has lived for the last half century. We assume some of the most peculiar and temporary of our late advantages as natural, permanent, and to be depended on, and we lay our plans accordingly. On this sandy and false foundation we scheme for social improvement and dress our political platforms, pursue our animosities and particular ambitions, and feel ourselves with enough margin in hand to foster, not assuage, civil conflict in the European family. Moved by insane delusion and reckless self-regard, the German people overturned the foundations on which we all lived and built. But the spokesmen of the French and British peoples have run the risk of completing the ruin which Germany began, by a Peace which, if it is carried into effect, must impair yet further, when it might have restored, the delicate, complicated organization, already shaken and broken by war, through which alone the European peoples can employ themselves and live.

In England the outward aspect of life does not yet teach us to feel or realize in the least that an age is over. We are busy picking up the threads of our life where we dropped them, with this difference only, that many of us seem a good deal richer than we were before. Where we spent millions before the war, we have now learnt that we can spend hundreds of millions and apparently not suffer for it. Evidently we did not exploit to the utmost the possibilities of our economic life. We look, therefore, not only to a return to the comforts of 1914, but to an immense broadening and intensification of them. All classes alike thus build their plans, the rich to spend more and save less, the poor to spend more and work less.

But perhaps it is only in England (and America) that it is possible to be so unconscious. In continental Europe the earth heaves and no one but is aware of the rumblings. There it is not just a matter of extravagance or "labor troubles"; but of life and death, of starvation and existence, and of the fearful convulsions of a dying civilization. . . .

In Paris, where those connected with the Supreme Economic Council received almost hourly the reports of the misery, disorder, and decaying organization of all Central and Eastern Europe, allied and enemy alike, and learnt from the lips of the financial representatives of Germany and Austria unanswerable evidence of the terrible exhaustion of their countries, an occasional visit to the hot, dry room in the President's house, where the Four fulfilled their destinies in empty and arid intrigue, only added to the sense of nightmare. Yet there in Paris the problems of Europe were terrible and clamant, and an occasional return to the vast unconcern of London a little disconcerting. For in London these questions were very far away, and our own lesser problems alone troubling. London believed that Paris was making a great confusion of its business, but remained uninterested. In this spirit the British people received the Treaty without reading it. But it was under the influence of Paris, not London, that this book has been written by one who, though an Englishman, feels himself a European also, and, because of too vivid recent experience, cannot disinterest himself from the further unfolding of the great historic drama of these days which will destroy great institutions, but may also create a new world.

CHAPTER II. EUROPE BEFORE THE WAR

Before 1870 different parts of the small continent of Europe had specialized in their own products; but, taken as a whole, it was substantially self-subsistent. And its population was adjusted to this state of affairs.

After 1870 there was developed on a large scale an unprecedented situation, and the economic condition of Europe became during the next fifty years unstable and peculiar. The pressure of population on food, which had already been balanced by the accessibility of supplies from America, became for the first time in recorded history definitely reversed. As numbers increased, food was actually easier to secure. Larger proportional returns from an increasing scale of production became true of agriculture as well as industry. With the growth of the European population there were more emigrants on the one hand to till the soil of the new countries, and, on the other, more workmen were available in Europe to prepare the industrial products and capital goods which were to maintain the emigrant populations in their new homes, and to build the railways and ships which were to make accessible to Europe food and raw products from distant sources. Up to about 1900 a unit of labor applied to industry yielded year by year a purchasing power over an increasing quantity of food. It is possible that about the year 1900 this process began to be reversed, and a diminishing yield of Nature to man's effort was beginning to reassert itself. But the tendency of cereals to rise in real cost was balanced by other improvements; and— one of many novelties—the resources of tropical Africa then for the first time came into large employ, and a great traffic in oil-seeds began to bring to the table of Europe in a newer and cheaper form one of the essential foodstuffs of mankind. In this economic Eldorado, in this economic Utopia, as the earlier economists would have deemed it, most of us were brought up.

That happy age lost sight of a view of the world which filled with deep-seated melancholy the founders of our Political Economy. Before the eighteenth century mankind entertained no false hopes. To lay the illusions which grew popular at that age's latter end, Malthus disclosed a Devil. For half a century all serious economical writers held that Devil in clear prospect. For the next half century he was chained up and out of sight. Now perhaps we have loosed him again.

What an extraordinary episode in the economic progress of man that age was which came to an end in August, 1914! The greater part of the population, it is true, worked hard and lived at a low standard of comfort, yet were, to all appearances, reasonably contented with this lot. But escape was possible, for any man of capacity or character at all exceeding the average, into the middle and upper classes, for whom life offered, at a low cost and with the least trouble, conveniences, comforts, and amenities beyond the compass of the richest and most powerful monarchs of other ages. The inhabitant of London could order by telephone, sipping his morning tea in bed, the various products of the whole earth, in such quantity as he might see fit, and reasonably expect their early delivery upon his doorstep; he could at the same moment and by the same means adventure his wealth in the natural resources and new enterprises of any quarter of the world, and share, without exertion or even trouble, in their prospective fruits and advantages; or he could decide to couple the security of his fortunes with the good faith of the townspeople of any substantial municipality in any continent that fancy or information might recommend. He could secure, forthwith, if he wished it, cheap and comfortable means of transit to any country or climate without passport or other formality, could despatch his servant to the neighboring office of a bank for such supply of the precious metals as might seem convenient, and could then proceed abroad to foreign quarters, without knowledge of their religion, language, or customs, bearing coined wealth upon his person, and would consider himself greatly aggrieved and much surprised at the least interference. But, most important of all, he regarded this state of affairs as normal, certain, and permanent, except in the direction of further improvement, and any deviation from it as aberrant, scandalous, and avoidable. The projects and politics of militarism and imperialism, of racial and cultural rivalries, of monopolies, restrictions, and exclusion, which were to play the serpent in this paradise, were little more than the amusements of his daily newspaper, and appeared to exercise almost no influence at all on the ordinary course of social and economic life, the internationalization of which was nearly complete in practice. . . .

Much . . . might be said in an attempt to portray the economic peculiarities of the Europe of 1914. I have selected for emphasis the three or four greatest factors of instability, the instability of an excessive population dependent for its livelihood on a complicated and artificial organization, the psychological instability of the labouring and capitalist classes, and the instability of Europe's claim, coupled with the completeness of her dependence, on the food supplies of the New World.

The war had so shaken this system as to endanger the life of Europe altogether. A great part of the Continent was sick and dying; its population was greatly in excess of the numbers for which a livelihood was available; its organization was destroyed, its transport system ruptured, and its food supplies terribly impaired.

It was the task of the Peace Conference to honor engagements and to satisfy justice; but not less to re-establish life and to heal wounds. These tasks were dictated as much by prudence as by the magnanimity which the wisdom of antiquity approved in victors. . . .

It happens, however, that it is not only an ideal question that is at issue. My purpose in this book is to show that the Carthaginian Peace is not *practically* right or possible. Although the school of thought from which it springs is aware of the economic factor, it overlooks, nevertheless, the deeper economic tendencies which are to govern the future. The clock cannot be set back. You cannot restore Central Europe to 1870 without setting up such strains in the European structure and letting loose such human and spiritual forces as, pushing beyond frontiers and races, will overwhelm not only you and your "guarantees," but your institutions, and the existing order of your society. . . .

CHAPTER VI. EUROPE AFTER THE TREATY

This chapter must be one of pessimism. The Treaty includes no provisions for the economic rehabilitation of Europe,—nothing to make the defeated Central Empires into good neighbors, nothing to stabilize the new States of Europe, nothing to reclaim Russia; nor does it promote in any way a compact of economic solidarity amongst the Allies themselves; no arrangement was reached at Paris for restoring the disordered finances of France and Italy, or to adjust the systems of the Old World and the New.

The Council of Four paid no attention to these issues, being preoccupied with others,—Clemenceau to crush the economic life of his enemy, Lloyd George to do a deal and bring home something which would pass muster for a week, the President to do nothing that was not just and right. It is an extraordinary fact that the fundamental economic problems of a Europe starving and disintegrating before their eyes, was the one question in which it was impossible to arouse the interest of the Four. Reparations was their main excursion into the economic field, and they settled it as a problem of theology, of politics, of electoral chicane, from every point of view except that of the economic future of the States whose destiny they were handling.

I leave, from this point onwards, Paris, the Conference, and the Treaty, briefly to consider the present situation of Europe, as the War and the Peace have made it; and it will no longer be part of my purpose to distinguish between the inevitable fruits of the War and the avoidable misfortunes of the Peace.

The essential facts of the situation, as I see them, are expressed simply. Europe consists of the densest aggregation of population in the history of the world. This population is accustomed to a relatively high standard of life, in which, even now, some sections of it anticipate improvement rather than deterioration. In relation to other continents Europe is not self-sufficient; in particular it cannot feed itself. Internally the population is not evenly distributed, but much of it is crowded into a relatively small number of dense industrial centers. This population secured for itself a livelihood before the war, without much margin of surplus, by means of a delicate and immensely complicated organization, of which the foundations were supported by coal, iron, transport, and an unbroken supply of imported food and raw materials from other continents. By the destruction of this organization and the interruption of the stream of supplies, a part of this population is deprived of its means of livelihood. Emigration is not open to the redundant surplus. For it would take years to transport them overseas, even, which is not the case, if countries could be found which were ready to receive them. The danger confronting us, therefore, is the rapid depression of the standard of life of the European populations to a point which will mean actual starvation for some (a point which is already reached in Russia and approximately reached in Austria). Men will not always die quietly. For starvation, which brings to some lethargy and a helpless despair, drives other temperaments to the nervous instability of hysteria and to a mad despair. And these in their distress may overturn the remnants of organization, and submerge civilization itself in their attempts to satisfy desperately the overwhelming needs of the individual. This is the danger against which all our resources and courage and idealism must now co-operate. . . .

The significant features of the immediate situation can be grouped under three heads: first, the absolute falling off, for the time being, in Europe's internal productivity; second, the breakdown of transport and exchange by means of which its products could be conveyed where they were most wanted; and third, the inability of Europe to purchase its usual supplies from overseas.

The decrease of productivity cannot easily be estimated, and may be the subject of exaggeration. But the *prima facie* evidence of it is overwhelming, and this factor has been the main burden of Mr. Hoover's well-considered warnings. A variety of causes have produced it;—violent and prolonged internal disorder as in Russia and Hungary; the creation of new governments and their inexperience in the readjustment of economic relations, as in Poland and Czecho-Slovakia; the loss throughout the Continent of efficient labor, through the casualties of war or the continuance of mobilization; the falling-off in efficiency through continued underfeeding in the Central Empires; the exhaustion of the soil from lack of the usual applications of artificial manures throughout the course of the war; the unsettlement of the mind of the laboring classes on the fundamental issues of their times. But above all (to quote Mr. Hoover) "there is a great relaxation of effort as the reflex of physical exhaustion of large sections of the population from privation and the mental and physical strain of the war." Many persons are for one reason or another out of employment altogether. According to Mr. Hoover, a summary of the unemployment bureaus in Europe in July, 1919, showed that 15,000,000 families were receiving unemployment allowances in one form or another, and were being paid in the main by a constant inflation of currency. In Germany there is the added deterrent to labor and to capital (in so far as the Reparation terms are taken literally), that anything, which they may produce beyond the barest level of subsistence, will for years to come be taken away from them. . . .

What then is our picture of Europe? A country population able to support life on the fruits of its own agricultural production but without the accustomed surplus for the towns, and also (as a result of the lack of imported materials and so of variety and amount in the saleable manufactures of the towns) without the usual incentives to market food in return for other wares; an industrial population unable to keep its strength for lack of food, unable to earn a livelihood for lack of materials, and so unable to make good by imports from abroad the failure of productivity at home. Yet, according to Mr. Hoover, "a rough estimate would indicate that the population of Europe is at least 100,000,000 greater than can be supported without imports, and must live by the production and distribution of exports." . . .

We are . . . faced in Europe with the spectacle of an extraordinary weakness on the part of the great capitalist class, which has emerged from the industrial triumphs of the nineteenth century, and seemed a very few years ago our all-powerful master. The terror and personal timidity of the individuals of this class is now so great, their confidence in their place in society and in their necessity to the social organism so diminished, that they are the easy victims of intimidation. This was not so in England twenty-five years ago, any more than it is now in the United States. Then the capitalists believed in themselves, in their value to society, in the propriety of their continued existence in the full enjoyment of their riches and the unlimited exercise of their power. Now they tremble before every insult;—call them pro-Germans, international financiers, or profiteers, and they will give you any ransom you choose to ask not to speak of them so harshly. They allow themselves to be ruined and altogether undone by their own instruments, governments of their own making, and a press of which they are the proprietors. Perhaps it is historically true that no order of society ever perishes save by its own hand. In the complexer world of Western Europe the Immanent Will may achieve its ends more subtly and bring in the revolution no less inevitably through a Klotz [1] or a George [2] than by the intellectualisms, too ruthless and self-conscious for us, of the bloodthirsty philosophers of Russia.

The inflationism of the currency systems of Europe has proceeded to extraordinary lengths. The various belligerent Governments, unable, or too timid or too short-sighted to secure from loans or taxes the resources they required, have printed notes for the balance. In Russia and Austria-Hungary this process has reached a point where for the purposes of foreign trade the currency is practically valueless. The Polish mark can be bought for about three cents and the Austrian crown for less than two cents, but they cannot be sold at all. The German mark is worth less than four cents on the exchanges. In most of the other countries of Eastern and South-Eastern Europe the real position is nearly as bad. The currency of Italy has fallen to little more than a half of its nominal value in spite of its being still subject to some degree of regulation; French currency maintains an uncertain market; and even sterling is seriously diminished in present value and impaired in its future prospects. . . .

There are . . . three separate obstacles to the revival of trade: a maladjustment between internal prices and international prices, a lack of individual credit abroad wherewith to buy the raw materials needed to secure the working capital and to re-start the circle of exchange, and a disordered currency system which renders credit operations hazardous or impossible quite apart from the ordinary risks of commerce. . . .

---

[1] Financial adviser to Clemenceau.　　　[2] Lloyd George.

All these influences combine not merely to prevent Europe from supplying immediately a sufficient stream of exports to pay for the goods she needs to import, but they impair her credit for securing the working capital required to re-start the circle of exchange, and, also, by swinging the forces of economic law yet further from equilibrium rather than towards it, they favor a continuance of the present conditions instead of a recovery from them. An inefficient, unemployed, disorganized Europe faces us, torn by internal strife and international hate, fighting, starving, pillaging, and lying. What warrant is there for a picture of less somber colors?

I have paid little heed in this book to Russia, Hungary, or Austria. There the miseries of life and the disintegration of society are too notorious to require analysis; and these countries are already experiencing the actuality of what for the rest of Europe is still in the realm of prediction. Yet they comprehend a vast territory and a great population, and are an extant example of how much man can suffer and how far society can decay. Above all, they are the signal to us of how in the final catastrophe the malady of the body passes over into malady of the mind. Economic privation proceeds by easy stages, and so long as men suffer it patiently the outside world cares little. Physical efficiency and resistance to disease slowly diminish, but life proceeds somehow, until the limit of human endurance is reached at last and counsels of despair and madness stir the sufferers from the lethargy which precedes the crisis. Then man shakes himself, and the bonds of custom are loosed. The power of ideas is sovereign, and he listens to whatever instruction of hope, illusion, or revenge is carried to him on the air. As I write, the flames of Russian Bolshevism seem, for the moment at least, to have burnt themselves out, and the peoples of Central and Eastern Europe are held in a dreadful torpor. The lately gathered harvest keeps off the worst privations, and Peace has been declared at Paris. But winter approaches. Men will have nothing to look forward to to nourish hopes on. There will be little fuel to moderate the rigors of the season or to comfort the starved bodies of the town-dwellers.

But who can say how much is endurable, or in what direction men will seek at last to escape from their misfortunes?

CHAPTER VII. REMEDIES

It is difficult to maintain true perspective in large affairs. I have criticized the work of Paris, and have depicted in somber colors the condition and the prospects of Europe. This is one aspect of the position and, I believe, a true one. But in so complex a phenomenon the prognostics do not all point one way; and we may make the error of expecting consequences to follow too swiftly and too inevitably from what perhaps are not *all* the relevant causes. The blackness of the prospect itself leads us to doubt its accuracy; our imagination is dulled rather than stimulated by too woeful a narration and our minds rebound from what is felt "too bad to be true." But before the reader allows himself to be too much swayed by these natural reflections, and before I lead him, as is the intention of this chapter, toward remedies and ameliorations and the discovery of happier tendencies, let him redress the balance of his thought by recalling two contrasts—England and Russia, of which the one may encourage his optimism too much, but the other should remind him that catastrophes can still happen, and that modern society is not immune from the very greatest evils. . . .

What then is to be done? . . . The opportunity was missed at Paris during the six months which followed the Armistice, and nothing we can do now can repair the mischief wrought at that time. Great privations and great risks to society have become unavoidable. All that is now open to us is to redirect, so far as lies in our power, the fundamental economic tendencies which underlie the events of the hour, so that they promote the re-establishment of prosperity and order, instead of leading us deeper into misfortune.

We must first escape from the atmosphere and the methods of Paris. Those who controlled the Conference may bow before the gusts of popular opinion, but they will never lead us out of our troubles. It is hardly to be supposed that the Council of Four can retrace their steps, even if they wished to do so. The replacement of the existing Governments of Europe is, therefore, an almost indispensable preliminary. . . .

Economic frontiers were tolerable as long as an immense territory was included in a few great Empires; but they will not be tolerable when the Empires of Germany, Austria-Hungary, Russia, and Turkey have been partitioned between some twenty independent authorities. A Free Trade Union, comprising the whole of Central, Eastern, and South-Eastern Europe, Siberia, Turkey, and (I should hope) the United Kingdom, Egypt, and India, might do as much for the peace and prosperity of the world as the League of Nations itself. Belgium, Holland, Scandinavia, and Switzerland might be expected to adhere to it shortly. And it would be greatly to be desired by their friends that France and Italy also should see their way to adhesion.

It would be objected, I suppose, by some critics that such an arrangement might go some way in effect towards realizing the former German dream of Mittel-Europa. If other countries were so foolish as to remain outside the Union and to leave to Germany all its advantages, there might be some truth in this. But an economic system, to which every one had the opportunity of belonging and which gave special privilege to none, is surely absolutely free from the objections of a privileged and avowedly imperialistic scheme of exclusion and discrimination. Our attitude to these criticisms must be determined by our whole moral and emotional reaction to the future of international relations and the Peace of the World. If we take the view that for at least a generation to come Germany cannot be trusted with even a modicum of prosperity, that while all our recent Allies are angels of light, all our recent enemies, Germans, Austrians, Hungarians, and the rest, are children of the devil, that year by year Germany must be kept impoverished and her children starved and crippled, and that she must be ringed round by enemies; then we shall reject all the proposals of this chapter, and particularly those which may assist Germany to regain a part of her former material prosperity and find a means of livelihood for the industrial population of her towns. But if this view of nations and of their relation to one another is adopted by the democracies of Western Europe, and is financed by the United States, heaven help us all. If we aim deliberately at the impoverishment of Central Europe, vengeance, I dare predict, will not limp. Nothing can then delay for very long that final civil war between the forces of Reaction and the despairing convulsions of Revolution, before which the horrors of the late German war will fade into nothing, and which will destroy, whoever is victor, the civilization and the progress of our generation. Even though the result disappoint us, must we not base our actions on better expectations, and believe that the prosperity and happiness of one country promotes that of others, that the solidarity of man is not a fiction, and that nations can still afford to treat other nations as fellow-creatures? . . .

There is no answer to these objections as matters are now. If I had influence at the United States Treasury, I would not lend a penny to a single one of the present Governments of Europe. They are not to be trusted with resources they would devote to the furtherance of policies in repugnance to which, in spite of the President's failure to assert either the might or the ideals of the people of the United States, the Republican and the Democratic parties are probably united. But if, as we must pray they will, the souls of the European peoples turn away this winter from the false idols which have survived the war that created them, and substitute in their hearts for the hatred and the nationalism, which now possess them, thoughts and hopes of the happiness and solidarity of the European family,—then should natural piety and filial love impel the American people to put on one side all the smaller objections of private advantage and to complete the work, that they began in saving Europe from the tyranny of organized force, by saving her from herself. And even if the conversion is not fully accomplished, and some parties only in each of the European countries have espoused a policy of reconciliation, America can still point the way and hold up the hands of the party of peace by having a plan and a condition on which she will give her aid to the work of renewing life.

The impulse which, we are told, is now strong in the mind of the United States to be quit of the turmoil, the complication, the violence, the expense, and, above all, the unintelligibility of the European problems, is easily understood. No one can feel more intensely than the writer how natural it is to retort to the folly and impracticability of the European statesmen,—Rot, then, in your own malice, and we will go our way—

> Remote from Europe; from her blasted hopes;
> Her fields of carnage, and polluted air.

But if America recalls for a moment what Europe has meant to her and still means to her, what Europe, the mother of art and of knowledge, in spite of everything, still is and still will be, will she not reject these counsels of indifference and isolation, and interest herself in what may prove decisive issues for the progress and civilization of all mankind? . . .

I see few signs of sudden or dramatic developments anywhere. Riots and revolutions there may be, but not such, at present, as to have fundamental significance. Against political tyranny and injustice Revolution is a weapon. But what counsels of hope can Revolution offer to sufferers from economic privation, which does not arise out of the injustices of distribution but is general? The only safeguard against Revolution in Central Europe is indeed the fact that, even to the minds of men who are desperate, Revolution offers no prospect of improvement whatever. There may, therefore, be ahead of us a long, silent process of semi-starvation, and of a gradual, steady lowering of the standards of life and comfort. The bankruptcy and decay of Europe, if we allow it to proceed, will affect every one in the long-run, but perhaps not in a way that is striking or immediate.

This has one fortunate side. We may still have time to reconsider our courses and to view the world with new eyes. For the immediate future events are taking charge, and the near destiny of Europe is no longer in the hands of any man. The events of the coming year will not be shaped by the deliberate acts of statesmen, but by the hidden currents, flowing continually beneath the surface of political history, of which no one can predict the outcome. In one way only can we influence these hidden currents,—by setting in motion those forces of instruction and imagination which change *opinion*. The assertion of truth, the unveiling of illusion, the dissipation of hate, the enlargement and instruction of men's hearts and minds, must be the means.

In this autumn of 1919, in which I write, we are at the dead season of our fortunes. The reaction from the exertions, the fears, and the sufferings of the past five years is at its height. Our power of feeling or caring beyond the immediate questions of our own material well-being is temporarily eclipsed. The greatest events outside our own direct experience and the most dreadful anticipations cannot move us.

> In each human heart terror survives
> The ruin it has gorged: the loftiest fear
> All that they would disdain to think were true:
> Hypocrisy and custom make their minds
> The fanes of many a worship, now outworn.
> They dare not devise good for man's estate,
> And yet they know not that they do not dare.
> The good want power but to weep barren tears.
> The powerful goodness want: worse need for them.
> The wise want love; and those who love want wisdom;
> And all best things are thus confused to ill.
> Many are strong and rich, and would be just,
> But live among their suffering fellow-men
> As if none felt: they know not what they do.

We have been moved already beyond endurance, and need rest. Never in the lifetime of men now living has the universal element in the soul of man burnt so dimly.

For these reasons the true voice of the new generation has not yet spoken, and silent opinion is not yet formed. To the formation of the general opinion of the future I dedicate this book.

ERNST TROELTSCH

WHATEVER the nature of the peace Germany might have imposed, the fact remains that many Germans of the highest responsibility believed at the war's end that Germany would receive a fair peace on the basis of Wilson's Fourteen Points and his earlier plea for "peace without victory." To some extent this conviction helped speed the German decision to ask for an armistice in 1918. The subsequent treatment of Germany at Versailles shocked the Germans and left behind the bitterest feelings of betrayal and, even worse, of longing for revenge.

Among leading German intellectuals at the time who were aroused by the demand that Germany accept full guilt for starting the war was Ernst Troeltsch (1865–1923), a contemporary and colleague of Max Weber. Troeltsch had been educated at Erlangen, Berlin, and Göttingen. He then went on to high academic posts in theology at Bonn and Heidelberg and eventually to a professorship in philosophy at Berlin. At Heidelberg, Troeltsch became friendly with Max Weber and his most famous work *The Social Teachings of the Christian Churches* (1912) in many respects reflects a Weberian interest in the sociology of religion. The more Troeltsch became interested in the historical conditions under which religious and theological changes took place the more difficult it was for him to find a place for the claims of the transcendent truth of Christian doctrines.

Troeltsch, like Weber, had a deep and informed interest in German politics. He was a thorough democrat and in 1919 was elected to the Prussian diet. He then joined the Prussian ministry of education and greatly influenced educational and religious policies in the nation. Not long after the Treaty of Versailles there appeared his posthumously published *Spektator-Briefen* (1924), in which he commented with great keenness on postwar life in Germany and Europe.

This selection dealing with the question of German war guilt has been translated from that volume by Benjamin K. Bennett.

"SPECTATOR" LETTERS

THE DOGMA OF GUILT
(19 June 1919)

The aspect [of the Versailles Treaty] which makes itself most conspicuous is the tremendous importance of the so-called guilt question. Only in so far as it was possible, on the basis of the priority of Germany's formal declaration of war and of the German invasion of Belgium, to convince the world of Germany's exclusive responsibility for the war, did this kind of treaty become possible. Formally, it reads like a moral inquisition while, substantially, it is an imperialistic monstrosity (similar to Rome's treatment of Carthage), made possible by the treacherous use of the Fourteen Points and by Germany's revolutionary self-disarmament. The justified demands for help in the rebuilding of badly damaged France and Belgium were recognized in the German counter-proposals, so that I need not speak of them here. But the Holy Alliance, which is just about as holy as the old one of a hundred years ago and which mouths moral slogans with just about as much justification, did not agree; its answer was essentially: let the heretic be burned. Here lie hidden the deepest of political, sociological, popular psychological and technical reasons and expedients, on whose basis this world division and confiscation of property would appear in the form of an inquisition.

A huge worldwide machinery of suggestion was built upon the belief in German guilt and responsibility for a war which, but for its guilty acts, could have been avoided. The effect of this suggestion upon all neutrals and small states was enormously increased by Germany's fateful act of policy and strategy, the invasion of Belgium, although this invasion, as Bethmann-Hollweg's book has made abundantly clear, was demonstrably *not* the cause of England's declaration of war. The suggestion enabled governments to fill their resisting peoples with war-fever and to make them stand firm, even while committing the most atrocious acts of violence. To keep one's word to the heretic was unnecessary; to accept his word, impossible; and to show him any consideration, a crime against humanity. By this means was, above all, American idealism stirred up and convinced of the intimate connection between Germany's crime against civilization and her old-fashioned autocratic system of government. At the same time, every attempt of Germany to defend herself against these ideas in America was strangled by leaving the control of German mail to England. But these formed only a part of the material which lies before us here. Now that Germany had been set us as the guilty party, as a criminal, all her military actions and all the accompanying destruction took on the character of outrageous brutalities and crimes, which did not, as in the case of the Entente, grow out of a justified war but which were rather the consequences of a thievish, godless act of violence, consequences which did nothing but further reveal and confirm the character of all German action. In addition, the chain of events brought it about that Germany's initial successes yielded her Belgium and northern France, whose truly horrible sufferings were therefore regarded not as a result of war, but rather as the results of German dementedness and malice. It followed then that every act of violence and destruction which was not absolutely necessary assumed a thousand-fold importance.

Such was the case of the U-boat war, which Germany adopted as a measure unforeseen by hitherto existing international law. The difference between undersea warfare and the slowly, undramatically effective blockade was this: that the former, rather, conspicuously and shockingly destroyed goods and men and had by nature to strike both friend and foe, thus exhibiting itself as, in fact, a highly difficult and suspect style of war. But it was regarded by others neither as a German political error nor as an act of self-defense against the starvation blockade, but rather as outrageous murder and insane destruction of goods, as an outpouring of the whole warlike, world-destroying German spirit. The case of zeppelins and long-range cannon was no different. In this way, the further progress of the war only intensified and broadened the complaints. But then, even in the face of the new revolutionary government, which was in no way responsible for "Caesarism," even in the face of a completely enfeebled Germany during the armistice, these complaints were maintained. In this way, every attempt at negotiation could be denied, every explanation and every policy could still be mistrusted "on principle"; in this way, the treaty could be prepared in complete secrecy, despite all "democratic ideals," and imposed with no negotiation upon the Germans, like a verdict. Then whatever was wanted could be demanded, partly as "punishment," partly as "lawful restitution for damages," partly as "insurance" against such a horribly dangerous people. Precisely for this reason was the most practically absurd and most morally outrageous thing demanded: the turning over of the "guilty ones." For their being turned over and judged is the seal on the theory of Germany's guilt, without which theory her enemies' war-effort could not have lasted and this treaty could not have been conceived. In addition, this demand enables our enemies to calm the gradually awakening and rising suspicion in their own ranks, where workers and liberals are beginning to recognize the monstrousness of this treaty. Likewise, it is hoped that German socialism will be robbed of its dangerous power to kindle ideas, in that it is described as the spiritual heir and essentially unchanged successor of the old government and is at the same time, by means of the "punitive conditions," materially enchained or even strangled. Finally, from this guilt is also concluded the necessity for a period of penitence and purification, during which Germany is to remain shut out of the League of Nations and, unmolested by her, the Entente is to divide up the world. The confusing reaction to this moral polemic within the German people itself, the destruction of self-respect, the evoking of the confessions of German guilt by means of which weak souls have sought to lighten their fate—all this is only a secondary effect, but a very important secondary effect. The solicitation of confessions of guilt as conditions of milder punishment has been used very much as the promise of Wilson's Fourteen Points was used to solicit self-disarmament. . . .

But now—and this is not purely a question of historical perspective—how was the establishment of such a dogma possible? First, as we can assert with today's insight, because of Germany's fear of beginning her military build-up too late and losing an important head start, and because of this resulting error in Germany's policy: that she declared war formally herself instead of letting the guns begin to fire of their own accord, which, in view of General Rennenkampf's now well-known army order, would certainly have occurred. Military authorities assure us that such a patient wait would then have been possible. The second point concerns the most fateful German act, the Belgian invasion, which, according to the single German military plan developed in 1913–14, seemed to have become necessary. In earlier years there had been several alternative plans. . . .

But this alone would not have given the guilt legend its power. The most essential precondition was actually this: that the legend was readily believed. The German was already hated to such an extent that the most derogatory thing said about him was the most believable and no longer required any actual proof. As far as the reasons for this hatred of Germans are concerned, Max Scheler, in his well-known book, has made a clarification in which he underemphasizes only the senseless activity involved in the whole complex of imperial speeches, pan-Germanic writings, the naval league and the Bülow-Tirpitz policy. Moreover, one must especially not forget the Anglo-Saxon characteristic of never doing anything without moral justification and of never asserting one's own interests except where one is assured of their moral superiority. This characteristic is a vestige of the old Puritanic mentality which uses its moral rectitude with infinite severity, but also with the constant intention that this rectitude give it a good conscience on the road to power and profit. Profit and rectitude *always* coincide for the Puritan. It is the infinite self-righteousness of Calvinism that we now smell on the breath of an entire world. But if we explain, with great "realism" and with petty pride in our honesty, that *everything* moral in politics is only excuse and camouflage for politics itself, for questions of power and interest, then we shall be working in the worst possible way against this self-righteousness. For in so doing we should confirm all of our antagonist's propositions for him and ourselves write the verdict of extermination. Such a verdict has in fact been written a thousand times over by the war publicity and industrial literature of Germany. Calvinist self-righteousness is not simply cant; among the Anglo-Saxons, it combines personally, with reasonable honesty and, above all, with great mass-psychological effectiveness, with a remarkable sense for business and power—so much could have been learned from Troeltsch's [1] book on *The Social Teachings of the Christian Churches*. But how many among us bother, in their enlightened state, to take such spiritual matters seriously?

The worst and most unfortunate thing of all, however, was German war policy itself. It allowed itself to be seduced by initial successes, and then by renewed successes in critical situations, into going beyond the original goals of preserving stability and of pure defense. After Falkenhayn and Ludendorff, a full-fledged General Staff policy took over; the management associations and the publicity-befuddled masses demanded ever greater acquisitions. Military methods now assumed several times the harshness that would have been absolutely necessary. Humanity and justice were officially regarded as sentimentalities, and to advocate a peaceful settlement was everywhere considered a sign of weakness. Political leadership was shaky and powerless and was at last broken up completely by the General Staff. The military and the political were never held together and balanced by the Kaiser, least of all at this critical moment. The nation broke in two. The proof of the Germans' will to conquest, of their guilt for the war, and of their evil military practices was now, by means of the Entente's relentless campaign of suggestion, quite easily furnished to the entire world. Moreover, both within and without Germany, our ethical integrity was sinking, so that the experiences of occupied territories everywhere, in the east and in the west, awakened hatred for the Germans. Our ruling classes hadn't the slightest talent for occupation and the treatment of occupied territories. All this lent such growth to the guilt dogma that our antagonists could at last dare scornfully to reject the request for an international and impartial settlement. The dogma of German guilt is as well established in the modern inquisition as the existence of the devil was in the medieval inquisition—and what else can it appear but an unheard-of insolence, when the heretic himself casts doubt upon the dogma?

Still one more factor was important: journalistic technique. Just as, in this war, the over-all atmosphere of technology destroyed all sense and reason and inflated reasonable military actions to the point of pure madness, likewise the technology of creating opinions and attitudes, as developed in the nations fighting for democracy, celebrated candidly monstrous and stunning triumphs. The complete isolation of the Central Powers and the all-out campaign of suggestion created in the entire world a mentality to which Germany was utterly inimical, and made Germany appear, regardless of

---

[1] When it was first published in the "Kunstwart" (Art observer) this essay was signed with the pseudonym "Spectator."

whether she be democratic or monarchic, as an absolute moral horror and a danger to humanity. Avenarius' books have gruesomely illuminated some of the tricks employed to this end. On our side, people believed it possible to neutralize such attacks by simple counter-assertions and, for the rest, continued to operate by means of military command and the pressure of authority. But the masses could not, or at least not for any long period of time, be manipulated by this sort of "enlightenment." One of the heads of this enlightenment-campaign asked me once about the reasons for his movement's ineffectiveness. When I said that all this enlightenment failed utterly to take mass psychology into account, he answered simply that psychology did not exist for him—only patriotism existed and, in cases of need, force. The enemy understood journalistic techniques incomparably better. And we, as must not be forgotten, presented him with an inexhaustible supply of raw material to work on, in the form of our presumption and stupidity, and the incautious and injudicious spouting of all our secret wishes and ideas. We refused any longer to believe in the power of moral ideas or in their military effectiveness; thus, we placed these weapons in the enemy's hands, heedless of whether or not he would use them fairly.

Such things must be recognized, in order that the treaty's conditions be merely understood.

III THE RUSSIAN REVOLUTIONS

REFORM UNDER THE TSARS

RUSSIAN HISTORY after the Emancipation of the Serfs (1863) is characterized by a rising variegated reform ferment. One of the principal organizations coming into conflict with the regime was an institution created (in 1864) by the tsar himself, the zemstvos, assemblies elected by landlords and peasant communes. The tsar never intended that they should become, as they did, platforms for a progressive opposition or that they should really share in the general government of the country. The provincial governors vetoed reformist zemstvo decrees, and the tsar forbade the zemstvos to combine for common purposes.

Another anti-tsarist group was the Narodnaya Volya, or People's Will, a circle of revolutionary intellectuals and workingmen formed in 1879. Its principal program for a constituent assembly elected by universal suffrage was publicized by propaganda, a wave of assassinations of prominent tsarist officials, and the dynamiting of trains and bridges. Tsar Alexander II escaped death in 1880, only to be assassinated the next year. The Narodnaya Volya at once reiterated its demands, unsuccessfully, in a letter to Alexander III.

Russia's severe defeat in the war with Japan in 1904 brought a fresh revolutionary wave. On January 9, 1905, an unarmed procession of petitioning workers, headed by a priest named Gapon, was fired upon by the tsar's troops. This "Bloody Sunday" marked the beginning of the revolution of 1905.

After months of alternating conciliation and terror by the tsar, in December, 1905, the first legislative assembly, or Duma, was convened, on the basis of a very limited suffrage. The Duma, however, did not prove docile enough and was dispersed in the summer of 1906.

The first selection below, on the zemstvos, is from the 1912 edition of Mackenzie Wallace's *Russia* (1st ed., 1877). The section on the Narodniks is taken from J. H. Robinson and C. A. Beard, *Readings in Modern European History* (Boston: Ginn and Co., 1909), Vol. II. The two readings on the Revolution of 1905 are from J. Mavor, *Economic History of Russia* (2d ed., New York: E. P. Dutton and Co., 1925), Vol. II, and *The Memoirs of Count Witte,* translated by Abraham Yarmolinsky (Garden City: Doubleday, Page and Co., 1921).

❧

THE ZEMSTVO AND LOCAL SELF-GOVERNMENT

MY PERSONAL ACQUAINTANCE with this interesting institution dates from 1870. Very soon after my arrival at Novgorod in that year, I made the acquaintance of a gentleman who was described to me as "the president of the provincial Zemstvo bureau," and finding him amiable and communicative, I suggested that he might give me some information regarding the institution of which he was the chief local representative. . . .

The Zemstvo is a kind of local administration which supplements the action of the rural Communes, and takes cognisance of those higher public wants which individual Communes cannot possibly satisfy. Its principal duties are to keep the roads and bridges in proper repair, to provide means of conveyance for the rural police and other officials, to look after primary education and sanitary affairs, to watch the state of the crops and take measures against approaching famine, and, in short, to undertake, within certain clearly defined limits, whatever seems likely to increase the material and moral well-being of the population. In form the institution is Parliamentary—that is to say, it consists of an assembly of deputies which meets regularly once a year, and of a permanent executive bureau elected by the Assembly from among its members. If the Assembly be regarded as a local Parliament, the bureau corresponds to the Cabinet. . . . Once every three years the deputies are elected in certain fixed proportions by the landed proprietors, the rural Communes, and the municipal corporations. Every province (*gubérniya*) and each of the districts (*uyézdy*) into which the province is sub-divided has such an assembly and such a bureau.

Not long after my arrival in Novgorod I had the opportunity of being present at a District Assembly. In the ballroom of the "Club de la Noblesse" I found thirty or forty men seated round a long table covered with green cloth. Before each member lay sheets of paper for the purpose of taking notes, and before the president—the Marshal of Noblesse for the district—stood a small handbell, which he rang vigorously at the commencement of the proceedings and on all occasions when he wished to obtain silence. To the right and left of the president sat the members of the executive (*upráva*), armed with piles of written and printed documents, from which they read long and tedious extracts, till the majority of the audience took to yawning and one or two of the members positively went to sleep. At the close of each of these reports the president rang his bell—presumably for the purpose of awakening the sleepers— and inquired whether anyone had remarks to make on what had just been read. Generally someone had remarks to make, and not unfrequently a discussion ensued. When any decided difference of opinion appeared, a vote was taken by handing round a sheet of paper, or by the simpler method of requesting the Ayes to stand up and the Noes to sit still.

What surprised me most in this assembly was that it was composed partly of nobles and partly of peasants—the latter being decidedly in the majority— and that no trace of antagonism seemed to exist between the two classes. Landed proprietors and their ci-devant serfs, emancipated only ten years before, evidently met for the moment on a footing of equality. The discussions were carried on chiefly by the nobles, but on more than one occasion peasant members rose to speak, and their remarks, always clear, practical, and to the point, were invariably listened to with respectful attention. Instead of that violent antagonism which might have been expected, considering the constitution of the Assembly, there was too much unanimity—a fact indicating plainly that the majority of the members did not take a very deep interest in the matters presented to them.

This assembly for the district was held in the month of September. At the beginning of December the Assembly for the Province met, and during nearly three weeks I was daily present at its deliberations. In general character and mode of procedure it resembled closely the District Assembly. Its chief peculiarities were that its members were chosen, not by the primary electors, but by the assemblies of the ten districts which compose the province, and that it took cognisance merely of those matters which concerned more than one district. Besides this, the peasant deputies were very few in number—a fact which somewhat surprised me, because I was aware that, according to the law, the peasant members of the District Assemblies were eligible, like those of the other classes. The explanation is that the District Assemblies choose their most active members to represent them in the Provincial Assemblies, and consequently the choice generally falls on landed proprietors. To this arrangement the peasants make no objection, for attendance at the Provincial Assemblies demands a considerable pecuniary outlay, and payment of the deputies is expressly prohibited by law. . . .

Even within its proper sphere, as defined by law, the Zemstvo has not accomplished what was expected of it. The country has not been covered with a network of macadamised roads, and the bridges are by no means as safe as could be desired. Village schools and infirmaries are still far below the requirements of the population. Little or nothing has been done for the development of trade or manufactures; and the villages remain very much what they were under the old Administration. Meanwhile the local rates have been rising with alarming rapidity; and many people draw from all this the conclusion that the Zemstvo is a worthless institution which has increased the taxation without conferring any corresponding benefit on the country. . . .

The Zemstvo has, however, done much more than the majority of its critics admit. It fulfils tolerably well, without scandalous peculation and jobbery, its commonplace, every-day duties, and it has created a new and more equitable system of rating by which landed proprietors and house-owners are made to bear their share of the public burdens. It has done a very great deal to provide medical aid and primary education for the common people, and it has improved wonderfully the condition of the hospitals, lunatic asylums, and other benevolent institutions committed to its charge. In its efforts to aid the peasantry it has helped to improve the native breeds of horses and cattle, and it has created a system of obligatory fire insurance, together with means for preventing and extinguishing fires in the villages—a most important matter in a country where the peasants live in wooden houses and big fires are fearfully frequent. After neglecting for a good many years the essential question as to how the peasants' means of subsistence can be increased, it has latterly . . . helped them to obtain improved agricultural implements and better seed, encouraged the formation of small credit associations and savings banks, and appointed agricultural inspectors to teach them how they may introduce modest improvements within their limited means. At the same time, in many districts it has endeavoured to assist the home industries which are threatened with annihilation by the big factories, and whenever measures have been proposed for the benefit of the rural population, such as the lowering of the land-redemption payments and the creation of the Peasant Land Bank, it has invariably given them its cordial support.

If you ask a zealous member of the Zemstvo why it has not done more he will probably tell you that it is because its activity has been constantly restricted and counteracted by the Government. The Assemblies were obliged to accept as presidents the Marshals of Noblesse, many of whom were men of antiquated ideas and retrograde principles. At every turn the more enlightened, more active members found themselves opposed, thwarted, and finally checkmated by the Imperial officials. . . .

LETTER OF THE REVOLUTIONARY EXECUTIVE COMMITTEE TO TSAR ALEXANDER III, 1881

March 10, 1881

YOUR MAJESTY:

Although the Executive Committee understands fully the grief that you must experience at this moment, it believes that it has no right to yield to the feeling of natural delicacy which would perhaps dictate the postponement of the following explanation to another time. There is something higher than the most legitimate human feeling, and that is, duty to one's country,—the duty for which a citizen must sacrifice himself and his own feelings, and even the feelings of others. In obedience to this all-powerful duty we have decided to address you at once, waiting for nothing, as will wait for nothing the historical process that threatens us with rivers of blood and the most terrible convulsions. . . .

You are aware, your Majesty, that the government of the late Tsar could not be reproached with a lack of energy. It hanged the innocent and the guilty, and filled prisons and remote provinces with exiles. Scores of so-called "leaders" were captured and hanged, and died with the courage and tranquillity of martyrs; but the movement did not cease,—on the contrary it grew and strengthened. The revolutionary movement, your Majesty, is not dependent upon any particular individuals; it is a process of the social organism; and the scaffolds raised for its more energetic exponents are as powerless to save the outgrown order of things as the cross that was erected for the Redeemer was powerless to save the ancient world from the triumph of Christianity. The government, of course, may yet capture and hang an immense number of separate individuals, it may break up a great number of separate revolutionary groups; but all this will not change, in the slightest degree, the condition of affairs. . . .

A dispassionate glance at the grievous decade through which we have just passed will enable us to forecast accurately the future progress of the revolutionary movement, provided the policy of the government does not change. The movement will continue to grow and extend; deeds of a terroristic nature will increase in frequency and intensity. Meanwhile the number of the discontented in the country will grow larger and larger; confidence in the government, on the part of the people, will decline; and the idea of revolution—of its possibility and inevitability—will establish itself in Russia more and more firmly. A terrible explosion, a bloody chaos, a revolutionary earthquake throughout Russia, will complete the destruction of the old order of things. Do not mistake this for a mere phrase. We understand better than any one else can how lamentable is the waste of so much talent and energy—the loss, in bloody skirmishes and in the work of destruction, of so much strength which, under other conditions, might have been expended in creative labor and in the development of the intelligence, the welfare, and the civil life of the Russian people. Whence proceeds this lamentable necessity for bloody conflict?

It arises, your Majesty, from the lack in Russia of a real government in the true sense of that word. A government, in the very nature of things, should only give outward form to the aspirations of the people and effect to the people's will. But with us—excuse the expression—the government has degenerated into a mere coterie, and deserves the name of a usurping "gang" much more than does the Executive Committee.

Whatever may be the intentions of the Tsar, the actions of the government have nothing in common with the popular welfare or popular aspirations. The government has brought Russia to such a pass that, at the present time, the masses of the people are in a state of pauperism and ruin; are subjected to the most humiliating surveillance, even at their own domestic hearths; and are powerless even to regulate their own communal and social affairs. The protection of the law and of the government is enjoyed only by the extortionist and the exploiter, and the most exasperating robbery goes unpunished. But, on the other hand, what a terrible fate awaits the man who sincerely considers the general good! You know very well, your Majesty, that it is not only socialists who are exiled and prosecuted.

These are the reasons why the Russian government exerts no moral influence and has no support among the people. These are the reasons why Russia brings forth so many revolutionists. These are the reasons why even such a deed as killing a Tsar excites in the minds of a majority of the people only gladness and sympathy. Yes, your Majesty! Do not be deceived by the reports of flatterers and sycophants; Tsaricide is popular in Russia.

From such a state of affairs there can be only two modes of escape: either a revolution,—absolutely inevitable and not to be averted by any punishments; or a voluntary turning of the supreme power to the people. In the interest of our native land, in the hope of preventing the useless waste of energy, in the hope of averting the terrible miseries that always accompany revolution, the Executive Committee approaches your Majesty with the advice to take the second course. Be assured, so soon as the supreme power ceases to rule arbitrarily, so soon as it firmly resolves to accede to the demands of the people's conscience and consciousness, you may, without fear, discharge the spies that disgrace the administration, send your guards back to their barracks, and burn the scaffolds that are demoralizing the people. The Executive Committee will voluntarily terminate its own existence, and the organizations formed about it will disperse, in order that their members may devote themselves to the work of promoting culture among the people of their native land.

We address your Majesty as those who have discarded all prejudices, and who have suppressed the distrust of you created by the actions of the government throughout a century. We forget that you are the representative of the authority that has so often deceived and that has so injured the people. We address you as a citizen and as an honest man. We hope that the feeling of personal exasperation will not extinguish in your mind your consciousness of your duties and your desire to know the truth. We also might feel exasperation. You have lost your father. We have lost not only our fathers, but our brothers, our wives, our children, and our dearest friends. We are nevertheless ready to suppress personal feeling if it be demanded by the welfare of Russia. We expect the same from you.

We set no conditions for you; do not let our proposition irritate you. The conditions that are prerequisite to a change from revolutionary activity to peaceful labor are created, not by us, but by history. These conditions are, in our opinion, two.

1. A general amnesty to cover all past political crimes; for the reason that they were not crimes but fulfillments of civil duty.

2. The summoning of representatives of the whole Russian people to examine the existing framework of social and governmental life, and to remodel it in accordance with the people's wishes.

We regard it as necessary, however, to remind you that the legalization of the supreme power, by the representatives of the people, can be valid only in case the elections are perfectly free. We declare solemnly, before the people of our native land and before the whole world, that our party will submit unconditionally to the decisions of a National Assembly elected in the manner above indicated, and that we will not allow ourselves, in future, to offer violent resistance to any government that the National Assembly may sanction.

And now, your Majesty, decide! Before you are two courses, and you are to make your choice between them. We can only trust that your intelligence and conscience may suggest to you the only decision that is compatible with the welfare of Russia, with your own dignity, and with your duty to your native land.

THE EXECUTIVE COMMITTEE

FATHER GAPON'S PETITION TO NICHOLAS II

SIRE,—We, working men and inhabitants of St. Petersburg of various classes, our wives and our children and our helpless old parents, come to Thee, Sire, to seek for truth and defence. We have become beggars; we have been oppressed; we are burdened by toil beyond our powers; we are scoffed at; we are not recognized as human beings; we are treated as slaves who must suffer their bitter fate and who must keep silence. We suffered, but we are pushed farther into the den of beggary, lawlessness, and ignorance. We are choked by despotism and irresponsibility, and we are breathless. We have no more power, Sire, the limit of patience has been reached. There has arrived for us that tremendous moment when death is better than the continuation of intolerable tortures. We have left off working, and we have declared to the masters that we shall not begin to work until they comply with our demands. We beg but little; we desire only that without which life is not life, but hard labour and eternal torture. The first request which we made was that our masters should discuss our needs with us; but this they refused, on the ground that no right to make this request is recognized by law. They also declared to be illegal our requests to diminish the working hours to eight hours daily, to agree with us about the prices for our work, to consider our misunderstandings with the inferior administration of the mills, to increase the wages for the labour of women and of general labourers, so that the minimum daily wage should be one ruble per day, to abolish overtime work, to give us medical attention without insulting us, to arrange the workshops so that it might be possible to work there, and not find in them death from awful draughts and from rain and snow. All these requests appeared to be, in the opinion of our masters and of the factory and mill administrations, illegal. Every one of our requests was a crime, and the desire to improve our condition was regarded by them as impertinence, and as offensive to them.

Sire, here are many thousands of us, and all are human beings only in appearance. In reality in us, as in all Russian people, there is not recognized any human right, not even the right of speaking, thinking, meeting, discussing our needs, taking measures for the improvement of our condition. We have been enslaved, and enslaved under the auspices of Thy officials, with their assistance, and with their co-operation. Every one of us who dares to raise a voice in defence of working-class and popular interests is thrown into jail or is sent into banishment. For the possession of good hearts and sensitive souls we are punished as for crimes. Even to pity a beaten man—a man tortured and without rights—means to commit a heavy crime. All the people—working men as well as peasants—are handed over to the discretion of the officials of the Government, who are thieves of the property of the State—robbers who not only take no care of the interests of the people, but who trample these interests under their feet. The Government officials have brought the country to complete destruction, have involved it in a detestable war, and have further and further led it to ruin. We working men have no voice in the expenditure of the enormous amounts raised from us in taxes. We do not know even where and for what is spent the money collected from a beggared people. The people are deprived of the possibility of expressing their desires, and they now demand that they be allowed to take part in the introduction of taxes and in the expenditure of them.

The working men are deprived of the possibility of organizing themselves in unions for the defence of their interests. . . .

Russia is too great. Its necessities are too various and numerous for officials alone to rule it. National representation is indispensable. It is indispensable that people should assist and should rule themselves. To them only are known their real necessities. Do not reject their assistance, accept it, order immediately the convocation of representatives of the Russian land from all ranks, including representatives from the working men. Let there be capitalists as well as working men—official and priest, doctor and teacher—let all, whatever they may be, elect their representatives. Let everyone be equal and free in the right of election, and for this purpose order that the elections for the Constitutional Assembly be carried on under the condition of universal, equal, and secret voting. This is the most capital of our requests. In it and upon it everything is based. This is the principal and only plaster for our painful wounds, without which our wounds will fester and bring us rapidly near to death. Yet one measure alone cannot heal our wounds. Other measures are also indispensable. Directly and openly as to a Father, we speak to Thee, Sire, about them in person, for all the toiling classes of Russia. The following are indispensable:

I. Measures against the ignorance and rightlessness of the Russian people:

1. The immediate release and return of all who have suffered for political and religious convictions, for strikes, and national peasant disorders.

2. The immediate declaration of freedom and of the inviolability of the person—freedom of speech and press, freedom of meetings, and freedom of conscience in religion.

3. Universal and compulsory elementary education of the people at the charge of the State.

4. Responsibility of the Ministers before the people and guarantee that the Government will be law-abiding.

5. Equality before the law of all without exception.

6. Separation of the Church from the State.

II. Measures against the poverty of the people:

1. Abolition of indirect taxes and the substitution of a progressive income tax.

2. Abolition of the Redemption Instalments, cheap credit, and gradual transference of the land to the people.

3. The orders for the military and naval ministries should be fulfilled in Russia, and not abroad.

4. The cessation of the war by the will of the people.

III. Measures against the oppression of labour:

1. Abolition of the factory inspectorships.

2. Institution at factories and mills of permanent committees of elected workers, which, together with the administration (of the factories) would consider the complaints of individual workers. Discharge of working men should not take place otherwise than by resolution of this committee.

3. Freedom of organization of co-operative societies of consumers and of labour trade unions immediately.

4. Eight-hours working day and regulation of overtime working.

5. Freedom of the struggle of labour against capital immediately.

6. Normal wages immediately.

7. Participation of working-class representatives in the working out of projects of law upon workmen's State insurance immediately. . . .

CONSTITUTIONAL MANIFESTO OF OCTOBER, 1905

UNREST AND DISTURBANCES in the capitals and in many regions of our Empire fill our heart with a great and heavy grief. The welfare of the Russian Sovereign is inseparable from the welfare of the people, and their sorrow is his sorrow. The unrest now arisen may cause a profound disorder in the masses and become a menace to the integrity and unity of the Russian State. The great vow of Imperial service enjoins us to strive with all the might of our reason and authority to put an end within the shortest possible time to this unrest so perilous to the State. Having ordered the proper authorities to take measures for the suppression of the direct manifestations of disorder, rioting, and violence, and for the protection of peaceful people who seek to fulfil in peace the duties incumbent upon them, We, in order to carry out more effectively the measures outlined by us for the pacification of the country, have found it necessary to unify the activity of the higher Government agencies.

We impose upon the Government the obligation to execute our inflexible will:

1. To grant the population the unshakable foundations of civic freedom on the basis of real personal inviolability, freedom of conscience, of speech, of assemblage, and of association.

2. Without stopping the appointed elections to the Imperial Duma, to admit to participation in the Duma those classes of the population which have hitherto been deprived of the franchise, in so far as this is feasible in the brief period remaining before the convening of the Duma, leaving the further development of the principle of general suffrage to the new legislative order (i.e., the Duma and Imperial Council established by the law of August 6, 1905).

3. To establish it as an unshakable rule that no law can become effective without the sanction of the Imperial Duma and that the people's elected representatives should be guaranteed a real participation in the control over the lawfulness of the authorities appointed by us.

We call upon all the faithful sons of Russia to remember their duty to their country, to lend assistance in putting an end to the unprecedented disturbances and together with us make every effort to restore quiet and peace in our native land. . . .

THE TSAR'S DISSOLUTION OF THE FIRST DUMA

WE SUMMONED the representatives of the nation by our will to the work of productive legislation. Confiding firmly in divine clemency and believing in the great and brilliant future of our people, we confidently anticipated benefits for the country from their labors. We proposed great reforms in all departments of the national life. We have always devoted our greatest care to the removal of the ignorance of the people by the light of instruction, and to the removal of their burdens by improving the conditions of agricultural work.

A cruel disappointment has befallen our expectations. The representatives of the nation, instead of applying themselves to the work of productive legislation, have strayed into spheres beyond their competence, and have been making inquiries into the acts of local authorities established by ourselves, and have been making comments upon the imperfections of the fundamental laws, which can only be modified by our imperial will. In short, the representatives of the nation have undertaken really illegal acts, such as the appeal by the Duma to the nation.

The peasants, disturbed by such anomalies, and seeing no hope of the amelioration of their lot, have resorted in a number of districts to open pillage and the destruction of other people's property, and to disobedience of the law and of the legal authorities. But our subjects ought to remember that an improvement in the lot of the people is only possible under conditions of perfect order and tranquillity. We shall not permit arbitrary or illegal acts, and we shall impose our imperial will on the disobedient by all the power of the State.

We appeal to all well-disposed Russians to combine for the maintenance of legal authority and the restoration of peace in our dear fatherland. May calm be reestablished once more in Russia, and may God help us to accomplish the chiefest of our tasks, the improvement of the lot of the peasant. Our will on this point is unalterable. The Russian husbandman, in case his land is too small to maintain him, shall be supplied, without prejudice to the property of others, with legitimate and honest means for enlarging his holdings. The representatives of the other classes will, at our request, devote all their efforts to the promotion of this great undertaking which will be given a definitely legal form by a future Duma.

In dissolving the Duma we confirm our immutable intention of maintaining this institution, and in conformity with this intention we fix March 5, 1907, as the date of the convocation of a new Duma by a ukase addressed to the Senate. With unshakable faith in divine clemency and in the good sense of the Russian people, we shall expect from the new Duma the realization of our efforts and their promotion of legislation in accordance with the requirements of a regenerated Russia.

Faithful sons of Russia, your Tsar calls upon you as a father upon his children to unite with him for the regeneration of our holy fatherland. We believe that giants in thought and action will appear, and that, thanks to their assiduous efforts, the glory of Russia will continue to shine.

LEON TROTSKY

LEON TROTSKY (1879–1940) was the adopted name of Leo Davidovitch Bronstein. Of the three most famous names in modern Communism—Lenin and Stalin being the other two—Trotsky had the most brilliant mind. His *History of the Russian Revolution,* for all its distortions, is one of the great histories written in the twentieth century.

Its author was a largely self-educated son of a Russian Jewish farmer. At the age of seventeen, Trotsky was already a Marxist and revolutionary. He was arrested by the tsarist police several times and eventually was sent to Siberia from which, in 1902, he escaped into exile. For the next fifteen years he traveled, wrote and edited; revolutionary conspiracy was his life. France, Belgium, Germany, England, Austria, the United States were all his bases from time to time, and Lenin was his constant colleague and correspondent. In these years Trotsky developed the theory of "the permanent revolution," postulating that a bourgeois revolution in Russia would be converted into a proletarian revolution which, in turn, would spread from Russia to the entire world. His and Lenin's long conspiratorial work brought results in Russia in 1917, not, however, against tsarist autocracy but against the democratic regime headed by Kerensky.

The great revolution against the tsar came in March, 1917. The country had been at war with Germany for two and a half years. Grave defeats and near collapse behind the lines brought deep dissatisfaction with the tsarist government among all classes of the population.

On March 11, 1917, a strike in Petrograd flared into revolution which quickly spread throughout the country. The tsar abdicated and a provisional government was set up under Prince Lvov. Lvov wanted to continue the war on the Allied side and to preserve the monarchy after having clipped away its former absolutist powers. Under these circumstances the arrival through German connivance of Lenin in Russia in April was of extreme importance. From exile in Switzerland, Lenin had carried on bitter opposition to the war, and had continued to organize the Bolsheviks to prepare to take power.

Lenin and Trotsky provoked a series of bitter clashes between the Provisional government, on the one hand, and the Soviets, on the other. The Soviets were committees and councils set up by factory workers and soldiers to organize administration after the collapse of the tsarist regime. In the Soviets, of course, the actual Communists played a large part. After a general rising in Petrograd in November, 1917, the Provisional government was deposed and power passed into the hands of the Communist party and the Soviets. Soon afterwards, in January, 1918, Lenin and his troops dismissed the only democratically elected representative assembly Russia has ever known. The Bolsheviks did not possess a majority, and were determined on dictatorial rule in any case.

In these months and in later years, Trotsky played an outstanding role, greater certainly than Stalin's. He helped negotiate the Treaty of Brest-Litovsk (1918) ending the unpopular and exhausting war with Germany. But although foreign affairs remained his special charge and interest, he was more famous for building the Red Army which by 1921 had succeeded in clearing Russia of foreign and domestic troops opposed to the Bolsheviks. After Lenin's death in 1924, although Lenin himself would probably have preferred Trotsky to Stalin as his successor, Trotsky lost out to Stalin in a long, bitter, and ideologically complex struggle. It is doubtful, however, despite the opinions of some Trotskyites, that Russia would not have become a totalitarian state if Trotsky had won. For years before 1924, in theory and practice, Trotsky was already totalitarian; at best his own rule might not have been marked by the sheer irrationality and megalomania of the Stalinist era.

Finally exiled from Russia in 1929, Trotsky wandered abroad for the next decade in Turkey, France, Norway, and Mexico, pursued in both fact and fantasy by Stalin's agents. He became a legendary figure with a near fanatic, if tiny, following in many nations outside Russia. In exile he resumed his brilliant writing, defending his ideas of permanent revolution and warning that Stalinism represented a betrayal of the revolution. *My Life* (1930) and *Stalin* (an unfinished book, 1946) were two principal works in addition to the great history of the revolution published in three volumes in 1932. In 1940 Trotsky was assassinated in his retreat near Mexico City by an associate whom many believe to have been sent by Stalin.

This selection comes from Trotsky's *The History of the Russian Revolution* (New York: Simon and Schuster, 1932). The dates used by Trotsky are based on the Russian calendar (October = the Western November).

THE HISTORY OF THE RUSSIAN REVOLUTION

THE CONQUEST OF THE CAPITAL

All is changed and yet all remains as before. The revolution has shaken the country, deepened the split, frightened some, embittered others, but not yet wiped out a thing or replaced it. Imperial St. Petersburg seems drowned in a sleeply lethargy rather than dead. The revolution has stuck little red flags in the hands of the cast-iron monuments of the monarchy. Great red streamers are hanging down the fronts of the government buildings. But the palaces, the ministries, the headquarters, seem to be living a life entirely apart from those red banners, tolerably faded, moreover, by the autumn rains. The two-headed eagles with the scepter of empire have been torn down where possible, but oftener draped or hastily painted over. They seem to be lurking there. All the old Russia is lurking, its jaws set in rage.

The slight figures of the militia-men at the street corners remind one of the revolution that has wiped out the old "Pharaohs," who used to stand there like live monuments. Moreover Russia has now for almost two months been called a republic. And the tzar's family is in Tobolsk. Yes, the February whirlwind has left its traces. But the tzarist generals remain generals, the senators senatorialize, the privy councillors defend their dignity, the Table of Precedence is still in effect. Colored hat-bands and cockades recall the bureaucratic hierarchy; yellow buttons with an eagle still distinguish the student. And yet more important—the landlords are still landlords, no end of the war is in sight, the Allied diplomats are impudently jerking official Russia along on a string.

All remains as before and yet nobody knows himself. The aristocratic quarters feel that they have been moved out into the backyard; the quarters of the liberal bourgeoisie have moved nearer the aristocracy. From being a patriotic myth, the Russian people have become an awful reality. Everything is billowing and shaking under foot. Mysticism flares up with sharpened force in those circles which not long ago were making fun of the superstitions of the monarchy.

Brokers, lawyers, ballerinas are cursing the oncoming eclipse of public morals. Faith in the Constituent Assembly is evaporating day by day. Gorky in his newspaper is prophesying the approaching downfall of culture. The flight from raving and hungry Petrograd to a more peaceful and well-fed province, on the increase since the July days, now becomes a stampede. Respectable families who have not succeeded in getting away from the capital, try in vain to insulate themselves from reality behind stone wall and under iron roof. But the echoes of the storm penetrate on every side: through the market, where everything is getting dear and nothing to be had; through the respectable press, which is turning into one yelp of hatred and fear; through the seething streets where from time to time shootings are to be heard under the windows; and finally through the back entrance, through the servants, who are no longer humbly submissive. It is here that the revolution strikes home to the most sensitive spot. That obstreperousness of the household slaves destroys utterly the stability of the family régime.

Nevertheless the everyday routine defends itself with all its might. Schoolboys are still studying the old text-books, functionaries drawing up the same useless papers, poets scribbling the verses that nobody reads, nurses telling the fairy-tales about Ivan Tzarevich. The nobility's and merchants' daughters, coming in from the provinces, are studying music or hunting husbands. The same old cannon on the wall of the Peter and Paul fortress continues to announce the noon hour. A new ballet is going on in the Mariinsky theater, and the Minister of Foreign Affairs, Tereshchenko, stronger on choreography than diplomacy, finds time, we may assume, to admire the steel toes of the ballerina and thus demonstrate the stability of the régime.

The remnants of the old banquet are still very plentiful and everything can be had for big money. The Guard officers still click their spurs accurately and go after adventures. Wild parties are in progress in the private dining rooms of expensive restaurants. The shutting-off of the electric lights at midnight does not prevent the flourishing of gambling clubs where champagne sparkles by candlelight, where illustrious peculators swindle no less illustrious German spies, where monarchist conspirators call the bets of Semitic smugglers, and where the astronomical figures of the stakes played for indicate both the scale of debauchery and the scale of inflation. . . .

Smolny [1] is more and more firmly and imperiously giving commands, the passionate sympathy of the masses is lifting her up. However, the central leadership grasps directly only the topmost links of that revolutionary system which as a connected whole is destined to achieve the change. The most important processes are taking place below, and somehow of their own accord. The factories and barracks are the chief forges of history in these days and nights. As in February, the Vyborg district focusses the basic forces of the revolution. But it has today a thing it lacked in February—its own powerful organization open and universally recognized. From the dwellings, the factory lunch-rooms, the clubs, the barracks, all threads lead to the house numbered 33 Samsonevsky Prospect, where are located the district Committee of the Bolsheviks, the Vyborg soviet, and the military headquarters. The district militia is fusing with the Red Guard. The district is wholly in the control of the workers. If the government should raid Smolny, the Vyborg district alone could re-establish a center and guarantee the further offensive. . . .

In Smolny, whence the compromisist Executive Committee had managed to steal away to the headquarters of the government staff, there were now concentrated the heads of all the revolutionary organizations led by the Bolsheviks. Here assembled on that day [October, 24] the all-important meeting of the Central Committee of the Bolsheviks to take the final decision before striking the blow. Eleven members were present. Lenin had not yet turned up from his refuge in the Vyborg district. Zinoviev also was absent from the session. According to the temperamental expression of Dzerzhinsky, he was "hiding and taking no part in the party work." Kamenev, on the other hand, although sharing the views of Zinoviev, was very active in the headquarters of the insurrection. Stalin was not present at the session. Generally

---

[1] Headquarters of the executive committee of the Soviet after July, 1917.

speaking he did not appear at Smolny, spending his time in the editorial office of the central organ. The session, as always, was held under the chairmanship of Sverdlov. The official minutes of the session are scant, but they indicate everything essential. For characterizing the leading participants in the revolution, and the distribution of functions among them, they are irreplaceable.

It was a question of taking full possession of Petrograd in the next twenty-four hours. That meant to seize those political and technical institutions which were still in the hands of the government. The Congress of Soviets must hold its session under the soviet power. The practical measures of the nocturnal assault had been worked out, or were being worked out, by the Military Revolutionary Committee and the Military Organizations of the Bolsheviks. The Central Committee was to underline the final points. . . .

The Peter and Paul fortress, won over politically only yesterday, is today completely taken possession of by the Military Revolution Committee. The machine gun crew, the most revolutionary unit, is being brought into fighting trim. A mighty work of cleaning the Colt machine guns is in progress —there are eighty of them. Machine guns are set up on the fortress wall to command the quay and the Troitsky bridge. The sentry guard at the gates is reinforced. Patrols are sent out into the surrounding districts. . . .

It was now possible to rely upon the fortress with tranquil confidence. Weapons were given out from the arsenal without hindrance. At Smolny, in the Factory and Shop Committee room, delegates from the plants stood in line to get orders for rifles. The capital had seen many queues during the war years—now it saw rifle-queues for the first time. Trucks from all the districts of the city were driving up to the arsenal. "You would hardly have recognized the Peter and Paul fortress," writes the worker Skorinko. "Its renowned silence was broken by the chugging automobiles, shouts, and the creak of wagons. There was a special bustle in the storehouses. . . . Here too they led by us the first prisoners, officers and junkers."

The meeting in the Cirque Moderne had another result. The bicycle men who had been guarding the Winter Palace since July withdrew, announcing that they would no longer consent to protect the government. That was a heavy blow. The bicycle men had to be replaced by junkers. The military support of the government was more and more reducing itself to the officers' schools—a thing which not only narrowed it extremely, but also conclusively revealed its social constitution. . . .

After Kerensky's speech at the Pre-Parliament the [government] authorities tried to broaden their offensive. The railroad stations were occupied by detachments of junkers. Pickets were posted at the big street-crossings and

ordered to requisition the private automobiles not turned over to headquarters. By three o'clock in the afternoon the bridges were raised, except
for the Dvortsovy which remained open under heavy guard for the movement of the junkers. This measure, adopted by the monarchy at all critical
moments and for the last time in the February days, was dictated by fear
of the worker's districts. The raising of the bridges was received by the population as an official announcement of the beginning of the insurrection. The
headquarters of the districts concerned immediately answered this military
act of the government in their own way by sending armed detachments to
the bridges. Smolny had only to develop the initiative. This struggle for the
bridges assumed the character of a test for both sides. Parties of armed
workers and soldiers brought pressure to bear on the junkers and Cossacks,
now persuading and now threatening. The guard finally yielded without
hazarding a straight-out fight. Some of the bridges were raised and lowered
several times.

The *Aurora* received a direct order from the Military Revolutionary Committee: "With all means at your command restore movement on the
Nikolaevsky Bridge." The commander of the cruiser at first refused to carry
out the order, but after a symbolic arrest of himself and all his officers
obediently brought the ship to the bridge. Cordons of sailors spread out along
both quays. By the time the *Aurora* had dropped anchor before the bridge,
relates Korkov, the tracks of the junkers were already cold. The sailors
themselves lowered the bridge and posted guards. Only Dvortsovy bridge
remained several hours in the hands of the government patrols. . . .

The tactical plans for the conquest of the capital were worked out chiefly
by the staff of the Military Organization of the Bolsheviks. Officers of the
general staff would have found many faults in them, but military academi-
cians do not customarily take part in the preparation of a revolutionary insurrection. The essentials at any rate were taken care of. The city was divided
into military divisions, each subordinate to the nearest headquarters. At the
most important points companies of the Red Guard were concentrated in
coordination with the neighboring military units, where companies were
awake and ready. The goal of each separate operation, and the forces for it,
were indicated in advance. All those taking part in the insurrection from
top to bottom—in this lay its power, in this also at times its Achilles' heel—
were imbued with absolute confidence that the victory was going to be won
without casualties.

The main operation began at two o'clock in the morning. Small military
parties, usually with a nucleus of armed workers or sailors under the leadership of commissars, occupied simultaneously, or in regular order, the rail-

road stations, the lighting plant, the munition and food stores, the water-
works, Dvortsovy bridge, the Telephone Exchange, the State Bank, the big
printing-plants. The Telegraph Station and the Post Office were completely
taken over. Reliable guards were placed everywhere. . . .

The commander of the district reported that night to general headquarters and the headquarters of the northern front over the military wire:
"The situation in Petrograd is frightful. There are no street demonstrations
or disorders, but a regulated seizure of institutions, railroad stations, also
arrests, is in progress. . . . The junkers' patrols are surrendering without
resistance. . . . We have no guarantee that there will not be an attempt to
seize the Provisional Government." Polkovnikov was right: they had no
guarantee of that.

In military circles the rumor was going round that agents of the Military
Revolutionary Committee had stolen from the desk of the Petrograd commandant the password for the sentries of the garrison. That was not at all
improbable. The insurrection had many friends among the lower personnel
of all institutions. Nevertheless this tale about stealing the password is
apparently a legend which arose in the hostile camp to explain the too
humiliating ease with which the Bolshevik patrols got possession of the
city. . . .

It is difficult to determine the number of forces directly engaged in this
nocturnal seizure of the capital—and this not only because nobody counted
them or noted them down, but also because of the character of the operations. Reserves of the second and third order almost merged with the garrison as a whole. But it was only occasionally necessary to have recourse to the
reserves. A few thousand Red Guards, two or three thousand sailors—to-
morrow with the arrivals from Kronstadt and Helsingfors there will be
about treble the number—a score of infantry companies: such were the
forces of the first and second order with whose aid the insurrectionists occupied the governmental high points of the capital. . . .

Step by step we have tried to follow in this book the development of the
October insurrection: the sharpening discontent of the worker masses, the
coming over of the soviets to the Bolshevik banners, the indignation of the
army, the campaign of the peasants against the landlords, the flood-tide of
the national movement, the growing fear and distraction of the possessing
and ruling classes, and finally the struggle for the insurrection within the
Bolshevik party. The final act of the revolution seems, after all this, too
brief, too dry, too business-like—somehow out of correspondence with the
historic scope of the events. The reader experiences a kind of disappointment. He is like a mountain climber, who, thinking the main difficulties are

still ahead, suddenly discovers that he is already on the summit or almost there. Where is the insurrection? There is no picture of the insurrection. The events do not form themselves into a picture. A series of small operations, calculated and prepared in advance, remain separated one from another both in space and time. A unity of thought and aim unites them, but they do not fuse in the struggle itself. There is no action of great masses. There are no dramatic encounters with the troops. There is nothing of all that which imaginations brought up upon the facts of history associate with the idea of insurrection.

The general character of the revolution in the capital subsequently moved Masaryk, among many others, to write: "The October revolution . . . was anything but a popular mass movement. That revolution was the act of leaders working from above and behind the scenes." As a matter of fact it was the most popular mass-insurrection in all history. The workers had no need to come out into the public square in order to fuse together: they were already politically and morally one single whole without that. The soldiers were even forbidden to leave their barracks without permission: upon that point the order of the Military Revolutionary Committee fell in with the order of Polkovnikov. But those invisible masses were marching more than ever before in step with the events. The factories and barracks never lost connection for a minute with the district headquarters, nor the districts with Smolny. The Red Guard detachments felt at their back the support of the factories. The soldier squad returning to the barracks found the new shifts ready. Only with heavy reserves behind them could revolutionary detachments go about their work with such confidence. The scattered government patrols, in contrast, being convinced in advance of their own isolation, renounced the very idea of resistance. The bourgeois classes had expected barricades, flaming conflagrations, looting, rivers of blood. In reality a silence reigned more terrible than all the thunders of the world. The social ground shifted noiselessly like a revolving stage, bringing forward the popular masses, carrying away to limbo the rulers of yesterday. . . .

At 2:35 in the afternoon—the foreign journalists looked at their watches, the Russians were too busy—an emergency session of the Petrograd Soviet was opened with a report by Trotsky, who in the name of the Military Revolutionary Committee announced that the Provisional Government no longer existed. "They told us that an insurrection would drown the revolution in torrents of blood. . . . We do not know of a single casualty." There is no example in history of a revolutionary movement involving such gigantic masses being so bloodless. "The Winter Palace is not yet taken, but its fate will be settled in the course of the next few minutes." The following twelve hours were to show that this prediction was too optimistic.

Trotsky said: "Troops have been moved against Petrograd from the front; it is necessary at once to send commissars of the soviets to the front, and throughout the country, to make known that the revolution has occurred." Voices from the small right sector: "You are anticipating the will of the Congress of Soviets." The speaker answered: "The will of the Congress has been anticipated by the colossal fact of an insurrection of the Petrograd workers and soldiers. It now remains only to develop our victory."

Lenin, who appeared here publicly for the first time after emerging from underground, briefly outlined the program of the revolution: To break up the old governmental apparatus; to create a new system of administration through the soviets; to take measures for the immediate cessation of war, relying upon revolutionary movements in other countries; to abolish the landlords' property rights and thus win the confidence of the peasants; to establish workers' control over production. "The third Russian revolution," he said, "must in the end lead to the victory of socialism." . . .

THE CAPTURE OF THE WINTER PALACE

Shortly after six the Winter Palace [Headquarters of the Kerensky government] was at last solidly surrounded by the troops of the Military Revolutionary Committee. There was no longer any passage either for reinforcements or for individuals.

From the direction of Konnogvardeisky Boulevard, the Admiralty Quay, Morskaia Street, Nevsky Prospect, Mars Field, Milliony Street and Dvortsovy Quay, the oval of the besiegers thickened and contracted. Imposing cordons extended from the iron fences of the Winter Palace garden, still in the hands of the besieged, from the arch between Palace Square and Morskaia Street, from the canal by the Hermitage, from the corners of the Admiralty, and the Nevsky nearby the palace. Peter and Paul fortress frowned threateningly from the other side of the river. The *Aurora* looked in from the Neva with her six-inch guns. Destroyers steamed back and forth patrolling the river. The insurrection looked at that moment like a military maneuver in the grand style.

On Palace Square, cleared by the junkers three hours before, armored automobiles now appeared and occupied the entrances and exits. Their old patriotic names were still visible on the armor under the new designations painted hastily in red. Under the protection of these steel monsters the attackers felt more and more confident on the square. One of the armored cars approached the main entrance of the palace, disarmed the junkers guarding it, and withdrew unhindered. . . .

That part of the palace adjoining the Hermitage is already filled with the enemy. The junkers make an attempt to come at them from the rear. In the corridors phantasmagoric meetings and clashes take place. All are armed to the teeth. Lifted hands hold revolvers. Hand-grenades hang from belts. But nobody shoots and nobody throws a grenade. For they and their enemy are so mixed together that they cannot drag themselves apart. Never mind: the fate of the palace is already decided.

Workers, sailors, soldiers are pushing up from outside in chains and groups, flinging the junkers from the barricades, bursting through the court, stumbling into the junkers on the staircase, crowding them back, toppling them over, driving them upstairs. Another wave comes on behind. The square pours into the court. The court pours into the palace, and floods up and down stairways and through corridors. On the befouled parquets, among mattresses and chunks of bread, people, rifles, hand-grenades are wallowing. The conquerors find out that Kerensky is not there, and a momentary pang of disappointment interrupts their furious joy. Antonov and Chudnovsky are now in the palace. Where is the government? That is the door—there where the junkers stand frozen in the last pose of resistance. The head sentry rushes to the ministers with a question: Are we commanded to resist to the end? No, no, the ministers do not command that. After all, the palace is taken. There is no need of bloodshed. We must yield to force. The ministers desire to surrender with dignity, and sit at the table in imitation of a session of the government. The commandant has already surrendered the palace, negotiating for the lives of the junkers, against which in any case nobody had made the slightest attempt. Antonov refuses to enter into any negotiations whatever.

The junkers at the last guarded doors were disarmed. The victors burst into the room of the ministers. "In front of the crowd and trying to hold back the onpressing ranks strode a rather small, unimpressive man. His clothes were in disorder, a wide-brimmed hat askew on his head, eyeglasses balanced uncertainly on his nose, but his eyes gleamed with the joy of victory and spite against the conquered." In these annihilating strokes the conquered have described Antonov. It is not hard to believe that his clothes and his hat were in disorder: It is sufficient to remember the nocturnal journey through the puddles of the Peter and Paul fortress. The joy of victory might also doubtless have been read in his eyes; but hardly any spite against the conquered in those eyes. I announce to you, members of the Provisional Government, that you are under arrest—exclaimed Antonov in the name of the Military Revolutionary Committee. The clock then pointed to 2:10 in the morning of October 26. . . .

THE OCTOBER INSURRECTION

In October the government of Kerensky, having irrevocably lost the soul of the soldier, still clung to the commanding summits. In its hands the headquarters, the banks, the telephone, were only the façade of power. When they should come into the hands of the soviets, they would guarantee the conquest of complete power. Such was the situation on the eve of the insurrection, and it decided the forms of activity during the last twenty-four hours.

Demonstrations, street fights, barricades—everything comprised in the usual idea of insurrection—were almost entirely absent. The revolution had no need of solving a problem already solved. The seizure of the governmental machine could be carried through according to plan with the help of comparatively small armed detachments guided from a single center. The barracks, the fortress, the storehouses, all those enterprises in which workers and soldiers functioned, could be taken possession of by their own internal forces. But the Winter Palace, the Pre-Parliament, the district headquarters, the ministries, the military schools, could not be captured from within. This was true also of the telephone, the telegraph, the Post Office and the State Bank. The workers in these institutions, although of little weight in the general combination of forces, nevertheless ruled within their four walls, and these were, moreover, strongly guarded with sentries. It was necessary to penetrate these bureaucratic high points from without. Political conquest was here replaced by forcible seizure. But since the preceding crowding-out of the government from its military bases had made resistance almost impossible, this military seizure of the final commanding heights passed off as a general rule without conflicts.

To be sure, the thing was not after all settled without fighting. The Winter Palace had to be taken by storm. But the very fact that the resistance of the government came down to a defense of the Winter Palace, clearly defines the place occupied by October 25th in the whole course of the struggle. The Winter Palace was the last redoubt of a régime politically shattered during its eight months' existence, and conclusively disarmed during the preceding two weeks. . . .

The October revolution can be correctly understood only if you do not limit your field of vision to its final link. During the last days of February the chess game of insurrection was played out from the first move to the last—that is to the surrender of the enemy. At the end of October the main part of the game was already in the past. And on the day of insurrection it remained to solve only a rather narrow problem: mate in two moves. The period of revolution, therefore, must be considered to extend from the 9th of October, when the conflict about the garrison began, or from the 12th, when the resolution was passed to create a Military Revolutionary Committee. The enveloping maneuver extended over more than two weeks. The more decisive part of it lasted five to six days—from the birth of the Military Revolutionary Committee to the capture of the Winter Palace. During this whole period hundreds of thousands of workers and soldiers took direct action, defensive in form, but aggressive in essence. The final stage, when the insurrectionaries at last threw off the qualifications of the dual power with its dubious legality and defensive phraseology, occupied exactly twenty-four hours: from 2 o'clock on the night of the 25th to 2 o'clock on the night of the 26th. During this period the Military Revolutionary Committee openly employed arms for the conquest of the city and the capture of the government. In these operations, generally speaking, as many forces took part as were needed to solve the limited problem—hardly more than 25 or 30 thousand at the most. . . .

THE CONGRESS OF THE SOVIET DICTATORSHIP

The Congress opened its [second] session at nine o'clock in the evening. "The picture on the whole was but little different from yesterday—fewer weapons, less of a jam." Sukhanov, now no longer a delegate, was able to find himself a free seat as one of the public. This session was to decide the questions of peace, land and government. Only three questions: end the war, give the land to the people, establish a socialist dictatorship. Kamenev began with a report of the work done by the praesidium during the day: the death penalty at the front introduced by Kerensky abolished; complete freedom of agitation restored; orders given for the liberation of soldiers imprisoned for political convictions, and members of land committees; all the commissars of the Provisional Government removed from office; orders given to arrest and deliver Kerensky and Kornilov. The Congress approved and ratified these measures.

Again some remnants of remnants took the floor, to the impatient disapproval of the hall. One group announced that they were withdrawing "at the moment of victory of the insurrection and not at the moment of its defeat." Others bragged of the fact that they had decided to remain. A representative of the Donetz miners urged immediate measures to prevent Kaledin from cutting the north off from coal. Some time must pass, however, before the revolution learns to take measures of such scope. Finally it became possible to take up the first point on the order of the day.

Lenin, whom the Congress has not yet seen, is given the floor for a report on peace. His appearance in the tribune evokes a tumultuous greeting. The trench delegates gaze with all their eyes at this mysterious being whom they had been taught to hate and whom they have learned without seeing him to love. "Now Lenin, gripping the edges of the reading-stand, let little winking eyes travel over the crowd as he stood there waiting, apparently oblivious to the long-rolling ovation, which lasted several minutes. When it was finished, he said simply, 'We shall now proceed to construct the socialist order.'"

DECREES OF THE BOLSHEVIK REVOLUTION

I N A SERIES of decrees, the new Bolshevik government of 1918 proclaimed the measures which were to be the first foundations of its rule. The Military Revolutionary Committee (whose Proclamation is the first of the following selections) was an organ of the Petrograd Soviet. It was set up for the special purpose of organizing and carrying out the uprising of November against the Provisional government. The "Declaration of the Rights of the Russian People" was worked out by Josef Stalin, people's commissar for nationalities. Under the tsarist regime there had been much rivalry and bitterness between peoples composing the empire; and many nationalities, such as the Poles and Finns, had been held in subjection for centuries. The new government aimed to put an end to this friction and to appeal to all nationalities to defend the regime.

The texts of the decrees are taken from John Reed, *Ten Days That Shook the World* (New York: International Publishers, 1919) and J. Bunyan and H. H. Fisher, *The Bolshevik Revolution 1917–1918* (Stanford: Stanford University Press, 1934).

PROCLAMATION OF THE MILITARY REVOLUTIONARY COMMITTEE (NOVEMBER 8, 1917)

To All Army Committees and All Soviets of Soldiers' Deputies.

The Petrograd garrison has overturned the Government of Kerensky, which had risen against the Revolution and the People. . . . In sending this news to the Front and the country, the Military Revolutionary Committee requests all soldiers to keep vigilant watch on the conduct of officers. Officers who do not frankly and openly declare for the Revolution should be immediately arrested as enemies.

The Petrograd Soviet interprets the programme of the new Government as: immediate proposals of a general democratic peace, the immediate transfer of great landed estates to the peasants, and the honest convocation of the Constituent Assembly. The people's revolutionary Army must not permit troops of doubtful morale to be sent to Petrograd. Act by means of arguments, by means of moral suasion—but if that fails, halt the movement of troops by implacable force.

The present order must be immediately read to all military units of every branch of the service. Whoever keeps the knowledge of this order from the soldier-masses . . . commits a serious crime against the Revolution, and will be punished with all the rigour of revolutionary law.

Soldiers! For peace, bread, land, and popular government! . . .

DECLARATION OF THE RIGHTS OF THE RUSSIAN PEOPLE (NOVEMBER 15, 1917)

THE OCTOBER REVOLUTION of the workers and peasants has begun under the common banner of deliverance.

The peasants have been freed from the yoke of the great landed proprietors, for there is no more private property in land—it is abolished.

The soldiers and sailors have been freed from the power of autocratic generals; the generals henceforth will be elected and removable at pleasure. The workers have been freed from the caprices and the arbitrariness of the capitalists, for starting from today control will be established by the workers over the workshops and the factories.

There remain but the peoples of Russia, who have been forbearing and have bided their time under the yoke and the arbitrariness, and whom it is necessary immediately to enfranchise and liberate.

In the epoch of Czarism, the peoples of Russia were aroused against each other. The results of this policy are known: massacres and pogroms on one side, enslaving of peoples on the other.

There can be no return to this shameful policy. Today it must be replaced by a voluntary and honest policy of union of the peoples of Russia.

In the epoch of imperialism, after the February revolution, when power passed into the hands of the Cadet bourgeoisie, the policy of incitation was replaced by a dastardly policy of distrust of the peoples of Russia, a policy of chicanery and provocation covering itself by the words of "liberty" and of "equality" of peoples. The results of this policy are known: increase of the antagonism between nationalities, lack of mutual confidence.

This unworthy policy of lies and mistrust, of chicanery and provocation must be definitely ended. It must be replaced today by an open and honest policy, leading to a complete mutual confidence of the peoples of Russia.

It is only thanks to such a confidence that the honest and solid union of all the peoples of Russia can be formed.

It is only thanks to such a union that the workers and peasants of Russia can be welded into a revolutionary force capable of defending itself against every attack on the part of the imperialist and annexationist bourgeoisie.

Starting on this principle, the first congress of soviets, in the month of June of this year, proclaimed the right of the peoples of Russia to self-determination.

The second congress of soviets in the month of October last confirmed this right in a more decisive and more precise fashion.

Executing the will of these soviets, the council of the people's commissaries has resolved to be guided in the question of nationalities by the following principles:

1. The equality and sovereignty of the peoples of Russia.

2. The right of the peoples of Russia to dispose of their own fate, even to separation and the establishment of an independent state.

3. Abolition of all privileges and limitations, national or religious.

4. Free development of national minorities and ethnographic groups inhabiting Russian territory.

Decrees will be prepared immediately after the creation of a commission on nationalities.

In the name of the Russian Republic,

The People's Commissary for Nationalities:
IOUSSIF DJOUGACHVILI STALIN
The President of the Council of the People's Commissaries:
V. ULIANOV

NATIONALIZATION OF BANKS
(DECEMBER 27, 1917)

IN THE INTERESTS of a proper organization of the national economy, a thorough eradication of bank speculation and a complete emancipation of the toiling masses from exploitation by the banking capitalists, and in order to found a single unified State Bank for the Russian Republic which shall serve the interests of the people and the poorest classes, the Central Executive Committee decrees that:

1. Banking is hereby declared a state monopoly.

2. All existing private joint-stock banks and other banking houses are to become a part of the State Bank.

3. Assets and liabilities of establishments in the process of liquidation will be assumed by the State Bank.

4. The manner of the amalgamation of private banks with the State Bank will be determined by a special decree.

VLADIMIR ILYICH LENIN

THE NAME of Lenin (Vladimir Ilyich Ulyanov, 1870–1924) stands second only to that of Marx in the history of socialist theory and is without a recognized equal in the story of communist practice. Since the Revolution of 1917 the "teachings of history" to which Marxists have appealed have been largely those lessons taught by Lenin under the impact of the epoch-making events in which he was the chief actor. To be sure, Leninism has become the subject of various and often divergent interpretations, but wherever the need for authority is strong among Communists it is Lenin's name which is invoked.

Born in Russia and a lawyer by profession, Lenin after 1893 devoted himself to a career of agitation on behalf of socialism. In 1896 he was imprisoned, and from 1897 to 1900 he was a political exile in Siberia. From 1900 until 1917 he was in Russia for only two years—at the time of the Revolution of 1905. Nevertheless, he was continuously one of the leaders in the anti-tsarist movement, and the acknowledged leader of the majority (Bolshevik) faction of Russian socialists, before and after their overthrow of the democratic Kerensky regime in November, 1917.

Having already provided the basic precepts of Bolshevik conspiratorial strategy in *What Is To Be Done?* (1902), Lenin logically was led to consider the role of the tightly disciplined party once capitalism had been overthrown. To what degree were the weapons used to overthrow capitalism legitimate in the building of socialism? In *The State and Revolution* (1917) Lenin draws together the results of his analysis of the downfall of capitalism and his program for Communist organization, emphasizing the concept of "the dictatorship of the proletariat, the organization of the vanguard of the oppressed as the ruling class for the purpose of crushing the oppressor." *The State and Revolution* is one of the fundamental works in the body of Bolshevik ideology, explaining as it does the dictatorship of the proletariat (that is the Bolshevik state) in the progress toward an ultimately classless society. Begun in the summer of 1917, it was never finished. The November Revolution called Lenin to put his theories into action.

Convinced that only he and like-minded Bolsheviks carried history with them, Lenin, once in power, tried to justify despotic and seemingly contradictory policies and actions. For this he was criticized by communists and socialists in the Soviet Union, Europe, and America. The chief criticism was against the continued strengthening of dictatorial power in the Communist party elite, at the expense of the soviets (councils), labor unions, and all other social and political groups. One of the most brilliant of Lenin's critics was Karl Kautsky (1854–1938) the leader of an important circle of German Marxists. Kautsky regarded the socialist revolution as the start of rapid democratization of the state and public authority. Almost as soon as the Bolsheviks seized power, Kautsky criticized the practice of proletarian dictatorship. His work, *The Dictatorship of the Proletariat* (1918) called forth Lenin's reply *The Proletarian Revolution and the Renegade Kautsky*

(1918), an important extension of the ideas in *The State and Revolution,* which, unlike the latter, was written when power was already in Lenin's hand.

By 1921 luck, Bolshevik fervor, and a divided opposition had removed the obstacles to consolidating Lenin's control of Russia. With foreign enemies and domestic opposition beaten, Lenin turned to rebuilding the shattered soviet economy. His New Economic Policy, permitting some revival and growth of production for private profit, seemed fundamentally at variance with Marxist theory. Lenin called his critics' insistence on purity of doctrine, when expediency dictated a departure from strict ideology, "left-wing infantilism." But the fact remains that Marxist doctrine was already becoming a mere rhetoric, justifying whatever policy the Communist party leadership decided to pursue. In the years to come the party itself was to veer between a harsh left-wing and a soft right-wing "line," both always justified with elaborate ideological explanations. Lenin and his successors were seemingly undisturbed by the blatant contradictions between actions and theory or between today's policy and "line" and yesteryear's.

The first selection from Lenin is taken from *The State and Revolution* (London: George Allen and Unwin, 1919). It is followed by extracts from *The Proletarian Revolution and the Renegade Kautsky* (New York: International Publishers, 1934), and *Left-Wing Communism: an Infantile Disorder* (New York: International Publishers, 1934).

$$\mathcal{C}$$

THE STATE AND REVOLUTION

Class Society and the State

THE "WITHERING AWAY" OF THE STATE AND VIOLENT REVOLUTION

ENGELS' WORDS regarding the "withering away" of the state enjoy such popularity, they are so often quoted, and they show so clearly the essence of the usual adulteration by means of which Marxism is made to look like opportunism, that we must dwell on them in detail. Let us quote the whole passage from which they are taken.

The proletariat seizes state power, and then transforms the means of production into state property. But in doing this, it puts an end to itself as the proletariat, it puts an end to all class differences and class antagonisms, it puts an end also to the state as the state. Former society, moving in class antagonisms, had need of the state, that is, an organisation of the exploiting class at each period for the maintenance of its external conditions of production; therefore, in particular, for the forcible holding down of the exploited class in the conditions of oppression (slavery, bondage or serfdom, wage-labour) determined by the existing mode of production. The state was the official representative of society as a whole, its embodiment in a visible corporate body; but it was this only in so far as it was the state of that class which itself, in its epoch, represented society as a whole: in ancient times, the state of the slave-owning citizens; in the Middle Ages, of the feudal nobility; in our epoch, of the bourgeoisie. When ultimately it becomes really representative of society as a whole, it makes itself superfluous. As soon as there is no longer any class of society to be held in subjection; as soon as, along with class domination and the struggle for individual existence based on the former anarchy of production, the collisions and excesses arising from these have also been abolished, there is nothing more to be repressed, and a special repressive force, a state, is no longer necessary. The first act in which the state really comes forward as the representative of society as a whole—the seizure of the means of production in the name of society—is at the same time its last independent act as a state. The interference of a state power in social relations becomes superfluous in one sphere after another, and then becomes dormant of itself. Government over persons is replaced by the administration of things and the direction of the processes of production. The state is not "abolished," *it withers away*. It is from this standpoint that we must appraise the phrase "people's free state"—both its justification at times for agitational purposes, and its ultimate scientific inadequacy—and also the demand of the so-called Anarchists that the state should be abolished overnight.

Without fear of committing an error, it may be said that of this argument by Engels so singularly rich in ideas, only one point has become an integral part of Socialist thought among modern Socialist parties, namely, that, unlike the Anarchist doctrine of the "abolition" of the state, according to Marx the state "withers away." To emasculate Marxism in such a manner is to reduce it to opportunism, for such an "interpretation" only leaves the hazy conception of a slow, even, gradual change, free from leaps and storms, free from revolution. The current popular conception, if one may say so, of the "withering away" of the state undoubtedly means a slurring over, if not a negation, of revolution.

Yet, such an "interpretation" is the crudest distortion of Marxism, which is advantageous only to the bourgeoisie; in point of theory, it is based on a disregard for the most important circumstances and considerations pointed out in the very passage summarising Engels' ideas, which we have just quoted in full.

In the first place, Engels at the very outset of his argument says that, in assuming state power, the proletariat by that very act "puts an end to the state as the state." One is "not accustomed" to reflect on what this really means. Generally, it is either ignored altogether, or it is considered as a piece of "Hegelian weakness" on Engels' part. As a matter of fact, however, these words express succinctly the experience of one of the greatest proletarian revolutions—the Paris Commune of 1871, of which we shall speak in greater detail in its proper place. As a matter of fact, Engels speaks here of the destruction of the bourgeois state by the proletarian revolution, while the words about its withering away refer to the remains of *proletarian* statehood *after* the Socalist revolution. The bourgeois state does not "wither away," according to Engels, but is "put an end to" by the proletariat in the course of the revolution. What withers away after the revolution is the proletarian state or semi-state.

Secondly, the state is a "special repressive force." This splendid and extremely profound definition of Engels' is given by him here with complete lucidity. It follows from this that the "special repressive force" of the bourgeoisie for the suppression of the proletariat, of the millions of workers by a handful of the rich, must be replaced by a "special repressive force" of the proletariat for the suppression of the bourgeoisie (the dictatorship of the proletariat). It is just this that constitutes the destruction of "the state as the state." It is just this that constitutes the "act" of "the seizure of the means of production in the name of society." And it is obvious that such a substitution of one (proletarian) "special repressive force" for another (bourgeois) "special repressive force" can in no way take place in the form of a "withering away."

Thirdly, as to the "withering away" or, more expressively and colourfully, as to the state "becoming dormant," Engels refers quite clearly and definitely to the period *after* "the seizure of the means of production [by the state] in the name of society," that is, *after* the Socialist revolution. We all know that the political form of the "state" at that time is complete democracy. But it never enters the head of any of the opportunists who shamelessly distort Marx that when Engels speaks here of the state "withering away," or "becoming dormant," he speaks of *democracy*. At first sight this seems very strange. But it is "unintelligible" only to one who has not reflected on the fact that democracy is *also* a state and that, consequently, democracy will *also* disappear when the state disappears. The bourgeois state can only be "put an end to" by a revolution. The state in general, *i.e.,* most complete democracy, can only "wither away."

Fourthly, having formulated his famous proposition that "the state withers away," Engels at once explains concretely that this proposition is directed equally against the opportunists and the Anarchists. In doing this, however, Engels puts in the first place that conclusion from his proposition about the "withering away" of the state which is directed against the opportunists. . . .

The "people's free state" was a demand in the programme of the German Social-Democrats and their current slogan in the 'seventies. There is no political substance in this slogan other than a pompous middle-class circumlocution of the idea of democracy. In so far as it referred in a lawful manner to a democratic republic, Engels was prepared to "justify" its use "at times" from a propaganda point of view. But this slogan was opportunist, for it not only expressed an exaggerated view of the attractiveness of bourgeois democracy, but also a lack of understanding of the Socialist criticism of every state in general. We are in favour of a democratic republic as the best form of the state for the proletariat under capitalism, but we have no right to forget that wage slavery is the lot of the people even in the most democratic bourgeois republic. Furthermore, every state is a "special repressive force" for the suppression of the oppressed class. Consequently, *no* state is either "free" or a "people's state." Marx and Engels explained this repeatedly to their party comrades in the 'seventies.

Fifthly, in the same work of Engels, from which every one remembers his argument on the "withering away" of the state, there is also a disquisition on the significance of a violent revolution. The historical analysis of its rôle becomes, with Engels, a veritable panegyric on violent revolution. This, of course, "no one remembers"; to talk or even to think of the importance of this idea is not considered good form by contemporary Socialist parties, and in the daily propaganda and agitation among the masses it plays no part whatever. Yet it is indissolubly bound up with the "withering away" of the state in one harmonious whole.

Here is Engels' argument:

That force, however, plays another rôle (other than that of a diabolical power) in history, a revolutionary rôle; that, in the words of Marx, it is the midwife of every old society which is pregnant with the new; that it is the instrument with whose aid social movement forces its way through and shatters the dead, fossilised political forms—of this there is not a word in Herr Dühring. It is only with sighs and groans that he admits the possibility that force will perhaps be necessary for the overthrow of the economic system of exploitation—unfortunately! because all use of force, forsooth, demoralises the person who uses it. And this in spite of the immense moral and spiritual impetus which has resulted from every victorious revolution! And this in Germany, where a violent collision—which indeed may be forced on the people—would at least have the advantage of wiping out the servility which has permeated the national consciousness as a result of the humiliation of the Thirty Years' War. And this parson's mode of thought—lifeless, insipid and impotent—claims to impose itself on the most revolutionary party which history has known?

How can this panegyric on violent revolution, which Engels insistently brought to the attention of the German Social-Democrats between 1878 and 1894, *i.e.,* right to the time of his death, be combined with the theory of the "withering away" of the state to form one doctrine? . . .

We have already said above and shall show more fully later that the teaching of Marx and Engels regarding the inevitability of a violent revolution refers to the bourgeois state. It *cannot* be replaced by the proletarian state (the dictatorship of the proletariat) through "withering away," but, as a general rule, only through a violent revolution. The panegyric sung in its honour by Engels and fully corresponding to the repeated declarations of Marx (remember the concluding passages of the *Poverty of Philosophy* and the *Communist Manifesto,* with its proud and open declaration of the inevitability of a violent revolution; remember Marx's *Critique of the Gotha Programme* of 1875 in which, almost thirty years later, he mercilessly castigates the opportunist character of that programme)—this praise is by no means a mere "impulse," a mere declamation, or a polemical sally. The necessity of systematically fostering among the masses *this* and just this point of view about violent revolution lies at the root of the *whole* of Marx's and Engels' teaching. The neglect of such propaganda and agitation by both the present predominant social-chauvinist and the Kautskyist currents brings their betrayal of Marx's and Engels' teaching into prominent relief.

The replacement of the bourgeois by the proletarian state is impossible without a violent revolution. The abolition of the proletarian state, *i.e.,* of all states, is only possible through "withering away." . . .

The Economic Base of the Withering Away of the State

A MOST DETAILED elucidation of this question is given by Marx in his *Critique of the Gotha Programme.* The polemical part of this remarkable work, consisting of a criticism of Lassalleanism, has, so to speak, overshadowed its positive part, namely, the analysis of the connection between the development of Communism and the withering away of the state.

FORMULATION OF THE QUESTION BY MARX

The whole theory of Marx is an application of the theory of evolution—in its most consistent, complete, well considered and fruitful form—to modern capitalism. It was natural for Marx to raise the question of applying this theory both to the *coming* collapse of capitalism and to the *future* evolution of *future* Communism.

On the basis of what *data* can the future evolution of future Communism be considered?

On the basis of the fact that *it has its origin* in capitalism, that it develops historically from capitalism, that it is the result of the action of a social force to which capitalism *has given birth.* There is no shadow of an attempt on Marx's part to conjure up a Utopia, to make idle guesses about that which cannot be known. Marx treats the question of Communism in the same way as a naturalist would treat the question of the evolution of, say, a new biological species, if he knew that such and such was its origin, and such and such the direction in which it changed. . . .

The first fact that has been established with complete exactness by the whole theory of evolution, by science as a whole—a fact which the Utopians forgot, and which is forgotten by the present-day opportunists who are afraid of the Socialist revolution—is that, historically, there must undoubtedly be a special stage or epoch of *transition* from capitalism to Communism.

TRANSITION FROM CAPITALISM TO COMMUNISM

Between capitalist and Communist society [Marx continues] lies the period of the revolutionary transformation of the former into the latter. To this also corresponds a political transition period, in which the state can be no other than *the revolutionary dictatorship of the proletariat.*

This conclusion Marx bases on an analysis of the rôle played by the proletariat in modern capitalist society, on the data concerning the evolution of this society, and on the irreconcilability of the opposing interests of the proletariat and the bourgeoisie.

Earlier the question was put thus: to attain its emancipation, the proletariat must overthrow the bourgeoisie, conquer political power and establish its own revolutionary dictatorship.

Now the question is put somewhat differently: the transition from capitalist society, developing towards Communism, towards a Communist society, is impossible without a "political transition period," and the state in this period can only be the revolutionary dictatorship of the proletariat.

What, then, is the relation of this dictatorship to democracy?

We have seen that the *Communist Manifesto* simply places side by side the two ideas: the "transformation of the proletariat into the ruling class" and the "establishment of democracy." On the basis of all that has been said above, one can define more exactly how democracy changes in the transition from capitalism to Communism.

In capitalist society, under the conditions most favourable to its development, we have more or less complete democracy in the democratic republic. But this democracy is always bound by the narrow framework of capitalist exploitation, and consequently always remains, in reality, a democracy for the minority, only for the possessing classes, only for the rich. Freedom in capitalist society always remains just about the same as it was in the ancient Greek republics: freedom for the slave-owners. The modern wage-slaves, owing to the conditions of capitalist exploitation, are so much crushed by want and poverty that "democracy is nothing to them," "politics is nothing to them";

that, in the ordinary peaceful course of events, the majority of the population is debarred from participating in social and political life.

The correctness of this statement is perhaps most clearly proved by Germany, just because in this state constitutional legality lasted and remained stable for a remarkably long time—for nearly half a century (1871–1914)—and because Social-Democracy in Germany during that time was able to achieve far more than in other countries in "utilising legality," and was able to organise into a political party a larger proportion of the working class than anywhere else in the world.

What, then, is this largest proportion of politically conscious and active wage-slaves that has so far been observed in capitalist society? One million members of the Social-Democratic Party—out of fifteen million wage-workers! Three million organised in trade unions—out of fifteen million!

Democracy for an insignificant minority, democracy for the rich—that is the democracy of capitalist society. If we look more closely into the mechanism of capitalist democracy, everywhere, both in the "petty"—so-called petty—details of the suffrage (residential qualification, exclusion of women, etc.), and in the technique of the representative institutions, in the actual obstacles to the right of assembly (public buildings are not for "beggars"!), in the purely capitalist organisation of the daily press, etc., etc.—on all sides we see restriction after restriction upon democracy. These restrictions, exceptions, exclusions, obstacles for the poor, seem slight, especially in the eyes of one who has himself never known want and has never been in close contact with the oppressed classes in their mass life (and nine-tenths, if not ninety-nine hundredths, of the bourgeois publicists and politicians are of this class), but in their sum total these restrictions exclude and squeeze out the poor from politics and from an active share in democracy.

Marx splendidly grasped this *essence* of capitalist democracy, when, in analysing the experience of the Commune, he said that the oppressed were allowed, once every few years, to decide which particular representatives of the oppressing class should be in parliament to represent and repress them!

But from this capitalist democracy—inevitably narrow, subtly rejecting the poor, and therefore hypocritical and false to the core—progress does not march onward, simply, smoothly and directly, to "greater and greater democracy," as the liberal professors and petty-bourgeois opportunists would have us believe. No, progress marches onward, *i.e.,* towards Communism, through the dictatorship of the proletariat; it cannot do otherwise, for there is no one else and no other way to *break the resistance* of the capitalist exploiters.

But the dictatorship of the proletariat—*i.e.,* the organisation of the vanguard of the oppressed as the ruling class for the purpose of crushing the oppressors —cannot produce merely an expansion of democracy. *Together* with an immense expansion of democracy which *for the first time* becomes democracy for the poor, democracy for the people, and not democracy for the rich folk, the dictatorship of the proletariat produces a series of restrictions of liberty in the case of the oppressors, the exploiters, the capitalists. We must crush them in order to free humanity from wage-slavery; their resistance must be broken by force; it is clear that where there is suppression there is also violence, there is no liberty, no democracy.

Engels expressed this splendidly in his letter to Bebel when he said, as the reader will remember, that "as long as the proletariat still *needs* the state, it needs it not in the interests of freedom, but for the purpose of crushing its antagonists; and as soon as it becomes possible to speak of freedom, then the state, as such, ceases to exist."

Democracy for the vast majority of the people, and suppression by force, *i.e.,* exclusion from democracy, of the exploiters and oppressors of the people —this is the modification of democracy during the *transition* from capitalism to Communism. . . .

Thus, in capitalist society, we have a democracy that is curtailed, poor, false; a democracy only for the rich, for the minority. The dictatorship of the proletariat, the period of transition to Communism, will, for the first time, produce democracy for the people, for the majority, side by side with the necessary suppression of the minority—the exploiters. Communism alone is capable of giving a really complete democracy, and the more complete it is the more quickly will it become unnecessary and wither away of itself.

In other words: under capitalism we have a state in the proper sense of the word, that is, special machinery for the suppression of one class by another, and of the majority by the minority at that. Naturally, for the successful discharge of such a task as the systematic suppression by the exploiting minority of the exploited majority, the greatest ferocity and savagery of suppression are required, seas of blood are required, through which mankind is marching in slavery, serfdom, and wage-labour.

Again, during the *transition* from capitalism to Communism, suppression is *still* necessary; but it is the suppression of the minority of exploiters by the majority of exploited. A special apparatus, special machinery for suppression, the "state," is *still* necessary, but this is now a transitional state, no longer a state in the usual sense, for the suppression of the minority of exploiters, by the majority of the wage slaves *of yesterday,* is a matter comparatively so easy, simple and natural that it will cost far less bloodshed than the suppression of the risings of slaves, serfs or wage labourers, and will cost mankind far less. This is compatible with the diffusion of democracy among such an over-whelming majority of the population, that the need for *special machinery* of suppression will begin to disappear. The exploiters are, naturally, unable to suppress the people without a most complex machinery for performing this task; but *the people* can suppress the exploiters even with very simple "machinery," almost without any "machinery," without any special apparatus, by the simple *organisation of the armed masses* (such as the Soviets of Work-ers' and Soldiers' Deputies, we may remark, anticipating a little).

Finally, only Communism renders the state absolutely unnecessary, for there is *no one* to be suppressed—"no one" in the sense of a *class,* in the sense of a systematic struggle with a definite section of the population. We are not Utopians, and we do not in the least deny the possibility and inevitability of excesses on the part of *individual persons,* nor the need to suppress *such* ex-cesses. But, in the first place, no special machinery, no special apparatus of repression is needed for this; this will be done by the armed people itself, as simply and as readily as any crowd of civilised people, even in modern so-ciety, parts a pair of combatants or does not allow a woman to be outraged. And, secondly, we know that the fundamental social cause of excesses which consist in violating the rules of social life is the exploitation of the masses, their want and their poverty. With the removal of this chief cause, excesses will inevitably begin to *"wither away."* We do not know how quickly and in what succession, but we know that they will wither away. With their withering away, the state will also *wither away.*

Without going into Utopias, Marx defined more fully what can *now* be defined regarding this future, namely, the difference between the lower and higher phases (degrees, stages) of Communist society.

FIRST PHASE OF COMMUNIST SOCIETY

The first phase of Communism . . . still cannot produce justice and equality; differences, and unjust differences, in wealth will still exist, but the *exploitation* of man by man will have become impossible, because it will be impossible to seize as private property the *means of production,* the fac-tories, machines, land, and so on. In tearing down Lassalle's petty-bourgeois, confused phrase about "equality" and "justice" *in general,* Marx shows the *course of development* of Communist society, which is forced at first to de-stroy *only* the "injustice" that consists in the means of production having been seized by private individuals, and which *is not capable* of destroying at once the further injustice consisting in the distribution of the articles of con-sumption "according to work performed" (and not according to need).

The vulgar economists, including the bourgeois professors and also "our"

Tugan-Baranovsky, constantly reproach the Socialists with forgetting the inequality of people and with "dreaming" of destroying this inequality. Such a reproach, as we see, only proves the extreme ignorance of the gentlemen propounding bourgeois ideology.

Marx not only takes into account with the greatest accuracy the inevitable inequality of men; he also takes into account the fact that the mere conversion of the means of production into the common property of the whole of society ("Socialism" in the generally accepted sense of the word) *does not remove* the defects of distribution and the inequality of "bourgeois right" which *continue to rule* as long as the products are divided "according to work performed."

But these defects—Marx continues—are unavoidable in the first phase of Communist society, when, after long travail, it first emerges from capitalist society. Justice can never rise superior to the economic conditions of society and the cultural development conditioned by them.

And so, in the first phase of Communist society (generally called Socialism) "bourgeois right" is *not* abolished in its entirety, but only in part, only in proportion to the economic transformation so far attained, *i.e.,* only in respect of the means of production. "Bourgeois right" recognises them as the private property of separate individuals. Socialism converts them into common property. *To that extent,* and to that extent alone, does "bourgeois right" disappear.

However, it continues to exist as far as its other part is concerned; it remains in the capacity of regulator (determining factor) distributing the products and allotting labour among the members of society. "He who does not work, shall not eat"—this Socialist principle is *already* realised; "for an equal quantity of labour, an equal quantity of products"—this Socialist principle is also *already* realised. However, this is not yet Communism, and this does not abolish "bourgeois right," which gives to unequal individuals, in return for an unequal (in reality unequal) amount of work, an equal quantity of products.

This is a "defect," says Marx, but it is unavoidable during the first phase of Communism; for, if we are not to fall into Utopianism, we cannot imagine that, having overthrown capitalism, people will at once learn to work for society *without any standards of right;* indeed, the abolition of capitalism *does not immediately lay* the economic foundations for *such* a change.

And there is no other standard yet than that of "bourgeois right." To this extent, therefore, a form of state is still necessary, which, while maintaining public ownership of the means of production, would preserve the equality of labour and equality in the distribution of products.

The state is withering away in so far as there are no longer any capitalists, any classes, and, consequently, no *class* can be suppressed.

But the state has not yet altogether withered away, since there still remains the protection of "bourgeois right" which sanctifies actual inequality. For the complete extinction of the state, complete Communism is necessary.

HIGHER PHASE OF COMMUNIST SOCIETY

Marx continues:

In a higher phase of communist society, when the enslaving subordination of individuals in the division of labour has disappeared, and with it also the antagonism between mental and physical labour; when labour has become not only a means of living, but itself the first necessity of life; when, along with the all-round development of individuals, the productive forces too have grown, and all the springs of social wealth are flowing more freely—it is only at that stage that it will be possible to pass completely beyond the narrow horizon of bourgeois rights, and for society to inscribe on its banners: from each according to his ability; to each according to his needs!

Only now can we appreciate the full correctness of Engels' remarks in which he mercilessly ridiculed all the absurdity of combining the words "freedom" and "state." While the state exists there is no freedom. When there is freedom, there will be no state.

The economic basis for the complete withering away of the state is that high stage of development of Communism when the antagonism between mental and physical labour disappears, that is to say, when one of the principal sources of modern *social* inequality disappears—a source, moreover, which it is impossible to remove immediately by the mere conversion of the means of production into public property, by the mere expropriation of the capitalists.

This expropriation will make a gigantic development of the productive forces *possible*. And seeing how incredibly, even now, capitalism *retards* this development, how much progress could be made even on the basis of modern technique at the level it has reached, we have a right to say, with the fullest confidence, that the expropriation of the capitalists will inevitably result in a gigantic development of the productive forces of human society. But how rapidly this development will go forward, how soon it will reach the point of breaking away from the division of labour, of removing the antagonism between mental and physical labour, of transforming work into the "first necessity of life"—this we do not and *cannot* know.

Consequently, we have a right to speak solely of the inevitable withering away of the state, emphasising the protracted nature of this process and its dependence upon the rapidity of development of the *higher phase* of Communism; leaving quite open the question of lengths of time, or the concrete forms of withering away, since material for the solution of such questions is *not available*.

The state will be able to wither away completely when society has realised the rule: "From each according to his ability; to each according to his needs," *i.e.,* when people have become accustomed to observe the fundamental rules of social life, and their labour is so productive, that they voluntarily work *according to their ability*. "The narrow horizon of bourgeois rights," which compels one to calculate, with the hard-heartedness of a Shylock, whether he has not worked half an hour more than another, whether he is not getting less pay than another—this narrow horizon will then be left behind. There will then be no need for any exact calculation by society of the quantity of products to be distributed to each of its members; each will take freely "according to his needs."

From the bourgeois point of view, it is easy to declare such a social order "a pure Utopia," and to sneer at the Socialists for promising each the right to receive from society, without any control of the labour of the individual citizen, any quantity of truffles, automobiles, pianos, etc. Even now, most bourgeois "savants" deliver themselves of such sneers, thereby displaying at once their ignorance and their self-seeking defence of capitalism.

Ignorance—for it has never entered the head of any Socialist to "promise" that the highest phase of Communism will arrive; while the great Socialists, in *foreseeing* its arrival, presupposed both a productivity of labour unlike the present and a person not like the present man in the street, capable of spoiling, without reflection, like the seminary students in Pomyalovsky's book, the stores of social wealth, and of demanding the impossible.

Until the "higher" phase of Communism arrives, the Socialists demand the *strictest* control, *by society and by the state,* of the quantity of labour and the quantity of consumption; only this control must *start* with the expropriation of the capitalists, with the control of the workers over the capitalists, and must be carried out, not by a state of bureaucrats, but by a state of *armed workers. . . .*

And here we come to that question of the scientific difference between Socialism and Communism, upon which Engels touched in his above-quoted discussion on the incorrectness of the name "Social-Democrat." The political difference between the first, or lower, and the higher phase of Communism will in time, no doubt, be tremendous; but it would be ridiculous to emphasise it now, under capitalism, and only, perhaps, some isolated Anarchist could invest it with primary importance. . . .

But the scientific difference between Socialism and Communism is clear. What is generally called Socialism was termed by Marx the "first" or lower phase of Communist society. In so far as the means of production become *public* property, the word "Communism" is also applicable here, providing we do not forget that it is *not* full Communism. The great significance of Marx's elucidations consists in this: that here, too, he consistently applies materialist dialectics, the doctrine of evolution, looking upon Communism as something which evolves *out of* capitalism. Instead of artificial, "elaborate," scholastic definitions and profitless disquisitions on the meaning of words (what Socialism is, what Communism is), Marx gives an analysis of what may be called stages in the economic ripeness of Communism.

In its first phase or first stage Communism *cannot* as yet be economically ripe and entirely free of all tradition and of all taint of capitalism. Hence the interesting phenomenon of Communism retaining, in its first phase, "the narrow horizon of bourgeois rights." Bourgeois rights, with respect to distribution of articles of *consumption,* inevitably presupposes, of course, the existence of the *bourgeois state,* for rights are nothing without an apparatus capable of *enforcing* the observance of the rights.

Consequently, for a certain time not only bourgeois rights, but even the bourgeois state remains under Communism, without the bourgeoisie!

This may look like a paradox, or simply a dialectical puzzle for which Marxism is often blamed by people who would not make the least effort to study its extraordinarily profound content.

But, as a matter of fact, the old surviving in the new confronts us in life at every step, in nature as well as in society. Marx did not smuggle a scrap of "bourgeois" rights into Communism of his own accord; he indicated what is economically and politically inevitable in a society issuing *from the womb* of capitalism.

Democracy is of great importance for the working class in its struggle for freedom against the capitalists. But democracy is by no means a limit one may not overstep; it is only one of the stages in the course of development from feudalism to capitalism, and from capitalism to Communism.

Democracy means equality. The great significance of the struggle of the proletariat for equality, and the significance of equality as a slogan, are apparent, if we correctly interpret it as meaning the abolition of *classes.* But democracy means only *formal* equality. Immediately after the attainment of equality for all members of society *in respect of* the ownership of the means of production, that is, of equality of labour and equality of wages, there will inevitably arise before humanity the question of going further from formal equality to real equality, *i.e.,* to realising the rule, "From each according to his ability; to each according to his needs." By what stages, by means of what practical measures humanity will proceed to this higher aim

—this we do not and cannot know. But it is important to realise how infinitely mendacious is the usual bourgeois presentation of Socialism as something lifeless, petrified, fixed once for all, whereas in reality, it is *only* with Socialism that there will commence a rapid, genuine, real mass advance, in which first the *majority* and then the whole of the population will take part —an advance in all domains of social and individual life.

Democracy is a form of the state—one of its varieties. Consequently, like every state, it consists in organised, systematic application of force against human beings. This on the one hand. On the other hand, however, it signifies the formal recognition of the equality of all citizens, the equal right of all to determine the structure and administration of the state. This, in turn, is connected with the fact that, at a certain stage in the development of democracy, it first rallies the proletariat as a revolutionary class against capitalism, and gives it an opportunity to crush, to smash to bits, to wipe off the face of the earth the bourgeois state machinery—even its republican variety: the standing army, the police, and bureaucracy; then it substitutes for all this a *more* democratic, but still a state machinery in the shape of armed masses of workers, which becomes transformed into universal participation of the people in the militia.

Here "quantity turns into quality": *such* a degree of democracy is bound up with the abandonment of the framework of bourgeois society, and the beginning of its Socialist reconstruction. If *every one* really takes part in the administration of the state, capitalism cannot retain its hold. In its turn, capitalism, as it develops, itself creates *prerequisites* for "every one" *to be able* really to take part in the administration of the state. Among such prerequisites are: universal literacy, already realised in most of the advanced capitalist countries, then the "training and disciplining" of millions of workers by the huge, complex, and socialised apparatus of the post-office, the railways, the big factories, large-scale commerce, banking, etc., etc.

With such *economic* prerequisites it is perfectly possible, immediately, within twenty-four hours after the overthrow of the capitalists and bureaucrats, to replace them, in the control of production and distribution, in the business of *control* of labour and products, by the armed workers, by the whole people in arms. (The question of control and accounting must not be confused with the question of the scientifically educated staff of engineers, agronomists and so on. These gentlemen work today, obeying the capitalists; they will work even better tomorrow, obeying the armed workers.)

Accounting and control—these are the *chief* things necessary for the organising and correct functioning of the *first phase* of Communist society. *All* citizens are here transformed into hired employees of the state, which is made up of the armed workers. *All* citizens become employees and workers of *one* national state "syndicate." All that is required is that they should work equally, should regularly do their share of work, and should receive equal pay. The accounting and control necessary for this have been *simplified* by capitalism to the utmost, till they have become the extraordinarily simple operations of watching, recording and issuing receipts, within the reach of anybody who can read and write and knows the first four rules of arithmetic.

When the *majority* of the people begin everywhere to keep such accounts and maintain such control over the capitalists (now converted into employees) and over the intellectual gentry, who still retain capitalist habits, this control will really become universal, general, national; and there will be no way of getting away from it, there will be "nowhere to go."

The whole of society will have become one office and one factory, with equal work and equal pay.

But this "factory" discipline, which the proletariat will extend to the whole of society after the defeat of the capitalists and the overthrow of the exploiters, is by no means our ideal, or our final aim. It is but a *foothold* necessary for the radical cleansing of society of all the hideousness and foulness of capitalist exploitation, *in order to advance further.*

From the moment when all members of society, or even only the overwhelming majority, have learned how to govern the state *themselves,* have taken this business into their own hands, have "established" control over the insignificant minority of capitalists, over the gentry with capitalist leanings, and the workers thoroughly demoralised by capitalism—from this moment the need for any government begins to disappear. The more complete the democracy, the nearer the moment when it begins to be unnecessary. The more democratic the "state" consisting of armed workers, which is "no longer a state in the proper sense of the word," the more rapidly does *every* state begin to wither away.

For when *all* have learned to manage, and independently are actually managing by themselves social production, keeping accounts, controlling the idlers, the gentlefolk, the swindlers and similar "guardians of capitalist traditions," then the escape from this national accounting and control will inevitably become so increasingly difficult, such a rare exception, and will probably be accompanied by such swift and severe punishment (for the armed workers are men of practical life, not sentimental intellectuals, and they will scarcely allow any one to trifle with them), that very soon the *necessity* of observing the simple, fundamental rules of every-day social life in common will have become a *habit.*

The door will then be wide open for the transition from the first phase of Communist society to its higher phase, and along with it to the complete withering away of the state.

THE PROLETARIAN REVOLUTION AND THE RENEGADE KAUTSKY

THE SOVIETS are the Russian form of the proletarian dictatorship. . . .

The passages from Kautsky's argument which I have just quoted in full represent the crux of the whole question about the Soviets. This crux is the question: should the Soviets aspire to become state organisations (in April, 1917, the Bolsheviks put forward the slogan: "All Power to the Soviets," and at the Party Conference held in the same month they declared that they were not satisfied with a bourgeois parliamentary republic, but demanded a workers' and peasants' republic of the Paris Commune type, or Soviet type), or, should the Soviets not strive for this, should they refrain from taking political power in their hands, refrain from becoming state organisations and remain the "militant organisations of one class" (as Martov expressed it, plausibly concealing under this innocent desire the fact that under Menshevik leadership the Soviets were instruments for the subjection of the workers to the bourgeoisie)?

Kautsky slavishly repeats Martov's words, takes up fragments of the theoretical controversy between the Bolsheviks and the Mensheviks and uncritically and senselessly transplants them to the general theoretical and European field. The result is such a muddle as to provoke Homeric laughter in every class-conscious Russian worker who hears of these arguments of Kautsky.

And when we explain what the question at issue is every worker in Europe (except a handful of inveterate social-imperialists) will greet Kautsky with the same outburst of laughter.

Kautsky has rendered Martov a backhanded service by reducing his mistake to obvious absurdity. Let us see what Kautsky's argument amounts to.

The Soviets embrace all wage workers. The old methods of the economic and political struggle of the proletariat are inadequate against finance capital. The Soviets have a great role to play in the future, and not only in Russia. They will play a decisive role in the great decisive battles between capital and labour in Europe. This is what Kautsky says.

Excellent. But will not the "decisive battles between capital and labour" decide the question as to which of the two classes will possess political power?

Nothing of the kind, God forbid!

Organisations which embrace all the wage workers must not become state organisations in the "decisive" battles.

But what is the state?

The state is nothing but a machine for the suppression of one class by another.

Thus, the oppressed class, the vanguard of all the toilers and of the exploited in modern society, must strive towards the "decisive battles between capital and labour," but must not touch the machine by means of which capital oppresses labour! It must not break up that machine! It must not make use of its all-embracing organisation for the purpose of suppressing the exploiters!

Excellent, magnificent, Mr. Kautsky! "We" recognise the class war, in the same way as all liberals recognise it, i.e., without the overthrow of the bourgeoisie!

This is where Kautsky's complete rupture with Marxism and socialism becomes obvious. Practically, it is desertion to the camp of the bourgeoisie which is prepared to concede to everything except the transformation of the organisations of the class which it oppresses into state organisations. Kautsky can no longer save his position of trying to reconcile everything and to avoid all profound contradiction by means of phrases.

Kautsky either rejects the transfer of political power to the working class; or he concedes that the working class may take over the old bourgeois state machine, but does not concede that it must break up, smash that machine and replace it by a new, proletarian one. Whichever way Kautsky's arguments are "interpreted" or "explained," his break with Marxism and his desertion to the bourgeoisie are obvious.

Already in the Communist Manifesto, in describing what sort of state the victorious working class needs, Marx wrote: "A state, that is, the proletariat organised as the ruling class."

Now a man who claims that he is still a Marxist comes on the scene and declares that the proletariat, organised to a man and waging the "decisive battle" against capital, must not transform its class organisation into a state organisation! Here Kautsky has betrayed that "superstitious faith in the state" which, in Germany, as Engels wrote as far back as 1891, "had permeated the minds of the bourgeoisie, and even of many workers." Workers, fight! Our philistine "agrees" to this (as every bourgeois "agrees," since the workers are fighting all the same and the only thing that worries him is finding the means to blunt the edge of their sword). Fight, but don't dare to win! Don't destroy the state machine of the bourgeoisie; don't put proletarian "state organisation" in the place of the bourgeois "state organisation"!

Whoever sincerely shares the Marxian view that the state is nothing but a machine for the suppression of one class by another, and who has at all reflected upon this truth, could never have reached the absurd conclusion that the proletarian organisations capable of defeating finance capital must not become transformed into state organisations. It was this point that betrayed the petty bourgeois who believed that "after all is said and done" the state is something that is outside of class, or stands above class. Why, indeed, should the proletariat, "one class," be permitted to wage determined war against capital, which rules not only over the proletariat, but over the whole people, over the whole of the petty bourgeoisie, over the whole of the peasantry, but why should this proletariat, this "one class" not be permitted to transform its organisation into a state organisation? Because the petty bourgeois is afraid of the class struggle, and does not carry it to its logical conclusion, to its main object. . . .

Kautsky admits that the Soviets are an excellent fighting organisation of the proletariat, and that they have a great future before them. But that being the case, Kautsky's position collapses like a house of cards, or like the dreams of a petty-bourgeois who believes that the acute struggle between the proletariat and the bourgeoisie can be avoided. For revolution is a continuous desperate struggle, and the proletariat is the vanguard class of all the oppressed, the focus and centre of all the aspirations of all the oppressed who are striving for emancipation! Naturally, therefore, the Soviets, as the organ of struggle of the oppressed masses, reflected and expressed the moods and changes of opinions of these masses ever so much more quickly, more fully, and more faithfully, than any other institution (that, incidentally, is one of the reasons why Soviet democracy is the highest type of democracy).

In the period between March 13 (February 28) and November 7 (October 25), 1917, the Soviets managed to convene two All-Russian Congresses of representatives of the overwhelming majority of the population of Russia, of all the workers and soldiers, and 70 or 80 per cent of all the peasantry; not to speak of the vast number of local, district, urban, provincial, and regional congresses. During this period, the bourgeoisie did not succeed in convening a single institution that represented the majority of the people (except that obvious sham and mockery called the "Democratic Conference," which enraged the proletariat).

The Constituent Assembly reflected the same mood of the masses and the same political groups as was reflected by the first (June) All-Russian Congress of Soviets. At the time the Constituent Assembly was convened (January 1918), the Second and Third Congresses of Soviets met (in November [October] 1917, and January 1918 respectively) and both demonstrated as clearly as clear can be that the masses had swung to the Left, had become revolutionised, had turned away from the Mensheviks and the Socialist-

Revolutionaries, and had passed over to the side of the Bolsheviks; that is, had turned away from petty-bourgeois leadership, from the illusion that it was possible to reach a compromise with the bourgeoisie, and joined the proletarian revolutionary struggle for the overthrow of the bourgeoisie.

Hence, even the external history of the Soviets shows that the dispersal of the Constituent Assembly was inevitable and that it was a reactionary body.

But Kautsky sticks firmly to his motto: Let "pure democracy" prevail though the revolution perish and the bourgeoisie triumph over the proletariat! Fiat justitia, pereat mundus! [1] . . .

Let the contemptible, scoundrelly renegades, amidst the applause of the bourgeoisie and social-chauvinists, abuse our Soviet constitution for disfranchising the exploiters. This is good, because it will accelerate and deepen the split between the revolutionary workers of Europe and the Scheidemanns and Kautskys, the Renaudels and Longuets, the Hendersons and Mac-Donalds, and all the old leaders of and old traitors to socialism.

The masses of the oppressed classes, the class-conscious and honest revolutionary proletarian leaders, will be on our side. It will be sufficient for such proletarians and such masses to become acquainted with our Soviet constitution for them to say at once: "These are indeed our people, theirs is a real workers' party; theirs is a real workers' government, for it does not deceive the workers by talking about reforms in the way the leaders enumerated have done; it is really fighting the exploiters, it is really bringing about a revolution, it is really fighting for the complete emancipation of the working class."

The fact that after twelve months' "experience" the Soviets are depriving the exploiters of the franchise shows that the Soviets are really organisations of the oppressed masses and not of social-imperialists and social pacifists who have sold themselves to the bourgeoisie.

The fact that the Soviets have disfranchised the exploiters, shows that they are not organs of petty-bourgeois compromise with the capitalists, not organs of parliamentary chatter (of the Kautskys, the Longuets and the Mac-Donalds), but organs of the genuinely revolutionary proletariat who are waging a life and death struggle against the exploiters.

"Kautsky's pamphlet is almost unknown here," a well-informed comrade in Berlin wrote to me a few days ago (today is October 30). I would advise our ambassadors in Germany and Switzerland not to stint a thousand or so in buying up this book and distributing it gratis among the class-conscious workers in order to trample this "European"—read: imperialist and re-

[1] Let justice be done though the world perishes.

formist—Social-Democracy, which has long been a "stinking corpse," in the mud.

LEFT WING COMMUNISM: AN INFANTILE DISORDER

ONE OF THE BASIC PREREQUISITES FOR THE SUCCESS OF THE BOLSHEVIKS

Bolshevism, as a trend of political thought and as a political party, has existed since 1903. Only the history of Bolshevism during the whole period of its existence can satisfactorily explain why it was able to build up and maintain, under most difficult conditions, the iron discipline necessary for the victory of the proletariat.

And first of all, the question arises: how is the discipline of the revolutionary party of the proletariat maintained? How is it tested? How is it reinforced? First, by the class consciousness of the proletarian vanguard and by its devotion to the revolution, by its firmness, self-sacrifice, and heroism. Secondly, by its ability to link itself with, to keep in close touch with, and, to a certain degree, if you will, merge itself with the broadest masses of the toilers—primarily with the proletarian but also with the non-proletarian toiling masses. Thirdly, by the correctness of the political leadership exercised by this vanguard and by the correctness of its political strategy and tactics, provided that the broadest masses become convinced of this correctness by their own experience. Without these conditions discipline in a revolutionary party that is really capable of being a party of the advanced class, whose mission it is to overthrow the bourgeoisie and to transform the whole of society, cannot be achieved. Without these conditions all attempts to establish discipline are inevitably transformed into trifling phrase-mongering and empty gestures. On the other hand, these conditions cannot arise all at once. They are created only through prolonged effort and hard-won experience. Their creation is facilitated only by correct revolutionary theory, which in its turn is not a dogma but assumes complete shape only in close connection with the practical activity of a truly mass and truly revolutionary movement.

If in 1917–1920, under the greatest difficulties, Bolshevism could build up and successfully carry out the strictest centralisation and iron discipline, it was due simply to a number of historical peculiarities of Russia.

On the one hand, Bolshevism arose in 1903 on the very firm foundation of Marxian theory. And the correctness of this—and only this—revolutionary theory has been proved not only by the experience of all countries during the entire nineteenth century but particularly by the experience of the wanderings and vacillations, the mistakes and disappointments of revolutionary thought in Russia. For almost half a century—approximately between the 'forties and 'nineties of last century—advanced thinkers in Russia, under the oppression of an unprecedented, savage and reactionary tsarism, sought eagerly for the correct revolutionary theory, following each and every "last word" in Europe and America in this sphere with astonishing diligence and thoroughness. Russia achieved Marxism, as the only correct revolutionary theory, virtually through suffering, by a half century of unprecedented torments and sacrifice, of unprecedented revolutionary heroism, incredible energy, painstaking search and study, testing in practice, disappointments, checking, and comparison with European experience. Thanks to the emigration enforced by tsarism, revolutionary Russia, in the second half of the nineteenth century, possessed such a wealth of international connections and such excellent information about world forms and theories of the revolutionary movement as no other country in the world possessed.

On the one hand, having arisen on this granite theoretical foundation, Bolshevism passed through fifteen years (1903-1917) of practical history which, in wealth of experience, has had no equal anywhere else in the world. For no other country during these fifteen years had anything even approximating this revolutionary experience, this rapid and varied succession of different forms of the movement—legal and illegal, peaceful and stormy, open and underground, small circles and mass movements, parliamentary and terrorist. In no other country was there concentrated during so short a period of time such a wealth of forms, shades and methods of struggle involving all classes of modern society, and, moreover, of a struggle which, owing to the backwardness of the country, and the heavy yoke of tsarism, was maturing with exceptional rapidity and assimilating most eagerly and successfully the corresponding "last word" of American and European political experience.

"LEFT" COMMUNISM IN GERMANY: LEADERS—PARTY—CLASS—MASSES

The German Communists, of whom we must now speak, call themselves not "Left," but, if I am not mistaken, the "opposition on principle." That they exhibit all the symptoms of the "infantile disorder of Leftism" will be seen from what follows.

A pamphlet, written from the standpoint of this opposition and entitled *The Split in the Communist Party of Germany* (the Spartacus League), issued by "the local group in Frankfurt-am-Main," sets forth concisely, clearly, briefly, and in highest relief the substance of the views of this opposition. A few quotations will suffice to acquaint the reader with the essential points:

The Communist Party is the party of the most determined class struggle. . . .
Politically, this transition period (between capitalism and socialism) is the period of the proletarian dictatorship. . . .
The question arises: Who should be the vehicle of this dictatorship, the Communist Party or the Proletarian Class? . . . Should we, on principle, strive towards the dictatorship of the Communist Party or the dictatorship of the proletarian class? . . .

Further, the author of the pamphlet accuses the "C.C." [2] of the Communist Party of Germany of seeking a way to a coalition with the Independent Social-Democratic Party of Germany, of putting to the fore "the question of recognising in principle all political means" of struggle, including parliamentarism, only for the purpose of concealing its main and real intention, viz., coalition with the Independents. And he goes on to say:

The opposition has chosen another road. It is of the opinion that the question of the rule of the Communist Party and of its dictatorship is only a question of tactics. At all events, the rule of the Communist Party is the final form of all party rule. On principle, we must strive towards the dictatorship of the proletarian class. And all Party measures, its organisation, methods of struggle, its strategy and tactics should be adapted to this end. Accordingly, it is necessary to reject most decisively all compromise with other parties, all reversion to parliamentary forms of struggle, which have become historically and politically obsolete, all policy of manoeuvring and compromise. . . . Specifically proletarian methods of revolutionary struggle must be strongly emphasised. In order to embrace the broadest proletarian circles and strata, which will have to take part in the revolutionary struggle under the leadership of the Communist Party, there must be created new forms of organisation upon the broadest foundations and within the widest limits. The rallying point for all revolutionary elements is the Workers' Union, which is built up on the basis of factory organisations. In this union all workers must unite who followed the slogan, "Leave the trade unions!" Here the fighting proletariat is being formed into the broadest battle ranks. Recognition of the class struggle, the Soviet system, and the dictatorship is sufficient for admittance. All further political training of the fighting masses and political orientation in the struggle is the task of the Communist Party, which is outside the Workers' Union.
Consequently, two Communist Parties are arrayed one against the other:
One, a party of leaders, which strives to organise the revolutionary struggle and direct it from above, which resorts to compromises and parliamentarism, in order to create a situation which would enable it to enter a coalition government in whose hands the dictatorship would rest.

[2] Central Committee.

The other is a mass party, which relies upon the upsurge of the revolutionary struggle from below, which knows and employs but a single method in the struggle, a method that leads clearly to the goal, and which rejects all parliamentary and opportunist methods. This single method is the method of the unequivocal overthrow of the bourgeoisie, for the purpose of establishing the proletarian class dictatorship, for the realisation of socialism. . . .

There—the dictatorship of leaders; here—the dictatorship of the masses:—this is our slogan.

Such are the most essential postulates that characterise the views of the opposition of the German Communist Party.

Any Bolshevik who has consciously participated in, or has closely observed, the development of Bolshevism since 1903 will at once say after reading these arguments: "What old and familiar rubbish! What 'Left' childishness!"

But let us look at these arguments a little more closely.

The very presentation of the question—"dictatorship of the Party or dictatorship of the class, dictatorship (Party) of the leaders or dictatorship (Party) of the masses?"—is evidence of the most incredible and hopeless confusion of mind. People try very hard to invent something extraordinary, and in their effort to be wise they become ridiculous. Everyone knows that the masses are divided into classes; that masses can be contrasted to classes only by contrasting the overwhelming majority in general, without dividing them according to their position in the social system of production, to categories occupying a definite position in the social system of production; that in modern civilised countries, at least, classes are usually, and in the majority of cases, led by political parties; that political parties, as a general rule, are directed by more or less stable groups composed of the most authoritative, influential, and experienced members who are elected to the most responsible positions and are called leaders. All this is ABC. All this is simple and clear. What was the use then, in place of this, of all this rigmarole, this new Volapük? Apparently, on the one hand, these people got confused in a serious situation in which the rapid alternation of legal and illegal existence of the Party disturbs the usual normal, simple relations between leaders, parties, and classes. In Germany, as in other European countries, people had become too much accustomed to legality, to the free and regular election of "leaders" at regular Party conventions, to convenient methods of testing the class composition of the Party by parliamentary elections, meetings, the press, the mood of the trade unions and other organisations, etc. When, instead of this customary procedure, it became necessary, in consequence of the extremely rapid advance of the revolution and the spread of civil war, to change quickly from legality to illegality, to combine the two, and adopt "inconvenient" and "undemocratic" methods of singling out or constituting or preserving "groups of leaders"—people lost their heads and began to invent supernatural nonsense. Probably the Dutch "Tribunists"—who had the misfortune to be born in a small country with traditions, and under conditions of particularly privileged and stable legality, who had never experienced the change from legality to illegality—became confused, lost their heads, and helped these absurd inventions. . . .

To go so far in this matter as to draw a contrast in general between the dictatorship of the masses and the dictatorship of the leaders, is ridiculously absurd and stupid. What is particularly funny is that actually, in place of the old leaders who hold commonsense views on ordinary matters, new leaders are put forth (under cover of the slogan, "Down with the leaders!") who talk supernatural nonsense and confusion. Such are Lauffenberg, Wolffheim, Horner, Karl Schröder, Friedrich Wendel, and Karl Erler in Germany. The attempts of the latter to make the question "more profound" and to proclaim that political parties in general are unnecessary and "bourgeois," are such Herculean pillars of absurdity that one can only shrug one's shoulders. In truth, a small mistake can always be transformed into a monstrously big one, if the small mistake is persisted in, if profound reasons are given for it and if it is carried to its "logical conclusion."

Repudiation of party and of party discipline—this is what the opposition amounts to. And this is tantamount to completely disarming the proletariat for the benefit of the bourgeoisie. It is the equivalent to precisely that petty-bourgeois diffuseness, instability, incapacity for sustained effort, unity and organised action, which, if indulged in, must inevitably destroy every proletarian revolutionary movement. From the standpoint of communism, repudiation of party means leaping from the eve of the collapse of capitalism (in Germany), not to the initial, or middle, but to the highest phase of communism. We in Russia, (in the third year after the overthrow of the bourgeoisie) are taking the first steps in the transition from capitalism to socialism, or the lowest stage of communism. Everywhere, classes have remained and will remain for years after the conquest of power by the proletariat. Perhaps in England, where there is no peasantry (but where, nevertheless, there are small proprietors!), the period will be shorter. The abolition of classes not only means driving out landlords and capitalists—that we accomplished with comparative ease—it means also getting rid of the small commodity producers, and they cannot be driven out or crushed; we must live in harmony with them; they can (and must) be remoulded and re-educated, but this can be done only by very prolonged, slow, cautious organisational work. They encircle the proletariat on every side with a petty-bourgeois atmosphere, which impregnates and corrupts the proletariat and causes constant relapses among the proletariat into petty-bourgeois spinelessness, disintegration, individualism and alternate moods of exaltation and dejection. The strictest centralisation and discipline is required in the political party of the proletariat in order to counteract this, in order that the organisation role of the proletariat (and this is its principal role) may be fulfilled correctly, successfully, victoriously. The dictatorship of the proletariat is a persistent struggle—sanguinary and bloodless, violent and peaceful, military and economic, educational and administrative—against the forces of traditions of the old society. The force of habit of millions and of tens of millions is a terrible force. Without an iron party steeled in the struggle, without a party enjoying the confidence of all who are honest in the given class, without a party capable of keeping track of and influencing the mood of the masses, it is impossible to conduct such a struggle successfully. It is a thousand times easier to vanquish the centralised big bourgeoisie than to "vanquish" millions and millions of small proprietors, who by their everyday, imperceptible, elusive, demoralising activity achieve the very results desired by the bourgeoisie and which restore the bourgeoisie. Whoever in the least weakens the iron discipline of the party of the proletariat (especially during its dictatorship) actually aids the bourgeoisie against the proletariat. . . .

The interrelations between leaders—Party—class—masses, as well as the relation of the dictatorship of the proletariat and its Party to the trade unions, now present themselves concretely in Russia in the following form. The dictatorship is exercised by the proletariat which is organised in the Soviets and is led by the Communist Party (Bolsheviks), which, according to the data of the last Party Congress (April 1920), has 611,000 members. Membership fluctuated considerably both before and after the October Revolution, and even in 1918 and 1919 was considerably less than it is now. We are afraid of an excessive growth of the Party, as careerists and charlatans, who deserve only to be shot, inevitably strive to attach themselves to the ruling party. The last time we opened wide the doors of the Party—for workers and peasants only—was in the days (winter, 1919) when Yudenich was a few versts from Petrograd and Denikin was in Orel (about 350 versts from Moscow), that is, when the Soviet Republic was in desperate, mortal danger, and when adventurers, careerists, charlatans and unreliable persons in general could not possibly count on making a profitable career (they had more reason to expect the gallows and torture) by joining the Communists. The Party, which holds annual congresses (the last on the basis of one delegate for each 1,000 members), is directed by a Central Committee of nineteen elected at the congress, while the current work in Moscow has to be carried on by still smaller bodies, viz., the so-called "Orgburo" (Organisation Bureau) and "Politburo" (Political Bureau), which are elected at the plenary sessions of the Central Committee, five members of the Central Committee in each bureau. This, then, looks like a real "oligarchy." Not a single important political or organisational question is decided by any state institution in our republic without the guiding instructions of the Central Committee of the Party.

In its work the Party relies directly on the trade unions, which, at present, according to the data of the last congress (April 1920), have over 4,000,000 members, and which, formally, are non-Party. In reality, all the controlling bodies of the overwhelming majority of the unions, and primarily, of course, of the All-Russian general trade union centre or bureau (All-Russian Central Council of Trade Unions) consist of Communists, who secure the carrying out of all the instructions of the Party. Thus, on the whole, we have a formally non-Communist, flexible, relatively wide, and very powerful proletarian apparatus, by means of which the Party is closely linked up with the class and with the masses, and by means of which, under the leadership of the Party, the class dictatorship of the class is realised. Without close contact with the trade unions, without their hearty support and self-sacrificing work not only in economic but also in military construction, it would, of course, have been impossible to govern the country and to maintain the dictatorship for two months, let alone two years. Of course, in practice, this close contact calls for very complicated and varied work in the form of propaganda, agitation, timely and frequent conferences not only with the leading but also with the influential trade union workers generally; it calls for determined struggle against the Mensheviks, who still have a certain, though very small, number of adherents, whom they teach all possible counter-revolutionary tricks, from the ideological defence of (bourgeois) democracy and the preaching of the "independence" of the trade unions (independence—from the proletarian state!) to the sabotaging of proletarian discipline, etc., etc.

We consider that contact with the "masses" through trade unions is not enough. Our practical experience during the course of the revolution has given rise to non-Party workers' and peasants' conferences, and we strive by every means to support, develop, and extend these institutions in order to be able to watch the mood of the masses, to come closer to them, to respond to their demands, to promote the best of their workers to state posts, etc. In a recent decree on the transformation of the People's Commissariat for State

Control into the Workers' and Peasants' inspection non-Party conferences of this kind are granted the right to elect members of the State Control to undertake various investigations, etc.

Then, of course, all the work of the Party is carried on through the Soviets, which unite the toiling masses irrespective of occupation. The Uyezd congresses of Soviets are institutions more democratic than any in the best democratic republics of the bourgeois world; and through these congresses (whose proceedings are followed by the Party with the closest attention), as well as by continuously sending class-conscious workers to various posts in the rural districts, the rôle of the proletariat as leader of the peasantry is fulfilled, the dictatorship of the urban proletariat is realised and systematic struggle against the bourgeois, rich, exploiting and profiteering peasantry is waged.

Such is the general mechanism of the proletarian state power viewed "from above," from the standpoint of the practical realisation of the dictatorship. It is to be hoped that the leader will understand why, to a Russian Bolshevik well acquainted with this mechanism and who for twenty-five years has watched its growth from small, illegal, underground circles, all talk about "from above" or "from below," about "the dictatorship of leaders" or "the dictatorship of the masses," cannot but appear to be ridiculous, childish nonsense, something like discussion whether the left leg or the right arm is more useful to man.

THE COMMUNIST INTERNATIONAL

As EARLY as 1915 Lenin foresaw that a world victory for Bolshevism would require an international organization to direct, coordinate, and discipline national Communist parties. Both the First World War and preoccupation with the overthrow of the Kerensky regime prevented any immediate attempts to create a general staff for international Communism. After the Bolshevik victory in Russia, prisoners of war were indoctrinated before being released, and immediately after the armistice Lenin and his cohorts quickly organized a Third International, the First International having disbanded in the 1870s and the Second International, founded in 1889, having resisted Bolshevization.

The new organization met, auspiciously enough, in Moscow, in 1919. Various departments were established, officers were elected, and the first of many appeals and manifestoes to the world's "working people" was released. Plans were laid to extend the Bolshevik Revolution at once to central Europe, England, and the United States. Revolts and short-lived Communist governments followed in Hungary and Bavaria. Their failure resulted in the calling of a second congress of the Third International in July, 1920. Again, a number of manifestoes was issued to the world. Although the Bolsheviks still clearly proclaimed their intention to revolutionize the world, their tactics had been changed along the lines laid out in this selection.

In order to speed these plans, a world-wide propaganda campaign was launched with Moscow as the center of the drive. From its beginnings the International was intended as the basis of a future Soviet world government. Its executive committee, though seemingly independent, was in fact completely subservient to the leaders of the Russian Communist party. Ever since 1920, in one form or another, whether its utterances have been strident or seemingly calm in tone, there has existed a large Soviet-dominated world apparatus dedicated to the final overthrow of non-Sovietized peoples and governments everywhere. The manifesto presented here is not merely the ravings of harmless fanatics, but one of a number of carefully considered strategies for continuous war against the free world.

The following selection comes from *The Communist International, 1919–1943: Documents*, edited by Jane Degras (London: Oxford University Press, 1956).

THESES ON THE BASIC TASKS OF THE COMMUNIST INTERNATIONAL ADOPTED BY THE SECOND COMINTERN CONGRESS

1. It is characteristic of the present moment in the development of the international communist movement that in all capitalist countries the best

representatives of the revolutionary proletariat have reached a thorough understanding of the most important principles of the Communist International, the dictatorship of the proletariat and the Soviet power, and that they have enthusiastically come over to the side of the Communist International. It is a still bigger and more important step forward that everywhere, not only among the broadest masses of the urban proletariat, but also among the more advanced rural workers, unreserved sympathy with these most important principles is clearly apparent.

On the other hand, two errors or weaknesses have emerged in this international movement, which is growing with such unusual rapidity. One very serious mistake, which is of the greatest immediate danger to the success of the cause of proletarian emancipation, arises from the fact that some of the old leaders and old parties of the Second International, in part half unconsciously yielding to the wishes and the pressure of the masses, in part deceiving them in order to maintain their former role as agents and assistants of the bourgeoisie within the workers' movement, proclaim their conditional or even unconditional adherence to the Communist International, while in fact they remain, in all their practical party activities and political performances, on the level of the Second International. Such a state of affairs is quite intolerable, for it creates confusion among the masses, hampers the formation and development of a strong communist party, diminishes respect for the Communist International, and threatens a repetition of the treachery committed by the Hungarian social-democrats, who hastened to don the red garb of communism. Another, but far less important error, which is rather a growing sickness in the movement, consists in the anxiety to be "radical"; this leads to an incorrect appreciation of the role and tasks of the party in relation to the class and the masses and of the obligation of revolutionary communists to work in bourgeois parliaments and reactionary trade unions.

It is the duty of communists not to hush up the weaknesses of their movement, but to criticize them openly, in order the more quickly and thoroughly to eradicate them. For this purpose it is necessary, firstly, to define the concepts of "proletarian dictatorship" and "Soviet power" more concretely, using, in particular, practical experience; secondly, to state in what the immediate preparatory work for the realization of these slogans can and should consist in all countries; thirdly, to indicate ways and means of curing our movement of its defects.

THE NATURE OF PROLETARIAN DICTATORSHIP AND SOVIET POWER

2. The victory of socialism (as the first stage of communism) over capitalism requires the proletariat, as the only truly revolutionary class, to carry out

the following three tasks. First: to overthrow the exploiters, and above all others the bourgeoisie, as their chief economic and political representatives; to crush their resistance, to make impossible any attempt on their part to restore the capitalist yoke and wage-slavery. Second: to attract not only the entire proletariat, or its overwhelming majority, but also the entire mass of working people and of those exploited by capital, and to bring them into position behind the revolutionary vanguard of the proletariat, the communist party; to educate, organize, train, and discipline them in the course of unflagging, bold, and relentless struggle against the exploiters; to rescue this overwhelming majority of the population in all capitalist countries from dependence on the bourgeoisie; to instill in them, through practical experience, belief in the leading role of the proletariat and of its revolutionary vanguard. The third task consists in neutralizing, in making harmless, the inevitable waverings between bourgeoisie and proletariat, between bourgeois democracy and Soviet power, of the class of small proprietors in agriculture, in industry, and in trade, a class which is still fairly numerous in all advanced countries, even though they do not form the majority of the population, and also in neutralizing the vacillations among that section of the intellectuals and white-collar workers associated with this class.

The first and second tasks are independent in character, and each requires special measures to be taken in regard to both the exploiters and the exploited. The third follows from the first two, and requires only a skillful, timely, and flexible combination of the measures designed for the first two, according to the concrete circumstances of each particular case of vacillation.

3. In the concrete situation created throughout the entire world, and particularly in the most advanced, most powerful, most enlightened and free capitalist States, by militarism, imperialism, the oppression of the colonies and weak countries, the imperialist world slaughter and the Versailles "peace," any concession to the idea that the capitalists will peacefully submit to the will of the exploited majority, the idea of a peaceful reformist transition to socialism, is not merely proof of extreme petty-bourgeois stupidity, but is a direct deception of the workers, a gilding of capitalist wage-slavery, a concealment of the truth. The truth is this, that the bourgeoisie, even the most enlightened and democratic, already shrink from no fraud and no crime, nor from the murder of millions of workers and peasants, to save private property in the means of production. Only the forcible overthrow of the bourgeoisie, the seizure of their property, the destruction of the entire bourgeois State machine from top to bottom—parliamentary, judicial, military, bureaucratic, administrative, municipal, etc.—going as far as the exile or internment of the most dangerous and stubborn exploiters, keeping a

strict watch over them to combat the inevitable attempts at resistance and to restore capitalist slavery—only by such measures can the real submission of the entire exploiting class be attained and secured.

There is another idea which whitewashes capitalism and bourgeois democracy and deceives the workers: that is the opinion common among the old parties and old leaders of the Second International, that the majority of the working people and the exploited are able, in the conditions of capitalist slavery and under the yoke of the bourgeoisie—which assumes countless different forms, both more refined and more cruel and ruthless the more civilized the country is—to acquire for themselves a completely clear socialist consciousness, firm socialist convictions and attitudes. In reality the education, training, and organization of the working and exploited masses under the influence and guidance of communists, their liberation from egoism, from sectionalism, from the vices and weaknesses engendered by private property, their transformation into a free union of free workers—all that is possible only in the actual course of the most acute class struggles, only when the vanguard of the proletariat, supported by all or by a majority of this class, which is the only revolutionary class, has overthrown and suppressed the exploiters, freed the exploited from their position of slavery and improved their conditions of life at the expense of the expropriated capitalists.

4. To win victory over capitalism there must be the right relation between the communist party, as leader, the revolutionary class, the proletariat, on the one hand, and the masses, that is, all the working people and the exploited, on the other. Only if the communist party is really the vanguard of the revolutionary class, if it includes all the best representatives of that class, if it consists of thoroughly conscious and devoted communists, trained and steeled by the experiences of stubborn revolutionary struggle, only if the party has been able to tie itself indissolubly to the entire life of its class and hence to the entire masses of the exploited, and enjoys the complete confidence of that class and those masses, only then is the party in a position to lead the proletariat in the unrelenting, decisive, last battle against all the forces of capitalism. On the other hand, it is only under the leadership of such a party that the proletariat is able to develop the full force of its revolutionary assault—which, because of the economic structure of capitalist society, is immeasurably greater than would correspond with the proportion of the total population represented by the proletariat—and to nullify the inevitable apathy and in part also the resistance of the small minority of the labour aristocracy, the old trade union and co-operative leaders, etc., corrupted by capitalism. Finally, it is only when the masses, i.e., all the working and exploited people, are really liberated from the yoke of the bourgeoisie

and the bourgeois State machine, and have been given the opportunity to organize themselves freely in Soviets, that they will be able in their millions, for the first time in history, to develop all the initiative and energy suppressed by capitalism. Only when the Soviets have become the sole machinery of State can there be real participation in government by the entire mass of the exploited, who, even under the most enlightened and free bourgeois democracy, have in reality always been ninety-nine per cent excluded from participation in government. Only in the Soviets do the exploited masses begin to learn, not from books but from their own practical experience, how to set about the work of socialist construction, of the creation of a new social discipline, a free union of free workers.

PREPARATION FOR THE DICTATORSHIP OF THE PROLETARIAT; WORK THAT MUST BE CARRIED OUT EVERYWHERE WITHOUT DELAY

5. It is a distinguishing feature of the present moment in the development of the international communist movement that in the great majority of capitalist countries the preparations of the proletariat to bring its dictatorship into being have not been completed, indeed in many cases have not even been systematically begun. It does not follow that the proletarian revolution is impossible in the immediate future. It is quite possible, for the entire economic and political situation is unusually rich in inflammable material and in reasons for its suddenly catching fire. A further prerequisite of revolution, apart from the preparation of the proletariat, namely, a general state of crisis in all ruling and all bourgeois parties, is also present. But from what has been said it follows that for the communist parties the immediate task is to accelerate the revolution, taking care not to provoke it artificially before adequate preparations have been made. The preparation of the proletariat for the revolution must be promoted by action. On the other hand the history of many socialist parties, previously referred to, makes it essential to see that recognition of the dictatorship of the proletariat does not remain an empty word.

From the standpoint of the international proletarian movement, therefore, the chief task of the communist parties at the present moment is to rally the scattered communist forces, to create a united communist party in each country (or the consolidation and regeneration of the parties already in existence), to multiply tenfold the work of preparing the proletariat for the conquest of State power in the form of the dictatorship of the proletariat. The socialist work usually done by groups and parties which recognize the dictatorship of the proletariat has not yet by a long way been subjected to that radical transformation and regeneration which are essential if it is to be regarded as communist work, corresponding to the tasks on the eve of the proletarian dictatorship.

6. The conquest of political power by the proletariat does not put an end to its class struggle against the bourgeoisie; on the contrary, it makes this struggle particularly comprehensive, acute, and unrelenting. Because the struggle has reached a pitch of the utmost intensity, all groups, parties, and active participants in the workers' movement which are wholly or partly reformist or "centrist" in character move inevitably either to the side of the bourgeoisie or to the side of the waverers, or (what is most dangerous) they join the unreliable friends of the victorious proletariat. That is why preparation for the dictatorship of the proletariat requires not only an intensified struggle against reformist and "centrist" tendencies, but also a change in the character of that struggle. It must not be restricted to explaining the incorrectness of these tendencies, but must mercilessly and ruthlessly expose every leading individual in the workers' movement who displays these tendencies, for otherwise the proletariat cannot learn with whom to act in the decisive struggle against the bourgeoisie. This struggle is of such a character that it may at any moment replace the weapon of criticism by the criticism of weapons, and, as experience has already shown, it not only may, but does. Any inconsistency or weakness in exposing those who turn out to be reformists or "centrists" directly increases the danger of the overthrow of the power of the proletariat by the bourgeoisie, who will tomorrow make use of what today seems to shortsighted people nothing but a "theoretical difference of opinion."

7. In particular it is not enough to be content with the usual rejection in principle of any co-operation between proletariat and bourgeoisie, any "class collaboration." In conditions of the proletarian dictatorship—which will never be able to abolish private property completely at one blow—the simple defence of "freedom" and "equality" changes, while private property in the means of production is maintained, into "co-operation" with the bourgeoisie, which directly undermines the power of the working class. For the dictatorship of the proletariat means that the entire apparatus of State power is used to establish and secure "unfreedom" for the exploiters to carry on their work of oppression and exploitation, "inequality" between property owners (that is, those who appropriate for their own use the means of production created by social labour) and the propertyless. What seems, before the victory of the proletariat, nothing but a theoretical difference of opinion about "democracy" inevitably becomes, on the morrow of victory, a question to be decided by force of arms. Consequently, without a fundamental change in the entire character of the struggle against the "centrists" and the "defenders of

democracy" even a preliminary preparation of the masses for the realization of the proletarian dictatorship is impossible.

8. The dictatorship of the proletariat is the most determined form of the class struggle of the proletariat against the bourgeoisie. This struggle can only be successful if the revolutionary vanguard is supported by the overwhelming majority of the proletariat. Preparation for the proletarian dictatorship therefore demands not only explaining the bourgeois character of any kind of reformism, any defence of democracy that involves the maintenance of private property in the means of production, not merely exposing those tendencies which mean in fact that the bourgeoisie are defended within the workers' movement; it also requires that the old leaders shall be replaced by communists in absolutely every kind of proletarian organization, not only political, but also trade union, co-operative, educational, etc. The longer bourgeois democracy has prevailed in a country, the more complete and well established it is, the more successful have the bourgeoisie of that country been in getting into those leading positions people who are reared in bourgeois democracy, saturated in its attitudes and prejudices, and very frequently bribed by it, whether directly or indirectly. These representatives of the labour aristocracy, or of workers who have become bourgeois in outlook, must be pushed out of all their positions a hundred times more boldly than ever before, and replaced even by inexperienced workers, so long as they are closely tied to the exploited masses and enjoy their confidence in the struggle against the exploiters. The dictatorship of the proletariat will make it necessary to appoint such inexperienced workers to the most responsible offices of State, otherwise the power of the workers' government will be ineffective and will not be supported by the masses.

9. The dictatorship of the proletariat is the most complete realization of the leadership of all working and exploited people, who have been enslaved, downtrodden, oppressed, intimidated, disunited, and deceived by the capitalist class, by the one class which the entire history of capitalism has prepared for this leading part. Consequently the work of preparing for the dictatorship of the proletariat must be everywhere undertaken without delay, along the following lines:

In all organizations, unions and associations of the working and exploited masses without exception, first in the proletarian and then in the non-proletarian (political, trade union, military, co-operative, educational, sport, etc.), groups or cells of communists must be formed, chiefly open in character, but also secret, the latter being obligatory wherever their dissolution, or the arrest or deportation of their members by the bourgeoisie, is likely; these cells, closely connected with each other and with the party centre, shall pool their experience, carry on propaganda, agitation, and organizational work, adapting themselves to absolutely every sphere of public life and to every kind and group of the working masses, and by this varied work systematically train themselves, the party, the class, and the masses.

In this connection it is of the utmost importance to work out and to develop the methods necessary for all these activities: the leaders or responsible representatives hopelessly corrupted by petty-bourgeois or imperialist prejudices must be mercilessly exposed and driven out of the workers' movement. In regard to the masses, however, who, particularly after the imperialist slaughter, are largely inclined to give a hearing to and to accept the theory of the necessity of the rule of the proletariat as the only way out of capitalist slavery, particular patience and caution must be shown in studying and allowing for the peculiarities and particular psychological features of every section, every occupation, etc.

10. There is one communist group or cell which deserves the party's particular attention and care; that is the parliamentary fraction, the group of members of parliament, deputies to bourgeois representative bodies (particularly in central, but also in local and municipal government). These bodies are of particularly great importance in the eyes of the backward working masses saturated in petty-bourgeois prejudices. Therefore communists must from that very tribune carry on the work of propaganda, agitation, and organization, and explain to the masses why it was legitimate in Russia (and in due course will be legitimate in any country) for the Soviet congress to dissolve the bourgeois parliament. On the other hand the entire course of bourgeois democracy has turned parliament, particularly in the advanced countries, into the main or one of the main centres for incredible swindles, for the financial and political deception of the people, for careerism, hypocrisy, and the oppression of the working people. That is why the burning hatred of parliament felt by the best representatives of the revolutionary proletariat is fully justified. That is why communist parties, and all parties of the Communist International—particularly if they were founded not by breakaways from the old parties, and in protracted and stubborn struggles with them, but as a result of the old parties going over (often in appearance only) to new political positions—must be specially strict in their attitude to their parliamentary fractions. The fractions must be completely subject to the control and direction of the committee of the party; they must consist largely of revolutionary workers; their speeches in parliament must be carefully analysed from the communist standpoint in the party press and at party meetings; members of parliament must be detailed for agitational

work among the masses, and any member of the fraction who shows Second International tendencies must be expelled.

11. One of the chief difficulties encountered by the revolutionary workers' movement in the advanced capitalist countries arises from the fact that capital, thanks to colonial possessions and the surplus profits of finance capital etc., is able to detach a comparatively broad and stable stratum, the labour aristocracy, which is a small minority of the working class. They enjoy good wages and are most deeply imbued with a narrow craft spirit and with petty-bourgeois and imperialist prejudices. They represent the real social "pillars" of the Second International of reformists and "centrists," and at the present moment are almost the sole social mainstay of the bourgeoisie. It is impossible even to begin to prepare the proletariat for the overthrow of the bourgeoisie without an immediate, systematic, comprehensive, and open struggle against this stratum which—as experience has already clearly demonstrated—will undoubtedly provide the bourgeois white guard with not a few recruits after the victory of the proletariat. All parties adhering to the Communist International must, at whatever cost, carry through the slogan "deeper into the masses," "closer contact with the masses," meaning by the masses all working people and all who are exploited by capital, particularly those who are least organized and least enlightened, most deeply oppressed and least accessible to organization.

The proletariat becomes revolutionary only in so far as it does not lock itself up in narrow craft limits, only in so far as it takes part in all activities and all spheres of public life as leader of all the working and exploited masses, and it is impossible for it to achieve its dictatorship if it is not ready and able to make the greatest sacrifices for the sake of victory over the bourgeoisie. In this respect Russia's experience is of both theoretical and practical significance. There the proletariat could not have established its dictatorship, could not have won the respect and confidence of all the working masses, if it had not made greater sacrifices and suffered greater hunger than any other section of the masses, in the most difficult periods of attack, of war, and of the blockade by the world bourgeoisie.

The communist party and the entire advanced proletariat must, in particular, give all-round and self-denying support to the broad and spontaneous mass strike movement, which alone is able really to rouse the masses under the yoke of capital, to get them into action, to educate and organize them, and to foster in them complete confidence in the leading role of the revolutionary proletariat. Without this preparation no dictatorship of the proletariat is possible, and people who come out openly against strikes, like

Kautsky in Germany and Turati in Italy, can in no circumstances be tolerated in parties which adhere to the Communist International. This of course applies in still greater degree to the trade union and parliamentary leaders who often betray the workers by using the experience of strikes to preach reformism and not revolution, for example Jouhaux in France, Gompers in America, J. H. Thomas in England.

12. In all countries, even the freest, most "legal" and most "peaceful"— that is, where the class struggle is least acute—the time has come when it is imperative for every communist party systematically to combine legal with illegal work, legal with illegal organization. For even in the most enlightened and free countries with the most "solid" bourgeois-democratic regime the governments are already beginning, despite their own false and hypocritical statements, to keep regular secret lists of communists, to resort to violations of their own constitution, to half-secret and secret support of the white guards, and to the murder of communists in every country, to secret preparation for the arrest of communists, to smuggling *agents provocateurs* into communist circles, etc. Only the most reactionary petty-bourgeois, however fine the "democratic" and pacifist phrases he may use, can deny these facts or the conclusion which necessarily follows from them—the necessity for all communist parties to establish without delay illegal organizations to carry on systematic illegal work and make thorough preparations for the day when bourgeois persecution comes out into the open. This illegal work is particularly necessary in the army, the navy, and the police, for after the great imperialist slaughter all governments have begun to fear national armies which are open to the worker and the peasant, and have begun in secret to single out from among the troops detachments recruited from the bourgeoisie and provided with special and technically superior equipment.

On the other hand it is also necessary, in all cases without exception, not to restrict oneself to illegal work but to carry out legal work, to overcome all obstacles, to found legal press organs and legal organizations under the most varied names, and when necessary to change the names frequently. This is being done by the illegal communist parties in Finland and Hungary, and to some extent in Germany, Poland, Latvia, etc. This must also be done by the IWW in America, and by all legal communist parties, if the public prosecutor finds it convenient to use decisions of the congresses of the Communist International to start persecuting them.

The imperative necessity, as a matter of principle, of combining illegal with legal work, is determined not merely by the totality of the special features of the present period, on the eve of the proletarian dictatorship, but also by the need to demonstrate to the bourgeoisie that there is not and cannot be any sphere of activity which the communists cannot conquer, and still more by the existence everywhere of broad strata of the proletariat, and even more of the non-proletarian working and exploited masses, who still have faith in bourgeois-democratic legality and whom it is very important for us to convince of the contrary.

13. The position of the workers' press in the most advanced capitalist countries shows particularly clearly both the entire mendacity of freedom and equality in a bourgeois democracy, and the necessity of systematic combination of legal and illegal work. In both defeated Germany and victorious America the entire power of the bourgeois State apparatus, and all the tricks of its financial tycoons, are used to deprive the workers of their press—prosecution in the courts and the arrest (even the murder by hired assassins) of its editors, the prohibition of distribution through the post, refusal of paper supplies, etc. Moreover, the news reports which are necessary for a daily paper are controlled by bourgeois press agencies, and the advertisements without which a large newspaper cannot pay its way are at the "free" disposition of capitalists. In these ways, by fraud and by the pressure of capital and of bourgeois rule, the bourgeoisie deprive the revolutionary proletariat of its press.

To combat this the communist parties must start a new kind of periodical press for mass distribution among the workers; first, legal publications which, without calling themselves communist or referring to their adherence to the party, must learn to take advantage of the slightest legal opportunities, as the Bolsheviks did after 1905 under the Tsar; secondly, illegal papers, even if they are only very small and are published only irregularly, but which can be reproduced in small printing shops by the workers (either secretly, or if the movement has become strong enough, by the revolutionary seizure of printing presses), and which give the proletariat revolutionary information and revolutionary watchwords.

Without a revolutionary struggle for the freedom of the communist press which carries the masses along with it, preparation for the dictatorship of the proletariat is impossible.

CORRECTING THE POLICY AND PARTLY ALSO THE COMPOSITION OF THE PARTIES WHICH HAVE JOINED OR WISH TO JOIN THE COMMUNIST INTERNATIONAL

14. The degree to which the proletariat in the countries which are most important from the standpoint of world economy and world politics is prepared for the realization of its dictatorship is indicated with the greatest objectivity and precision by the breakaway of the most influential parties in the

Second International—the French Socialist Party, the Independent Social-Democratic Party of Germany, the Independent Labour Party in England, the American Socialist Party—from that yellow International, and by their decision to adhere conditionally to the Communist International. This shows that not only the vanguard of the majority of the revolutionary proletariat, convinced by the course of events, have begun to come over to our side. The chief thing now is to know how to make this change complete and to consolidate what has been attained in lasting organizational form, so that progress can be made along the whole line without any hesitation.

15. The entire activity of the parties mentioned (to which the Swiss Socialist Party will most probably be added) shows, and their periodical press clearly confirms, that this activity is not yet communist and not infrequently is frankly incompatible with the basic principles of the Communist International, namely, recognition of the dictatorship of the proletariat and of Soviet power instead of bourgeois democracy.

Therefore the second congress of the Communist International has decided that it does not consider it possible to accept these parties immediately; that it approves the answer given by the ECCI[1] to the German "Independents," that it confirms its readiness to conduct negotiations with any party which leaves the Second International and wishes to approach the Communist International; that it grants delegates of such parties a consultative voice at all its congresses and conferences; that it makes the following conditions for the complete unification of these (and similar) parties with the Communist International:

(i) Publication of all decisions of all congresses of the Communist International and of its Executive Committee in all the party's periodicals.

(ii) Discussion of these decisions at special meetings of all sections or local groups of the party.

(iii) The convening, after such discussion, of a special congress of the party to draw the conclusions. This congress must be called as early as possible and in any case not later than four months after the second congress of the Communist International.

(iv) The party to be cleansed of all elements which continue to act in the spirit of the Second International.

(v) All party periodicals to be put in the hands of exclusively communist editorial boards.

(vi) Parties which now wish to enter the Communist International but have not yet made a radical break with their old tactics must ensure that two-thirds of the membership of their central committees and central bodies

[1] Executive Committee of the Communist International.

consist of comrades who, before the second congress, came out openly in favour of adherence to the Communist International. Exceptions can be made only with the consent of the ECCI.

(vii) Members of the party who reject the conditions and theses adopted by the Communist International must be expelled. The same applies to members of the extraordinary congress.

The second congress of the Communist International instructs the Executive Committee to accept the parties mentioned, and similar parties, into the Communist International, after satisfying itself that all these conditions have really been fulfilled and the party's activity has become communist in character.

16. As to the question how communists, who are now in the minority, should behave when they occupy responsible positions in the said parties, the second congress of the Communist International has decided that, in view of the present rapid growth in the revolutionary spirit of the masses, it is not desirable for communists to leave these parties so long as they have the opportunity of working in them for the recognition of the proletarian dictatorship and the Soviet power, and of criticizing the opportunists and centrists who still remain in these parties. Whenever the left wing of a centrist party has become strong enough, and the development of the communist movement requires it, it may leave the party in a body and form a communist party.

At the same time the second congress of the Communist International is in favour of the affiliation of communist or sympathizing groups and organizations in England to the Labour Party, although the Labour Party belongs to the Second International. For so long as this party allows the organizations affiliated to it their present freedom of criticism and freedom to engage in propaganda, agitation, and organization for the proletarian dictatorship and the Soviet power, so long as this party retains the character of an association of all trade union organizations of the working class, communists must do everything they can, and even make certain organizational compromises, to have the possibility of exercising influence on the broad working masses, of exposing their opportunist leaders from a high tribune visible to the masses, of accelerating the transference of political power from the direct representatives of the bourgeoisie to the "labour lieutenants of the capitalist class," in order to cure the masses quickly of their last illusions on this score.

17. As to the Italian Socialist Party, the second congress of the Communist International recognizes that the revision of the programme decided on at the Bologna congress of this party last year marks a very im-

portant stage in this party's road to communism, and that the proposals put forward by the Turin section to the National Council of the party and published in *L'Ordine Nuovo* of 8 May 1920 are in conformity with all the basic principles of the Communist International. The congress requests the Italian Socialist Party at its next congress, which is to be held in accordance with its own statutes and the conditions of admission to the Communist International, to examine the said proposals and all the decisions of the two congresses of the Communist International, particularly with respect to the parliamentary fraction, the trade unions, and non-communist elements in the party.

18. The second congress of the Communist International judges as incorrect the views about the relation of the party to the class and the masses, about communist party participation in bourgeois parliaments and in reactionary trade unions held and defended in their most thoroughgoing form by the Communist Labour Party of Germany (KAPD), and in part by the Communist Party of Switzerland, and in *Der Kommunismus,* organ of the East European secretariat of the Communist International in Vienna, by some Dutch comrades, and by some communist organizations in England, for example the Socialist Workers' Federation and the Shop Stewards' Committee, and by the IWW in America; these views have been refuted in detail in special resolutions of the second congress. Nevertheless the second congress of the Communist International considers both possible and desirable the immediate affiliation to the Communist International of such of these organizations as have not yet officially joined, for in these cases—particularly the IWW in America and Australia, and the shop stewards in England, we are dealing with a profoundly proletarian mass movement, whose principles really correspond to the basic principles of the Communist International. In such organizations the incorrect views about participation in bourgeois parliaments derive not so much from the influence of members of bourgeois origin, who bring their basically petty-bourgeois outlook into the movement—an outlook which anarchists often share—as from the lack of political experience of thoroughly revolutionary proletarians who are closely bound to the masses.

The second congress of the Communist International therefore requests all communist organizations and groups in the Anglo-Saxon countries, even if the IWW and the shop stewards should not immediately join, to pursue a friendly policy towards these organizations, to draw closer to them and to the masses who sympathize with them, and to explain to them, in the light of the experiences of all revolutions and particularly of the three Russian revolutions of the twentieth century, in a most friendly way the incorrectness of their views in this respect, and not to desist from repeated attempts to unite with these organizations into a single communist party.

19. In this connection the congress directs the attention of all comrades, particularly in the Latin and Anglo-Saxon countries, to the deep theoretical cleavage that has been taking place since the war among anarchists throughout the world on the question of their attitude to the proletarian dictatorship and the Soviet power. The proletarian elements, who were frequently driven to anarchism by a wholly natural hatred of the opportunism and reformism of the parties of the Second International, have a particularly good grasp of these principles, which is growing as they become more familiar with the experience of Russia, Finland, Hungary, Latvia, Poland, and Germany.

The congress therefore thinks it the duty of all comrades to support to the utmost the movement of all mass proletarian elements from anarchism towards the Communist International. The congress declares that the success of the work of genuine communist parties can be measured among other things by the extent to which they succeed in attracting from anarchism to their side all the mass proletarian elements.

IV CROSSCURRENTS: 1918–1929

LABOUR AND THE NEW SOCIAL ORDER

As THE First World War neared its end, men in both Europe and America sensed that Western civilization was on the verge of fundamental social changes. The capitalist and democratic institutions that had been patched together in the nineteenth century could no longer be counted on to arouse deep loyalty; a mood of alienation and criticism had set in. The Bolshevik triumph in Russia and the potentially revolutionary conditions in central Europe seemed to augur the birth of a new age. Repressive measures against pacifists and radicals in the United States and other nations suggested the great insecurity of the old holders of power in the face of possible uprisings or radical reforms.

In England the Labour party, already about a generation old, turned its attention to the problems of postwar reconstruction. A firm alliance among trades unions, the cooperative movement, and intellectuals had been created to serve as a basis for Labour's peaceful search for power. Sidney Webb, the leading intellectual in the Labour party, went to work on a postwar program for Labour in connection with drafting a new party constitution openly favoring the "common ownership of the means of production."

Webb's draft program, which was circulated in 1917, became a topic for well-founded excited debate and discussion. After adaptation as a Labour party policy in June, 1918, *Labour and the New Social Order* became the basis of all subsequent reform proposals and, with the great Labour triumph in England in 1945, the agenda for a peaceful but dramatic revolution. In Webb's document were the essentials of the later doctrines of "full employment," of the necessity of public works in time of distress, of public ownership under a more democratic parliament with guarantees of individual and trade-union freedom, and many other features of future socialist and nonsocialist welfare states. It is noteworthy that although the manifesto of 1918 represented the triumph of the Fabian Society's evolutionary socialist approach to the ills of capitalist society, Webb still cautiously avoided the words "socialization" and "nationalization" in his draft; he wrote instead of "common ownership."

This extract is taken from *Labour and the New Social Order* (London: The Labour Party, 1918).

LABOUR AND THE NEW SOCIAL ORDER

THE END OF A CIVILISATION

The view of the Labour Party is that what has to be reconstructed after the war is not this or that Government Department, or this or that piece of social machinery; but, so far as Britain is concerned, society itself. The individual worker, or for that matter the individual statesman, immersed in daily routine—like the individual soldier in a battle—easily fails to understand the magnitude and far-reaching importance of what is taking place around him. How does it fit together as a whole? How does it look from a distance? Count Okuma, one of the oldest, most experienced and ablest of the statesmen of Japan, watching the present conflict from the other side of the globe, declares it to be nothing less than the death of European civilisation. Just as in the past the civilisations of Babylon, Egypt, Greece, Carthage and the great Roman Empire have been successively destroyed, so, in the judgment of this detached observer, the civilisation of all Europe is even now receiving its death-blow. We of the Labour Party can so far agree in this estimate as to recognise, in the present world catastrophe, if not the death, in Europe, of civilisation itself, at any rate the culmination and collapse of a distinctive industrial civilisation, which the workers will not seek to reconstruct. At such times of crisis it is easier to slip into ruin than to progress into higher forms of organisation. That is the problem as it presents itself to the Labour Party to-day.

What this war is consuming is not merely the security, the homes, the livelihood and the lives of millions of innocent families, and an enormous proportion of all the accumulated wealth of the world, but also the very basis of the peculiar social order in which it has arisen. The individualist system of capitalist production, based on the private ownership and competitive administration of land and capital, which has in the past couple of centuries become the dominant form, with its reckless "profiteering" and wage-slavery; with its glorification of the unhampered struggle for the means of life and its hypocritical pretence of the "survival of the fittest"; with the monstrous inequality of circumstances which it produces and the degradation and brutalisation, both moral and spiritual, resulting therefrom, may, we hope, indeed have received a death-blow. With it must go the political system and ideas in which it naturally found expression. We of the Labour Party, whether in opposition or in due time called upon to form an Administration, will certainly lend no hand to its revival. On the contrary, we shall do our utmost to see that it is buried with the millions whom it has done to death. If we in Britain are to escape from the decay of civilisation itself, which the Japanese statesman foresees, we must ensure that what is presently to be built up is a new social order, based not on fighting but on fraternity —not on the competitive struggle for the means of bare life, but on a deliberately planned co-operation in production and distribution for the benefit of all who participate by hand or by brain—not on the utmost possible inequality of riches, but on a systematic approach towards a healthy equality of material circumstances for every person born into the world— not on an enforced dominion over subject nations, subject races, subject Colonies, subject classes, or a subject sex, but, in industry as well as in government, on that equal freedom, that general consciousness of consent, and that widest possible participation in power, both economic and political, which is characteristic of a true Democracy. No one to-day can help noticing how very far from efficient the capitalist system has been proved to be, with its stimulus of private profit and its evil shadow of wages driven down by competition often below subsistence level. The Labour Party recognises that it is vital, for any genuine social reconstruction, to increase the nation's aggregate annual production, not of profit or dividend, but of useful commodities and services; that this increased productivity is obviously not to be sought in reducing the means of subsistence of the workers, whether by hand or by brain, nor yet in lengthening their hours of work, for neither "sweating" nor "driving" can be made the basis of lasting prosperity, but in (a) the socialisation of industry so as to secure the elimination of every kind of inefficiency and waste; (b) the application both of more honest determination to produce the very best, and of more science and intelligence to every branch of the nation's work; together with (c) an improvement in social, political, and industrial organisation; and (d) the indispensable marshalling of the nation's resources so that each need is met in the order of, and in proportion to, its real national importance. We do not, of course, pretend that it is possible, even after the drastic clearing away that is now going on, to build society anew in a year or two of feverish "Reconstruction." What the Labour Party intends to satisfy itself about is that each brick that it helps to lay shall go to erect the structure that it intends, and no other.

THE PILLARS OF THE HOUSE

The Four Pillars of the House that we propose to erect, resting upon the common foundation of the Democratic control of society in all its activities, may be termed, respectively:

(a) The Universal Enforcement of the National Minimum;
(b) The Democratic Control of Industry;
(c) The Revolution in National Finance; and
(d) The Surplus Wealth for the Common Good.

The various detailed proposals of the Labour Party, herein briefly summarised, rest on these four pillars, and can best be appreciated in connection with them.

THE UNIVERSAL ENFORCEMENT OF A NATIONAL MINIMUM

The first principle of the Labour Party—in significant contrast with those of the Capitalist System, whether expressed by the Liberal or by the Conservative Party—is the securing to every member of the community, in good times and bad alike (and not only to the strong and able, the well-born or the fortunate), of all the requisites of healthy life and worthy citizenship. This is in no sense a "class" proposal. Such an amount of social protection of the individual, however poor and lowly, from birth to death, is, as the economist now knows, as indispensable to fruitful co-operation as it is to successful combination; and it affords the only complete safeguard against that insidious Degradation of the Standard of Life, which is the worst economic and social calamity to which any community can be subjected. We are members one of another. No man liveth to himself alone. If any, even the humblest, is made to suffer, the whole community and every one of us, whether or not we recognise the fact, is thereby injured. Generation after generation this has been the corner-stone of the faith of Labour. It will be the guiding principle of any Labour Government.

THE LEGISLATIVE REGULATION OF EMPLOYMENT

Thus it is that the Labour Party to-day stands for the universal application of the Policy of the National Minimum, to which (as embodied in the successive elaboration of the Factory, Mines, Railways, Shops, Merchant Shipping, Trade Boards, and Truck Acts, the Public Health, Housing, and Education Acts, and the Minimum Wage Acts) the spokesmen of Labour have already gained the support of the enlightened statesmen and economists of the world. All these laws purporting to prevent any Degradation of the Standard of Life need considerable improvement and extension before they can fulfil their purpose of securing to every worker, by hand or by brain, at least the prescribed Minimum of Health, Education, Leisure, and Subsistence, whilst their administration leaves much to be desired. . . .

The legal minimum (which will need revision according to the level of prices, and which ought to be the very lowest statutory base line for the least skilled adult workers, men or women, in any occupation, in all parts of the United Kingdom) must be not less than enough to provide all the requirements of a full development of body, mind, and character, from which the nation has no right to exclude any class or section whatsoever.

SECURING EMPLOYMENT FOR ALL

The Labour Party insists—as no other political party has thought fit to do —that what the soldiers and sailors will most seriously look to, is not the sum of money doled out to them, but the provision made for ensuring such of them as are not wholly disabled situations appropriate to their capacities and desires, and that the obligation to find suitable employment in productive work for all these men and women rests upon the Government for the time being. The work of re-settling the disbanded soldiers and discharged munition workers into new situations is a national obligation; and the Labour Party emphatically protests against it being regarded as a matter for private charity. It strongly objects to this public duty being handed over either to committees of philanthropists or benevolent societies, or to any of the military or recruiting authorities. The policy of the Labour Party in this matter is to make the utmost use of the Trade Unions, and equally, for the brainworkers, of the various Professional Associations. In view of the fact that, in any trade, the best organisation for placing men in situations is a national Trade Union having local Branches throughout the kingdom, every soldier and every munition worker should be allowed, if he chooses, to have a duplicate of his industrial discharge notice sent, one month before the date fixed for his discharge, to the Secretary of the Trade Union to which he belongs or wishes to belong. Apart from this use of the Trade Union (and a corresponding use of the Professional Association) the Government must, of course, avail itself of some such public machinery as that of the Employment Exchanges; but before the existing Exchanges (which will need to be greatly extended) can receive the co-operation and support of the organised Labour Movement, without which their operations can never be fully successful, it is imperative that they should be drastically reformed, on the lines laid down in the Demobilisation Report of the "Labour After the War" Joint Committee; and, in particular, that each Exchange should be placed effectively under the supervision and control of a Joint Committee of Employers and Trade Unionists in equal numbers.

The responsibility of the Government for the time being, in the grave industrial crisis that demobilisation will produce, goes, however, far beyond the eight million men and women whom the various Departments will suddenly discharge from their own service. The effect of this peremptory discharge on all the other workers has also to be taken into account. To the Labour Party it will seem the supreme concern of the Government of the day to see to it that there shall be, as a result of the gigantic "General Post" which it will itself have deliberately set going, nowhere any Degradation of the Standard of Life. The Government has pledged itself to restore the Trade Union conditions and "pre-war practices" of the workshop, which the Trade Unions patriotically gave up at the direct request of the Government itself, and to secure this restoration by effective statutory provisions; and this solemn pledge must be fulfilled, of course, in the spirit as well as in the letter. If it is considered that some of the rules, conditions, and customs are, in the industrial reorganisation that is contemplated, inconsistent with the highest development of production, or injurious to other sections of workers, it is for the Government, as responsible for the fulfilment of the pledge, to submit for discussion to the trade unions concerned alternative proposals for securing the standard wage and normal day, protecting the workers from unemployment, and maintaining the position and dignity of the crafts. The Labour Party, moreover, holds it to be the duty of the Government of the day to take all necessary steps to prevent the Standard Rates of Wages, in any trade or occupation whatsoever, from suffering any reduction, relatively to the contemporary cost of living. Unfortunately, the present Government, like the Liberal and Conservative Parties, so far refuses to speak on this important matter with any clear voice. We claim that it should be a cardinal point of Government policy to make it plain to every capitalist employer that any attempt to reduce the customary rates of wages when peace comes, for women no less than for men, or to take advantage of the dislocation of demobilisation to worsen the conditions of employment in any grade whatsoever, will certainly lead to embittered industrial strife, which will be in the highest degree detrimental to the national interests; and that the Government of the day must not hesitate to take all necessary steps to avert such a calamity. In the great impending crisis the Government of the day should not only, as the greatest employer of both brainworkers and manual workers, set a good example in this respect, but should also actively seek to influence private employers by proclaiming in advance that it will not itself attempt to lower the Standard Rates of conditions in public employment; by announcing that it will insist on the most rigorous observance of the Fair Wages Clause in all public contracts, and by explicitly recommending every Local Authority to adopt the same policy. . . .

Nothing is more dangerous to the Standard of Life, or so destructive of those minimum conditions of healthy existence, which must in the interests of the community be assured to every worker, than any widespread or continued unemployment. It has always been a fundamental principle of the Labour Party (a point on which, singularly enough, it has not been followed by either of the other political parties) that, in a modern industrial community, it is one of the foremost obligations of the Government to find, for every willing worker, whether by hand or by brain, productive work at Standard Rates.

It is accordingly the duty of the Government to adopt a policy of deliberately and systematically preventing the occurrence of unemployment, instead of (as heretofore) letting unemployment occur, and then seeking, vainly and expensively, to relieve the unemployed. It is now known that the Government can, if it chooses, arrange the public works and the orders of National Departments and Local Authorities in such a way as to maintain the aggregate demand for labour in the whole kingdom (including that of capitalist employers) approximately at a uniform level from year to year; and it is therefore a primary obligation of the Government to prevent any considerable or widespread fluctuations in the total numbers employed in times of good or bad trade. But this is not all. In order to prepare for the possibility of there being any unemployment, either in the course of demobilisation or in the first years of peace, it is essential that the Government should make all necessary preparations for putting instantly in hand, directly or through the Local Authorities, such urgently needed public works as (a) the rehousing of the population alike in rural districts, mining villages, and town slums, to the extent, possibly, of a million new cottages and an outlay of 300 millions sterling; (b) the immediate making-good of the shortage of schools, training colleges, &c., and the engagement of the necessary additional teaching, clerical, and administrative staffs; (c) new roads; (d) light railways; (e) the unification and reorganisation of the railway and canal system; (f) afforestation; (g) the reclamation of land; (h) the development and better equipment of our ports and harbours; (i) the opening up of access to land by co-operative small holdings and in other practicable ways. Moreover, in order to relieve any pressure of an overstocked labour market, the opportunity should be taken, if unemployment should threaten to become widespread, (a) immediately to raise the school-leaving age to sixteen; (b) greatly to increase the number of scholarships and bursaries for Secondary and Higher Education; and (c) substantially to shorten the hours of labour of all young persons, even to a greater extent than the seven or eight hours per week contemplated in the new Education Act, in order to enable them to attend technical and other classes in the daytime. Finally, wherever practicable, the hours of adult labour should be reduced to not more than forty-eight per week, without reduction of the Standard Rates of Wages. There can be no economic or other justification for keeping any man or woman to work for long hours, or at overtime, whilst others are unemployed.

SOCIAL INSURANCE AGAINST UNEMPLOYMENT

In so far as the Government fails to prevent Unemployment—whenever it finds it impossible to discover for any willing worker, man or woman, a suitable situation at the Standard Rate—the Labour Party holds that the Government must, in the interest of the community as a whole, provide him or her with adequate maintenance, either with such arrangements for honourable employment or with such useful training as may be found practicable, according to age, health and previous occupation.

THE DEMOCRATIC CONTROL OF INDUSTRY

Unlike the Conservative and Liberal Parties, the Labour Party insists on Democracy in industry as well as in government. It demands the progressive elimination from the control of industry of the private capitalist, individual or joint-stock; and the setting free of all who work, whether by hand or by brain, for the service of the community, and of the community only. And the Labour Party refuses absolutely to believe that the British people will permanently tolerate any reconstruction or perpetuation of the disorganisation, waste and inefficiency involved in the abandonment of British industry to a jostling crowd of separate private employers, with their minds bent, not on the service of the community, but—by the very law of their being—only on the utmost possible profiteering. What the nation needs is undoubtedly a great bound onward in its aggregate productivity. But this cannot be secured merely by pressing the manual workers to more strenuous toil, or even by encouraging the "Captains of Industry" to a less wasteful organisation of their several enterprises on a profit-making basis. What the Labour Party looks to is a genuinely scientific reorganisation of the nation's industry, no longer deflected by individual profiteering, on the basis of the Common Ownership of the Means of Production; the equitable sharing of the proceeds among all who participate in any capacity and only among these, and the adoption, in particular services and occupations, of those systems and methods of administration and control that may be found, in practice, best to promote, not profiteering, but the public interest.

IMMEDIATE NATIONALISATION

The Labour Party stands not merely for the principle of the Common Ownership of the nation's land, to be applied as suitable opportunities occur, but also, specifically, for the immediate Nationalisation of Railways, Mines and the production of Electrical Power. We hold that the very foundation of any successful reorganisation of British Industry must necessarily be found in the provision of the utmost facilities for transport and communication, the production of power at the cheapest possible rate and the most economical supply of both electrical energy and coal to every corner of the kingdom. Hence the Labour Party stands, unhesitatingly, for the National Ownership and Administration of the Railways and Canals, and their union, along with Harbours and Roads, and the Posts and Telegraphs—not to say also the great lines of steamers which could at once be owned, if not immediately directly managed in detail, by the Government—in a united national service of Communication and Transport; to be worked, unhampered by capitalist, private or purely local interests (and with a steadily increasing participation of the organised workers in the management, both central and local), exclusively for the common good. . . .

But the sphere of immediate Nationalisation is not restricted to these great industries. We shall never succeed in putting the gigantic system of Health Insurance on a proper footing, or secure a clear field for the beneficent work of the Friendly Societies, or gain a free hand for the necessary development of the urgently called for Ministry of Health and the Local Public Health Service, until the nation expropriates the profit-making Industrial Insurance Companies, which now so tyrannously exploit the people with their wasteful house-to-house Industrial Life Assurance. Only by such an expropriation of Life Assurance Companies can we secure the universal provision, free from the burdensome toll of weekly pence, of the indispensable Funeral Benefit. Nor is it in any sense a "class" measure. Only by the assumption by a State Department of the whole business of Life Assurance can the millions of policy-holders of all classes be completely protected against the possibly calamitous results of the depreciation of securities and suspension of bonuses which the war is causing. Only by this means can the great staff of insurance agents find their proper place as Civil Servants, with equitable conditions of employment, compensation for any disturbance and security of tenure, in a nationally organised public service for the discharge of the steadily increasing functions of the Government in Vital Statistics and Social Insurance.

LOCAL GOVERNMENT

The Labour Party is alive to the evils of centralisation and the drawbacks of bureaucracy. To counteract these disadvantages it intends that the fullest possible scope shall be given, in all branches of social reconstruction, to the democratically elected local governing bodies. It holds that whilst the central Government Departments should assist with information and grants in aid, the local authorities should be given a free hand to develop their own services, over and above the prescribed national minimum, in whatever way they choose; that they should be empowered to obtain capital from the Government at cost price, and to acquire land cheaply and expeditiously, for any of the functions with which they are entrusted. The Labour Party holds, moreover, that the municipalities and County Councils should not confine themselves to the necessarily costly services of education, sanitation, and police, and the functions to be taken over from the Boards of Guardians, nor yet rest content with acquiring control of the local water, gas, electricity, and tramways, but that they should greatly extend their enterprises in housing and town planning, parks, and public libraries, the provision of music and the organisation of popular recreation, and also that they should be empowered to undertake, not only the retailing of coal, but also other services of common utility, particularly the local supply of milk, where this is not already fully and satisfactorily organised by a co-operative society. Further, that in view of the great and growing importance of local government, the Labour Party thinks it high time that the Councillors should again be required to submit themselves for election, and that a system of Proportional Representation should be adopted; that, on the first election, at any rate, the whole of each Council should vacate their seats, and that, in order to throw the position open to all persons, rich or poor, all Councillors should be provided with payment for any necessary travelling expenses, and for the time spent on the public service.

By far the most important function of the Local Authorities is the administration of Education. The first step to social reconstruction must be a genuine nationalisation of education, which shall get rid of all class distinctions and privileges, and bring effectively within the reach, not only of every boy and girl, but also of every adult citizen, all the training, physical, mental and moral, literary, technical, and artistic of which he is capable.

The Labour Party cannot be satisfied with a system which condemns the great bulk of the children to merely the elements of schooling with accommodation and equipment inferior to that of the secondary schools, in classes too large for efficient instruction, under teachers of whom at least one-third are insufficiently trained; which denies to the great majority of the teachers in the kingdom, whether in elementary or in secondary schools (and notably to most of the women), alike any opportunity for all-round culture as well as for training in their art, an adequate wage, reasonable prospects of advancement, and suitable superannuation allowances; and which, notwithstanding what is yet done by way of scholarships for exceptional talent, still reserves the endowed secondary schools, and even more the Universities, for the most part, to the sons and daughters of a small privileged class, whilst contemplating nothing better than eight or ten weeks a year continuation schooling up to 18 for 90 per cent. of the youth of the nation.

The Labour Party accordingly asks for a systematic reorganisation of the whole educational system, from the nursery school to the University, on the basis of (a) social equality, (b) the provision for each age, for child, youth, and adult, of the best and most varied education of which it is capable, with whatever provision by way of maintenance is needed to enable the students to obtain full advantage of the instruction provided; (c) the educational institutions, irrespective of social class or wealth, to be planned, equipped, and staffed according to their several functions, up to the same high level for elementary, secondary, or University teaching, with regard solely to the greatest possible educational efficiency, but without any military training; and (d) the recognition of the teaching profession, without distinction of grade, as one of the most valuable to the community.

AGRICULTURE AND RURAL LIFE

In no part of the present social order has there been a greater failure than in agriculture and rural life. The Labour Party regards the present arrangements for the production and distribution of food in this country, and the life to which many thousands of country dwellers are condemned, as nothing short of a national disgrace, and as needing to be radically altered without delay. What is essential is that the Government should resume control of the nation's agricultural land, and ensure its utilisation not for rent, not for game, not for the social amenity of a small social class, not even for obtaining the largest percentage on the capital employed, but solely with a view to the production of the largest possible proportion of the foodstuffs required by the population of these islands under conditions allowing of a good life to the rural population, with complete security for the farmer's enterprise, yet not requiring the consumer to pay a price exceeding that for which foodstuffs can be brought from other lands. To the Labour Party it seems that this end can probably best be attained by a combination of (a) national farms, administered on a large scale, with the utmost use of machinery; (b) small holdings made accessible to practical agriculturists; (c) municipal enterprises in agriculture, in conjunction with municipal institutions of various kinds, milk depots, sewage works etc.; (d) farms let to co-operative societies and other tenants, under covenants requiring the kind of cultivation desired, with universal protection, by insurance, against the losses due to bad seasons. Under all systems the agricultural labourer must be secured a healthy and commodious cottage, with sufficient garden ground, the opportunity of getting an accessible allotment, and, when he so desires, a small holding, together with a wage continuously adequate for the full development of body, mind, and character.

But the greatest financial loss now occurs in the distribution of the product. The Labour Party suggests that the distribution of foodstuffs in the towns—from milk and meat to bread and vegetables—should, with equitable compensation for all interests expropriated and persons displaced, be taken out of the hands of the present multiplicity of dealers and shopkeepers, and organised by consumers' co-operative societies and the local authorities working in conjunction, solely with an eye to the common good.

THE SURPLUS FOR THE COMMON GOOD

In the disposal of the surplus above the Standard of Life society has hitherto gone as far wrong as in its neglect to secure the necessary basis of any genuine industrial efficiency or social order. We have allowed the riches of our mines, the rental value of the lands superior to the margin of cultivation, the extra profits of the fortunate capitalists, even the material outcome of scientific discoveries—which ought by now to have made this Britain of ours immune from class poverty or from any widespread destitution—to be absorbed by individual proprietors; and then devoted very largely to the senseless luxury of an idle rich class. Against this misappropriation of the wealth of the community, the Labour Party—speaking in the interests not of the wage-earners alone, but of every grade and section of producers by hand or by brain, not to mention also those of the generations that are to succeed us, and of the permanent welfare of the community—emphatically protests. Our main Pillar of the House that the Labour Party intends to build is the future appropriation of the Surplus, not to the enlargement of any individual fortune, but to the Common Good. It is from this constantly arising Surplus (to be secured, on the one hand, by Nationalisation and Municipalisation and, on the other, by the steeply graduated Taxation of Private Income and Riches) that will have to be found the new capital which the community day by day needs for the perpetual improvement and increase of its various enterprises, for which we shall decline to be dependent on the usury-exacting financiers. It is from the same source that has to be defrayed the public provision for the Sick and Infirm of all kinds (including that for Maternity and Infancy) which is still so scandalously insufficient; for the Aged and those prematurely incapacitated by accident or disease, now in many ways so imperfectly cared for; for the education alike of children, of adolescents and of adults, in which the Labour Party demands a genuine equality of opportunity, overcoming all differences of material circumstances; and for the organisation of public improvements of all kinds, including the brightening of the lives of those now condemned to almost ceaseless toil, and a great development of the means of recreation. From the same source must come the greatly increased public provision that the Labour Party will insist on being made for scientific investigation and original research, in every branch of knowledge, not to say also for the promotion of music, literature and fine art, which have been under Capitalism so greatly neglected, and upon which, so the Labour Party holds, any real development of civilisation fundamentally depends. Society, like the individual, does not live by bread alone—does not exist only for perpetual wealth production. It is in the proposal for this appropriation of every surplus for the Common Good —in the vision of its resolute use for the building up of the community as a whole instead of for the magnification of individual fortunes—that the Labour Party, as the Party of the Producers by hand or by brain, most distinctively marks itself off from the older political parties, standing, as these do, essentially for the maintenance, unimpaired, of the perpetual private mortgage upon the annual product of the nation that is involved in the individual ownership of land and capital.

MORE LIGHT—BUT ALSO MORE WARMTH!

The Labour Party is far from assuming that it possesses a key to open all locks; or that any policy which it can formulate will solve all the problems that beset us. But we deem it important to ourselves as well as to those who may, on the one hand, wish to join the Party, or, on the other, to take up arms against it, to make quite clear and definite our aim and purpose. The Labour Party wants that aim and purpose, as set forth in the preceding pages, with all its might. It calls for more warmth in politics, for much less apathetic acquiescence in the miseries that exist, for none of the cynicism that saps the life of leisure. On the other hand, the Labour Party has no belief in any of the problems of the world being solved by Good Will alone. Good Will without knowledge is Warmth without Light. Especially in all the complexities of politics, in the still undeveloped Science of Society, the Labour Party stands for increased study, for the scientific investigation of each succeeding problem, for the deliberate organisation of research, and for a much more rapid dissemination among the whole people of all the science that exists. And it is perhaps specially the Labour Party that has the duty of placing this Advancement of Science in the forefront of its political programme. What the Labour Party stands for in all fields of life is, essentially, Democratic Co-operation; and Co-operation involves a common purpose which can be agreed to; a common plan which can be explained and discussed, and such a measure of success in the adaptation of means to ends as will ensure a common satisfaction. An autocratic Sultan may govern without science if his whim is law. A Plutocratic Party may choose to ignore science, if it is heedless whether its pretended solutions of social problems that may win political triumphs ultimately succeed or fail. But no Labour Party can hope to maintain its position unless its proposals are, in fact, the outcome of the best Political Science of its time; or to fulfil its purpose unless that science is continually wresting new fields from human ignorance. Hence, although the Purpose of the Labour Party must, by the law of its being, remain for all time unchanged, its Policy and its Programme will, we hope, undergo a perpetual development, as knowledge grows, and as new phases of the social problem present themselves, in a continually finer adjustment of our measures to our ends. If Law is the Mother of Freedom, Science, to the Labour Party, must be the Parent of Law.

ARTHUR MOELLER VAN DEN BRUCK

THE POLITICAL AND SOCIAL chaos which followed defeat in the First World War left many Europeans disillusioned and with no sense of direction. The institutions to which Germans had anchored their ideals and ambitions were swept away. Militarism was defeated and monarchy discredited: their colonies and alliances, their power and prestige were gone.

This disaster needed explaining. Some Germans, who believed that the German mistake had been the failure to adopt Western liberalism, put their hope in the Weimar Republic. Others blamed the former enemy, Versailles, perfidious allies, or traitors within the gates. Still others blamed Germany's lack of unity, the absence of a sense of common destiny among the German people, and the modern political and social ideals that fostered social diversity.

Among the latter was Arthur Moeller van den Bruck (1876–1925), who called himself a "revolutionary conservative." He despised liberalism because it set the individual before the "Folk." He hated England and the West. He inveighed against the "boisterous mediocrity of the bourgeoisie who behave so shamefully." He attacked Marxism because the theory of class war divided and weakened the nation. In Germany's numerous political parties, he discerned the signs of German decay. For government by coalition or compromise he had only contempt.

Upon his release from military service in the First World War, Moeller wrote *Das Dritte Reich* (*The Third Reich*), first published in 1923. In it he proposed the establishment of a third party to be above parties, whose program would be national and social, embracing and uniting all German people. Only thus, he thought, could Germany's destiny be fulfilled, and Germany's Third Empire be established—a mystical successor to the Holy Roman Empire and to the Second Reich of Bismarck and the Kaiser. Although Moeller's book is replete with phraseology and ideology common to Nazi works, the Nazis themselves considered him "bloodless and artificial."

Moeller was a mystic, a student of Hegel, an admirer of Nietzsche, but apparently misunderstood them as much as he misunderstood himself. "Germans," he wrote, "are only too prone to abandon themselves to self-deception. The thought of a 'Third Reich' might well be the most fatal of all the illusions to which they have ever yielded. . . . Germany might perish of her Third Reich dream. . . . The beast in man is threatening."

How right he was, he never knew. Perhaps he was afraid of his own idea, or despaired of ever realizing it. He killed himself in 1925.

The following excerpts are taken from a condensed translation, *Germany's Third Reich,* by E. O. Lorimer (London: George Allen and Unwin, 1934).

THE THIRD REICH

THE ATTEMPT this book makes was not possible from any party standpoint; it ranges over all our political problems, from the extreme Left to the extreme Right. It is written from the standpoint of a Third Party, which is already in being. Only such an attempt could address itself to the nation while attacking all the parties; could reveal the disorder and discord into which the parties have long since fatefully fallen and which has spread from them through our whole political life; could reach that lofty spiritual plane of political philosophy which the parties have forsaken, but which must for the nation's sake be maintained, which the conservative must preserve and the revolutionary must take by storm.

Instead of government by party we offer the ideal of the *Third Empire*. It is an old German conception and a great one. It arose when our First Empire fell; it was early quickened by the thought of a millennium; but its underlying thought has always been a future which should be not the end of all things but the dawn of a German Age in which the German People would for the first time fulfil their destiny on earth.

In the years which followed the collapse of our Second Empire, we have had experience of Germans; we have seen that the nation's worst enemy is herself: her trustfulness, her casualness, her credulity, her inborn, fate-fraught, apparently unshakable, optimism. The German people were scarcely defeated —as never a people was defeated before in history—than the mood asserted itself: "We shall come up again all right!" We heard German fools saying: "We have no fears for Germany!" We saw German dreamers nod their heads in assent: "Nothing can happen to me!" . . .

There are Germans who assure us that the Empire which rose out of the ruins on the Ninth of November is already the Third Empire, democratic, republican, logically complete. These are our opportunists and eudaemonists. There are other Germans who confess their disappointment but trust to the "reasonableness" of history. These are our rationalists and pacifists. They all draw their conclusions from the premises of their party-political or utopian wishes, but not from the premises of the reality which surrounds us. They will not realize that we are a fettered and maltreated nation, perhaps on the very verge of dissolution. Our reality connotes the triumph of all the nations of the earth over the German nation; the primacy in our country of parliamentism after the western model—and party rule. If the *Third Empire* is ever to come it will not beneficently fall from heaven. If the *Third Empire* is to put an end to strife it will not be born in a peace of philosophic dreaming. The *Third Empire* will be an empire of organization in the midst of European chaos. The occupation of the Ruhr and its consequences worked a change in the minds of men. It was the first thing that made the nation think. It opened up the possibility of liberation for a betrayed people. It seemed about to put an end to the "policy of fulfilment" which had been merely party politics disguised as foreign policy. It threw us back on our own power of decision. It restored our will. Parliamentism has become an institution of our public life, whose chief function would appear to be—in the name of the people—to enfeeble all political demands and all national passions. . . .

A suspicion broods over the country that the nation has suffered betrayal.

Not the betrayal of Versailles. That is sufficiently self-evident: the Fourteen Points became the four hundred and forty articles of the Peace Treaty, signed and sealed by the Founder of Peace [1] himself.

These other betrayals arose from the abuse of ideals for a selfish end. Our enemies saw that they could not do better for themselves than by persuading us to abandon, in the cause of peace, a war which we had not yet won; they saw that it would be best of all if they could induce some Germans themselves to persuade us into accepting these ideals. Whether we concentrate attention on the betrayers or the betrayed, we find ourselves in a peculiar atmosphere where high-falutin' principles are talked of: while a deal is being put through.

Our opponents exploited this peculiar atmosphere for their own advantage and to our injury. The atmosphere to which we allude is charged with a dangerous mental infection, the carriers of which enjoy an immunity which enables them to ruin their victim. It is the disintegrating atmosphere of liberalism, which spreads moral disease amongst nations, and ruins the nation whom it dominates. This deadly liberalism is not to be conceived as being the prerogative of any one political party. It originated in a general European party to which it owes its name, but it subsequently exercised its baneful influence on all parties and blurred the distinctions between them: it created the familiar figure of the professional party leader.

The principle of liberalism is to have no fixed principle and to contend that this is in itself a principle. . . .

Modern liberalism had its roots where the individual shook off the conventions of the middle ages. The liberal afterwards claimed to have freed himself from them. This freedom of his was an illusion.

The conventions of the middle ages were achievements, the achievements of

---

[1] President Wilson.

Church and State, the constructive Gothic achievements which for ten centuries prevented the disintegration of the ancient world. These were the mighty achievements which denoted what—on an immensely smaller scale and applied to far more trivial things—is now styled "progress." The men to whom these achievements were due, were rooted in these conventions, which also were of their creation. The conventions of the middle ages were the mighty foundations of mighty activities. No one prated of liberty, because everyone creatively possessed it: as will in action.

A disintegrating generation succeeded to this great inheritance. Humanism brought men the consciousness of human dignity. The renaissance imposed on individualism moderation, form, a classic attitude. The men of the renaissance drew from the literature of classical antiquity the forces which they felt they required as models. In the certain assurance that life must have a firm foundation if it was not to fall asunder, the men of the renaissance made a last effort at linking up with the past.

Men retain their creative power, however, only as long as the nations are creative. The nations were now developing a society which was divorced from the people. Monumental art was yielding its place to mere decoration. Recent centuries have achieved results in chemistry, mathematics, astronomy and most lately in sociology. But they have not produced men with the insight to see that all these are only partial glimpses into nature. They have made scientific research an end in itself, which is to turn an imaginary searchlight on to an imagined truth. This they have called enlightenment.

Man was committed to his reason, and reason was self-sufficient. Revelation was replaced by experiment. Men no longer perceived and felt; they only observed. They no longer drew dogmatic conclusions as faith had done. They no longer drew visionary conclusions like the mystic. They drew no idealist conclusions like the humanists; they drew critical conclusions: "there are no inborn ideas"—"there is no God"—"man is not free." Negatives all! "What discoveries!" they cried. They failed to see that they were tilting only against nomenclature, while the phenomena remained. They did not dream that all their speculations dealt only with the foreground of things while the background remained more and more incomprehensible. In the pride of his reason the man of enlightenment claimed the right to cast adrift from all conventions. He did so, reckless of the consequence. He committed life to a reason abandoned to her own devices. He knew what he was doing. Or did he not? He did the reasonable thing. Or not? We must ask of the liberals who as the party of enlightenment took over the justification of the age of reason. . . .

Marx had offered to men accustomed for tens of centuries to live for and by ideas, the lure of his materialist thought and his materialist conception of history. Movements, however, beget counter-movements. When Marxism was swamped in democratic chaos, Nietzsche with his conception of aristocracy came again to the fore.

Nietzsche foresaw an age of intense reflection that would set in after "the terrible earthquake." But he warned us that it would be an age of "new questions," eternal questions as he wished them heroically understood, conservative questions as we should rather call them. And amongst these questions he reckoned the proletarian question. Nietzsche was of course the enemy of everything that was amorphous mass and not subordination, order, organization. He felt himself to be the rehabilitation of rank amongst men in an age "of universal suffrage, that is to say where everyone has the right to sit in judgment on everybody and everything." He spoke of "the terrible consequences of equality" and said "our whole sociology recognizes no instinct but that of the herd: that is to say the sum total of cyphers where every cypher has an equal right, nay a duty, to be a cypher."

Nietzsche knew that democracy is only the superficial phenomenon of a dying society. The proletariat on the other hand was intimately related to the problem of the renewal of the human race from below. He said of the German people that they had no To-day, but only a Yesterday and a To-morrow. He saw that this future must somehow include the proletariat and he recognized that socialism (not the mere doctrine of socialism, but a vital socialism that is the expression of an uplift of humanity) was an elemental problem that could neither be evaded nor ignored.

There are two sides to socialism: on the negative side a complete levelling of human values would lead to their complete devaluation; on the positive side it might form the substructure of a new system of new values. Nietzsche saw first the negative side when he explained the nihilist movement (in which he included the socialistic) as the moral, ascetic legacy of Christianity; Christianity being for him "the will to deny life." On its other side, however, socialism is the will to accept life. Its demand is: a real place in the world for the proletariat—a material place of course, for as yet the proletariat knows nothing of ideals—a place in an economically-regulated world, since the proletariat as yet lives a merely animal existence. But Nietzsche's final thought is of a millennium. He envisages not the abrogation of law but its fulfilment; and he sees the state as the guarantor of law. "That the feeling for social values should for the moment predominate," he notes, "is natural and right: a substructure must be established which will ultimately make a stronger race possible. . . . The lower species must be conceived as the humble basis on which a higher species can take its stand and can live for its own tasks." . . .

It is intolerable that the nation should have permanently under its feet a proletariat that shares its speech, its history and its fate, without forming an integral part of it. The masses are quick to perceive that they cannot fend for themselves, that someone must take charge of them. But individuals rise from the masses and raise the masses with them. These new individuals—and still more their sons and their sons' sons—bring to the nation proletarian forces, at first materialist and amorphous enough, but which later, as they become incorporated into the life of the nation and absorb its spirit, are shaped and spiritualized. Such was Nietzsche's conception of the proletariat. He thought of its duties as well as its rights. He was thinking of human dignity when he adjured the working man to remember: "Workmen must learn to feel as soldiers do. A regular salary, but no wages." Or, as he expresses it elsewhere: "There must be no relation between pay and accomplishment. Each individual, according to his gifts, must be so placed that he does the best that it is in him to do." Himself an aristocrat, he gave a nobler interpretation to communism when he foresaw a future "in which the highest good and the highest happiness is common to the hearts of all," when he prophesied and extolled "a time when the word 'common' shall cease to carry a stigma." For equality—with the terrible levelling-down that it implies—Nietzsche thus substituted equality of rights on a higher, and more moral plane. He demanded that the proletarian should be given the right of entry into that kingdom of values which had hitherto been barred to him. He recognized only one measure for human values and he demanded that the proletarian also should attain it. . . .

The Third Party wills the Third Empire.

The Third Party stands for the continuity of history.

The Third Party is the party of all who wish to see Germany preserved for the German people. . . .

To-day we call this resolution not conservative but nationalist.

This nationalist will desires to conserve all that in Germany is worth conserving. It wills to preserve Germany for Germany's sake: and it knows what it wills.

The nationalist does not say, as the patriot does, that Germany is worth preserving because she is German. For him the nation is not an end in itself.

The nationalist's dreams are of the future. He is a conservative because he knows that there can be no future which has not its roots in the past. He is also a politician because he knows that past and future can only be secure if the nation is secure in the present.

But his thoughts range beyond the present. If we concentrate exclusively on the past, we might easily imagine that German history is closed. It is nowhere written that a people has a right to life eternal. For every people the hour at length strikes when they perish either by murder or by suicide. No more glorious end could be conceived for a great people than to perish in a World War where a world in arms overcame one single country. . . .

Our old, enduring mission is a continuation of the task of Austria, and Prussia and the Bismarckian Empire. We can only fulfil our task towards the east if we feel our rear protected in the West. Our most immediate and most German task is to make ourselves free. Fr. W. Foerster called Bismarck the greatest blunder in our history. But Bismarck, the founder of our Second Empire survives his work, and lives to be the founder also of Germany's Third Empire. . . .

Time and history have liquidated the state. Only the nation remains: only from the nation can a new mystery spring: the love of country.

The state that has fallen had made patriotism an item in our educational curriculum. In the cultural decay of the nineteenth century, however, more especially of the Wilhelmine period, education was degraded more and more to serve the ends of career, of social position, of economic advantage. Hence the inevitable failure of our patriotic education.

The crumbling state threatened to bury the nation in its ruins. But there has arisen a hope of salvation: a conservative-revolutionary movement of nationalism. It seeks to save the nation's life; it seeks to make good what had been omitted: to permit the nation to take a share in determining its own destinies.

Nationalism seeks to secure for the nation a democratic participation in which the proletarian shall also have a share.

The ideals of a nationalist movement differ as greatly from the ideals of a merely formal democracy as from the ideals of a class-conscious proletariat— above all in this: that it is a movement from above and not from below. Participation implies consciousness of the values which are to be shared. This consciousness can never be imparted unless a movement of ready acceptance comes from below; it must, however, be imparted from above.

The democrat, who always leans towards cosmopolitan points of view, and still more the proletarian who hankers after international trains of thought, both like to toy with the thought that there exists a neutral sphere in which the differences between the values of one people and of another vanish. The nationalist on the other hand holds that its own peculiar values are the most characteristic and precious possession of a nation, the very breath of its being. These give a nation form and personality; they cannot be transferred or interchanged.

In no country are the values so mysterious; so incomprehensible and uncomprehended as in Germany: so imperfectly-developed, fragmentary and yet complete; now most intimate confessions, now wild stormings of heaven; tender or powerful; earth-born or sublime; utterly realistic or entirely space-defying; to all appearance the expression of irreconcilables and incompatibles. But in no country are they more closely and fatefully bound up with the history of the nation: they are the countenance and the mirror and the tragic confession of the German who has created them amidst the contradictions of his history—not for himself, but for the nation.

In no country have these values tended so definitely towards a unity—a unity which we have never enjoyed since our First Empire, a unity which in our Second Empire we failed to achieve—

A unity which it must be the task of our Third Empire to establish. The antitheses of our history will remain, but it is reserved for our Third Empire to bring our values to their fulfilment.

We must have the strength to live in antitheses.

German history is full of fresh starts for new goals.

We never reached any goal. When we did reach one of the goals we had set ourselves, we reached it accidentally and with a bound and for a moment, only to fall back from it the more completely. But we pulled ourselves together and chose another goal—frequently an old one over again—and tried again with new strength. . . .

The greatness of a man is: to be something more than his mere self.

The greatness of a nation is: to be something greater than itself, to be able to communicate something of itself; to possess something that it can communicate.

In this ambition all great Germans fulfilled their tasks on earth, and left the issue to eternity. They often did not emphasise their German nationality in their work; yet it was there: enshrined, unintentionally, securely, self-evidently, and they could rest secure that its influence would not belie it. But if they were asked whence their strength came to which their work was owed, they forthwith confessed their German nationality. And when their people were in danger they rallied to them.

Side by side with this, however, there has always existed a fatal German weakness to fall under the spell of foreign modes of thought, to prefer foreign opinions to our own and to run off to salute the flag of every foreign philosophy. German ideologues talk to-day of a supernational mission by which they mean a renunciation of nationality—and boast of this betrayal as something characteristically German. These are the people who as revolutionaries confused the idea of political peace with the philosophical ideal of world peace. Even to-day, after the experiences of the Ruhr and the Rhine and Saar, there are German communists so hardened in their enlightened world-revolutionary doctrines that they will not admit that the class war idea is not only "national in form" (which Marx admitted), but also (which Marx repudiated as bourgeois) "national in content."

Engels spoke of the "spirit of servility" which still clung to us from the days of our many petty states, and he hoped that a revolution would cure us of it. He was thinking of this spirit of servility as something in our domestic politics: a spirit of vassalage which a free people no longer owed to princes who had forfeited their royalty. It would be a most desirable result of the Revolution if it could teach us to think of this spirit of servility in relation to our foreign politics: a false spirit of admiration which we now owe to no other nation—since ten of them stood against us and seven and twenty of them betrayed us. It would be good if this experience made us humbler towards ourselves and haughtier in our bearing to the foe.

We have had our warning—an experience unique in our history. We know that we can only live with our supernational mission if we as a nation are secure. All our values owe their origin to the German nation's fight for spiritual and intellectual self-preservation. If we had not maintained ourselves politically as a nation we should never have possessed anything to communicate to other nations; we should have been scattered and crushed at other nations' will. If our credulity is such as to let us still trust the European benevolence of our enemies our fate is sealed.

The thought of enduring peace is in very truth the thought of the Third Empire.

But it must be fought for, and the Empire must be maintained. . . .

German nationalism is the champion of the Final Empire: ever promised, never fulfilled.

It is the peculiar prerogative of the German people for which other peoples vie with us. In the World War the peoples fought against the Empire-for-the-sake-of-the-empire, the Empire-for-the-sake-of-world-hegemony, in which we claimed our very material share. Each of these nations wanted an empire of its own: a sphere and empire of Latin or Anglo-Saxon or Pan-Slav thought. They annihilated our material empire. They still tremble before its political shadow.

But they had to leave our Empire standing. There is only *One Empire*, as there is only *One Church*. Anything else that claims the title may be a state or a community or a sect. There exists only *the Empire*.

German nationalism fights for the possible Empire. The German nationalist to-day as a German remains for ever a mystic, as a politician he has turned sceptic.

He knows that nations can only realize the idea committed to their charge in proportion as they maintain themselves and assert themselves in history.

The German nationalist is in no danger of falling under the spell of ideology for the sake of ideology. He sees through the humbug of the fine words with which the peoples who conquered us ascribed a world mission to themselves. He knows that within the radius of these peoples' civilization, which they so complacently describe as western, humanity has not risen but has sunk.

In the midst of this sinking world, which is the victorious world of to-day, the German seeks his salvation. He seeks to preserve those imperishable values, which are imperishable in their own right. He seeks to secure their permanence in the world by recapturing the rank to which their defenders are entitled. At the same time he is fighting for the cause of Europe, for every European influence that radiates from Germany as the centre of Europe.

We are not thinking of the Europe of To-day which is too contemptible to have any value. We are thinking of the Europe of Yesterday and whatever thereof may be salvaged for To-morrow. We are thinking of the Germany of All Time, the Germany of a two-thousand-year past, the Germany of an eternal present which dwells in the spirit, but must be secured in reality and can only so be politically secured.

The ape and tiger in man are threatening. The shadow of Africa falls across Europe. It is our task to be guardians on the threshold of values.

BENITO MUSSOLINI

BENITO MUSSOLINI (1883–1945), the son of a blacksmith and of a school-teacher, was successively a schoolteacher, an unemployed laborer, the editor of the leading Socialist daily, the founder of the "anti-Socialist" Fascist party, the dictator of Italy, a key actor in Europe's dramatic parley at Munich, and a puppet of Hitler in the rapidly shrinking remainders of German-occupied Italy after 1943.

Before the First World War he had led the extreme revolutionary wing of Socialism to a split with the "reformists" who advocated some degree of collaboration with the government and the nation rather than the international class struggle. He was in turn expelled from the party when he advocated Italy's participation in the war against Germany and Austria, and he founded a new organization (Fasces of Revolutionary Action) early in 1915. In 1919 he established the ultranationalist National Fascist Party which waged a violent struggle against left-wing parties. While still proclaiming the "popular," "anti-bourgeois," and social reformist character of his movement, Mussolini was now deriving most of his support from conservatives. In October, 1922, his illegal military formations (Blackshirts) enabled him to capture power. Between 1922 and 1940 Mussolini built up what he called a "totalitarian" state, and led it to clamorous if superficial imperialistic triumphs in Africa in the face of the hesitant policy of the democracies. He crushed the organized opposition which had brought him close to defeat in 1923 and 1924, but he wasted away in the pursuit of megalomaniac ambitions the meager resources of his country, which had been on the way to recovery following the First World War. The Second World War bared the political and military weakness of the regime. After the Allied invasion of Sicily in 1943, Mussolini was ousted and imprisoned by the king whom he had made an emperor. Rescued by German troops, "Il Duce" saw his last regime crumble under the combined blows of Allied troops and Italian patriot forces. He himself was shot in April, 1945, by partisans.

The analysis of Fascist doctrine below, signed by Mussolini, was actually prepared by the Fascist philosopher, Giovanni Gentile. The article is the rationalization of an opportunistic movement which failed to penetrate the national life as deeply as did Hitlerism in Germany and Stalinism in Russia, for Mussolini turned from delusion to delusion and from system to system. He was cynical enough to fight for any cause that might lead him to power, and imaginative enough to believe in his idea of the moment. In both his "theories" and his achievements there was, beneath a flashy exterior of Fascist construction, poverty, disease, brutality, and death.

The first of the following selections is from Volume XIV of the *Enciclopedia Italiana* (1932); the second is from a speech delivered in 1933.

THE POLITICAL AND SOCIAL DOCTRINE OF FASCISM

WHEN, in the now distant March of 1919, I summoned a meeting at Milan through the columns of the *Popolo d'Italia* of the surviving members of the Interventionist Party who had themselves been in action, and who had followed me since the creation of the Fascist Revolutionary Party (which took place in the January of 1915), I had no specific doctrinal attitude in my mind. I had a living experience of one doctrine only—that of Socialism, from 1903–4 to the winter of 1914—that is to say, about a decade: and from Socialism itself, even though I had taken part in the movement first as a member of the rank and file and then later as a leader, yet I had no experience of its doctrine in practice. My own doctrine, even in this period, had always been a doctrine of action. A unanimous, universally accepted theory of Socialism did not exist after 1905, when the revisionist movement began in Germany under the leadership of Bernstein, while under pressure of the tendencies of the time, a Left Revolutionary movement also appeared, which though never getting further than talk in Italy, in Russian Socialistic circles laid the foundations of Bolshevism. Reformation, Revolution, Centralization—already the echoes of these terms are spent—while in the great stream of Fascism are to be found ideas which began with Sorel, Péguy, with Lagardelle in the "Mouvement Socialiste," and with the Italian trades-union movement which throughout the period 1904–14 was sounding a new note in Italian Socialist circles (already weakened by the betrayal of Giolitti) through Olivetti's *Pagine Libre,* Orano's *La Lupa,* and Enrico Leone's *Divenire Sociale.*

After the War, in 1919, Socialism was already dead as a doctrine: it existed only as a hatred. There remained to it only one possibility of action, especially in Italy, reprisals against those who had desired the War and who must now be made to "expiate" its results. The *Popolo d'Italia* was then given the subtitle of "The newspaper of ex-service men and producers," and the word producers was already the expression of a mental attitude. Fascism was not the nursling of a doctrine worked out beforehand with detailed elaboration; it was born of the need for action and it was itself from the beginning practical rather than theoretical; it was not merely another political party but, even in the first two years, in opposition to all political parties as such, and itself a living movement. The name which I then gave to the organization fixed its character. And yet, if one were to re-read, in the now dusty columns of that date, the report of the meeting in which the *Fasci Italiani di combattimento* [1]

---

[1] [*Italian combatant groups.*]

were constituted, one would there find no ordered expression of doctrine, but a series of aphorisms, anticipations, and aspirations which, when refined by time from the original ore, were destined after some years to develop into an ordered series of doctrinal concepts, forming the Fascist political doctrine—different from all others either of the past or the present day.

"If the bourgeoisie," I said then, "think that they will find lightning-conductors in us, they are the more deceived; we must start work at once. . . . We want to accustom the working-class to real and effectual leadership, and also to convince them that it is no easy thing to direct an industry or a commercial enterprise successfully. . . . We shall combat every retrograde idea, technical or spiritual. . . . When the succession to the seat of government is open, we must not be unwilling to fight for it. We must make haste; when the present régime breaks down, we must be ready at once to take its place. It is we who have the right to the succession, because it was we who forced the country into the War, and led her to victory. The present method of political representation cannot suffice, we must have a representation direct from the individuals concerned. It may be objected against this program that it is a return to the conception of the corporation, but that is no matter. . . . Therefore, I desire that this assembly shall accept the revindication of national trades-unionism from the economic point of view." . . .

And above all, Fascism, the more it considers and observes the future and the development of humanity quite apart from political considerations of the moment, believes neither in the possibility nor the utility of perpetual peace. It thus repudiates the doctrine of Pacifism—born of a renunciation of the struggle and an act of cowardice in the face of sacrifice. War alone brings up to its highest tension all human energy and puts the stamp of nobility upon the peoples who have the courage to meet it. All other trials are substitutes, which never really put men into the position where they have to make the great decision—the alternative of life or death. Thus a doctrine which is founded upon this harmful postulate of peace is hostile to Fascism. And thus hostile to the spirit of Fascism, though accepted for what use they can be in dealing with particular political situations, are all the international leagues and societies which, as history will show, can be scattered to the winds when once strong national feeling is aroused by any motive—sentimental, ideal, or practical. . . .

Such a conception of life makes Fascism the complete opposite of that doctrine, the base of so-called scientific and Marxian Socialism, the materialist conception of history; according to which the history of human civilization can be explained simply through the conflict of interests among the various social groups and by the change and development in the means and instruments of production. That the changes in the economic field—new discoveries of raw materials, new methods of working them, and the inventions of science—have their importance no one can deny; but that these factors are sufficient to explain the history of humanity excluding all others is an absurd delusion. Fascism, now and always, believes in holiness and in heroism; that is to say, in actions influenced by no economic motive, direct or indirect. And if the economic conception of history be denied, according to which theory men are no more than puppets, carried to and fro by the waves of chance, while the real directing forces are quite out of their control, it follows that the existence of an unchangeable and unchanging class-war is also denied— the natural progeny of the economic conception of history. And above all Fascism denies that class-war can be the preponderant force in the transformation of society. These two fundamental concepts of Socialism being thus refuted, nothing is left of it but the sentimental aspiration—as old as humanity itself—towards a social convention in which the sorrows and sufferings of the humblest shall be alleviated. But here again Fascism repudiates the conception of "economic" happiness, to be realized by Socialism and, as it were, at a given moment in economic evolution to assure to everyone the maximum of well-being. Fascism denies the materialist conception of happiness as a possibility, and abandons it to its inventors, the economists of the first half of the nineteenth century: that is to say, Fascism denies the validity of the equation, well-being–happiness, which would reduce men to the level of animals, caring for one thing only—to be fat and well-fed—and would thus degrade humanity to a purely physical existence.

After Socialism, Fascism combats the whole complex system of democratic ideology, and repudiates it, whether in its theoretical premises or in its practical application. Fascism denies that the majority, by the simple fact that it is a majority, can direct human society; it denies that numbers alone can govern by means of a periodical consultation, and it affirms the immutable, beneficial, and fruitful inequality of mankind, which can never be permanently leveled through the mere operation of a mechanical process such as universal suffrage. The democratic régime may be defined as from time to time giving the people the illusion of sovereignty, while the real effective sovereignty lies in the hands of other concealed and irresponsible forces. Democracy is a régime nominally without a king, but it is ruled by many kings—more absolute, tyrannical, and ruinous than one sole king, even though a tyrant. This explains why Fascism, having first in 1922 (for reasons of expediency) assumed an attitude tending towards republicanism, renounced this point of

view before the march to Rome; being convinced that the question of political form is not today of prime importance, and after having studied the examples of monarchies and republics past and present reached the conclusion
that monarchy or republicanism are not to be judged, as it were, by an absolute standard; but that they represent forms in which the evolution—political,
historical, traditional, or psychological—of a particular country has expressed
itself. . . .

Fascism has taken up an attitude of complete opposition to the doctrines of
Liberalism, both in the political field and the field of economics. There should
be no undue exaggeration (simply with the object of immediate success in
controversy) of the importance of Liberalism in the last century, nor should
what was but one among many theories which appeared in that period be put
forward as a religion for humanity for all time, present and to come. Liberalism only flourished for half a century. . . .

Fascism uses in its construction whatever elements in the Liberal, Social, or
Democratic doctrines still have a living value; it maintains what may be
called the certainties which we owe to history, but it rejects all the rest—
that is to say, the conception that there can be any doctrine of unquestioned
efficacy for all times and all peoples. Given that the nineteenth century was
the century of Socialism, of Liberalism, and of Democracy, it does not necessarily follow that the twentieth century must also be a century of Socialism,
Liberalism, and Democracy: political doctrines pass, but humanity remains;
and it may rather be expected that this will be a century of authority, a century of the Left, a century of Fascism. For if the nineteenth century was a
century of individualism (Liberalism always signifying individualism) it may
be expected that this will be the century of collectivism, and hence the century
of the State. . . .

In 1929, at the first five-yearly assembly of the Fascist régime, I said:

"For us Fascists, the State is not merely a guardian, preoccupied solely with
the duty of assuring the personal safety of the citizens; nor is it an organization with purely material aims, such as to guarantee a certain level of well-
being and peaceful conditions of life; for a mere council of administration
would be sufficient to realize such objects. Nor is it a purely political creation,
divorced from all contact with the complex material reality which makes up
the life of the individual and the life of the people as a whole. The State, as
conceived of and as created by Fascism, is a spiritual and moral fact in itself,
since its political, juridical, and economic organization of the nation is a
concrete thing: and such an organization must be in its origins and development a manifestation of the spirit. The State is the guarantor of security both

internal and external, but it is also the custodian and transmitter of the spirit of the people, as it has grown up through the centuries in language, in customs, and in faith. And the State is not only a living reality of the present, it is also linked with the past and above all with the future, and thus transcending the brief limits of individual life, it represents the immanent spirit of the nation. The forms in which States express themselves may change, but the necessity for such forms is eternal. It is the State which educates its citizens in civic virtue, gives them a consciousness of their mission and welds them into unity; harmonizing their various interests through justice, and transmitting to future generations the mental conquests of science, of art, of law and the solidarity of humanity. It leads men from primitive tribal life to that highest expression of human power which is Empire: it links up through the centuries the names of those of its members who have died for its existence and in obedience to its laws, it holds up the memory of the leaders who have increased its territory and the geniuses who have illumined it with glory as an example to be followed by future generations. When the conception of the State declines, and disunifying and centrifugal tendencies prevail, whether of individuals or of particular groups, the nations where such phenomena appear are in their decline." From 1929 until today, evolution, both political and economic, has everywhere gone to prove the validity of these doctrinal premises. . . .

For Fascism, the growth of empire, that is to say the expansion of the nation, is an essential manifestation of vitality, and its opposite a sign of decadence. Peoples which are rising, or rising again after a period of decadence, are always imperialist; any renunciation is a sign of decay and of death. Fascism is the doctrine best adapted to represent the tendencies and the aspirations of a people, like the people of Italy, who are rising again after many centuries of abasement and foreign servitude. But empire demands discipline, the coordination of all forces and a deeply felt sense of duty and sacrifice: this fact explains many aspects of the practical working of the régime, the character of many forces in the State, and the necessarily severe measures which must be taken against those who would oppose this spontaneous and inevitable movement of Italy in the twentieth century, and would oppose it by recalling the outworn ideology of the nineteenth century—repudiated wheresoever there has been the courage to undertake great experiments of social and political transformation: for never before has the nation stood more in need of authority, of direction, and of order. If every age has its own characteristic doctrine, there are a thousand signs which point to Fascism as the characteristic doctrine of our time. For if a doctrine must be a living thing, this is proved by the fact that Fascism has created a living faith; and that this faith is very powerful in the minds of men, is demonstrated by those who have suffered and died for it.

Fascism has henceforth in the world the universality of all those doctrines which, in realizing themselves, have represented a stage in the history of the human spirit.

THE CORPORATE STATE

ON OCTOBER 16 of the Tenth Year, before the thousands of Party officers gathered in the Piazza Venezia at Rome for the celebration of the tenth anniversary, I asked: Is this crisis that has tortured us for four years—we have now lived through one month of the fifth—is this crisis *in* our system or *of* it? A grave question, a question which can not be answered immediately. To answer it, it is necessary to reflect, to reflect long and to arm oneself with facts. Today I reply: The crisis has penetrated the system so profoundly that it has become a crisis *of* the system. It is no longer a mere lesion, it is a constitutional disease. Today we can assert that the capitalistic method of production has been superseded, and with it the theory of liberal economics that illustrated and defended it.

I want to trace for you in broad outline the history of capitalism in the last century, which might be called the century of capitalism. But first of all, what is capitalism? We do not need to confuse capitalism and the bourgeoisie. The bourgeoisie is something else. It is a mode of being that may be great or petty, heroic or philistine. Capitalism, on the contrary, is a particular type of production, it is a system of industrial production. In its perfect expression capitalism is a system of mass production for mass consumption, by mass finances, that is, by issuing incorporated capital, both national and international. Capitalism is therefore industrial and has not shown great importance in the field of agriculture.

I would distinguish three periods in the history of capitalism: the dynamic period, the static period, and the decadent period. The dynamic period extends from 1830 to 1870. It coincides with the introduction of the power-loom and the appearance of the steam-engine, the rise of the factory. The factory is the typical manifestation of industrial capitalism. This is the period of big margins, and hence the law of free competition and the struggle of all against all had full play. The fallen and the dead are picked up by the Red Cross. In this period, too, there are crises, but they are clinical crises, not long or universal. . . .

What took place in America we should perhaps not call heroic. That is a word we must reserve for affairs of a strictly military nature; but the conquest of the Far West was certainly difficult and exacting and had the risks and the losses of a great conquest.

This dynamic period of capitalism lasted from the appearance of the steam-engine to the opening of the Suez Canal. Forty years. During these forty years the State was an onlooker, took no part, and the theorists of liberalism said to it: You have only one duty—to see that your existence should not even be suspected in the realm of economics. The better the government, the less it concerns itself with the problems of the economic system. Hence the economic system in all its manifestations was limited only by the penal code and the code of commerce.

But after 1870 this period changes. No longer the struggle for existence, free competition, survival of the strongest. We notice the first symptoms of weariness and decline in the capitalistic world. The era of cartels, of syndicates, of consortiums, of "trusts." . . .

Having arrived at this point, super-capitalism draws its inspiration and its justification from a Utopian dream, the dream of unlimited consumption. The ideal of super-capitalism would be the standardization of human life from the cradle to the grave. Super-capitalism would like to have all babies born uniform in size so that cradles could be standardized; they want all children to like the same toys; they want all men to wear the same livery, all to read the same books, all to have the same tastes in the movies, all, in short, to become a so-called utilitarian machine. This is not a caprice, but it is the logic of events, for only in this way can super-capitalism project its plans. When did capitalistic enterprise cease to be an economic fact? When its dimensions made of it a social fact.

And this is precisely the moment in which capitalistic enterprise, finding itself in difficulty, pitched itself straight into the arms of the State, and this is the moment in which State intervention was born and since when it has become more and more necessary. And those who had ignored it, now sought it frantically. We have reached the point where if in all the nations of Europe the State should go to sleep for twenty-four hours, that interval would be enough to precipitate disaster. There is no longer any economic field in which the State can not interfere. If, purely hypothetically, we wanted to give way to this current capitalism, we should fly into State capitalism, which is nothing else but State socialism up-side-down; we should arrive in one way or another at the exercise of national economy!

This is the crisis of the capitalistic system taken in its universal significance. But for us there is a specific crisis which we face particularly as Italians and Europeans. It is a European crisis, typically European. Europe is no longer the continent that directs human civilization. To this dramatic conclusion men must come who think for themselves and for others. There was a time when Europe was the political, spiritual, and economic leader of the world. Politically dominant by means of her political institutions. Spiritually by means of all that the spirit of Europe had produced throughout the centuries. Economically because it was the only continent completely industrialized. But, across the Atlantic, a great industrial and capitalistic enterprise has developed. In the Far East is Japan which, having made a contact with Europe through the war of 1905, is encroaching on the big markets of the West. Here is the political problem. I talk of politics here because this Assembly, too, is strictly political. Europe can still try to regain the leadership of universal civilization if she finds a "minimum" of political unity. We must carry on as heretofore. Europe's political goal can not be achieved unless certain grave injustices are first rectified.

We have come to an extremely serious point in this situation: the League of Nations has lost everything that gave it political significance or historical importance. Even the country that invented it has failed to join it. Russia, the United States, Japan, and Germany are absent. This League of Nations was founded on one of those principles that sound very beautiful at first but when considered and analyzed and taken apart reveal their absurdity. What other diplomatic means exist that can re-establish contacts among the nations? Locarno? Locarno is another matter. Locarno has nothing to do with disarmament; that is no way out. A great silence has reigned of late concerning the Four Power Pact. Nobody talks of it, but everybody thinks about it. It is precisely for this reason that we do not intend to start over again or to speed up a situation that is bound to mature logically and inevitably.

Let us ask ourselves now: Is Italy a capitalistic nation? You have never asked this question? If by capitalism one means that totality of manners, customs, and technical progress now common to all the nations, it can be said that Italy, too, is capitalistic. But if we go into the subject and examine the situation from a statistical point of view, that is, from the mass of different economic groups of our population, we have the facts in the case which will permit us to say that Italy is not a capitalistic nation in the current meaning of that word.

April 21, 1931 there were 2,943,000 farmers on their own land; 858,000 tenant-farmers. There were 1,631,000 share-croppers; and the other farmers, farm-hands, and agricultural day-laborers numbered 2,475,000. The total of the population directly and immediately dependent on agriculture is 7,900,000. There are 523,000 industrialists; 841,000 merchants; 724,000 artisans, dependent or independent; 4,283,000 wage earners; 849,000 domestic servants and porters; the armed forces of the state number 541,000, including, of course, the police force. In the professions and liberal arts there are 553,000; public and private office employees, 905,000. The total in this and the above groups is 17,000,000. There are few landed proprietors and large landowners in Italy —201,000; 1,945,000 students; 11,244,000 housewives. Then there is the item called other non-professional occupations—1,295,000—an item which can be interpreted in various ways.

You see at once from this picture that the economic life of Italy is varied, complex, and can not be defined according to one pattern. Furthermore the industrialists, who make up the imposing number of 523,000, almost all operate either small or medium-sized concerns. The small concern may go from a minimum of 50 employees to a maximum of 500. From 500 to five or six thousand is the medium-sized industry; above that is big industry, and only here and there does Italian industry overflow into super-capitalism.

This survey demonstrates also how wrong Karl Marx was, who, following his own apocalyptic schemes, pretended that human society could be divided into two classes neatly distinguished from each other and eternally irreconcilable. Italy, in my opinion, must remain a nation of mixed economy, with a strong agriculture, which is the base of all, inasmuch as it is true that what little revival of industry there has been of late has been due, according to the unanimous opinion of those who have studied the matter, to the respectable yields of agriculture in these years. A healthy small or medium sized industry, a bank that does not engage in speculation, a commerce that performs its irreplaceable duty of distributing merchandise to consumers rapidly and reasonably.

In my statements presented last evening, the Corporation is defined as we understand it and intend to create it, and its purposes too are defined. I said the Corporation was created in view of the development of the wealth, the political power, and the welfare of the Italian people. These three elements interact. Political power creates wealth, and wealth in its turn reinforces political power.

I want to call your attention to what I said was the aim of the Corporation, the welfare of the Italian people. It is necessary that at any given time these institutions which we have created should be felt and recognized directly by the masses as instruments through which they can raise their standard of living. It is necessary that at a given time the workman and the farm-laborer should be able to say to himself: if today my status is improved, I owe it to the institutions which the Fascist Revolution has created. In all societies there is inevitable poverty. There is a group of persons who live on the margin of society; special institutions deal with them. However, that which should trouble us is the poverty of strong and honest men who are earnestly looking for work in vain. We must see to it that Italian workmen, in whom we are interested as Italians, workmen, and Fascists, feel that we are not creating institutions only to give form to our doctrines, but we are creating institutions that must sometime show positive, concrete, practical, and tangible results. . . .

On January 13, 1923, when the Grand Council was created, superficial thinkers may have thought, only one more institute. On the contrary. On that day we buried political liberalism. With the Militia, the armed guard of the Party and the Revolution, with the establishment of the Grand Council, the supreme organ of the Revolution, we dealt the death-blow to the whole theory and practice of liberalism; we definitely set out on the road of revolution.

Today we are burying economic liberalism. The corporation will function on economic ground as the Grand Council and the Militia function on political ground. Corporatism is economics disciplined and therefore controlled, for discipline without control is unthinkable. Corporatism supersedes socialism and supersedes liberalism; it creates a new synthesis.

One fact is symptomatic—a fact we have perhaps thought too little about: that the decline of capitalism coincides with the decline of socialism. All the socialist parties in Europe are in fragments. I am not speaking only of Italy and Germany, but also of the other countries. Evidently these two phenomena —I do not claim that they are necessarily connected logically—were nevertheless historically simultaneous. This is why the corporate economy takes its rise at the very juncture in history when those two concurrent phenomena, capitalism and socialism, have given all they can give. From each we inherit what was vital in it. We have rejected the theory of the economic man, the liberal theory, and we go up in the air every time we hear anybody talk of labor as a commodity. The economic man does not exist; the whole man exists, being political, economic, and religious, saint and soldier. Today we are taking a decisive new step in the path of the Revolution. . . .

There is no doubt that, given the general crisis of capitalism, some of the solutions of Corporatism will become imperative everywhere. But to carry on a complete, full, integral, revolutionary Corporatism three conditions are necessary. A single party which flanks economic discipline with political discipline and which is over and above conflicting interests, binding all together in a common faith. This is not enough. After a single party you have to have a totalitarian state, that is, a state that absorbs within itself, in order to transform and invigorate them, all the energy, all the interests, all the hopes of a people. This is still not enough. The third and last and most important condition: there must be a time of the highest moral vigor.

We live in this time of high moral vigor. This is why, step by step, we give strength and consistency to all our dreams, translating all our doctrine into fact. How can it be denied that this our Fascist period is one of the highest moral vigor? Nobody can deny it. These are the times when arms have been crowned with victory, when human institutions are being regenerated, when lands are being redeemed and cities founded.

R. H. TAWNEY

AMONG RECENT English historians few rank higher than Richard Henry Tawney (1880–). Best known perhaps for his *Religion and the Rise of Capitalism* (1926), Tawney has been a lifelong socialist. The sources of his criticism of social privilege, however, are English and evangelical, rather than continental and Marxist. With an intellectual lineage stretching back three centuries to the radical "Levellers" of the Puritan revolution, Tawney has been as loyal to democratic government as he has been antagonistic to what he called the "religion of inequality." He has been active in the practical work of building English socialism while making his reputation in the world of scholarship. Government investigations, adult education, and Labour party activities have all enlisted his aid.

Tawney's early work, *The Agrarian Problem in the Sixteenth Century* (1912), influenced the views of two generations of historians on the origins of that important English social group, the gentry. Even more influential and more revealing of Tawney's presuppositions was *Religion and the Rise of Capitalism* in which Tawney, like Max Weber, tried to analyze the influence of early Protestant ideals on an intensified capitalism. Despite his socialism, Tawney refused to give paramount or exclusive importance to economic motives as a source of religious change. In his view, it was Calvinism or Puritanism that stimulated a rising capitalist spirit rather than capitalist accumulation that caused men to revolt against Catholicism.

In 1920 Tawney published his influential and deeply felt indictment of *The Acquisitive Society*. It is in the English tradition of Christian and humanitarian criticism of industrial society but it is not marred by a fusty medievalism or an elitist psychology. Tawney asked that the enjoyment of property and the direction of industry be regarded not as absolute rights but as "functions" to be judged by successful contributions to social well-being. Although he believed that public ownership of major industries was probably unavoidable if a system of rewards commensurate with efforts was to work, his theory did not logically preclude private ownership, so long as it proved socially responsible.

This selection comes from *The Acquisitive Society* (London: G. Bell and Sons, 1920).

THE ACQUISITIVE SOCIETY

IX. THE NEW CONDITION OF EFFICIENCY

It is not only for the sake of the producers, on whom the old industrial order weighed most heavily, that a new industrial order is needed. It is needed for the sake of the consumers, because the ability on which the old industrial order prided itself most and which is flaunted most as an argument against change, the ability to serve them effectively, is itself visibly breaking down. It is breaking down at what was always its most vulnerable point, the control of the human beings whom, with characteristic indifference to all but their economic significance, it distilled for its own purposes into an abstraction called "Labour." The first symptom of economic collapses has usually been in the past—the failure of customary stimuli to evoke their customary response in human effort.

(a) *The Passing of Authority from the Capitalist.* Till that failure is recognized and industry reorganized so that new stimuli may have free play, the collapse will not correct itself, but, doubtless with spasmodic revivals and flickering energy, will continue and accelerate. The cause of it is simple. It is that those whose business it is to direct economic activity are increasingly incapable of directing the men upon whom economic activity depends. The fault is not that of individuals, but of a system, of Industrialism itself. During the greater part of the nineteenth century industry was driven by two forces, hunger and fear, and the employer commanded them both. He could grant or withold employment as he pleased. If men revolted against his terms he could dismiss them, and, if they were dismissed, what confronted them was starvation or the workhouse. Authority was centralized; its instruments were passive; the one thing which they dreaded was unemployment. And since they could neither prevent its occurrence nor do more than a little to mitigate its horrors when it occurred, they submitted to a discipline which they could not resist, and industry pursued its course through their passive acquiescence in a power which could crush them individually if they attempted to oppose it.

That system might be lauded as efficient, or denounced as inhuman. But, at least, as its admirers were never tired of pointing out, it worked. And, like the Prussian State, which alike in its virtues and deficiencies it not a little resembled, as long as it worked it survived denunciations of its methods, as a strong man will throw off a disease. But to-day it is ceasing to have even the qualities of its defects. It is ceasing to be efficient. It no longer secures the ever-increasing output of wealth which it offered in its golden prime, and which enabled it to silence criticism by an imposing spectacle of material success. Though it still works, it works unevenly, amid constant friction and jolts and stoppages, without the confidence of the public and without full confidence even in itself. It is a tyrant who must intrigue and cajole where formerly he commanded, a gaoler who, if not yet deprived of the whip, dare only administer moderate chastisement, and who, though he still protests that he alone can keep the treadmill moving and get the corn ground, is compelled to surrender so much of his authority as to make it questionable whether he is worth his keep.

For the instruments through which Capitalism exercised discipline are one by one being taken from it. It cannot pay what wages it likes or work what hours it likes. For several years it has been obliged to accept the control of prices and profits. In well-organized industries the power of arbitrary dismissal, the very center of its authority, is being shaken, because men will no longer tolerate a system which makes their livelihood dependent on the caprices of an individual. In all industries alike the time is not far distant when the dread of starvation can no longer be used to cow dissatisfied workers into submission, because the public will no longer allow involuntary unemployment to result in starvation.

The last point is of crucial importance. It is the control of the workers' will through the control of his livelihood which has been in the past the master weapon of economic tyranny. Both its champions and its opponents know it. In 1919, when the world of Labour was in motion, there were some employers who looked to the inevitable recurrence of bad trade "to teach them reason." Now that bad trade has come, and with it the misery of unemployment, there are some employers who say that the immediate loss will be more than counterbalanced if the lesson which the older generation had learned, and which was half forgotten during the war, is impressed upon the young men who grew up between 1914 and 1920. Let them once realise what it is not to be wanted, and, except for an occasional outburst, they will come to heel for the rest of their lives.

The calculation is superficial, since the fear of unemployment is one potent cause of industrial *malaise* and of the slackening of production. The building operative whose job is drawing towards its close, and who in the past has had to tramp the streets for months in search of another, may think that he has a duty to his employer, but he reflects that he has a prior duty to his wife and children. So he "makes the job last"; and he is right. As an expedient for the moment, however, unemployment may be an effective weapon—providing that the young men will follow their fathers' example, and treat it as the act of God, not as a disease accompanying a particular type of industrial organization. But will they? It is too early yet to answer that question. It seems clear, however, that the whole repulsive body of assumptions, which made it seem natural to use the mass of workers as instruments to be picked up when there was work and to be laid aside when there was not, is finding increasing difficulty in meeting the criticism directed against it. In the impressive words of Lord Shaw, "If men were merely the spare parts of an industrial machine, this callous reckoning might be appropriate; but Society will not much longer tolerate employment of human beings on those lines."

What the trade unions are beginning to demand, and what they are likely to demand with increasing insistence in the future, is that their members shall be treated as "on the strength" of their respective industries, and that, if an industry requires workers when it is busy, it shall accumulate in good times the reserves needed to maintain those workers when it is slack. The Building Guilds have adopted that principle. The Committee of employers and trade unionists presided over by Mr. Foster recommended a scheme which was, in essence, the same. The striking programme submitted by Mr. Bevin to the Transport Workers' Federation proposes that the whole of the 125,000 workers to be registered as members of the industry shall be guaranteed a regular wage of £4 a week throughout the year, provided they present themselves for employment, and that the cost shall be met by a levy of 4d. a ton on imports and exports. The provisions for "contracting out" under the Unemployment Insurance Act, unsatisfactory as they are, are a step towards the adoption of schemes which will treat the payment of regular wages to the workers in each industry, work or play, as part of the normal "costs" which the return to the industry must cover. Now that the principle of maintenance has been recognized, however inadequately, by legislation, its application is likely to be extended from the exiguous benefit at present provided to the payment of a sum which will, in effect, be a standing wage, payable in bad times as in good, to all workers normally engaged in each industry.

In proportion as that result is achieved, Capitalism will be unable to appeal to the terror of unemployment which has been in the past its most powerful instrument of economic discipline. And its prestige will vanish with its power. Indeed it is vanishing already. For if Capitalism is losing its control of men's bodies, still more has it lost its command of their minds. The product of a civilization which regarded "the poor" as the instruments, at worst of the luxuries, at best of the virtues, of the rich, its psychological foundation fifty years ago was an ignorance in the mass of mankind which led them to reverence as wisdom the very follies of their masters, and an almost animal incapacity for responsibility. Education and experience have destroyed the passivity which was the condition of the perpetuation of industrial government in the hands of an oligarchy of private capitalists. The workman of to-day has as little belief in the intellectual superiority of many of those who direct industry as he has in the morality of the system. It appears to him to be not only oppressive, but wasteful, unintelligent, and inefficient. In the light of his own experience in the factory and the mine, he regards the claim of the capitalist to be the self-appointed guardian of public interests as a piece of sanctimonious hypocrisy. For he sees every day that efficiency is sacrificed to short-sighted financial interests; and while as a man he is outraged by the inhumanity of the industrial order, as a professional who knows the difference between good work and bad he has a growing contempt at once for its misplaced parsimony and its misplaced extravagance, for the whole apparatus of adulteration, advertisement and quackery which seems inseparable from the pursuit of profit as the main standard of industrial success.

So, Capitalism no longer secures strenuous work by fear, for it is ceasing to be formidable. And it cannot secure it by respect, for it has ceased to be respected. And the very victories by which it seeks to reassert its waning prestige are more disastrous than defeats. Employers may congratulate themselves that they have maintained intact their right to freedom of management, or opposed successfully a demand for public ownership, or broken a movement for higher wages and shorter hours. But what is success in a trade dispute or in a political struggle is often a defeat in the workshop. The workmen may have lost, but it does not follow that their employers, still less than the public, which is principally composed of workmen, have won.

For the object of industry is to produce goods, and to produce them at the lowest cost in human effort. But there is no alchemy which will secure efficient production from the resentment or distrust of men who feel contempt for the order under which they work. It is a commonplace that credit is the foundation of industry. But credit is a matter of psychology, and the workman has his psychology as well as the capitalist. If confidence is necessary to the investment of capital, confidence is not less necessary to the effective performance of labour by men whose sole livelihood depends on it. If they are not yet strong enough to impose their will, they are strong enough to resist when their masters would impose theirs. They may work rather than strike. But they will work to escape dismissal, not for the greater glory of a system in which they do not believe; and if they are dismissed, those who take their place will do the same.

That this is one cause of a low output has been stated both by employers and workers in the building industry, and by the representatives of the miners before the Coal Commission. It was reiterated with impressive emphasis by Mr. Justice Sankey. Nor is it seriously contested by employers themselves. What else, indeed, do their repeated denunciations of "restriction of output" mean, except that they have failed to organize industry so as to secure the efficient service which it is their special function to provide? Nor is it appropriate to the situation to indulge in full-blooded denunciations of the "selfishness" of the working classes. "To draw an indictment against a whole nation" is a procedure which is as impossible in industry as it is in politics. Institutions must be adapted to human nature, not human nature to institutions. If the effect of the industrial system is such that a large and increasing number of men and women find that it offers them no adequate motive for economic effort, it is mere pedantry to denounce men and women instead of amending the system.

Thus the time has come when absolutism in industry may still win battles, but loses the campaign, and loses it on the very ground of economic efficiency which was of its own selection. In the period of transition, while economic activity is distracted by the struggle between those who have the name and habit of power, but no longer the full reality of it, and those who are daily winning more of the reality of power but are not yet its recognized repositories, it is the consumer who suffers. He has neither the service of docile obedience, nor the service of intelligent co-operation. For slavery will work—as long as the slaves will let it; and freedom will work when men have learned to be free; but what will not work is a combination of the two. So the public goes short of coal, not only because of the technical deficiencies of the system under which it is raised and distributed, but because the system itself has lost its driving force—because the mine owners can no longer persuade the miners into producing more dividends for themselves and more royalties for the owners of minerals, while the public cannot appeal to them to put their whole power into serving itself, because it has chosen that they should be the servants, not of itself, but of shareholders.

And this dilemma is not, as some suppose, temporary, the aftermath of war, or peculiar to the coal industry, as though the miners alone were the children of sin which in the last two years they have been described to be. It is permanent; it has spread far; and, as sleeping spirits are stirred into life by education and one industry after another develops a strong corporate consciousness, it will spread further. Nor will it be resolved by lamentations or menaces or denunciations of leaders whose only significance is that they say openly what plain men feel privately. For the matter at bottom is one of psychology. What has happened is that the motives on which the industrial system relied for several generations to secure efficiency, secure it no longer. And it is as impossible to restore them, to revive by mere exhortation the complex of hopes and fears and ignorance and patient credulity and passive acquiescence, which together made men, fifty years ago, plastic instruments in the hands of industrialism, as to restore innocence to any others of those who have eaten of the tree of knowledge.

The ideal of some intelligent and respectable business men, the restoration of the golden sixties, when workmen were docile and confiding, and trade unions were still half illegal, and foreign competition meant English competition in foreign countries, and prices were rising a little and not rising too much, is the one Utopia which can never be realized. The King may walk naked as long as his courtiers protest that he is clad; but when a child or a fool has broken the spell a tailor is more important than all their admiration. If the public, which suffers from the slackening of economic activity, desires to end its *malaise,* it will not laud as admirable and all-sufficient the operation of motives which are plainly ceasing to move. It will seek to liberate new motives and to enlist them in its service. It will endeavour to find an alternative to incentives which were always degrading, to those who used them as much as to those upon whom they were used, and which now are adequate incentives no longer. And the alternative to the discipline which Capitalism exercised through its instruments of unemployment and starvation is the self-discipline of responsibility and professional pride. . . .

The truth is that we ought radically to revise the presuppositions as to human motives on which current presentations of economic theory are ordinarily founded, and in terms of which the discussion of economic questions is usually carried on. The assumption that the stimulus of imminent personal want is either the only spur, or a sufficient spur, to productive effort is a relic of a crude psychology which has little warrant either in past history or in present experience. It derives what plausibility it possesses from a confusion between work in the sense of the lowest *quantum* of activity needed to escape actual starvation, and the work which is given, irrespective of the fact that elementary wants may already have been satisfied, through the natural disposition of ordinary men to maintain, and of extraordinary men to improve upon, the level of exertion accepted as reasonable by the public opinion of the group of which they are members. It is the old difference, forgotten by society as often as it is learned, between the labour of the free man and that of the slave. Economic fear may secure the minimum effort needed to escape economic penalties. What, however, has made progress possible in the past, and what, it may be suggested, matters to the world to-day, is not the bare minimum which is required to avoid actual want, but the capacity of men to bring to bear upon their tasks a degree of energy which, while it can be stimulated by economic incentives, yields results far in excess of any which are necessary merely to avoid the extremes of hunger or destitution.

That capacity is a matter of training, tradition and habit, at least as much as of pecuniary stimulus, and the ability to raise it of a professional association representing the public opinion of a group of workers is, therefore, considerable. Once industry has been liberated from its subservience to the interests of the functionless property-owner, it is in this sphere that trade unions may be expected increasingly to find their functions. Its importance both for the general interests of the community and for the special interests of particular groups of workers can hardly be exaggerated. Technical knowledge and managerial skill are likely to be available as readily for a committee appointed by the workers in an industry as for a committee appointed, as now, by the shareholders. But it is more evident to-day that the crux of the economic situation is not the technical deficiencies of industrial organization, but the growing inability of those who direct industry to command the active goodwill of the *personnel*. Their co-operation is promised by the conversion of industry into a profession serving the public, and promised, as far as can be judged, by that alone.

Nor is the assumption of the new and often disagreeable obligations of internal discipline and public responsibility one which trade unionism can afford, once the change is accomplished, to shirk, however alien they may be to its present traditions. For ultimately, if by slow degrees, power follows the ability to wield it; authority goes with function. The workers cannot have it both ways. They must choose whether to assume the responsibility for industrial discipline and become free, or to repudiate it and continue to be serfs. If, organized as professional bodies, they can provide a more effective service than that which is now, with increasing difficulty, extorted by the agents of capital, they will have made good their hold upon the future. If they cannot, they will remain among the less calculable instruments of production which many of them are to-day. The instinct of mankind warns it against accepting at their face value spiritual demands which cannot justify themselves by practical achievements. And the road along which the organized workers, like any other class, must climb to power, starts from the provision of a more effective economic service than their masters, as their grip upon industry becomes increasingly vacillating and uncertain, are able to supply.

RECENT ECONOMIC CHANGES

THE SENTIMENTAL VIEW of the 1920s as a golden age of ease and pleasures overlooks the great unevenness of the "prosperity decade." In the United States, agriculture, coal mining, the textile industry, and the railroads were in continuous or recurrent difficulties and there were several moderate to severe business downturns between 1918 and 1929. Together with the decline of old taboos and the rise of a new personal freedom and leisure a wave of fervent narrow puritanism swept out of the nation's small towns and rural areas, bringing a revivified Ku Klux Klan, hyperpatriotism, and anti-intellectualism. Prosperity itself, where it did exist, was based increasingly on overextended credit, inflated stock market prices, and a questionable speculative temperament. "Welfare-capitalism" in the form of company unions was often another name for hostility to an independent labor movement. It is thus no surprise that in 1924 a national reform party in America could take five million votes from the two major party candidates. But after 1926 over-all increases in productivity, the radio and automobile revolutions, and the tendency of the nation to base its view of itself on the news reports from booming industrial and financial centers tended to obscure dangers and shortcomings.

In 1928 Herbert Hoover, an apostle of business freedom and scientific management, was elected President. Anti-Catholicism may have helped to defeat Hoover's opponent Al Smith, but prosperity, to which both parties were pledged, would probably have defeated the Democratic party in any case.

A series of White House-sponsored surveys of the national economy was initiated in 1921. These led in January, 1928 to a study of recent economic changes, chaired initially by Hoover, then secretary of commerce. The investigation enlisted the efforts of some of the nation's biggest businessmen, conservative labor leaders, and orthodox economists. The committee was to make "a critical appraisal of the factors of stability and instability . . . suggesting rather than developing recommendations." Predominantly, the report ratified the view that all was basically sound and hopeful in the American economy. The optimistic survey was released in the fall of 1929 but on October 29 the New York Stock Exchange had its famous, disastrous "crash," only six months after Hoover had heralded the coming of permanent prosperity to the nation.

The following selection is taken from the introduction to the report written by Edwin F. Gay of the National Bureau of Economic Research. The report was printed in two volumes as *Recent Economic Changes in the United States* (New York: McGraw-Hill, 1929).

RECENT ECONOMIC CHANGES
IN THE UNITED STATES

INTRODUCTION

There is a measure of truth in the statement that the perspective of distance is analogous to that of time. The foreign observer imports his own preconceptions, and from the nature of his situation is likely to be inaccurate as to details, but he sees things in the mass. He generalizes on inadequate data, as must the historian, but it is often instructive to see through his eyes. What to the native is negligible matter of daily use and wont is lifted by the intelligent foreigner to the plane of a national characteristic or an important trend of social development. There have been many such travelers in the United States since the beginning of its history, and diverse have been their observations, but never has the flow of visitors and comment been so great as in recent years. Inquirers and writers from many countries, official and unofficial, literary folk and technicians, business men and representatives of labor, have come singly and in groups. During the last six or seven years, books, reports and articles, in many languages, describing, explaining or criticizing the economic and social situation in the United States, have appeared in unparalleled quantity. This has been heralded as the new Discovery of America.

Foreign Opinions.—Despite much divergence of opinion among these contemporaneous observers as to causes and conditions, there is marked unanimity as to the fact which is chiefly responsible for this extraordinary interest. They agree that of late there has been an "immense advance in America." [1] Our visitors are "impressed, everywhere and every day, by the evidences of an ebullient prosperity and a confidence in the future." [2] Even a skeptical Australian journalist who begins by doubting the very fact for which all other visitors are seeking the cause, namely the existence of high wages in the United States, ends by saying that "America has been experiencing a period of unusual industrial prosperity. Millions of people have found their earnings increasing at a more rapid rate than their standard of living." [3] The critical German trade-unionists, in their careful report, believe that American prosperity has within it the seeds of its later undoing, but they bear witness to the high earnings and effectiveness of the American worker, his

[1] Sir Josiah Stamp, *Some Economic Factors in Modern Life* (1929), p. 121.
[2] Ramsay Muir, *America the Golden* (1927), p. 1.
[3] H. G. Adam, *An Australian Looks at America* (1928), pp. 35, 116.

mobility and freedom from class antagonism, and above all to the prevalent well-being and optimism of Americans in general. A German industrialist declares that, with an economic supremacy characterized by high wages and machine progress, the United States has become "the first power of the world." [4]

The consensus of foreign opinion concerning the present great American prosperity is evident to any student of this recent literature. But, though it might be interesting, it would certainly be a difficult and time-consuming task to trace all the divergences of point of view and the differing degrees of emphasis as to the causes of that prosperity. Some of the travelers have returned home to spread the gospel of mass production, of automatic machinery and conveyers. But *Fordismus* and *Rationalisierung,* the slogans of these evangelists, have also been acrimoniously criticised. Ramsay Muir asserts, indeed, that "the methods of mass-production have not been introduced, and cannot be introduced, in the greater part even of American industry," but he elsewhere lays stress upon the factors of great natural resources and a great domestic free-trade market which have made mass production possible for the United States. England, by contrast, lives "by supplying the needs of world-wide markets, infinitely variegated," and must therefore make quality, not quantity, its aim. Dr. Heinrich Ludwig complains that his German compatriots have, since the war, studied American industry too superficially. Ford, he declares, is not typical of the new management methods in the United States, and scientific management (*Rationalisierung*) has been misconceived in Europe as concerned primarily with mechanical equipment. It is not American technique but American psychology which should be studied. Its chief characteristics, he asserts, are optimism tempered by statistics and experiment; its aim is stabilization; the secret of American success is its study of the market.

America has become the arsenal whence weapons are drawn for both sides of embittered argument. It is, for instance, to some European protectionists a demonstration of the benefits of a high protective tariff; to other writers it is a proof in its free-trade continental market of the correctness of the commercial principles urged by the *laissez-faire* economists; and it is also a reinforcing support to the advocates of a European *Zoll-Verein*. Its high wages are both the cause and the result of its prosperity. The labor situation of the United States, so puzzling to the foreign workers who are surprised at the friendly working spirit in American labor-relations, furnishes grounds both for attack and defense in respect to trade-union policy. Some observers em-

[4] Carl Köttgen, *Das Wirtschaftliche Amerika* (3d ed., 1926), p. iii.

phasize American individualism, others our spirit of co-operation, our "unconscious socialism," [5] while one economist shrewdly remarks that the pioneer's struggle with the wilderness simultaneously developed both of these apparently incompatible traits. We are assured that America is a land of contrasts, with great diversity of regions and races, and also that it is the home of a nation remarkable for its uniformity of tastes and its passion for standardization. Its people are massed increasingly in monotonous repetitive machine-labor; yet they show high intelligence and mobility in a free field for ambition. The condition of the farmer in the United States is called by Ramsay Muir one of the "spots on the sun" of the American heaven, and he thinks that in American agriculture, "there seems to be an arrest of development." [6] But a German writer, not less observant, works out a coefficient of welfare higher for the United States than for Germany on the basis of the fact that while in Germany 43.3 per cent of the gainfully employed are required to feed its population, in the United States 29 per cent suffices to perform the same service. The agricultural production per man in the United States, he states, is 2.46 times greater than in Germany. Not counting tractors and other agricultural machinery which have brought such an accession of power and wealth-production to the American farmer, in the item of horses alone he finds the number per agriculturist in the United States to be 3.7 times that of Germany. To him, agricultural America seems "a blessed country." [7]

It is needless to enlarge on the numerous clashes in the testimony of the foreign observers. It is more to the point to indicate that, despite their varying origins and predilections, there is a considerable degree of concurrence, although with differing emphasis, regarding certain main factors in the recent economic and social experience of this country. These factors may here be briefly summarized.

1. The natural resources of the United States are unrivaled, especially those which are fundamental to modern large-scale industrialism. There is not only a continental width of fertile land, but there exist also marvelous deposits of coal, petroleum, iron and other essential minerals. The more critical of the foreign visitors are inclined to stress these bountiful gifts of nature, others weight more heavily the energy and organization which has utilized them.

2. In this vast expanse of territory, historically so recently opened to European migration and settlement, labor is relatively scarce and wages are relatively high. The situation may be tersely stated, that "because American

[5] Julius Hirsch, *Das Amerikanische Wirtschaftswunder* (1926), p. 229.
[6] Muir, *America the Golden*, pp. 16–19.
[7] Köttgen, *Das Wirtschaftliche Amerika*, pp. 9–15.

resources are abundant, they are wasted; because American labor is dear, it is economized." [8] In the present undeveloped state of international wage statistics, it is natural that estimates of the higher range of American wages should vary. André Siegfried, in his somewhat impressionistic manner, says they are "often ten times as much as those of even a European," [9] while the more conservative German trade-unionists put the American wage level at about three times that of Germany and real wages two and a half times as high. But the European writers agree that there is in the United States a markedly higher standard of living and that this profoundly influences the American outlook.

3. In consequence of the juxtaposition of rich resources and an inadequate labor supply, there has resulted a progressive development of labor-supplementing machine equipment, in agriculture, transportation, and industry, and also a remarkable utilization of power. To some, this seems to be the chief explanation of the greater productivity of the American wage earner and hence of his higher standard of living.

4. Many observers hold that of even greater importance than the technical progress is the great domestic market, untrammeled by barriers of tariffs, language, or tradition of local or national jealousies. The resulting "mass consumption" makes mass production possible and profitable. The nation-wide market necessitates expanding agencies of distribution which are highly remunerative to their originators and which absorb a growing proportion of the gainfully employed. The character of the unified American market frequently leads to foreign comment on its surprising uniformity of demand. The American business man, according to a French point of view, "has standardized the individual in order to be better able to standardize manufacture." [10]

5. The problem of correlating abundant resources, expensive labor, and unsurpassed machine equipment, to serve the greatest of markets, has put a high premium on management and organizing capacity. Scientific management in industry and commerce, apparently the resultant of emerging pressures, is thought by many of the foreigners writing on recent economic changes in the United States to be the chief contribution which this country is making to economic welfare and to be the key to its success. It is seen that the American effort is aimed at the "optimum" result, the proper balance of all the many factors in a business enterprise. The preoccupation of the old-time manager with wages has given way to a concern for the manifold ele-

[8] L. Chiozza Money, *L'Europe Nouvelle,* IX (1926), 1528.
[9] André Siegfried, *America Comes of Age* (1927), p. 160.
[10] Pichot and Fournier, "Communication sur le voyage aux États-Unis," *Bulletin de la Chambre de Commerce de Paris,* July 7, 1928.

ments entering into unit costs. Such far-sighted management is becoming highly specialized; a new profession is entering into the structure of American industry.

6. In order to obtain the effective utilization of the worker's effort and to lower costs, American management has begun more systematically to improve industrial relations. It seeks to reduce the turnover of labor and the friction of labor troubles which disturb the smooth-running mechanism of industry. In a number of the larger concerns departments have been established to study and to deal with this problem, and this new specialization of personnel management has attracted favorable foreign attention. Some observers regard "the achievement of industrial peace between labor, capital and management" [11] as among the leading causes of American prosperity. But even those who speak in cooler tone agree that a great improvement in industrial relations has been effected. It is generally recognized that there has been a voluntary assumption by employers of heavy social charges in the establishment of benefits of various kinds, and there has continued since the war a considerable interest in plans for workers' representation. A corresponding shift in the labor-union attitude has also taken place which differentiates the American labor movement from that found in any other country. The new labor-union policy recognizes not the identity but the mutuality of interest between the two parties to the labor contract. This approach to better understanding on both sides is itself a sign of general change in the temper of the industrial community. The human aspects of the relationships of management not only with labor, but also with customers, competitors, and the public, are more stressed in word and in practice. There is a growing sense of social responsibility.

7. A related factor in American economic efficiency is the openmindedness of American management. Many visitors note with appreciation the freedom of access and information which they have found. "What is raising the whole standard of management in the United States is the habit among employers of discussing their problems openly among themselves, of comparing the methods of one industry with those of another, and of founding associations for research and conference. . . . They are not afraid to teach each other or too proud to learn from each other." [12] They are giving increasing support to scientific research and looking with respect upon university training.

8. Emphasis is unanimously laid upon the dominant national trait of

---

[11] P. A. Molteno, "The Causes and Extent of American Prosperity," *Contemporary Review,* August, 1927.

[12] "American Industry and Its Significance," *Round Table* (London), XVII (1926), 264.

optimistic energy, as an underlying element in these various phenomena of American economic activity. The individual in America is mobile as to place and calling; he is moving upward. He sometimes appears docile, but is because he is tolerant of social inconveniences which his experience tells him are only incidental and temporary. The way to education and to promotion is wide open; indeed many ladders to advancement are available and their rungs are all intact, so that he may climb who will. We are told that this is the inheritance of the frontier; in spite of the fact that the agricultural frontier has disappeared, our visitors find still strongly persistent the same characteristic spirit of indomitable hopefulness. . . .

It will serve our present purpose to point out that most of the eight significant features of the existing economic conditions in the United States upon which we have found our foreign visitors in substantial agreement are also characteristic of former major periods of prosperity in our history. The fundamental conditions of our existence on this continent have thus far remained substantially unchanged, and the responses have therefore been similar, not so much in external form as in their essential character. Even the successive maladjustments of economic growth show, behind their external dissimilarities, an underlying likeness. With superabundant natural resources, for example, we have always been open to the charge of wastefulness, and this is easily explicable, but with insufficient man power it seems, at first thought, curious that we are now and have ever been wasteful of human life. That we should permit the rate of accident and crime to remain so much higher than in other civilized nations may spring from the reckless forcefulness with which we have attacked the difficulties of expansion. But there was a sign of change in the fundamental conditions of our national life when there emerged the conservation movement for the natural resources, and the slogan "safety first" for human life. Another serious maladjustment has been constantly observable in the extreme to which we have carried the swings of prosperity and business depression, the fierce bursts of speculative activity and the sharp reactions. Again, our environment and its needs may help to explain this feverish pulse-beat; yet here also another slogan, "stability," may be symptomatic of coming fundamental change. It is, furthermore, highly characteristic of all our periods of expansion that the rapidity and vigor of growth of some elements is so great as seriously to unbalance the whole organism. Each previous phase of prosperity has had its flourishing "new" industries, a different group each time, and each period has seen, or failed to see, other suffering members seeking readjustment or reduced to atrophy. With each successive advance, for instance, there has remained a farm problem and agrarian discontent somewhere in the rear. These rough dislocations in the past have made us exceptionally prone to scrap machinery and men. But quick adaptation and rapid mutation, perhaps biologically useful, our industrial society is now commencing to regard with more social concern.

The shiftings of psychological attitude, here indicated, seem to suggest that something distinctly different from our former experience is taking place. The chief characteristics of the present economic phase, agreed upon by our numerous visitors from abroad, are, it is true, evolved logically from what has preceded, and we are still finding answers along similar lines to a similarly constructed problem. But there seem now to be differences of degree which approach differences in kind. In this sense we may say that the unprecedented utilization of power and its wide dispersion by automobile and tractor, in which this country leads the way, is a new addition of enormous potentiality to our resources. With the general increase of wealth, the growth in the number of millionaires has been accompanied by a remarkable rise in the real wages of industrial workers, and a wide diffusion of investments. The profession of management is clearly emerging, and there is visible an increasing professional spirit in business, which springs from and entails recognized social responsibilities. The "self-policing" of business, with its codes of ethics, has been assisted by the recent development of trade-associations and the increasing influence of research and professional education. The strength and stability of our financial structure, both governmental and commercial, is of modern growth. The great corporate development of business enterprise, well marked in the fourth period of expansion, has gone on to new heights. It may be creating, as some think, a new type of social organization, but in any case the open-mindedness of the public, and of the state which is its instrument, toward this growing power of business corporations appears to be novel in American history.

Here are the beginnings of new answers to the old problem. But more than this. Some of the basic elements of the problem are evidently in process of change. The resources of the country, still enormous, are no longer regarded as limitless; the labor of the world is no longer invited freely to exploit them. The capital flow has turned outward; private and public interests and responsibilities have a new world-wide scope. These changes must have far-reaching consequences and entail further and more perplexing adjustments.

V THE GREAT DEPRESSION

WILLIAM H. BEVERIDGE

WHEN IT BEGAN, the "crash" of 1929 seemed to be another of the periodic crises which had marked the history of capitalism. But as it deepened, its intensity exceeded that of any of its predecessors, except possibly the depression of the 1890s. It lasted longer, recovery was slower, and unlike earlier depressions it affected virtually the whole world. It neither originated in one country nor were its repercussions confined to any particular nation or class. From the very outset it was an international catastrophe which hit all nations, including the Soviet Union. (The first Russian Five-Year Plan was based upon certain expectations as to imports of foreign capital goods for which Russia intended to pay by the proceeds of her exports. The depression abroad led to a contraction of Russian exports which made it impossible to carry out her import plan and thus endangered the fulfillment of the Five-Year Plan as a whole.) In the United States alone, the decline of output and employment was estimated to have caused a loss of perhaps $200 billion of potential national income from 1929 to 1937.

However, the consequences of the Great Depression went far beyond even great financial losses. Economic depressions not only disrupt economic life but also affect the state of public health, mortality, crime, alcoholism, the marriage rate, and so on. Even more far-reaching are the psychological, political, and international effects of a serious breakdown of major national economies. It will probably never be possible to evaluate accurately the social losses which resulted from the economic instability and recurrent unemployment which after 1929 deeply frustrated the hopes of millions of individuals in many countries. It is in this sense that it is possible to say that the Great Depression of 1929 was a turning point in the economic and political history of Europe. Europe and, indeed, the world are still preoccupied with remedying the political damage caused by this social crisis and its repercussions. The depression of the 1930s helps to account for the growth of European communism and the success of the Nazi movement in Germany. Any explanation of the latter must take into consideration the experiences of prolonged unemployment which hit the German people after the postwar inflation and erased whatever savings had been accumulated by the middle class. Elsewhere in Europe, and in the United States, the crisis accelerated the tendencies to state intervention in both the national and international markets that had formerly been operated largely by private individuals and corporations. The confidence of people in private capitalism and the confidence of the great business classes in themselves never returned to their former heights.

The following selection is designed to illustrate some of the economic and psychological effects of the Great Depression. It is from William H. Beveridge, *Full Employment in a Free Society* (New York: W. W. Norton, 1945), one of the many reports and documents prepared in Europe and America as the Second World War neared its end and as people and governments resolved not to permit a recurrence of the conditions that led to the tragic waste of the years after 1929.

FULL EMPLOYMENT IN A FREE SOCIETY

THE GREAT DEPRESSION of 1931–32 was in itself of the same type as previous depressions. Although more severe than anything previously experienced and though its effects in Britain were increased by structural unemployment due to the secular decline of overseas demand, the cyclical movement from 1929 to 1938 is a lineal descendant of the successive fluctuations which have brought insecurity to all advanced industrial countries with an unplanned market economy ever since industry took its modern form. So far as the United States is concerned, there is no reason for confidence or even for hope that the economic system which produced this depression, if left to itself, will fail to reproduce similar depressions in future. So far as Britain is concerned, while there was after the first World War a special factor of failure of overseas demand, there is equally no assurance that other special factors will not recur and if added to cyclical fluctuation will produce intolerable unemployment.

Though it is clear that unemployment between the two wars in Britain and in America was worse than it was before the first World War, we are not in a position really to say how bad things were before 1914 because there is no full record. . . .

While the main evil of unemployment is in its social and human effects upon the persons unemployed and upon the relations between citizens, the purely material loss of material wealth involved in it is serious. If the unused labour resources of Britain between the two wars could have been brought into use it would have been possible without any further change to increase the total output of the community by approximately one-eighth. . . .

Statistics of unemployment are not just statistics. Economic arguments about unemployment are not arguments in the air. In my first study of unemployment thirty-five years ago, I illustrated the statistical record and the economic argument by an extract from the life story of one of the early labour leaders and Members of Parliament, Mr. Will Crooks. The story is so little out of date while fear of unemployment remains, that it may fitly be repeated here. It tells how, after tramping in search of work from London to Liverpool and back again, Crooks decided to try to find work outside his own trade of cooper. He went down to the docks, where by the aid of a friendly foreman he got occasional jobs as a casual labourer.

One typical day of tramping for work in London he described to me thus:

"I first went down to the riverside at Shadwell. No work to be had there. Then I called at another home and got two slices of bread in paper and walked eight miles to a cooper's yard in Tottenham. All in vain. I dragged myself back to Clerkenwell. Still no luck. Then I turned homewards in despair. By the time I reached Stepney I was dead beat.

"That year I know I walked in London till my limbs ached again. I remember returning home once by way of Tidal Basin, and turning into Victoria Docks so utterly exhausted that I sank down on a coil of rope and slept for hours."

Work came at last in an unexpected way. He was returning home after another empty day when he hailed a carman and asked for a lift.

"All right, mate, jump up," was the response.

As they sat chatting side by side, the carman learned that his companion was seeking work.

"What's yer trade?" he enquired.

"A cooper."

"Why, the governor wants a cooper."

So instead of dropping off at Poplar, Crooks accompanied the carman to the works. . . . That work was a stepping-stone to another and better job at Wandsworth. . . . Crooks was never out of work again in his life. . . .

Nothing wearies one more than walking about hunting for employment which is not to be had. It is far harder than real work. The uncertainty, the despair, when you reach a place only to discover that your journey is fruitless are frightful. I've known a man say: "Which way shall I go to-day?" Having no earthly idea which way to take, he tosses up a button. If the button comes down on one side he tracks east; if on the other, he tracks west.

In repeating this story, in 1909, I added the comment, "Nothing can better illustrate the waste of time, energy and shoe leather involved in the personal search for employment. This is the lottery which industrial disorganization makes of the workman's life. This is the process as to which comfortable ignorance has so often assured us: 'The men know where to look for work all right, they know. Lord bless you! *they* know!' "

To-day the same or worse statistics could be illustrated by countless human tales, from many sources:

The depression and apathy which finally settles down in many of the homes of these long-unemployed men lies at the root of most of the problems which are connected with unemployment. It is one of the reasons why they fail to get back to work. It is one of the reasons why the majority of them "have not the heart" for clubs or activities of other kinds, and it is one of the reasons why their homes seem so poverty stricken. "I don't know how it is," said a young married woman in Blackburn, "but these last few years since I've been out of the mills I don't seem able to take trouble, somehow; I've got no spirit for anything. But I didn't use to be like that." One of us who saw her had little doubt "how it was." The woman looked thin and ill, and it was clear that what food there was was going to the children. . . .

My chief trouble is the monotony of a long spell of unemployment . . . monotonous and insufficient food and having nothing to do all day after the garden is done, kill all a man's interest in life. . . . Perhaps I miss cigarettes most, and I hate being chained to the home most. There is no substitute for work. . . . There is nothing I can do to keep myself efficient; odd repairs in a house are no substitute for constructional work on a steam engine. (A skilled millwright aged 49.)

The wife works while I look after the home. . . . I earned good wages (£4 a week) for years and we had saved fifty pounds when I lost my job. We have none of that fifty pounds to-day. . . . Any long spell of unemployment leaves you with little to be proud of and much to be ashamed of. Our child is still too young to realize that it is her mother who works. We carefully keep her from knowing it. (A skilled wire-drawer aged 32.)

My husband is a good man and he does a lot for me in the house. . . . But he is a changed man these last two years. He never complains, but I wish he would. It makes me unhappy to find him becoming quieter and quieter, when I know what he must be feeling. If I had someone to talk to about my troubles I should feel much better. But having to keep them to myself, as my husband does, makes everything so much worse. We quarrel far more now than we have ever done in our lives before. We would both rather be dead than go on like this. . . . He has been out of work so long now that I do not think that he will get his Old Age Pension when he is sixty-five for he will not have enough stamps on his Health Insurance Cards. . . . That will be our greatest disappointment. (A Derbyshire miner's wife aged 66, he being 62.)

The passages just quoted describe people past their first youth or with domestic ties that might limit their availability for work. But the statistics of unemployment are not confined to such people. They cover many tens of thousands in the first flush of manhood and womanhood. From a survey of *Disinherited Youth*, made under the auspices of the Carnegie United Kingdom Trustees during the years 1936–9, the following passages are taken:

From the very start of their industrial life, at fourteen, they had experienced unemployment, so that even the youngest of them at age eighteen, were personalities that had matured, during those very important and impressionable four years against a background of unemployment, in some cases slight, in other cases entirely devoid of any pattern of work as a part of life. (Page 65.)

One young man described his feeling while unemployed as "living death." Many more may have felt this, but could not express it. Unemployment due to conditions of world trade, or technological changes in industrial organization, meant nothing to them. Such explanations left them cold. What mattered to most of them was that they were fit and able for work and wanted it badly, not so much as an end in itself as a means to an end. They needed the money, their homes needed the money, and it would be money earned by their own effort. One young wife put it thus: "Somehow when it's money that your man has worked for, it goes further."

Unemployment was a new and strange feature in the lives of a few. They were anxious and alert. They expressed their youthful impatience with the slow moving queues and hurriedly left the Employment Exchange after "signing on." Others, however, had acquired the art of patience. They had longer and more frequently recurring experiences of unemployment. With drooping shoulders and slouching feet they moved as a defeated and dispirited army. They gave their names, signed the necessary forms and shuffled out of the Exchange. This, twice a week, was the only disciplined routine with which they had to comply. (Pages 5-6.)

I am still unemployed and have no prospects. I have come to the stage when I think I will never find employment. I am glad you still take an interest in me as it is good to know someone is interested in the welfare of the unemployed. (Page 6, W.B., aged 22.)

I was an apprentice engineer and during the depression (1931) I was paid off. I got the offer of my job back but I was working then as a labourer and getting 30s. a week. I just couldn't go back to my apprentice's wage of 15s. I'm sorry now that I didn't. (Page 13.)

To tell you the truth I don't look for work now. You've got about as much chance of picking up a job nowadays as of winning the Irish Sweep. (Page 14.)

A number of the men married during the period of the Enquiry. One talked with them first as single men and then, later, as married men, and the urge to make fresh attempts "for the wife's sake" was noticeable. But one or two short spells of temporary or casual employment soon brought about a change of attitude. The young wife soon found that this fluctuation between a few days' wages and a few day's unemployment allowance instead of a regular, if minimum, weekly sum for total unemployment, upset any plan of expenditure she might make. One young mother told how, when her husband got the offer of a job, she had immediately to go and get him a pair of heavy working boots and pay them up by instalments. He thought the job would last at least a fortnight and with two weeks' pay she could manage to pay them up in full. The job lasted four days. It took her many weeks to return to her planned budget. Such a simple happening as this throws light on part of the reason for the married man's unemployment. (Page 27.)

The central problem of the lives of most of these young men is one of maintenance of self-respect. Rightly, they feel a need to take their places in society, achieving in their own right the means of living. Much of their conduct, irrational and unreasonable to outward seeming, becomes understandable if regarded in its perspective, as part of a struggle for the retention of self-respect. The attitude of many men who refuse training—a problem discussed in a later chapter—has its origin here; similarly, their resentment at being "messed about" can be understood for what it really is—an essay in self-respect. They have no function in society. They are the unwanted hangers-on of a community in the life of which they are unable to play their full part. (Page 80.)

The facts that in certain parts of Britain even young adaptable people could find no employment and the disastrous effects upon them of prolonged idleness have been described already as among the worst blots on our record between the two wars. In the United States the position was no better: "The difficulty of youth in finding jobs has emerged as one of the most serious problems of depression. It is estimated that youth constituted a third of all the unemployed during the thirties and that at least one-third of all the employable youth were unable to find jobs." This estimate of wasted youth in the United States is no hasty judgment; it is confirmed by numerous local surveys. The record of where youth stands in free democracies in times of peace is in poignant contrast to what is required of youth in war, and to the call to youth made by the German dictator in preparing war. But this judgment of uselessness that is passed so widely on adaptable youth, the unplanned market economy of the past in Britain and in America must itself be judged and stands condemned.

Statistics of unemployment mean rows of men and women, not of figures only. The three million or so unemployed of 1932 means three million lives being wasted in idleness, growing despair and numbing indifference. Behind these three million individuals seeking an outlet for their energies and not finding it, are their wives and families making hopeless shift with want, losing their birth-right of healthy development, wondering whether they should have been born. Beyond the men and women actually unemployed at any moment, are the millions more in work at that moment but never knowing how long that work or any work for them may last. Unemployment in the ten years before this war meant unused resources in Britain to the extent of at least £500,000,000 per year. That was the additional wealth we might have had if we had used instead of wasting our powers. But the loss of material wealth is the least of the evils of unemployment, insignificant by comparison to the other evils. Even with that loss, Britain was still one of the richest countries of the world. If that unemployment could have been divided evenly over the whole people as leisure, we should have been as rich and altogether happier; we should have had a standard of living with which few countries could compare. The greatest evil of unemployment is not the loss of additional material wealth which we might have with full employment. There are two greater evils: first, that unemployment makes men seem useless, not wanted, without a country; second, that unemployment makes men live in fear and that from fear springs hate.

So long as chronic mass unemployment seems possible, each man appears as the enemy of his fellows in a scramble for jobs. So long as there is a scramble for jobs it is idle to deplore the inevitable growth of jealous restrictions, of demarcations, of organized or voluntary limitations of output, of resistance to technical advance. By this scramble are fostered many still uglier growths— hatred of foreigners, hatred of Jews, enmity between the sexes. Failure to use our productive powers is the source of an interminable succession of evils. When that failure has been overcome, the way will be open to progress in unity without fear.

The necessity of preventing the return of mass unemployment is a recurrent theme in nearly all that has been written on reconstruction problems in Britain after the war, from whatever angle it is written. "Unemployment such as darkened the world between the two wars, must not recur." "There must be no return to the disastrous waste of man-power which characterized the period between the wars." "This is the issue which in the years after the war, more than any other, will make or break the reputation of any minister of any government." Yet, as Sir John Anderson remarked exactly a year ago when discussing Assumption C of the Beveridge Report, "There is no question whether we can achieve full employment; we must achieve it. It is the central factor which will determine the pattern of national life after the war, including, perhaps, the fate of democratic institutions." The same thoughts find utterance in America: "Never again will doles and subsistence levels be tolerated." "The liberty of a democracy is not safe if its business system does not provide employment and produce and distribute goods in such a way as to sustain an acceptable standard of living."

The necessity of preventing after this war a return to the mass unemployment between the two wars is formally admitted by all. The possibility of doing so, if we are prepared to will the means as well as the end, is not open to reasonable doubt. Depressions of trade are not like earthquakes or cyclones; they are man-made. In the course of relieving unemployment, all industrial countries, but particularly Britain, have acquired much knowledge as to its causes. Though there remain some unsolved problems, the conditions without which mass unemployment cannot be prevented are known and the main lines for remedial action are clear. Finally, the experience of the two wars has shown that it is possible to have a human society in which every man's effort is wanted and none need stand idle and unpaid.

The doubt is not as to the possibility of achieving full employment but as to the possibility of achieving it without the surrender of other things that are even more precious. Some things which are more precious than full employment, that is to say, some of the essential British liberties, are surrendered in war. But it can be shown that this surrender is required by the special nature of the war objective, and not by the full employment which is incidental to war. This surrender of essential liberties would not be required for full employment in peace and should be refused. The Policy for Full Employment set out in this Report preserves all the essential British liberties; it rejects rationing, which forbids the free spending of personal income; it rejects direction of men and women to compulsory tasks; it rejects prohibition of strikes and lock-outs. The policy preserves also other liberties which, if less essential, are deeply rooted in Britain, including collective bargaining to determine wages, and private enterprise in a large sector of industry; it preserves these lesser liberties, subject to the degree of responsibility with which they are exercised. The policy preserves possibility of change, the springs of progress and the way to rising standards of life. It is not open to the criticism that it would destroy essential liberties or lead to stagnation. Is it open to any other serious objection? It will be convenient to name some of the possible objections and give brief answers.

There are some who will say that full employment, combined with unemployment insurance, will remove the incentive of effort which depends on fear of starvation. The answer is that for civilized human beings ambition and desire for service are adequate incentives. It may be that cattle must be driven by fear. Men can and should be led by hope. The policy set out in this Report is not one of stagnation or forced equality. It does not give security for life in a particular job; it gives only the opportunity of exercising one's gifts and energies in generous rather than in ungenerous rivalry with one's fellows.

There are some who will say that the great development of State activity involved in the policy proposed here will destroy the "little man," that is to say the small, independent business. The answer is that the policy does nothing of the sort, unless risk of bankruptcy in trade depressions is essential to the existence and happiness of the "little man." The policy is simply one of setting up sufficient demand. It involves, as an implication, control of monopolies to prevent exploitation of the demand and supervision of large concerns in order to plan investment. It does not touch the "little man" at all; he can work to meet the demand like any other. He will find more scope than before, once strong demand has eliminated the slumps in which so many small businesses in the past have come to grief.

There are some who will object to the proposals of this Report on the ground that they involve an extension of the activities of Government and a consequent increase in the number of civil servants. That the proposals do involve action by Government in fields which in the past have been left wholly to private enterprise is true; the justification for this lies in the failures of the past. In certain industries men may find themselves working directly for the community in place of being the employees of a monster business corporation. In all industries, the managers of large undertakings may find themselves both regulated and assisted in keeping what they do—in investment, in the location of industry, in price policy—in accord with national interest. But there is nothing in all the proposals of this Report to involve greater inter-ference in the private lives of the mass of the people. On the contrary, not only will all the war time restrictions on consumption and choice of work vanish with war, but many of the previous interferences with private lives will be ended. There will be no unemployment assistance subject to a means test; the 8,000 officials of the Unemployment Assistance Board in 1938 will become unnecessary for that work. So, too, a substantial proportion of the 28,000 peace-time officials of the Ministry of Labour, that is to say, those en-gaged in paying or calculating unemployment benefit, will find that occupa-tion gone, though it may be hoped that most of these will render still better service in preventing unemployment by organizing the labour market. A full employment policy involves more public control over a limited class of busi-ness undertakers, and less control over the private lives of the mass of the people. It may in the end mean fewer bureaucrats, not more.

There may be some who will say that in the emphasis laid in this Report on the need for organizing the labour market the Report treats labour as a com-modity, in conflict with the opening declaration of the Charter adopted by the International Labour Conference in Philadelphia in May, 1944. There is no conflict. The Philadelphia declaration that labour is not a commodity can-not mean that men should not be free to sell their labour as men sell com-modities. In a free community the right to sell or to refrain from selling one's labour by hand or brain and to bargain as to the terms on which it should be used is essential. This makes important the question of how those who desire to sell their labour and those who, whether for private profit or as representa-tives of a public authority, desire to buy the labour, shall be brought together. In concerning itself with these matters, the Report does not treat men them-selves as a commodity; it treats them, as the Philadelphia declaration demands, as an end and not as a means; it proposes a fundamental difference to be established between the position of those who desire to sell their labour and the position of all other sellers. Only for labour should the market always be a seller's market. It should not be that always for any particular commodity.

There are some who will say that the policy of this Report subordinates the individual to the State. The answer is that this criticism directly reverses the truth. If the State is regarded as more important than the individual, it may be reasonable to sacrifice the individual in mass unemployment to the progress and prosperity of his more fortunate fellows, as he is sacrificed in war by the dictators for their power and dominion or that of the race. If, on the other hand, the State is regarded as existing for the individual, a State which fails, in respect of many millions of individuals, to ensure them any opportunity of service and earning according to their powers or the possibility of a life free from the indignities and inquisitions of relief, is a State which has failed in a primary duty. Acceptance by the State of responsibility for full employment is the final necessary demonstration that the State exists for the citizens —for all the citizens—and not for itself or for a privileged class.

There are some who will say that the policy of this Report is a mere palliative which will block the way to further reforms like socialism or communism. The answer is that the policy does not block the way to these or other reforms, if they are good in themselves. It is a policy directed against one particular evil and includes steps which must be taken under any economic system which preserves essential liberties, in order to deal with that evil. The case for socialization of the means of production must be argued in the main on other grounds, of efficiency of production or of social justice. The Policy for Full Employment is in essence that the State takes responsibility for seeing that while any human needs are unsatisfied, they are converted into effective demand. This leaves open to argument on its merits the question whether production to meet that effective demand should be undertaken under conditions of private enterprise guided by profit, or of social enterprise working directly for use, or of a combination of these methods. . . .

Twice in this century the onset of cyclical depression has been arrested by the outbreak of war, just after the culmination of an upward movement of the trade cycle. After the boom of 1913 employment had already begun to fall in 1914. After the half-hearted boom of 1937 employment fell in 1938. In each case an incipient depression was stopped or reversed, but it needed a war to bring this about. The test of statesmanship in the near future lies in finding a way to avoid depressions without plunging into war.

That is the aim and hope of this Report. We cure unemployment for the sake of waging war. We ought to decide to cure unemployment without war. We cure unemployment in war, because war gives us a common objective that is recognized by all, an objective so vital that it must be attained without regard to cost, in life, leisure, privileges or material resources. The cure of unemployment in peace depends on finding a common objective for peace that will be equally compelling on our efforts. The suggestion of this Report is that we should find that common objective in determination to make a Britain free of the giant evils of Want, Disease, Ignorance and Squalor. We cure unemployment through hate of Hitler; we ought to cure it through hate of these giant evils. We should make these in peace our common enemy, changing the direction and the speed rather than the concentration and strength of our effort. Whether we can do this, depends upon the degree to which social conscience becomes the driving force in our national life. We should regard Want, Disease, Ignorance and Squalor as common enemies of all of us, not as enemies with whom each individual may seek a separate peace, escaping himself to personal prosperity while leaving his fellows in their clutches. That is the meaning of social conscience; that one should refuse to make a separate peace with social evil. Social conscience, when the barbarous tyranny abroad has ended, should drive us to take up different arms in a new war against Want, Disease, Ignorance, and Squalor at home.

Want, arising mainly through unemployment and other interruptions of earnings, to a less extent through large families, is the subject of my earlier Report on Social Insurance. It could, without question, be abolished by the whole-hearted acceptance of the main principles of that Report. The worst feature of Want in Britain shortly before this war was its concentration upon children. Wages were not and probably could not be adjusted in any way to family responsibilities; the various social insurance schemes for providing income when wages failed either ignored family responsibilities entirely—as in health insurance or workmen's compensation—or made inadequate provision for them—as in unemployment insurance. By consequence there followed a sinister concentration of Want on those who would suffer from it most helplessly and most harmfully. Nearly half of all the persons discovered in Want by the social surveys of British cities between the wars were children under fifteen. Nearly half of all the working-class children in the country were born into Want. It is certain on general principles and can be shown by experiment that the bodies and minds of children respond directly and automatically to better environment, that the citizens of the future will grow up taller, stronger, abler, if in childhood all of them have had good feeding, clothing, housing and physical training. Want and its concentration on children between the wars represented a destruction of human capital none the less real because it did not enter into any economic calculus. The decision to destroy Want should be taken at once, for its own sake, to free Britain from a needless scandal and a wasting sore. That decision would deliver at the same time the first blow in the war against Idleness. The redistribution of income that is involved in abolishing Want by Social Insurance and children's allowances will of itself be a potent force in helping to maintain demand for the products of industry, and so in preventing unemployment.

Disease is in part a subject of my earlier Report on Social Insurance and Allied Services. But on this side the Report is limited to proposing that medical treatment of all kinds should be secured to all persons, free of all charge on treatment, and to discussing some of the general issues involved in the proposal. The acceptance of this proposal, announced by the Government in the Parliamentary Debate on that Report in February, 1943, forms the starting-point of the White Paper on the National Health Service which was published in March, 1944. This White Paper, outlining for discussion with the medical profession, the hospitals and the local authorities concerned, a scheme for the organization of a comprehensive health service free for all, opens the way to a revolution in the health of the people. Removal of any economic barrier between patient and treatment is an essential negative step for bringing avoidable disease to an end. But while essential, it is only a small part of all that is required. There is needed an immense positive extension both of preventive treatment and of curative treatment, through more and more hospitals, more and more doctors, dentists and other practitioners. There is needed, as an essential part of the attack on disease, a good policy of nutrition carried through by the wisdom of the State in using science. Here is a large field for communal outlay, using resources for purposes of high priority, in preserving the health and vigour of all.

Ignorance is an evil weed, which dictators may cultivate among their dupes, but which no democracy can afford among its citizens. Attack on it involves an immense programme of building schools, training and employing teachers, providing scholarships to fit opportunity to young ability wherever it is found. The first essential steps for that have been taken in the framing and introduction of the new Education Bill; there remains the task of pressing the attack on Ignorance with vigour and speed on all fronts. Learning should not end with school. Learning and life must be kept together throughout life; democracies will not be well governed till that is done. Later study should be open to all, and money, teaching and opportunities must be found for that as well. In the development of education lies the most important, if not the most urgent, of all the tasks of reconstruction. The needs of civilized men are illimitable, because they include the wise, happy enjoyment of leisure.

Squalor means the bad conditions of life for a large part of our people which have followed through the unplanned disorderly growth of cities, through our spoiling more and more country by building towns without building good towns, through our continuing to build inadequate, ill-equipped homes that multiply needlessly the housewife's toil. The greatest opportunity open in this country for raising the general standard of living lies in better housing, for it is in their homes and in the surroundings of their homes that the greatest disparities between different sections of the community persist to-day.

Better housing means not merely better houses but houses in the right environment, in the right relation to places of work and recreation and communal activity. Town and country planning must come before housing, and such planning, as one enquiry after another has shown, is impossible, until we resolve justly but firmly the problem of land values. Here is the greatest urgency of all. The attack on Squalor cannot wait, but it must be a planned attack. The war will leave a yawning gap, which must be filled without delay by building more homes. We must have housing at once but we must have town and country planning before housing.

The Policy for Full Employment outlined in this Report is a policy of spending and doing. It is a policy of common action. If we attack with determination, unity and clear aim the four giant evils of Want, Disease, Ignorance and Squalor, we shall destroy in the process their confederate—the fifth giant of Idleness enforced by mass unemployment. The carrying out of the policy depends on the positive acceptance of a new responsibility by the State, that of ensuring adequate demand for the products of industry, however industry itself may be organized. The policy preserves all the essential British liberties; it uses Britain's political advantages to carry through a task which can be carried through only by the power of the State. These political advantages are great and should be used. The constitution of Britain concentrates in the Government of the day the great power without which the problems of a great society cannot be solved. It makes the use of that power subject to continual scrutiny by the citizens and their representatives, and the power itself to recall; the essence of democracy is effective means of changing the Government without shooting. Finally, Britain has a public service, central and local, second to none in the world for efficiency, integrity and devotion to duty. Through these advantages, Britain has a chance of showing, sooner and more easily than any other large nation, that democracy can order peace as well as war better than the dictators do. The British people can win full employment while remaining free.

But they have to win it, not wait for it. Full employment, like social security, must be won by a democracy; it cannot be forced on a democracy or given to a democracy. It is not a thing to be promised or not promised by a Government, to be given or withheld as from Olympian heights. It is something that the British democracy should direct its Government to secure, at all costs save the surrender of the essential liberties. Who can doubt that full employment is worth winning, at any cost less than surrender of those liberties? If full employment is not won and kept, no liberties are secure, for to many they will not seem worth while.

EDMUND WILSON

THE CAREER OF Edmund Wilson, America's foremost literary critic, exemplifies the changing moods and interest of recent American intellectual life. Bohemian rebel in the 1920s, student of Marxism in the depression decade and of American traditions after the Second World War, Wilson has played each of his roles with much success. His work has helped establish new critical interest in F. Scott Fitzgerald, Henry James, the Russian poet Pushkin, and Jane Austen, among many others. Whether the subject is the Marxist tradition, the Dead Sea Scrolls, or the Iroquois Indians, a new Wilson book usually arouses wide interest, for readers will find in it the most direct as well as one of the most learned engagements between author and subject in modern criticism.

Wilson was born in 1895 and was reared in New Jersey. His family was of old native stock but his father, a lawyer, was one of a generation of skillful and sensitive young men who found that their simple republican heritage was at variance with the venal atmosphere of America after the Civil War. Edmund Wilson, Junior, was educated at a private school and then at Princeton, where he was friendly with F. Scott Fitzgerald. His father's dismay at post-Appomatox America was similar to the son's response to America of the 1920s. During the notable flowering of American letters inspired by the political disillusionment of that decade, Wilson, working both as a magazine columnist and as a free-lance writer, published many essays and reviews. They continuously exemplify the value a sense of alienation can have for a man of talent and taste. The pieces from those years were later collected in *The Shores of Light* (1952) and *The American Earthquake* (1958). These books recreate, as few chronicles of the era do, the intellectual excitement and wide range of interests of Wilson's contemporaries in Greenwich Village or Paris, the two chief retreats of exiles from the world of big business and stand-pat government.

With the onset of the Great Depression, Wilson's interest in political subjects became broader. By 1931 the "crash" was bringing him and other exiles at home or abroad to turn to political subjects and social reform. In both the United States and Western Europe many intellectuals found an explanation of what had gone wrong and a program for reconstruction in variants of Marxism. The existing small groups of American Marxists and Communists suddenly acquired many new and distinguished members.

His 1931 essay that follows was one of the first of the calls to action that were to become so common during the next five years. It is taken from *The Shores of Light* (New York: Doubleday, 1952).

AN APPEAL TO PROGRESSIVES

It seems to me impossible today . . . to continue to believe in the salvation of our society by the gradual and natural approximation to socialism . . . called progressivism, but which has more generally come to be known as liberalism. That benevolent and intelligent capitalism on which liberals have always counted has not merely not materialized to the extent of accepting socialism—it has not even been able to prevent a national economic disaster of proportions which neither capitalists nor liberals foresaw and which they both now profess themselves unable to explain. There are today in the United States, according to the census director, something like nine million men out of work; our cities are scenes of privation and misery on a scale which sickens the imagination; our agricultural life is bankrupt; our industry, in shifting to the South, has reverted almost to the horrible conditions, before the Factory Acts, of the England of a hundred years ago, and the fight of the unions there for recognition is all to begin again; so many banks are failing that the newspapers do not dare to print the truth about them. And when we look to South America or to the European countries west of Russia, we see only the same economic chaos, the same lack of capacity or will to deal with it, and the same resultant suffering. May we not well fear that what has broken down, in the course of one catastrophic year, is not simply the machinery of representative government but the capitalist system itself?—and that, even with the best intentions, it may be henceforward impossible for capitalism to guarantee not merely social justice but even security and order? May we not fear lest our American society, in spite of its apparently greater homogeneity, be liable, through sheer inefficiency, the heritage of political corruption, to collapse in the long run as ignominiously as the feudal regimes of old France and Russia?

The capitalist Americans of the twentieth century are certainly more kindly and democratic than the landlords of the feudal age; but, on the other hand, the capitalist system makes it very much easier for people not to realize what they are doing, not to know about the danger and the hardship, the despair and the humiliation, that their way of life implies for others. The feudal lord might flog or kill his serfs, but he was dealing directly with the human realities as the stockholder or the banker is not. The feudal master might be arrogant and cruel, but his arrogance and cruelty were open, accepted as necessities imposed or enjoyed as privileges conferred by superior social position. But the chivalrous Southerner whose interest is mounting up in the bank that lends money to the textile mill is no more conscious that he has helped pull the trigger that murdered Ella May Wiggins than the cultivated Bostonian knows that the money that reaches his pocket from the shares in the South Braintree shoe company in which his broker has recommended his investing has on its way helped turn on the switch that electrocuted Sacco and Vanzetti. Mr. Lawrence Dennis, late of Seligman, has recently written . . . of the queer and unenviable lot of the bond salesmen, who, taking over their bonds on trust from the bankers and selling them to customers who take them on trust, do not assume any professional responsibility and never touch at any point the realities of the things with which they are dealing. Not only are the people in a capitalist society very often completely ignorant as to what their incomes come from; it is actually sometimes impossible for them to find this out. And as long as a fair proportion of the bankers, the manufacturers, the middle men, the merchants and the workers whom their capital and machines keep busy are able to make a little more money than before, no matter how unscrupulously or short-sightedly, we are able, as a nation, to maintain our belief in our prosperity and even in our happiness.

That is what has been happening in the period which has just now come to a close. The liberal Stuart Chase tried to make us see this situation in his little book called *Prosperity: Fact or Myth?* published in 1929, on the eve of the stock-market crash. Between 1922 and 1928, he tells us, the average income in the United States was increased twenty percent, but this left the average annual wage in 1929 "well below $1,500." Through this whole period the coal, textile, shoe, leather, shipbuilding and railroad-equipment industries were all doing more or less badly and the people employed in them were hanging on to the bare edge of subsistence; the farmers became more and more impoverished; the mergers and the new machinery were throwing more and more people out of work; and the radio and motor industries, on which the illusion of prosperity depended, were prospering at the expense of selling these articles to many people who didn't need them. The salesmen and advertisers had had to begin to break down the "sales resistance" of their public: it was no longer a question merely of persuading people of the attractiveness of one's wares but of combating a positive antagonism to them. The sales departments resorted to both inspirational and scientific methods, but when the public began to come to from the industrial opium-dream, the motor-car industry was suddenly sunk and the rest of American business went with it. May we not ask ourselves whether it is possible, in the conditions of our capitalist society, for any further spectacular appearance of revival to be anything more than a spurt depending on the overinflation, equally senseless and mischievous, of some other inessential industry?—an inflation just as sure to end in another abject disaster?

In any case, American optimism has taken a serious beating; the national morale is weak. The energy and the faith for a fresh start seem now not to be forthcoming: a dreadful apathy, unsureness and discouragement is felt to have fallen upon us. It is as if we were afraid to go on with what we were doing before or as if we had no longer the heart for it. I want to suggest that the present depression may be nothing less than one of the turning-points in our history, our first real crisis since the Civil War. The Americans at the present time seem to be experiencing not merely an economic breakdown but a distinct psychological change. From the time of the Civil War on, all our enthusiasm and creative energy went into the development of our tremendous resources. This development had two aspects: one was the exploration of the continent and the engineering feats involved in reclaiming it; the other the amassing of gigantic fortunes. Today the discoveries have all been made: we no longer look toward the West, as the Europeans once looked to America, as to a world of untold treasures and wonders—and the excitement of mastering new seacoasts, new rivers, forests, prairies and mountains seems now completely spent. This was already true at the time of the European War (when, incidentally, we were running into a business depression), but the war gave us a new objective—new discoveries, the discovery of Europe; new heroic stunts of engineering, the transportation of our army to France. Since the end of the war, however, we have, as a people, had nothing to carry us along except the momentum of money-making. We have been trying still to find in it the exhilaration of the money-making of our earlier period, which had been largely the exhilaration of the wildness and size of the continent—the breaking it in to the harness of the railroads, the stumbling upon sudden riches. But during these last years our hope and our faith have all been put behind the speed of mass production, behind stupendous campaigns of advertising, behind cyclones of salesmanship. Our buoyancy had been becoming hysterical. And the reaction from an hysterical exhilaration is a slump into despondency and inertia. What we have lost is, it may be, not merely our way in the economic labyrinth but our conviction of the value of what we were doing. Money-making and the kind of advantages which a money-making society provides for money to buy are not enough to satisfy humanity—neither is a system like ours in which everyone is out for himself and devil take the hindmost, with no common purpose and little common culture to give life stability and sense. Our idolization of our aviators—our extravagant excitement over Lindbergh and our romantic admiration (now beginning to cool off) for Byrd—has been like a last desperate burst of American idealism, a last impulse to dissociate our national soul from a precipitate progress that was taking us from automobiles and radios straight through electric refrigerators to Tom Thumb golf courses.

The old American ideal and legend of the poor boy who gets to be a millionaire, which gradually came to take the place of the poor boy who got to be President, has today lost almost all its glamor. Not only do people not hope to be Hoover—they do not even hope so often as they did to be Carnegie or Henry Ford. The romance of the legend of the poor boy was the romance of the old democratic chance, of the career open to the talents —but the realities of a millionaire society have turned out to be the monstrosities of capitalism: the children of the successful poor boy get lazy and sick on their father's money, and the poor boys who afterwards arrive on the scene discover that—with the crippling of the grain market, the elimination of the factory worker by the development of the machine and the decimation of the white-collar class, even though sometimes well on their way to getting in on the big money themselves, by enormous business mergers— the career is no longer open to the extent that had originally been hoped. What began as the libertarian adventure of eighteenth-century middle-class democracy seems to have ended in the cul de sac of an antiquated economic system. And capitalist-minded as the Americans have now become, they seem to feel they are in a cul de sac. It is as if they did not dare to go on. In spite of the fundamental absurdity of so much of what we have lately been doing, we are considerably better educated and more intelligent than we once were, and since the war we have been closer to Europe. The Buicks and Cadillacs, the bad gin and Scotch, the radio concerts interrupted by advertising talks, the golf and bridge of the suburban household, which the bond salesman can get for his money, can hardly compensate him for daily work of a kind in which it is utterly impossible to imagine a normal human being taking satisfaction or pride—and the bond salesman is the type of the whole urban office class. The brokers and bankers who are shooting themselves and jumping out of windows have been disheartened by the precariousness of their profession—but would they be killing themselves if they loved it? Who today, in fact, in the United States, can really love our meaningless life, where the manufacturer raises the workers' wages only in order to create a demand for the gadgets which for better or worse he happens to have an interest in selling them, while agriculture goes hang, and science and art are left to be exploited by the commercial laboratories, the market for commercial art illustration and the New York publishers' racket, or to be fed in a haphazard way by a dole from the fortunes of rich men who have been conscience-stricken or simply overpowered at finding themselves at the end of their careers with enough money on their hands to buy out an old-fashioned empire?

We liberals have professed not to love it, yet we have tried to believe in it, none the less. In a country where money changes hands so often and social position fluctuates so easily, where the minds of the working class have seemed largely to have been absorbed into the psychology of the middle class, we have been unable to believe in the Marxist doctrine that capitalism must eventually give rise to class warfare, and we have perhaps never taken sufficiently seriously Karl Marx's prediction that for many years to come the stupid automatic acquisitive instinct of humanity would still be so far ahead of its capacity for intelligent and disinterested behavior that the system of private enterprise would never even be able to run itself with foresight enough to avoid a wreck. It used to be pointed out that in America our support of this system was indestructible, since the stock market made it possible for anybody who had been able to save a little money to become a capitalist himself, with interests presumably identical with those of J. P. Morgan and Charlie Schwab. But can we expect that to be true in the future? —and even if people persist in aspiring to be stock-market capitalists, should they be encouraged in this or even left to their luck? Should they not rather be shown that their interests are incompatible with capitalism itself?

Yet the truth is that we liberals and progressives have been betting on capitalism—and that most of our heroes and allies, heterodox professors like Dewey and Beard, survivors of the old republican tradition like Woodrow Wilson and Justice Holmes, able and well-educated labor organizers like the officers of the Amalgamated, intelligent journalists like Lippmann and Chase, though all sincere and outspoken democrats, have been betting on capitalism, too. And now, in the abyss of starvation and bankruptcy into which the country has fallen, with no sign of any political leadership which will be able to pull us out, our liberalism seems to have little to offer beyond a discreet recommendation of public ownership of water power and certain other public utilities, a cordial feeling that labor ought to organize in a non-social-revolutionary way and a protest, invariably ineffective, against a few of the more obviously atrocious of the jailings, beatings-up and murders with which the industrialists have been trying to keep the working class docile.

Doesn't this program today seem rather inadequate? We liberals have always insisted on the desirability of a planned society—the phrase "social control" has been our blessed Mesopotamian word. If this means anything, does it not mean socialism? And should we not do well to make this plain? It may be said that at the present time it is utopian in America to talk about socialism; but with the kind of administrations that the country has lately been getting, do not all progressive proposals, however reasonable or modest, seem utopian? Is it not obvious . . . that a government like our present one is incapable of acting in good faith in even the simple matter of preserving the water power which is supposed to be operated for the general benefit from being exploited by private profiteers? Our society has finally produced in its specialized professional politicians one of the most useless and obnoxious groups which has perhaps ever disgraced human history—a group that seems unique among governing classes in having managed to be corrupt, uncultivated and incompetent all at once. We know that we are not even able to depend on them today to protect us against the frankly disreputable race of blackmailers, thieves and assassins who dominate our municipal life. We know that we cannot even complain that the racketeers are breaking the laws which are supposed to be guaranteed by the government, because the government differs little from the racketeers. How can we expect them, then, to check the relatively respectable scoundrels who merely rob us of the public utilities by more or less legalistic means?

Yet, as I say, it may be true that, with the present breakdown, we have come to the end of something, and that we are ready to start on a different tack. If we look back through the depressions of the last fifty years, we see that through every one of them there always remained something for which the Americans could still legitimately feel ambition or enthusiasm, something to challenge the national spirit and appeal to the national imagination. . . . [But] the future is as blank in the United States today as the situation is desperate: the President seems so inhibited by dread of encouraging subversive forces and by faith in the capacity of the capitalist system to right itself and survive that it is impossible for him to act, and when he tries to, he is deadlocked by Congress; nor have the industrialists or the financiers come forward with any constructive proposal. But this very blindness of the outlook may mean that we are looking in the wrong direction and that help may be coming from some other quarter. In the meantime, one gets the impression that the people who don't deal in ideas are doing more thinking at the present time than the professional ideologues.

The minds of the general public have, furthermore, been more affected by the example of Soviet Russia than is easily grasped by anyone who has been in the habit of assuming that it is only the radical or liberal who understands what Russia is up to, and that the ordinary American citizen is bound to be stupidly prejudiced against the Soviet system. During the NEP period in Russia, the capitalist powers were relieved to feel that the Russians had been forced to recognize the impracticability of Communism and were quietly returning to laissez faire. But with the inauguration of the Five-Year-Plan to eliminate capitalist business in Russia, the aspect of things changed. The apparent success of the plan has had its effect on all classes in all the rest of the world—on the Americans, surely, not least. In the course of this winter of our capitalist quandary, the Soviets have been emerging from the back pages of the New York newspapers and are now given much and prominent space—even to interviews with Stalin's mother; and behind what one reads on the subject in even the reactionary papers, one feels as much admiration as resentment. After all, the great Communist project is distinguished by almost all the features that Americans have been taught to glorify—the extreme of efficiency and economy combined with the ideal of a herculean program—like a Liberty Loan drive—to put over by concerted action to the tune of impassioned boosting. The Russians, furthermore, on their own side, have been studying American methods: they have imported a thousand American engineers and put them at the head of enormous enterprises with practically a free hand, and one would not be at all surprised to hear that Mr. Edward L. Bernays had been in Moscow at the time of the recent trial. We have already, in spite of the Treasury regulation, been doing a good deal of trading with Russia, and an important New York bank was at one time on the point of advancing to the Soviets the loan that has been advocated by this magazine [*New Republic*].

The Communists in the United States assume that, by their very nature, neither our government nor our business is capable of learning anything from or of associating itself with the Soviets. They believe that a war against Russia is inevitable. They believe, moreover, that they themselves constitute a trained compact minority which, at the moment when American capitalism shall have finally broken down completely and been left helpless in its ignorance and anarchic selfishness, will be able to step in and man the works. To liberals, this idea has always sounded absurd, but who will say that it is entirely fantastic today when the machine is so badly in need of repairs, and one can see no political group in any position of power that has either a sensible plan or even good intentions? I believe that if the American radicals and progressives who repudiate the Marxist dogma and the strategy of the Communist Party still hope to accomplish anything valuable, they must take Communism away from the Communists, and take it without ambiguities, asserting that their ultimate goal is the ownership by the government of the means of production. If we want to prove the Communists wrong, if we want to demonstrate that the virtue has not gone out of American democracy, if we want to confute the Marxist cynicism implied by "economic laws" the catastrophic outcome of which is, after all, predicted only on an assumption of the incurable swinishness and inertia of human nature—if we seriously want to do this, an American opposition must not be afraid to dynamite the old conceptions and shibboleths and to substitute new ones as shocking as necessary. Who knows but they may seem less shocking to the ordinary suffering public than to us shibboleth-experts ourselves? When John Dos Passos proposed last summer that what was really needed in the United States was a publicity expert like Ivy Lee to familiarize the public with the idea of Communism and induce people at least to remain neutral toward Communist agitation instead of clapping all the Communists in jail, the suggestion, to some, sounded comic. Yet Dos Passos at once had a letter from a publicity man in San Francisco, who said that the same idea had recently occurred to him and that he would like nothing better than a chance to carry it out. There are some signs that the liberals are having ideas as well as the publicity men: Stuart Chase has said lately that the past year may represent "the end of an epoch" and has offered a set of suggestions for rescuing the economic structure, and John Dewey has just proposed to Senator Norris that he lead a new political party. The extreme illiberalism of the post-Wilsonian period has had the effect of discouraging liberals. We have gone on complaining and recommending, but with a vigor that has tended to diminish in proportion as we came to be conscious that people were not listening to us. Who knows but, if we spoke out now with confidence and boldness, we might find our public at last?

FRANKLIN D. ROOSEVELT

Although born to aristocratic wealth and prestige, Franklin D. Roosevelt (1882–1945) is known to history as the chief architect of the "third American revolution"—the New Deal.

Roosevelt went from a family estate at Hyde Park, New York, to the Groton School, Harvard, and Columbia Law School. His early political career was more perfunctory, however, than might have been expected. Like many younger men who came to political maturity in America about 1910, Roosevelt was touched by the reform enthusiasm of the age, although he was a Wilsonian Democrat rather than a supporter of his distant cousin Theodore Roosevelt, a Republican. He was a state senator, assistant secretary of the navy under Wilson, and the Democratic nominee for vice president in 1920. Warren G. Harding's sweeping victory over the Democratic presidential nominee James M. Cox seemed to doom the young Roosevelt to political obscurity.

A year later, on a summer vacation, Roosevelt contracted poliomyelitis. For the next seven years he battled the effects of the disease. He recovered sufficiently to re-enter politics in 1928, but he was badly crippled for the rest of his life, and carefully minimized his lameness before the public. Between 1928 and 1932 Roosevelt served as governor of New York, compiling a modest reform record, which, however, along with most of his public pronouncements of that time, did not foreshadow the revolution that he was to lead when he was elected President at the depths of the Great Depression in 1932.

Historians are closer to agreement on the effects of the New Deal than on the motives and ideals that inspired it. The Roosevelt years fundamentally altered the role of the federal government in the national economy and made the nation's politicians more conscious than ever before of the claims and interests of working people, small farmers, and minority groups. In its own time, however, Roosevelt's New Deal was all things to all men; experiment is the word enthusiasts use to describe it; others speak of mere expediency. Although the New Deal did not cure the economic ills of the depression it both revived faith in and increased the powers of democratic government at a time when free institutions elsewhere in the world were close to exhaustion. At the heart of the history of the New Deal there still lies the mystery of Roosevelt himself, that baffling combination of master politician, patrician humanitarian, and Machiavellian.

The first selection comes from that period of the New Deal when the government's strategy shifted. After first entrusting economic recovery to the nation's business interests, Roosevelt moved to create mass purchasing power directly and to reduce both privilege and social blight. By 1935 the failures of the early New Deal had helped the cause of a number of demagogues in the nation. The possible defection of voters to them, as well as the growing evidence of the misfiring of early plans for economic recovery, elicited the more radical economic and social program that undoubtedly helped bring Roosevelt his great re-election victory in 1936.

The extracts from Roosevelt's speeches are taken from *The Public Papers and Addresses of Franklin D. Roosevelt* (New York: Random House, 1938).

ANNUAL MESSAGE TO CONGRESS, JANUARY 4, 1935

Mr. President, Mr. Speaker, Members of the Senate and of the House of Representatives: . . .

We have undertaken a new order of things: yet we progress to it under the framework and in the spirit and intent of the American Constitution. We have proceeded throughout the nation a measurable distance on the road towards this new order. Materially, I can report to you substantial benefits to our agricultural population, increased industrial activity, and profits to our merchants. Of equal moment, there is evident a restoration of that spirit of confidence and faith which marks the American character. Let him who, for speculative profit or partisan purpose, without just warrant would seek to disturb or dispel this assurance, take heed before he assumes responsibility for any act which slows our onward steps. . . .

Let us, for a moment, strip from our simple purpose the confusion that results from a multiplicity of detail and from millions of written and spoken words.

We find our population suffering from old inequalities, little changed by past sporadic remedies. In spite of our efforts and in spite of our talk, we have not weeded out the over-privileged and we have not effectively lifted up the under-privileged. Both of these manifestations of injustice have retarded happiness. No wise man has any intention of destroying what is known as the profit motive: because by the profit motive we mean the right by work to earn a decent livelihood for ourselves and for our families.

We have, however, a clear mandate from the people, that Americans must forswear that conception of the acquisition of wealth which, through excessive profits, creates undue private power over private affairs and, to our misfortune, over public affairs as well. In building toward this end, we do not destroy ambition nor do we seek to divide our wealth into equal shares on stated occasions. We continue to recognize the greater ability of some to earn more than others. But we do assert that the ambition of the individual to obtain for him and his a proper security, a reasonable leisure, and a decent living throughout life, is an ambition to be preferred to the appetite for great wealth and great power.

I recall to your attention my Message to the Congress last June in which I said—"among our objectives I place the security of the men, women and children of the nation first." That remains our first and continuing task; and in a very real sense every major legislative enactment of this Congress should be a component part of it.

In defining immediate factors which enter into our quest, I have spoken to the Congress and the people of three great divisions:

1. The security of a livelihood through the better use of the national resources of the land in which we live.
2. The security against the major hazards and vicissitudes of life.
3. The security of decent homes.

I am now ready to submit to the Congress a broad program designed ultimately to establish all three of these factors of security—a program which because of many lost years will take many future years to fulfill.

A study of our national resources, more comprehensive than any previously made, shows the vast amount of necessary and practicable work which needs to be done for the development and preservation of our natural wealth for the enjoyment and advantage of our people in generations to come. The sound use of land and water is far more comprehensive than the mere planting of trees, building of dams, distributing of electricity or retirement of sub-marginal land. It recognizes that stranded populations, either in the country or the city, cannot have security under the conditions that now surround them.

To this end we are ready to begin to meet this problem—the intelligent care of population throughout our nation, in accordance with an intelligent distribution of the means of livelihood for that population. A definite program for putting people to work, of which I shall speak in a moment, is a component part of this greater program of security of livelihood through the better use of our national resources.

Closely related to the broad problem of livelihood is that of security against the major hazards of life. Here also a comprehensive survey of what has been attempted or accomplished in many nations and in many States proves to me that the time has come for action by the National Government. I shall send to you, in a few days, definite recommendations based on these studies. These recommendations will cover the broad subjects of unemployment insurance and old age insurance, of benefits for children, for mothers, for the handicapped, for maternity care and for other aspects of dependency and illness where a beginning can now be made.

The third factor—better homes for our people—has also been the subject of experimentation and study. Here, too, the first practical steps can be made through the proposals which I shall suggest in relation to giving work to the unemployed.

Whatever we plan and whatever we do should be in the light of these three clear objectives of security. We cannot afford to lose valuable time in haphazard public policies which cannot find a place in the broad outlines of these major purposes. In that spirit I come to an immediate issue made for us by hard and inescapable circumstance—the task of putting people to work. In the spring of 1933 the issue of destitution seemed to stand apart; today, in the light of our experience and our new national policy, we find we can put people to work in ways which conform to, initiate and carry forward the broad principles of that policy.

The first objectives of emergency legislation of 1933 were, to relieve destitution, to make it possible for industry to operate in a more rational and orderly fashion, and to put behind industrial recovery the impulse of large expenditures in government undertakings. The purpose of the National Industrial Recovery Act to provide work for more people succeeded in a substantial manner within the first few months of its life, and the Act has continued to maintain employment gains and greatly improved working conditions in industry.

The program of public works provided for in the Recovery Act launched the Federal government into a task for which there was little time to make preparation and little American experience to follow. Great employment has been given and is being given by these works.

More than two billions of dollars have also been expended in direct relief to the destitute. Local agencies of necessity determined the recipients of this form of relief. With inevitable exceptions the funds were spent by them with reasonable efficiency and as a result actual want of food and clothing in the great majority of cases has been overcome.

But the stark fact before us is that great numbers still remain unemployed.

A large proportion of these unemployed and their dependents have been forced on the relief rolls. The burden on the Federal government has grown with great rapidity. We have here a human as well as an economic problem. When humane considerations are concerned, Americans give them precedence. The lessons of history, confirmed by the evidence immediately before me, show conclusively that continued dependence upon relief induces a spiritual and moral disintegration fundamentally destructive to the national fibre. To dole out relief in this way is to administer a narcotic, a subtle destroyer of the human spirit. It is inimical to the dictates of sound policy, it is in violation of the traditions of America. Work must be found for able bodied but destitute workers.

The Federal government must and shall quit this business of relief.

I am not willing that the vitality of our people be further sapped by the giving of cash, of market baskets, of a few hours of weekly work cutting grass, raking leaves or picking up papers in the public parks. We must preserve not only the bodies of the unemployed from destitution but also their self-respect, their self-reliance and courage and determination. This decision brings me to the problem of what the government should do with approximately five million unemployed now on the relief rolls.

About one million and a half of these belong to the group which in the past was dependent upon local welfare efforts. Most of them are unable for one reason or another to maintain themselves independently—for the most part, through no fault of their own. Such people, in the days before the great depression, were cared for by local efforts—by states, by counties, by towns, by cities, by churches and by private welfare agencies. It is my thought that in the future they must be cared for as they were before. I stand ready through my own personal efforts, and through the public influence of the office that I hold, to help these local agencies to get the means necessary to assume this burden.

The security legislation which I shall propose to the Congress will, I am confident, be of assistance to local effort in the care of this type of cases. Local responsibility can and will be resumed, for, after all, common sense tells us that the wealth necessary for this task existed and still exists in the local community, and the dictates of sound administration require that this responsibility be in the first instance a local one.

There are however an additional three and one half million employable people who are on relief. With them the problem is different and the responsibility is different. This group was the victim of a nationwide depression caused by conditions which were not local but national. The Federal government is the only governmental agency with sufficient power and credit to meet this situation. We have assumed this task and we shall not shrink from it in the future. It is a duty dictated by every intelligent consideration of national policy to ask you to make it possible for the United States to give employment to all of these three and one half million employable people now on relief, pending their absorption in a rising tide of private employment.

It is my thought that with the exception of certain of the normal public building operations of the government, all emergency public works shall be united in a single new and greatly enlarged plan.

With the establishment of this new system we can supersede the Federal Emergency Relief Administration with a co-ordinated authority which will be charged with the orderly liquidation of our present relief activities and the substitution of a national chart for the giving of work. . . .

Ever since the adjournment of the 73rd Congress, the Administration has been studying from every angle the possibility and the practicability of new forms of employment. As a result of these studies I have arrived at certain very definite convictions as to the amount of money that will be necessary for the sort of public projects that I have described. I shall submit these figures in my budget message. I assure you now they will be within the sound credit of the government.

The work itself will cover a wide field including clearance of slums, which for adequate reasons cannot be undertaken by private capital; in rural housing of several kinds, where, again, private capital is unable to function; in rural electrification; in the reforestation of the great watersheds of the nation; in an intensified program to prevent soil erosion and to reclaim blighted areas; in improving existing road systems and in constructing national highways designed to handle modern traffic; in the elimination of grade crossings; in the extension and enlargement of the successful work of the Civilian Conservation Corps; in non-Federal work, mostly self-liquidating and highly useful to local divisions of government; and on many other projects which the nation needs and cannot afford to neglect.

CAMPAIGN SPEECH, CHICAGO, OCTOBER 14, 1936

Mr. Chairman, Governor Horner, Mayor Kelly, my friends of the great State of Illinois:

I seem to have been here before.

Four years ago I dropped into this city from the airways—an old friend come in a new way—to accept in this hall the nomination for the Presidency of the United States. I came to a Chicago fighting with its back to the wall —factories closed, markets silent, banks shaky, ships and trains empty. Today those factories sing the song of industry—markets hum with bustling movement, banks are secure, ships and trains are running full. Once again it is a Chicago that smiles. And with Chicago a whole nation that had not been cheerful for years is full of cheer once more.

On this trip I have talked to farmers, I have talked to miners, I have talked to industrial workers—and in all that I have seen and heard one fact has been clear as crystal—that they are part and parcel of a rounded whole, and that none of them can succeed in their chosen occupations if those in the other occupations fall or fail in their prosperity. I have driven that point home.

And tonight, in this center of business of America, I give the same message to the business men of America—to those who make and sell the processed goods the Nation uses and to the men and women who work for them.

To them I say:

Do you have a deposit in the bank? It is safer today than it has ever been in our history. It is guaranteed. Last October first marked the end of the first full year in 55 years without a single failure of a national bank in the United States. Isn't that on the credit side of the government's account with you?

Are you an investor? Your stocks and bonds are up to a five and six year high level.

Are you a merchant? Your markets have the precious lifeblood of purchasing power. Your customers on the farms have better incomes and smaller debts. Your customers in the cities have more jobs, surer jobs, better jobs. Didn't your government have something to do with this?

Are you in industry? Industrial earnings, industrial profits are the highest in four, six, or even seven years! Bankruptcies are at a new low. Your government takes some credit for that.

Are you in railroads? Freight loadings are steadily going up and so are passenger receipts because, for one reason, your government made the railroads cut rates and make money.

Are you a middleman in the great stream of farm products? The meat and grain that move through your yards and elevators have a steadier supply, a steadier demand and steadier prices than you have known for years. And your government is trying to keep it that way.

Now, my friends, some people say that all this recovery has just happened. But in a complicated modern world recoveries from depressions do not just happen. The years from 1929 to 1933 when we waited for recovery just to happen, proves the point.

But in 1933, after March 4th, we did not wait—we acted. Behind the growing recovery of today is a story of deliberate government acceptance of responsibility to save business—to save the American system of private enterprise and economic democracy—a record unequaled by any modern government in history. . . .

Because we cherished our system of private property and free enterprise and were determined to preserve it as the foundation of our traditional

American system, we recalled the warning of Thomas Jefferson that "widespread poverty and concentrated wealth cannot long endure side by side in a democracy."

And so our job was to preserve the American ideal of economic as well as political democracy, against the abuse of concentration of economic power that had been insidiously growing up among us in the last fifty years, particularly during the twelve years of preceding Administrations. Free economic enterprise was being weeded out at an alarming pace.

During those years of false prosperity one business after another, one small corporation after another, their resources depleted, had failed or had fallen into the lap of a bigger competitor.

A dangerous thing was happening. More than half of the corporate wealth of the country had come under the control of less than two hundred big corporations. That is not all. These huge corporations in some cases did not even try to compete with each other. They themselves were tied together by interlocking directors, interlocking bankers and interlocking lawyers.

This concentration of wealth and power has been built upon other people's money, other people's business, other people's labor. Under this concentration independent business was allowed to exist only by sufferance. It has been a menace to the social system as well as the economic system which we call American Democracy.

As a matter of practical fact, there is no excuse for it in the cold terms of industrial efficiency.

There is no excuse for it from the point of view of the average investor.

There is no excuse for it from the point of view of the independent business man.

I believe, I have always believed, and I always will believe in private enterprise as the backbone of economic well-being in the United States.

But I know, and you know, and every independent business man who has had to struggle against the competition of monopolies knows, that this concentration of economic power in all-embracing corporations does not represent private enterprise as we Americans cherish it and propose to foster it. On the contrary, it represents private enterprise which has become a kind of private government and is a power unto itself—a regimentation of other people's money and other people's lives.

Back in Kansas I spoke about bogey-men and fairy tales which the real Republican leaders, many of whom are part of this concentrated power, are using to spread fear among the American people.

You good people have heard about these fairy tales and bogey-men too.

You have heard about how antagonistic to business this Administration is supposed to be. You have heard all about the dangers which the business of America is supposed to be facing if this Administration continues.

My friends, the answer to that is the record of what we have done. It was this Administration which saved the system of private profit and free enterprise after it had been dragged to the brink of ruin by these same leaders who now try to scare you.

Look at the advance in private business in the last three and a half years; and read there what we think about private business.

Today for the first time in seven years the banker, the storekeeper, the small factory owner, the industrialist, can all sit back and enjoy the company of their own ledgers. They are in the black. That is where we want them to be; that is where our policies aim that they shall be; that is where we intend them to be in the days to come.

Some of these people really forget how sick they were. But I know how sick they were. I have their fever charts. I know how the knees of all of our rugged individualists were trembling four years ago and how their hearts fluttered. They came to Washington in great numbers. Washington did not look like a dangerous bureaucracy to them then. No, it looked like an emergency hospital. And all of these distinguished patients wanted two things—a quick hypodermic to end the pain and they wanted a course of treatment to cure the disease. They wanted them in a hurry, and we gave them both. And now, my friends, most of the patients seem to be doing very nicely. Some of them are even well enough to throw their crutches at the doctor.

I believe in individualism. I believe in it in the arts, sciences and professions. I believe in it in business. I believe in individualism in all these things—up to the point where the individualist starts to operate at the expense of society. And the overwhelming majority of American business men do not believe in it beyond that point. We have all suffered in the past from individualism run wild—society has suffered and business has suffered.

And so, believing in the solvency of business, the solvency of farmers and the solvency of workers, I believe also in the solvency of Government. Your Government is solvent.

The net Federal debt today is lower in proportion to the income of the Nation and in proportion to the wealth of the Nation than it was on March 4, 1933.

And in the future it will become lower still because with the rising tide of national income and national wealth, the very causes of our emergency spending are starting to disappear, Government expenditures are coming down, and Government income is going up. And so, my friends, the opportunities for private enterprise will continue to expand.

The people of America have no quarrel with business. They insist only that the power of concentrated wealth shall not be abused.

We have come through a hard struggle to preserve democracy in America. Where other nations in other parts of the world have lost that fight, we have won it.

The businessmen of America and all other citizens have joined in a firm resolve to hold the fruits of that victory—to cling to the old ideals, to cling to the old fundamentals upon which America has grown great.

JOHN DEWEY

THE RELEASE of individuals from the frustrations and log jams of the Great Depression seemed to depend on a number of positive public policies. John Dewey (1859–1952), one of the most influential modern American liberals, envisaged a program of welfare-state activities even before 1929. The crisis in America in the 1930s sharpened the pertinency of his ideas. Dewey believed he had combined the best aspects of the two classic formulations of liberty: the view of liberty as the absence of restraint and the view of liberty as perfect obedience to perfect law. Dewey's philosophy of democracy is different from that of most of his predecessors of the nineteenth century by virtue of the greater importance he attaches to free inquiry and to the scientific method of testing and reformulating hypotheses in the light of discoverable facts. Liberty and equality were for him not absolute endowments of individuals, but the relative rewards of democratic society. The democratic process of spreading public responsibility over progressively wider areas demands the extensive fostering of the powers of free thought and independent judgment.

For many day-to-day social problems Dewey relied less on government than on "voluntary associations." Schools, laboratories, unions, lobbies, any cooperative attempt at achieving some common good—not possessed exclusively, but shared with still wider groups—these are the institutions of democracy. Government is democratic insofar as it is responsive to these many groups with their diversified interests, regulating where necessary, in the hope of striking a balance between what seems a present general good and the legitimate needs of private associations.

The first of the following selections appeared in the magazine section of the New York *Times,* February 23, 1936. It was Dewey's restatement in summary form of the views expressed in his *Liberalism and Social Action,* which had appeared some months earlier. Dewey's conception of democracy came at least in part from his experience with educational practice and administration and has in turn contributed tremendously to the reshaping of American educational aims and methods. The second selection is taken from his speech before the National Education Association, 1937, and was published in *School and Society,* April, 1937, under the title "Democracy and Educational Administration."

LIBERALISM AND SOCIAL ACTION

LIBERALISM as a conscious and aggressive movement arose in Great Britain as two different streams flowed into one. One of these streams was the humanitarian and philanthropic zeal that became so active late in the eighteenth century and that in various forms is still a mighty current. It was expressed in the feeling that man is his brother's keeper and that the world is full of suffering and evil that are caused by failure to recognize this fact. . . .

The other great stream that entered into the formation of liberalism sprang from the stimulus to manufacturing and trade that came from the application of steam to industry. The great intellectual leader of this moment was Adam Smith. . . . While the two streams came together, they never coalesced. Although the humanitarian movement expressed itself most actively in personal and voluntary effort, it was far from averse to employing governmental agencies to achieve its reforms. Most of them, in fact, like abolition of the slave trade, prison reform, removal of abuses attending the labor of women and children, could not be effected without some intervention on the part of government.

The whole movement toward what is known as social legislation with its slogan of social justice derives from this source and involves more and more appeal to governmental action. Hence there was from the beginning an inner split in liberalism. Any attempt to define liberalism in terms of one or the other of its two strains will be vehemently denied by those attached to the other strain.

Historically, the split was embodied in the person of one of the chief representatives of nineteenth-century liberalism, Jeremy Bentham. Whether he was aware of it or not, his leading principle, that of the greatest happiness of the greatest number, was derived from the philanthropic and humanitarian movement. But when it came to the realization of this goal, he ranked himself, with some exceptions, such as public health and public education, with laissez-faire liberalism.

He was strong for political action to reform abuses of judicial procedure, of law-making and methods of electing law-makers, but he regarded the abuses to be corrected as the product of the failure of government in the past to confine itself to its proper sphere. When the abuses of governmental action by government were once removed, he believed that the free play of individual initiative and effort would furnish the sure road to progress and to producing the greatest happiness of the greatest number.

As I have indicated, the inner breach in liberalism has never been healed. On the Continent, so-called liberal parties have been almost universally the political representatives of big industry, banking and commerce. In Great Britain, true to the spirit of tradition and compromise so strong in English affairs, liberalism has been a mixture of the two strains, leaning now in one direction and now in another.

In the United States liberalism has been identified largely with the idea of the use of governmental agencies to remedy evils from which the less-fortunate classes suffer. It was "forward-looking" in the Progressive movement; it lies, nominally at least, behind Square Deals and New Deals. It has favored employer-liability acts, laws regulating hours and conditions of labor, anti-sweatshop legislation, supplementation of private charity by public relief and public works, generous appropriations for public schools, graded higher taxation of larger incomes and of inheritances; in general, when there has been a conflict between labor and employers it has sided with labor.

Its philosophy has rarely been clear cut. But so far as it has had a philosophy it has been that government should regularly intervene to help equalize conditions between the wealthy and the poor, between the overprivileged and the underprivileged. For this reason liberals of the other, or laissez-faire, school have always attacked it as pink socialism, as disguised radicalism; while at the present time the favorite charge is that it is instigated, of all places in the world, from Moscow.

As a matter of fact, up to this time in this country political liberalism has never attempted to change the fundamental conditions of the economic system or to do more than ameliorate the estate in which the mass of human beings live. For this reason liberalism at present is under more violent attack from radicals than from conservatives. In the mouth of radicals liberalism is a term of hissing and reproach.

In spite of the extreme clash, both schools of liberalism profess devotion to the same ultimate ideal and goal. The slogan of both schools is the utmost possible liberty of the individual. The difference between them concerns the province in which liberty and individuality are most important and the means by which they are to be realized. One has only to read any outgiving of the adherents of laissez-faire liberalism to see that it is the liberty of the entrepreneur in business undertakings which they prize and which they come close to identifying with the heart of all liberty.

To the spokesmen of the Liberty League and to ex-President Hoover in his doctrine of rugged individualism, any governmental action that interferes with this particular kind of liberty is an attack upon liberty itself. The ruggedness, independence, initiative and vigor of individuals upon which they set chief store is that of the individuals who have come to the top in the existing economic system of finance capitalism. They are exposed to the charge of identifying the meaning of liberty and of rugged individualism with the maintenance of the system under which they have prospered.

The charge is given force by the fact that they have for the most part supported the system of protective tariffs, against which original simon-pure laissez-faire liberals directed some of their most violent attacks. The author of the phrase "rugged individualism" used the government to come to the aid of industry when it was in straits by means of the Reconstruction Finance Corporation, and, as far as I know, the opponents of governmental intervention made no protest in this flagrant case of governmental interference with the free course of private industry.

The most vocal spokesmen for this special form of liberty have never attacked land monopoly and if they think at all about Henry George, think of him as one of the subversive and dangerous radicals. They have themselves built up financial and industrial systems so concentrated as to be semi-monopolies or monopolies proper.

Liberals of the other school are those who point to things like those just mentioned and who assert that the system of industry for private profit without regard to social consequences has had in fact a most unfavorable effect upon the real liberty of the mass of individuals.

Their conception of what I called the province of liberty and individuality is broader and more generous than is that of those who come forward as the self-appointed champions of liberty. They think that liberty is something that affects every aspect and phase of human life, liberty of thought, of expression, of cultural opportunity, and that it is not to be had, even in the economic sphere, without a degree of security that is denied to millions by the present economic system.

They point out that industry, banking and commerce have reached a point where there is no such thing as merely private initiative and enterprise. For the consequences of private business enterprise affect so many persons and in such deep and enduring ways that all business is affected with a public interest. Since the consequences of business are social, society must itself look after, by means of increased organized control, the industrial and financial causes of these consequences.

There is, accordingly, no doubt in my own mind that laissez-faire liberalism is played out, largely because of the fruits of its own policies. Any system that cannot provide elementary security for millions has no claim to the title of being organized in behalf of liberty and the development of individuals. Any person and any movement whose interest in these ends is genuine and not a cover for personal advantage and power must put primary emphasis in thought and action upon the means of their attainment.

At present those means lie in the direction of increased social control and increased collectivism of effort. Humane liberalism in order to save itself must cease to deal with symptoms and go to the causes of which inequalities and oppressions are but the symptoms. In order to endure under present conditions, liberalism must become radical in the sense that, instead of using social power to ameliorate the evil consequences of the existing system, it shall use social power to change the system.

Radicalism in the minds of many, however, both among its professed adherents and its bitter enemies, is identified with a particular method of changing the system. To them, it means the change of the present system by violent overthrow. Radicalism of this sort is opposed to liberalism and liberalism is opposed to it. For liberalism both by its history and by its own nature is committed to democratic methods of effecting social change.

The idea of forcing men to be free is an old idea, but by nature it is opposed to freedom. Freedom is not something that can be handed to men as a gift from outside, whether by old-fashioned dynastic benevolent despotisms or by new-fashioned dictatorships, whether of the proletarian or of the Fascist order. It is something which can be had only as individuals participate in winning it, and this fact, rather than some particular political mechanism, is the essence of democratic liberalism.

The denial of the democratic method of achieving social control is in part the product of sheer impatience and romantic longing for a short-cut which if it were taken would defeat its own end. It is in part the fruit of the Russian revolution, oblivious of the fact that Russia never had any democratic tradition in its whole history and was accustomed to dictatorial rule in a way that is foreign to the spirit of every Western country. In part, it is the product of the capture of the machinery of democratic legislation and administration by the dominant economic power, known for short as plutocracy or "the interests."

Discontent with democracy as it operates under conditions of exploitation by special interests has justification. But the notion that the remedy is violence and a civil war between classes is a counsel of despair. If the method of violence and civil war be adopted the end will be either fascism, open and undisguised, or the common ruin of both parties to the struggle. The democratic method of social change is slow; it labors under many and serious handicaps imposed by the undemocratic character of what passes for democracy. But it is the method of liberalism, with its belief that liberty is the means as well as the goal and that only through the development of individuals in their voluntary cooperation with one another can the development of individuality be made secure and enduring.

DEMOCRACY

DEMOCRACY is much broader than a special political form, a method of conducting government, of making laws and carrying on governmental administration by means of popular suffrage and elected officers. It is that, of course. But it is something broader and deeper than that. The political and governmental phase of democracy is a means, the best means so far found, for realizing ends that lie in the wide domain of human relationships and the development of human personality. It is, as we often say, though perhaps without appreciating all that is involved in the saying, a way of life, social and individual. The key-note of democracy as a way of life may be expressed, it seems to me, as the necessity for the participation of every mature human being in formation of the values that regulate the living of men together: which is necessary from the standpoint of both the general social welfare and the full development of human beings as individuals.

Universal suffrage, recurring elections, responsibility of those who are in political power to the voters, and the other factors of democratic government are means that have been found expedient for realizing democracy as the truly human way of living. They are not a final end and a final value. They are to be judged on the basis of their contribution to an end. It is a form of idolatry to erect means into the end which they serve. Democratic political forms are simply the best means that human wit has devised up to a special time in history. But they rest back upon the idea that no man or limited set of men is wise enough or good enough to rule others without their consent; the positive meaning of this statement is that all those who are affected by social institutions must have a share in producing and managing them. The two facts that each one is influenced in what he does and enjoys and in what he becomes by the institutions under which he lives, and that therefore he shall have, in a democracy, a voice in shaping them, are the passive and active sides of the same fact.

The development of political democracy came about through substitution of the method of mutual consultation and voluntary agreement for the method of subordination of the many to the few enforced from above. Social arrangements which involve fixed subordination are maintained by coercion. The coercion need not be physical. There have existed, for short periods, benevolent despotisms. But coercion of some sort there has been; perhaps economic, certainly psychological and moral. The very fact of exclusion from participation is a subtle form of suppression. It gives individuals no opportunity to reflect and decide upon what is good for them. Others who are supposed to be wiser and who in any case have more power decide the question for them and also decide the methods and means by which subjects may arrive at the enjoyment of what is good for them. This form of coercion and suppression is more subtle and more effective than is overt intimidation and restraint. When it is habitual and embodied in social institutions, it seems the normal and natural state of affairs. The mass usually become unaware that they have a claim to a development of their own powers. Their experience is so restricted that they are not conscious of restriction. It is part of the democratic conception that they as individuals are not the only sufferers, but that the whole social body is deprived of the potential resources that should be at its service. The individuals of the submerged mass may not be very wise. But there is one thing they are wiser about than anybody else can be, and that is where the shoe pinches, the troubles they suffer from.

The foundation of democracy is faith in the capacities of human nature; faith in human intelligence and in the power of pooled and cooperative experience. It is not belief that these things are complete but that if given a show they will grow and be able to generate progressively the knowledge and wisdom needed to guide collective action. Every autocratic and authoritarian scheme of social action rests on a belief that the needed intelligence is confined to a superior few, who because of inherent natural gifts are endowed with the ability and the right to control the conduct of others; laying down principles and rules and directing the ways in which they are carried out. It would be foolish to deny that much can be said for this point of view. It is that which controlled human relations in social groups for much the greater part of human history. The democratic faith has emerged very, very recently in the history of mankind. Even where democracies now exist, men's minds and feelings are still permeated with ideals about leadership imposed from above, ideas that develop in the long early history of mankind. After democratic political institutions were nominally established, beliefs and ways of looking at life and of acting that originated when men and women were externally controlled and subjected to arbitrary power, persisted in the family, the church, business and the school, and experience shows that as long as they persist there, political democracy is not secure.

Belief in equality is an element of the democratic credo. It is not, however, belief in equality of natural endowments. Those who proclaimed the idea of equality did not suppose they were enunciating a psychological doctrine, but a legal and political one. All individuals are entitled to equality of treatment by law and in its administration. Each one is affected equally in quality if not in quantity by the institutions under which he lives and has an equal right to express his judgment, although the weight of his judgment may not be equal in amount when it enters into the pooled result to that of others. In short, each one is equally an individual and entitled to equal opportunity of development of his own capacities, be they large or small in range. Moreover, each has needs of his own, as significant to him as those of others are to them. The very fact of natural and psychological inequality is all the more reason for establishment by law of equality of opportunity, since otherwise the former becomes a means of oppression of the less gifted.

While what we call intelligence be distributed in unequal amounts, it is the democratic faith that it is sufficiently general so that each individual has something to contribute, whose value can be assessed only as it enters into the final pooled intelligence constituted by the contributions of all. Every authoritarian scheme, on the contrary, assumes that its value may be assessed by some *prior* principle, if not of family and birth or race and color or possession of material wealth, then by the position and rank a person occupies in the existing social scheme. The democratic faith in equality is the faith that each individual shall have the chance and opportunity to contribute whatever he is capable of contributing and that the value of his contribution be decided by its place and function in the organized total of similar contributions, not on the basis of prior status of any kind whatever.

I have emphasized in what precedes the importance of the effective release of intelligence in connection with personal experience in the democratic way of living. I have done so purposely because democracy is so often and so naturally associated in our minds with freedom of *action*, forgetting the importance of freed intelligence which is necessary to direct and to warrant freedom of action. Unless freedom of individual action has intelligence and informed conviction back of it, its manifestation is almost sure to result in confusion and disorder. The democratic idea of freedom is not the right of each individual to *do* as he pleases, even if it be qualified by adding "provided he does not interfere with the same freedom on the part of others." While the idea is not always, not often enough, expressed in words, the basic freedom is that of freedom of *mind* and of whatever degree of freedom of action and experience is necessary to produce freedom of intelligence. The modes of freedom guaranteed in the Bill of Rights are all of this nature: Freedom of belief and conscience, of expression of opinion, of assembly for discussion and conference, of the press as an organ of communication. They are guaranteed because without them individuals are not free to develop and society is deprived of what they might contribute. . . .

There is some kind of government, of control, wherever affairs that concern a number of persons who act together are engaged in. It is a superficial view that holds government is located in Washington and Albany. There is government in the family, in business, in the church, in every social group. There are regulations, due to custom if not to enactment, that settle how individuals in a group act in connection with one another.

It is a disputed question of theory and practice just how far a democratic political government should go in control of the conditions of action within special groups. At the present time, for example, there are those who think the federal and state governments leave too much freedom of independent action to industrial and financial groups, and there are others who think the government is going altogether too far at the present time. I do not need to discuss this phase of the problem, much less to try to settle it. But it must be pointed out that if the methods of regulation and administration in vogue in the conduct of secondary social groups are non-democratic, whether directly or indirectly or both, there is bound to be an unfavorable reaction back into the habits of feeling, thought and action of citizenship in the broadest sense of that word. The way in which any organized social interest is controlled necessarily plays an important part in forming the dispositions and tastes, the attitudes, interests, purposes and desires, of those engaged in carrying on the activities of the group. For illustration, I do not need to do more than point to the moral, emotional and intellectual effect upon both employers and laborers of the existing industrial system. Just what the effects specifically are is a matter about which we know very little. But I suppose that every one who reflects upon the subject admits that it is impossible that the ways in which activities are carried on for the greater part of the waking hours of the day; and the way in which the share of individuals are involved in the management of affairs in such a matter as gaining a livelihood and attaining material and social security, can not but be a highly important factor in shaping personal dispositions; in short, forming character and intelligence.

In the broad and final sense all institutions are educational in the sense that they operate to form the attitudes, dispositions, abilities and disabilities that constitute a concrete personality. The principle applies with special force to the school. For it is the main business of the family and the school to influence directly the formation and growth of attitudes and dispositions, emotional, intellectual and moral. Whether this educative process is carried on in a predominantly democratic or non-democratic way becomes, therefore, a question of transcendent importance not only for education itself but for its final effect upon all the interests and activities of a society that is committed to the democratic way of life. . . .

There are certain corollaries which clarify the meaning of the issue. Absence of participation tends to produce lack of interest and concern on the part of those shut out. The result is a corresponding lack of effective responsibility. Automatically and unconsciously, if not consciously, the feeling develops, "This is none of our affair; it is the business of those at the top; let that particular set of Georges do what needs to be done." The countries in which autocratic government prevails are just those in which there is least public spirit and the greatest indifference to matters of general as distinct from personal concern. Can we expect a different kind of psychology to actuate teachers? Where there is little power, there is correspondingly little sense of positive responsibility. It is enough to do what one is told to do sufficiently well to escape flagrant unfavorable notice. About larger matters, a spirit of passivity is engendered. In some cases, indifference passes into evasion of duties when not directly under the eye of a supervisor; in other cases, a carping, rebellious spirit is engendered. . . .

It still is also true that incapacity to assume the responsibilities involved in having a voice in shaping policies is bred and increased by conditions in which that responsibility is denied. I suppose there has never been an autocrat, big or little, who did not justify his conduct on the ground of the unfitness of his subjects to take part in government. . . . What the argument for democracy implies is that the best way to produce initiative and constructive power is to exercise it. Power, as well as interest, comes by use and practice. Moreover, the argument from incapacity proves too much. If it is so great as to be a permanent bar, then teachers can not be expected to have the intelligence and skill that are necessary to execute the directions given them. The delicate and difficult task of developing character and good judgment in the young needs every stimulus and inspiration possible. It is impossible that the work should not be better done when teachers have that understanding of what they are doing that comes from having shared in forming its guiding ideas. . . .

The fundamental beliefs and practices of democracy are now challenged as they never have been before. In some nations they are more than challenged. They are ruthlessly and systematically destroyed. Everywhere there are waves of criticism and doubt as to whether democracy can meet pressing problems of order and security. The causes for the destruction of political democracy in countries where it was nominally established are complex. But of one thing I think we may be sure. Wherever it has fallen it was too exclusively political in nature. It had not become part of the bone and blood of the people in daily conduct of its life. Democratic forms were limited to Parliament, elections and combats between parties. What is happening proves conclusively, I think, that unless democratic habits of thought and action are part of the fiber of a people, political democracy is insecure. It can not stand in isolation. It must be buttressed by the presence of democratic methods in all social relationships. The relations that exist in educational institutions are second only in importance in this respect to those which exist in industry and business, perhaps not even to them. . . .

VI TOTALITARIAN LIFE AND THE WAR AGAINST FASCISM

ADOLF HITLER

Adolf Hitler was born in Austria in 1889 and committed suicide in besieged Berlin in 1945. He had been an unsuccessful painter and building worker before 1914 and a corporal in the First World War. The dismal failure of an attempted revolt against the Weimar Republic in 1923 discredited him and led to a short term of imprisonment, during which he began writing a book of wild political reflections—*Mein Kampf* (1925)—advocating savage violence, political dishonesty, and unrestricted imperialism. Its simplistic analysis and its vengefulness attracted to him half-educated, economically ruined men and women smarting under Germany's defeat and the humiliations of 1918–19. His hatred of the Communists and his call for armed revenge persuaded many wealthy industrialists to finance him and many army officers to place hope in him as the Führer (leader). Hitler attained supreme power legally when Hindenburg, president of the Weimar Republic, made him reich chancellor (January 30, 1933) after his party had won the largest number of parliamentary seats, although not a majority, in a free if tumultuous election.

There followed twelve increasingly nightmarish years culminating in total war against Europe and the deliberate mass murder of millions of Europeans, principally Jews. An apocalyptic rhetoric of the Aryan "master race" and its "new order" which was to last for the next thousand years disguised Hitler's attempts to destroy all law and to substitute for law the will of the party and its Führer. By June, 1940, Hitler had gobbled up most of Europe and seemed to many unbeatable. Five years later he was dead in the flaming ruins of his capital and his shattered Third Reich was overrun by Western and Soviet troops.

The following selection is from Hitler's speech to the German workers, December 10, 1940, at the Rheinmetall-Borsig armament works in Berlin.

TO THE GERMAN WORKERS

Fellow countrymen, workers of germany: Nowadays I do not speak very often. In the first place I have little time for speaking, and in the second place I believe that this is a time for action rather than speech. We are involved in a conflict in which more than the victory of only one country or the other is at stake; it is rather a war of two opposing worlds. I shall try to give you, as far as possible in the time at my disposal, an insight into the essential reasons underlying this conflict. I shall, however, confine myself to Western Europe only. The peoples who are primarily affected—eighty-five million Germans, forty-six million Britishers, forty-five million Italians, and about thirty-seven million Frenchmen—are the cores of the states who were or still are opposed in war. If I make a comparison between the living conditions of these peoples the following facts become evident:

Forty-six million Britishers dominate and govern approximately sixteen million square miles of the surface of the earth. Thirty-seven million Frenchmen dominate and govern a combined area of approximately four million square miles. Forty-five million Italians possess, taking into consideration only those territories in any way capable of being utilized, an area of scarcely one hundred and ninety thousand square miles. Eighty-five million Germans possess as their living space scarcely two hundred and thirty-two thousand square miles. That is to say: eighty-five million Germans own only two hundred and thirty-two thousand square miles on which they must live their lives and forty-six million Britishers possess sixteen million square miles.

Now, my fellow countrymen, this world has not been so divided up by Providence or Almighty God. This allocation has been made by man himself. The land was parcelled out for the most part during the last three hundred years, that is, during the period in which, unfortunately, the German people were helpless and torn by internal dissension. . . .

The second people that failed to receive their fair share in this distribution, namely the Italians, experienced and suffered a similar fate. Torn by internal conflicts, devoid of unity, split up into numerous small states, this people also dissipated all their energy in internal strife. Nor was Italy able to obtain even the natural position in the Mediterranean which was her due. . . .

You all know the situation in which we found ourselves eight years ago. Our people were on the verge of collapse. Seven million were unemployed. About six and a half million were on part-time work; our economic system was threatened by disintegration; agriculture faced ruination; trade and industry were at a standstill and shipping was paralyzed. It was easy to foresee the time when the seven million unemployed would necessarily become eight, nine or ten millions. The number of working people became fewer and fewer, while on the other hand the number of unemployed—who had to be kept on relief—became greater and greater. In other words, even those who were still working could not benefit from the fruits of their labor to the fullest extent, for each had to support a non-worker besides himself. Whether this was done by social legislation or in the form of charity made no difference. When a worker has to nourish and support another who does not work, neither will have enough in the long run. There will be too little to live on, even though they do not starve.

For us, therefore, national unity was one of the essential conditions if we were to coordinate the powers inherent in the German nation properly, to make the German people conscious of their own greatness, realize their strength, recognize and present their vital claims, and seek national unity by an appeal to reason.

I know that I have not been successful everywhere. For nearly fifteen years of my struggle I was the target of two opposing sides. One side reproached me: "You want to drag us who belong to the intelligentsia and to the upper classes down to the level of the others. That is impossible. We are educated people. In addition to that, we are wealthy and cultured. We cannot accept this."

These people were incapable of listening to reason; even today there are some who cannot be converted. However, on the whole the number of those who realize that the lack of unity in our national structure would sooner or later lead to the destruction of all classes, has become greater and greater.

I also met with opposition from the other side. They said: "We have our class consciousness." However I was obliged to take the stand that in the existing situation we could not afford to make experiments. It certainly would have been simple to eliminate the intelligentsia. Such a process could be carried out at once. But we would have to wait fifty or perhaps a hundred years for the gap to refill—and such a period would mean the destruction of the nation. For how can our people, its three hundred and sixty per square mile, exist at all if they do not employ every ounce of brain power and physical strength to wrest from their soil what they need? This distinguishes us from the others. In Canada, for example, there are 2.6 persons per square mile; in other countries perhaps 16, 18, 20 or 26 persons. Well, my fellow countrymen, no matter how stupidly one managed one's affairs in such a country, a decent living would still be possible.

Here in Germany, however, there are 360 persons per square mile. The others cannot manage with 26 persons per square mile, but we must manage with 360. This is the task we face. That is why I expressed this view in 1933: "We *must* solve these problems and, therefore, we *shall* solve them." Of course that was not easy; everything could not be done immediately. . . .

It has been a tremendous task. The establishment of a German community was the first item on the program in 1933. The second item was the elimination of foreign oppression as expressed in the Treaty of Versailles, which also prevented our attaining national unity, forbade large sections of our people to unite and robbed us of our possessions in the world, our German colonies.

The second item on the program was, therefore, the struggle against Versailles. No one can say that I express this opinion for the first time today. I expressed it, my fellow countrymen, in the days following the Great War when, still a soldier, I made my first appearance in the political arena. My first address was a speech against the collapse, against the Treaty of Versailles, and for the reestablishment of a powerful German Reich. That was the beginning of my work. What I have brought about since then does not represent a new aim but the oldest aim. It is the primary reason for the conflict in which we find ourselves today. The rest of the world did not want our inner unity, because they knew that, once it was achieved, the vital claim of our masses could be realized. They wanted to maintain the dictate of Versailles in which they saw a second peace of Westphalia. However, there is still another reason. I have stated that the world was unequally divided. American observers and Englishmen have found a wonderful expression for this fact: They say there are two kinds of peoples—the "haves" and the "have-nots." "We, the British, are the 'haves.' It is a fact that we possess sixteen million square miles. And we Americans are also 'haves,' and so are we Frenchmen. The others—they are simply the 'have-nots.' He who *has* nothing *receives* nothing. He shall remain what he is. He who has is not willing to share it."

All my life I have been a "have-not." At home I was a "have-not." I regard myself as belonging to them and have always fought exclusively for them. I defended them and, therefore, I stand before the world as their representative. I shall never recognize the claim of the others to that which they have taken by force. Under no circumstances can I acknowledge this claim with regard to that which has been taken from us. It is interesting to examine the life of these rich people. In this Anglo-French world there exists, as it were, democracy, which means the rule of the people by the people. Now the people must possess some means of giving expression to their thoughts or their wishes. Examining this problem more closely, we see that the people themselves have originally no convictions of their own. Their convictions are formed, of course, just as everywhere else. The decisive question is who enlightens the people, who educates them? In those countries, it is actually capital that rules; that is, nothing more than a clique of a few hundred men who possess untold wealth and, as a consequence of the peculiar structure of their national life, are more or less independent and free. They say: "Here we have liberty." By this they mean, above all, an uncontrolled economy, and by an uncontrolled economy, the freedom not only to acquire capital but to make absolutely free use of it. That means freedom from national control or control by the people both in the acquisition of capital and in its employment. This is really what they mean when they speak of liberty. These capitalists create their own press and then speak of the "freedom of the press."

In reality, every one of the newspapers has a master, and in every case this master is the capitalist, the owner. This master, not the editor, is the one who directs the policy of the paper. If the editor tries to write other than what suits the master, he is ousted the next day. This press, which is the absolutely submissive and characterless slave of the owners, molds public opinion. Public opinion thus mobilized by them is, in its turn, split up into political parties. The difference between these parties is as small as it formerly was in Germany. You know them, of course—the old parties. They were always one and the same. In Britain matters are usually so arranged that families are divided up, one member being a conservative, another a liberal and a third belonging to the labor party. Actually, all three sit together as members of the family, decide upon their common attitude and determine it. A further point is that the "elected people" actually form a community which operates and controls all these organizations. For this reason, the opposition in England is really always the same, for on all essential matters in which the opposition has to make itself felt, the parties are always in agreement. They have one and the same conviction and through the medium of the press mold public opinion along corresponding lines. One might well believe that in these countries of liberty and riches, the people must possess an unlimited degree of prosperity. But no! On the contrary, it is precisely in these countries that the distress of the masses is greater than anywhere else. Such is the case in "rich Britain."

She controls sixteen million square miles. In India, for example, a hundred million colonial workers with a wretched standard of living must labor for her. One might think perhaps, that at least in England itself every person must have his share of these riches. By no means! In that country class distinction is the crassest imaginable. There is poverty—incredible poverty—on the one side, and equally incredible wealth on the other. They have not solved a single problem. The workmen of that country which possesses more than one-sixth of the globe and of the world's natural resources dwell in misery, and the masses of the people are poorly clad. In a country which ought to have more than enough bread and every sort of fruit, we find millions of the lower classes who have not even enough to fill their stomachs, and go about hungry. A nation which could provide work for the whole world must acknowledge the fact that it cannot even abolish unemployment at home. For decades this rich Britain has had two and a half million unemployed; rich America, ten to thirteen millions, year after year; France six, seven and eight hundred thousand. . . .

It is self-evident that where this democracy rules, the people as such are not taken into consideration at all. The only thing that matters is the existence of a few hundred gigantic capitalists who own all the factories and their stock and, through them, control the people. The masses of the people do not interest them in the least. They are interested in them just as were our bourgeois parties in former times—only when elections are being held, when they need votes. Otherwise, the life of the masses is a matter of complete indifference to them.

To this must be added the difference in education. Is it not ludicrous to hear a member of the British Labor Party—who, of course, as a member of the Opposition is officially paid by the government—say: "When the war is over, we will do something in social respects."

It is the members of Parliament who are the directors of the business concerns—just as used to be the case with us. But we have abolished all that. A member of the Reichstag cannot belong to a Board of Directors, except as a purely honorary member. He is prohibited from accepting any emolument, financial or otherwise. This is not the case in other countries.

They reply: "That is why our form of government is sacred to us." I can well believe it, for that form of government certainly pays very well. But whether it is sacred to the mass of the people as well is another matter.

The people as a whole definitely suffer. I do not consider it possible in the long run for one man to work and toil for a whole year in return for ridiculous wages, while another jumps into an express train once a year and pockets enormous sums. Such conditions are a disgrace. On the other hand, we National Socialists equally oppose the theory that all men are equals. Today, when a man of genius makes some astounding invention and enormously benefits his country by his brains, we pay him his due, for he has really accomplished something and been of use to his country. However, we hope to make it impossible for idle drones to inhabit this country.

I could continue to cite examples indefinitely. The fact remains that two worlds are face to face with one another. Our opponents are quite right when they say: "Nothing can reconcile us to the National Socialist world." How could a narrow-minded capitalist ever agree to my principles? It would be easier for the Devil to go to church and cross himself with holy water than for these people to comprehend the ideas which are accepted facts to us today. But we have solved our problems. . . .

My dear friends, if I had stated publicly eight or nine years ago: "In seven or eight years the problem of how to provide work for the unemployed will be solved, and the problem then will be where to find workers," I should have harmed my cause. Every one would have declared: "The man is mad. It is useless to talk to him, much less to support him. Nobody should vote for him. He is a fantastic creature." Today, however, all this has come true. Today, the only question for us is where to find workers. That, my fellow countrymen, is the blessing which work brings.

Work alone can create new work; money cannot create work. Work alone can create values, values with which to reward those who work. The work of one man makes it possible for another to live and continue to work. And when we have mobilized the working capacity of our people to its utmost, each individual worker will receive more and more of the world's goods.

We have incorporated seven million unemployed into our economic system; we have transformed another six millions from part-time into full-time workers; we are even working over-time. And all this is paid for in cash in Reichsmarks which maintained their value in peacetime. In wartime we had to ration its purchasing capacity, not in order to devalue it, but simply to earmark a portion of our industry for war production to guide us to victory in the struggle for the future of Germany. . . .

You know, my comrades, that I have destroyed nothing in Germany. I have always proceeded very carefully, because I believe—as I have already said —that we cannot afford to wreck anything. I am proud that the revolution of 1933 was brought to pass without breaking a single windowpane. Nevertheless, we have wrought enormous changes.

I wish to put before you a few basic facts: The first is that in the capitalistic democratic world the most important principle of economy is that the people exist for trade and industry, and that these in turn exist for capital. We have reversed this principle by making capital exist for trade and industry, and trade and industry exist for the people. *In other words, the people come first.* Everything else is but a means to this end. When an economic system is not capable of feeding and clothing a people, then it is bad, regardless of whether a few hundred people say: "As far as I am concerned it is good, excellent; my dividends are splendid."

However, the dividends do not interest me at all. Here we have drawn the line. They may then retort: "Well, look here, that is just what we mean. You jeopardize liberty."

Yes, certainly, we jeopardize the liberty to profiteer at the expense of the community, and, if necessary, we even abolish it. British capitalists, to mention only one instance, can pocket dividends of 76, 80, 95, 140 and even 160 per cent from their armament industry. Naturally they say: "If the German methods grow apace and should prove victorious, this sort of thing will stop."

They are perfectly right. I should never tolerate such a state of affairs. In my eyes, a 6 per cent dividend is sufficient. Even from this 6 per cent we deduct one-half and, as for the rest, we must have definite proof that it is invested in the interest of the country as a whole. In other words, no individual has the right to dispose arbitrarily of money which ought to be invested for the good of the country. If he disposes of it sensibly, well and good; if not, the National Socialist state will intervene. . . .

In Germany, the people, without any doubt, decide their existence. They determine the principles of their government. In fact it has been possible in this country to incorporate many of the broad masses into the National Socialist Party, that gigantic organization embracing millions and having millions of officials drawn from the people themselves. This principle is extended to the highest ranks.

For the first time in German history, we have a state which has absolutely abolished all social prejudices in regard to political appointments as well as in private life. I myself am the best proof of this. Just imagine: I am not even a lawyer, and yet I am your Fuehrer! . . .

Opposed to this there stands a completely different world. In that world the highest ideals are the struggle for wealth, for capital, for family possessions, for personal egoism; everything else is merely a means to such ends. Two worlds confront each other today. We know perfectly well that if we are defeated in this war it would not only be the end of our National Socialist work of reconstruction, but the end of the German people as a whole. For without its powers of coordination, the German people would starve. Today the masses dependent on us number 120 or 130 millions, of which 85 millions alone are our own people. We remain ever aware of this fact.

On the other hand, that other world says: "If we lose, our world-wide capitalistic system will collapse. For it is we who save hoarded gold. It is lying in our cellars and will lose its value. If the idea that work is the decisive factor spreads abroad, what will happen to us? We shall have bought our gold in vain. Our whole claim to world dominion can then no longer be maintained. The people will do away with their dynasties of high finance. They will present their social claims, and the whole world system will be overthrown."

I can well understand that they declare: "Let us prevent this at all costs; it must be prevented." They can see exactly how our nation has been reconstructed. You see it clearly. For instance, there we see a state ruled by a numerically small upper class. They send their sons to their own schools, to Eton. We have Adolf Hitler Schools or national political educational establishments. On the one hand, the sons of plutocrats, financial magnates; on the other, the children of the people. Etonians and Harrovians exclusively in leading positions over there; in this country, men of the people in charge of the State.

These are the two worlds. I grant that one of the two must succumb. Yes, one or the other. But if we were to succumb, the German people would succumb with us. If the other were to succumb, I am convinced that the nations will become free for the first time. We are not fighting individual Englishmen or Frenchmen. We have nothing against them. For years I proclaimed this as the aim of my foreign policy. We demanded nothing of them, nothing at all. When they started the war they could not say: "We are doing so because the Germans asked this or that of us." They said, on the contrary: "We are declaring war on you because the German system of Government does not suit us; because we fear it might spread to our own people." For that reason they are carrying on this war. They wanted to blast the German nation back to the time of Versailles, to the indescribable misery of those days. But they have made a great mistake.

If in this war everything points to the fact that gold is fighting against work, capitalism against peoples, and reaction against the progress of humanity, then work, the peoples and progress will be victorious. Even the support of the Jewish race will not avail the others.

I have seen this coming for years. What did I ask of the other world? Nothing but the right for Germans to reunite and the restoration of all that had been taken from them—nothing which would have meant a loss to the other nations. How often have I stretched out my hand to them? Ever since I came into power. I had not the slightest wish to rearm.

For what do armaments mean? They absorb so much labor. It was I who regarded work as being of decisive importance, who wished to employ the working capacity of Germany for other plans. I think the news is already out that, after all, I have some fairly important plans in my mind, vast and splendid plans for my people. It is my ambition to make the German people rich and to make the German homeland beautiful. I want the standard of living of the individual raised. I want us to have the most beautiful and the finest civilization. I should like the theatre—in fact, the whole of German civilization—to benefit all the people and not to exist only for the upper ten thousand, as is the case in England.

The plans which we had in mind were tremendous, and I needed workers in order to realize them. Armament only deprives me of workers. *I made proposals to limit armaments. I was ridiculed. The only answer I received was "no." I proposed the limitation of certain types of armament. That was refused. I proposed that airplanes should be altogether eliminated from warfare. That also was refused. I suggested that bombers should be limited. That was refused.* They said: "That is just how we wish to force our regime upon you."

I am not a man who does things by halves. If it becomes necessary for me to defend myself, I defend myself with unlimited zeal. When I saw that the same old warmongers of the World War in Britain were mobilizing once more against the great new German revival, I realized that this struggle would have to be fought once more, that the other side did not want peace. . . .

When this war is ended, Germany will set to work in earnest. A great "Awake!" will sound throughout the country. Then the German nation will stop manufacturing cannon and will embark on peaceful occupations and the new work of reconstruction for the millions. Then we shall show the world for the first time who is the real master, capitalism or work. Out of this work will grow the great German Reich of which great poets have dreamed. It will be the Germany to which every one of her sons will cling with fanatical devotion, because she will provide a home even for the poorest. She will teach everyone the meaning of life.

Should any one say to me: "These are mere fantastic dreams, mere visions," I can only reply that when I set out on my course in 1919 as an unknown, nameless soldier I built my hopes of the future upon a most vivid imagination. Yet all has come true.

What I am planning or aiming at today is nothing compared to what I have already accomplished and achieved. It will be achieved sooner and more definitely than everything already achieved. The road from an unknown and nameless person to Fuehrer of the German nation was harder than will be the way from Fuehrer of the German nation to creator of the coming peace.

I had to fight and struggle for fifteen years for your confidence. Today, thanks to your confidence, I fight and struggle for Germany. Some day we shall once more struggle together in confidence for this great Reich of peace, work, prosperity and culture which we intend to establish and shall establish. Thank you.

NAZISM IN ACTION

T HE MARK left by Nazism in action is deep throughout Europe, and it will take a long time to repair the moral and material ruin left by the German "New Order." The Nazi concentration camps, torture houses, and gas chambers were inspected by thousands of Allied soldiers and civilians; press correspondents and newsreels revealed the facts to the world. That these atrocities did not deter the overwhelming majority of Germans from remaining at least impassive under Hitler's regime was one of the most distressing discoveries of 1945.

The selection that follows is taken from the records of the trial of Nazi leaders by the Allies at Nuremberg, in the United States State Department publication *Trial of War Criminals* (Washington: Government Printing Office, 1945).

INDICTMENT OF NAZI INDIVIDUALS AND OR-GANIZATIONS BY THE INTERNATIONAL MILITARY TRIBUNAL

Count One—The Common Plan or Conspiracy

STATEMENT OF THE OFFENSE

All the defendants, with divers other persons, during a period of years preceding 8th May, 1945, participated as leaders, organizers, instigators or accomplices in the formulation or execution of a common plan or conspiracy to commit, or which involved the commission of, Crimes against Peace, War Crimes, and Crimes against Humanity, as defined in the Charter of this Tribunal, and, in accordance with the provisions of the Charter, are individually responsible for their own acts and for all acts committed by any persons in the execution of such plan or conspiracy. The common plan or conspiracy embraced the commission of Crimes against Peace, in that the defendants planned, prepared, initiated and waged wars of aggression, which were also wars in violation of international treaties, agreements or assurances. In the development and course of the common plan or conspiracy it came to embrace the commission of War Crimes, in that it contemplated, and the defendants determined upon and carried out, ruthless wars against countries and populations, in violation of the rules and customs of war, including as typical and systematic means by which the wars were prosecuted, murder, ill-treatment, deportation for slave labor and for other purposes of civilian populations of occupied territories, murder and ill-treatment of prisoners of war and of persons on the high seas, the taking and killing of hostages, the plunder of public and private property, the wanton destruction of cities, towns, and villages, and devastation not justified by military necessity. The common plan or conspiracy contemplated and came to embrace as typical and systematic means, and the defendants determined upon and committed, Crimes against Humanity, both within Germany and within occupied territories, including murder, extermination, enslavement, deportation, and other inhumane acts committed against civilian populations before and during the war, and persecutions on political, racial or religious grounds, in execution of the plan for preparing and prosecuting aggressive or illegal wars, many of such acts and persecutions being violations of the domestic laws of the countries where perpetrated. . . .

Count Two—Crimes against Peace

STATEMENT OF THE OFFENSE

All the defendants, with divers other persons, during a period of years preceding 8th May, 1945, participated in the planning, preparation, initiation and waging of wars of aggression, which were also wars in violation of international treaties, agreements and assurances.

PARTICULARS OF THE WARS PLANNED, PREPARED, INITIATED AND WAGED

(A) The wars referred to in the Statement of Offense in this Count Two of the Indictment and the dates of their initiation were the following: against Poland, 1st September, 1939; against the United Kingdom and France, 3rd September, 1939; against Denmark and Norway, 9th April, 1940; against Belgium, the Netherlands and Luxembourg, 10th May, 1940; against Yugoslavia and Greece, 6th April, 1941; against the U. S. S. R., 22nd June, 1941; and against the United States of America, 11th December, 1941. . . .

Count Three—War Crimes

STATEMENT OF THE OFFENSE

All the defendants committed War Crimes between 1st September, 1939, and 8th May, 1945, in Germany and in all those countries and territories occupied by the German armed forces since 1st September, 1939, and in Austria, Czechoslovakia, and Italy, and on the High Seas.

All the defendants, acting in concert with others, formulated and executed a common plan or conspiracy to commit War Crimes as defined in Article 6 (b) of the Charter. This plan involved, among other things, the practice of "total war" including methods of combat and of military occupation in direct conflict with the laws and customs of war, and the commission of crimes perpetrated on the field of battle during encounters with enemy armies, and against prisoners of war, and in occupied territories against the civilian population of such territories.

The said War Crimes were committed by the defendants and by other persons for whose acts the defendants are responsible (under Article 6 of the Charter) as such other persons when committing the said War Crimes performed their acts in execution of a common plan and conspiracy to commit the said War Crimes, in the formulation and execution of which plan and conspiracy all the defendants participated as leaders, organizers, instigators and accomplices.

These methods and crimes constituted violations of international conventions, of internal penal laws and of the general principles of criminal law as derived from the criminal law of all civilized nations, and were involved in and part of a systematic course of conduct.

(A) Murder and Ill-treatment of Civilian Populations of or in Occupied Territory and on the High Seas

Throughout the period of their occupation of territories overrun by their armed forces, defendants, for the purpose of systematically terrorizing the inhabitants, murdered and tortured civilians, and ill-treated them, and imprisoned them without legal process.

The murders and ill-treatment were carried out by divers means, including shooting, hanging, gassing, starvation, gross over-crowding, systematic undernutrition, systematic imposition of labor tasks beyond the strength of those ordered to carry them out, inadequate provision of surgical and medical services, kickings, beatings, brutality and torture of all kinds, including the use of hot irons and pulling out of finger nails and the performance of experiments by means of operations and otherwise on living human subjects. In some occupied territories the defendants interfered with religious services, persecuted members of the clergy and monastic orders, and expropriated church property. They conducted deliberate and systematic genocide, viz., the extermination of racial and national groups, against the civilian populations of certain occupied territories in order to destroy particular races and classes of people and national, racial or religious groups, particularly Jews, Poles and Gypsies and others.

Civilians were systematically subjected to tortures of all kinds, with the object of obtaining information. Civilians of occupied countries were subjected systematically to "protective arrests" whereby they were arrested and imprisoned without any trial and any of the ordinary protections of the law, and they were imprisoned under the most unhealthy and inhumane conditions.

In the concentration camps were many prisoners who were classified "Nacht und Nebel." These were entirely cut off from the world and were allowed neither to receive nor to send letters. They disappeared without trace and no announcement of their fate was ever made by the German authorities. . . .

Such murder and ill-treatment took place in concentration camps and similar establishments set up by the defendants, and particularly in the concentration camps set up at Belsen, Buchenwald, Dachau, Breendonck, Grini, Natzweiler, Ravensbrück, Vught and Amersfoort, and in numerous cities, towns and villages, including Oradour sur Glane, Trondheim and Oslo.

Crimes committed in France or against French citizens took the following forms:—

Arbitrary arrests were carried out under political or racial pretexts; they were both individual and collective; notably in Paris (round-up of the 18th Arrondissement by the Field Gendarmerie, round-up of the Jewish population of the 11th Arrondissement in August, 1941, round-up of Jewish intellectuals in December, 1941, round-up in July, 1942); at Clermont-Ferrand (round-up of professors and students of the University of Strasbourg, who were taken to Clermont-Ferrand on 25th November, 1943); at Lyons, at Marseilles (round-up of 40,000 persons in January, 1943); at Grenoble (round-up on 24th December, 1943); at Cluny (round-up on 24th December, 1944); at Figeac (round-up in May, 1944); at Saint Pol de Leon (round-up in July, 1944); at Locminé (round-up on 3rd July, 1944); at Eyzieux (round-up in May, 1944) and at Moussey (round-up in September, 1944). These arrests were followed by brutal treatment and tortures carried out by the most diverse methods, such as immersion in icy water, asphyxiation, torture of the limbs, and the use of instruments of torture, such as the iron helmet and electric current, and practiced in all the prisons of France, notably in Paris, Lyons, Marseilles, Rennes, Metz, Clermont-Ferrand, Toulouse, Nice, Grenoble, Annecy, Anas, Bethune, Lille, Loos, Valenciennes, Nancy, Troyes and Caen, and in the torture chambers fitted up at the Gestapo centers.

In the concentration camps, the health regime, and the labor regime, were such that the rate of mortality (alleged to be from natural causes) attained enormous proportions, for instance:—

1. Out of a convoy of 230 French women deported from Compiégne to Auschwitz in January, 1943, 180 died of exhaustion by the end of four months.

2. 143 Frenchmen died of exhaustion between 23rd March and 6th May, 1943, in Block 8 at Dachau.

3. 1,797 Frenchmen died of exhaustion between 21st November, 1943, and 15th March, 1945, in the Block at Dora.

4. 465 Frenchmen died of general debility in November, 1944, at Dora.

5. 22,761 deportees died of exhaustion at Buchenwald between 1st January, 1943, and 15th April, 1945.

6. 11,560 detainees died of exhaustion at Dachau Camp (most of them in Block 30 reserved for the sick and infirm) between 1st January and 15th April, 1945.

7. 780 priests died of exhaustion at Mauthausen.

8. Out of 2,200 Frenchmen registered at Flossenburg Camp, 1,600 died from supposedly natural causes.

Methods used for the work of extermination in concentration camps were: —bad treatment, pseudo-scientific experiments (sterilization of women at Auschwitz and at Ravensbrück, study of the evolution of cancer of the womb at Auschwitz, of typhus at Buchenwald, anatomical research at Natzweiller, heart injections at Buchenwald, bone grafting and muscular excisions at Ravensbrück, etc.), gas chambers, gas wagons and crematory ovens. Of 228,-000 French political and racial deportees in concentration camps, only 28,000 survived.

In France also systematic extermination was practiced, notably at Asq on 1st April, 1944, at Colpo on 22nd July, 1944, at Buget sur Tarn on 6th July, 1944, and on 17th August, 1944, at Pluvignier on 8th July, 1944, at Rennes on 8th June, 1944, at Grenoble on 8th July, 1944, at Saint Flour on 10th June, 1944, at Ruisnes on 10th July, 1944, at Nimes, at Tulle, and at Nice, where, in July, 1944, the victims of torture were exposed to the population, and at Oradour sur Glane where the entire village population was shot or burned alive in the church.

The many charnel pits give proof of anonymous massacres. Most notable of these are the charnel pits of Paris (Cascade du Bois de Boulogne), Lyons, Saint Genies Laval, Besançon, Petit Saint Bernard, Aulnat, Caen, Port Louis, Charleval, Fontainebleau, Bouconne, Gabaudet, L'hermitage Lorges, Morlaas, Bordelongue, Signe.

In the course of a premeditated campaign of terrorism, initiated in Denmark by the Germans in the latter part of 1943, 600 Danish subjects were murdered and, in addition, throughout the German occupation of Denmark, large numbers of Danish subjects were subjected to torture and ill-treatment of all sorts. In addition, approximately 500 Danish subjects were murdered, by torture and otherwise, in German prisons and concentration camps.

In Belgium between 1940 and 1944 tortures by various means, but identical in each place, were carried out at Brussels, Liége, Mons, Ghent, Namur, Antwerp, Tournai, Arlon, Charleroi and Dinant.

At Vught, in Holland, when the camp was evacuated about 400 persons were murdered by shooting.

In Luxembourg, during the German occupation, 500 persons were murdered and, in addition, another 521 were illegally executed, by order of such special tribunals as the so-called "Sondergericht." Many more persons in Luxembourg were subjected to torture and mistreatment by the Gestapo. Not less than 4,000 Luxembourg nationals were imprisoned during the period of German occupation, and of these at least 400 were murdered.

Between March, 1944, and April, 1945, in Italy, at least 7,500 men, women and children, ranging in years from infancy to extreme old age were murdered by the German soldiery at Civitella, in the Ardeatine Caves in Rome, and at other places. . . .

About 1,500,000 persons were exterminated in Maidanek and about 4,000,-000 persons were exterminated in Auschwitz, among whom were citizens of Poland, the U. S. S. R., the United States of America, Great Britain, Czechoslovakia, France and other countries.

In the Lwow region and in the city of Lwow the Germans exterminated about 700,000 Soviet people, including 70 persons in the field of the arts, science and technology, and also citizens of the U. S. A., Great Britain, Czechoslovakia, Yugoslavia and Holland, brought to this region from other concentration camps.

In the Jewish ghetto from 7th September, 1941, to 6th July, 1943, over 133,-000 persons were tortured and shot.

Mass shooting of the population occurred in suberbs of the city and in the Livenitz forest.

In the Ganov camp 200,000 peaceful citizens were exterminated. The most refined methods of cruelty were employed in this extermination, such as disembowelling and the freezing of human beings in tubs of water. Mass shootings took place to the accompaniment of the music of an orchestra recruited from the persons interned.

Beginning with June, 1943, the Germans carried out measures to hide the evidence of their crimes. They exhumed and burned corpses, and they crushed the bones with machines and used them for fertilizer.

At the beginning of 1944 in the Ozarichi region of the Bielorussian S. S. R., before liberation by the Red Army, the Germans established three concentration camps without shelters, to which they committed tens of thousands of persons from the neighboring territories. They brought many people to these camps from typhus hospitals intentionally, for the purpose of infecting the other persons interned and for spreading the disease in territories from which the Germans were being driven by the Red Army. In these camps there were many murders and crimes.

In the Esthonian S. S. R. they shot tens of thousands of persons and in one day alone, 19th September, 1944, in Camp Kloga, the Germans shot 2,000 peaceful citizens. They burned the bodies on bonfires.

In the Lithuanian S. S. R. there were mass killings of Soviet citizens, namely: in Panerai at least 100,000; in Kaunas more than 70,000; in Alitus about 60,000; in Prenai more than 3,000; in Villiampol about 8,000; in Mariampol about 7,000; in Trakai and neighboring towns 37,640.

In the Latvian S. S. R. 577,000 persons were murdered.

As a result of the whole system of internal order maintained in all camps, the interned persons were doomed to die.

In a secret instruction entitled "the internal regime in concentration camps," signed personally by Himmler in 1941 severe measures of punishment were set forth for the internees. Masses of prisoners of war were shot, or died from the cold and torture. . . .

(E) PLUNDER OF PUBLIC AND PRIVATE PROPERTY

The Defendants ruthlessly exploited the people and the material resources of the countries they occupied, in order to strengthen the Nazi war machine, to depopulate and impoverish the rest of Europe, to enrich themselves and their adherents, and to promote German economic supremacy over Europe.

The Defendants engaged in the following acts and practices, among others:

1. They degraded the standard of life of the people of occupied countries and caused starvation, by stripping occupied countries of foodstuffs for removal to Germany.

2. They seized raw materials and industrial machinery in all of the occupied countries, removed them to Germany and used them in the interest of the German war effort and the German economy.

3. In all the occupied countries, in varying degrees, they confiscated businesses, plants and other property.

4. In an attempt to give color of legality to illegal acquisitions of property, they forced owners of property to go through the forms of "voluntary" and "legal" transfers.

5. They established comprehensive controls over the economies of all of the occupied countries and directed their resources, their production and their labor in the interests of the German war economy, depriving the local populations of the products of essential industries.

6. By a variety of financial mechanisms, they despoiled all of the occupied

countries of essential commodities and accumulated wealth, debased the local currency systems and disrupted the local economies. They financed extensive purchases in occupied countries through clearing arrangements by which they exacted loans from the occupied countries. They imposed occupation levies, exacted financial contributions, and issued occupation currency, far in excess of occupation costs. They used these excess funds to finance the purchase of business properties and supplies in the occupied countries.

7. They abrogated the rights of the local populations in the occupied portions of the USSR and in Poland and in other countries to develop or manage agricultural and industrial properties, and reserved this area for exclusive settlement, development, and ownership by Germans and their so-called racial brethren.

8. In further development of their plan of criminal exploitation, they destroyed industrial cities, cultural monuments, scientific institutions, and property of all types in the occupied territories to eliminate the possibility of competition with Germany.

9. From their program of terror, slavery, spoliation and organized outrage, the Nazi conspirators created an instrument for the personal profit and aggrandizement of themselves and their adherents. They secured for themselves and their adherents:

(a) Positions in administration of business involving power, influence and lucrative perquisites.

(b) The use of cheap forced labor.

(c) The acquisition on advantageous terms of foreign properties, business interests, and raw materials.

(d) The basis for the industrial supremacy of Germany.

These acts were contrary to International Conventions, particularly Articles 46 to 56 inclusive of the Hague Regulations, 1907, the laws and customs of war, the general principles of criminal law as derived from the criminal laws of all civilized nations, the internal penal laws of the countries in which such crimes were committed and to Article 6 (b) of the Charter. . . .

Count Four—Crimes against Humanity

STATEMENT OF THE OFFENSE. . . .

(A) MURDER, EXTERMINATION, ENSLAVEMENT, DEPORTATION AND OTHER INHUMANE ACTS COMMITTED AGAINST CIVILIAN POPULATIONS BEFORE AND DURING THE WAR

For the purposes set out above, the defendants adopted a policy of persecution, repression, and extermination of all civilians in Germany who were, or who were believed to [be], or who were believed likely to become, hostile to the Nazi Government and the common plan or conspiracy described in Count One. They imprisoned such persons without judicial process, holding them in "protective custody" and concentration camps, and subjected them to persecution, degradation, despoilment, enslavement, torture and murder.

Special courts were established to carry out the will of the conspirators; favored branches or agencies of the State and Party were permitted to operate outside the range even of nazified law and to crush all tendencies and elements which were considered "undesirable." The various concentration camps included Buchenwald, which was established in 1933 and Dachau, which was established in 1934. At these and other camps the civilians were put to slave labor, and murdered and ill-treated by divers means, including those set out in Count Three above, and these acts and policies were continued and extended to the occupied countries after the 1st September, 1939, and until 8th May, 1945.

    (B) PERSECUTION ON POLITICAL, RACIAL AND RELIGIOUS GROUNDS IN EXE-
        CUTION OF AND IN CONNECTION WITH THE COMMON PLAN MENTIONED
        IN COUNT ONE

As above stated, in execution of and in connection with the common plan mentioned in Count One, opponents of the German Government were exterminated and persecuted. These persecutions were directed against Jews. They were also directed against persons whose political belief or spiritual aspirations were deemed to be in conflict with the aims of the Nazis.

Jews were systematically persecuted since 1933; they were deprived of their liberty, thrown into concentration camps where they were murdered and ill-treated. Their property was confiscated. Hundreds of thousands of Jews were so treated before the 1st September, 1939.

Since the 1st September, 1939, the persecution of the Jews was redoubled; millions of Jews from Germany and from the occupied Western Countries were sent to the Eastern Countries for extermination.

Particulars by way of example and without prejudice to the production of evidence of other cases are as follows:

The Nazis murdered amongst others Chancellor Dollfuss, the Social Democrat Breitscheid and the Communist Thaelmann. They imprisoned in concentration camps numerous political and religious personages, for example Chancellor Schuschnigg and Pastor Niemöller.

In November, 1938 by orders of the Chief of the Gestapo, anti-Jewish demonstrations all over Germany took place. Jewish property was destroyed, 30,000 Jews were arrested and sent to concentration camps and their property confiscated.

Under Paragraph VIII A, above, millions of the persons there mentioned as having been murdered and ill-treated were Jews.

Among other mass murders of Jews were the following:

At Kislovdosk all Jews were made to give up their property: 2,000 were shot in an anti-tank ditch at Mineraliye Vodi: 4,300 other Jews were shot in the same ditch.

60,000 Jews were shot on an island on the Dvina near Riga.

20,000 Jews were shot at Lutsk.

32,000 Jews were shot at Sarny.

60,000 Jews were shot at Kiev and Dniepropetrovsk.

Thousands of Jews were gassed weekly by means of gas-wagons which broke down from overwork.

As the Germans retreated before the Soviet Army they exterminated Jews rather than allow them to be liberated. Many concentration camps and ghettos were set up in which Jews were incarcerated and tortured, starved, subjected to merciless atrocities and finally exterminated.

About 70,000 Jews were exterminated in Yugoslavia. . . .

JOSEPH STALIN

UNLIKE LENIN, and unlike his own principal rival Leon Trotsky, Joseph Stalin (1879–1953) did not come from middle-class forebears, but was born the son of a poor Georgian cobbler. He was originally destined for the Orthodox priesthood, but was expelled for insubordination and radicalism in 1896 from a theological seminary in Tiflis. At the age of fifteen, he joined an underground revolutionary movement of Marxists. Stalin remained a fighter; his assumed name (his real name was Dzhugashvili) means "man of steel." In 1903, after the split within the Russian Social Democratic party, Stalin joined with the Bolshevik, or revolutionary majority, wing. He first met Lenin in 1905. Subsequently Stalin engaged in the relentless struggle against the tsarist regime. Before the outbreak of the First World War he was imprisoned several times and finally exiled to Siberia. In 1910 he helped found the Communist party's newspaper, *Pravda*. More prominent Bolsheviks like Lenin and Trotsky spent years of exile abroad before and during the First World War, but Stalin ventured into Western Europe on only a few occasions to attend secret revolutionary meetings. While not negligible, his role in the October Revolution of 1917 was less prominent than later official Soviet biographies have asserted. His intellectual contributions to Marxist theory were inferior to those of his early Politburo colleagues. In the first council of commissars after the Revolution, Stalin received the modest post of commissar of nationalities, while his rival, Trotsky, as commissar for foreign affairs and organizer of the Red army, emerged beside Lenin as the second most powerful figure of the Revolution.

Stalin, an indefatigable administrator, became secretary-general of the Soviet Communist party in 1922, a position of decisive importance, and held it until his death. In the struggle for power which followed Lenin's death in 1924, Stalin quickly overshadowed all his rivals. Trotsky, coming to view Stalin as a "rightist" for his then lenient policies toward the peasantry and for his rejection of intensified revolutionary activities abroad, sank into impotence, was dismissed as war commissar, was exiled in 1929, and died in Mexico at the hands of an assassin in 1940.

Stalin's victory over his opposition—involving the liquidation of many of his "Old Bolshevik" associates in the 1930s—had a decisive effect upon the subsequent course of Russian history. Retaining party leadership, he acquired, after 1939, unchallenged power in the government. Touted in official Soviet circles as a Marxist theoretician, scientist, music and art critic, and infallible prophet of Bolshevik world revolution, he was never successfully challenged within the orbit of established Communism—except by Yugoslavia's Marshal Tito in 1948. Stalin died in March, 1953, and was succeeded as premier by Georgi Malenkov.

The following selection is from the abridged text of Stalin's report to the Special Eighth All-Union Congress of Soviets, delivered on November 25, 1936, during a discussion of the new Soviet constitution.

THE NEW SOVIET CONSTITUTION

THE CONSTITUTION COMMISSION was to introduce changes into the Constitution operating at present, which was adopted in 1924, taking into account the changes in the life of the U.S.S.R. in the direction of socialism brought about in the period from 1924 to our days.

What changes have occurred in the life of the U.S.S.R. during the period 1924-1936?

That was the first period of the New Economic Policy, when Soviet power permitted a certain revival of capitalism, along with the general development of socialism, when it calculated that, in the process of competition between the two economic systems—the capitalist and the socialist—it would organize the superiority of the socialist system over the capitalist system.

The task was, in the process of this competition, to consolidate the position of socialism, to attain the liquidation of the capitalist elements and consummate the victory of the socialist system as the basic system of national economy.

At that time our industry presented an unenviable picture, especially heavy industry. True, it was recovering little by little, but it had not yet raised its output to anywhere near the pre-war level.

It was based on the old, backward, scanty technique. It was developing, of course, in the direction of socialism. At that time the share of the socialist sector formed about 80 per cent of our industry. But still the sector of capitalism held at least 20 per cent of industry in its hands.

Our agriculture presented a still more unenviable picture. It is true that the landlord class had already been done away with, but as compared to that class, the agricultural capitalist kulak class still formed a rather important force.

Agriculture as a whole at that time resembled a boundless ocean of small individual peasant farms with their backward medieval technique. There were in formation isolated points and little islands in this ocean, collective farms and state farms which, strictly speaking, were not yet of any really serious importance in our national economy.

The collective farms and state farms were weak, while the kulaks were still in their strength. At that time we did not talk about the liquidation of kulaks, but of restricting them.

The same thing can be said of the goods turnover of the country. The socialist sector of goods turnover amounted to some 50–60 per cent, no more, while all the rest was occupied by merchants, speculators and other private traders.

Such was the picture of our economy in 1924.

What have we in 1936?

While previously we had the first period of the New Economic Policy, the beginning of the New Economic Policy, a certain revival of capitalism, today we have the end of the New Economic Policy, the period of the complete liquidation of capitalism in all spheres of national economy.

Let us start from the fact that our industry during this period has grown into a gigantic force. Now it is no longer possible to call it weak and badly equipped technically. On the contrary, it is now based on new, rich and modern technique, with a strongly developed heavy industry and still more strongly developed machine-building industry.

Most important is the fact that capitalism has been completely expelled from the sphere of our industry, and the socialist form of production is now the system which alone dominates the sphere of our industry.

The fact that in volume of production our present socialist industry exceeds pre-war industry more than seven-fold cannot be regarded as a trifle.

In the sphere of agriculture, instead of an ocean of small individual peasant farms with weak technique and a preponderance of kulaks, we now have mechanized production conducted on the largest scale anywhere in the world, equipped with modern technique in the form of an all-embracing system of collective and state farms.

Everyone knows the kulaks in agriculture have been liquidated and that the small individual peasant farm sector with its backward medieval technique now occupies an insignificant place. The share of individual farms in agriculture, as far as sown area is concerned, now comprises no more than two to three per cent.

One cannot but note the fact that the collective farms now have at their disposal 316,000 tractors with a total of 5,700,000 horsepower, and, together with the state farms, they possess over 400,000 tractors with 7,580,000 horsepower.

As for distribution throughout the country, the merchants and speculators are now completely expelled from this sphere. The whole field of distribution is now in the hands of the state, the cooperative societies and the collective farms.

A new Soviet trade has come into being and it is a trade without speculators, a trade without capitalists.

THE NEW SOCIETY

Thus the complete victory of the socialist system in all spheres of the national economy is now a fact. This means that exploitation of man by man is abolished—liquidated—while the socialist ownership of the implements and means of production is established as the unshakable basis of our Soviet society.

As a result of all these changes in the national economy of the U.S.S.R., we have now a new socialist economy, knowing neither crises nor unemployment, neither poverty nor ruin, and giving to the citizens every possibility to live prosperous and cultured lives.

Such, in the main, are the changes which took place in our economy during the period from 1924 to 1936. Corresponding to these changes in the sphere of the economy of the U.S.S.R., the class structure of our society has also changed. As is known, the landlord class had already been liquidated as a result of the victorious conclusion of the Civil War.

As for the other exploiting classes, they share the fate of the landlord class. The capitalist class has ceased to exist in the sphere of industry. The kulak class has ceased to exist in the sphere of agriculture. The merchants and speculators have ceased to exist in the sphere of distribution. In this way, all exploiting classes are proved to have been liquidated.

The working class has remained. The peasant class has remained. The intellectuals have remained. But it would be mistaken to think these social groups have undergone no changes during this period, that they remained what they were, say, in the period of capitalism.

Take, for example, the working class of the U.S.S.R. It is often called "the proletariat" through old habit. But what is the proletariat? The proletariat is a class exploited by the capitalists.

But as is well known, the capitalist class is already liquidated in our country, the implements and means of production have been taken from the capitalists and transferred to the leading power of the state, which is the working class.

Consequently, there no longer exists a capitalist class which could exploit the working class.

Consequently our working class is not only not bereft of the implements and means of production, but, on the contrary, possesses them in conjunction with the whole people. And since it possesses these and the capitalist class is liquidated, all possibility of exploiting the working class is precluded. Is it possible after this to call our working class a "proletariat"?

It is clearly impossible. Marx said:

"In order that the proletariat may emancipate itself, it must smash the capitalist class, take the implements and means of production from the capitalists and abolish the conditions of production which create the proletariat."

Can it be said that the working class of the U.S.S.R. has already achieved these conditions for its emancipation?

Undoubtedly it can and should be said.

What does this mean? It means that the proletariat of the U.S.S.R. has become transformed into an entirely new class, into the working class of the U.S.S.R., which has abolished the capitalist system of economy and has established the socialist ownership of implements and means of production and is directing Soviet society along the path to communism. As you see, the working class of the U.S.S.R. is an entirely new working class, freed from exploitation and having no counterpart in the history of mankind.

Now, let us pass to the question of the peasantry. It is customary to say that the peasantry is a class of small producers, with atomized members, scattered over the face of the whole country, plowing their lonely furrows on their small farms with backward technique, slaves of private property, exploited with impunity by landlords, kulaks, merchants, speculators, usurers, etc. Indeed, the peasantry in capitalist countries, bearing in mind the main mass, is such a class.

Can it be said that our present-day peasantry, the Soviet peasantry, in the mass, resembles such a peasantry?

No, this cannot be said. We no longer have such a peasantry in our country. Our Soviet peasantry is an entirely new peasantry. We no longer have landlords and kulaks, merchants and usurers to exploit peasants. Consequently our peasantry is a peasantry freed from exploitation. Further, the overwhelming majority of our peasantry is collective farm peasantry, *i.e.,* it bases its work and its possessions not on individual labor and backward technique but on collective labor and modern technique.

Finally, the economy of our peasantry is not based on private property but on collective property, which grew up on the basis of collective labor. As you see, the Soviet peasantry is an entirely new peasantry, having no counterpart in the history of mankind.

Finally, let us pass to the question of the intellectual, the question of engineering and technical workers, the workers on the cultural front, office employees generally, etc. They too have undergone great changes during the past period. There is no longer the old conservative intelligentsia which tried to place itself above classes, but, in fact, as a mass, served the landlords and capitalists. Our Soviet intelligentsia is bound by all its roots to the working class and the peasantry.

First, the composition of the intelligentsia has changed. The offspring of the nobility and of the bourgeoisie comprise a small percentage of our

Soviet intelligentsia. Eighty to ninety per cent of the Soviet intelligentsia come from the working class, the peasantry and other strata of the toiling population.

Finally, the very nature of the activities of the intelligentsia changes. Formerly it had to serve the rich classes, for it could do nothing else. Now it must serve the people, for the exploiting classes have ceased to exist. And precisely for that reason it is now an equal member of Soviet society, in which, pulling together jointly with the workers and peasants, it is building the new classless socialist society.

As you see, this is an entirely new working class intelligentsia, for which you will not find a counterpart in any country on the globe.

Such are the changes which have taken place in the recent period in the class structure of Soviet society.

What do these changes signify?

They signify, first, that the dividing line between the working class and the peasantry, as well as that between these classes and the intelligentsia, is becoming obliterated and that the old class exclusiveness is disappearing. This means that the distance between these social groups is more and more diminishing.

They signify, secondly, that the economic contradictions between these social groups is subsiding, is becoming obliterated.

They signify, finally, that the political contradictions between them are also subsiding, becoming obliterated.

Such is the position concerning the changes in the sphere of class structure in the U.S.S.R.

The picture of the changes in social life in the U.S.S.R. would be incomplete without a few words regarding the changes in another sphere. I have in mind the sphere of national interrelations within the U.S.S.R. As is well known, the Soviet Union comprises about sixty nations, national groups and nationalities. The Soviet state is a multi-national state. Clearly the question of the interrelations among peoples of the U.S.S.R. cannot but be of first rate importance to us.

The Union of Soviet Socialist Republics was formed, as is well known, in 1922 at the First Congress of Soviets of the U.S.S.R. It was formed on the principles of equality and free will of the peoples of the U.S.S.R. The Constitution now in force, adopted in 1924, is the first Constitution of the U.S.S.R.

That was a period when the relations among the peoples had not yet been settled, as they should have been, when the survivals of mistrust towards the Russians had not yet disappeared, when the centrifugal forces still continued to operate. Under these conditions it was necessary to establish fraternal cooperation of peoples on the basis of economic, political and military mutual aid, uniting them in one union, a multi-national state.

The Soviet power could not but see the difficulties of this. It had before it the unsuccessful experiments and unfortunate experience of multi-national states in bourgeois countries. It had before it the abortive experience of old Austria-Hungary. Nevertheless it decided to make the experiment of creating a multi-national state, for it knew that a multi-national state which came into being on the basis of socialism is bound to pass every possible test. Fourteen years have passed since then, a period sufficiently long to verify the experiment. What is the result?

The period that has passed undoubtedly shows that the experiment in forming a multi-national state created on the basis of socialism has been entirely successful. This is an undoubted victory of Lenin's national policy.

How is this victory to be explained?

The very absence of the exploiting classes which are the principal organizers of strife among the nationalities, the absence of exploitation, breeding mutual distrust and fanning nationalist passions, the fact that the power is held by the working class, which is the enemy of all enslavement and the faithful bearer of ideas of internationalism, the materialization in reality of mutual aid of the peoples in all fields of economic and social life, and finally the high development of the national culture of the peoples of the U.S.S.R., culture that is national in form and socialist in content—as a result of all these and similar factors, the peoples of the U.S.S.R. have radically changed their characteristics. Their feeling of mutual distrust has disappeared. The feeling of mutual friendship has developed, and thus fraternal cooperation of the peoples has been established in the system of a single union state.

As a result, we now have a fully formed multi-national socialist state, which has passed all tests and which has a stability which any national state in any part of the world may well envy.

Such are the changes that have taken place during the past period in the sphere of relationships among the nationalities of the U.S.S.R. Such is the sum total of the changes in the sphere of economic and social-political life in the U.S.S.R. which have taken place in the period from 1924 to 1936.

THE NEW CONSTITUTION

How are these changes in the life of the U.S.S.R. reflected in the draft of the new Constitution?

In other words, what are the main specific features of the draft Constitution submitted for consideration at the present congress?

The Constitution Commission was instructed to introduce changes in the text of the 1924 Constitution. The work of the Constitution Commission resulted in a new text of a Constitution, in a draft of a new Constitution for the U.S.S.R.

In drafting the new Constitution, the Constitution Commission took as a point of departure that the Constitution must not be confused with a program. That means, there is an essential difference between a program and a constitution. Whereas a program speaks of what does not yet exist, and of what should still be achieved and won in the future, a constitution deals with the present.

Two examples for illustration:

Our Soviet society succeeded in achieving socialism, in the main, and has created a socialist order, *i.e.,* has achieved what is otherwise called among Marxists the first or lower phase of communism, that is, socialism.

It is known that the fundamental principle of this phase of communism is the formula: "From each according to his abilities; to each according to his deeds."

Should our Constitution reflect this fact, the winning of socialism?

Should it be based on this victory?

Undoubtedly it should. It should because for the U.S.S.R. socialism is something already achieved, already won.

But Soviet society has not yet succeeded in bringing about the highest phase of communism where the ruling principle will be the formula: "From each according to his abilities; to each according to his needs," although it sets itself the aim of achieving the materialization of this higher phase, full communism, in the future.

Can our Constitution be based on the higher phase? On communism which does not yet exist and which has still to be won?

No, it cannot, unless it wants to become a program or a declaration about future conquests.

Such is the framework our Constitution presents at this historical moment.

Thus the draft of the new Constitution sums up the path already traversed, sums up the gains already achieved. Consequently it is the record and legislative enactment of what has been achieved and won in fact.

This constitutes the first specific feature of the draft of the new Constitution of the U.S.S.R.

To continue:

The constitutions of bourgeois countries are usually taken as a point of departure for the conviction that the capitalist system is unshakable. The main bases of these constitutions form the principles of capitalism, and are its principal mainstays, namely: private ownership of land, forests, factories, shops and other implements and means of production; exploitation of man by man and the existence of exploiters and exploited; insecurity for the toiling majority at one pole of society and luxury for the non-toiling but well-secured minority at the other pole, etc.

They rest on these and similar mainstays of capitalism. They reflect them, they fix them by legislation.

Unlike these, the draft of the new Constitution of the U.S.S.R. proceeds from the fact of the abolition of the capitalist system, from the fact of the victory of the socialist system in the U.S.S.R.

The main foundation of the draft of the new Constitution of the U.S.S.R is formed of the principles of socialism and its chief mainstays, already won and put into practice, namely, the socialist ownership of land, forests, factories, shops and other implements and means of production; abolition of exploitation and exploiting classes; abolition of poverty for the majority and luxury for the minority; abolition of unemployment; work as an obligation and duty and the honor of every able-bodied citizen according to the formula: "He who does not work, neither shall he eat," *i.e.,* the right of every citizen to receive guaranteed work; the right to rest and leisure; the right to education, etc.

The draft of the new Constitution rests on these.

To continue: Bourgeois constitutions tacitly proceed from the premise that society consists of antagonistic classes, of classes which own wealth and classes which do not own wealth; that whatever party comes to power in the state guidance of society (dictatorship) must belong to the bourgeoisie; that the constitution is needed to consolidate the social order desired by and for the advantage of the propertied classes.

Unlike the bourgeois constitutions, the draft of the new Constitution of the U.S.S.R. proceeds from the fact that antagonistic classes no longer exist in our society, that our society consists of two friendly classes: the workers and peasants, that precisely these toiling classes are in power, that the state guidance of society (dictatorship) belongs to the working class as the advanced class of society, that the Constitution is needed to consolidate the social order desired by and of advantage to the toilers.

Such is the third specific feature of the draft of the new Constitution.

To continue: Bourgeois constitutions tacitly proceed from the premise that nations and races cannot be equal, that there are nations with full rights and nations not possessing full rights; that in addition there is a third category of nations or races, for example, in colonies, which have still fewer rights than those which do not possess full rights. This means that at bottom all these constitutions are nationalistic, *i.e.,* constitutions of ruling nations.

As distinct from these constitutions the draft of the New Constitution of the U.S.S.R. is, on the contrary, profoundly international. It proceeds from the premise that all nations and races have equal rights. It proceeds from the premise that color or language differences, differences in cultural level or the level of state development as well as any other difference among nations and races, cannot serve as grounds for jutifying national inequality of rights.

It proceeds from the premise that all nations and races irrespective of their past or present position, irrespective of their strength or weakness, must enjoy equal rights in all spheres, economic, social, state and the cultural life of society.

Such is the fourth feature of the draft of the new Constitution.

The fifth specific feature of the draft of the new Constitution is its consistent and fully sustained democracy.

From the viewpoint of democracy, the bourgeois constitutions may be divided into two groups. One group of constitutions openly denies or virtually negates equality of the rights of citizens and democratic liberties. The other group of constitutions willingly accepts and even advertises democratic principles, but in doing so makes such reservations and restrictions that democratic rights and liberties prove to be utterly mutilated.

They talk about equal suffrage for all citizens but immediately limit it by residential, educational and even by property qualifications. They talk about equal rights of citizens, but immediately make the reservation that this does not apply to women, or only partly applies to them, etc.

A specific feature of the draft of the new Constitution of the U.S.S.R. is that it is free from such reservations and restrictions.

Active and passive citizens do not exist for it; for it all citizens are active. It recognizes no difference in the rights of men and women, "of fixed abode" and "without fixed abode," with property or without property, educated or uneducated.

For it all citizens are equal in their rights. Neither property status nor national origin, nor sex, nor official standing, but only the personal capabilities and personal labor of every citizen determine his position in society.

Finally, there is one other specific feature in the draft of the new Constitution.

Bourgeois constitutions usually limit themselves to recording the formal rights of citizens without concerning themselves about the conditions for exercising these rights, about the possibility of exercising them, the means of exercising them. They speak about equality of citizens but forget that real equality between master and workman, between landlord and peasants, is impossible if the former enjoy wealth and political weight in society, while the latter are deprived of both; if the former are exploiters and the latter are exploited.

Or again: they speak of free speech, freedom of assemblage and of the press, but forget that all these liberties may become empty sound for the working class if the latter is deprived of the possibility of having at its command suitable premises for meetings, good printshops, sufficient quantity of paper, etc.

A specific feature of the draft of the new Constitution is that it does not limit itself to recording formal rights of citizens, but transfers the center of gravity to questions of the guarantee of these rights, to the question of the means of exercising them.

It does not merely proclaim the equality of the rights of citizens but ensures them by legislative enactment of the fact of liquidation of the regime of exploitation, by the fact of liberation of citizens from any exploitation.

It not only proclaims the right to work, but ensures it by legislative enactment of the fact of non-existence of crises in Soviet society, and the fact of abolition of unemployment. It not merely proclaims democratic liberties but guarantees them in legislative enactments by providing definite material facilities.

It is clear, therefore, that the democracy of the new Constitution is not the "usual" and "generally recognized" democracy in general, but socialist democracy.

Such are the principal specific features of the draft of the new Constitution of the U.S.S.R. Such is the reflection in the draft of the new Constitution of the mutations and changes in economic and social-political life in the U.S.S.R. which were brought about in the period from 1924 to 1936. . . .

[Stalin here considers the arguments of several groups of critics.]

Finally, there is one more group of critics. Whereas the preceding group charges that the draft Constitution renounced the dictatorship of the working class, this group, on the contrary, charges that the draft makes no change in the existing position of the U.S.S.R.; that it leaves the dictatorship of the working class intact, does not provide for freedom of political parties, and preserves the present leading position of the Communist Party of the U.S.S.R. And, at the same time, this group of critics believes that the absence of freedom for parties in the U.S.S.R. is an indication of the violation of the fundamental principles of democracy.

I must admit the draft of the new Constitution really does leave in force the regime of the dictatorship of the working class, and also leaves unchanged the present leading position of the Communist Party of the U.S.S.R.

If our venerable critics regard this as a shortcoming of the draft Constitution, this can only be regretted. We Bolsheviks, however, consider this as a merit of the draft Constitution. As for freedom for various political parties, we here adhere to somewhat different views.

The party is part of the class, its vanguard section. Several parties and consequently freedom of parties can only exist in a society where antagonistic classes exist whose interests are hostile and irreconcilable, where there are capitalists and workers, landlords and peasants, kulaks and poor peasants.

But in the U.S.S.R. there are no longer such classes as capitalists, landlords, kulaks, etc. In the U.S.S.R. there are only two classes, workers and peasants, whose interests not only are not antagonistic but, on the contrary, amicable. Consequently there are no grounds for the existence of several parties, and therefore for the existence of freedom of such parties in the U.S.S.R. There are grounds for only one party, the Communist Party, in the U.S.S.R. Only one party can exist, the Communist Party, which boldly defends the interests of the workers and peasants to the very end. And there can hardly be any doubt about the fact that it defends the interests of these classes.

They talk about democracy. But what is democracy? Democracy in capitalist countries where there are antagonistic classes is in the last analysis the democracy for the strong, democracy for the propertied minority. Democracy in the U.S.S.R., on the contrary, is democracy for all. But from this it follows that the principles of democracy are violated not by the draft of the new Constitution of the U.S.S.R. but by the bourgeois constitutions.

That is why I think that the Constitution of the U.S.S.R. is the only thoroughly democratic constitution in the world.

And that is how matters stand with regard to the bourgeois criticism of the draft of the new Constitution of the U.S.S.R.

THE PURGE OF BUKHARIN

Almost coincident with his final victory over Leon Trotsky in 1929, Joseph Stalin introduced Trotsky's earlier program of massive industrialization and the forced collectivization of agriculture as official Soviet policy. By 1933 the program and terrible famine had killed five to ten million Russians. The liquidation of the kulaks (independent farmers) as a class sent another ten million citizens into forced labor. Stalin's violence and brutality during this "era of socialist construction" lost him the loyalty of so many party members that by 1934 he no longer had a majority of party Communists with him. As early as 1932 he had tried to start a purge but could not obtain support. But with astute planning and plotting of unsurpassed viciousness Stalin crushed all opposition. He had the opposition leader Sergei Kirov murdered and the head of the secret police replaced. The new chief, Nikolai Yezhov, then began, on Stalin's orders, the Great Purges (1936–38) often called the *Yezhovshchina*. An entire generation of Communist leaders was wiped out. Indictments prepared in advance were commonly used, the worst tortures were applied, and incredible "confessions" of crimes against the regime were made—from plotting with Trotsky to accepting pay from Nazi Germany.

Revelations made after Stalin's death indicated that 70 percent of the central committee of the party was shot and that 1,108 of the 1,966 delegates to the 17th party congress were arrested. Lenin's old comrades from years before the Bolshevik revolution went to their deaths, but so did hundreds of those who had supported Stalin in his climb to power after Lenin's death. The present-day Soviet leadership includes men who stood by Stalin and shared with him the rewards of this blood bath. For example, the only two party secretaries who did not fall at the time were Andrei Zhdanov (who is still a high Soviet official) and Nikita Khrushchev.

Nothing in the purges stunned the world as much as the deliberately staged public trials of the greatest of the old Bolsheviks, Kamenev, Zinoviev, Rykov, and Bukharin. These men had been at the center of Soviet power since the revolution, but now Stalin had marked them for death. The astonishing thing about the trials was the dramatic revelations of terrible crimes by these leaders—crimes which in fact they had not committed. That they had been tortured only partly explains their performance. The confessions give a profitable insight into the minds of totalitarian leaders who, schooled to believe in "the necessities of history" and the all powerful wisdom of the party, can be prevailed upon to confess because the revolution needs victims. Exactly what inspired the confessions of the old Bolsheviks may never be known, although psychologists, novelists, and social scientists have debated the matter for more than a generation.

The climax of the purge trials was reached in March, 1938, when Nikolai Bukharin, famous party theoretician and former editor of *Pravda,* arose to make his last plea before the military collegium of the Supreme Court of the U.S.S.R.

Bukharin's confession is also known as Bukharin's testament. It helps reveal the ideals of loyalty to the state that led him to accept his death as a contribution to the revolution's success. Perhaps he never understood that force and power, the means of the revolution for Lenin, had for Stalin become the ends.

This selection comes from the English translation *Report of Court Proceedings in the Case of the Anti-Soviet Bloc of Rights and Trotskyites* (Moscow, 1938).

❧

THE PURGE OF BUKHARIN

Report of Court Proceedings in the Case of the Anti-Soviet "Bloc of Rights and Trotskyites"

INDICTMENT in the case of N. I. Bukharin, A. I. Rykov, G. G. Yagoda, N. N. Krestinsky, K. G. Rakovsky, A. P. Rosengoltz, V. I. Ivanov, M. A. Chernov, G. F. Grinko, I. A. Zelensky, S. A. Bessonov, A. Ikramov, F. Khodjayev, V. F. Sharangovich, P. T. Zubarev, P. P. Bulanov, L. G. Levin, D. D. Pletnev, I. N. Kazakov, V. A. Maximov-Dikovsky and P. P. Kryuchkov, accused of having on the instructions of the intelligence services of foreign states hostile to the Soviet Union formed a conspiratorial group named the "bloc of Rights and Trotskyites" with the object of espionage on behalf of foreign states, wrecking, diversionist and terrorist activities, undermining the military power of the U.S.S.R., provoking a military attack by these states on the U.S.S.R., dismembering the U.S.S.R. and severing from it the Ukraine, Byelorussia, the Central Asiatic Republics, Georgia, Armenia, Azerbaijan, and the Maritime Region of the Far East for the benefit of the aforementioned foreign states, and lastly, with the object of overthrowing the Socialist social and state system existing in the U.S.S.R. and of restoring capitalism, of restoring the power of the bourgeoisie.

The investigation instituted by the organs of the People's Commissariat of Internal Affairs has established that on the instructions of the intelligence services of foreign states hostile to the U.S.S.R. the accused in the present case organized a conspiratorial group named the "bloc of Rights and Trotskyites," the object of which was to overthrow the Socialist social and state system existing in the U.S.S.R., to restore capitalism and the power of the bourgeoisie in the U.S.S.R., to dismember the U.S.S.R. and to sever from it for the benefit of the aforementioned states the Ukraine, Byelorussia, the Central Asiatic Republics, Georgia, Armenia, Azerbaijan and the Maritime Region.

The investigation has established that the "bloc of Rights and Trotskyites" united within its ranks underground anti-Soviet groups of Trotskyites, Rights, Zinovievites, Mensheviks, Socialist-Revolutionaries and bourgeois nationalists of the Ukraine, Byelorussia, Georgia, Armenia, Azerbaijan and the Central Asiatic Republics, which is corroborated by the materials not only of the present investigation, but also by the materials of the trials which have taken place in various parts of the U.S.S.R., and, in particular, the trial of the group of military conspirators—Tukhachevsky and others— who were convicted by a Special Session of the Supreme Court of the U.S.S.R. on June 11, 1937, and of the trial of the Georgian bourgeois nationalist group of Mdivani, Okudjava and others, who were convicted by the Supreme Court of the Georgian Soviet Socialist Republic on July 9, 1937.

Lacking all support within the U.S.S.R., the members of the "bloc of Rights and Trotskyites" in their struggle against the Socialist social and state system existing in the U.S.S.R. and for seizing power placed all their hopes exclusively upon the armed assistance of foreign aggressors, who promised the conspirators this assistance on the condition that the U.S.S.R. was to be dismembered and that the Ukraine, the Maritime Region, Byelorussia, the Central Asiatic Republics, Georgia, Armenia and Azerbaijan were to be severed from the U.S.S.R.

This agreement between the "bloc of Rights and Trotskyites" and the representatives of the aforementioned foreign states was facilitated by the fact that many of the leading participants of this conspiracy had long been agents of foreign intelligence services and had for many years carried on espionage activities on behalf of these intelligence services.

This applies first of all to one of the inspirers of the conspiracy, enemy of the people Trotsky. His connection with the Gestapo was exhaustively proved at the trials of the Trotskyite-Zinovievite Terrorist Centre in August 1936, and of the Anti-Soviet Trotskyite Centre in January 1937.

However, the materials in the possession of the investigating authorities in the present case establish that the connections between enemy of the people Trotsky and the German political police and intelligence services of other countries were established at a much earlier date. The investigation has definitely established that Trotsky has been connected with the German intelligence service since 1921, and with the British Intelligence Service since 1926.

As far as the accused in the present case are concerned, a considerable number of them, on their own confession, have been espionage agents of foreign intelligence services for a long period of time. . . .

The leaders of the "bloc of Rights and Trotskyites," including Rykov, Bukharin and others accused in the present case, were fully informed of the espionage connections of their accomplices and did everything to encourage the expansion of these espionage connections.

All this sufficiently explains why these gentlemen, being in the service of foreign intelligence services, so readily agreed to the dismemberment of the U.S.S.R. and to the severance of whole regions and republics from it for the benefit of foreign states.

Agreement between the "bloc of Rights and Trotskyites" and foreign intelligence services was also facilitated by the fact that several of the conspirators accused in the present case had been provocateurs and agents of the tsarist secret police.

Having wormed their way into responsible posts in the Soviet state, these provocateurs, however, never ceased to fear the exposure of the crimes they had committed against the working class, against the cause of Socialism. Constantly in fear of exposure, these participants in the conspiracy saw their only hope of safety in the overthrow of the Soviet power, in the destruction of the Soviet system and in the restoration of the power of the landlords and capitalists, in whose interests they had sold themselves to the tsarist secret police, and under whose rule alone they could feel safe. . . .

The investigation has established that as far back as 1918, directly after the October Revolution, at the time of the conclusion of the Peace of Brest-Litovsk, Bukharin and his group of so-called "Left Communists," and Trotsky and his group, together with the "Left" Socialist-Revolutionaries, hatched a plot against V. I. Lenin, J. V. Stalin and J. M. Sverdlov, and forming a new government consisting of Bukharinites—who as a blind at that time called themselves "Left Communists"—of Trotskyites and of "Left" Socialist-Revolutionaries. . . .

The President: We shall now proceed to the interrogation of the accused Bukharin.

Bukharin: I have a request to make to the Court on the following two points: firstly, to give me the opportunity of freely presenting my case to the Court, and, secondly, to permit me at the beginning of my statement to dwell more or less, as far as time will permit, on an analysis of the ideological and political stand of the criminal "bloc of Rights and Trotskyites," for the following reasons: firstly, because comparatively little has been said about it, secondly, because it has a certain public interest, and thirdly, because Citizen the Public Prosecutor put this question at the previous session, if I am not mistaken.

Vyshinsky: If the accused Bukharin intends in any way to restrict the right of the State Prosecutor to put him questions in the course of his explanations, I think that Comrade the President should explain to Bukharin that the right of the Prosecutor to put questions is based on law. I therefore ask that this request should be denied, as provided in the Code of Criminal Procedure.

Bukharin: That is not what I meant by my request.

The President: The first question to the accused Bukharin: Do you confirm the testimony you gave at the preliminary investigation about your anti-Soviet activities?

Bukharin: I confirm my testimony fully and entirely.

The President: What do you wish to say about your anti-Soviet activities? And Comrade the Procurator is entitled to put questions.

Vyshinsky: Allow me to begin the interrogation of the accused Bukharin. Formulate briefly what exactly it is you plead guilty to.

Bukharin: Firstly, to belonging to the counter-revolutionary "bloc of Rights and Trotskyites."

Vyshinsky: Since what year?

Bukharin: From the moment the bloc was formed. Even before that, I plead guilty to belonging to the counter-revolutionary organization of the Rights.

Vyshinsky: Since what year?

Bukharin: Roughly since 1928. I plead guilty to being one of the outstanding leaders of this "bloc of Rights and Trotskyites." Consequently, I plead guilty to what directly follows from this, the sum total of crimes committed by this counter-revolutionary organization, irrespective of whether or not I knew of, whether or not I took a direct part, in any particular act. Because I am responsible as one of the leaders and not as a cog of this counter-revolutionary organization.

Vyshinsky: What aims were pursued by this counter-revolutionary organization?

Bukharin: This counter-revolutionary organization, to formulate it briefly . . .

Vyshinsky: Yes, briefly for the present.

Bukharin: The principal aim it pursued although, so to speak, it did not fully realize it, and did not dot all the "i's"—was essentially the aim of restoring capitalist relations in the U.S.S.R.

Vyshinsky: The overthrow of the Soviet power?

Bukharin: The overthrow of the Soviet power was a means to this end.

Vyshinsky: By means of?

Bukharin: As is known . . .

Vyshinsky: By means of a forcible overthrow?

Bukharin: Yes, by means of the forcible overthrow of this power.

Vyshinsky: With the help of?

Bukharin: With the help of all the difficulties encountered by the Soviet power, in particular, with the help of a war which prognostically was in prospect.

Vyshinsky: Which was prognostically in prospect, with whose help?

Bukharin: With the help of foreign states.

Vyshinsky: On condition?

Bukharin: On condition, to put it concretely, of a number of concessions.

Vyshinsky: To the extent of . . .

Bukharin: To the extent of the cession of territory.

Vyshinsky: That is?

Bukharin: If all the "i's" are dotted—on condition of the dismemberment of the U.S.S.R.

Vyshinsky: The severance of whole regions and republics from the U.S.S.R.?

Bukharin: Yes.

Vyshinsky: For example?

Bukharin: The Ukraine, the Maritime Region, Byelorussia.

Vyshinsky: In whose favour?

Bukharin: In favour of the corresponding states, whose geographical and political . . .

Vyshinsky: Which exactly?

Bukharin: In favour of Germany, in favour of Japan, and partly in favour of England.

Vyshinsky: So, that was the agreement with the circles concerned? I know of one agreement which the bloc had.

Bukharin: Yes, the bloc had an agreement. . . .

Vyshinsky: That fully satisfies me.

The President: You have no more questions to put to Bukharin for the present?

Vyshinsky: Not for the present.

The President: I must explain to the accused Bukharin that it is not a speech for the defence he must make, nor a last plea.

Bukharin: I understand that.

The President: And so, if you want to say anything about your criminal anti-Soviet activities, you may do so.

Bukharin: I want to deal with the subject of the restoration of capitalism. May I?

Vyshinsky: Of course, that is your chief speciality.

Bukharin: I want first to deal with ideological positions, not in the sense of declining responsibility for practical, criminal counter-revolutionary activities. I have not the slightest desire that the proletarian Court should conceive such an opinion. I want to reply to the question which Citizen the State Prosecutor put to Rakovsky, namely, for the sake of what did the "bloc of Rights and Trotskyites" carry on such a criminal struggle against the Soviet power. I realize that I am not a lecturer and must not preach a sermon here, but that I am an accused person who must bear responsibility as a criminal, facing the Court of the proletarian country. But just because it seems to me that this trial is of public importance, and because this question has been dealt with extremely little, I thought that it would be useful to dwell on the program which has never been written down anywhere, on the practical program of the "bloc of Rights and Trotskyites," and to decipher one formula, namely, what is meant by the restoration of capitalism, in the way it was visualized and conceived in the circles of the "bloc of Rights and Trotskyites." I repeat that in desiring to dwell upon this aspect of the matter I have no wish to disclaim responsibility for various practical things, for my counter-revolutionary crimes. But I want to say that I was not one of the cogs of counter-revolution, but one of the leaders of counter-revolution; and as one of the leaders I play and answer in a far greater degree, bear far greater responsibility than any of the cogs. And so I cannot be suspected of wanting to wriggle out of or repudiate responsibility, even if I were not a member of the Right and Trotskyite organization. The Court and the public opinion of our country, like the public opinion of other countries, as far as progressive mankind is concerned, can judge how people sank to such depths, how we all became rabid counter-revolutionaries, traitors to the Socialist fatherland, and how we turned into spies, terrorists and restorers of capitalism, and what, in the end, were the ideas and political standpoint of the "bloc of Rights and Trotskyites." We embarked on treachery, crime and treason. But for the sake of what did we embark on this? We turned into an insurrectionary band, we organized terrorist groups, engaged in wrecking activities, wanted to overthrow the valiant leadership of Stalin, the Soviet government of the proletariat.

One of the very widespread replies is that through the logic of the struggle we were forced to become counter-revolutionaries, plotters and traitors, that we were led to the shame, to the crime, that has brought us into the criminal dock. I need not say that such things do not happen in public life; here there is a logic, the logic of the struggle is combined with the methods of the struggle, with the platform.

I want to dwell on these facts, although I am convinced that actually such a terminology may sound rather strange in relation to such criminal activities, but nevertheless it seems important to me to dwell on this.

It has been proved many times, and repeated tens of thousands of times, that the Right deviation, from the moment of its inception, when it was still in an embryo, from the moment of its inception set itself the aim of restoring capitalism. I do not intend to speak about this. I want to speak of another aspect of the matter, from a far more important standpoint, from the objective side of this matter, because here there arises the problem of accountability and judgment from the standpoint of the crimes revealed in Court, all the more so because I am one of the leaders in the dock. We must here start from the beginning.

The Right counter-revolutionaries seemed at first to be a "deviation"; they seemed at first glance to be people who began with discontent in connection with collectivization, in connection with industrialization, with the fact, as they claimed, that industrialization was destroying production. This, at a first glance, seemed to be the chief thing. Then the Ryutin platform appeared. When all the state machines, when all the means, when all the best forces were flung into the industrialization of the country, into collectivization, we found ourselves, literally in twenty-four hours, on the other shore, we found ourselves with the kulaks, with the counter-revolutionaries, we found ourselves with the capitalist remnants which still existed at the time in the sphere of trade. Hence it follows that the basic meaning, the judgment, from the subjective standpoint, is clear. Here we went through a very interesting process, an over-estimation of individual enterprise, a crawling over to its idealization, the idealization of the property-owner. Such was the evolution. Our program was—the prosperous peasant farm of the individual, but in fact the kulak became an end in itself. We were ironical about the collective farms. We, the counter-revolutionary plotters, came at that time more and more to display the psychology that collective farms were music of the future. What was necessary was to develop rich property-owners. This was the tremendous change that took place in our standpoint and psychology. In 1917 it would never have occurred to any members of the Party, myself included, to pity Whiteguards who had been killed; yet in the period of the liquidation of the kulaks, in 1929–30, we pitied the expropriated kulaks, from so-called humanitarian motives. To whom would it have occurred in 1919 to blame the dislocation of our economic life on the Bolsheviks, and not on sabotage? To nobody. It would have sounded as frank and open treason. Yet I myself in 1928 invented the formula about the military-feudal exploitation of the peasantry, that is, I put the blame for the costs of the class struggle not on the class which was hostile to the proletariat, but on the leaders of the proletariat itself. This was already a swing of 180 degrees. This meant that ideological and political platforms grew into counter-revolutionary platforms. Kulak farming and kulak interests actually became a point of program. The logic of the struggle led to the logic of ideas and to a change of our psychology, to the counter-revolutionizing of our aims.

Take industry. At first we raised an outcry over over-industrialization, about over-straining the budget, and so on. But as a matter of fact this was a program demand, it was the ideal of a kulak agrarian country with an industrial appendage. And psychologically? Psychologically, we, who at one time had advocated Socialist industrialism, began to regard with a shrug of the shoulders, with irony, and with anger at bottom, our huge, gigantically growing factories as monstrous gluttons which consumed everything, deprived the broad masses of articles of consumption, and represented a certain danger. The heroic efforts of the foremost workers . . .

The President: Accused Bukharin, you have again not understood me. You are not making your last plea now. You are asked to testify to your anti-Soviet, counter-revolutionary activities, but you are giving us a lecture. In your last plea you may say whatever you like. I am explaining this to you for the third time.

Bukharin: Then permit me very briefly . . .

Vyshinsky: Tell me, accused Bukharin, how all this took shape in practice in your anti-Soviet activities.

Bukharin: Then permit me to enumerate certain points of program. And then I will immediately pass on to relate my practical counter-revolutionary activities. May I, Citizen the President?

The President: Only more briefly, if you please. You will have an opportunity to make a speech as your own Counsel for Defence.

Bukharin: This is not my defence, it is my self-accusation. I have not said a single word in my defence. If my program stand were to be formulated practically, it would be, in the economic sphere, state capitalism, the prosperous muzhik individual, the curtailment of the collective farms, foreign concessions, surrender of the monopoly of foreign trade, and, as a result— the restoration of capitalism in the country.

Vyshinsky: What did your aims amount to? What general prognosis did you make?

Bukharin: The prognosis was that there would be a heavy list towards capitalism.

Vyshinsky: And what transpired?

Bukharin: What transpired was quite different.

Vyshinsky: What transpired was the complete victory of Socialism.

Bukharin: The complete victory of Socialism.

Vyshinsky: And the complete collapse of your prognosis.

Bukharin: And the complete collapse of our prognosis. Inside the country our actual program—this I think must be said with all emphasis—was a lapse into bourgeois-democratic freedom, coalition, because from the bloc with the Mensheviks, Socialist-Revolutionaries, and the like, it follows that there would be freedom of parties, freedom of coalition, and follows quite logically from the combination of forces for struggle, because if allies are chosen for overthrowing the government, on the day after the possible victory they would be partners in power. A lapse not only into the ways of bourgeois-democratic freedom, but in the political sense into ways where there are undoubtedly elements of Caesarism.

Vyshinsky: Say fascism simply.

Bukharin: Since in the circles of the "bloc of Rights and Trotskyites" there was an ideological orientation towards the kulaks and at the same time an orientation towards a "palace revolution" and a coup d'état, towards a military conspiracy and a praetorian guard of counter-revolutionaries, this is nothing other than elements of fascism.

Since the features of state capitalism about which I spoke operate in the sphere of economics . . .

Vyshinsky: In short, you lapsed into outright rabid fascism.

Bukharin: Yes, that is correct, although we did not dot all the "i's." That is the formulation characterizing us as conspirators, restorers of capitalism, true from all points of view. And quite naturally, this was accompanied by a disintegration and degeneration of the whole ideology, our entire practice and methods of struggle.

Now permit me to go straight on with an account of my criminal activity. . . .

EVENING SESSION, MARCH 12, 1938

The Commandant of the Court: The Court is coming, please rise.

The President: Please be seated. The session is resumed. Accused Bukharin, you may make your last plea.

Bukharin: Citizen President and Citizen Judges, I fully agree with Citizen the Procurator regarding the significance of the trial, at which were exposed our dastardly crimes, the crimes committed by the "bloc of Rights and Trotskyites," one of whose leaders I was, and for all the activities of which I bear responsibility.

This trial, which is the concluding one of a series of trials, has exposed all the crimes and the treasonable activities, it has exposed the historical significance and the roots of our struggle against the Party and the Soviet government. . . .

It seems to me that when some of the West European and American intellectuals begin to entertain doubts and vacillations in connection with the trials taking place in the U.S.S.R., this is primarily due to the fact that these people do not understand the radical distinction, namely, that in our country the antagonist, the enemy, has at the same time a divided, a dual mind. And I think that this is the first thing to be understood.

I take the liberty of dwelling on these questions because I had considerable contacts with these upper intellectuals abroad, especially among scientists, and I must explain to them what every Young Pioneer in the Soviet Union knows.

Repentance is often attributed to diverse and absolutely absurd things like Thibetan powders and the like. I must say of myself that in prison, where I was confined for over a year, I worked, and retained my clarity of mind. This will serve to refute by facts all fables and absurd counter-revolutionary tales.

Hypnotism is suggested. But I conducted my own defence in Court from the legal standpoint too, orientated myself on the spot, argued with the State Prosecutor; and anybody, even a man who has little experience in this branch of medicine, must admit that hypnotism of this kind is altogether impossible.

This repentance is often attributed to the Dostoyevsky mind, to the specific properties of the soul ("l'âme slave" as it is called), and this can be said of types like Alyosha Karamazov, the hero of the "Idiot" and other Dostoyevsky characters, who are prepared to stand up in the public square and cry: "Beat me, Orthodox Christians, I am a villain!"

But that is not the case here at all. "L'âme slave" and the psychology of Dostoyevsky characters are a thing of the remote past in our country, or exist perhaps only on the outskirts of small provincial towns, if they do even there. On the contrary, such a psychology is to be found in Western Europe.

I shall now speak of myself, of the reasons for my repentance. Of course, it must be admitted that incriminating evidence plays a very important part. For three months I refused to say anything. Then I began to testify. Why? Because while in prison I made a revaluation of my entire past. For when you ask yourself: "If you must die, what are you dying for?"—an absolutely black vacuity suddenly rises before you with startling vividness. There was nothing to die for, if one wanted to die unrepented. And, on the contrary, everything positive that glistens in the Soviet Union acquires new dimensions in a man's mind. This in the end disarmed me completely and led me to bend my knees before the Party and the country. And when you ask yourself: "Very well, suppose you do not die; suppose by some miracle you remain alive, again what for? Isolated from everybody, an enemy of the people, in an inhuman position, completely isolated from everything that constitutes the essence of life . . ." And at once the same reply arises. And at such moments, Citizens Judges, everything personal, all the personal incrustation, all the rancour, pride, and a number of other things, fall away, disappear. And, in addition, when the reverberations of the broad international struggle reach your ear, all this in its entirety does its work, and the result is the complete internal moral victory of the U.S.S.R. over its kneeling opponents. I happened by chance to get Feuchtwanger's book from the prison library. There he refers to the trials of the Trotskyites. It produced a profound impression on me; but I must say that Feuchtwanger did not get at the core of the matter. He stopped half way, not everything was clear to him; when, as a matter of fact, everything is clear. World history is a world court of judgment: A number of groups of Trotskyite leaders went bankrupt and have been cast into the pit. That is true. But you cannot do what Feuchtwanger does in relation to Trotsky in particular, when he places him on the same plane as Stalin. Here his arguments are absolutely false. For in reality the whole country stands behind Stalin; he is the hope of the world; he is a creator. Napoleon once said that fate is politics. The fate of Trotsky is counter-revolutionary politics.

I am about to finish. I am perhaps speaking for the last time in my life.

I am explaining how I came to realize the necessity of capitulating to the investigating authorities and to you, Citizens Judges. We came out against the joy of the new life with the most criminal methods of struggle. I refute the accusation of having plotted against the life of Vladimir Ilyich, but my counter-revolutionary confederates, and I at their head, endeavoured to murder Lenin's cause, which is being carried on with such tremendous success by Stalin. The logic of this struggle led us step by step into the blackest quagmire. And it has once more been proved that departure from the position of Bolshevism means siding with political counter-revolutionary banditry. Counter-revolutionary banditry has now been smashed, we have been smashed, and we repent our frightful crimes.

The point, of course, is not this repentance, or my personal repentance in particular. The Court can pass its verdict without it. The confession of the accused is not essential. The confession of the accused is a medieval principle of jurisprudence. But here we also have the internal demolition of the forces of counter-revolution. And one must be a Trotsky not to lay down one's arms.

I feel it my duty to say here that in the parallelogram of forces which went to make up the counter-revolutionary tactics, Trotsky was the principal motive force. And the most acute methods—terrorism, espionage, the dismemberment of the U.S.S.R., and wrecking—proceeded primarily from this source.

I may infer a priori that Trotsky and my other allies in crime, as well as the Second International, all the more since I discussed this with Nikolayevsky, will endeavour to defend us, especially and particularly myself. I reject this defence, because I am kneeling before the country, before the Party, before the whole people. The monstrousness of my crimes is immeasurable especially in the new stage of the struggle of the U.S.S.R. May this trial be the last severe lesson, and may the great might of the U.S.S.R. become clear to all. Let it be clear to all that the counter-revolutionary thesis of the national limitedness of the U.S.S.R. has remained suspended in the air like a wretched rag. Everybody perceives the wise leadership of the country that is ensured by Stalin.

It is in the consciousness of this that I await the verdict. What matters is not the personal feelings of a repentant enemy, but the flourishing progress of the U.S.S.R. and its international importance.

NEVILLE CHAMBERLAIN

Arthur Neville Chamberlain (1869–1940) was the son of Joseph Chamberlain, the influential English imperialist statesman who served as colonial secretary at the end of the nineteenth century. Like his father, Neville Chamberlain started his political career in the city of Birmingham. He entered Parliament as a Conservative in 1918 but rose very rapidly to cabinet service. He was chancellor of the exchequer in 1923 and served thereafter in that and other posts under Conservative governments until 1937. Stanley Baldwin then resigned and Chamberlain succeeded him as prime minister.

His achievement in that office is still debated. In his own time he was regarded by some as a savior of European peace and a protector against Bolshevism and by others as a dishonest coward who placated the Fascist dictators to save English business interests. Chamberlain is still widely considered the symbol of "appeasement" and of the futility of attempts to make settlements with totalitarian leaders such as he arranged in late 1938. Even before that fateful date, however, the Chamberlain government had recognized Italy's war conquests in Africa and had sent only formal protests against Hitler's annexation of Austria. Chamberlain's motives are difficult to understand. Basically, he seems never to have taken the true gauge of Hitler and Mussolini. His background as a Christian gentleman and English businessman had failed to prepare him adequately for the new era of totalitarian politics then breaking on the world. The paths he followed, furthermore, had been marked out for him by his old chief Stanley Baldwin, and the feeble British armed strength he inherited in 1937 gave him little bargaining power with Hitler (although it is now known that Hitler himself lacked the military strength he claimed he had at the time of the meeting).

In the summer of 1938 Hitler threatened to annex German-speaking border regions in Czechoslovakia to the Third Reich. Hitler's terrible shouts and subsequent calm words about "my last demand" set in motion intense diplomatic activity at the end of the summer. By mid-September war seemed very near but, after Chamberlain had gone to Germany to deal personally with Hitler, a meeting of the major Western powers was arranged at Munich for September 29–30. England and France backed down on their obligations to the Czechs, acquiesced in Hitler's annexation of the Sudetenland in Czechoslovakia, and accepted Hitler's guarantee, backed by the word of his recent ally Mussolini, that he would make no further territorial demands. Chamberlain flew home to announce a triumph for "peace in our time" and to defend his actions in the speech to the House of Commons which is given here.

By the next spring Hitler had seized all of Czechoslovakia. England, still under Chamberlain, had started serious rearmament and had given guarantees to Poland. In fulfillment of those promises, but thereby admitting the futility of the Munich policy, Chamberlain took England into war against Germany when Hitler invaded Poland in September, 1939.

Chamberlain managed to hold power until early 1940 but Hitler's victory in Norway virtually ended his career. He resigned the prime ministership to a leading critic of Munich, Winston Churchill, on May 10, 1940. Chamberlain stayed on in the cabinet for a few months but died shortly after his final resignation from the government in October. He was that pathetic figure, a man who had tried to do right by the best light known to him but who had earned only misunderstanding and contempt.

Chamberlain's speech to the House of Commons comes from *Parliamentary Debates*, 339 H. C. Deb, 5s (London: His Majesty's Stationery Office, 1938).

REPORT ON THE MUNICH CONFERENCE, OCTOBER 3, 1938

WHEN the House met last Wednesday we were all under the shadow of an imminent menace. A war more stark and terrible than had ever taken place before seemed to be staring us in the face. Before I had sat down a message had come which gave us new hope that peace might yet be saved. That day, or a few days later, we joined in joy and thankfulness that the prayers of millions had been answered.

Our anxiety has been lifted from our hearts. On the members of the Cabinet the strain of responsibility has been for weeks almost overwhelming. Some of us, I have no doubt, will carry the marks of it for the rest of our days.

Necessarily, the weight fell heavier upon some shoulders than upon others. While all bore their parts, I would like here and now to pay a special tribute of gratitude and praise to the man upon whom fell the first brunt of those decisions which had to be taken day by day and almost hour by hour —to the courage and patience and the wisdom of the Foreign Secretary [Viscount Halifax]. His lofty conception of his duty, not only to this country but to all humanity, dominated us all and sustained us through the darkest hours.

Before I come to describe the agreement which was signed at Munich in the early hours of Friday morning, I would like to remind the House of two things which I think it is very essential not to forget when these terms are being considered.

The first is this. We did not go there to decide whether the predominantly German areas in the Sudetenland should be passed over to the German Reich. That had been decided already when the Czechoslovak government accepted the Anglo-French proposal. [Ironical Labor cheers.] What we had to discuss was the method, the conditions and the time of the transfer of the territory.

The second point we have to remember is that time was one of the essential factors. All the elements were present on the spot for the outbreak of a conflict which might have precipitated a catastrophe. There were considerable quantities of arms which were by no means confined to regularly organized forces and, therefore, it was essential that we should quickly reach a conclusion so that this painful and difficult operation of transfer might be carried out, beginning at the earliest moment and concluded as soon as was consistent with ordinary procedure, in order that we might avoid the possibility of something which might have rendered all our attempts at a peaceful solution useless. . . .

Now, in giving a verdict upon the agreement, we should do well to avoid describing it as a personal or a national triumph for anybody. The real triumph is that it has shown that the representatives of four great powers can find it possible to agree on a way of carrying out a difficult and delicate operation by discussion instead of by loss of life. They have averted a catastrophe which would have ended civilization as we have known it.

Relief of our escape from this great peril of war has everywhere been mingled in this country with profound feelings of—[Labor cries of "shame! shame!"]

I have nothing to be ashamed of. [Loud cheers from government supporters.]

Those who have may hang their heads.

We must all feel profound sympathy for a small and gallant nation in the hour of their national grief and loss. I say in the name of this House and of the people of this country that Czechoslovakia has earned our admiration and respect for her restraint and dignity, for her magnificent discipline in the face of such a trial as few nations have been called upon to suffer.

General Syrovy [Jan Syrovy, Premier of Czechoslovakia] said the other night in his broadcast that his government could have decided to stand up against over-powering forces but it would have meant the deaths of millions. The army whose courage no man has ever questioned have obeyed the order of their president as they would have equally obeyed had he told them to march to the trenches.

It is my hope and my belief that under the new system of guaranties the new Czechoslovakia will find a greater security than it has enjoyed hitherto. We must recognize that she has been put in a position where she has got to reconstruct her own economy. In doing so she must encounter difficulties which it would be practically impossible for her to solve alone.

We have received from the Czechoslovak government through their minister in London an appeal to help them to raise a loan of £30,000,000 [$150,000,000] by a British government guaranty. [Cheers.] I believe that the House will feel with the government that that is an appeal which should meet with a sympathetic and even generous response.

So far as we have yet been able to ascertain, the Czechoslovak government has not as yet addressed any similar request to any government and it is evident that the terms and conditions of a guaranteed loan and what governments should participate in it cannot be decided immediately. Evidently this is one of those cases where the old proverb applies, that "He who gives quickly gives twice."

Would members opposite [Labor interruptions] kindly allow me to continue this rather important part of my speech without these continual interruptions which distract attention and make it difficult for the House to take in exactly what I am saying.

His Majesty's Government are informing the Czechoslovak government that we are prepared immediately to arrange for an advance of £10,000,000 ($50,000,000) to be at that government's disposal for their urgent needs. [Ministerial cheers.]

How this advance will be related to the final figure that may be decided upon later is for future consideration. Manifestly, all this depends upon many factors which cannot now be determined.

The precise character of the problem will want expert examination in which we shall, if desired, be very willing to be associated and during the coming weeks the resulting situation and its needs can be more fully explored. What we feel to be required and justified now is that the action I have mentioned should be taken without any delay so as to assist the Czechoslovak state in the crisis of its difficulties.

The Chancellor of the Exchequer, on behalf of the government, has addressed a letter to the Bank of England requesting the bank to provide the necessary credit of £10,000,000, and, when the House resumes its sittings in November Parliament will be asked to pass the necessary legislation to reimburse the bank from the Exchequer. [Ministerial cheers.]

I pass from that subject and would like to say a few words in respect of the various other participants besides ourselves in the proceedings at Munich.

Hard things have been said about the German Chancellor today and in the past, but I do feel that the House ought to recognize the difficulty for a man in that position to take back such an emphatic declaration as he had already made and to recognize that in consenting, even though it were only at the last minute, to discuss with the representatives of other powers those things which he had declared he had already decided once and for all, was a real contribution on his part. [Ministerial cheers and opposition cries of "Why?"]

As regards Signor Mussolini, his contribution was certainly notable, and perhaps decisive. It was on his suggestion that the final stages of mobilization were postponed for twenty-four hours, to give us an opportunity of discussing the situation, and I wish to say that at the conference itself both he and the Italian Foreign Secretary, Count Ciano, were most helpful in the discussion.

It was they who, very early in the proceedings, produced a memorandum which [French Premier] Daladier and I were able to accept as a basis of discussion. [Ironical opposition laughter and ministerial cheers.]

I think Europe and the world has reason to be grateful to the head of the Italian government for contributing to a peaceful solution. [Ministerial cheers.]

Daladier had in some respects the most difficult task of the whole four of us, because of the special relations uniting his country and Czechoslovakia, and I should like to say that his courage and his readiness to take responsibility, his pertinacity and his unfailing good humor were unvarying and invaluable throughout the whole of our discussions.

There is one other power which was not represented at the conference, but which we felt to be exercising a constantly increasing influence. I refer, of course, to the United States. [Ministerial cheers.]

These messages of President Roosevelt, so firmly yet so persuasively phrased, showed how the voice of the most powerful nation in the world could make itself heard across 3,000 miles of ocean to sway the minds of men in Europe. [Ministerial cheers.]

In my view, the strongest force of all was the unmistakable sense of unanimity among the peoples of the world that war somehow must be averted.

Therein the peoples of the British Empire were at one with those of Germany, France and Italy. Their anxieties, their intense desire for peace, pervaded the whole atmosphere of the conference, and I believe that that and not threats made possible the concessions which we were able to get. [Cheers.]

Throughout these discussions the governments of the dominions have been kept in closest touch with the march of events by telegraph and by personal contact. I would like to say how greatly I was encouraged on each of the journeys I made to Germany by knowledge that I went with the good wishes of the governments of the dominions. [Cheers.] They shared all our anxieties and all our hopes. They rejoiced with us when peace was preserved. With us, they looked forward to further efforts to consolidate what has been won.

Ever since I assumed my present office my main purpose has been to work for the pacification of Europe, [cheers] for the removal of those suspicions and animosities which have so long poisoned the air.

The path that leads to peace is a long one and bristles with obstacles. This question of Czechoslovakia is the latest and perhaps the most dangerous. Now that we have got past it I feel that it may be possible to make further progress along the road to sanity.

Mr. Duff Cooper [Alfred Duff Cooper, resigned first lord of the admiralty], has alluded in somewhat bitter terms to my conversation last Friday morning with Herr Hitler. I do not know why that conversation should give rise to suspicion, still less to criticism. [Ministerial cheers.]

I ended it with no pact. I made no new commitments. There is no secret understanding. Our conversation was hostile to no other nations.

The object of that conversation for which I asked was to try to extend a little further the personal contact which I had established with Herr Hitler, which I believed to be essential to modern diplomacy.

Finally, there are the noncommittal conversations carried on on my part with a view to seeing whether there could be points in common between the head of a democratic government and the ruler of a totalitarian state. You see the result. [Cheers.]

A declaration which has been published and in which Mr. Duff Cooper finds so much ground for suspicion. What does it say? [A Labor member, "Nothing."]

The first paragraph says, "That we agree in recognizing that the question of Anglo-German relations is of first importance to the two countries and to Europe."

Will any one deny that?

The second is an expression of opinion only. It says we regard the agreement signed and the Anglo-German naval agreement as symbolic of the desire of our two peoples never to go to war with one another again. [Cheers.]

Does any one doubt that that is the desire of the people? [Cheers.]

[The Prime Minister then read the last paragraph of the declaration suggesting that Germany and Britain might continue their efforts to remove all possible sources of differences.]

Is there any one who will stand up and condemn that sentence? I believe that there are many who will feel with me that in this declaration signed by the German Chancellor and myself there is something more than a pious expression of opinion.

In our relations with other countries everything depends upon there being sincerity and good-will on both sides. [Cheers.] I believe there is sincerity and good-will on both sides. That is why the significance goes far beyond its actual words.

If there is one lesson which I think we have to learn from the events of the last week, it is this: Peace is not to be obtained by sitting still and waiting for it to come. [Cheers.] It requires active and positive effort.

I know I shall have plenty of critics who will say I have been guilty of facile optimism and that the better plan would have been to disbelieve every word by rulers of other great states of Europe.

I am too much a realist to believe that we are going to achieve our purpose in a day. We have only laid the foundations of peace. The superstructure is not even begun.

For a long period now we have been engaged in this country in a great program of rearmament which is daily increasing in pace and volume. Let no one think because we have signed this agreement between the four powers at Munich we can afford to relax our efforts [cheers] or call a halt in our armaments at this moment.

Disarmament on the part of this country will never be unilateral again. We have tried that once and we very nearly brought ourselves into disaster.

If disarmament is to come at all it must come by steps and it must come with the agreement and active cooperation of other countries. Until we know that we can obtain that cooperation, until we agree on the actual steps which are to be taken, we must remain on guard.

When, only a little while ago, we had to call upon people in this country to begin to take those steps which will be necessary if an emergency should come upon us, we saw a magnificent spirit displayed by the naval reserves, the territorial army, the auxiliary air force and the observers corps which obeyed the summons to mobilize so quickly and so readily. We must remember that most of these men gave up their peacetime work at a moment's notice to serve their country.

We would like to thank them. We would like to thank also the employers who accepted the inevitable inconvenience of mobilization. I know that they will show the same spirit of patriotic cooperation by taking back all their former employees when they are demobilized.

I know, though the crisis has passed, they must still feel proud at the thought that they are employing men upon whom the state can rely if a crisis should occur.

Well, we must renew our determination to build up the deficiencies which yet remain in our armaments and in our defensive precautions so that we may be able to be ready to defend ourselves and make our diplomacy effective [Labor laughter]. Yes, I am a realist. Nevertheless, I say with a sense of relief that I do see fresh opportunity of approaching this subject of disarmament opening up before us.

I believe they are at least as hopeful today as they have been at any previous time. It is to such tasks—the winning back of confidence, the gradual removal of hostility between nations till they feel that they can safely discard their weapons one by one—it is to such tasks that I would wish to devote what energy and time may be left to me before I hand over my office to younger men [cheers].

WINSTON CHURCHILL

WINSTON CHURCHILL (1874–   ) is regarded by many observers as the greatest Western statesman of the first half of the twentieth century. Although politics has been his master passion, Churchill has earned a reputation in many other fields, chiefly in biography and history.

Churchill was born near Oxford at Blenheim Palace, the family home built in the eighteenth century by a grateful nation for his soldier-ancestor John Churchill, first duke of Marlborough. Winston Churchill's father was a younger brother of the then duke and his mother was an American. Ties of blood have thus strengthened Churchill's belief in the common destiny of the Anglo-American peoples.

Churchill was educated at Harrow and Sandhurst. He left the British army and became a soldier of fortune in the late 1890s in Cuba, India, and the Sudan. During the the Boer War in South Africa (1899), while serving as a war correspondent, he was captured by the Boers but escaped. In 1900 he entered Parliament and five years later was appointed to the first of the many government posts that he was to hold. Between 1911 and 1915, as first lord of the admiralty, he reorganized and rebuilt the royal navy so that it was able to maintain an effective blockade and to confine the German fleet during the war to coastal waters. He resigned in 1915 after the failure of a brilliantly conceived invasion of Turkey. After 1918 Churchill favored and helped sponsor the small Western forces sent to Russia to crush the Bolsheviks but clashed with his prime minister, Lloyd George, about the intervention. In the 1920s he held several government positions, chief among them that of chancellor of the exchequer (1924–29). From 1929 to 1939 he was in the House of Commons, but not in the government. Increasingly, he warned that war would come if Hitler was not stopped. The following selection is his radio address to America after the Munich settlement. It summarizes his reading of the events of the decade.

When war finally came in 1939 Churchill, although long a critic of Chamberlain, had to be offered a cabinet post, and he returned to the admiralty. From here he was called to greatness and the fulfillment of his highest ambition, the prime ministry, in May, 1940. There followed the five heroic years of the war during which Churchill rallied the free world from the darkness of near defeat. In a cherished, long-sought alliance of the United States and the British empire and with the aid of exiled governments he helped break Fascist tyranny. In July, 1945, while he was attending the conference at Potsdam to settle remaining issues of peace and war among the United States, Great Britain, and the Soviet Union, Churchill's Conservatives lost a general election and Churchill had to resign his leadership.

In subsequent years he worked on his six-volume history of the war, which was followed by a four-volume chronicle of the English-speaking peoples. He remained in the House of Commons as leader of the opposition to the peaceful Socialist revolution. In 1946 Churchill carried forward his forebodings of the last year of the war and warned the world that Russia had placed an "iron curtain" around her conquered territories in Eastern Europe. Five years later he was again prime minister after a Conservative victory. The British empire which he had often pledged to maintain had almost disappeared; England itself was essentially a socialist state, accepted as such, in the main, even by the Conservatives; and the Western world which Churchill had already warned to seek federal union was being hard pressed by a growingly confident Soviet Union. In 1953, however, Churchill was able to greet a second Queen Elizabeth to the throne. He resigned the prime ministership due to age in 1955 but refused, as he had before, elevation to the House of Lords. He preferred to remain what many regard as the greatest of the Commoners of his time.

Churchill's speech on the Munich Crisis comes from *Vital Speeches,* V (November 1, 1938).

THE LIGHTS ARE GOING OUT

Broadcast to the United States on the Munich Crisis
October 16, 1938

I AVAIL MYSELF with relief of the opportunity of speaking to the people of the United States. I do not know how long such liberties will be allowed. The stations of uncensored expression are closing down. The lights are going out. But there is still time for those to whom parliamentary government means something to consult together.

Let me, then, speak in earnest. The American people have, it seems to me, formed a true judgment upon the disaster which has befallen Europe. They realize, perhaps more clearly than the French and British public have yet done, the far-reaching consequences of the abandonment and ruin of the Czechoslovak Republic.

I hold to the opinion, expressed some months ago, that if, in April, May or June, Great Britain, France and Russia had jointly declared that they would act together upon Nazi Germany if Herr Hitler committed an act of unprovoked aggression against this small State, and if they had told Poland, Yugoslavia and Rumania what they meant to do in good time and had invited them to join the combination of peace-defending powers—in that case I hold that the German dictator would have been confronted with such a formidable array that he would have been deterred from his purpose.

This also would have been an opportunity for all the peace-loving and moderate forces in Germany, together with the heads of the German Army, to make a great effort to reestablish something like sane and civilized conditions in their own country.

If the risks of war which were undergone by France and Britain at the last moment had been boldly faced in good time, and if plain declarations had been made and meant, how different would our prospects be today!

But all these backward speculations are useless. It is no use using hard words among friends about the past and reproaching one another for what cannot be recalled. It is the future, not the past, that demands our early and anxious thought. We must recognize that the parliamentary democracies and liberal peace forces have everywhere sustained a defeat which leaves them weakened, morally and physically, to cope with dangers which have vastly grown.

But the cause of freedom has in it a recuperative power and virtue which can draw out from misfortune new hope and new strength.

If ever there was a time when men and women who cherished the ideals of the founders of the British and American Constitutions should take earnest counsel with one another, that time is now.

All the world wishes for peace and security. It is their heart's desire. Have we gained it? That is what we ask. Have we gained it by the sacrifice of the Czechoslovak Republic?

Here was the model democratic State of Central Europe, a country where minorities were treated better than anywhere else. That has been deserted, destroyed, and is now being digested.

The question which is of interest to a lot of ordinary people, common people, is whether this destruction of the Czechoslovak Republic will bring up to the world a blessing or a curse.

We must hope it will bring a blessing. We must all hope that after we have averted our gaze for a while from the forces of subjugation and liquidation, every one will breathe more freely; that if the load will be taken off our chest, that we shall be able to say to ourselves, "Well, that is out of the way anyway anyhow. Now let's get on with our regular daily life."

But are these hopes well founded? Or are we merely making the best of what we have not the face and the virtue to stop? That is the question that the English-speaking people in all our lands must ask themselves today and they must ask themselves this question, "Is this the end or is there more to come?" And there is another question which arises out of this, "Can peace, good-will and confidence be built upon some mission of wrong-doing backed by force?" One may put this question in the largest form: "Has any benefit or progress ever been achieved by the human race through submission to organized and calculated violence?" That is put in the largest way.

As we look back over the long story of the nations, we must see on the contrary that their glory has been founded upon the spirit of resistance to tyranny and injustice, especially when these evils seem to be backed by heavier force.

Since the dawn of the Christian era a certain way of life has slowly been shaping itself among the Western peoples and certain standards of conduct and government have come to be esteemed. After many miseries and prolonged confusion, there arose into the broad light of day the conception of the right of the individual, his right to be consulted in the government of his country, his right to criticize or oppose the government of his country, his right to invoke the law of the land, even against the State itself. Independent courts of justice were created, the law enforced and thus was assured, of course, throughout the English-speaking world, and in France by the stern lessons of the Revolution, what Kipling called, "Leave to live by no man's leave underneath the law."

Now it seems to me, and I dare say to many of you, that all that makes existence precious to man and all that confers honor and health upon the State.

But we are confronted with another theme. It is not a new theme; it leaps upon us from the Dark Ages—racial persecution, religious intolerance, deprivation of free speech, the conception of the citizen as a mere soulless fraction of the State.

To this has been added the cult of war. Children are to be taught in their early schooling the delights and profits of conquest and aggression. An almighty community has been drawn painfully by severe privation into a warlike frame. They are held in this condition, which they relish no more than we, by a party organization several millions strong who derive all kind of profits from the upkeep of the regime.

Like the Communists, the Nazis tolerate no opinion but their own. Like the Communists, they feed on hatred. Like the Communists, they must seek from time to time, and always, mark you, at shorter intervals, a new prize, a new victim. The dictator in all his pride is held in the grip of his party regime. He can go forward; he cannot go back. He must blood his hounds and show them sport, or else be destroyed by them. All strong without, he is all weak within.

As Byron wrote a hundred years ago: "These pagan things of sabre sway, with fronts of brass and feet of clay."

No one must, however, underrate the power and efficiency of a totalitarian State, where the whole population of a great country—amiable, goodhearted, peace-loving people—are gripped by the neck and by the hair by a

Communist or Nazi tyranny, for they are the same things spelled in different ways. In such a State the rulers for the time being can exercise a power for the purposes of war and external domination before which the ordinary free, parliamentary societies are admittedly at a grievous practical disadvantage. We have to recognize this.

But then on top of all comes this wonderful agent of the air, which our century has discovered but of which, alas! mankind has so far proved unworthy.

This air menace, with its claim to torture and terrorize the women and children, the civil population, all the humble people in neighboring countries —this combination, pray mark me, this combination of medieval passion, of the weapons of modern science and the blackmailing power of bombing— this combination is the most monstrous challenge to peace, order and fertile progress that has appeared in the world since the Mongol invasions of the thirteenth century.

The culminating question to which I have been leading in these few words, these preliminary remarks—the culminating question is whether the world, as we have known it, the great hopeful world before the war, the world having increasing scope of enjoyment for the common man, the world with honor, traditions and expanding science—whether this world should meet this menace by submission or by resistance—there is the question. Let us see, then, whether the means of resistance remain to us today.

The renown of France, gallant France, is dimmed. In spite of her brave, efficient army, her influence is profoundly diminished. No one has a right to say that Britain, for all her blundering, has broken her word. Indeed, when it was too late, she was better than her word. Nevertheless, Europe lies at this moment abashed and distracted before the triumphant assertions of dictatorial power. You see it in many directions.

In the Spanish Peninsula, a purely Spanish quarrel has been carried by the intervention—or shall I say the non-intervention, to quote the current jargon? —by the non-intervention of dictators the Spanish quarrel by this intervention has been raised into the region of a world war. But it is not only in Europe that these oppressions prevail.

China has been torn to pieces by a military clique in Japan. The poor tormented Chinese people there are making a brave and stubborn defense— God help them.

The ancient Empire of Ethiopia has been overrun. The Ethiopians were taught to look to the sanctity of the public law. They were even prevented from buying weapons while time remained. They were referred to the tribunal of many nations gathered in majestic union. But all failed. They were deceived. And now they are winning back their right to life by beginning again from the bottom—a struggle in primordial life.

Even in South America the Nazi regime, thriving under the Monroe Doctrine, begins to undermine the fabric of Brazilian society.

Such is the scene. Far away, happily protected by the Atlantic and Pacific Oceans, to you, the people of the United States, to whom I now have the chance to speak—you are the spectators, and, may I add, the increasingly involved spectators, of these tragedies and crimes. We are left in no doubt where American interests and sympathies lie, but let me ask this, since I have the moment, let me ask you this: Will you wait until British freedom and independence have succumbed and then take up the cause when it is three-quarters over, and take it up, as you will have to, when it is yours alone?

I hear them say in the United States that because England and France have failed to do their duty, therefore the American people can wash their hands of the whole business. This may be the feeling of many people, but there is no sense in it. If things have got much worse, all the more must we try to cope with them. For after all, there are the remaining forces of civilization. They are overwhelming. If only they were united in a common conception of right and duty, there could be no war.

On the contrary, the German people—industrious, faithful, valiant—but alas, lacking in the proper spirit of civic independence—the German people, if liberated from their present nightmare, will take their honorable place in the vanguard of human society.

Alexander the Great remarked that the people of Asia were slain because they had not learned to pronounce the word "no." We cannot let that be the epitaph of the English-speaking peoples or of parliamentary democracy or of France, or of the many surviving liberal States of Europe!

There, in one single word, is the resolve which the forces of freedom and progress, of tolerance and good-will—there is the resolve which they should take. It is not within the power of one nation, however formidably armed, still less is it within the power of a small group of men, violent, ruthless men, who have always cast their eyes back over their shoulders—it is not within their power to try to fetter the forward march of human destiny.

We have preponderant world forces upon our side. They have but to be combined and obeyed. France must start, Britain must start, America must start. If through an earnest desire for peace we have placed ourselves at a disadvantage, we must make up for it by redoubled exertion and, if need be, by fortitude in suffering.

We shall no doubt arm. Britain, casting away the habits of centuries, will decree national service for her citizens. The British people will stand erect and will face whatever may be coming. But, my friends, these instrumentalities, as President Wilson called them, are not sufficient by themselves. We must add to them the power of ideals.

People say, many people, we ought not to allow ourselves to be drawn into a purely theoretical antagonism between Nazidom and democracy, but the antagonism is here now. It governs our lives. It is this very combination of spiritual and moral ideas which gives free countries a great part of their strength.

You see these dictators on their pedestal, surrounded by their soldiers and the truncheons of their police. On all sides they are guarded by masses around them and airplanes, fortifications and the like. They boast and vaunt themselves before the world. Yet in their hearts there is unspeakable fear. They are afraid of words and thoughts, words spoken abroad, hopes stirring at home, all the more powerful because forbidden. These terrors—a little mouse, a little tiny mouse of thought, appears in the room, and even the mighty potentates are thrown into a panic.

They make frantic efforts to bar out thoughts and words. They are afraid of the workings of the human mind. Airplanes—they can manufacture these in large quantities, but how are they to quell the natural promptings of human nature, which, after all these centuries of trial and progress, have become the armory of potent and indestructible knowledge?

Dictatorship, the fetish worship of one man, against which the British and American Constitutions have elaborated their provisions—dictatorship cannot be a part of any—a state of society where men may not speak their mind, where children denounce their parents to the police, where a business man or small shopkeeper ruins his competitor by telling tales about his private opinion—such a state of society cannot long endure if it is brought continually in contact with the healthy outside world.

The life of civilized progress with its currency and cooperation, with its dignities and joys, has often, as history shows, been blotted out, but I hold the belief that we have now at least got far enough ahead of barbarism to control it. And to avert it. If only we realize what is afoot and make up our minds in good time. Of course, we shall do it in the end. We shall surely do it. And how much harder our toil for every day's delay!

That is what I have to say to you on this occasion. And let me say, is this a call to war? Does anyone pretend that preparations for resistance against aggression amount to unleashing of war? There, indeed, is a sorry tale. I declare it to be the sole guarantee of peace, the finest and the surest prospect of peace—swift organized gathering of forces to confront not only military but moral aggression, the resolute and sober acceptance of their duty by the English-speaking peoples and by all nations, great and small—and they are many—who wish to walk with them.

Their faithful and zealous comradeship, armed, effectual—this would, almost between night and morning, clear the path of progress and banish from all our lives the fear which already darkens God's sunlight to hundreds of millions of men.

CHESTER WILMOT

FIFTEEN YEARS after the end of the Second World War comparatively few books had been published about the causes of the conflict. The First World War had been such a shock to civilized men that almost before it ended writers were at work trying to understand how the high hopes of their generation had been so awesomely frustrated. But throughout the 1930s many men already sobered by the first war felt certain that the rise of German totalitarianism would bring another great struggle. The recurrent question about the second war was less how did it start but how did it end on so solemn a note, with Communist totalitarianism in control of the very great areas of Europe that Britain and France had fought to save from Nazi tyranny.

The memoirs and diaries of the leaders of the Second World War have been gone over assiduously by scholars looking for an explanation of its tragic and paradoxical results. Of the works published thus far few have aroused as much interest as Chester Wilmot's *The Struggle for Europe*.

Wilmot (1911–54) was born and educated in Australia. He served during the war as a correspondent for the Australian and then the British radio networks. In 1945–46 he was special correspondent for the BBC at the Nuremberg trials of Nazi leaders. In 1947 he completed a volume in the Australian Official History of the Second World War and in 1952, the year in which he published *The Struggle for Europe*, he was appointed military correspondent for *The Observer*, an influential London weekend newspaper. Two years later Wilmot's seemingly brilliant future career was cut short when he was killed in an airplane crash.

The argument provoked by Wilmot's book turned, as the book itself did, on the assessment of Soviet intentions during the war. Those trying to defend the Allied leaders, especially the Americans, against charges of naïveté, stupidity, or worse, claimed that hindsight was always easier than foresight. There was, it was also alleged, nothing intrinsically wrong with the agreements made with Russia during the war, for they had seemed to assure peace, if Russia had supported them. The opponents of this view claimed that foresight as to Soviet intentions was not difficult in wartime and that several high and responsible Western officials had indeed sounded warnings, even during the war. These, and the long-known Soviet record of duplicity, should have put the West on guard to prevent a Soviet "presence" in Central Europe by the war's end.

This selection is the text of a BBC broadcast in 1952 during which Wilmot presented the main themes of his recently published book. It is taken from *The Listener*, XLVIII (February 7, 1952).

THE CONDUCT OF THE WAR

IN THE HISTORY of the past ten years, there is, I think, a peculiar irony. In January 1942, when Mr. Churchill was in Washington for the first time as Prime Minister, the greatest worry for him and for the President was the fear that Russia and China might collapse or come to terms with the enemy. But in January 1952, it was the new-found power of Russia and China that provided the main problems for discussion when Mr. Churchill made his most recent visit to the White House. In Russia's case, of course, this power is the direct result of the victory the United Nations gained over Germany and Japan, but what I want to do is to consider how this came about, and to what extent it was the result of the policy pursued by the Western Allies during the war. I think this is an appropriate moment to re-examine our conduct of the war, and, in doing so, I want to reconstruct the background of some of the major war-time decisions, in the hope of finding out how it was the Anglo-American alliance worked in practice, and why, for all our victories in the field, we failed to gain a more tolerable peace. How was it that in the process of crushing Nazi Germany and liberating western Europe, we allowed the Soviet Union to gain control of eastern Europe, and to become the dominant power on the Continent? Was this inevitable?

COULD RUSSIA SURVIVE?

In December 1941, when Mr. Churchill went to Washington, Hitler was master of Europe. His armies were on the outskirts of Leningrad and Moscow. He had nothing to fear in the west, since nearly all the immediate resources of Britain and the United States were engaged in containing the Japanese. Japan was in command of far eastern waters and it was not impossible that the Axis Powers would join forces in the Indian Ocean, for there was little the west could do to prevent Russia going down. In the first half of 1942 the Western Allies were to lose two ships for every one they could build, and as long as these losses continued they could not bring any substantial forces into action in Europe. Of course we were confident that Germany would eventually be defeated, but few of us dreamt that Russia might emerge as the mightiest power in Europe. What concerned us then was not Russia's expansion, but her very survival.

It seemed that Stalin's regime had been shaken to its roots, not only by military defeat but by the series of disastrous political miscalculations which had begun when Russia and Germany had signed their pact of non-aggression on the eve of the war. At that time—in August 1939—Stalin appears to have believed that he was turning Hitler westward, into a war of attrition with the Western Powers—a war which would leave Europe vulnerable to communist penetration. But Hitler gained such a tremendous victory in the west for the very reason that he was able to concentrate all his forces on one front. While 130 German divisions were engaged in the Battle of France, Hitler had only seven divisions in Poland, watching the Red Army. Stalin was naturally alarmed by this victory, and he took prompt advantage of Germany's weakness in the east. He already had possession of eastern Poland, and now he absorbed the little Baltic States and demanded that Rumania should surrender her northern provinces—Bessarabia and Bukovina. Hitler advised the Rumanians to give way, but he proceeded to treble his forces in Poland, and to warn the Kremlin that henceforth Germany would guarantee Rumania's territorial integrity.

At this stage—with France defeated and the British expelled from the Continent—Hitler was ready to come to terms with Britain, so that he could attack Russia without involving himself in that "war on two fronts" which he had sworn to avoid. With the Russians in Bessarabia, barely 100 miles from the Rumanian oilfields, Hitler dared not embark on a prolonged struggle with the British Commonwealth—and after his defeat in the Battle of Britain he knew this struggle would be prolonged. In the hope of escaping from this dilemma, Hitler made another approach to Russia. In November 1940, Molotov was invited to Berlin and there he was offered a substantial share in the "partition of the British Empire," which was, so Hitler said, "a gigantic world-wide estate in bankruptcy." Molotov's response was cautious and critical, and it revealed, I think, the historic continuity of Russian foreign policy. Ribbentrop suggested to Molotov that the four great totalitarian powers—Russia, Germany, Italy, and Japan—should divide the world between them and agree upon spheres of influence that would preclude the possibility of their coming into conflict with each other. Ribbentrop proposed that they should all "direct the momentum of their lebensraum expansion southward," since Russia by turning south would find, he said, "her natural outlet to the sea."

Molotov replied: "Which sea?" And in this question we have, I think, the real issue between the Soviet Union and Germany, for Molotov made it clear that Russia would not be satisfied merely with access to the Persian Gulf and the Indian Ocean. Her "natural outlet" was through the Black Sea and the Bosphorus into the Mediterranean; and so she would not give up her interest in Turkey, Bulgaria, and Rumania, nor for that matter in the Balkans generally, nor in Poland. "Paper agreements," said Molotov, "could not suffice for the Soviet Union; rather she would have to insist on effective guarantees for her security." By "effective guarantees" Molotov meant physical possession, or domination, of those strategic areas which lay within the sphere of Soviet ambitions.

Following this conference, Stalin "accepted in principle" the German proposal for a four-power alliance, but sought to impose conditions which would have made Hitler permanently dependent on the good graces of the Soviet Union for the supplies of oil he needed for the conquest of Britain. Stalin demanded control of the Bosphorus and the Dardanelles, and—perhaps more significant for us today—he asked Hitler to recognise the Persian Gulf area as "the centre of the aspirations of the Soviet Union."

In the week before Molotov's visit to Berlin Roosevelt had been re-elected President for a third term. This event convinced Hitler that the United States would eventually enter the war and that before this occurred he must do one of two things: either consolidate his position in the west by subduing Britain, or remove the threat in the east by defeating the Soviet Union. He could invade Russia with his existing war machine in 1941, but he could not invade Britain until he had fundamentally reorganised the Wehrmacht and the German war economy in order to place the main striking power in the hands of the Luftwaffe and the Navy. Yet this could not be done as long as he had to maintain in eastern Europe an army large enough to keep Russia neutral and to intimidate Stalin into delivering the oil and raw materials Germany would need for the war against Britain. Accordingly, when Goering and Raeder tried to persuade him to concentrate first on driving the British from the Mediterranean, Hitler replied: "In view of Russia's inclination to interfere in the affairs of the Balkans, we must at all costs eliminate the last remaining enemy on the Continent before coming to grips with Britain."

STALIN AT THE DINNER TABLE

Those words were spoken in December 1940. One year later it seemed that Hitler was on the point of achieving this purpose. He was, as I have said, master of Europe, and both Churchill and Roosevelt feared that Stalin might make a separate peace. White Russia and the Ukraine had been overrun; the Wehrmacht had been welcomed as a liberating army, and by December 4, 1941, its vanguard was fighting in the suburbs of Moscow within sight of the Kremlin. Inside the Kremlin that night Stalin gave a dinner. The guest of honour was the Polish Prime Minister, General Sikorski. "At the height of the party," says one of the General's colleagues, "when Sikorski believed he had found some mellowness in the man, Stalin turned to him and said: 'Now we will talk about the frontier between Poland and Russia.'"

So here, in the moment of apparent defeat, Stalin had his eye on the political objective, on the post-war territorial settlement. As the Red Army's fortunes fluctuated, Stalin varied his diplomatic tactics, but the long-term purpose of his grand strategy remained the same. Even now—with the Germans on the outskirts of Moscow—he sought to turn his immediate military weakness to ultimate political advantage. A fortnight later, when Mr. Eden visited Moscow—to prepare the way for a treaty of alliance between Britain and the Soviet Union—he was confronted with the blunt demand that the Western Allies must recognise the Russian frontiers as they had been when Germany invaded the Soviet Union. This demand was rejected by the President and the Prime Minister, since it would have meant giving Russia the territories she had acquired as a result of her pact with Hitler—namely, the little Baltic States, eastern Poland, and northern Rumania.

"WHEN THE TIME COMES WE WILL SPEAK"

For the first five months of 1942 Stalin and Molotov continued to press these claims, and at one stage Mr. Churchill was inclined to give way, so great was his fear that Russia would make a separate peace. But President Roosevelt refused on principle to give any war-time commitments about post-war frontiers. He was determined to avoid Woodrow Wilson's mistake of making commitments which Congress would not endorse, and in any case the Russian proposal was in direct conflict with the Atlantic Charter which the Soviet Union had accepted. Stalin withdrew his demand and changed his methods. During the next eighteen months these territorial claims were never mentioned, and at the Teheran conference—in December 1943—when Churchill raised the matter over dinner Stalin replied: "There is no need to speak now about Soviet desires, but when the time comes we will speak." That time would not come until the Red Army was in physical control of the areas that Russia wanted to annex, for then Stalin's possession might override Roosevelt's principle.

But in the spring of 1942, when the Western Powers stood firm on this frontier question, Molotov came to London and concluded an Anglo-Soviet treaty that contained no territorial concessions whatever. Nevertheless he did not return empty-handed from this visit to the west. In London he pleaded vehemently but in vain for the opening of a second front in France that year. In Washington he demanded "a straight answer," and he got it. The minutes of his discussions show that with General Marshall's full approval President Roosevelt "authorised Mr. Molotov to inform Mr. Stalin that we expect the formation of a second front this year"—1942. Having got this assurance, the shrewd Molotov proceeded to embody it in an official communiqué, which was interpreted everywhere as an Anglo-American commitment. It was not known then that the British Government had given Molotov an aide mémoire in which it pointed out the futility of launching a cross-Channel attack that was bound to fail, and added: "We can therefore give no promise in the matter." The Americans, on the other hand, had made what amounted to a promise.

As I examined the evidence of the next two years, I could not help feeling that this assurance lay uneasily on Roosevelt's conscience and left him at a moral disadvantage in his dealings with Stalin. It was a rash promise, given out of the generosity of the American heart and with an earnest desire to come to Russia's aid, but it was made without due regard for the harsh facts of the military situation. In the summer of 1942, the British argued that there were neither the troops nor the equipment nor the shipping for the Western Powers to carry out a major amphibious operation on the strongly defended Channel coast that year. This argument won the day. At the time, General Eisenhower thought he had seen "the blackest day in history," but since the war he has acknowledged that the British were right—and, of course, they were, if only because of the shortage of shipping.

There could be no second front in France that year, and yet the fatal promise had been made, and this promise led to another which seems to me to have been most unfortunate in its outcome. In January 1943, at Casablanca, the President and the Prime Minister issued their celebrated demand for unconditional surrender. At the time this was regarded as a "vote of self-confidence," but, after talking to some of those who were there, I am convinced that this demand was intended primarily as an assurance to Stalin. It was an assurance that, although the Western Powers could not open a second front even in 1943, they would never come to terms with Germany. The unconditional surrender formula was the President's brain-child, but we must bear equal responsibility for its proclamation. It was approved by the Prime Minister and by the British War Cabinet before it was announced. And yet I can find no evidence that there was any preliminary consideration of its probable impact on the resistance of the German people or their armed forces. Hitler himself, of course, had always intended to fight on, as he once said, "until five past midnight"; and his generals, almost without exception, would have fought with him in any case, since they were fighting for professional survival: they knew that the Allies were determined to destroy the German military class. But would the German troops and the German people have supported Hitler to the very end if we had not closed the door to any negotiations with any group of Germans?

There is ample evidence now that they would not. Even before Casablanca,

Goebbels had written in his private diary: "The more the English prophesy a disgraceful peace for Germany, the easier it is for me to toughen and harden German resistance." Goebbels made good use of "unconditional surrender," and by stiffening German resistance prolonged the war. . . . But the Allied demand had a further effect, which seems to me even more important. It meant that the war would not end until the Anglo-American armies and the Red Army met in the heart of Europe. It meant too that, if this were to happen, Germany would be destroyed politically; that there would be a political vacuum in central Europe—a vacuum which would be filled by Russian power. Moreover, the enforcement of unconditional surrender by Allied Armies of Occupation meant that the Russians, having advanced to the Elbe, would have a lawful reason for staying there, and for maintaining what would amount to occupation forces—not only in eastern Germany, but in the countries of eastern Europe through which their supply lines would run.

Thus, during 1943—in the year following Casablanca—since the Allied armies were to meet somewhere in Europe, the important questions, for the post-war world, were: where would the meeting place be; by what route would the converging forces come? We knew that the Russians would come —if they came at all—through Poland, but there was a long argument between the British and the Americans about the route or routes that the western armies should take. This difference of opinion was not new. It arose out of a strategic controversy which was already a year old and which was to drag on for two years longer. In January 1942, the President and the Prime Minister had agreed that they must concentrate first on the defeat of Germany. In April 1942, Mr. Churchill had accepted the American view that "the final blow against Germany must be delivered across the English Channel." On these two points there was full agreement: defeat Hitler first, and make the decisive attack from the west. But the British leaders always made this reservation: that the cross-Channel assault should not be undertaken unless it could be made in such strength that it was sure to succeed. How then was that success to be ensured? It was on this question that the two Allies differed fundamentally because their approaches to war were different.

The Americans, optimistic, self-confident, and impatient by nature, believed in the direct assault by the shortest route. To them the cross-Channel attack was primarily a matter of logistics—of resources. They argued that if the Germans in France were too strong, then the Allies should build up their forces in Britain until they had amassed the necessary superiority. They preferred to out-produce Hitler, rather than to out-manoeuvre him. The British, on the other hand, were instinctively opposed to making a head-on assault against the enemy's strongest rampart. They accepted the eventual necessity of a cross-Channel invasion, but they knew from long experience of European wars that the invader must first exploit the great mobility of sea power (and now air power) in order to keep the opposing forces dispersed and to counter the enemy's advantage of being able to move on interior lines. They wanted to win by manoeuvre, not by mass, and so they favoured a strategy of indirect approach. They were anxious to weaken the enemy in France by distraction—to expose his southern flank before assaulting his western front. And since it was unanimously agreed at Casablanca that there could be no cross-Channel attack that year, the British leaders were eager to extract the greatest advantage from the Mediterranean in 1943 as the prelude to the invasion of northern France in 1944.

AMERICAN SUSPICION OF BRITISH MOTIVES

They presented this view on grounds that were strictly military. But the American Chiefs of Staff were quite confident of their power to carry through the assault across the Channel without any preliminary diversions; so confident that they suspected the British of advocating the Mediterranean approach for sinister political reasons. The President's view was—and here I quote his own words—"I see no reason for putting the lives of American soldiers in jeopardy in order to protect real or fancied British interests on the European continent." Consequently, rather than continue operations in the Mediterranean, rather than strike at the "soft under-belly" of Europe in 1943, as Mr. Churchill wanted, the American Chiefs of Staff proposed to concentrate on the Pacific. They were prevented from doing this only because the President upheld the "Hitler first" strategy. Yet the pull to the far east continued and it resulted in an unhappy compromise. It was agreed at Casablanca that Eisenhower should invade Sicily as soon as he had cleared North Africa, but no plan was made for attacking Italy direct. In fact, the American Chiefs insisted that after the conquest of Sicily, priority in shipping and in landing craft should be given not to the Mediterranean but to the Pacific.

The result of this decision was that in July 1943, when Mussolini was driven from power, Eisenhower had not the resources to take advantage of this great political opportunity. It was six weeks before Eisenhower could assemble the forces to make a major landing on the Italian coast. In July Hitler had been willing to give up all Italy south of Florence, but when we failed to seize our chance, he reinforced the Italian front and was able to halt our armies well to the south of Rome throughout the winter. Nevertheless, the invasion of Italy did compel Hitler to disperse his strength and to withdraw forces from other fronts, as Mr. Churchill had predicted. A year later, when we invaded Normandy, the Germans had as many divisions in the Mediterranean as they had in the west. But this dividend lay in the future; the immediate impact was greatest not in the west but in the east.

THE CONSEQUENCES OF MUSSOLINI'S FALL

Shortly before Mussolini's downfall Hitler had launched a big offensive against the Russians at Kursk and had suffered a heavy defeat. Before he could recover—and rebuild his armoured reserves—Mussolini fell and Hitler had to send six of his best mobile divisions to Italy. These had no sooner left than the Red Army began its summer offensive and gained a quick break through. This was the more serious because Hitler had expressly forbidden the construction of a rearward defence line along the Dnieper. In the autumn of 1943 the Red Army broke this river barrier and liberated most of the Ukraine. And they did this at a time when the Anglo-American armies in Italy were checked by mud and mountains and by the divisions which Hitler had moved from Russia.

This was the strategic situation when the three Allied leaders met together for the first time at Teheran late in November 1943. At Teheran we see the direct relation between operations in the field and discussions at the conference table, for Stalin came with the political advantage of having just gained a great military victory, and also with another political advantage, which sprang from the attitude of President Roosevelt and his advisers to Russia on the one hand and to Britain on the other.

Before I define the attitude of the Americans to their allies, as I see it, let me say that I believe it was the President's personal leadership which kept the Grand Alliance together and carried it to victory; and that it was the massive development of America's economic and military power under his guidance which decided the fate of the Axis Powers, as Stalin himself admitted at Teheran. Nevertheless, it must be said that Roosevelt did misjudge his own capacity to deal with the Russians. In March 1942—in a cable to Churchill—Roosevelt said:

I know you will not mind my being brutally frank when I tell you that I think I can handle Stalin personally better than either your Foreign Office or my State Department. Stalin hates the guts of all your top people. He likes me better and I hope he will continue to do so.

Some time later—and before he went to Teheran—Roosevelt discussed his approach to Russia with William Bullitt, who had been American Ambassador in Moscow. To him the President said:

I have just a hunch that Stalin doesn't want anything but security for his country, and I think that if I give him everything I possibly can and ask nothing in return, noblesse oblige, he won't try to annex anything and will work for a world of democracy and peace.

And so, when he went to Teheran, the President was convinced that he could handle Stalin and that, once they met across the conference table, he would be able to win the Marshal's trust and friendship. This was not merely the view of "Roosevelt the visionary." In this I am sure he was fully supported by his political and military advisers. Like him, they believed that if only the Soviet Union could be induced to join the United Nations, it would not matter if the balance of power was destroyed. After a visit to Moscow late in 1943 the American Secretary of State, Cordell Hull, reported to Congress that, when the United Nations was established,

there would no longer be any need for spheres of influence, for alliances, for balance of power, or any of the other special arrangements by which, in the unhappy past, nations strove to safeguard their security or promote their interests.

Similarly, three months before the Teheran conference, the President's military advisers had prepared for him a memorandum in which they said:

Since Russia is the decisive factor in the war, she must be given every assistance and every effort must be made to obtain her friendship. Since, without doubt, Russia will dominate Europe on the defeat of the Axis, it is even more essential to develop and maintain the most friendly relations with Russia.

I do not quote these contemporary statements in any sense of criticism, for I believe the effort to win Russia's friendship had to be made and had to be made by the Americans. The source of Roosevelt's attitude was not merely personal. It was also historical—and national. The idea that they could "get along with" the Russians came easily to the Americans. The United States is the "great melting pot" and its people have shown an unrivalled capacity for absorbing into their own society a multitude of nationalities. Even after Yalta and Potsdam, we find the President's personal envoy, Harry Hopkins, writing this: "The Russians are a tenacious, determined people, who think and act just like you and I do." The same point was made by General Eisenhower, well after the war. "The ordinary Russian," he wrote, "seems to me to bear a marked similarity to what we call an 'average American.'" But Eisenhower went further than this in seeking common ground for friendship. He believed, so he wrote, that "in the past relations of America and Russia there was no cause to regard the future with pessimism," because "the two peoples had maintained an unbroken friendship," and because "both

were free from the stigma of colonial empire building by force." This was
the American way of saying that both peoples were free from original sin.
Of course, this was far from true of either country but it was believed, and
it coloured not merely the President's approach but the whole American attitude to Russia and to Britain. In American eyes Britain was an imperial
power, bearing the "colonial stigma," and Russia was not.

In his memoirs Cordell Hull says:

> We had definite ideas with respect to the future of the British colonial empire
> on which we differed from the British. It might be said that the future of that
> empire was no business of ours; but we felt that unless dependent peoples were
> assisted towards self-government and were given it . . . they would provide
> kernels of conflict.

That was the official view. Indeed, it is fair to say that the President was
determined to liberate not only the countries the Axis had occupied, but also
the colonies of the older imperial powers. He wanted to extend throughout
the colonial world the revolution that had started in 1776. This was the source
of Mr. Roosevelt's proposal that colonial territories should be placed under
international trusteeship. In Cairo, on the eve of the Teheran conference, he
proposed this solution for French Indo-China. Mr. Churchill replied that in
this case that country would be taken over by Chiang Kai-shek, but the
President assured him that Chiang had said he had no interest in Indo-
China. To this the Prime Minister answered: "Nonsense." Thereupon the
President said: "Winston, you have 400 years of acquisitive instinct in your
blood, and you just don't understand how a country may not want to acquire
land somewhere if they can get it." Recounting this incident to Edward
Stettinius, who became Secretary of State, the President said: "Remember,
Ed, the British will take land anywhere in the world, even if it's only rock or
a sandbar."

MR. CHURCHILL'S "REARGUARD ACTION"

And so, throughout the war, Mr. Churchill had to fight a rearguard action
against American critics of the British Empire—and on one occasion he declared publicly: "I have not become the King's first Minister in order to
preside over the liquidation of the British Empire." When Churchill made
this statement, at the Mansion House in November 1942, I wonder how
many of his hearers realised that he was directing his words primarily at the
man whom he was proud to acclaim as "the greatest American friend we
have ever known and the greatest champion of freedom who has ever
brought help and comfort from the new world to the old."

This, then, was the political background of the Teheran conference so far as the Americans were concerned: the belief that the Russians would play fair and that it was the British who were the real imperialists who had to be restrained. The Teheran conference began with a private meeting between Stalin, Roosevelt, and their interpreters. Here the President let it be known that he did not always agree with the British Prime Minister, and Stalin took the point. That evening he suggested that, in the interest of security, the President should move from the American Legation to the Soviet Embassy. When Roosevelt did so, Stalin gave up his own quarters and moved to a small cottage in the Embassy grounds. Then, at the first formal session, Stalin proposed that the President should act as chairman at all meetings, and thus with one move he brought Mr. Roosevelt halfway to his side of the conference table. At Teheran, and later at Yalta, the President was delighted to be in the chair, for he could then preserve greater freedom of action and avoid committing himself until he had heard the British and Russian views. But the President's eagerness to act as arbitrator meant that the Americans tended to take up an intermediate position, even on issues where the true interests of Britain and the United States were almost identical. In fact, at many of the sessions the assertion of what was really the Anglo-American point of view was left to the British alone, much to Mr. Churchill's annoyance.

CONFERENCE AT TEHERAN

This was very serious because no common Anglo-American policy had been agreed upon beforehand. I am told by those who were present at the first session in Teheran that Stalin was surprised and delighted to find that his Allies were in conflict about their military plans for 1944. And the immediate result was that western strategy was virtually settled by the Russians. The issue—as put by Roosevelt—was whether the Western Powers should stake everything on an early invasion of France, or should first exploit their opportunities in Italy and the eastern Mediterranean as a further prelude to the cross-Channel attack. Stalin replied, in effect, that what he wanted was the invasion of France from the west and the south, and the sooner the better. He did not favour any major operations by the Western Allies in the Balkan Peninsula, for this, he said, was "far from the heart of Germany." The Russian view prevailed, and thus Stalin ensured that Anglo-American military power would be employed to hasten the defeat of Germany without impinging upon Russia's political objectives in south-eastern Europe. Already the map of post-war Europe was being drawn, but in 1944 the Western Powers were given two chances militarily of preventing that map being drawn too much in favour of Russia. The first came after the fall of Rome and the second after the fall of Paris. In June 1944, General Alexander gained an overwhelming victory in Italy, but just when Hitler feared that all Italy was lost and that the Allies would leap the Adriatic to reinforce Tito's partisans in Yugoslavia, Alexander's triumphant advance was checked. And for what purpose? So that seven of his divisions and a major part of his air force and all the amphibious resources of the Mediterranean command could be used for the invasion of southern France. Mr. Churchill and the British Chiefs of Staff fought until the last minute against this plan, but they were overruled. The result was, however, that from early July until mid-August—during six invaluable weeks of summer campaigning while the struggle in the Normandy bridgehead was at its height and while the Russian summer offensive was in full spate—the Allied assault along the whole southern flank of Europe was brought almost to a standstill, so that we could go into southern France.

At this point I must clear up a possible misunderstanding. At no time did the Prime Minister or his Chiefs of Staff suggest that the major offensive against Germany could or should be launched through southern Europe. But Mr. Churchill did believe in 1944 that if the existing resources of the Mediterranean area were employed in the Balkans they would contribute substantially to the winning of the war, by distracting German divisions from France; and would enhance the prospects of winning the peace, by re-establishing democratic influence in central and southeastern Europe.

This chance was lost but a second opportunity developed, as I have said, after the Allied victory in Normandy had brought about the liberation of Paris. The great controversy that developed then between General Eisenhower and Field-Marshal Montgomery centred on the question whether the Allies should advance to the Rhine on a broad front or should make a single, concentrated thrust to the Ruhr. General Eisenhower's "broad front" policy prevailed—to the amazement of the German High Command. The German records show that for the defence of the Ruhr at the end of September 1944, the Germans had only 239 tanks—fewer tanks than there were in Britain after Dunkirk! It has been said in criticism of Montgomery that Eisenhower had not the supplies to support his single thrust. But we now know from the figures of tonnage actually delivered to all parts of the front that this was not the case; and, anyway, at the time General Eisenhower believed he had sufficient supplies to support his broad advance. Then it has been said—by General Eisenhower himself—that there was "a considerable reserve in the heart of Germany." But again this was not the argument used at the time. We now know from the German records that there was in fact no reserve, and that the divisions which Hitler threw into his Ardennes offensive three months later had yet to be created or rebuilt or transferred from the east.

But whatever the merits of this great controversy about Allied strategy, I am quite convinced that the Ardennes offensive was the direct result of the "broad front" policy. It was General Eisenhower's attempt to attack in so many places that left the Allied line vulnerable in the Ardennes, and gave Hitler his chance. At the time we were alarmed at the military consequences of this attack, but its real significance was political, because Hitler's object was to split the Grand Alliance and make the Western Allies conclude a compromise peace. At the start of the Ardennes offensive Hitler told his generals:

Never in history was there a coalition like that of our enemies, composed of such heterogeneous elements with such divergent aims. . . . Even now these states are at loggerheads, and, if we can deliver a few more heavy blows, then this artificially bolstered common front may suddenly collapse with a gigantic clap of thunder.

Believing this, he took the risk of stripping the eastern front in order to mount that offensive in the west that drove the Americans back almost to the Meuse, and this enabled the Red Army to break through the weakened German line in Poland and to advance from the Vistula to the Oder in the first few weeks of 1945, on the eve of the Yalta conference.

The timing of this Yalta conference was most significant. On the day before the Germans attacked in the Ardennes, the Prime Minister told the House of Commons: "It has been impossible to arrange any meeting of the three Great Powers." A week later, when Hitler's armies were driving for the Meuse, apparently unchecked, Stalin sent word to Washington that he would meet the President and Prime Minister at Yalta in the new year. Even Stalin can hardly have expected that the turn of events would swing the balance of power so quickly or so far in his favour. But in fact, when the Yalta conference began, early in February, the Russians were within forty-five miles of Berlin, and the Western Allies were little nearer the German capital than they had been in September 1944, or, for that matter, in September 1939. The occasion had now come for Stalin to "speak about Soviet desires." And how opportune it was, for the Yalta conference opened on the morrow of a severe Anglo-American reverse, at the moment of a great Russian victory, and at a time of acute discord between the Western Allies. The main source of that discord was the open and official American criticism of British policy in the Balkans, and particularly in Greece, where Mr. Churchill had intervened to forestall the Greek communists.

On their way to the Crimea the President, the Prime Minister, and the Combined Chiefs of Staff had a brief meeting at Malta, and there the British were dismayed to find that their American colleagues were less suspicious of Russia's post-war intentions than they were of Britain's. Once again the President declined to agree in advance upon a common policy. He was still anxious—as his own Secretary of State has revealed—to avoid giving the Russians any cause to think they were dealing with an Anglo-American alliance. This, I feel, is the key to the understanding of Yalta.

—AND AT YALTA

At this conference the President had two major objectives so far as Stalin was concerned: to bring Russia into the United Nations and into the war against Japan. He was prepared to pay a high price for Soviet co-operation, and the price he paid was high—especially in the far east. I want to look closely at this bargain that was made about Russia's entry into the war against Japan, because it is an excellent example of Stalin's technique, and it is a reminder of the importance of Anglo-American unity. Take this last point first. These discussions at Yalta were conducted on a strictly Russo-American basis by Stalin and Roosevelt. The Prime Minister did not take part, for the Americans had always insisted that the Pacific war was their affair. When Mr. Churchill found what had been agreed, he was, I understand, gravely disturbed—and well he might have been, for this is what had happened.

In October 1943, Stalin had told Cordell Hull that, when Germany was defeated, Russia would join in the war against Japan, and he had made no conditions. At Teheran, a month later, Stalin had repeated this assurance to the President himself, again with no conditions. But Mr. Roosevelt had then spontaneously offered to restore to Russia the rights that the Tsars had enjoyed in the Manchurian port of Dairen. This gesture encouraged Stalin to impose a price, and later in 1944—when we hardly needed Russian help against Japan—he announced that certain political demands would have to be met before Russia could enter the Japanese war. At Yalta Stalin made these demands known and they meant in effect that the Soviet Union would have a free hand in Outer Mongolia and Manchuria, and thus would become the political heir of Japan in north China and Korea. President Roosevelt accepted these demands even though they were made at the expense of his ally, China, and without her knowledge or consent.

That was serious enough, but the consequences of this bargain extended well beyond the far east, for it involved the sacrifice of those very principles that the President had always striven to uphold. By this bargain Mr. Roosevelt undermined his own moral authority in relation to Stalin. So far he had always refused to make any post-war territorial commitments or to recognise any spheres of influence. But now, having agreed to the infringement of China's sovereignty—without her consent—how could he defend the sovereignty of Poland? Having abandoned his principles in Asia, he could not expect to be allowed to apply them in Europe, not against a realist like Stalin.

A CLEAR ROAD INTO EASTERN EUROPE

At Yalta Stalin refused even to discuss the fate of the little Baltic States; he enforced his demand for eastern Poland; and he insisted on annexing northern Rumania, and thus got control of the mouth of the Danube. By securing these territories—that Roosevelt and Churchill had once denied him—Stalin secured a clear road into eastern Europe.

The negotiations which brought about this result lasted more than a week, but the full drama of Yalta is lost if we study this conference subject by subject, as a list of items on an agenda. It must be examined chronologically— hour by hour—for then the discussions are revealed for what they were, a series of moves in a game of diplomatic chess. And what emerges from this is the remarkable persistence of the Russians. In the end, Stalin gave way on those questions that did not require him to make any material sacrifice or surrender. But on all issues where the direct, physical interests of Russia were at stake he was most adamant and demanding. For instance, he eventually agreed that France should take part in the occupation of Germany, but, when it came to the matter of reparations, he fought to the end for the inclusion in the protocol of a precise and substantial figure defining Russia's share. He refused to modify his political or territorial claims on Poland, but he glibly signed the President's "Declaration on Liberated Europe," thus pledging the Soviet Union to uphold the independence of small nations. By signing this declaration Stalin surrendered nothing, for he could break it whenever he wanted—and he did. Before the President and the Prime Minister could even report to their legislatures about Yalta, Mr. Vyshinsky had arrived in Rumania to demand the dismissal of the all-party government and to secure the appointment of the Rumanian communist leader as Prime Minister. Thus within a month of Yalta the "Declaration on Liberated Europe" had become another "scrap of paper" and Stalin had set up the first of the satellite puppet governments.

This open breach of the Yalta Agreement was soon followed by others— almost as flagrant. By the start of April 1945 relations between Washington and Moscow were decidedly strained. Roosevelt was upbraiding Stalin over

Soviet policy in Rumania and Poland. Stalin, in turn, was accusing the Western Allies of negotiating a separate peace. This charge was particularly galling to the President, and, on April 4, he said in a cable to Stalin: "Frankly I cannot avoid a feeling of bitter resentment toward your informers whoever they are for such vile misrepresentations of my actions or those of my trusted subordinates."

By this time General Eisenhower's armies were well across the Rhine, but the Russian were held up on the Oder. Accordingly, Mr. Churchill proposed that Eisenhower should drive hard for Berlin and secure a bargaining position from which to insist that the Soviet Union must honour the promises she had made. There was no agreement, military or political, to prevent Eisenhower going to Berlin, but his main concern was not the German capital: it was the so-called Southern Redoubt, for the Americans feared that Hitler and the S.S. might make a prolonged stand in the Bavarian Alps. This view was strongly challenged by Mr. Churchill, by the British Chiefs of Staff, and by Field-Marshal Montgomery. But Eisenhower was supported by his own Chiefs of Staff. General Marshall, cabling to London, said:

The single objective should be quick and complete victory. Such psychological and political advantages as would result from the possible capture of Berlin ahead of the Russians should not override the imperative military consideration which, in our opinion, is the destruction of the German Armed Forces.

This policy triumphed and the Americans were halted on the Elbe while the Russians took Berlin. They were also stopped on the frontier of Czechoslovakia, because Stalin objected when Eisenhower proposed to march into Prague. Thus, the three great capitals of central Europe—Berlin, Prague, and Vienna—were all liberated from Nazi rule by the Red Army, and communist Russia gained both position and prestige which Stalin soon turned to his own advantage—especially in Czechoslovakia. But the real test of the balance of power in post-war Europe arose over Poland and it was decided within a few weeks of Germany's collapse. In July 1945, when the Allied leaders met at Potsdam, the Prime Minister and President Truman were confronted with a double fait accompli. At Yalta Stalin had agreed to the reorganisation of the provisional Polish Government "on a more democratic basis." Before Potsdam, the Russians arrested, on charges of espionage, sixteen prominent Polish democrats who had been promised safe conduct to Moscow for consultation. At Yalta Stalin had agreed that the demarcation of Poland's western frontier should be settled at the peace conference. Before Potsdam, he authorised the Poles to take over the administration of eastern Germany as far as the line of the Oder and the Neisse. And both these pre-emptive moves were carried through without any reference to London or Washington. One final illustration: during the Potsdam conference, so the story goes, Mr. Churchill reported a protest from the Vatican about the treatment of the Catholic Church in Poland. Stalin listened while the protest was translated and then said: "How many divisions has the Pope got?" With that question Stalin underlined the moral of the situation the war had produced, which surely was that when the balance of power is destroyed it is force, not justice, that prevails.

And now to sum up: it seems to me that the two most serious miscalculations of the second world war both concerned the Soviet Union: Hitler's miscalculation of Russia's military strength, and Roosevelt's miscalculation of Russia's political ambition. These two errors of judgment gave Stalin the opportunity of establishing the Soviet Union as the dominant power in Europe, and he was able to clinch that opportunity because he succeeded in defeating both his enemies and his friends.

WHAT THE AMERICANS FORGOT

Today we have good reason to regret President Roosevelt's misjudgment of Stalin, and to regret the opportunities which America's military leaders sacrificed by their refusal to take account of political factors in determining strategy. The Americans regret this themselves. In fact, General Bradley, the present Chairman of the American Joint Chiefs of Staff, in his memoirs says quite frankly:

At times we forgot that wars are fought for the resolution of political conflicts, and in the ground campaign for Europe we sometimes overlooked political considerations of vast importance.

At the same time we have good reason to be thankful that Franklin Roosevelt led the American people out of isolation and involved the New World —as Mr. Churchill has said—"inexorably and irrevocably in the fortunes of the Old." In the process some grave mistakes were made, but this was inevitable.

VII THE PROBLEM OF PEACE IN A REVOLUTIONARY WORLD

WENDELL L. WILLKIE

DESPITE THE FACT that in August, 1939, the Soviet Union had dumfounded the nations of the West by concluding a non-aggression treaty with its enemy, Nazi Germany, after Hitler's invasion of Russia in 1941 hopes for peaceful and happy relations with the Stalinist regime at the war's end rose in the West. Much planning for the postwar world was based on these hopes. Indeed, Franklin D. Roosevelt seemed to believe that the greatest future threat to peace and justice might come from resurgent British and French imperialism. As for the Soviet Union, the President was convinced, at least until late 1944, that he could handle Stalin, that the Soviet leader's war aims were limited merely to guaranteeing future Russian security, and that his professed intentions could be trusted. Roosevelt's optimism was generally shared inside his administration, in important circles in the Republican party, and among the educated public.

Of all the books praising "our noble Russian allies" and predicting a great era of progress after the war, few were more typical and more popular than Wendell L. Willkie's *One World*. The author was an energetic and intelligent public utilities executive who had managed by astute planning to capture the Republican nomination for the Presidency from party professionals in 1940. Willkie had become a Republican after Roosevelt's victory in 1936 but he belonged to the liberal and internationalist wing of his party. In 1940 he ran a lively campaign against Roosevelt's bid for a third term but was defeated. He returned to a private law practice in New York and in 1942, with White House help, he arranged a trip around the world to analyze the course of the war and the possibilities of the peace that was to come. In 1943, he published the results of his trip in *One World,* later dubbed "Gullible's Travels" by Winston Churchill. It was an immense success. In two months it sold more than a million copies and its total sales exceeded two million. It was translated into sixteen foreign languages. The optimistic author lived at a furious pace and taxed himself severely in his efforts to win his party as well as the public away from isolationism. The year after *One World* appeared Willkie died in New York at the age of fifty-two.

The following selection is from *One World* (New York: Simon and Schuster, 1943).

ONE WORLD

I HAD NOT GONE to Russia to remember the past. Besides my concrete assignments for the President, I had gone determined to find an answer for myself to the actual problems posed for our generation of Americans by the simple fact that the Soviet Union, whether we like it or not, exists.

Some of these answers I believe I found, at least to my own satisfaction. I can sum up the three most important in a few sentences.

First, Russia is an effective society. It works. It has survival value. The record of Soviet resistance to Hitler has been proof enough of this to most of us, but I must admit in all frankness that I was not prepared to believe before I went to Russia what I now know about its strength as a going organization of men and women.

Second, Russia is our ally in this war. The Russians, more sorely tested by Hitler's might even than the British, have met the test magnificently. Their hatred of Fascism and the Nazi system is real and deep and bitter. And this hatred makes them determined to eliminate Hitler and exterminate the Nazi blight from Europe and the world.

Third, we must work with Russia after the war. At least it seems to me that there can be no continued peace unless we learn to do so. . . .

Among the leaders I met and talked to at any great length were Viacheslav Molotov, the Foreign Minister, Andrei Vishinsky and Solomon Lozovsky, his assistants, Marshal Voroshilov, the former Commissar of Defense, Anastas Mikoyan, Commissar of Supply and head of the Soviet foreign-trade apparatus. Each of these is an educated man, interested in the foreign world, completely unlike in manner, appearance, and speech from the uncouth, wild Bolshevik of our cartoons.

In Kuibishev, at a dinner given for me by Mr. Vishinsky, who was the chief state prosecutor in all the grim treason trials of four and five years ago, I caught myself studying his white hair, his professor's face, and his quiet, almost studious manner, and wondering if this could possibly be the same man who had purged some of the oldest heroes of the Russian Revolution on charges of murder and betrayal of their country.

Whenever the talk of these men ran to peace, to what the world must be prepared to do after the war is over, they talked with statesmanship and real understanding.

Since I have returned to the United States, Mr. Stalin has defined the program, as he sees it, of the Anglo-American-Soviet coalition in the European war. These are the goals he calls for:

"Abolition of racial exclusiveness, equality of nations and integrity of their territories, liberation of enslaved nations and restoration of their sovereign rights, the right of every nation to arrange its affairs as it wishes, economic aid to nations that have suffered and assistance to them in attaining their material welfare, restoration of democratic liberties, the destruction of the Hitlerite regime."

We may ask: does Stalin mean what he says? Some will point out that only two years ago Russia was in an alliance of expediency with Germany. I make no defense of expediency, military, political, temporary, or otherwise. For I believe the moral losses of expediency always far outweigh the temporary gains. And I believe that every drop of blood saved through expediency will be paid for by twenty drawn by the sword. But a Russian, feeling that by the German alliance his country was buying time, might well remind the democracies of Munich, and of the seven million tons of the best grade of scrap iron the United States shipped to Japan between 1937 and 1940.

Perhaps we can better measure the good faith of Stalin's statement in the light of the millions of Russians who have already died defending their fatherland and of the sixty million who have become slaves of the Nazis; in those other millions of Russian men and women who are working feverishly sixty-six hours a week in factories and mines to forge and produce instruments of war for the fighters at the front; and in the effort that went into the almost miraculous movement of great factories, hundreds of miles, that they might operate, uninterrupted, beyond Nazi reach. For it is in the attitude of the people that we may find the best interpretation of Stalin's purpose.

Many among the democracies fear and mistrust Soviet Russia. They dread the inroads of an economic order that would be destructive of their own. Such fear is weakness. Russia is neither going to eat us nor seduce us. That is—and this is something for us to think about—that is, unless our democratic institutions and our free economy become so frail through abuse and failure in practice as to make us soft and vulnerable. The best answer to Communism is a living, vibrant, fearless democracy—economic, social, and political. All we need to do is to stand up and perform according to our professed ideals. Then those ideals will be safe.

No, we do not need to fear Russia. We need to learn to work with her against our common enemy, Hitler. We need to learn to work with her in the world after the war. For Russia is a dynamic country, a vital new society, a force that cannot be bypassed in any future world. . . .

What is Russian going to do? Is she going to be the new disturber of the peace? Is she going to demand conditions at the end of the war that will make it impossible to re-establish Europe on a decent peaceful road? Is she going to attempt to infiltrate other countries with her economic and social philosophy?

Frankly, I don't think anyone knows the answers to these questions; I doubt if even Mr. Stalin knows all the answers.

Obviously, it would be ridiculous for me to attempt to say what Russia is going to do. This much, however, I do know to be true: there are 200,000,000 subjects of the U.S.S.R.; they control the largest single land mass in the world under one government; they have almost inexhaustible supplies of timber, iron, coal, oil, which are, practically speaking, unexploited; through elaborate systems of hospitalization and public-health organizations the Russian people are one of the healthiest peoples in the world, living in a vigorous, stimulating climate; in the last twenty-five years, through a widespread, drastic educational system, a large percentage have become literate and tens of thousands technically trained; and from the topmost official to the most insignificant farm or factory worker the Russians are fanatically devoted to Russia and supercharged with the dream of its future development.

I don't know the answers to all the questions about Russia, but there's one other thing I know: that such a force, such a power, such a people cannot be ignored or disposed of with a high hat or a lifting of the skirt. We cannot act as if we were housewives going into an A & P store, picking and choosing among the groceries displayed; taking this, leaving that. The plain fact is: we have no choice in the matter. Russia will be reckoned with. That is the reason why I am constantly telling my fellow Americans: work in ever-closer co-operation with the Russians while we are joined together in the common purpose of defeating a common enemy. Learn all we can about them and let them learn about us.

There's still another thing I know: geographically, from a trade standpoint, in their similarity of approach to many problems, the Russians and the Americans should get along together. The industrialization of Russia will require a limitless amount of American products, and Russia has unlimited natural resources that we need. The Russians, like us, are a hardy, direct people and have great admiration for everything in America, except the capitalistic system. And, frankly, there are many things in Russia that we can admire—its vigor, its vast dreams, its energy, its tenacity of purpose. No one could be more opposed to the Communist doctrine than I am, for I am completely opposed to any system that leads to absolutism. But I have never understood why it should be assumed that in any possible contact between Communism and democracy, democracy should go down.

So let me say once more: I believe it is possible for Russia and America, perhaps the most powerful countries in the world, to work together for the economic welfare and the peace of the world. At least, knowing that there can be no enduring peace, no economic stability, unless the two work together, there is nothing I ever wanted more to believe. And so deep is my faith in the fundamental rightness of our free economic and political institutions that I am convinced they will survive any such working together. . . .

America must choose one of three courses after this war: narrow nationalism, which inevitably means the ultimate loss of our own liberty; international imperialism, which means the sacrifice of some other nation's liberty; or the creation of a world in which there shall be an equality of opportunity for every race and every nation. I am convinced the American people will choose, by overwhelming majority, the last of these courses. To make this choice effective, we must win not only the war, but also the peace, and we must start winning it now.

To win this peace three things seem to me necessary—first, we must plan now for peace on a world basis; second, the world must be free, politically and economically, for nations and for men, that peace may exist in it; third, America must play an active, constructive part in freeing it and keeping its peace.

When I say that peace must be planned on a world basis, I mean quite literally that it must embrace the earth. Continents and oceans are plainly only parts of a whole, seen, as I have seen them, from the air. England and America are parts. Russia and China, Egypt, Syria and Turkey, Iraq and Iran are also parts. And it is inescapable that there can be no peace for any part of the world unless the foundations of peace are made secure throughout all parts of the world.

This cannot be accomplished by mere declarations of our leaders, as in an Atlantic Charter. Its accomplishment depends primarily upon acceptance by the peoples of the world. For if the failure to reach international understanding after the last war taught us anything it taught us this: even if war leaders apparently agree upon generalized principles and slogans while the war is being fought, when they come to the peace table they make their own interpretations of their previous declarations. So unless today, while the war is being fought, the people of the United States and of Great Britain, of Russia and of China, and of all the other United Nations, fundamentally agree on their purposes, fine and idealistic expressions of hope such as those of the Atlantic Charter will live merely to mock us as have Mr. Wilson's Fourteen Points. The Four Freedoms will not be accomplished by the declarations of those momentarily in power. They will become real only if the people of the world forge them into actuality.

When I say that in order to have peace this world must be free, I am only reporting that a great process has started which no man—certainly not Hitler—can stop. Men and women all over the world are on the march, physically, intellectually, and spiritually. After centuries of ignorant and dull compliance, hundreds of millions of people in eastern Europe and Asia have opened the books. Old fears no longer frighten them. They are no longer willing to be Eastern slaves for Western profits. They are beginning to know that men's welfare throughout the world is interdependent. They are resolved, as we must be, that there is no more place for imperialism within their own society than in the society of nations. The big house on the hill surrounded by mud huts has lost its awesome charm.

Our Western world and our presumed supremacy are now on trial. Our boasting and our big talk leave Asia cold. Men and women in Russia and China and in the Middle East are conscious now of their own potential strength. They are coming to know that many of the decisions about the future of the world lie in their hands. And they intend that these decisions shall leave the peoples of each nation free from foreign domination, free for economic, social, and spiritual growth.

Economic freedom is as important as political freedom. Not only must people have access to what other peoples produce, but their own products must in turn have some chance of reaching men all over the world. There will be no peace, there will be no real development, there will be no economic stability, unless we find the method by which we can begin to break down the unnecessary trade barriers hampering the flow of goods. Obviously, the sudden and uncompromising abolition of tariffs after the war could only result in disaster. But obviously, also, one of the freedoms we are fighting for is freedom to trade. I know there are many men, particularly in America, where our standard of living exceeds the standard of living in the rest of the world, who are genuinely alarmed at such a prospect, who believe that any such process will only lessen our own standard of living. The reverse of this is true.

Many reasons may be assigned for the amazing economic development of the United States. The abundance of our national resources, the freedom of our political institutions, and the character of our population have all undoubtedly contributed. But in my judgment the greatest factor has been the fact that by the happenstance of good fortune there was created here in America the largest area in the world in which there were no barriers to the exchange of goods and ideas.

And I should like to point out to those who are fearful one inescapable fact. In view of the astronomical figures our national debt will assume by the end of this war, and in a world reduced in size by industrial and transportation developments, even our present standard of living in America cannot be maintained unless the exchange of goods flows more freely over the whole world. It is also inescapably true that to raise the standard of living of any man anywhere in the world is to raise the standard of living by some slight degree of every man everywhere in the world.

Finally, when I say that this world demands the full participation of a self-confident America, I am only passing on an invitation which the peoples of the East have given us. They would like the United States and the other United Nations to be partners with them in this grand adventure. They want us to join them in creating a new society of independent nations, free alike of the economic injustices of the West and the political malpractices of the East. But as partners in that great new combination they want us neither hesitant, incompetent, nor afraid. They want partners who will not hesitate to speak out for the correction of injustice anywhere in the world.

Our allies in the East know that we intend to pour out our resources in this war. But they expect us now—not after the war—to use the enormous power of our giving to promote liberty and justice. Other peoples, not yet fighting, are waiting no less eagerly for us to accept the most challenging opportunity of all history—the chance to help create a new society in which men and women the world around can live and grow invigorated by independence and freedom.

GEORGE F. KENNAN

B Y THE EARLY WINTER of 1946 it had become apparent that wartime hopes for future good relations between the West and the Soviet Union had been chimerical. That spring Winston Churchill had given his warning about the "iron curtain" across Eastern Europe and at the diplomatic tables what was to become a familiar and frustrating pattern of Soviet intransigence and hostility had emerged. The foreign offices in the West went busily to work drafting long-term plans to fight a cold war. In July, 1947, there appeared an article, "The Sources of Soviet Conduct" in the American quarterly *Foreign Affairs*. It was signed "X." The article was soon regarded as a sketch of the probable basis for Western political strategy in the cold war and its author became known. He was George F. Kennan, American career diplomat. Since the publication of his essay Kennan has been regarded by many people as one of the principal Western students of Soviet foreign policy.

Kennan was born in Wisconsin in 1904 and was educated at Princeton, class of 1925. He joined the United States Foreign Service after graduation and remained in the diplomatic service for more than twenty-five years. He held posts in Switzerland, Germany, and the Baltic countries, before going to the Soviet Union in 1933 on the opening of formal diplomatic relations between the United States and the Stalin government. In the next dozen years he acquired a wide variety of diplomatic experience in Russia and Europe. In 1946 he was brought to Washington to use his knowledge in planning foreign policy and in 1947, when he published his famous article, he became head of the State Department's policy planning staff. In 1950 he took a leave of absence to write and study at the Institute for Advanced Study at Princeton. The following year he published the influential book *American Diplomacy: 1900–1950*, an attempt to analyze the major suppositions behind a half century of United States foreign policy and to assess their adequacy in the light of the probable needs of the cold war.

In 1952 Kennan was appointed ambassador to the Soviet Union but was soon declared *persona non grata* by Moscow and thus did not hold his post for long. Kennan has since spent little time in government service and has been at work in Princeton on a multi-volumed history of Soviet-American diplomatic relations.

This selection is taken from *Foreign Affairs* 25 (July, 1947).

THE SOURCES OF SOVIET CONDUCT

T HE OUTSTANDING circumstance concerning the Soviet regime is that down to the present day [the] process of political consolidation has never been completed and the men in the Kremlin have continued to be predominantly absorbed with the struggle to secure and make absolute the power which they seized in November 1917. They have endeavored to secure it primarily against forces at home, within Soviet society itself. But they have also endeavored to secure it against the outside world. For ideology . . . taught them that the outside world was hostile and that it was their duty eventually to overthrow the political forces beyond their borders. The powerful hands of Russian history and tradition reached up to sustain them in this feeling. Finally, their own aggressive intransigence with respect to the outside world began to find its own reaction; and they were soon forced, to use another Gibbonesque phrase, "to chastise the contumacy" which they themselves had provoked. It is an undeniable privilege of every man to prove himself right in the thesis that the world is his enemy; for if he reiterates it frequently enough and makes it the background of his conduct he is bound eventually to be right.

Now it lies in the nature of the mental world of the Soviet leaders, as well as in the character of their ideology, that no opposition to them can be officially recognized as having any merit or justification whatsoever. Such opposition can flow, in theory, only from the hostile and incorrigible forces of dying capitalism. As long as remnants of capitalism were officially recognized as existing in Russia, it was possible to place on them, as an internal element, part of the blame for the maintenance of a dictatorial form of society. But as these remnants were liquidated, little by little, this justification fell away; and when it was indicated officially that they had been finally destroyed, it disappeared altogether. And this fact created one of the most basic of the compulsions which came to act upon the Soviet regime: since capitalism no longer existed in Russia and since it could not be admitted that there could be serious or widespread opposition to the Kremlin springing spontaneously from the liberated masses under its authority, it became necessary to justify the retention of the dictatorship by stressing the menace of capitalism abroad.

This began at an early date. In 1924, Stalin specifically defended the retention of the "organs of suppression," meaning, among others, the army and the secret police, on the ground that "as long as there is a capitalist encirclement there will be danger of intervention with all consequences that flow from that danger." In accordance with that theory, and from that time on, all internal opposition forces in Russia have consistently been portrayed as the agents of foreign forces of reaction antagonistic to Soviet power.

By the same token, tremendous emphasis has been placed on the original Communist thesis of a basic antagonism between the capitalist and Socialist worlds. It is clear, from many indications, that this emphasis is not founded in reality. The real facts concerning it have been confused by the existence abroad of genuine resentment provoked by Soviet philosophy and tactics and occasionally by the existence of great centers of military power, notably the Nazi regime in Germany and the Japanese Government of the late 1930's, which did indeed have aggressive designs against the Soviet Union. But there is ample evidence that the stress laid in Moscow on the menace confronting Soviet society from the world outside its borders is founded not in the realities of foreign antagonism but in the necessity of explaining away the maintenance of dictatorial authority at home.

Now the maintenance of this pattern of Soviet power, namely, the pursuit of unlimited authority domestically, accompanied by the cultivation of the semi-myth of implacable foreign hostility, has gone far to shape the actual machinery of Soviet power as we know it today. Internal organs of administration which did not serve this purpose withered on the vine. Organs which did serve this purpose became vastly swollen. The security of Soviet power came to rest on the iron discipline of the Party, on the severity and ubiquity of the secret police, and on the uncompromising economic monopolism of the state. The "organs of suppression," in which the Soviet leaders had sought security from rival forces, became in large measure the masters of those whom they were designed to serve. Today the major part of the structure of Soviet power is committed to the perfection of the dictatorship and to the maintenance of the concept of Russia as in a state of siege, with the enemy lowering beyond the walls. And the millions of human beings who form that part of the structure of power must defend at all costs this concept of Russia's position, for without it they are themselves superfluous.

As things stand today, the rulers can no longer dream of parting with these organs of suppression. The quest for absolute power, pursued now for nearly three decades with a ruthlessness unparalleled (in scope at least) in modern times, has again produced internally, as it did externally, its own reaction. The excesses of the police apparatus have fanned the potential opposition to the regime into something far greater and more dangerous than it could have been before those excesses began.

But least of all can the rulers dispense with the fiction by which the maintenance of dictatorial power has been defended. For this fiction has been canonized in Soviet philosophy by the excesses already committed in its name; and it is now anchored in the Soviet structure of thought by bonds far greater than those of mere ideology.

II

So much for the historical background. What does it spell in terms of the political personality of Soviet power as we know it today?

Of the original ideology, nothing has been officially junked. Belief is maintained in the basic badness of capitalism, in the inevitability of its destruction, in the obligation of the proletariat to assist in that destruction and to take power into its own hands. But stress has come to be laid primarily on those concepts which relate most specifically to the Soviet regime itself: to its position as the sole truly Socialist regime in a dark and misguided world, and to the relationships of power within it.

The first of these concepts is that of the innate antagonism between capitalism and Socialism. We have seen how deeply that concept has become imbedded in foundations of Soviet power. It has profound implications for Russia's conduct as a member of international society. It means that there can never be on Moscow's side any sincere assumption of a community of aims between the Soviet Union and powers which are regarded as capitalist. It must invariably be assumed in Moscow that the aims of the capitalist world are antagonistic to the Soviet regime and, therefore, to the interests of the peoples it controls. If the Soviet Government occasionally sets its signature to documents which would indicate the contrary, this is to be regarded as a tactical maneuver permissible in dealing with the enemy (who is without honor) and should be taken in the spirit of *caveat emptor*. Basically, the antagonism remains. It is postulated. And from it flow many of the phenomena which we find disturbing in the Kremlin's conduct of foreign policy: the secretiveness, the lack of frankness, the duplicity, the war suspiciousness, and the basic unfriendliness of purpose. These phenomena are there to stay, for the foreseeable future. There can be variations of degree and of emphasis. When there is something the Russians want from us, one or the other of these features of their policy may be thrust temporarily into the background; and when that happens there will always be Americans who will leap forward with gleeful announcements that "the Russians have changed," and some who will even try to take credit for having brought about such "changes." But we should not be misled by tactical maneuvers. These characteristics of Soviet policy, like the postulate from which they flow, are basic to the internal nature of Soviet power, and will be with us, whether in the foreground or the background, until the internal nature of Soviet power is changed.

This means that we are going to continue for a long time to find the Russians difficult to deal with. It does not mean that they should be considered as embarked upon a do-or-die program to overthrow our society by a given date. The theory of the inevitability of the eventual fall of capitalism has the fortunate connotation that there is no hurry about it. The forces of progress can take their time in preparing the final *coup de grâce*. Meanwhile, what is vital is that the "Socialist fatherland"—that oasis of power which has been already won for Socialism in the person of the Soviet Union—should be cherished and defended by all good Communists at home and abroad, its fortunes promoted, its enemies badgered and confounded. The promotion of premature, "adventuristic" revolutionary projects abroad which might embarrass Soviet power in any way would be an inexcusable, even a counter-revolutionary act. The cause of Socialism is the support and promotion of Soviet power, as defined in Moscow.

This brings us to the second of the concepts important to contemporary Soviet outlook. That is the infallibility of the Kremlin. The Soviet concept of power, which permits no focal points of organization outside the Party itself, requires that the Party leadership remain in theory the sole repository of truth. For if truth were to be found elsewhere, there would be justification for its expression in organized activity. But it is precisely that which the Kremlin cannot and will not permit.

The leadership of the Communist Party is therefore always right, and has been always right ever since in 1929 Stalin formalized his personal power by announcing that decisions of the Politburo were being taken unanimously.

On the principle of infallibility there rests the iron discipline of the Communist Party. In fact, the two concepts are mutually self-supporting. Perfect discipline requires recognition of infallibility. Infallibility requires the observance of discipline. And the two together go far to determine the behaviorism of the entire Soviet apparatus of power. But their effect cannot be understood unless a third factor be taken into account: namely, the fact that the leadership is at liberty to put forward for tactical purposes any particular thesis which it finds useful to the cause at any particular moment and to require the faithful and unquestioning acceptance of that thesis by the members of the movement as a whole. This means that truth is not a constant but is actually created, for all intents and purposes, by the Soviet leaders themselves. It may vary from week to week, from month to month. It is nothing absolute and immutable—nothing which flows from objective reality. It is only the most recent manifestation of the wisdom of those in whom the ultimate wisdom is supposed to reside, because they represent the logic of history. The accumulative effect of these factors is to give to the whole subordinate apparatus of Soviet power an unshakeable stubbornness and steadfastness in its orientation. This orientation can be changed at will by the Kremlin but by no other power. Once a given party line has been laid down on a given issue of current policy, the whole Soviet governmental machine, including the mechanism of diplomacy, moves inexorably along the prescribed path, like a persistent toy automobile wound up and headed in a given direction, stopping only when it meets with some unanswerable force. The individuals who are the components of this machine are unamenable to argument or reason which comes to them from outside sources. Their whole training has taught them to mistrust and discount the glib persuasiveness of the outside world. Like the white dog before the phonograph, they hear only the "master's voice." And if they are to be called off from the purposes last dictated to them, it is the master who must call them off. Thus the foreign representative cannot hope that his words will make any impression on them. The most that he can hope is that they will be transmitted to those at the top, who are capable of changing the party line. But even those are not likely to be swayed by any normal logic in the words of the bourgeois representative. Since there can be no appeal to common purposes, there can be no appeal to common mental approaches. For this reason, facts speak louder than words to the ears of the Kremlin; and words carry the greatest weight when they have the ring of reflecting, or being backed up by, facts of unchallengeable validity. . . .

In these circumstances it is clear that the main element of any United States policy toward the Soviet Union must be that of a long-term, patient but firm and vigilant containment of Russian expansive tendencies. It is important to note, however, that such a policy has nothing to do with outward histrionics: with threats or blustering or superfluous gestures of outward "toughness." While the Kremlin is basically flexible in its reaction to political realities, it is by no means unamenable to considerations of prestige. Like almost any other government, it can be placed by tactless and threatening gestures in a position where it cannot afford to yield even though this might be dictated by its sense of realism. The Russian leaders are keen judges of human psychology, and as such they are highly conscious that loss of temper and of self-control is never a source of strength in political affairs. They are quick to exploit such evidences of weakness. For these reasons, it is a *sine qua non* of successful dealing with Russia that the foreign government in question should remain at all times cool and collected and that its demands on Russian policy should be put forward in such a manner as to leave the way open for a compliance not too detrimental to Russian prestige.

III

In the light of the above, it will be clearly seen that the Soviet pressure against the free institutions of the Western world is something that can be contained by the adroit and vigilant application of counter-force at a series of constantly shifting geographical and political points, corresponding to the shifts and maneuvers of Soviet policy, but which cannot be charmed or talked out of existence. The Russians look forward to a duel of infinite duration, and they see that already they have scored great successes. It must be borne in mind that there was a time when the Communist Party represented far more of a minority in the sphere of Russian national life than Soviet power today represents in the world community. . . .

IV

It is clear that the United States cannot expect in the foreseeable future to enjoy political intimacy with the Soviet regime. It must continue to regard the Soviet Union as a rival, not a partner, in the political arena. It must continue to expect that Soviet policies will reflect no abstract love of peace and stability, no real faith in the possibility of a permanent happy coexistence of the Socialist and capitalist worlds, but rather a cautious, persistent pressure toward the disruption and weakening of all rival influence and rival power.

Balanced against this are the facts that Russia, as opposed to the Western world in general, is still by far the weaker party, that Soviet policy is highly flexible, and that Soviet society may well contain deficiencies which will eventually weaken its own total potential. This would of itself warrant the United States entering with reasonable confidence upon a policy of firm containment, designed to confront the Russians with unalterable counterforce at every point where they show signs of encroaching upon the interests of a peaceful and stable world.

But in actuality the possibilities for American policy are by no means limited to holding the line and hoping for the best. It is entirely possible for the United States to influence by its actions the internal developments, both within Russia and throughout the international Communist movement, by which Russian policy is largely determined. This is not only a question of the modest measure of informational activity which this government can conduct in the Soviet Union and elsewhere, although that, too, is important. It is rather a question of the degree to which the United States can create among the peoples of the world generally the impression of a country which knows what it wants, which is coping successfully with the problems of its internal life and with the responsibilities of a World Power, and which has a spiritual vitality capable of holding its own among the major ideological currents of the time. To the extent that such an impression can be created and maintained, the aims of Russian Communism must appear sterile and quixotic, the hopes and enthusiasm of Moscow's supporters must wane, and added strain must be imposed on the Kremlin's foreign policies. For the palsied decrepitude of the capitalist world is the keystone of Communist philosophy. Even the failure of the United States to experience the early economic depression which the ravens of the Red Square have been predicting with such complacent confidence since hostilities ceased would have deep and important repercussions throughout the Communist world.

By the same token, exhibitions of indecision, disunity and internal disintegration within this country have an exhilarating effect on the whole Communist movement. At each evidence of these tendencies, a thrill of hope and excitement goes through the Communist world; a new jauntiness can be noted in the Moscow tread; new groups of foreign supporters climb on to what they can only view as the band wagon of international politics; and Russian pressure increases all along the line in international affairs.

It would be an exaggeration to say that American behavior unassisted and alone could exercise a power of life and death over the Communist movement and bring about the early fall of Soviet power in Russia. But the United States has it in its power to increase enormously the strains under which Soviet policy must operate, to force upon the Kremlin a far greater degree of moderation and circumspection than it has had to observe in recent years, and in this way to promote tendencies which must eventually find their outlet in either the break-up or the gradual mellowing of Soviet power. For no mystical, Messianic movement—and particularly not that of the Kremlin— can face frustration indefinitely without eventually adjusting itself in one way or another to the logic of that state of affairs.

Thus the decision will really fall in large measure in this country itself. The issue of Soviet-American relations is in essence a test of the over-all worth of the United States as a nation among nations. To avoid destruction the United States need only measure up to its own best traditions and prove itself worthy of preservation as a great nation.

Surely, there was never a fairer test of national quality than this. In the light of these circumstances, the thoughtful observer of Russian-American relations will find no cause for complaint in the Kremlin's challenge to American society. He will rather experience a certain gratitude to a Providence which, by providing the American people with this implacable challenge, has made their entire security as a nation dependent on their pulling themselves together and accepting the responsibilities of moral and political leadership that history plainly intended them to bear.

NIKITA S. KHRUSHCHEV

Not until after Stalin's death under mysterious circumstances in 1953 did the Western public begin to hear much of Nikita Sergeyevich Khrushchev (1894–). Their easiest first measure of the man was taken from the fact that he was among the small handful of higher Communist officials who profited from Stalin's purges in the 1930s.

Before his recent rise to power Khrushchev, the son of a miner, had been principally concerned with party matters in the Ukraine, his birthplace. He was a common laborer until the First World War when he was drafted into the tsarist army. After the Bolshevik revolution he joined the Communist party and fought in the Red army. At the end of the Civil War in 1921 he became a party official in the Ukraine and about 1930 he moved to Moscow for important party work, including the supervision of the construction of the famous Moscow subway. In 1938, in the era of the great purges, he was appointed first secretary of the party in the Ukraine to direct Stalin's purges there. He spent the next eleven years in the Ukraine in the highest political and military posts, an obedient and successful servant of Stalinist policies. He was thus directly responsible for the ruthless murders of perhaps millions of Ukranians suspected of nationalist tendencies. In 1949 he was recalled to Moscow to direct a massive collectivization of agriculture.

Within six months after Stalin's death Khrushchev was named to the all-important post from which Stalin had built his power, first secretary of the Communist party of the U.S.S.R. Khrushchev continued to be interested in agricultural policy but took an active role in the struggle for leadership after Stalin's death. As Stalin's closest underlings maneuvered for supremacy, Khrushchev carefully built his own position and by mid-1954 he was recognized as the coming principal figure in the Soviet Union. By 1955 his prestige was only less than Premier Bulganin's at the Geneva "summit" meetings with Western leaders. Auspiciously enough, it was Khrushchev who had nominated Bulganin for the premiership. Within two years the nominator had succeeded the nominee.

In February, 1956, the 20th Party Congress met in Moscow. For three years the party leaders had been trying to outdistance each other and to make a more manageable system out of Stalin's erratic personal tyranny. The congress was the first since Stalin's death but only the third since 1934. For a little under a generation Russia had been under one-man rule but now the principle of "collective leadership" was affirmed. It is probable that Khrushchev's subsequent rise to preeminence and semi-adulation has not brought him either the power or the prestige of Stalin. His famous speech at the 20th Party Congress must be understood as an attempt to dissociate himself from his Stalinist heritage. It is noteworthy, however, that Stalin's policies against the Soviet people were not attacked in Khrushchev's speech but only Stalin's violation of "socialist legality" against Communist party leaders.

The following selection is from Khrushchev's long address, sometimes called "Crimes of the Stalin Era," but formally the *Special Report to the 20th Congress of the Communist Party of the Soviet Union,* Closed session, February 24–25, 1956. The English text was made available by the American magazine *The New Leader* in pamphlet form.

CRIMES OF THE STALIN ERA

COMRADES: In the report of the Central Committee of the party at the 20th Congress, in a number of speeches by delegates to the Congress, as also formerly during the plenary CC/CPSU [Central Committee of the Communist Party of the Soviet Union] sessions, quite a lot has been said about the cult of the individual and about its harmful consequences.

After Stalin's death the Central Committee of the party began to implement a policy of explaining concisely and consistently that it is impermissible and foreign to the spirit of Marxism-Leninism to elevate one person, to transform him into a superman possessing supernatural characteristics, akin to those of a god. Such a man supposedly knows everything, sees everything, thinks for everyone, can do anything, is infallible in his behavior.

Such a belief about a man, and specifically about Stalin, was cultivated among us for many years.

The objective of the present report is not a thorough evaluation of Stalin's life and activity. Concerning Stalin's merits, an entirely sufficient number of books, pamphlets and studies had already been written in his lifetime. The role of Stalin in the preparation and execution of the Socialist Revolution, in the Civil War, and in the fight for the construction of socialism in our country, is universally known. Everyone knows this well.

At present, we are concerned with a question which has immense importance for the party now and for the future—with how the cult of the person of Stalin has been gradually growing, the cult which became at a certain specific stage the source of a whole series of exceedingly serious and grave perversions of party principles, of party democracy, of revolutionary legality. . . .

We have to consider seriously and analyze correctly this matter in order that we may preclude any possibility of a repetition in any form whatever of what took place during the life of Stalin, who absolutely did not tolerate collegiality in leadership and in work, and who practiced brutal violence, not only toward everything which opposed him, but also toward that which seemed, to his capricious and despotic character, contrary to his concepts.

Stalin acted not through persuasion, explanation and patient cooperation with people, but by imposing his concepts and demanding absolute submission to his opinion. Whoever opposed this concept or tried to prove his viewpoint and the correctness of his position was doomed to removal from the leading collective and to subsequent moral and physical annihilation. This was especially true during the period following the 17th Party Congress, when many prominent party leaders and rank-and-file party workers, honest and dedicated to the cause of Communism, fell victim to Stalin's despotism. . . .

Worth noting is the fact that, even during the progress of the furious ideological fight against the Trotskyites, the Zinovievites, the Bukharinites and others, extreme repressive measures were not used against them. The fight was on ideological grounds. But some years later, when socialism in our country was fundamentally constructed, when the exploiting classes were generally liquidated, when the Soviet social structure had radically changed, when the social basis for political movements and groups hostile to the party had violently contracted, when the ideological opponents of the party were long since defeated politically—then the repression against them began.

It was precisely during this period (1935-1937-1938) that the practice of mass repression through the Government apparatus was born, first against the enemies of Leninism—Trotskyites, Zinovievites, Bukharinites, long since politically defeated by the party—and subsequently also against many honest Communists, against those party cadres who had borne the heavy load of the Civil War and the first and most difficult years of industrialization and collectivization, who actively fought against the Trotskyites and the rightists for the Leninist party line.

Stalin originated the concept "enemy of the people." This term automatically rendered it unnecessary that the ideological errors of a man or men engaged in a controversy be proven; this term made possible the usage of the most cruel repression, violating all norms of revolutionary legality, against anyone who in any way disagreed with Stalin, against those who were only suspected of hostile intent, against those who had bad reputations. This concept "enemy of the people" actually eliminated the possibility of any kind of ideological fight or the making of one's views known on this or that issue, even those of a practical character. In the main, and in actuality, the only proof of guilt used, against all norms of current legal science, was the "confession" of the accused himself; and, as subsequent probing proved, "confessions" were acquired through physical pressures against the accused. This led to glaring violations of revolutionary legality and to the fact that many entirely innocent persons, who in the past had defended the party line, became victims.

We must assert that, in regard to those persons who in their time had opposed the party line, there were often no sufficiently serious reasons for their physical annihilation. The formula "enemy of the people" was specifically introduced for the purpose of physically annihilating such individuals.

It is a fact that many persons who were later annihilated as enemies of the party and people had worked with Lenin during his life. Some of these persons had made errors during Lenin's life, but, despite this, Lenin benefited by their work; he corrected them and he did everything possible to retain them in the ranks of the party; he induced them to follow him. . . .

Lenin's traits—patient work with people, stubborn and painstaking education of them, the ability to induce people to follow him without using compulsion, but rather through the ideological influence on them of the whole collective—were entirely foreign to Stalin. He discarded the Leninist method of convincing and educating, he abandoned the method of ideological struggle for that of administrative violence, mass repressions and terror. He acted on an increasingly larger scale and more stubbornly through punitive organs, at the same time often violating all existing norms of morality and of Soviet laws.

Arbitrary behavior by one person encouraged and permitted arbitrariness in others. Mass arrests and deportations of many thousands of people, execution without trial and without normal investigation created conditions of insecurity, fear and even desperation.

This, of course, did not contribute toward unity of the party ranks and of all strata of working people, but, on the contrary, brought about annihilation and the expulsion from the party of workers who were loyal but inconvenient to Stalin. . . .

Let us take the example of the Trotskyites. At present, after a sufficiently long historical period, we can speak about the fight with the Trotskyites with complete calm and can analyze this matter with sufficient objectivity. After all, around Trotsky were people whose origin cannot by any means be traced to bourgeois society. Part of them belonged to the party intelligentsia and a certain part were recruited from among the workers. We can name many individuals who, in their time, joined the Trotskyites; however, these same individuals took an active part in the workers' movement before the Revolution, during the Socialist October Revolution itself, and also in the consolidation of the victory of this greatest of revolutions. Many of them broke with Trotskyism and returned to Leninist positions. Was it necessary to annihilate such people? We are deeply convinced that, had Lenin lived, such an extreme method would not have been used against any of them. . . .

Stalin, on the other hand, used extreme methods and mass repressions at a time when the Revolution was already victorious, when the Soviet state was strengthened, when the exploiting classes were already liquidated and socialist relations were rooted solidly in all phases of national economy, when our party was politically consolidated and had strengthened itself both numerically and ideologically.

It is clear that here Stalin showed in a whole series of cases his intolerance, his brutality and his abuse of power. Instead of proving his political correctness and mobilizing the masses, he often chose the path of repression and physical annihilation, not only against actual enemies, but also against individuals who had not committed any crimes against the party and the Soviet Government. Here we see no wisdom but only a demonstration of the brutal force which had once so alarmed V. I. Lenin.

Lately, especially after the unmasking of the Beria gang, the Central Committee looked into a series of matters fabricated by this gang. This revealed a very ugly picture of brutal willfulness connected with the incorrect behavior of Stalin. As facts prove, Stalin, using his unlimited power, allowed himself many abuses, acting in the name of the Central Committee, not asking for the opinion of the Committee members nor even of the members of the Central Committee's Political Bureau; often he did not inform them about his personal decisions concerning very important party and government matters. . . .

Whereas, during the first few years after Lenin's death, party congresses and Central Committee plenums took place more or less regularly, later, when Stalin began increasingly to abuse his power, these principles were brutally violated. This was especially evident during the last 15 years of his life. Was it a normal situation when over 13 years elapsed between the 18th and 19th Party Congresses, years during which our party and our country had experienced so many important events? These events demanded categorically that the party should have passed resolutions pertaining to the country's defense during the Patriotic War [Second World War] and to peacetime construction after the war. Even after the end of the war a Congress was not convened for over seven years. Central Committee plenums were hardly ever called. It should be sufficient to mention that during all the years of the Patriotic War not a single Central Committee plenum took place. It is true that there was an attempt to call a Central Committee plenum in October 1941, when Central Committee members from the whole country were called to Moscow. They waited two days for the opening of the plenum, but in vain. Stalin did not even want to meet and talk to the Central Committee members. This fact shows how demoralized Stalin was in the first months of the war and how haughtily and disdainfully he treated the Central Committee members.

In practice, Stalin ignored the norms of party life and trampled on the Leninist principle of collective party leadership.

Having at its disposal numerous data showing brutal willfulness toward party cadres, the Central Committee has created a party commission under the control of the Central Committee Presidium; it was charged with investigating what made possible the mass repressions against the majority of the Central Committee members and candidates elected at the 17th Congress of the All-Union Communist Party (Bolsheviks).

The commission has become acquainted with a large quantity of materials in the NKVD archives and with other documents, and has established many facts pertaining to the fabrication of cases against Communists, to false accusations, to glaring abuses of socialist legality, which resulted in the death of innocent people. It became apparent that many party, Soviet and economic activists, who were branded in 1937–1938 as "enemies," were actually never enemies, spies, wreckers, etc., but were always honest Communists; they were only so stigmatized and, often, no longer able to bear barbaric tortures, they charged themselves (at the order of the investigative judges—falsifiers) with all kinds of grave and unlikely crimes.

The commission has presented to the Central Committee Presidium lengthy and documented materials pertaining to mass repressions against the delegates to the 17th Party Congress and against members of the Central Committee elected at that Congress. These materials have been studied by the Presidium of the Central Committee.

It was determined that of the 139 members and candidates of the party's Central Committee who were elected at the 17th Congress, 98 persons, i.e., 70 per cent were arrested and shot (mostly in 1937–1938). (Indignation in the hall.) What was the composition of the delegates to the 17th Congress? It is known that 80 per cent of the voting participants of the 17th Congress joined the party during the years of conspiracy before the Revolution and during the civil war; this means before 1921. By social origin the basic mass of the delegates to the Congress were workers (60 per cent of the voting members).

For this reason, it was inconceivable that a congress so composed would have elected a Central Committee a majority of whom would prove to be enemies of the party. The only reason why 70 per cent of the Central Committee members and candidates elected at the 17th Congress were branded as enemies of the party and of the people was because honest Communists were slandered, accusations against them were fabricated, and revolutionary legality was gravely undermined.

The same fate met not only the Central Committee members but also the majority of the delegates to the 17th Party Congress. Of 1,966 delegates with either voting or advisory rights, 1,108 were arrested on charges of anti-revolutionary crimes, i.e., decidedly more than a majority. This very fact shows how absurd, wild and contrary to common sense were the charges of counterrevolutionary crimes made out, as we now see, against a majority of participants in the 17th Party Congress. (Indignation in the hall.)

We should recall that the 17th Party Congress is historically known as the Congress of Victors. Delegates to the Congress were active participants in the building of our socialist state; many of them suffered and fought for party interests during the pre-Revolutionary years in the conspiracy and at the civil-war fronts; they fought their enemies valiantly and often nervelessly looked into the face of death.

How, then, can we believe that such people could prove to be "two-faced" and had joined the camps of the enemies of socialism during the era after the political liquidation of Zinovievities, Trotskyites and rightists and after the great accomplishments of socialist construction? This was the result of the abuse of power by Stalin, who began to use mass terror against the party cadres.

What is the reason that mass repressions against activists increased more and more after the 17th Party Congress? It was because at that time Stalin had so elevated himself above the party and above the nation that he ceased to consider either the Central Committee or the party.

While he still reckoned with the opinion of the collective before the 17th Congress, after the complete political liquidation of the Trotskyites, Zinovievites and Bukharinites, when as a result of that fight and socialist victories the party achieved unity, Stalin ceased to an even greater degree to consider the members of the party's Central Committee and even the members of the Political Bureau. Stalin thought that now he could decide all things alone and all he needed were statisticians; he treated all others in such a way that they could only listen to and praise him.

After the criminal murder of Sergei M. Kirov, mass repressions and brutal acts of violation of socialist legality began. On the evening of December 1, 1934 on Stalin's initiative (without the approval of the Political Bureau—which was passed two days later, casually), the Secretary of the Presidium of the Central Executive Committee, Yenukidze, signed the following directive:

"1. Investigative agencies are directed to speed up the cases of those accused of the preparation or execution of acts of terror.

"2. Judicial organs are directed not to hold up the execution of death sentences pertaining to crimes of this category in order to consider the possibility of pardon, because the Presidium of the Central Executive Committee of the USSR does not consider as possible the receiving of petitions of this sort.

"3. The organs of the Commissariat of Internal Affairs are directed to execute the death sentences against criminals of the above-mentioned categories immediately after the passage of sentences."

This directive became the basis for mass acts of abuse against socialist legality. During many of the fabricated court cases, the accused were charged with "the preparation" of terroristic acts; this deprived them of any possibility that their cases might be re-examined, even when they stated before the court that their "confessions" were secured by force, and when, in a convincing manner, they disproved the accusations against them. . . .

Mass repressions grew tremendously from the end of 1936 after a telegram from Stalin and [Andrei] Zhdanov, dated from Sochi on September 25, 1936, was addressed to Kaganovich, Molotov and other members of the Political Bureau. The content of the telegram was as follows:

"We deem it absolutely necessary and urgent that Comrade Yezhov be nominated to the post of People's Commissar for Internal Affairs. Yagoda has definitely proved himself to be incapable of unmasking the Trotskyite-Zinovievite bloc. The OGPU is four years behind in this matter. This is noted by all party workers and by the majority of the representatives of the NKVD."

Strictly speaking, we should stress that Stalin did not meet with, and, therefore, could not know the opinion of party workers.

This Stalinist formulation that the "NKVD is four years behind" in applying mass repression and that there is a necessity for "catching up" with the neglected work directly pushed the NKVD workers on the path of mass arrests and executions. . . .

The mass repressions at this time were made under the slogan of a fight against the Trotskyites. Did the Trotskyites at this time actually constitute such a danger to our party and to the Soviet state? We should recall that in 1927, on the eve of the 15th Party Congress, only some 4,000 votes were cast for the Trotskyite-Zinovievite opposition while there were 724,000 for the party line. During the 10 years which passed between the 15th Party Congress and the February-March Central Committee plenum, Trotskyism was completely disarmed; many former Trotskyites had changed their former views and worked in the various sectors building socialism. It is clear that in the situation of socialist victory there was no basis for mass terror in the country. . . .

Stalin deviated from [the] clear and plain precepts of Lenin. Stalin put the party and the NKVD up to the use of mass terror when the exploiting classes had been liquidated in our country and when there were no serious reasons for the use of extraordinary mass terror.

This terror was not actually directed at the remnants of the defeated exploiting classes but against the honest workers of the party and of the Soviet state; against them were made lying, slanderous and absurd accusations concerning "two-facedness," "espionage," "sabotage," preparation of fictitious "plots," etc.

At the February-March Central Committee plenum in 1937 many members actually questioned the rightness of the established course regarding mass repressions under the pretext of combating "two-facedness."

Comrade Postyshev most ably expressed these doubts. He said: "I have philosophized that the severe years of fighting have passed. Party members who have lost their backbones have broken down or have joined the camp of the enemy; healthy elements have fought for the party. These were the years of industrialization and collectivization. I never thought it possible that after this severe era had passed Karpov and people like him would find themselves in the camp of the enemy. (Karpov was a worker in the Ukrainian Central Committee whom Postyshev knew well.) And now, according to the testimony, it appears that Karpov was recruited in 1934 by the Trotskyites. I do not personally believe that in 1934 an honest party member who had trod the long road of unrelenting fight against enemies for the party and for socialism would now be in the camp of the enemies. I do not believe it. . . . I cannot imagine how it would be possible to travel with the party during the difficult years and then, in 1934, join the Trotskyites. It is an odd thing. . . ." (Movement in the hall.)

Using Stalin's formulation, namely, that the closer we are to socialism the more enemies we will have, and using the resolution of the February-March Central Committee plenum passed on the basis of Yezhov's report, the *provocateurs* who had infiltrated the state-security organs together with conscienceless careerists began to protect with the party name the mass terror against party cadres, cadres of the Soviet state and the ordinary Soviet citizens. It should suffice to say that the number of arrests based on charges of counterrevolutionary crimes had grown ten times between 1936 and 1937.

It is known that brutal willfulness was practiced against leading party workers. The party statute, approved at the 17th Party Congress, was based on Leninist principles expressed at the 10th Party Congress. It stated that, in order to apply an extreme method such as exclusion from the party against a Central Committee member, against a Central Committee candidate and against a member of the Party Control Commission, "it is necessary to call a Central Committee plenum and to invite to the plenum all Central Committee candidate members and all members of the Party Control Commission"; only if two-thirds of the members of such a general assembly of responsible party leaders find it necessary, only then can a Central Committee member or candidate be expelled.

The majority of the Central Committee members and candidates elected at the 17th Congress and arrested in 1937–1938 were expelled from the party illegally through the brutal abuse of the party statute, because the question of their expulsion was never studied at the Central Committee plenum.

Now, when the cases of some of these so-called "spies" and "saboteurs" were examined, it was found that all their cases were fabricated. Confessions of guilt of many arrested and charged with enemy activity were gained with the help of cruel and inhuman tortures.

At the same time, Stalin, as we have been informed by members of the Political Bureau of that time, did not show them the statements of many accused political activists when they retracted their confessions before the military tribunal and asked for an objective examination of their cases. There were many such declarations and Stalin doubtless knew of them.

The Central Committee considers it absolutely necessary to inform the Congress of many such fabricated "cases" against the members of the party's Central Committee elected at the 17th Party Congress.

An example of vile provocation of odious falsification and of criminal violation of revolutionary legality is the case of the former candidate for the Central Committee Political Bureau, one of the most eminent workers of the party and of the Soviet Government, Comrade Eikhe, who was a party member since 1905. (Commotion in the hall.)

Comrade Eikhe was arrested on April 29, 1938 on the basis of slanderous materials, without the sanction of the Prosecutor of the USSR, which was finally received 15 months after the arrest.

Investigation of Eikhe's case was made in a manner which most brutally violated Soviet legality and was accompanied by willfulness and falsification.

Eikhe was forced under torture to sign ahead of time a protocol of his confession prepared by the investigative judges, in which he and several other eminent party workers were accused of anti-soviet activity.

On October 1, 1939 Eikhe sent his declaration to Stalin in which he categorically denied his guilt and asked for an examination of his case. In the declaration he wrote: "There is no more bitter misery than to sit in the jail of a government for which I have always fought." . . .

On February 2, 1940 Eikhe was brought before the court. Here he did not confess any guilt and said as follows:

"In all the so-called confessions of mine there is not one letter written by me with the exception of my signatures under the protocols, which were forced from me. I have made my confession under pressure from the investigative judge, who from the time of my arrest tormented me. After that I began to write all this nonsense. . . . The most important thing for me is to tell the court, the party and Stalin that I am not guilty. I have never been guilty of any conspiracy. I will die believing in the truth of party policy as I have believed in it during my whole life."

On February 4 Eikhe was shot. (Indignation in the hall.)

It has been definitely established now that Eikhe's case was fabricated; he has been posthumously rehabilitated. . . .

Many thousands of honest and innocent Communists have died as a result of this monstrous falsification of such "cases," as a result of the fact that all kinds of slanderous "confessions" were accepted, and as a result of the practice of forcing accusations against oneself and others. In the same manner were fabricated the "cases" against eminent party and state workers—Kossior, Chubar, Postyshev, Kosarev and others.

In those years repressions on a mass scale were applied which were based on nothing tangible and which resulted in heavy cadre losses to the party.

The vicious practice was condoned of having the NKVD prepare lists of persons whose cases were under the jurisdiction of the Military Collegium and whose sentences were prepared in advance. Yezhov would send these lists to Stalin personally for his approval of the proposed punishment. In 1937–1938, 383 such lists containing the names of many thousands of party, Soviet, Komsomol, Army and economic workers were sent to Stalin. He approved these lists.

A large part of these cases are being reviewed now and a great part of them are being voided because they were baseless and falsified. Suffice it to say that from 1954 to the present time the Military Collegium of the Supreme Court has rehabilitated 7,679 persons, many of whom were rehabilitated posthumously. . . .

Only because our party has at its disposal such great moral-political strength was it possible for it to survive the difficult events in 1937–1938 and to educate new cadres. There is, however, no doubt that our march forward toward socialism and toward the preparation of the country's defense would have been much more successful were it not for the tremendous loss in the cadres suffered as a result of the baseless and false mass of repressions in 1937–1938. . . .

Facts prove that many abuses were made on Stalin's orders without reckoning with any norms of party and Soviet legality. Stalin was a very distrustful man, sickly suspicious; we know this from our work with him. He could look at a man and say: "Why are your eyes so shifty today?" or "Why are you turning so much today and avoiding to look me directly in the eyes?" The sickly suspicion created in him a general distrust even toward eminent party workers whom he had known for years. Everywhere and in everything he saw "enemies," "two-facers" and "spies." Possessing unlimited power, he indulged in great willfulness and choked a person morally and physically. A situation was created where no one could express one's own will.

When Stalin said that one or another should be arrested, it was necessary to accept on faith that he was an "enemy of the people." Meanwhile, Beria's gang, which ran the organs of state security, outdid themselves in proving the guilt of the arrested and the truth of materials which it falsified. And what proofs were offered? The confessions of the arrested, and the investigative judges accepted these "confessions." And how is it possible that a person confesses to crimes which he has not committed? Only in one way—because of application of physical methods of pressuring him, tortures, bringing him to a state of unconsciousness, deprivation of his judgment, taking away of his human dignity. In this manner were "confessions" acquired. . . .

Very grievous consequences, especially in reference to the beginning of the war, followed Stalin's annihilation of many military commanders and political workers during 1937–1949 because of his suspiciousness and through slanderous accusations. During these years repressions were instituted against certain parts of military cadres beginning literally at the company and battalion commander level and extending to the higher military centers; during this time the cadre of leaders who had gained military experience in Spain and in the Far East was almost completely liquidated.

The policy of large-scale repression against the military cadres led also to undermining military discipline, because for several years officers of all ranks and even soldiers in the party and Komsomol cells were taught to "unmask" their superiors as hidden enemies. (Movement in the hall.) It is natural that this caused a negative influence on the state of military discipline in the first war period.

And, as you know, we had before the war excellent military cadres which were unquestionably loyal to the party and to the Fatherland. Suffice it to say that those of them who managed to survive, despite severe tortures to which they were subjected in the prisons, have from the first war days shown themselves real patriots and heroically fought for the glory of the Fatherland; I have here in mind such comrades as Rokossovsky (who, as you know, had been jailed), Gorbatov, Maretskov (who is a delegate at the present Congress), Podlas (he was an excellent commander who perished at the front), and many, many others. However, many such commanders perished in camps and jails and the Army saw them no more.

All this brought about the situation which existed at the beginning of the war and which was the great threat to our Fatherland. . . .

On one occasion after the war, during a meeting of Stalin with members of the Political Bureau, Anastas Ivanovich Mikoyan mentioned that Khrushchev must have been right when he telephoned concerning the Kharkov operation and that it was unfortunate that his suggestion had not been accepted.

You should have seen Stalin's fury! How could it be admitted that he, Stalin, had not been right! He is after all a "genius," and a genius cannot help but be right! Everyone can err, but Stalin considered that he never erred, that he was always right. He never acknowledged to anyone that he made any mistake, large or small, despite the fact that he made not a few mistakes in the matter of theory and in his practical activity. After the Party Congress we shall probably have to re-evaluate many wartime military operations and present them in their true light.

The tactics on which Stalin insisted without knowing the essence of the conduct of battle operations cost us much blood until we succeeded in stopping the opponent and going over to the offensive. . . .

Comrades, let us reach for some other facts. The Soviet Union is justly considered as a model of a multinational state because we have in practice assured the equality and friendship of all nations which live in our great Fatherland.

All the more monstrous are the acts whose initiator was Stalin and which are rude violations of the basic Leninist principles of the nationality policy of the Soviet state. We refer to the mass deportations from their native places of whole nations, together with all Communists and Komsomols without any exception; this deportation was not dictated by any military considerations.

Thus, already at the end of 1943, when there occurred a permanent breakthrough at the fronts of the Great Patriotic War benefiting the Soviet Union, a decision was taken and executed concerning the deportation of all the Karachai from the lands on which they lived.

In the same period, at the end of December 1943, the same lot befell the whole population of the Autonomous Kalmyk Republic. In March 1944, all the Chechen and Ingush peoples were deported and the Chechen-Ingush Autonomous Republic was liquidated. In April 1944, all Balkars were deported to faraway places from the territory of the Kabardino-Balkar Autonomous Republic and the Republic itself was renamed the Autonomous Kabardian Republic.

The Ukrainians avoided meeting this fate only because there were too many of them and there was no place to which to deport them. Otherwise, he would have deported them also. (Laughter and animation in the hall.) . . .

Let us also recall the "affairs of the doctor-plotters." (Animation in the hall.) Actually there was no "affair" outside of the declaration of the woman doctor Timashuk, who was probably influenced or ordered by someone (after all, she was an unofficial collaborator of the organs of state security) to write Stalin a letter in which she declared that doctors were applying supposedly improper methods of medical treatment.

Such a letter was sufficient for Stalin to reach an immediate conclusion that there are doctor-plotters in the Soviet Union. He issued orders to arrest a group of eminent Soviet medical specialists. He personally issued advice on the conduct of the investigation and the method of interrogation of the arrested persons. He said that the academician Vinogradov should be put in chains, another one should be beaten. Present at this Congress as a delegate is the former Minister of State Security, Comrade Ignatiev. Stalin told him curtly, "If you do not obtain confessions from the doctors we will shorten you by a head." (Tumult in the hall.)

Stalin personally called the investigative judge, gave him instructions, advised him on what investigative methods should be used; these methods were simple—beat, beat and, once again, beat.

Shortly after the doctors were arrested, we members of the Political Bureau received protocols with the doctors' confessions of guilt. After distributing these protocols, Stalin told us, "You are blind like young kittens; what will happen without me? The country will perish because you do not know how to recognize enemies."

The case was so presented that no one could verify the facts on which the investigation was based. There was no possibility of trying to verify facts by contacting those who had made the confessions of guilt.

We felt, however, that the case of the arrested doctors was questionable. We knew some of these people personally because they had once treated us. When we examined this "case" after Stalin's death, we found it to be fabricated from beginning to end.

This ignominious "case" was set up by Stalin; he did not, however, have the time in which to bring it to an end (as he conceived that end), and for this reason the doctors are still alive. Now they have all been rehabilitated; they are working in the same places they were working before; they treat top individuals, not excluding members of the Government; they have our full confidence; and they execute their duties honestly, as they did before. . . .

Comrades! The 20th Congress of the Communist Party of the Soviet Union has manifested with a new strength the unshakable unity of our party, its cohesiveness around the Central Committee, its resolute will to accomplish the great task of building communism. (Tumultuous applause.)

And the fact that we present in all their ramifications the basic problems of overcoming the cult of the individual which is alien to Marxism-Leninism, as well as the problem of liquidating its burdensome consequences, is an evidence of the great moral and political strength of our party. (Prolonged applause.)

We are absolutely certain that our party, armed with the historical resolutions of the 20th Congress, will lead the Soviet people along the Leninist path to new successes, to new victories. (Tumultuous, prolonged applause.)

Long live the victorious banner of our party—Leninism! (Tumultuous, prolonged applause ending in ovation. All rise.)

MILOVAN DJILAS

A MAJOR AIM of Soviet strategy during the Second World War was to end the war with Russian troops as deep in Europe as possible. Most of their line of furthest advance westward later became known as the Iron Curtain and behind it the Soviet armies and East European Communists effectuated their "people's revolutions." The difficulties of reconciling Soviet-dominated communist regimes with national aspirations and a spirit of criticism of totalitarian rule became apparent in East Europe within a few years after the war.

The only successful breakaway from Soviet control came in Yugoslavia in 1948 under the wartime leader and postwar dictator Marshal Tito. Although Tito's regime remained totalitarian and hostile to the West it was more intent on building Communism in Yugoslavia than on international expansion. Hemmed in as they were by Soviet satellites, the Yugoslavs, nevertheless, managed to maintain their independence and defiance of the Cominform, the slightly disguised postwar version of the Moscow-controlled former Communist International.

Among Tito's principal associates was Milovan Djilas (1911–), son of a Montenegrin army officer and a Serbian mother. While studying law and philosophy at the University of Belgrade in the 1920s, Djilas was already a Marxist. Soon he was active in Communist party work. In 1933 he was sent to prison for organizing demonstrations against the monarchy but resumed conspiratorial activity on his release. By 1934 he had met and had become a collaborator of Tito, then secretary-general of the Yugoslav Communists. Djilas joined the party's Politburo in 1940. During the war he was an important resistance leader and in 1944 met Stalin while on a mission to Moscow. At the war's end he was openly critical of Soviet actions in Yugoslavia and he helped Tito prepare the break of 1948. After national independence was secured Djilas became one of the principal officials of the nation, very near to Tito in influence and prestige.

Having broken with Moscow's imperialism, Djilas went on to criticize his own regime's totalitarian practices. In 1954 his outspokenness brought his downfall. Warnings from Tito, a suspended prison sentence, poverty, unemployment, and social ostracism had had no effect. Djilas' continued publication in the foreign press of anti-Communist views brought his arrest again in 1956. He was sent to jail for three years, but the publication in America of his book *The New Class* (1957) led Tito to extend his prison term by seven years.

As a contribution to a large, ever increasing literature by disaffected Communists *The New Class* has many familiar themes, but Djilas' former high position and his general theory of the growth of statist and undemocratic bureaucratic tendencies in all Communist regimes gives the work some distinction. *The New Class* also implies a fundamental change in Marxist outlook for it states that the abolition of capitalism by social ownership of the means of production is not sufficient guarantee against the growth of new tyrannies with their own privileges and parasitic functionaries.

The following selection is from *The New Class* (New York: Praeger, 1957).

THE NEW CLASS

EVERYTHING happened differently in the U.S.S.R. and other Communist countries from what the leaders—even such prominent ones as Lenin, Stalin, Trotsky, and Bukharin—anticipated. They expected that the state would rapidly wither away, that democracy would be strengthened. The reverse happened. They expected a rapid improvement in the standard of living—there has been scarcely any change in this respect and, in the sub-jugated East European countries, the standard has even declined. In every instance, the standard of living has failed to rise in proportion to the rate of industrialization, which was much more rapid. It was believed that the differ-ences between cities and villages, between intellectual and physical labor, would slowly disappear; instead these differences have increased. Communist anticipations in other areas—including their expectations for developments in the non-Communist world—have also failed to materialize.

The greatest illusion was that industrialization and collectivization in the U.S.S.R., and destruction of capitalist ownership, would result in a classless society. In 1936, when the new Constitution was promulgated, Stalin an-nounced that the "exploiting class" had ceased to exist. The capitalist and other classes of ancient origin had in fact been destroyed, but a new class, previously unknown to history, had been formed.

It is understandable that this class, like those before it, should believe that the establishment of its power would result in happiness and freedom for all men. The only difference between this and other classes was that it treated the delay in the realization of its illusions more crudely. It thus affirmed that its power was more complete than the power of any other class before in history, and its class illusions and prejudices were proportionally greater.

This new class, the bureaucracy, or more accurately the political bureauc-racy, has all the characteristics of earlier ones as well as some new char-acteristics of its own. Its origin had its special characteristics also, even though in essence it was similar to the beginnings of other classes.

Other classes, too, obtained their strength and power by the revolutionary path, destroying the political, social, and other orders they met in their way. However, almost without exception, these classes attained power *after* new economic patterns had taken shape in the old society. The case was the reverse with new classes in the Communist systems. It did not come to power to *complete* a new economic order but to *establish* its own, and, in so doing, to establish its power over society.

In earlier epochs the coming to power of some class, some part of a class, or of some party, was the final event resulting from its formation and its development. The reverse was true in the U.S.S.R. There the new class was definitely formed after it attained power. Its consciousness had to develop before its economic and physical powers, because the class had not taken root in the life of the nation. This class viewed its role in relation to the world from an idealistic point of view. Its practical possibilities were not diminished by this. In spite of its illusions, it represented an objective tendency towards industrialization. Its practical bent emanated from this tendency. The promise of an ideal world increased the faith in the ranks of the new class and sowed illusions among the masses. At the same time it inspired gigantic physical undertakings.

Because this new class had not been formed as a part of the economic and social life before it came to power, it could only be created in an organization of a special type, distinguished by a special discipline based on identical philosophic and ideological views of its members. A unity of belief and iron discipline was necessary to overcome its weaknesses.

The roots of the new class were implanted in a special party, of the Bolshevik type. Lenin was right in his view that his party was an exception in the history of human society, although he did not suspect that it would be the beginning of a new class.

To be more precise, the initiators of the new class are not found in the party of the Bolshevik type as a whole but in that stratum of professional revolutionaries who made up its core even before it attained power. It was not by accident that Lenin asserted after the failure of the 1905 revolution that only professional revolutionaries—men whose sole profession was revolutionary work—could build a new party of the Bolshevik type. It was still less accidental that even Stalin, the future creator of a new class, was the most outstanding example of such a professional revolutionary. The new ruling class has been gradually developing from this very narrow stratum of revolutionaries. These revolutionaries composed its core for a long period. Trotsky noted that in pre-revolutionary professional revolutionaries was the origin of the future Stalinist bureaucrat. What he did not detect was the beginning of a new class of owners and exploiters.

This is not to say that the new party and the new class are identical. The party, however, is the core of that class, and its base. It is very difficult, perhaps impossible, to define the limits of the new class and to identify its members. The new class may be said to be made up of those who have special privileges and economic preference because of the administrative monopoly they hold.

Since administration is unavoidable in society, necessary administrative functions may be coexistent with parasitic functions in the same person. Not every member of the party is a member of the new class, any more than every artisan or member of the city party was a bourgeois.

In loose terms, as the new class becomes stronger and attains a more perceptible physiognomy, the role of the party diminishes. The core and the basis of the new class is created in the party and at its top, as well as in the state political organs. The once live, compact party, full of initiative, is disappearing to become transformed into the traditional oligarchy of the new class, irresistibly drawing into its ranks those who aspire to join the new class and repressing those who have any ideals.

The party makes the class, but the class grows as a result and uses the party as a basis. The class grows stronger, while the party grows weaker; this is the inescapable fate of every Communist party in power.

If it were not materially interested in production or if it did not have within itself the potentialities for the creation of a new class, no party could act in so morally and ideologically foolhardy a fashion, let alone stay in power for long. Stalin declared, after the end of the First Five-Year Plan: "If we had not created the apparatus, we would have failed!" He should have substituted "new class" for the word "apparatus," and everything would have been clearer.

It seems unusual that a political party could be the beginning of a new class. Parties are generally the product of classes and strata which have become intellectually and economically strong. However, if one grasps the actual conditions in pre-revolutionary Russia and in other countries in which Communism prevailed over national forces, it will be clear that a party of this type is the product of specific opportunities and that there is nothing unusual or accidental in this being so. . . .

When Communist systems are being critically analyzed, it is considered that their fundamental distinction lies in the fact that a bureaucracy, organized in a special stratum, rules over the people. This is generally true. However, a more detailed analysis will show that only a special stratum of bureaucrats, those who are not administrative officials, make up the core of the governing bureaucracy, or, in my terminology, of the new class. This is actually a party or political bureaucracy. Other officials are only the apparatus under the control of the new class; the apparatus may be clumsy and slow but, no matter what, it must exist in every socialist society. It is sociologically possible to draw the borderline between the different types of officials, but in practice they are practically indistinguishable. This is true not only because the Communist system by its very nature is bureaucratic, but because Communists handle the various important administrative functions. In addition, the stratum of political bureaucrats cannot enjoy their privileges if they do not give crumbs from their tables to other bureaucratic categories.

It is important to note the fundamental differences between the political bureaucracies mentioned here and those which arise with every centralization in modern economy—especially centralizations that lead to collective forms of ownership such as monopolies, and also in nationalized industries in the West. . . .

While such functionaries have much in common with Communist bureaucrats, especially as regards "esprit de corps," they are not identical. Although state and other bureaucrats in non-Communist systems form a special stratum, they do not exercise authority as the Communists do. Bureaucrats in a non-Communist state have political masters, usually elected, or owners over them, while Communists have neither masters nor owners over them. The bureaucrats in a non-Communist state are officials in modern capitalist economy, while the Communists are something different and new: a new class.

As in other owning classes, the proof that it is a special class lies in its ownership and its special relations to other classes. In the same way, the class to which a member belongs is indicated by the material and other privileges which ownership brings to him.

As defined by Roman law, property constitutes the use, enjoyment, and disposition of material goods. The Communist political bureaucracy uses, enjoys, and disposes of nationalized property.

If we assume that membership in this bureaucracy or new owning class is predicated on the use of privileges inherent in ownership—in this instance nationalized material goods—then membership in the new party class, or political bureaucracy, is reflected in a larger income in material goods and privileges than society should normally grant for such functions. In practice, the ownership privilege of the new class manifests itself as an exclusive right, as a party monopoly, for the political bureaucracy to distribute the national income, to set wages, direct economic development, and dispose of nationalized and other property. This is the way it appears to the ordinary man who considers the Communist functionary as being very rich and as a man who does not have to work.

The ownership of private property has, for many reasons, proved to be unfavorable for the establishment of the new class's authority. Besides, the destruction of private ownership was necessary for the economic transformation of nations. The new class obtains its power, privileges, ideology, and its customs from one specific form of ownership—collective ownership—which the class administers and distributes in the name of the nation and society.

The new class maintains that ownership derives from a designated social relationship. This is the relationship between the monopolists of administration, who constitute a narrow and closed stratum, and the mass of producers (farmers, workers, and intelligentsia) who have no rights. However, this relationship is not valid since the Communist bureaucracy enjoys a monopoly over the distribution of material goods.

Every fundamental change in the social relationship between those who monopolize administration and those who work is inevitably reflected in the ownership relationship. Social and political relations and ownership—the totalitarianism of the government and the monopoly of authority—are being more fully brought into accord in Communism than in any other single system.

To divest Communists of their ownership rights would be to abolish them as a class. To compel them to relinquish their other social powers, so that workers may participate in sharing the profits of their work—which capitalists have had to permit as a result of strikes and parliamentary action—would mean that Communists were being deprived of their monopoly over property, ideology, and government. This would be the beginning of democracy and freedom in Communism, the end of Communist monopolism and totalitarianism. Until this happens, there can be no indication that important, fundamental changes are taking place in Communist systems, at least not in the eyes of men who think seriously about social progress.

The ownership privileges of the new class and membership in that class are the privileges of *administration*. This privilege extends from state administration and the administration of economic enterprises to that of sports and humanitarian organizations. Political, party, or so-called "general leadership" is executed by the core. This position of leadership carries privileges with it. In his *Stalin au pouvoir,* published in Paris in 1951, Orlov states that the average pay of a worker in the U.S.S.R. in 1935 was 1,800 rubles annually, while the pay and allowances of the secretary of a rayon committee amounted to 45,000 rubles annually. The situation has changed since then for both workers and party functionaries, but the essence remains the same. Other authors have arrived at the same conclusions. Discrepancies between the pay of workers and party functionaries are extreme; this could not be hidden from persons visiting the U.S.S.R. or other Communist countries in the past few years.

Other systems, too, have their professional politicians. One can think well or ill of them, but they must exist. Society cannot live without a state or a government, and therefore it cannot live without those who fight for it. However, there are fundamental differences between professional politicians in other systems and in the Communist system. In extreme cases, politicians in other systems use the government to secure privileges for themselves and their cohorts, or to favor the economic interests of one social stratum or another. The situation is different with the Communist system where the power and the government are identical with the use, enjoyment, and disposition of almost all the nation's goods. He who grabs power grabs privileges and indirectly grabs property. Consequently, in Communism, power or politics as a profession is the ideal of those who have the desire or the prospect of living as parasites at the expense of others.

Membership in the Communist Party before the Revolution meant sacrifice. Being a professional revolutionary was one of the highest honors. Now that the party has consolidated its power, party membership means that one belongs to a privileged class. And at the core of the party are the all-powerful exploiters and masters.

For a long time the Communist revolution and the Communist system have been concealing their real nature. The emergence of the new class has been concealed under socialist phraseology and, more important, under the new collective forms of property ownership. The so-called socialist ownership is a disguise for the real ownership by the political bureaucracy. And in the beginning this bureaucracy was in a hurry to complete industrialization, and hid its class composition under that guise. . . .

Although he did not realize it, Lenin started the organization of the new class. He established the party along Bolshevik lines and developed the theories of its unique and leading role in the building of a new society. This is but one aspect of his many-sided and gigantic work; it is the aspect which came about from his actions rather than his wishes. It is also the aspect which led the new class to revere him.

The real and direct originator of the new class, however, was Stalin. He was a man of quick reflexes and a tendency to coarse humor, not very educated nor a good speaker. But he was a relentless dogmatician and a great administrator, a Georgian who knew better than anyone else whither the new powers of Greater Russia were taking her. He created the new class by the use of the most barbaric means, not even sparing the class itself. It was inevitable that the new class which placed him at the top would later submit to his unbridled and brutal nature. He was the true leader of that class as long as the class was building itself up, and attaining power.

The new class was born in the revolutionary struggle in the Communist Party, but was developed in the industrial revolution. Without the revolution, without industry, the class's position would not have been secure and its power would have been limited.

While the country was being industrialized, Stalin began to introduce considerable variations in wages, at the same time allowing the development toward privileges to proceed. He thought that industrialization would come to nothing if the new class was not made materially interested in the process, by acquisition of some property for itself. Without industrialization the new class would find it difficult to hold its position, for it would have neither historical justification nor the material resources for its continued existence.

The increase in the membership of the party, or of the bureaucracy, was closely connected with this. In 1927, on the eve of industrialization, the Soviet Communist Party had 887,233 members. In 1934, at the end of the First Five-Year Plan, the membership had increased to 1,874,488. This was a phenomenon obviously connected with industrialization: the prospects for the new class and privileges for its members were improving. What is more, the privileges and the class were expanding more rapidly than industrialization itself. It is difficult to cite any statistics on this point, but the conclusion is self-evident for anyone who bears in mind that the standard of living has not kept pace with industrial production, while the new class actually seized the lion's share of the economic and other progress earned by the sacrifices and efforts of the masses.

The establishment of the new class did not proceed smoothly. It encountered bitter opposition from existing classes and from those revolutionaries who could not reconcile reality with the ideals of their struggle. In the U.S.S.R. the opposition of revolutionaries was most evident in the Trotsky-Stalin conflict. The conflict between Trotsky and Stalin, or between oppositionists in the party and Stalin, as well as the conflict between the regime and the peasantry, became more intense as industrialization advanced and the power and authority of the new class increased.

Trotsky, an excellent speaker, brilliant stylist, and skilled polemicist, a man cultured and of excellent intelligence, was deficient in only one quality: a sense of reality. He wanted to be a revolutionary in a period when life imposed the commonplace. He wished to revive a revolutionary party which was being transformed into something completely different, into a new class unconcerned with great ideals and interested only in the everyday pleasures of life. He expected action from a mass already tired by war, hunger, and death, at a time when the new class already strongly held the reins and had begun to experience the sweetness of privilege. Trotsky's fireworks lit up the distant heavens; but he could not rekindle the fires in weary men. He sharply noted the sorry aspect of the new phenomena but he did not grasp their meaning. In addition, he had never been a Bolshevik. This was his vice and his virtue. Attacking the party bureaucracy in the name of the revolution, he attacked the cult of the party and, although he was not conscious of it, the new class. . . .

In Stalin's victory Trotsky saw the Thermidoric reaction against the revolution, actually the bureaucratic corruption of the Soviet government and the revolutionary cause. Consequently, he understood and was deeply hurt by the amorality of Stalin's methods. Trotsky was the first, although he was not aware of it, who in the attempt to save the Communist movement discovered the essence of contemporary Communism. But he was not capable of seeing it through to the end. He supposed that this was only a momentary cropping up of bureaucracy, corrupting the party and the revolution and concluded that the solution was in a change at the top, in a "palace revolution." When a palace revolution actually took place after Stalin's death, it could be seen that the essence had not changed; something deeper and more lasting was involved. The Soviet Thermidor of Stalin had not only led to the installation of a government more despotic than the previous one, but also to the installation of a class. This was the continuation of that other violent foreign revolution which had inevitably borne and strengthened the new class. . . .

It would not be important to establish the fact that in contemporary Communism a new owning and exploiting class is involved and not merely a temporary dictatorship and an arbitrary bureaucracy, if some anti-Stalinist Communists including Trotsky as well as some Social Democrats had not depicted the ruling stratum as a passing bureaucratic phenomenon because of which this new ideal, classless society, still in its swaddling clothes, must suffer, just as bourgeois society had had to suffer under Cromwell's and Napoleon's despotism.

But the new class is really a new class, with a special composition and special power. By any scientific definition of a class, even the Marxist definition by which some classes are lower than others according to their specific position in production, we conclude that, in the U.S.S.R. and other Communist countries, a new class of owners and exploiters is in existence. The specific characteristic of this new class is its collective ownership. Communist theoreticians affirm, and some even believe, that Communism has arrived at collective ownership. . . .

The Communists did not invent collective ownership as such, but invented its all-encompassing character, more widely extended than in earlier epochs, even more extensive than in Pharaoh's Egypt. That is all that the Communists did.

The ownership of the new class, as well as its character, was formed over a period of time and was subjected to constant change during the process.

At first, only a small part of the nation felt the need for all economic powers to be placed in the hands of a political party for the purpose of aiding the industrial transformation. The party, acting as the *avant-garde* of the proletariat and as the "most enlightened power of socialism," pressed for this centralization which could be attained only by a change in ownership. The change was made in fact and in form through nationalization first of large enterprises and then of smaller ones. The abolition of private ownership was a prerequisite for industrialization, and for the beginning of the new class. However, without their special role as administrators over society and as distributors of property, the Communists could not transform themselves into a new class, nor could a new class be formed and permanently established. Gradually material goods were nationalized, but in fact, through its right to use, enjoy, and distribute these goods, they became the property of a discernible stratum of the party and the bureaucracy gathered around it.

In view of the significance of ownership for its power—and also of the fruits of ownership—the party bureaucracy cannot renounce the extension of its ownership even over small-scale production facilities. Because of its totalitarianism and monopolism, the new class finds itself unavoidably at war with everything which it does not administer or handle, and must deliberately aspire to destroy or conquer it. . . .

The fact that the seizure of property from other classes, especially from small owners, led to decreases in production and to chaos in the economy was of no consequence to the new class. Most important for the new class, as for every owner in history, was the attainment and consolidation of ownership. The class profited from the new property it had acquired even though the nation lost thereby. The collectivization of peasant holdings, which was economically unjustified, was unavoidable if the new class was to be securely installed in its power and its ownership. . . .

No bureaucracy alone could be so stubborn in its purposes and aims. Only those engaged in new forms of ownership, who tread the road to new forms of production, are capable of being so persistent.

GEORGE ORWELL

EORGE ORWELL (1903–50), called by one critic "the conscience of his generation," was the pen name of Eric Blair. He was born in India but educated at Eton as a scholarship student. While there his intellectual independence and obvious talent won the admiration of his fellows. After leaving Eton he went to Burma in 1922 as a police officer. There he saw at firsthand the paradoxes of modern imperialism that he later depicted so well in his essay "Shooting an Elephant." Fed up with the work of empire he returned to Europe in 1927 and lived, as one of his titles expressed it, "down and out in Paris and London." By 1935 he made a little money from his writing and moved from London into the country. Although Orwell was not the son of a working-class family, he knew poverty and the poor. This, his intellectual awareness, and an innate sense of justice made him a socialist.

Like many men of the left in the 1930s, Orwell recognized the stakes in the Spanish Civil War, the terrible struggle that started in 1936 as a battle between Fascist nationalist rebels and a then republican regime. Orwell went to Spain to fight for the republicans but he soon recognized that the Communists were out to use the republican cause for their own ends, a fact that many non-communist leftists approved or did not point out. Their attitude to Communism in Spain was a notable example of the mistake that Orwell later characterized as trying to be anti-fascist without being anti-totalitarian. Spain made him forever skeptical about the politically organized "left" but did not end his socialist sympathies. His report on the Spanish Civil War in *Homage to Catalonia* (1938) is perhaps the best account of the struggle and of the ambiguous relations of the left with the Communists.

Orwell first became known to the general public in 1945 when he published *Animal Farm,* a short parable of the Bolshevik revolution and a warning about other revolutions that may start out declaring that all men are created equal but end by proclaiming, "but some are more equal than others." By 1945 Orwell, never a robust person, was in wretched health. He was, however, on the road to fame and subsequently published several collections of essays which are among the best examples of prose written in the last generation.

Orwell's major work, however, was *1984,* a novel about the fully developed totalitarian state of the future in which human private destinies have been virtually abolished. The book was hailed in England and America as a still more brilliant attack on Soviet tyranny than *Animal Farm.* In fact, it was an examination of tendencies common to the entire world which could lead to the totally effective police state. After *1984* Orwell's health became rapidly worse and he died of tuberculosis in a nursing home in London at the age of 46.

In *1984* there is a mythical enemy of the state, modeled somewhat on Leon Trotsky. His name is Emmanuel Goldstein. There circulates underground a secret book purportedly written by Goldstein. "The book" alone can explain to men who have been deliberately denied a true history of the past how the twentieth century managed to produce so monstrous a society. The hero of the novel manages to secure a copy and it vindicates his feelings that his nightmare world is not the only life possible for men, but a dreadful and monstrous perversion. The account in the book is true but when the hero is caught by the secret police he learns that it has been deliberately put into circulation by the regime to trap people who have somehow escaped thought control.

This selection is an arrangement of principal parts of "The Notebooks of Emmanuel Goldstein" and has been edited from *1984* (New York: Harcourt, Brace, 1949).

&

1984

The Theory and Practice of Oligarchical Collectivism by Emmanuel Goldstein

CHAPTER I. IGNORANCE IS STRENGTH

Throughout recorded time, and probably since the end of the Neolithic Age, there have been three kinds of people in the world, the High, the Middle, and the Low. They have been subdivided in many ways, they have borne countless different names, and their relative numbers, as well as their attitude toward one another, have varied from age to age; but the essential structure of society has never altered. Even after enormous upheavals and seemingly irrevocable changes, the same pattern has always reasserted itself, just as a gyroscope will always return to equilibrium, however far it is pushed one way or another. . . .

The aims of these three groups are entirely irreconcilable. The aim of the High is to remain where they are. The aim of the Middle is to change places with the High. The aim of the Low, when they have an aim—for it is an abiding characteristic of the Low that they are too much crushed by drudgery to be more than intermittently conscious of anything outside their daily lives—is to abolish all distinctions and create a society in which all men shall be equal. Thus throughout history a struggle which is the same in its main outlines recurs over and over again. For long periods the High seem to be securely in power, but sooner or later there always comes a moment when they lose either their belief in themselves, or their capacity to govern efficiently, or both. They are then overthrown by the Middle, who enlist the Low on their side by pretending to them that they are fighting for liberty and justice. As soon as they have reached their objective, the Middle thrust the Low back into their old position of servitude, and themselves become the High. Presently a new Middle group splits off from one of the other groups, or from both of them, and the struggle begins over again. Of the three groups, only the Low are never even temporarily successful in achieving their aims. It would be an exaggeration to say that throughout history there has been no progress of a material kind. Even today, in a period of decline, the average human being is physically better off than he was a few centuries ago. But no advance in wealth, no softening of manners, no reform or revolution has ever brought human equality a millimeter nearer. From the point of view of the Low, no historic change has ever meant much more than a change in the name of their masters.

By the late nineteenth century the recurrence of this pattern had become obvious to many observers. There then arose schools of thinkers who interpreted history as a cyclical process and claimed to show that inequality was the unalterable law of human life. This doctrine, of course, had always had its adherents, but in the manner in which it was now put forward there was a significant change. In the past the need for a hierarchical form of society had been the doctrine specifically of the High. It had been preached by kings and aristocrats and by the priests, lawyers, and the like who were parasitical upon them, and it had generally been softened by promises of compensation in an imaginary world beyond the grave. The Middle, so long as it was struggling for power, had always made use of such terms as freedom, justice, and fraternity. Now, however, the concept of human brotherhood began to be assailed by people who were not yet in positions of command, but merely hoped to be so before long. In the past the Middle had made revolutions under the banner of equality, and then had established a fresh tyranny as soon as the old one was overthrown. The new Middle groups in effect proclaimed their tyranny beforehand. Socialism, a theory which appeared in the early nineteenth century, and was the last link in a chain of thought stretching back to the slave rebellions of antiquity, was still deeply infected by the Utopianism of past ages. But in each variant of Socialism that appeared from about 1900 onwards the aim of establishing liberty and equality was more and more openly abandoned. The new movements which appeared in the middle years of the century, Ingsoc in Oceania, Neo-Bolshevism in Eurasia, Death-worship, as it is commonly called, in Eastasia, had the conscious aim of perpetuating *un*freedom and *in*equality. These new movements, of course, grew out of the old ones and tended to keep their names and pay lip-service to their ideology. But the purpose of all of them was to arrest progress and freeze history at a chosen moment. The familiar pendulum swing was to happen once more, and then stop. As usual, the High were to be turned out by the Middle, who would then become the High; but this time, by conscious strategy, the High would be able to maintain their position permanently.

The new doctrines arose partly because of the accumulation of historical knowledge, and the growth of the historical sense, which had hardly existed before the nineteenth century. The cyclical movement of history was now intelligible, or appeared to be so; and if it was intelligible, then it was alterable. But the principal, underlying cause was that, as early as the beginning of the twentieth century, human equality had become technically possible. It was still true that men were not equal in their native talents and that functions had to be specialized in ways that favored some individuals against others; but there was no longer any real need for class distinctions or for large differences of wealth. In earlier ages, class distinctions had been not only inevitable but desirable. Inequality was the price of civilization. With the development of machine production, however, the case was altered. Even if it was still necessary for human beings to do different kinds of work, it was no longer necessary for them to live at different social or economic levels. Therefore, from the point of view of the new groups who were on the point of seizing power, human equality was no longer an ideal to be striven after, but a danger to be averted. In more primitive ages, when a just and peaceful society was in fact not possible, it had been fairly easy to believe in it. The idea of an earthly paradise in which men should live together in a state of brotherhood, without laws and without brute labor, had haunted the human imagination for thousands of years. And this vision had had a certain hold even on the groups who actually profited by each historic change. The heirs of the French, English, and American revolutions had partly believed in their own phrases about the rights of man, freedom of speech, equality before the law, and the like, and had even allowed their conduct to be influenced by them to some extent. But by the fourth decade of the twentieth century all the main currents of political thought were authoritarian. The earthly paradise had been discredited at exactly the moment when it became realizable. Every new political theory, by whatever name it called itself, led back to hierarchy and regimentation. And in the general hardening of outlook that set in round about 1930, practices which had been long abandoned, in some cases for hundreds of years—imprisonment without trial, the use of war prisoners as slaves, public executions, torture to extract confessions, the use of hostages and the deportation of whole populations—not only became common again, but were tolerated and even defended by people who considered themselves enlightened and progressive.

It was only after a decade of national wars, civil wars, revolutions and counterrevolutions in all parts of the world that Ingsoc and its rivals emerged as fully worked-out political theories. But they had been foreshadowed by the various systems, generally called totalitarian, which had appeared earlier in the century, and the main outlines of the world which would emerge from the prevailing chaos had long been obvious. What kind of people would control this world had been equally obvious. The new aristocracy was made up for the most part of bureaucrats, scientists, technicians, trade-union organizers, publicity experts, sociologists, teachers, journalists, and professional politicians. These people, whose origins lay in the salaried middle class and the upper grades of the working class, had been shaped and brought together by the barren world of monopoly industry and centralized government. As compared with their opposite numbers in past ages, they were less avaricious, less tempted by luxury, hungrier for pure power, and, above all, more conscious of what they were doing and more intent on crushing opposition. This last difference was cardinal. By comparison with that existing today, all the tyrannies of the past were half-hearted and inefficient. The ruling groups were always infected to some extent by liberal ideas, and were content to leave loose ends everywhere, to regard only the overt act, and to be uninterested in what their subjects were thinking. Even the Catholic Church of the Middle Ages was tolerant by modern standards. Part of the reason for this was that in the past no government had the power to keep its citizens under constant surveillance. The invention of print, however, made it easier to manipulate public opinion, and the film and the radio carried the process further. With the development of television and the technical advance which made it possible to receive and transmit simultaneously on the same instrument, private life came to an end. Every citizen, or at least every citizen important enough to be worth watching, could be kept for twenty-four hours a day under the eyes of the police and in the sound of official propaganda, with all other channels of communication closed. The possibility of enforcing not only complete obedience to the will of the State, but complete uniformity of opinion on all subjects, now existed for the first time.

After the revolutionary period of the Fifties and Sixties, society regrouped itself, as always, into High, Middle, and Low. But the new High group, unlike all its forerunners, did not act upon instinct but knew what was needed to safeguard its position. It had long been realized that the only secure basis for oligarchy is collectivism. Wealth and privilege are most easily defended when they are possessed jointly. The so-called "abolition of private property" which took place in the middle years of the century meant, in effect, the concentration of property in far fewer hands than before; but with this difference, that the new owners were a group instead of a mass of individuals.

Individually, no member of the Party owns anything, except petty personal belongings. Collectively, the Party owns everything in Oceania, because it controls everything and disposes of the products as it thinks fit. In the years following the Revolution it was able to step into this commanding position almost unopposed, because the whole process was represented as an act of collectivization. It had always been assumed that if the capitalist class were expropriated, Socialism must follow; and unquestionably the capitalists had been expropriated. Factories, mines, land, houses, transport—everything had been taken away from them; and since these things were no longer private property, it followed that they must be public property. Ingsoc, which grew out of earlier Socialist movement and inherited its phraseology, has in fact carried out the main item in the Socialist program, with the result, foreseen and intended beforehand, that economic inequality has been made permanent.

But the problems of perpetuating a hierarchical society go deeper than this. There are only four ways in which a ruling group can fall from power. Either it is conquered from without, or it governs so inefficiently that the masses are stirred to revolt, or it allows a strong and discontented Middle Group to come into being, or its loses its own self-confidence and willingness to govern. These causes do not operate singly, and as a rule all four of them are present in some degree. A ruling class which could guard against all of them would remain in power permanently. Ultimately the determining factor is the mental attitude of the ruling class itself.

After the middle of the present century, the first danger had in reality disappeared. Each of the three powers which now divide the world is in fact unconquerable, and could only become conquerable through slow demographic changes which a government with wide powers can easily avert. The second danger also, is only a theoretical one. The masses never revolt of their own accord, and they never revolt merely because they are oppressed. The recurrent economic crises of past times were totally unnecessary and are not now permitted to happen, but other and equally large dislocations can and do happen without having political results, because there is no way in which discontent can become articulate. As for the problem of overproduction, which has been latent in our society since the development of machine technique, it is solved by the device of continuous warfare . . . which is also useful in keying up public morale to the necessary pitch. From the point of view of our present rulers, therefore, the only genuine dangers are the splitting off of a new group of able, underemployed, power-hungry people, and the growth of liberalism and skepticism in their own ranks. The problem, that is to say, is educational. It is a problem of continuously mold-ing the consciousness both of the directing group and of the larger executive group that lies immediately below it. The consciousness of the masses needs only to be influenced in a negative way.

Given this background, one could infer, if one did not know it already, the general structure of Oceanic society. At the apex of the pyramid comes Big Brother. Big Brother is infallible and all-powerful. Every success, every achievement, every victory, every scientific discovery, all knowledge, all wisdom, all happiness, all virtue, are held to issue directly from his leadership and inspiration. Nobody has ever seen Big Brother. He is a face on the boardings, a voice on the telescreen. We may be reasonably sure that he will never die, and there is already considerable uncertainty as to when he was born. Big Brother is the guise in which the Party chooses to exhibit itself to the world. His function is to act as a focusing point for love, fear, and reverence, emotions which are more easily felt toward an individual than toward an organization. Below Big Brother comes the Inner Party, its numbers limited to six millions, or something less than two per cent of the population of Oceania. Below the Inner Party comes the Outer Party, which, if the Inner Party is described as the brain of the State, may be justly likened to the hands. Below that come the dumb masses whom we habitually refer to as "the proles," numbering perhaps eighty-five per cent of the population. In the terms of our earlier classification, the proles are the Low, for the slave populations of the equatorial lands, who pass constantly from conqueror to conqueror, are not a permanent or necessary part of the structure.

In principle, membership in these three groups is not hereditary. The child of Inner Party parents is in theory not born into the Inner Party. Admission to either branch of the party is by examination, taken at the age of sixteen. Nor is there any racial discrimination, or any marked domination of one province by another. Jews, Negroes, South Americans of pure Indian blood are to be found in the highest ranks of the Party, and the administrators of any area are always drawn from the inhabitants of that area. In no part of Oceania do the inhabitants have the feeling that they are a colonial population ruled from a distant capital. Oceania has no capital, and its titular head is a person whose whereabouts nobody knows. Except that English is the chief lingua franca and Newspeak its official language, it is not centralized in any way. Its rulers are not held together by blood ties but by adherence to a common doctrine. It is true that our society is stratified, and very rigidly stratified, on what at first sight appear to be hereditary lines. There is far less to-and-fro movement between the different groups than happened under capitalism or even in the pre-industrial ages. Between the two branches of the Party there is a certain amount of interchange, but only so much as will ensure that weaklings are excluded from the Inner Party and that ambitious members of the Outer Party are made harmless by allowing them to rise. Proletarians, in practice, are not allowed to graduate into the Party. The most gifted among them, who might possibly become nuclei of discontent, are simply marked down by the Thought Police and eliminated. But this state of affairs is not necessarily permanent, nor is it a matter of principle. The Party is not a class in the old sense of the word. It does not aim at transmitting power to its own children, as such; and if there were no other way of keeping the ablest people at the top, it would be perfectly prepared to recruit an entire new generation from the ranks of the proletariat. In the crucial years, the fact that the Party was not a hereditary body did a great deal to neutralize opposition. The older kind of Socialist, who had been trained to fight against something called "class Privilege," assumed that what is not hereditary cannot be permanent. He did not see that the continuity of an oligarchy need not be physical, nor did he pause to reflect that hereditary aristocracies have always been short-lived, whereas adoptive organizations such as the Catholic Church have sometimes lasted for hundreds or thousands of years. The essence of oligarchical rule is not father-to-son inheritance, but the persistence of a certain world-view and a certain way of life, imposed by the dead upon the living. A ruling group is a ruling group so long as it can nominate its successors. The Party is not concerned with perpetuating its blood but with perpetuating itself. Who wields power is not important, provided that the hierarchical structure remains always the same.

All the beliefs, habits, tastes, emotions, mental attitudes that characterize our time are really designed to sustain the mystique of the Party and prevent the true nature of present-day society from being perceived. Physical rebellion, or any preliminary move toward rebellion, is at present not possible. From the proletarians nothing is to be feared. Left to themselves, they will continue from generation to generation and from century to century, working, breeding, and dying, not only without any impulse to rebel, but without the power of grasping that the world could be other than it is. They could only become dangerous if the advance of industrial technique made it necessary to educate them more highly; but, since military and commercial rivalry are no longer important, the level of popular education is actually declining. What opinions the masses hold, or do not hold, is looked on as a matter of indifference. They can be granted intellectual liberty because they have no intellect. In a Party member, on the other hand, not even the smallest deviation of opinion on the most unimportant subject can be tolerated.

A Party member lives from birth to death under the eye of the Thought Police. Even when he is alone he can never be sure that he is alone. Wherever he may be, asleep or awake, working or resting, in his bath or in bed, he can be inspected without warning and without knowing that he is being inspected. Nothing that he does is indifferent. His friendships, his relaxations, his behavior toward his wife and children, his expression of his face when he is alone, the words he mutters in sleep, even the characteristic movements of his body, are all jealously scrutinized. Not only any actual misdemeanor, but any eccentricity, however small, any change of habits, any nervous mannerism that could possibly be the symptom of an inner struggle, is certain to be detected. He has no freedom of choice in any direction whatever. On the other hand, his actions are not regulated by law or by any clearly formulated code of behaviour. In Oceania there is no law. Thoughts and actions which, when detected, mean certain death are not formally forbidden, and the endless purges, arrests, tortures, imprisonments, and vaporizations are not inflicted as punishment for crimes which have actually been committed, but are merely the wiping-out of persons who might perhaps commit a crime at some time in the future. A Party member is required to have not only the right opinions, but the right instincts. Many of the beliefs and attitudes demanded of him are never plainly stated, and could not be stated without laying bare the contradictions inherent in Ingsoc. If he is a person naturally orthodox (In Newspeak, a *goodthinker*), he will in all circumstances know, without taking thought, what is the true belief or the desirable emotion. But in any case an elaborate mental training, undergone in childhood and grouping itself round the Newspeak words *crimestop, blackwhite,* and *doublethink,* makes him unwilling and unable to think too deeply on any subject whatever.

A Party member is expected to have no private emotions and no respites from enthusiasm. He is supposed to live in a continuous frenzy of hatred of foreign enemies and internal traitors, triumph over victories, and self-abasement before the power and wisdom of the Party. The discontents produced by his bare, unsatisfying life are deliberately turned outwards and dissipated by such devices as the Two Minutes Hate, and the speculations which might possibly induce a skeptical or rebellious attitude are killed in advance by his early acquired inner discipline. The first and simplest stage in the discipline, which can be taught even to young children, is called, in Newspeak, *crimestop. Crimestop* means the faculty of stopping short, as though by instinct, at the threshold of any dangerous thought. It includes the power of not grasping analogies, of failing to perceive logical errors, of misunderstanding the simplest arguments if they are inimical to Ingsoc, and of being bored or repelled by any train of thought which is capable of leading in a heretical direction. *Crimestop,* in short, means protective stupidity. But stupidity is not enough. On the contrary, orthodoxy in the full sense demands a control over one's own mental processes as complete as that of a contortionist over his body. Oceanic society rests ultimately on the belief that Big Brother is omnipotent and that the Party is infallible. But since in reality Big Brother is not omnipotent and the Party is not infallible, there is need for an unwearying moment-to-moment flexibility in the treatment of facts. The key word here is *blackwhite*. Like so many Newspeak words, this word has two mutually contradictory meanings. Applied to an opponent, it means the habit of impudently claiming that black is white, in contradiction of the plain facts. Applied to a Party member, it means a loyal willingness to say that black is white when Party discipline demands this. But it means also the ability to *believe* that black is white, and more, to *know* that black is white, and to forget that one has ever believed the contrary. This demands a continuous alteration of the past, made possible by the system of thought which really embraces all the rest, and which is known in Newspeak as *doublethink*.

The alteration of the past is necessary for two reasons, one of which is subsidiary and, so to speak, precautionary. The subsidiary reason is that the Party member, like the proletarian, tolerates present-day conditions partly because he has no standards of comparison. He must be cut off from the past, just as he must be cut off from foreign countries, because it is necessary for him to believe that he is better off than his ancestors and that the average level of material comfort is constantly rising. But by far the more important reason for the readjustment of the past is the need to safeguard the infallibility of the Party. It is not merely that speeches, statistics, and records of every kind must be constantly brought up to date in order to show that the predictions of the Party were in all cases right. It is also that no change in doctrine or in political alignment can ever be admitted. For to change one's mind, or even one's policy, is a confession of weakness. If, for example, Eurasia or Eastasia (whichever it may be) is the enemy today, then that country must always have been the enemy. And if the facts say otherwise, then the facts must be altered. Thus history is continuously rewritten. This day-to-day falsification of the past, carried out by the Ministry of Truth, is as necessary to the stability of the regime as the work of repression and espionage carried out by the Ministry of Love.

The mutability of the past is the central tenet of Ingsoc. Past events, it is argued, have no objective existence, but survive only in written records and in human memories. The past is whatever the records and the memories agree upon. And since the Party is in full control of all records, and in equally full control of the minds of its members, it follows that the past is whatever the Party chooses to make it. It also follows that though the past is alterable, it never has been altered in any specific instance. For when it has been recreated in whatever shape is needed at the moment, this new version *is* the past, and no different past can ever have existed. This holds good even when, as often happens, the same event has to be altered out of recognition several times in the course of a year. At all times the Party is in possession of absolute truth, and clearly the absolute can never have been different from what it is now. It will be seen that the control of the past depends above all on the training of memory. To make sure that all written records agree with the orthodoxy of the moment is merely a mechanical act. But it is also necessary to *remember* that events happened in the desired manner. And if it is necessary to rearrange one's memories or to tamper with written records, then it is necessary to *forget* that one has done so. The trick of doing this can be learned like any other mental technique. It is learned by the majority of Party members, and certainly by all who are intelligent as well as orthodox. In Oldspeak it is called, quite frankly, "reality control." In Newspeak it is called *doublethink,* though *doublethink* comprises much else as well.

Doublethink means the power of holding two contradictory beliefs in one's mind simultaneously, and accepting both of them. The Party intellectual knows in which direction his memories must be altered; he therefore knows that he is playing tricks with reality; but by the exercise of *doublethink* he also satisfies himself that reality is not violated. The process has to be conscious, or it would not be carried out with sufficient precision, but it also has to be unconscious, or it would bring with it a feeling of falsity and hence of guilt. *Doublethink* lies at the very heart of Ingsoc, since the essential act of the Party is to use conscious deception while retaining the firmness of purpose that goes with complete honesty. To tell deliberate lies while genuinely believing in them, to forget any fact that has become inconvenient, and then, when it becomes necessary again, to draw it back from oblivion for just so long as it is needed, to deny the existence of objective reality and all the while to take account of the reality which one denies—all this is indispensably necessary. Even in using the word *doublethink* it is necessary to exercise *doublethink*. For by using the word one admits that one is tampering with reality; and so on indefinitely, with the lie always one leap ahead of the truth. Ultimately it is by means of *doublethink* that the Party has been able —and may, for all we know, continue to be able for thousands of years—to arrest the course of history.

All past oligarchies have fallen from power either because they ossified or because they grew soft. Either they became stupid and arrogant, failed to adjust themselves to changing circumstances, and were overthrown, or they became liberal and cowardly, made concessions when they should have used force, and once again were overthrown. They fell, that is to say, either through consciousness or through unconsciousness. It is the achievement of the Party to have produced a system of thought in which both conditions can exist simultaneously. And upon no other intellectual basis could the dominion of the Party be made permanent. If one is to rule, and to continue ruling, one must be able to dislocate the sense of reality. For the secret of rulership is to combine a belief in one's own infallibility with the power to learn from past mistakes.

It need hardly be said that the subtlest practitioners of *doublethink* are those who invented *doublethink* and know that it is a vast system of mental cheating. In our society, those who have the best knowledge of what is happening are also those who are furthest from seeing the world as it is. In general, the greater the understanding, the greater the delusion: the more intelligent, the less sane. One clear illustration of this is the fact that war hysteria increases in intensity as one rises in the social scale. Those whose attitude toward the war is most nearly rational are the subject peoples of the disputed territories. To these people the war is simply a continuous calamity which sweeps to and fro over their bodies like a tidal wave. Which side is winning is a matter of complete indifference to them. They are aware that a change of overlordship means simply that they will be doing the same work as before for new masters who treat them in the same manner as the old ones. The slightly more favored workers whom we call "the proles" are only intermittently conscious of the war. When it is necessary they can be prodded into frenzies of fear and hatred, but when left to themselves they are capable of forgetting for long periods that the war is happening. It is in the ranks of the Party, and above all of the Inner Party, that the true war enthusiasm is found. World-conquest is believed in most firmly by those who know it to be impossible. This peculiar linking-together of opposites—knowledge with ignorance, cynicism with fanaticism—is one of the chief distinguishing marks of Oceanic society. The official ideology abounds with contradictions even where there is no practical reason for them. Thus, the Party rejects and vilifies every principle for which the Socialist movement originally stood, and it chooses to do this in the name of Socialism. It preaches a contempt for the working class unexampled for centuries past, and it dresses its members in a uniform which was at one time peculiar to manual workers and was adopted for that reason. It systematically undermines the solidarity of the family, and it calls its leaders by a name which is a direct appeal to the sentiment of family loyalty. Even the names of the four Ministries by which we are governed exhibit a sort of impudence in their deliberate reversal of the facts.

The Ministry of Peace concerns itself with war, the Ministry of Truth with lies, the Ministry of Love with torture, and the Ministry of Plenty with starvation. The contradictions are not accidental, nor do they result from ordinary hypocrisy: they are deliberate exercises in *doublethink*. For it is only by reconciling contradictions that power can be retained indefinitely. In no other way could the ancient cycle be broken. If human equality is to be forever averted—if the High, as we have called them, are to keep their places permanently—then the prevailing mental condition must be controlled insanity.

But there is one question which until this moment we have almost ignored. It is: *why* should human equality be averted? Supposing that the mechanics of the process have been rightly described, what is the motive for this huge, accurately planned effort to freeze history at a particular moment of time?

Here we reach the central secret. As we have seen, the mystique of the Party, and above all of the Inner Party, depends upon *doublethink*. But deeper than this lies the original motive, the never-questioned instinct that first led Thought Police, continuous warfare, and all the other necessary paraphernalia into existence afterwards.

GAMAL ABDAL NASSER

GAMAL ABDAL NASSER, premier of Egypt since 1954, like many of the leaders of new African and Asian nations is a son of a middle-class family. Born in Egypt in 1918, he was fortunate in having a father wealthy enough to educate him. After schooling in Cairo he entered in 1937 the Military College, where, an official biography states, "he was known for his outspokenness and his rebellion against colonialism." During his military training and in his first years of service in the army he met many of the young men who were to be colleagues in the 1952 coup against the corrupt and vicious regime of King Farouk.

In 1942 he became a teacher at the Military College and later attended the Army Staff College. At exactly what point in his career Nasser became a revolutionary is difficult to state. Like so many leaders of recent nationalist movements Nasser was a by-product of an empire. The foreign power, England, that had paramount influence in his country needed native administrators. But such men, once trained, understandably wish to remove all foreign and native officials who stand over them and in the way of their nation's freedom.

During the war that followed the establishment of Israel in 1948 Nasser participated bravely in key battles and was wounded. His chagrin at Egypt's humiliation during the war alienated him completely from Farouk's rule. Gathering together his old friends and newer colleagues from the war with Israel, on July 23, 1952, Nasser helped to overthrow Farouk and to install a revolutionary government. Nasser himself took the premiership two years later. He led the nation in 1956 to safeguard his seizure of the Suez Canal against English, French, and Israeli invaders.

To explain his calling Nasser wrote *Egypt's Liberation, the Philosophy of the Revolution.* The book is one of a number of testaments that were published following the overthrow of Western controls of Asian and African nations after the Second World War. Mixed with Nasser's wishes to bring "justice, progress, and stability" to a new nation, there are the messianism and intellectual naïveté of an indignant and authoritarian political enthusiast who aspires to lead other nations as well as his own against any resurgent Western imperialism.

In the Middle East Nasser's ambition to crush Israel and to unite the Moslem nations has not helped bring peace. Egypt's union with Syria in a new United Arab Republic sparked coups, murders, sabotage, and even American and British armed intervention in Lebanon and Jordan. Nasser's hostility to the West and his need for arms and loans have also made him more friendly toward the Soviet Union than his professions of neutrality in the cold war would lead one to expect. Nevertheless, his attitudes and his regime are examples of a wide variety of responses to the cold war by the new former colonial nations.

The following selection is from *Egypt's Liberation* (Washington, D.C.: Public Affairs Press, 1955).

EGYPT'S LIBERATION

FOR A LONG TIME I have been asking myself: Was it necessary for us, the Army, to do what we did on July 23, 1952?

I have already observed that the revolution marked the realization of a great hope felt by the people of Egypt since they began, in modern times, to think in terms of self-government and to demand that they have the final word in determining their own future. But if that is so, and if what happened on July 23rd was neither a military mutiny nor a popular uprising, why then was it entrusted to the Army, and not to other forces, to bring it about?

I have always been a confirmed believer in the ideal of the military service. It imposes one duty on the Army: that it should die on the frontiers of the motherland. Why did our Army find itself obliged to act in the capital of the motherland instead of on the frontiers?

Again, let me draw attention to the fact that the rout in Palestine, and the defective arms, and the crisis in the Officers' Club were not the real sources from which poured out the torrent: all these were only contributory factors to the speed of the flow; but, as I said before, they were never the real origin.

But why the Army? I have long asked myself this question; I asked it during the stages of hope, thinking and planning prior to July 23rd, and I have continued to ask it during the many stages of action since then.

There were various justifications before July 23rd which made it clear to us why it was necessary for us to do what we did. We used to say, "If the Army does not do this job, who will?" We also used to say, "We have been used by the Despot as a bogey to give the people nightmares; now it is high time that the bogey be turned against the Despot to shatter his own dreams." We said many other things, but we felt to the depth of our beings this was our soldier's duty and that if we failed to discharge it, we would be failing in the sacred trust placed in us.

I confess, however, that the full picture did not become clear in my mind until after a long period of trial after July 23rd. It was the details of this experience which filled in the details of the picture.

THE ROLE OF VANGUARD

I can testify that there were certain critical occasions since July 23rd when I accused myself, my comrades and the rest of the Army, of stupidity and madness for doing what we had done on that day.

Before July 23rd, I had imagined that the whole nation was ready and prepared, waiting for nothing but a vanguard to lead the charge against the battlements, whereupon it would fall in behind in serried ranks, ready for the sacred advance towards the great objective. And I had imagined that our role was to be this commando vanguard. I thought that this role would never take more than a few hours. Then immediately would come the sacred advance behind us of the serried ranks and the thunder of marching feet as the ordered advance proceeded towards the great objective. I heard all this in my imagination, but by sheer faith it seemed real and not the figment of imagination.

Then suddenly came reality after July 23rd. The vanguard performed its task and charged the battlements of tyranny. It threw out Farouk and then paused, waiting for the serried ranks to come up in their sacred advance toward the great objective.

SYMBOL OF THE REVOLUTION

For a long time it waited. Crowds did eventually come, and they came in endless droves—but how different is the reality from the dream! The masses that came were disunited, divided groups of stragglers. The sacred advance toward the great objective was stalled, and the picture that emerged on that day looked dark and ominous; it boded danger. At this moment I felt, with sorrow and bitterness, that the task of the vanguard, far from being completed, had only begun.

We needed order, but we found nothing behind us but chaos. We needed unity, but we found nothing behind us but dissension. We needed work, but we found behind us only indolence and sloth. It was from these facts, and no others, that the revolution coined its slogan.

WEAPON IN THE HANDS OF HATE

We were not yet ready. So we set about seeking the views of leaders of opinion and the experience of those who were experienced. Unfortunately we were not able to obtain very much.

Every man we questioned had nothing to recommend except to kill someone else. Every idea we listened to was nothing but an attack on some other idea. If we had gone along with everything we heard, we would have killed off all the people and torn down every idea, and there would have been nothing left for us to do but sit down among the corpses and ruins, bewailing our evil fortune and cursing our fate.

We were deluged with petitions and complaints by the thousands and hundreds of thousands, and had these complaints and petitions dealt with cases demanding justice or grievances calling for redress, this motive would have been understandable and logical. But most of the cases referred to us were no more or less than demands for revenge, as though the revolution had taken place in order to become a weapon in the hands of hatred and vindictiveness.

THE EVILS OF EGOTISM

If anyone had asked me in those days what I wanted most, I would have answered promptly: To hear an Egyptian speak fairly about another Egyptian. To sense that an Egyptian had opened his heart to pardon, forgiveness and love for his Egyptian brethren. To find an Egyptian who does not devote his time to tearing down the views of another Egyptian.

In addition to all this, there was a confirmed individual egotism. The word "I" was on every tongue. It was the solution to every difficulty, the cure for every ill. I had many times met eminent men—or so they were called by the press—of every political tendency and color, but when I would ask any of them about a problem in the hope he could supply a solution, I would never hear anything but "I."

Economic problems? He alone could understand them; as for the others, their knowledge on the subject was that of a crawling infant. Political issues? He alone was expert. No one else had gotten beyond the a-b-c's of politics. After meeting one of these people, I would go back in sorrow to my comrades and say, "It is no use. If I had asked this fellow about the fishing problems in the Hawaiian Islands, his only answer would be 'I.'"

DUTIES AND RESPONSIBILITIES

I remember visiting once one of our universities where I called the professors together and sat with them in order to benefit from their scholastic experience. Many of them spoke before me and at great length. It was unfortunate that none of them advanced any ideas; instead, each confined himself to advancing himself to me, pointing out his unique fitness for making miracles. Each of them kept glancing at me with the look of one who preferred me to all the treasures of earth and heaven.

I recall that I could not restrain myself, so I stood up and said, "Every one of us is able in his own way to perform a miracle. His primary duty is to bend every effort to his work. And if you, as university professors, were to think of your students' welfare, and consider them as you should, your basic work, you would be in a position to provide us with the fundamental strength to build up our motherland.

"Everyone must remain at his post, to which he should dedicate all his efforts. Do not look at us—we have been forced by circumstances to leave our posts in order to perform a sacred duty. If the motherland had no need for us other than to stay in the ranks of the Army as professional soldiers, we would have remained there."

THE COMPLETE PICTURE

I confess that this whole situation produced in me a psychological crisis; but the events that followed, and my reflections thereon, together with the real meaning I could adduce from them, tended to ease my distress and set me to seek a justification for this situation, which I found when the whole picture of the motherland's plight rose somewhat clearly before my eyes. This clarification, moreover, brought me the answer to the question which had long bothered me, namely: Was it necessary for us, the Army, to do what we did on July 23rd?

The answer is yes, beyond any subterfuge or equivocation. I can say now that we did not ourselves define the role given us to play; it was the history of our country which cast us in that role.

I can now state that we are going through two revolutions, not one revolution. Every people on earth goes through two revolutions: a political revolution by which it wrests the right to govern itself from the hand of tryanny, or from the army stationed upon its soil against its will; and a social revolution, involving the conflict of classes, which settles down when justice is secured for the citizens of the united nation.

Peoples preceding us on the path of human progress have passed through two revolutions, but they have not had to face both simultaneously; their revolutions, in fact, were centuries apart in time. For us, the terrible experience through which our people are going is that we are having both revolutions at the same time.

BETWEEN THE MILLSTONES

This terrible experience stems from the fact that both revolutions have attendant factors which clash and contradict violently. To be successful, the political revolution must unite all elements of the nation, build them solidly together and instill in them the spirit of self-sacrifice for the sake of the whole country. But one of the primary features of social revolution is that it shakes values and loosens principles, and sets the citizenry, as individuals and classes, to fighting each other. It gives free rein to corruption, doubt, hatred and egoism.

We are caught between the millstones of the two revolutions we are fated now to be going through. One revolution makes it obligatory that we unite and love one another, fighting side by side to achieve our ends; the other brings dissension upon us against our desires, causing us to hate each other and think only of ourselves.

Between these two millstones, for example, the 1919 revolution was lost; it was unable to make secure the results it should have achieved. The ranks which formed in 1919 and faced up to tyranny were soon scattered by the outbreak of strife and conflict between individuals and classes. The result was dismal failure. Tyranny tightened its grip afterwards, overtly by means of occupation troops, and covertly through its masked stooges led by Sultan Fuad and King Farouk after him. The people harvested nothing except self-doubt, evil, hatred and rancour between individuals and classes.

ONLY THE ARMY

The hope reposed in the 1919 revolution was thus dimmed. I say dimmed, but not extinguished, because the natural forces of resistance called into being by the great aspirations of our people did not cease to be active and to prepare for a new attempt.

This was the state of affairs which existed after the 1919 revolution, and which singled out the Army as the force to do the job. The situation demanded the existence of a force set in one cohesive framework, far removed from the conflict between individuals and classes, and drawn from the heart of the people: a force composed of men able to trust each other; a force with enough material strength at its disposal to guarantee a swift and decisive action.

These conditions could be met only by the Army.

In this way, as I have already remarked, it was not the Army which defined its role in the events that took place; the opposite is closer to the truth. The events and their ramifications defined the role of the Army in the great struggle to free the nation.

I have been aware since the beginning that our unity is dependent upon our full realization of the nature of circumstances in which we found ourselves, the historical circumstances of our country. For we could not alter the circumstances by the mere stroke of a pen, nor could we turn back the hands of the clock, or advance them—we could not control time. It was not within our power to stand on the road of history like a traffic policeman and hold up the passage of one revolution until the other had passed by in order to prevent a collision. The only thing possible to do was to act as best we could and try to avoid being ground between the millstones.

It was inevitable that we go through the two revolutions at the same time. When we moved along the path of the political revolution and dethroned Farouk, we took a similar step on the path of the social revolution by deciding to limit land ownership.

I continue to believe that the July 23rd revolution must maintain its initiative and ability to move swiftly in order to perform the miracle of traveling through two revolutions at the same time, however contradictory our resulting actions might at times appear.

When one of my comrades came to me saying, "You want unity to face the English, but at the same time you allow the treason courts to continue their work," I listened to him with our great crisis in mind, the crisis of the millstones—a revolution on the one hand which obliges us to unite in one phalanx and to forget the past, and on the other hand, another revolution which demands that we restore lost dignity to our moral values by not forgetting the past. I might have replied that our only salvation lies, as I said before, in maintaining our speed of movement and our initiative, and our ability to travel through two revolutions simultaneously.

This situation does not exist because I wished it, or because all those who participated in the revolution have wished it. It is brought about by the act of fate, the history of our people, and the stage it is passing through at the present time. . . .

As I see it, we were like a sick man who had been shut up in a closed room for a long time. The temperature of the closed room rose high until he was almost choked. All of a sudden a storm blew and shattered the door and windows. The currents of cold air rushed in and the perspiring sick body shivered with chill. The sick man was, to be sure, in need of a breath of air, but it was a powerful gale that blew over him. The frail and exhausted body succumbed to fever.

This was exactly what happened to our society. For us, it was a perilous experience, whereas the Europeans had evolved by an orderly process, gradually bridging the gap between the Renaissance which followed the Middle Ages and the nineteenth century. The stages of evolution there came naturally.

But with us everything came as new and strange. We had been living in isolation, cut off from the rest of the world, especially after the trade with the East had changed routes and traveled via the Cape of Good Hope. Then, suddenly we were coveted by the countries of Europe, since we became for them the bridge to be crossed for their colonies in the east and the south.

Waves of thoughts and ideas came over us while we were not yet developed enough to evaluate them. We were still living mentally in the captivity of the 13th century, in spite of a few manifestations of the nineteenth and afterwards of the twentieth century. Our minds tried to catch up with the caravan of human progress, although we were five centuries or more behind. The pace was fearful and the journey was exhausting.

There is no doubt that this situation is responsible for the lack of a strong and united public opinion in our country. The differences between individuals are great, and between generations they are still greater.

I used to complain that the people did not know what they wanted and could not agree on any program to be followed. Then I realized that I was demanding the impossible and that I had disregarded the circumstances of our society.

We live in a society that has not yet taken form. It is still fluid and agitated and has not yet settled down or taken a stabilized shape. It is in the process of an evolution, striving to catch up with those other nations that have preceded us on the road.

With no intention of flattering, I believe that our people have nonetheless achieved a miracle. It is quite possible that any other nation, under the same conditions, would have faded away, drowned by such currents as have but submerged us. But we have stood firm against the violent flood. It is true that we have almost lost our balance on certain occasions, but it is our destiny never to have fallen but that we rose again.

Sometimes I examine the conditions of an average Egyptian family among the thousands of families living in Cairo. It may be that the father is a turbaned farmer who has been born outside the city, in the heart of the countryside. The mother is a descendant of a Turkish family. The sons are being educated at an English style school, while the daughters attend schools run on the methods of the French. And all this is being backgrounded by a curious mixture of thirteenth and twentieth century ways of life.

I consider all this, and feel a deep understanding of the confusion that besets our national life and of the disorder from which we plan escape. Then I reflect: this society will develop form, consolidate and become a strong, homogeneous and unified whole. But first we must make ourselves ready to survive and make growth during the period of transition. . . .

Can we possibly ignore the fact that there is an African continent which Fate decreed us to be a part of, and that it is also decreed that a terrible struggle exists for its future—a struggle whose results will be either for us or against us, with or without our will? Can we further ignore the existence of an Islamic world, with which we are united by bonds created not only by religious belief, but also reinforced by historic realities? As I have said once, Fate is no jester.

It is not without significance that our country is situated west of Asia, in contiguity with the Arab states with whose existence our own is inter-woven. It is not without significance, too, that our country lies in northeast Africa, overlooking the Dark Continent, wherein rages a most tumultuous struggle between white colonizers and black inhabitants for control of its un-limited resources. Nor is it without significance that, when the Mongols swept away the ancient capitals of Islam, Islamic civilization and the Islamic heritage fell back on Egypt and took shelter there. Egypt protected them and saved them, while checking the onslaught of the Mongols at 'Ain Jalut. All these are fundamental realities with deep roots in our lives which we cannot—even if we try—escape or forget.

A ROLE IN SEARCH OF A HERO

I do not know why I recall, whenever I reach this point in my recollections as I meditate alone in my room, a famous tale by a great Italian poet, Luigi Pirandello—"Six Characters in Search of an Author." The pages of history are full of heroes who created for themselves roles of glorious valor which they played at decisive moments. Likewise the pages of history are also full of heroic and glorious roles which never found heroes to perform them. For some reason it seems to me that within the Arab circle there is a role, wandering aimlessly in search of a hero. And I do not know why it seems to me that this role, exhausted by its wanderings, has at last settled down, tired and weary, near the borders of our country and is beckoning to us to move, to take up its lines, to put on its costume, since no one else is qualified to play it.

NUMERICAL BALANCE OF POWER

. . . When I try to analyze the elements of our strength, there are three main sources which should first be taken into account.

The first of these sources is that we are a community of neighboring peoples linked by all the material and moral ties possible, and that we have characteristics and abilities and a civilization which have given rise to three holy religions—factors which cannot be ignored in the effort to build a secure and peaceful world. So much for the first source.

As for the second source of strength, it is our land itself and its position on the map—that important, strategic position which embraces the cross-roads of the world, the thoroughfare of its traders and the passageway of its armies.

There remains the third source: oil—a sinew of material civilization with-out which all its machines would cease to function. The great factories, producing every kind of goods; all the instruments of land, sea and air communication; all the weapons of war, from the mechanical bird above the clouds to the submarine beneath the waves—without oil, all would turn back to naked metal, covered with rust, incapable of motion or use.

Here I would like to pause for a moment to deal with the subject of oil. Perhaps its existence as a material necessity which has been established by facts and figures will afford a useful model for our analysis of the importance of the sources of strength in our country.

I read recently an article published by the University of Chicago on the world oil situation. It would be a good thing if every Arab could read it, grasp its implication, and see the great significance revealed by its statistics.

The article points out, for example, that in the Arab countries the effort to extract oil requires comparatively little capital. Oil companies spent 60 million dollars in Colombia, beginning in 1916, and did not discover a drop of oil until 1936. They spent $44 million in Venezuela, and did not get a drop of oil for 15 years. They spent $39 million in the Dutch Indies before they struck oil. According to the article, it all adds up to the fact that the cost of producing a barrel of oil in North America is 78 cents, in South America, 48 cents, but in the Arab countries the cost is only 10 cents.

The article further says that the center of world oil production has shifted from the United States, where oil wells are going dry, where the cost of land is going up and the wages of workers have risen, to the Arab area, where the fields are still virgin, where vast tracts of land continue to cost almost nothing, and where labor is comparatively cheap. Half the proved reserves of oil in the world lie beneath Arab soil, the remainder being divided among the United States, Russia, the Caribbean area and other sections of the globe.

It is a fact, too, that the average daily production per well is 11 barrels in the United States, 230 barrels in Venezuela, and 4,000 barrels in the Arab area. Have I made clear how great is the importance of this element of strength? I hope so.

So we are strong. Strong not in the loudness of our voices when we wail or shout for help, but rather when we remain silent and measure the extent of our ability to act; when we really understand the strength resulting from the ties binding us together, making our land a single region from which no part can withdraw, and of which no part, like an isolated island, can be defended without defense of the whole.

THE INTERIOR OF THE DARK CONTINENT

If we consider next the continent of Africa—I may say without exaggeration that we cannot, under any circumstances, however much we might desire it, remain aloof from the terrible and sanguinary conflict going on there today between five million whites and 200 million Africans. We cannot do so for an important and obvious reason: we are *in* Africa. The peoples of Africa will continue to look to us, who guard their northern gate, and who constitute their link with the outside world. We will never in any circumstances be able to relinquish our responsibility to support, with all our might, the spread of enlightenment and civilization to the remotest depths of the jungle.

There remains another important reason. It is that the Nile is the life artery of our country, bringing water from the heart of the continent.

As a final reason, the boundaries of our beloved brother, the Sudan, extend far into the depths of Africa, bringing into contiguity the politically sensitive regions in that area.

The Dark Continent is now the scene of a strange and excited turbulence: the white man, representing various European nations, is again trying to redivide the map of Africa. We shall not, in any circumstance, be able to stand idly by in the face of what is going on, in the false belief that it will not affect or concern us.

I will continue to dream of the day when I will find in Cairo a great African institute dedicated to unveiling to our view the dark reaches of the continent, to creating in our minds an enlightened African consciousness, and to sharing with others from all over the world the work of advancing the welfare of the peoples of this continent.

ISLAMIC PARLIAMENT

When I consider the 80 million Muslims in Indonesia, and the 50 million in China, and the millions in Malaya, Siam and Burma, and the nearly 100 million in Pakistan, and the more than 100 million in the Middle East, and the 40 million in the Soviet Union, together with the other millions in far-flung parts of the world—when I consider these hundreds of millions united by a single creed, I emerge with a sense of the tremendous possibilities which we might realize through the cooperation of all these Muslims, a cooperation going not beyond the bounds of their natural loyalty to their own countries, but nonetheless enabling them and their brothers in faith to wield power wisely and without limit.

And now I go back to that wandering mission in search of a hero to play it. Here is the role. Here are the lines, and here is the stage. We alone, by virtue of our place, can perform the role.

K. M. PANNIKAR

THE RETREAT of Western power from its former imperial territories after 1945 left behind a diverse heritage. Hatred for Western racism, imperialism, and capitalism was combined with the determination by native leaders to adopt the best Western techniques and programs to create strong and modern nations in former colonial areas. The actual diversity of these programs of nation-building precludes generalizations about the extent to which the West has much to fear or to admire in the new African and Asian countries. It is clear that any aggression against these nations would strengthen hostility to the West and increase the opportunities for the imperialistic Soviet Union to pose as a friend of oppressed people everywhere.

The so-called national revolutions were usually led by native intellectuals, soldiers, and administrators who had been given a consciousness of modernity, as well as their basic training in modern government by former Western masters. The freeing of the nations produced a large literature by these leaders assessing the nature of Western imperialism and announcing their programs for the future. Perhaps the most notable of these studies was written by the eminent Indian scholar and statesman, Kavalam Madhara Pannikar (1896–). Like Nehru and other important Indian leaders, Pannikar was born in India but finished his education in England. At Oxford he was the first Indian to obtain first class honors in history (1917) after which he returned to India, a university post, and the national struggle for freedom. Pannikar's political and diplomatic experience is too long and diverse to permit summary but he has served at the highest levels as an ambassador (China, France, Egypt), in the United Nations, and in the Indian states and national government. He has also been a leading student of Indian and Asian history, a newspaper editor, novelist, playwright, and poet.

His book *Asia and Western Dominance* has been received in the West as perhaps the outstanding attempt to take a long full view of the period 1492–1945, the five centuries during which Europe spread its power over the globe and then had to retreat. Pannikar's balanced assessment of the Western role in the East is remarkable in a man who for 30 years struggled to overthrow imperial power in order to win freedom for India.

The following selection is taken from the conclusion of *Asia and Western Dominance* (New York: John Day, 1954).

ASIA AND WESTERN DOMINANCE

THE PERIOD of maritime authority over Asia, beginning with Vasco da Gama's arrival and ending with the departure of the Western fleets from their bases on the Asian continent, covers an epoch of the highest significance to human development. The changes it directly brought about and the forces it generated in the countries of Asia in contact with Europe for a period of 450 years, and subjected to Western domination for over a century, have effected a transformation which touches practically every aspect of life in these countries . . . The social, political and economic conditions of Asian countries have undergone revolutionary changes as a result of these contacts and influences. Their religious and philosophical systems, the material set-up of their lives and their mental outlook have been affected to an extent which it is not possible for anyone to estimate now. Everywhere in Asia this prolonged contact has produced ferments, the possible effects of which cannot be foreseen.

Though it is impossible to anticipate what Asia will make of these influences in the future, and how the different Asian countries will transmute the experiences, ideas and institutions in the crucible of their racial characteristics, history and social tradition, there is no gainsaying the fact that the massiveness of the changes that have already taken place, the upsurges which have radically transformed their ancient societies, and the ideas that have modified their outlook involve a qualitative break with the past which justly entitles the changes to be described as revolutionary. The period of European control of the States of Asia is a dividing line in their history, for both by resistance and by adaptation they have had to call forth new vitality and consciously adapt themselves to new ideas by which alone they were able gradually to recover their independence and strength. . . .

The third phase of European relations with Asia, which begins with the middle of the nineteenth century, is the period of imperialism in the true sense of the word. The transformation is completed earliest in India, which provides the pattern for the rest, for the Dutch in Indonesia, for the French in Indo-China, for all the nations in respect of China. The imperialist relationship, involving large-scale capital investment, had the result of importing into Asia advanced technical skills and scientific knowledge. Railway construction, which was the main field of capital investment, required the importation of engineers. Rivers had to be spanned, tunnels had to be built, and the lines, once constructed, had to be maintained. Imported technical skill, except at the highest levels, became too costly, and as a result engineering colleges and schools became unavoidable. The spread of technical knowledge in the East, of which this is merely an example, was a necessary result of capital investment. It was not possible to keep Asian nationals out of this knowledge, for returns on capital depended on finding technical skill locally. In regard to industry also, a similar movement became noticeable. European industries established in Calcutta, Bombay and Shanghai had to depend, at least in their lower levels, on locally trained personnel. With the advancement of knowledge among local populations it became impossible to prevent Asian capital from encroaching on European industrial monopolies. In India, cotton mills began to spring up in Bombay and Ahmedabad. In Shanghai, which had become practically a European city, Chinese industrialists found no difficulty in setting up factories in imitation of European models. Railway construction in China, which was a subject of furious international competition, when it was first taken up, soon became an activity of the Chinese Government. Thus, in its primary characteristic, imperialism as an export of capital carried into Asia the seeds of its own destruction.

In its second aspect, that is territorial expansion for providing areas for exploitation, European imperialism in the nineteenth century, under the humanitarian impulses of the liberal movement, embarked on a policy of education, welfare schemes and even political training. Direct administration of vast populations naturally created new interests. The administrative authorities had no direct connection with or interest in trade, the officers being, at least according to English tradition, recruited from the middle classes with public school training. So in India, and to some extent in Indonesia, a contradiction developed within the structure of imperialism in which the administrative authorities were inclined to emphasize the welfare aspect of their work, while the commercial interests still considered the territories as areas for exploitation. . . . In fact political authority, combined with the humanitarian ideals of the era of peace, brought a sense of responsibility towards "the backward peoples." No danger to the supremacy of Europe was suspected as being inherent in this development, for even at the end of the nineteenth century the Europeans—even the most progressive among them—were convinced that their superiority was divinely ordained and was safe at least for centuries to come. The idea that the Chinese, weak, immobilized and without industrial potential, could stand up and fight the European within a measurable time, or that Indians could compete with the British in trade or industry, or that the hundreds of Indonesian islands could be united in opposition to the Dutch, would have sounded ludicrous to a European in the Augustan age of imperialism. Therefore the humanitarian ideal of educating the Asian people and of encouraging them to develop at least those skills which were necessary for the more effective discharge of the white man's mission, was pursued without any sense of fear.

Also, the complexities of direct administration of vast areas like India and Indonesia made it necessary to develop a large body of indigenous administrative personnel. In the period of imperialism this was unavoidable. The apparatus of modern States, run largely by local talent, had to be built up, providing the Asian peoples both with administrative training and with knowledge and understanding of the mechanism of modern government. This is particularly important, for one of the main differences between the earlier periods of history and the political systems that developed in the nineteenth and twentieth centuries lay in the vast administrative systems which touched every aspect of life which the State organizations of the nineteenth and twentieth centuries represented. In the eighteenth century, neither in Europe nor in Asia was there a Government which was also an administration in the present-day sense. In the latter half of the nineteenth century European countries, having had to deal with more and more complex problems of industry, commerce, social and economic welfare, organized the vast mechanism of modern administration, which neither Frederick the Great nor Napoleon could have conceived, and which earlier political thought would have resisted bitterly as encroachments on liberty. The Asian State-systems, though essentially bureaucratic and therefore "administrative" and not political, were, however, limited to land administration and defence. Neither Akbar nor Kang Hsi nor Hideyoshi had any conception of the State beyond that of collecting revenue, ensuring peace and fighting the enemies. After their time—the time of Akbar in India, Kang Hsi in China and Hideyoshi in Japan—the State idea had not developed. Thus in the middle of the nineteenth century Japan was still feudal, China was governed under an autocracy and the provincial viceroys were semi-independent officials directly under the Emperor, and in India even the British Government thought only of governing as little as possible and not interfering with the people. The administrative system which the Crown developed in India and which every colonial administration felt compelled to develop in its territory, provided not merely the first conception of the modern State to the Asian mind, but equipped it with the mechanism necessary to realize it in time. Even in regard to China, this is a development which has not received sufficient attention. The organization of the imperial customs department under Western leadership, and the growth of posts and telegraphs, provided China with the pattern of new administration.

The third aspect of territorial expansion—of the era of imperialism—was the popular sentiment of responsibility for "moral well-being" which found its most characteristic expression in the missionary work. The conscience of the people, especially of the Protestant countries, was aroused by the fact that in the areas directly governed by them or under their influence hundreds of millions lived and died without the chance of salvation. We have already seen the zeal and blind devotion of men like William Hudson Taylor, the founder of the China Inland Mission. He was only the most notable example among thousands of serious-minded, pious men who devoted themselves to the cause of evangelization and spent their lives in the different countries of Asia. Though the results of their religious activities were negligible and often led only to reactions which they least expected, their interest in the life and well-being of the common people, and their efforts to break down the barrier of race, had the benefit of bringing the West nearer to Asia. Also, their educational and medical work in the interior of India, China and Burma had far-reaching consequences.

It is necessary to emphasize that the contact between the peoples of the East with Europeans began really only in the era of imperialism. In the 300 and odd years that preceded it (from 1498 to 1858) this contact was limited, even in India, to narrow circles, and had not penetrated even into the ruling classes. With direct administration, development of educational systems, exploitation instead of trade, the contact gradually extended to different levels. Slowly Asian youths began to find their way to European seats of learning. We have seen how Japan began with a planned system of sending selected young men to understand the secrets of Europe. China's "first hundred" promoted by the Great Viceroy Tsang Kuo-fan was an abortive attempt in the same line. The first impulse which took young Indians across the seas was not to probe the mysteries of European life, but the more material consideration of a chance to compete in the Civil Service examinations. But soon this movement assumed immense proportions, and a large proportion of the students who went to Europe were dedicated to the study of such subjects as engineering, medicine, forestry, geology and chemistry, apart of course from law and social sciences. A similar movement took large numbers of Indo-Chinese students to Paris and Indonesians to Leyden. The prestige of German technical advances attracted a growing number of students to the universities of the Reich.

The period between 1870–1914 thus witnessed the first large-scale meeting of Asian and Western minds. The mental ferment that this contact caused in Asia cannot be dealt with simply as a challenge to the established traditions of the past which they represented; it also sowed the seed of the new thought which in time replaced the learning of the ancients and placed the Asian countries on the road to intellectual progress. The Asian countries again became scientifically minded. Their social thought took them beyond Confucius and Manu: their history began to take in the lessons of other countries. Besides all this, the essential point for our purpose is that in every one of the countries of Asia, the leadership in the movement which ultimately displaced European supremacy belonged to those who had been trained by the West under the aegis of imperialism. Not only Mahatma Gandhi and Jawaharlal Nehru, but the founders of the Indian National Congress and the successive generations of Congress leaders were trained in the West. In Japan, it is the group of explorers sent to the West by the Shogunate that led the movement for the reorganization of the State. In China, though the deposition of the Manchus was not the work of Western-educated people, the building up of the revolutionary movement that followed was led by men of Western training. In Indonesia, Indo-China, Burma and Ceylon it is the men and women educated in the West—the "Wogs" (Westernized Oriental gentlemen) as the European contemptuously called them—that provided the leadership.

It will thus be seen that in the relationship between the East and the West, the vital period which witnessed the realization of European ambitions and generated at the same time movements which led to its destruction was the period of Imperialism. . . .

In the case of Europe the position was very different from that of earlier foreign influences on Asian life. Though the Hindus, the Chinese and the Japanese liked to believe that their own cultures were superior they could not deny either the superiority of Western knowledge or the greater strength —though not the stability—of the European social and economic organization. They were convinced, after a short period of intoxication, that their own religious and moral systems were superior, but they had ample proofs to satisfy them that Europe was intellectually centuries ahead of them. European learning therefore earned the respect of all Asians during the whole century, and, what is more, European social and economic organization provided a norm which, in part, they accepted enthusiastically and, in part, was forced upon them by world conditions. This had never happened before, at least in the history of India and China. Five hundred years of Muslim authority in North India had not forced the Hindus to change their social ideas in regard to caste and untouchability—in fact, it had strengthened them. Hundreds of years of foreign rule had not forced the Chinese to question the validity of Confucian teachings, or doubt the canonical value of the *Book of Filial Piety*. Today, however, as a result of the contact with the West, untouchability has been abolished and caste no longer is king in India. Confucius has ceased to be the Most Holy One in China where the slogans of the youth movement execrate him. There is no doubt, therefore, that the changes that have been brought about in Asian life by the contact with Europe are radical and far-reaching, and will not disappear as many observers are inclined to think with the rise of a new Asian sentiment.

It would be useful at this point to examine the major features where Western influences are likely to be permanent, and the extent of these influences on Asian societies in general.

The first and perhaps the most abiding influence is in the sphere of law. In all Asian countries the legal systems have been fundamentally changed and reorganized according to the post-revolutionary conceptions of nineteenth-century Europe. The first country in which this change was introduced was India where, under the influence of Thomas Babington Macaulay, new legal principles were systematically introduced and applied. . . .

The imposing and truly magnificent legal structure, under which not only 360 million people of India but the millions in Pakistan and Burma have lived during the last 100 years, has changed the basis of society in a manner which few people realize. Though the personal laws of different communities may be different, the penal law is the same for all. This has been supplemented by a vast corpus of legislation, which has profoundly affected every kind of social relationship. The position of women in India, for example, has undergone changes which Hindu thought even fifty years ago would have considered revolutionary. Even the personal law of the Hindus in respect of their succession, inheritance, marriage, joint family and the rest of what may be called their special social organization, has been greatly modified by the legal systems now in force in India. There can be no going back on this— in any case to the old Hindu ideas. The transformation brought about by the new legal doctrines of the West is a permanent one and is likely to outlast the more spectacular changes in many other fields.

The transformation of legal systems is not confined to areas which were directly administered by colonial Powers like Indonesia, Indo-China and Burma. Japan voluntarily brought into force a modern system of law which has been in operation now for over half a century. It was on the strength of the liberal and modern character of its legal system and judicial administration that Japan was able to obtain the early abrogation of extra-territoriality in her Empire. In China, though the elaborate civil and criminal codes introduced by the Kuomintang have now been discarded, the tendency has not been to go back to the legal systems of the pre-revolutionary era but to introduce something which is considered even more progressive. At least in the realm of family relationships the new laws are more advanced than in any Western country.

Economic structures may break down, leading to widespread misery; political organizations may disappear under the impact of new revolutionary forces. In these spheres Asian societies may conceivably be thrown back after a period. But it is difficult to imagine how the basic ideas of the new legal systems could be changed so easily, unless civilization itself is extinguished in these areas. For such a pessimism there is no valid reason in countries like India, China and Japan where elaborate legal systems survived unimpaired even periods of dreadful confusion and anarchy. We may therefore assume that the great changes brought about in social relationships by the introduction and acceptance of new legal systems under the influence of Europe will be an abiding factor in the civilization of Asia.

It is not possible to speak with the same certainty about the political and social structures brought about as a result of the conflict with Europe. The forms of Government, the nature of political rights, democracy in its widest sense, local and municipal administrations—these may all disappear, change their character or survive only in attenuated and unrecognizable forms in certain areas. And yet at the present time they constitute the most spectacular change in Asia. No country in the East is now governed under a system of "Oriental despotism." Even Japan, where the divinely descended Emperor reigns in an unbroken line of succession, is now clothed with all the paraphernalia of a democratic constitution. In fact, the norm of Government in the East has become a republic. While in Europe there are still six sovereigns and a Grand Duchess, in non-Islamic Asia there are only three monarchies (Japan, Siam and Nepal), while all the nations which acquired their independence or threw off foreign domination have been proclaimed republics. India, Burma, Indonesia and China, seats of ancient empires and kingdoms, are all now republican governments. It may be a changing phase, for no political system can be considered permanent. But it is fairly certain that even if democratic institutions in Asia, as in some Latin American Republics, get metamorphosed into something quite different from their original shape and form, or do not develop in the spirit of genuine vigour, the principles of "Oriental despotism" will not come back. Hindu monarchies, though strictly secular, require the support of religion for their sanction. The Son of Heaven cannot be restored to the dragon throne without the people of China going back to the five principles of obedience, or keeping up the pretence of the mandate of heaven and of annual sacrifices to report on his work to the higher powers. In fact, "Oriental despotism" has at all times reflected certain ideas and principles accepted generally by the people. Those ideas and principles no longer find any acceptance. So, even if an Emperor by some miracle sits on a new peacock throne in the Red Fort at Delhi, or holds court in the Forbidden City, he cannot create among the people the same veneration which an unbroken tradition of monarchy creates among a people. Once the thread is broken the mystique of the doctrine also ceases.

So, while the new democratic institution in Asia may not last beyond a few generations or may become transformed quite early in replicas of "Liberian democracies," it would yet be true to say that the principles of government that Asia has accepted from the West constitute a major and qualitative change whose influence will penetrate far into the future. The new social structure has to be reflected in new political institutions. Further, the commercial economy resulting in the participation in world trade; industrialization, bringing along with it both the power of accumulated wealth and of organized labour; the growth of organized city life, different from that of the great capital towns of the past; all these, and numerous other factors, render a reversion to the old political structures, based as they were on a rural economy and on land tax, altogether out of the question. No doubt the political structures of the Asian countries, though they may now copy the institutions of the West, may in time evolve their own patterns which may not too closely follow the traditions of Europe. But any return to a purely Asian tradition is ruled out by the growth of social, economic and political forces which no country in Asia had to deal with in the past.

The growth of great cities, themselves centres of political and economic dynamism, is a result of European contacts, the immense significance of which has not been fully appreciated. There was a great urban life and culture previous to the arrival of Europeans in India, China and Japan. . . . But the towns and cities in India, when they were not great capitals, were merely great centres of population, sometimes important from the point of view of trade, often from the point of view of religious sanctity. They did not involve any civic tradition. The same was the case in China.

The new cities, which grew up as a result of European contacts, Bombay, Calcutta and Madras, Shanghai, Tientsin, Singapore, Colombo, Jakarta, etc., represent a new principle: the organization of the city as an independent unit. In Madras, Calcutta and Bombay we have the full paraphernalia of European city life, with sheriffs, mayors, corporations and aldermen. From this point of view, the organization of the Municipal Committee of Shanghai by the British merchants, and its phenomenal growth during a period of seventy years, may represent a greater and more far-reaching change than the control exercised by the foreigners on the imperial court. These cities, with others developed on their model, now constitute a major feature of Asian life. . . . It is the city that has created the wealthy middle classes in India, China and other Asian countries. The emergence of the middle classes as both leaders in political and economic life and as reservoirs of essential scientific skills, has been in the main the outcome of the new life in the cities. The possibility of the great cities surviving as centres of civilization, even if regression set in elsewhere inside the countries of Asia much in the same way as in Medieval Europe, cannot be overlooked, and if that happens the credit for the survival of the new life in the great cities will certainly belong to Europe.

Another point, one which arises directly out of Europe's long domination over Asia, is the integration of vast territories into great nation States of a kind unknown in the previous history of Asia. India, for instance, all through her long history, had never been welded together into a single State as she is now. Her territorial unity was in the past emphasized by the unity of Hinduism, by the similarity of Sanskrit culture and by a political impulse which led every leading Empire in India to undertake the task of conquering and bringing under one dominion the territory extending from the Himalayas to Cape Comorin. This relentless urge moved every dynasty of importance in the past; but it was never realized.

Even under the British, vast areas, amounting to nearly two-fifths of the territory of India, were under the rule of semi-independent princes. For the first time in history India has been integrated into a single State living under the same constitution and subject to the same laws. Unquestionably this was the result of a hundred years of British administration, which imposed a unity on the peoples of India, both by the machinery of Government which it created and by the forces of resistance to which it gave rise. Even more striking is the case of Indonesia. In the past these islands had never been united into a single political organization. Nor was it ever the dream of the great Empires of Java and Sumatra to weld the whole archipelago into one State. The Sailendra monarchs of Srivijaya, in the greatness of their maritime strength, never dreamed of claiming suzerainty even over the whole of Java, let alone Borneo, Moluccas and the innumerable islands of the Sundas. When the Europeans arrived in the islands there was no feeling of Indonesian unity. The present unity of the islands is therefore the result of the four hundred and fifty years of contact with Europe, and the political and economic ties created by the Dutch.

Even in regard to China, the resistance to Europe has brought about an integration of territory the importance of which cannot be overlooked. From the earliest times to the time of Kuomintang Revolution, the great provinces of China, though governed under the direct orders of the Emperor, were not subjected to uniform policies. . . . Even in matters relating to war, the whole Empire was never engaged. . . . It was only after the Kuomintang Revolution (1925–7) that the first effective steps were taken to convert China into a nation State with a proper central administration, a regular national army and defined national policies with regard to important matters. And yet, the Kuomintang was not wholly successful, as old-time war lords like a true product of Victorian culture, the dominance of Sanskrit traditions was clearly visible. He used every known Western form, drama, short story, lyrical poetry, essay; but the voice that spoke was of one nurtured on the epics of Vyasa and Valmiki, the poetry of Kalidasa and Jayadeva and the songs of Vidyapathi, Kabir and Mira. During the last thirty years, however, the literatures of the great Indian languages have undergone a revolutionary change. They are no longer concerned with the refinements of classical style. They borrow freely from all the literatures of the West, the drama from Ibsen, Shaw, Pirandello and Chekhov, the short story and the novel from their French and Russian masters, and poetry from the latest schools in Europe. No longer have they any concern with the lotus and the moon, the swans, the chatakas and other time-worn symbolisms of the past.

The new art forms, especially in prose, owe little or nothing to the earlier Indian traditions. It may in fact be said that the thought of Europe is at last being acclimatized in India by the popular literature of the last quarter-of-a-century. The social and political content of the new writing is essentially cosmopolitan, influenced widely by the breakdown of the old society in Europe and by the dynamism of Marxist thought in the widest sense. Also it is not only through literature in its creative aspect that this message is being spread. Weeklies, magazines, newspapers, cinema films and radio constitute the ever widening popularity of the new literature. "There is no writer under forty today," say Mulk Raj Anand, "who will deny that at one time or another he did not subscribe to the dominant influence of the Progressive Writers Association, which was formed in 1935. And the movement which this body generated has unleashed a tremendous amount of poetry and prose in which the conditions of our existence are constantly related to the extreme limit of possibilities." In fact, it is the New Life—not Europe—that finds its voice echoed in a thousand mouths.

This, few will deny, widens every day the gulf between the past and the present in Asia. It is the change in the language that is in many ways the most far-reaching transformation in Asia, for it is not merely the reflection of the changed mind but is in itself the instrument of continuing changes, for the new languages of Asia represent a new semantics, a new world of ideas and thought which is reaching a larger and larger circle every day.

Yen Hsi-shan in Shansi and the Muslim "Ma" war-lords in Kan
others refused to give more than nominal allegiance to the Central (
ment. But the forces of integration were at work, and the unific;
China, completed by the People's Republic, was but the consumm
the tendencies already in operation.

So far we have discussed the changes in the social and political ins
which arose directly from Asia's contact with Europe. A vaster and
more significant change is in the realm of ideas, which it is not pc
discuss in this treatise. What the introduction of modern science:
and wider knowledge of the world has done to the mind of /
supremely fascinating subject of inquiry. What the outcome of that !
tion will be no one is yet in a position to foresee or forecast. Ob\
has affected every aspect of life, religion, arts, language, processes
ing and speculative philosophies which had long held sway over 1
of men. If the Eastern religions and philosophies have not been disp
in fact are stronger today, it does not mean that they have not 1
profound changes. As against other religions and other philoso
have more than held their own; but they have also had to unde
transformations to resolve the conflicts which modern science,
rival religions, forced on them. Thus the new interpretations of
and Hinduism reflect in a large measure the influence of mo
mostly arising from contact with Europe.

Philosophy and religious thinking, however much they may ir
people in general, are the special interests of intellectuals. But
language, and it is here that the influence of Europe has been 1
able. From the great literatures of China, India and Japan to
languages spoken only by a few million people, everywhere tl
of the West overshadows past traditions. The Literary Revoluti(
(1918–21) will perhaps be considered in future a more signi
than the many revolutions that country has undergone in this
day in China the forms of writing which are followed show lit
fluence of the classics, and are modelled upon the literature of tl

The instance of India is even more significant. In the great
India there has been no revolutionary break with the past. In f
1914, though the Western forms of writing had taken deep ro
guages, and novels, short stories and dramas were popular and
hold on the public mind, it was the classical tradition that was s
In poetry especially, India, with its three thousand years (
heritance, clung to the forms and manner of Sanskrit classicisr
a great extent by the literary renaissance of the Middle Ages. E

HENRY A. KISSINGER

THE EXPLOSION of two atomic bombs over Japan at the end of the Second World War heralded a fundamental transformation in the nature of international politics. The subsequent improvement of atomic bombs and the successful development of hydrogen bombs and rockets by the United States and Soviet Russia made it probable that another major war would annihilate much of mankind and hideously poison those able to survive the blast and fire.

In the decade after 1945 diplomats and military men were engaged in a terrible double task—trying to prevent war and yet preparing for a war that people everywhere regarded with well-founded dread. War seemed impossible but political insecurity and tension increased national stockpiles of so-called total weapons. As a "nuclear stalemate" developed and as both sides in the cold war recognized that, at the margin, the worst might still come, Western and Communist governments tried to devise cold war strategies that would bring victory without carnage. Negotiations of the utmost complexity, technically and diplomatically, were carried on at all levels to lessen the danger involved in nuclear arms production and warfare.

As Soviet strategy seemed to shift to "peaceful" economic, ideological, and political conquest of the free world, there was danger that even this strategy or occasional small-scale military aggression would lead to "brush-fire" wars like the Korean conflict (1950–53). Clearly, if the nations were prepared to fight only nuclear wars or to regard any open aggression as a cause for general war, international tension would become unbearable and might indeed invite a preventive nuclear onslaught.

The continuous worried search by diplomats for release from the specter of the hydrogen bomb was accompanied by heated debate in the Western nations about defense strategy. Countless books, articles, speeches, and meetings advocated one military plan or another. In 1957 a young American political scientist, Henry A. Kissinger, published *Nuclear Weapons and Foreign Policy*. It was regarded by many as an outstanding statement of defense problems in the age of nuclear armaments and an equally pertinent plea for more diversified military preparedness by the West.

Kissinger was born in Germany in 1923, and came to America in 1938. He served with distinction in the American army in the Second World War. After the war he returned to Harvard from which he was graduated with the highest honors in 1950. His graduate work in political science at Harvard was equally distinguished and he joined the Harvard faculty in 1954. In the same year the Council on Foreign Relations named Kissinger to head a study by three committees of American responses to Soviet action. Kissinger's much-acclaimed work is actually a general concluding analysis based on the results of the inquiry. The author has also been an official policy consultant for the United States government and has published well-received books and articles on the Congress of Vienna, and on individual themes explored in his book on nuclear strategy.

This selection comes from *Nuclear Weapons and Foreign Policy* (New York: Harper and Brothers, 1957).

☙

NUCLEAR WEAPONS AND FOREIGN POLICY

IN GREEK MYTHOLOGY, the gods sometimes punished man by fulfilling his wishes too completely. It has remained for the nuclear age to experience the full irony of this penalty. Throughout history, humanity has suffered from a shortage of power and has concentrated all its efforts on developing new sources and special applications of it. It would have seemed unbelievable even fifty years ago that there could ever be an excess of power, that everything would depend on the ability to use it subtly and with discrimination.

Yet this is precisely the challenge of the nuclear age. Ever since the end of the second World War brought us not the peace we sought so earnestly, but an uneasy armistice, we have responded by what can best be described as a flight into technology: by devising ever more fearful weapons. The more powerful the weapons, however, the greater becomes the reluctance to use them. At a period of unparalleled military strength, President Dwight D. Eisenhower summed up the dilemma posed by the new weapons technology in the phrase "there is no alternative to peace."

It is only natural, of course, that an age which has known two world wars and an uneasy armistice since should have as its central problem the attainment of peace. It is paradoxical, however, that so much hope should concentrate on man's most destructive capabilities. We are told that the growth of the thermonuclear stockpiles has created a stalemate which makes war, if not too risky, at least unprofitable. The power of the new weapons technology is said to have brought about a tacit nonaggression treaty: a recognition that war is no longer a conceivable instrument of policy and that for this reason international disputes can be settled only by means of diplomacy. And it has been maintained that the peaceful uses of nuclear energy have made irrelevant many of the traditional motivations for wars of aggression because each major power can bring about a tremendous increase in its productive capacity without annexing either foreign territory or foreign labor.

These assertions fit in well with a national psychology which considers peace as the "normal" pattern of relations among states and which has few doubts that reasonable men can settle all differences by honest compromise. So much depends, however, on the correctness of such propositions that they must be subjected to close scrutiny. For if recourse to force has in fact become impossible, diplomacy too may lose its efficacy. Far from leading to a resolution of tensions, the inability to use force may perpetuate all disputes, however trivial. It may be a strange fulfillment of the hopes of centuries for universal peace, that, when finally realized, it should contribute to the demoralization of the international order and that diplomacy, so long considered the alternative to war, should emerge as its complement.

It is an illusion of posterity that past international settlements were brought about entirely by reasonableness and negotiating skill. In a society of "sovereign" states, a power can in the last resort vindicate its interpretation of justice or defend its "vital interests" only by the willingness to employ force. Even during the period of seemingly greatest harmony, it was understood that a negotiation which failed did not return matters to their starting point but might call other pressures into play. The motive force behind international settlements has always been a combination of the belief in the advantages of harmony and the fear of the consequences of proving obdurate. A renunciation of force, by eliminating the penalty for intransigence, will therefore place the international order at the mercy of its most ruthless or its most irresponsible member.

This becomes a particular problem in a revolutionary period like the present, because the distinguishing feature of revolution is the priority it gives to change over the requirement of harmony. Contemporary international relations would therefore be difficult at best, but they take on a special urgency because never have so many different revolutions occurred simultaneously. On the political plane, the postwar period has seen the emergence into nationhood of a large number of peoples hitherto under colonial rule. To integrate so many new states into the international community would not be a simple matter at any time; it has become increasingly formidable because many of the newly independent states continue to inject into their policies the revolutionary fervor that gained them independence. On the ideological plane, the contemporary ferment is fed by the rapidity with which ideas can be communicated and by the inherent impossibility of fulfilling the expectations aroused by revolutionary slogans. On the economic and social plane, millions are rebelling against standards of living as well as against social and racial barriers which had remained unchanged for centuries. And these problems, serious enough in themselves, are manipulated by the Sino-Soviet bloc which is determined to prevent the establishment of an equilibrium and which is organized to exploit all hopes and dissatisfactions for its own ends.

All these revolutions have been taking place, moreover, at a moment when international relationships have become truly global for the first time. Classical history was confined to the Mediterranean basin with little awareness of events in the rest of the world. In the Middle Ages, the policy of the European powers was conducted in almost complete isolation from that of the Asian empires. And when in the eighteenth and nineteenth centuries the European powers developed world-wide interests, they were enabled by the temporary passivity of the Asian states to conduct their affairs as an extension of European diplomacy. With modern technology, and in the face of the contemporary intellectual ferment, there are no longer any isolated areas, however. Any diplomatic or military move immediately involves world-wide consequences.

Statesmanship has never faced a more fearful challenge. Diplomacy is asked to overcome schisms unparalleled in scope and to do so at a moment when the willingness to utilize the traditional pressures available to it—even during periods of harmony—is constantly diminishing. To be sure, the contemporary revolution cannot be managed by force alone; it requires a consistent and bold program to identify ourselves with the aspirations of humanity. But when there is no penalty for irresponsibility, the pent-up frustrations of centuries may seek an outlet in the international field instead of in domestic construction. To the extent that recourse to force has become impossible, the restraints of the international order may disappear as well.

Moreover, whatever the possibilities of identifying ourselves with the aspirations of the rest of humanity, we are confronted by two revolutionary powers, the U.S.S.R. and Communist China, which pride themselves on their superior understanding of "objective" forces and to which policies unrelated to a plausible possibility of employing force seem either hypocrisy or stupidity. Because harmony between different social systems is explicitly rejected by Soviet doctrine, the renunciation of force in the face of it will create a vacuum into which the Soviet leadership can move with impunity. Because the Soviet rulers pride themselves on their ability to "see through" our protestations of peaceful intentions, our only possibility for affecting their actions resides in the possession of superior force. For the Soviet leadership has made every effort to retain its militancy. It has been careful to insist that no technological discovery, however powerful, can abolish the laws of history and that real peace is attainable only after the triumph of communism. "We will bury you," Nikita S. Khrushchev has said, and the democracies would have been spared much misery but for their penchant on insisting that dictators do not mean what they say. "Political power," Mao Tse-tung has said, "grows out of the barrel of a gun. . . . Yes . . . we are advocates of the omnipotence of the revolutionary war, which . . . is good and is Marxist."

The dilemma of the nuclear period can, therefore, be defined as follows: the enormity of modern weapons makes the thought of war repugnant, but the refusal to run any risks would amount to giving the Soviet rulers a blank check. At a time when we have never been stronger, we have had to learn that power which is not clearly related to the objectives for which it is to be employed may merely serve to paralyze the will. No more urgent task confronts American policy than to bring our power into balance with the issues for which we are most likely to have to contend. All the difficult choices which confront us—the nature of our weapons systems, the risks diplomacy can run—presuppose an ability on our part to assess the meaning of the new technology. . . .

The destructiveness and speed of modern weapons have ended our traditional invulnerability, and the polarization of power in the world has reduced our traditional margin of safety. The intermediary states having lost either the power or the will to resist aggression by themselves, we can no longer count on other powers to hold a line while we are assessing events and making up our minds on whether a threat has become unambiguous. Resistance to aggression henceforth is no longer a problem of our coming into a battle long in progress in order to tilt the scales, as was the case with our entry into World War I and World War II. It depends not only on our strength, but also on our ability to recognize aggression. In the nuclear age, by the time a threat has become unambiguous it may be too late to resist it.

Moreover, nuclear technology makes it possible, for the first time in history, to shift the balance of power solely through developments within the territory of another sovereign state. No conceivable acquisition of territory—not even the occupation of Western Europe—could have affected the strategic balance as profoundly as did the Soviet success in ending our atomic monopoly. Had a power in the past sought to achieve a comparable strategic transformation through territorial expansion, war would have been the inevitable consequence. But because the growth of nuclear technology took place within sovereign territory, it produced an armaments race as a substitute for war. And immediately before us is the prospect of many other powers upsetting the strategic balance in this manner. Within another fifteen years the diffusion of nuclear technology will make inevitable the possession of nuclear weapons by many now secondary states.

Finally, as the power of weapons has increased, the forms of attack have multiplied, not only militarily, but also politically and psychologically. The age of the hydrogen bomb is also the age of internal subversion, of intervention by "volunteers," of domination through political and psychological warfare.

In such circumstances, our notion of aggression as an unambiguous act and our concept of war as inevitably an all-out struggle have made it difficult to come to grips with our perils. Because the consequences of our weapons technology are so fearsome, we have not found it easy to define a *casus belli* which would leave no doubt concerning our moral justification to use force. We have been clear that we would resist aggression, the goal of which we have identified with world domination, and our military policy has prescribed all-out war for meeting this contingency. But, faced with the implications of our power, we have had to learn that world domination need not be aimed at directly by means of final showdown. Even Hitler's attack on the international order took the form of such issues as his claims to Danzig and the Polish Corridor, which at the time seemed to the United States not to warrant embarking on war. In the face of the methodical, almost imperceptible advances of the Kremlin, subtly adjusted so that no one of its individual steps seems "worth" an all-out war, it has become even more apparent that resistance to aggression depends importantly on the price that must be paid. The dilemma of our postwar policy can be described as the quest for the "pure" case of aggression, in which our military doctrine, the provocation and our principles would be in harmony.

We have, therefore, been vulnerable to Soviet maneuvers in two ways. Because we have considered the advantage of peace so self-evident, we have been tempted to treat each act of Soviet intransigence as if it were caused by a misunderstanding of our intentions or else by the malevolence of an individual. There is a measure of pathos in our continued efforts to discover "reasonable" motives for the Soviet leaders to cease being Bolsheviks: the opportunities to develop the resources of their own country, the unlimited possibilities of nuclear energy, or the advantages of expanding international trade. The Kremlin has been able to exploit this attitude by periodically launching policies of "peaceful coexistence," which inevitably raised the debate whether a "fundamental" shift has occurred in Soviet purposes, thus lulling us before the next onslaught. On the other hand, because our strategic doctrine recognized few intermediate points between total war and total peace, we have found it difficult, during periods of Soviet belligerency, to bring the risks of resistance into relationship with the issues which have actually been at stake. . . .

Nuclear weapons, only a short decade ago a difficult and delicate engineering feat, have now become plentiful. They can be produced in all sizes, from weapons of a fraction of the explosive power of the bombs used over Hiroshima and Nagasaki, to thermonuclear devices (popularly called H-bombs) which represent the same increase of explosive power over the Hiroshima bomb as the original atomic bomb did over the largest "blockbusters" of World War II: a thousandfold increase. The Hiroshima and Nagasaki bombs had an explosive equivalent of 20 thousand tons TNT (20 kilotons). Today "tactical" nuclear weapons as small as 100 tons of TNT equivalent have been developed. Thermonuclear devices exist which have an explosive equivalent of 20 million tons of TNT (20 megatons), and there is no upper limit: thermonuclear and nuclear weapons can be made of any desired explosive power. . . .

And the new technology is awesome. The lethal radius of the weapons dropped over Hiroshima and Nagasaki—the area within which destruction was total and the proportion of fatalities was in excess of 75 per cent—was 1½ miles. Their blast and heat effects destroyed or set fire to buildings within a radius of another 4.4 square miles in Hiroshima and 1.8 square miles in Nagasaki. The explosions of the first atomic bombs killed between 70 thousand and 80 thousand in Hiroshima and 35 thousand in Nagasaki; the direct injuries were between 100 thousand and 180 thousand in Hiroshima and between 50 thousand and 100 thousand in Nagasaki. The collateral effects of radiation may not become fully apparent for several decades.

For all their horror the atom bombs dropped on the two Japanese cities were puny compared to present weapons. The damage they caused was restricted to a relatively small area, and even the effects of radiation were generally confined to the area covered by heat and blast damage. The thermonuclear weapons, on the other hand, do not possess this relative measure of discrimination. Theoretically, their explosive power is unlimited. A 20 megaton weapon, which is easily within the range of our capabilities and will soon be within that of the Soviet Union, has a lethal radius of 8 miles; its area of total destruction is 48 square miles. Within that area at least 75 per cent of the population would be killed and all the remainder severely injured.

Nor are the damage and casualties exhausted by the direct effects. If it touches the ground, the fireball of a megaton weapon sucks up particles of earth and buildings and deposits them downwind as radioactive material. Depending on meteorological conditions, the radioactive fall-out may cover an area of 10,000 square miles or a territory larger than the state of New Jersey. A successful attack on fifty of the most important metropolitan areas of the United States would thus bring under fire 40 per cent of our population, 50 per cent of our key facilities and 60 per cent of our industry.

At this scale of catastrophe, it is clear that the nature of war has altered. Our traditional insistence on reserving our military effort for an unambiguous threat and then going all-out to defeat the enemy may lead to paralysis when total war augurs social disintegration even for the victor. During the period of our atomic monopoly, it was possible to rely on our nuclear stockpile to deter all forms of aggression because we could inflict punishment without fear of retaliation. But in the face of the newfound Soviet capability to inflict devastating damage on the United States, our reluctance to engage in an all-out war is certain to increase. To be sure, we shall continue to insist that we reject the notion of "peace at any price." The price of peace, however, cannot be determined in the abstract. The growth of the Soviet nuclear stockpile is certain to widen the line between what is considered "vital" and what is "peripheral" if we must weigh each objective against the destruction of New York or Detroit, of Los Angeles or Chicago.

It can be argued that the fear of all-out war is bound to be mutual, that the Soviet leaders will, therefore, share our reluctance to engage in any adventures which may involve this risk. But because each side may be equally deterred from engaging in all-out war, it makes all the difference which side can extricate itself from its dilemma only by initiating such a struggle. If the Soviet bloc can present its challenges in less than all-out form it may gain a crucial advantage. Every move on its part will then pose the appalling dilemma of whether we are willing to commit suicide to prevent encroachments, which do not, each in itself, seem to threaten our existence directly but which may be steps on the road to our ultimate destruction.

The growing Soviet nuclear stockpile, coupled with the diversification of nuclear technology, places precisely this possibility in the hands of the Soviet leadership. It can engage in military actions ranging from the employment of conventional forces to the use of "tactical" nuclear weapons of a size which will raise serious doubt as to whether they "warrant" the resort to all-out war. Every Soviet move of this nature will provide us with an incentive to defer a showdown to a more propitious moment or to a clearer provocation. An all-or-nothing military policy will, therefore, play into the hands of the Soviet strategy of ambiguity which seeks to upset the strategic balance by small degrees and which combines political, psychological and military pressures to induce the greatest degree of uncertainty and hesitation in the minds of the opponent. Moreover, to the extent that we become dependent on the most absolute applications of our power, even the secondary states may be able to blackmail us; because the force suitable for an all-out war is not really designed for dealing with local wars, or because we will be inhibited from using it by the fear of its impact on world opinion. . . .

The notion that a new war would inevitably start with a surprise attack on the United States has been basic to postwar United States strategic thought. Reinforced by the memory of Pearl Harbor, it has provided the background for our preponderant concern with the problem of all-out war. Thus a vicious circle has been set up. The more total the sanctions of our weapons technology have become, the more absolute we have imagined the provocation that would alone justify unleashing it. The more we have become convinced that a war would start with an attack on the continental United States, the more fearsome the strategy we have devised to resist it. In the process, we have not realized how abstract and one-sided the notion of a surprise attack has been, particularly at a time when the Soviet Union possessed neither a nuclear arsenal nor a long-range air force. We have failed to see how vulnerable it has left us to the preferred form of Soviet aggression: internal subversion and limited war. By concentrating on measures to defeat a Soviet attempt to neutralize us physically, we have given the Soviet leadership an opportunity to strive to neutralize us psychologically by so graduating their actions that the provocation would never seem "worth" an all-out war, the only form of war our doctrine took into account.

If our military doctrine in the immediate postwar period had difficulty in coming to grips with our most likely dangers, it had few doubts about the strategy for conducting any war that might break out. A war would be global and it would be won by our superior industrial potential. Since war would start with a surprise attack, our best defense lay in "our ability to strike back quickly with a counteroffensive, to neutralize the hostile attack at its source . . . by striking at the vitals of the aggressor." The doctrine of massive retaliation was far from new at the time Secretary John Foster Dulles proclaimed it.

The postulate that deterrence was to be achieved by strategic striking power and that victory depended on inflicting maximum destruction on the aggressor was never questioned. On the contrary, each service justified its requirements by the contribution it could make to a strategy of strategic bombing. . . . Even our alliances were justified primarily in terms of the air bases they afforded us.

Thus the strategy developed in the immediate postwar period did not depend on nuclear weapons. Rather it added them almost as an afterthought to a familiar military doctrine, as a more efficient explosive to destroy enemy industrial centers. There were several reasons for this: a feeling of moral revulsion about the destructiveness of nuclear weapons, a fear that the weapons, if flaunted, would make an understanding with the U.S.S.R. more difficult, and real uncertainty about the meaning of the new technology. Above all, the nuclear weapons were taken as another indication of our inherent technological superiority. At least subconsciously, it was felt that as long as we retained our atomic monopoly, we could not possibly be faced with an overt challenge. . . .

Our military policy was directed to only two contingencies: a direct attack on the United States and a direct attack on Western Europe. It offered no solutions either to Soviet moves in other areas or to the gradual overturning of the balance of power through subversion, guerrilla activity, or indeed the ending of our atomic monopoly. In fact, it denied that these were the concern of our military policy. In its insistence on a "pure" cause of war, it had developed a *casus belli,* surprise attack on the territorial United States, which did not happen to fit any of the issues actually in dispute, from the division of Germany, to the satellite orbit, to international control of the atom. This was the real gap between our military policy and our diplomacy. . . .

This was the strategy of a satisfied power, content with its place in the world, eager to enjoy its benefits undisturbed. Its defensiveness was a symptom of our desire to project the pattern of our domestic affairs abroad, to construct an international order animated entirely by the consciousness of the evident advantages of harmony. But the tragic element of our struggle with the U.S.S.R. resided in the insistence of the Soviet leaders on treating the protestations of our peaceful intentions as due to ignorance or hypocrisy, which caused them to seek to neutralize our power by all means. Thus the more we protested our horror of war, the more we removed the Soviet leaders' inhibitions against expanding their influence. Because we could think of no positive goals for which to contend (two of the national objectives listed by General Bradley concerned the preservation of the status quo and the other two dealt with economic matters), there was a quality of abstractness about our military planning which was only barely obscured by our concern with technical problems. "Everything the enemy has we must have bigger and better," said Representative Paul J. Kilday during the B-36 hearings, and his views reflected an attitude which inhibited consideration of doctrine by confusing it with our technological achievement. . . .

When reality clashes with our expectations of it, frustration is the inevitable consequence. For Korea caught us completely unprepared not only militarily but above all in doctrine. Our strategic thinking had defined but two causes of war: a surprise attack on the continental United States and military aggression against Western Europe. It had foreseen all-out war as the only solution, and it had relied on our industrial potential, backed by strategic air power, as the means to victory. Secretary Acheson's speech of January 12, 1950, which excluded Korea from our defensive perimeter, was no more than an application of fundamental United States strategy, no different in content and almost identical in language with a statement made by General Douglas MacArthur nine months previously. In an all-out war with the U.S.S.R. Korea was indeed outside our defensive perimeter, and its fate would depend on the outcome of a struggle fought in other theaters. As a result, the Korean war fitted no category of our strategic thought. It was not initiated by a surprise attack against the United States, nor directed against Europe, nor did it involve the U.S.S.R. It was a war to which an all-out strategy seemed peculiarly unsuited. It has been remarked more than once that had the Korean war not actually taken place, we would never have believed that it could have.

It was a courageous decision to resist an aggression so totally at variance with all previous planning. The penalty we paid for the one-sidedness of our doctrine, however, was the necessity for improvising a new strategy under the pressure of events, as well as a growing difficulty in harmonizing our political and military objectives. Throughout the Korean war we were inhibited by the consciousness that this was not the war for which we had prepared. The result was an endless conflict between the commanders who, being responsible for fighting the war, sought to apply literally the doctrine that victory means crushing the enemy, and the responsible officials in Washington who, in the light of their preconceptions and the global nature of their responsibilities, could only consider the Korean war a strategic diversion or a deliberate feint on the part of the adversary. . . .

The literalness of our notion of power is well expressed in our certainty that a war against the U.S.S.R. must necessarily take the form of a battle with the U.S.S.R., probably over Europe. This was the real bone of contention between MacArthur and his opponents, and it was also reflected in their disputes over the nature of preparedness. "You have got a war on your hands," MacArthur maintained, "and you can't just say, 'Let that war go on indefinitely while I prepare for some other war.' . . . Does your global plan for defense of this United States . . . consist of permitting war indefinitely to go on in the Pacific? . . . If you are not going to bring the war to a decisive conclusion, what does the preparedness mean?" The difficulty was, of course, that it was precisely the global nature of our defense plans which left us unprepared for the challenges of the Korean war. The assumption behind our military planning had been that our wars would be fought against a principal enemy and a major challenge, but that our forces-in-being need only be powerful enough to gain us the time to mobilize our industrial potential. This doctrine presupposed two related contingencies: that other powers would bear the initial brunt of aggression and that the threat would be unambiguous.

But in the aftermath of World War II, this doctrine was no longer adequate to the situation because the smaller states had lost either the strength or the will to resist by themselves. Since their ability to resist aggression had now come to depend on our willingness to commit our forces at the very beginning of any war and their decision to resist at all depended more and more on their confidence in our ability to act at once, our forces-in-being would have to be strong enough to absorb the first blows and to strike back effectively without delay. The quandary presented by a limited war turned out to be that its challenge was either not made by a principal enemy or that it did appear as an all-out challenge. In Korea the opponent was first a satellite of the third order and then Communist China. The attack was directed not against us or our installations, but against a remote area from which we had withdrawn our troops scarcely a year before. In such a situation, it is little wonder that our preoccupation with an all-out strategy caused us to consider the Korean war as an aberration and a strategic diversion. . . .

The importance of a strategy of intermediate objectives is now all the greater because of the changing nature of deterrence. The notion that deterrence can be achieved by only one of the two superpowers is no longer applicable, if it ever was. So long as the United States enjoyed an absolute atomic monopoly, even a small number of nuclear weapons exercised a powerful deterrent effect. Then we could protect many areas by the threat of massive retaliation. But, as the Soviet nuclear stockpile has grown, the American strategic problem has been transformed. No matter how vast our remaining margin in the number and refinement of weapons, henceforth not only they but we must fear them. In this situation deterrence can no longer be measured by absolute numbers of bombs or planes. To seek safety in numerical superiority, or even in superior destructiveness, may come close to a Maginot-line mentality—to seek in numbers a substitute for conception. Moreover, in many fields where our present weapons system is already adequate to its mission, new technological advances will add much less to our effective strength than to that of the Soviet bloc. This seems to be true for the Intercontinental Ballistic Missile and the atomic submarine. And when weapons can be made of any desired degree of destructiveness a point will be reached at which additional increments of destructive power yield diminishing returns. What is the sense in developing a weapon that can destroy a city twice over?

Thus for the first time in military history we are facing the prospect of a stalemate, despite the absolute superiority of one side in numbers of weapons and in their technology. It is a stalemate not so much in equality of power as in the assessment of risks; an uneasy balance which shifts from region to region with the importance which the contenders attach to each and with the alternatives which their strategy and their weapons systems present them. To be sure, the key to survival is the possession of an adequate retaliatory force. Without a powerful Strategic Air Force no other measures are possible. But all-out surprise attack does not exhaust the range of our perils;

although the greatest threat, it may, in fact, be the least likely danger. Mastery of the challenges of the nuclear age will depend on our ability to combine physical and psychological factors, to develop weapons systems which do not paralyze our will, and to devise strategies which permit us to shift the risks of counteraction to the other side. The pernicious aspect of the absence of doctrinal agreement among the services is that it tempts each of them to aim for absolute solutions in purely military terms. And it therefore inhibits the attempt to bridge the gap which has opened between power and the objectives for which power can be used.

A revolution cannot be mastered until it is understood. The temptation is always to seek to integrate it into familiar doctrine: to deny that a revolution is taking place. Nothing is more important, therefore, than to attempt an assessment of the technological revolution which we have witnessed in the past decade, in order to determine its impact on our, by now, traditional concepts of surprise attack, deterrence, coalition policy, and all-out war.

ANDRÉ MALRAUX

RCHAEOLOGIST, art-historian, soldier of fortune, novelist, government official—
these have been only the major callings of André Malraux (1901–   ), one
of the best known and most highly regarded of living French writers.
Malraux, Parisian by birth, was educated to become an oriental archaeologist and
he spent the years 1923–29 in the Far East, depicting in his first important novel,
The Conquerors (1928), the early stages of the Asian national revolutions of our
time. He himself fought in the Chinese revolutionary struggles of the 1920s and
was for a time an official in the Kuomintang. Malraux left China after the collapse of the revolution and traveled in the Middle East before returning to Paris
and the enthusiasms of the political left of the 1930s. In 1933 his novel, *Man's
Fate,* about the Chinese revolution of 1924, won the Goncourt Prize.

For the next six years Malraux wrote other novels and essays, worked on a
treatise on esthetics, did editorial work, went on an air expedition over the
Arabian desert, and, increasingly, became involved in "popular front" and Communist political causes. He organized an air corps for the Spanish republican
forces during the civil war (1936–39) against the Fascists, personally flying 65
sorties over the enemy lines and being wounded twice. From his experiences in
Spain Malraux wrote *Man's Hope* (1938), another well-received political novel.
In 1939 Malraux returned to Paris where he joined the tank corps as a private at
the start of the Second World War. He was captured by the Germans, escaped,
and became a guerrilla leader in the Resistance. He was wounded in 1944 in the
Normandy invasion but recovered and soon joined the forces of General Charles
De Gaulle, who had led the Free French during the war and who became provisional president of France after the peace of 1945. Malraux's Communist
sympathies had now been transformed into a strong anti-Soviet position.

Malraux has been continuously loyal to De Gaulle's plans for a revivified
democratic French political community. Since De Gaulle's call to power in 1958
as president of the Fifth Republic, Malraux has served in his government. Meanwhile, Malraux had also published his long awaited work on art history and
esthetics, known in English as *The Voices of Silence* (1953). Behind it lay 30
years of study and reflection. Like most of Malraux's writing its thematic and
conceptual brilliance rests on uneven or even dubious scholarship and on colorful
aperçus, rather than sustained logical argument.

One of the principal themes in the work is the effect modern technology and
communications have had in providing the world of the twentieth century with
a common culture derived from the entire world and the whole of man's past. The
sense of freedom and vitality in Malraux's conception of modern culture is unusual, for one of the paradoxes in Western civilization in the last generation has
been that the impressive increase in its technical, scientific, and industrial power
has failed to inspire any solid confidence in modern Western ideals among important Western intellectuals. Indeed, among many Western thinkers, defeatism

and a self-pitying skepticism run along with a recurrent conviction that in their time the future is to be seen everywhere except in the West.

The following selection is taken from a 1947 address by Malraux to a Gaullist rally in Paris. It is a typical Malraux performance, darting and fragmentary but yet a trenchant analysis of the faltering confidence of Europeans in Europe and of men of the West in the West. The speech is found in the appendix to the paperback version of *The Conquerors* (Boston: Beacon Press, 1956).

THE WEAKENING OF THE
EUROPEAN CONSCIENCE

THE EUROPEAN SPIRIT is the object of a double metamorphosis. Here, in our opinion, lies the drama of the twentieth century: While the political myth of internationalism is in its death throes, an unprecedented internationalization of culture is going on briskly.

All through the past century, from the times when Michelet raised his mighty voice to those of the mighty voice of Jaurès, a sort of evidence pointed out that, the less a man was bound to his country, the more man he would become. Here was neither baseness nor error: it was the form hope took at that period. Victor Hugo believed that the United States of Europe would develop by their own power and that they would be the prelude to the United States of the World. The fact is that the United States of Europe will come into being amid suffering and that the United States of the World are a long way off. . . .

What we have learned is that the vast disdainful gesture with which Russia is sweeping aside the song "The Internationale"—which will remain bound, whether Russia wills or no, to the eternal dream men have of justice—is scattering the dreams of the nineteenth century at one fell swoop. We know henceforth that we shall not be the more man by being the less Frenchman but that we shall thereby be simply the more Russian. For better or for worse, we are bound to the motherland. And we know we shall not create the European without her; whether we wish to or not, we must create the European upon her foundation.

While this immense hope was dying, while each man was being thrown back upon his native land, a profusion of works burst upon civilization. Music and the plastic arts had just invented their art of printing. Translations entered freely into every land: Colonel Lawrence went cheek by jowl with Benjamin Constant, and the Garnier foreign classics elbowed the Payot series.

Finally the cinema came to birth. And at present a Hindu woman seeing *Anna Karenina* may be weeping, as a Swedish actress and an American director express the Russian Tolstoy's idea of love. . . .

If we have united the dreams of the living but little, at least we have better united the dead.

And this evening, here in this hall, we can say without being ridiculous: "You, here present, are the first generation of mankind to inherit the world in its entirety."

How is such an inheritance possible? Let us be careful to notice that each of the vanished civilizations applies to but one portion of man. Medieval culture was primarily a culture of the heart; that of the eighteenth century, primarily a culture of the mind. From age to age, successive civilizations, appealing to successive elements in man, were successively superimposed; they are deeply embodied only in their heirs. Inheritance is always a metamorphosis. The true inheritor of Chartres, of course, is not the art of Saint Sulpice: it is Rembrandt. Michelangelo, believing he was reproducing antiquity, was actually producing Michelangelo.

What could those of whom our civilization was born have said to one another? It unites a Greek element, a Roman element, and a Biblical element, as we all know. But what exchange could there have been between Julius Caesar and the Prophet Elijah? An exchange of insults! In order that the dialogue of Christ and of Plato might truly come to birth, Montaigne had necessarily to be born.

The metamorphosis whence life is born is produced only within the inheritor.

Who lays claim to this metamorphosis today? The United States, the Soviet Union, and Europe. And let us at the outset discard the bunkum according to which cultures are at perpetual fisticuffs as States are. The example of Latin America suffices to prove how idiotic this is. At the present hour and without the slightest fighting, Latin America is busy reconciling what she wishes to receive from the Anglo-Saxon world and what she wishes to receive from the Latin. There are irreducible political conflicts, but it is absolutely false to state that conflicts of cultures are irreducible by definition. They may happen to be most seriously so or they may happen to be so not at all.

Let us spare ourselves that absurd Manicheism, that separation of angels friendly to the orator from demons hostile to the orator, which has become fashionable whenever America and Russia are discussed. What we think of Russian policy toward our country is clear. We think that the same forces which made Russia wager on France at the time of the Liberation are today making her wager implacably against France. And we intend to put matters to rights. But Stalin is of no more significance as against Dostoevsky than Moussorgsky's genius is a guarantee of Stalin's policy.

Let us first examine the claim of the United States to the cultural heritage of the world. In America there is no culture which elects to be specifically American. This is an invention by Europeans. Americans consider that a particular setting of life exists. They consider America as a country without roots, as an urban country; a country ignorant of that ancient and profound relation with trees and stones in which the oldest geniuses of China and the oldest geniuses of the Occident are united; a country that has the advantage over us of being able and willing to welcome with like heart all the heritages of the world; a country whose principal museum displays in one and the same room Roman statues facing our Occident from afar and Tang statues facing Chinese civilization from afar.

Yet a great culture, even on an epic scale, is not the studio of a superior antiquary. As soon as Europe is set aside, American culture is infinitely more a realm of knowledge than a realm of organic culture.

In another sense, America is at present endowing the arts of the masses—radio, cinema and press—with their proper accent.

Her art appears to us most specifically American when it is an art of the masses. And, after all, I dare say there is not such a great difference between the spirit of their *Life* magazine and our *Samedi Soir*. The simple truth is that there are more Americans than Frenchmen.

Finally America possesses its own particular romanticism. But, once again, is this romanticism specifically American? There is incontestably an American attitude toward the world which permanently reduces the latter to its romantic datum. But need I remind you that in *The Three Musketeers* Richelieu is a great man less because of what he made of France than because he apprised the King of the studs missing in the set His Majesty had given Anne of Austria? For the moment, America represents romanticism more than any other country, but she probably manifests this in terms of a country of masses. True culture ranges far beyond such problems.

What is the opinion of cultured Americans?

They believe that American culture is but one of the national cultures of Western civilization, and that there is no more difference between high American and high French culture than there is between high French culture and high British culture or what used to be high German culture. In Europe, we are not at all similar people! Believe me, the divergence between Behaviorism and Bergsonism is no less signal than the divergence between Bergson and Hegel. In a word, in relation to us on the cultural plane, America has never considered herself as a part of the world. She has always reckoned herself a part of our world.

There is less American art than there are American artists. We all observe the same systems of values; these do not possess all the essentials of Europe's past, but all that is essential in them harks back to Europe, I repeat: American culture, conceived as distinct from ours like Chinese culture, is purely and simply the invention of Europeans.

Any hypothesis of an American culture specifically opposed to ours depends precisely upon the extent of Europe's resignation.

It is difficult properly to consider Russia as a European country.

Saint Petersburg gave and Leningrad still gives the impression of a European "settlement," a vast imperial outpost of the West, complete with shops, barracks, and cupolas—a New Delhi of the North.

But to consider the Russians as Asians, as species of Chinese or Hindus—which is what their opponents have done since time was—is ludicrous. The truth, perhaps, is that we should not take geographical maps too seriously, and that Russia is neither in Europe nor Asia, but in Russia—just as Japan, where love and the army play such a great part, is neither in China nor in America.

Other European countries form parts of our culture on various levels and through exchanges. During certain centuries, Italy, Spain, France, Britain dominated that culture. All these lands have in common the cultural myth of Greece and Rome and the heritage of fifteen centuries of a common Christianity. Doubtless this last heritage, which in itself separates the Slavs of Bohemia from the Slavs of Russia, is of considerable import; and the heritage of Byzantium, for its part, has weighed so heavily upon Russia that Russian painting has never quite managed to shake it off and that Stalin nowadays evokes Basil II at least as much as Peter the Great.

Russia entered Western culture only in the nineteenth century, thanks to her musicians and novelists. At that, Dostoevsky is perhaps the only one among the latter who wished himself to be specifically Russian.

Indirectly, Ilya Ehrenburg replied to an interview I had given upon Atlantic civilization by asking: "Which is European: the atom bomb or Tolstoy?"

Let us, by your leave, not bother about the atomic bomb. If the Russians did not possess it at that time, it was not for want of having sought for it. And to present Stalin to us as the sort of fellow Gandhi was is sheer nonsense.

As for Tolstoy, which Tolstoy are we discussing? The author of *Anna Karenina* and of *War and Peace* not only belongs to Europe, but marks one of the summits of Western genius. According to a famous dictum, "it is ad-

visable not to spit into the springs at which we have slaked our thirst."
Moreover when he wrote his novels, Tolstoy wished to be European—
namely, in rivalry with Balzac.

But if we consider Count Leo Nikolaevich Tolstoy, who tried to live like
a kind of Christian Gandhi, who died in the snow like the hero of a by-line,
and who wrote that he "preferred a good pair of boots to Shakespeare," then
I think of one of the great illuminati of Byzantium. And, if I had at all costs
to compare him to another genius, it would be to Tagore, inseparable from
India, and writing in *The Home and the World* one of the great universal
novels; it would *not* be to Stendhal.

What separates Tolstoy most from us is very likely also what separates us
from Russia: his Oriental dogmatism. Stalin believes in his own truth and
that truth admits of no margin; but as soon as Tolstoy broke away from the
Occident, he believed no less fervently in his truth. And Dostoevsky's genius
applied itself throughout his lifetime to serve an indomitable necessity to
preach. Russia never experienced either a Renaissance or an Athens; she never
knew a Bacon or a Montaigne.

In Russia there is always one element that would be Sparta and another
that would be Byzantium. Sparta easily identifies itself with Europe, Byzantium does not. Today the frantic industrialization of this agricultural
land, attempted within a span of thirty years, manifests the most tremendous
effort of westernization that it has known since Peter the Great. "To catch
up with America and to outdo her!" But the greater this effort, the more
stoutly the Russian spirit defends itself.

It is not by chance that the Russian Communists attack Picasso. His painting challenges the very system upon which they base everything; willy-nilly
this painting represents the most acute presence of Europe.

In the realm of the spirit, everything that Russia terms "formalism," all
that she has deported or slain indefatigably for the last ten years, is Europe.
Painters, writers, animators of the screen, philosphers, musicians under suspicion are primarily suspected of undergoing the influence of a "moldering
Europe." Eisenstein, Babel, and Prokofiev are so many Europeans! The European spirit is a danger to a Pharaonic industry. The condemnation of
Picasso in Moscow is by no means an accident; it seeks to be a defense of the
five-year plans.

Depending upon whether they die in time or a little too late, artists are
buried with honors in the wall of the Kremlin or without honors at the foot
of a Siberian wall in a camp of deportees.

The true reason why Russia is not European has nothing to do with
geography; it is a matter of Russia's will.

I am not giving a course in the history of culture here. I shall not speak of Europe save in relation to the Soviet Union and to the United States. To-day Europe has two characteristics.

The first is her link between art and culture. These two fields are sep-arated in Russia by the dogmatism of thought. They are no less irreversibly separated in the United States because there the man of culture is not an artist: he is the university professor. An American writer—Hemingway, Faulkner—is not at all the equivalent of Gide or Valéry: he is the equivalent of Rouault or Braque. They are brilliant specialists of determined culture; they are neither men of History nor "ideologists."

The second characteristic, a particularly important one, is the will to transcendence. Watch out: Europe is that part of the world where Chartres, Michelangelo, Shakespeare, Rembrandt succeeded one another. Are we going to repudiate these—yes or no? No. Well then, we should know clearly what we are talking about.

It is as if we seemed to believe that we are unfortunates face to face with one immense culture which is called the American novelists and with another immense culture which is called—I do not quite know what—at best, say, the Russian musicians (which incidentally is not at all bad).

But finally, after all, one half of the world still looks to Europe, and Eu-rope alone answers its searching question. Who has taken Michelangelo's place? That light which others seek in her is the last glow of the light of Rembrandt; and the last great tremulous gesture which she believes ac-companies her values is still the heroic gesture of Michelangelo.

People object: "These are bourgeois agonies." But what on earth is this business of defining art by its conditioning?

Do not misunderstand me. I consider it fair for a Russian philosopher—who, by the way, has since gone to Siberia—to have said that "Plato's thought is inseparable from slavery." It is true that there is a historical datum of thought, a conditioning of thought. But the problem does not end here: it begins here. For, all in all, you people have read Plato! And surely you did so neither as slaves nor as owners of slaves.

No one in this room—neither myself nor anyone else—knows what feelings moved an Egyptian sculptor when he fashioned a statue of the Ancient Em-pire. Nevertheless we certainly gaze upon this statue with an admiration we did not go to seek amid the exaltation of bourgeois virtues. Here the prob-lem arises: it is precisely that of learning what assures the partial transcend-ence of dead cultures.

I am not speaking of eternity here: I am speaking of metamorphosis. Egypt has reappeared for us; it had disappeared for more than fifteen hun-dred years. Is the metamorphosis unforeseeable? Well then, we are face to face with a fundamental datum of civilization, which is the impossibility to foresee renaissances. At that, I prefer a world of unforeseeability to a world of imposture.

The present drama of Europe is the death of man. Ever since the atomic bomb, and even quite a while before, we understood that what the nineteenth century called "progress" exacted a heavy ransom. We understood that the world had once again become a dualistic world and that the immense hope without liabilities which man had set upon the future was no longer valid.

But it is not because the optimism of the nineteenth century no longer exists that there is no longer any human thought! Since when was will power founded upon an immediate optimism? If this were the case, there would never have been a Resistance movement before 1944. According to an old and illustrious phrase, "Hope is not necessary for an undertaking. . . ." You know the rest.

Ay, man must be founded anew but not upon old chromos. Europe is still defending the highest intellectual values in the world. To find this out, we need but suppose her to be dead. Let us imagine that on the site of what was once Florence or on the site of what was once Paris, we had reached the day when "the swaying and murmurous reeds shall bow down." Do you really believe it would take long before what these illustrious places meant would be reintegrated in the mind of man as sacred figures?

We are alone in having ceased to believe in Europe. The rest of the world still looks with a distant and timid veneration at these age-old hands which are fumbling in the shadows. . . .

If Europe no longer thinks in terms of freedom, but rather in terms of fate, it will not be for the first time. Things were going none too well when Michelangelo engraved upon the pedestal of his "Night" the words: "If it be to open thine eyes upon tyranny, mayest thou never awaken."

There is therefore no question of the submission of Europe. The devil take such tomfoolery! On the one hand, there is a hypothesis: Europe becomes a capital element in Atlantic civilization. On the other hand, there is a question: What becomes of Europe within the Soviet structure?

The Atlantic civilization calls to Europe and, in the matter of culture, still respects Europe; the Soviet structure despises Europe's past, detests her present, and accepts from her only a future in which exactly nothing remains of what she once was.

The values of Europe are threatened from within by techniques born of means that appeal to collective passions—the press, the cinema, the radio, and advertising—in a word, "means of propaganda." In lofty parlance, these are called "psychological techniques."

They are signally elaborated in the countries we have just mentioned. In

America they are chiefly devoted to the service of an economic system, and they tend to compel the individual to purchase some commodity. In Russia they are devoted to the service of a political system, and they tend to compel the citizen to adhere unreservedly to the ideology of the rulers, and, to that end, commit a man fully.

Let us not confuse the action of such techniques in their country of origin with their incidence of action upon Europe, and particularly upon France. The incidence of American psychotechnics upon our culture is secondary, that of Russian psychotechnics is, in intent, decisive.

Let us make sure here not to discuss a future culture to which Russian psychotechnics are forever referring. Let us face facts. The totality of Soviet technique in France, practically speaking, results today in a systematic organization of falsehoods chosen by reason of their efficacity. . . .

As for allies:

First, we have an ancient hoax, the Christian and ethical hoax. In France certain of the most profound elements of Stalinism have remained inseparable from the great Christian appeal. But we know now what such jokes are worth.

Secondly, we have the national hoax. This one embodies the whole Stalinist policy undertaken from the Cominform on. The point here is to prevent in all Western countries an economic recovery which runs the risk of drawing these countries toward the United States and Great Britain. For this purpose "the national defense of peoples threatened by America" must be invented.

To their recruitment of workers, the Stalinists seek to launch a vast bourgeois recruitment. Accordingly, they must establish a national ideology of which the Communist Party will become the active wing, as they call it. By these means, we would no longer be on a Russian footing or on the footing of a class versus class but on a footing which the Stalinists have already experienced during the Resistance—namely, the union of all sincerely national forces under a Communist false nose and whiskers to the benefit of Moscow.

Next comes the hoax of historical perspective. I repeat: it is high time to substitute the question "What actually is?" for the determination forever to explain the hidden significance, preferably historical, of what is. They expose the theory of Socialist realism in painting—and naturally it is as defensible as anything else. But what pictures do they produce? They do not produce Socialist realist canvases: they fashion icons of Stalin in the style of Déroulède.

To condemn Bernanos in the absolute in the name of a mythical proletariat might be defended if we were not compelled also to admire the edifying novels of Monsieur Garaudy. Ah, how many hopes have been betrayed, how

many insults and deaths have been inflicted, all to end up merely in changing
one set of edifying juvenile tales for another.

Then there is the celebrated hoax of revolutionary continuity. As we all
know, the gilt-edged marshals are the legitimate heirs of the leather-coated
companions of Lenin. Still, we should thrash this matter out. André Gide and
I happened to be requested to deliver to Hitler protests against the condemnation of Dimitrov, who was guiltless in the Reichstag fire. To us, this was a
great honor (and, I may add, we were not in a crowd!). When today Dimitrov is in power and has the guiltless Petkov hanged, who has changed—
Gide and myself, or Dimitrov?

In the beginning, Marxism recomposed the world according to the law of
freedom. The sentimental liberty of the individual played an immense part
in Lenin's Russia. Lenin had Chagall paint the frescoes in the Jewish Theater
of Moscow. Today, Stalinism reviles Chagall. Who has changed?

In its time one of my books, *Man's Fate,* interested not a few Russians.
Eisenstein was to make a film of it, with music by Shostakovich; Meyerhold
was to make a play of it, with music by Prokofiev. Is this a sufficiently long
procession to death and abjuration for a single work? I shall be informed
that I know nothing of dialectic; nor do convicts—and corpses, even less!

There were innumerable writers who broke away: Victor Serge, Gide,
Hemingway, Dos Passos, Mauriac, and how many others! It is false to say
that these breaks had anything whatever to do with the social problem. For
it was not understood that our "singing tomorrows" would become this howl
that rises from the Caspian to the White Sea, nor that their song would be
the song of the chain gang.

Standing here on this rostrum, we do not repudiate Spain. Let some
Stalinist rise on it some day to defend Trotsky!

In Russia, the problem is different. The country is closed, and, by that
token, cut off from the essentials of modern culture. It is that country today
in which everything must have happened. I quote from a text for school
children:

"It was a Russian schoolteacher, Ciolkowski, who formulated the theory
of jet propulsion. It was a Russian electrotechnician, Popov, who first invented the radio." (*Simlia Russkaia,* page 55.)

"In capitalist countries, instruction is a private activity and costs a great
deal. For very many young men and young women, it is an unattainable
desire and dream." (*Simlia Russkaia,* page 277.)

Ah well, let us leave it at that!

In the positive order of things, there remains a form of thought which
seeks to exalt solidarity, labor, and a certain messiahship with always the

same note of disdain on the part of the deliverers. Then there are psychological techniques destined to give a picture of the world and human feelings that will prove most favorable to Party action. Writers are engineers of "souls"! And how!

But for this purpose they invoke truth. Let us not forget that the greatest Russian newspaper is called "Pravda," or "Truth." Yet there are people who know the score. And here a rather interesting problem arises, to wit: upwards of what rank has a man today in Russia the right to be a liar? For Stalin knows as well as I do that education exists in France.

There are those who are in the game and those who are not. I believe this is worth thinking about, as is the contempt implicit in the psychological techniques. Whether it is a question of selling a cake of soap or of obtaining a ballot, no known psychological technique but is based upon contempt for the purchaser or the voter. Otherwise it would prove useless.

Here man himself is implicated; the system is a whole. Technique can exist without totalitarianism, but it follows the latter as ineluctably as the GPU, for without a police it is a vulnerable monster. For some years it was difficult to deny that Trotsky created the Red Army; in order that "L'Humanité" prove fully effective, the reader must not enjoy the possibility of reading an opposition newspaper.

There are no margins. That is why even partial disagreement of the artist with the system leads him to abjuration.

Here is where our essential problem appears: How can we prevent psychological techniques from destroying the quality of the mind? Even supposing there were ever a totalitarian art in the world, there is none left now. Christianity has no cathedrals any more: it builds Sainte Clotilde. And Russia, with her portraits of Stalin, offers the most conventionally bourgeois art. I said "supposing there were ever," because the masses have never been sensitive to art as such. (Both aristocracy and bourgeoisie are in this respect "masses.") I call artists those who are sensitive to the specific essence of an art; the others are sensitive to its sentimental values. There is no such thing as "the man who knows nothing about music"; there are those who love Mozart and those who love military marches. There is no such thing as "the man who knows nothing about painting"; there are those who love painting and those who love Detaille's *Dream* or pictures of cats in a basket. There is no such thing as "the man who knows nothing about poetry"; there are those interested in Shakespeare and those interested in sentimental songs. The difference between the two groups is that for the second group art is a means of sentimental expression.

At certain periods this sentimental expression may happen to embody a

very great art. This is what happened with Gothic art. The fusion of the
deepest feelings (love, the vulnerability of man's estate) with an appro-
priately plastic form can then produce an art of genius which appeals to
everyone. (There is something of the sort among the great Romantic individualists: Beethoven, Wagner to a slight extent, Michelangelo certainly,
Rembrandt, and even Victor Hugo.)

Whether a sentimental work is artistic or not, it is a fact; it is neither a
theory nor a principle. In political terms, then, our urgent problem is to
substitute the real creation of a democratic culture for the false appeal of
this or that totalitarian culture. The point is not to force art upon the masses
which are indifferent to it. The point is to open up the realm of culture to
all those who wish to reach it. In other words, the right to culture is purely
and simply the wish to accede to it.

We do not intend absurdly to establish a model of culture here, but to
bring to culture the means of maintaining, in its next metamorphosis, the
most lofty characteristics it attained among us.

We consider that the fundamental value of the European artist, during
the greatest epochs, from the sculptors of Chartres down to the great individualists, from Rembrandt to Victor Hugo, lies in the will to maintain art
and culture as the object of a conquest. To speak more clearly, I may say that
genius is a difference conquered, and that genius—be it Renoir's or that of a
Theban sculptor—begins as follows. A man, having looked since childhood
at a few admirable works which sufficed to divert him from the world, came
one day to feel that he was at odds with these forms, either because they were
not serene enough or because they were too serene. He determined to restrict
the world, and the very works of which he was born, within a truth, mysterious and incommunicable except through his work. This determination gave
rise to his genius. In other words, no genius was ever a copyist; there are no
servile geniuses. A truce to this talk of the great artisans of the Middle Ages.
Even in a civilization where all the artists were slaves, the imitator of forms
would still remain irreducible to the slave who might have discovered unknown forms. In art as in other fields, discovery is marked by a sort of
signature of genius, and this signature has not changed throughout the five
millenniums of history that we know.

If humanity bears an eternal scheme deep within, it is indeed that tragic
hesitation of the man who subsequently for centuries will be called an artist
—face to face with the work which he feels more deeply than any other,
which he admires as nobody else does, but which he alone in the world wishes
at the same time to destroy underhandedly.

Now if genius is a discovery, let us recognize that the resurrection of the past is founded upon this discovery. At the beginning of this speech I mentioned what a renaissance and what the inheritance of a culture might be. A culture is reborn when men of genius, seeking their own truth, draw from the depths of the centuries everything that once resembled that truth, even if they do not know that truth.

The Renaissance created Antiquity at least as much as Antiquity created the Renaissance. Negro fetishes no more created the Fauve school of painting than the Fauves created Negro fetishes. After all, the true heir to the art which has re-arisen in fifty years is not America, which places its masterpieces side by side, nor Russia, whose vast appeal of yore is satisfied at bargain rates by her new icons; it is that "formalist" school of Paris, whose resurrections of so many centuries resemble one immense family. Our adversary Picasso could best reply to "Pravda":

"I am perhaps, as you say, decadent and putrid. But if you knew how to look at my painting instead of admiring so many mustachioed icons, you would perceive that your pseudo-history is a little thing as against the surge of the generations, and that this ephemeral painting happens, like the Sumerian statues, to resuscitate a language forgotten for four millenniums."

Now this conquest is efficacious only through a free search. Everything opposed to the irreducible will to discovery belongs if not to the realm of death—for there is no death in art, and there is admittedly an Egyptian art —to the paralysis of the artist's most fruitful faculties.

We therefore proclaim the necessity of maintaining the freedom of this search against everything that intends to establish its direction beforehand. And mainly against methods of psychological action based upon an appeal to mass unconsciousness in order to further political ends.

First, we proclaim as values not the unconscious but conscience, not abandonment but will, not bluff but truth. (I know that somebody once upon a time asked: "What is truth?" In the field we are discussing, truth is whatever we can confirm.)

And next, liberty of discovery. All this, not with the idea of "to what goal?"—for we know nothing about that—but rather "starting from where?" as is the rule in contemporary sciences. Whether we want it or no, "the European will light his way with the torch he bears, even if it burns his hand."

Consequently, we wish to found these values upon the present. Any reactionary thought is centered upon the past, as we have long known; all Stalinist thought is centered upon a Hegelianism oriented by an uncontrollable future. What we primarily require is to find the present.

What we are here defending will be defended before the end of the century by all the great nations of the West. We wish to restore to France the part which she has already played several times before, during the Romanesque and Gothic periods as during the nineteenth century, and which imposed its accent upon Europe when it was at once that of audacity and that of freedom.

In the realm of the spirit, almost all of you are liberals. For us, the guarantee of political freedom and intellectual freedom does not lie in political liberalism, which is sentenced to death the moment it is faced with Stalinism. The guarantee of liberty is the strength of the State at the service of all its citizens.

When was France great? When she was not thrown back upon France. She is universalist. For the world, France as a great power is rather the France of the cathedrals or of the Revolution than the France of Louis XIV.

There are countries like Great Britain—and this may well redound to their honor—which are the mightier for being the lonelier. France was never greater than when she spoke for all men, and that is why her silence is heard so poignantly today.

What will become of mind and spirit? Well, it is you who shall fashion them.